EMPIRE OF PAIN

ALSO BY PATRICK RADDEN KEEFE

Say Nothing

The Snakehead

Chatter

EMPIRE OF PAIN

THE SECRET HISTORY
OF THE SACKLER DYNASTY

PATRICK RADDEN KEEFE

PICADOR

First published in the UK in paperback 2021 by Picador

This edition first published 2021 by Picador
an imprint of Pan Macmillan
The Smithson, 6 Briset Street, London EC1M 5NR
EU representative: Macmillan Publishers Ireland Ltd,
Mallard Lodge, Lansdowne Village, Dublin 4
Associated companies throughout the world
www.panmacmillan.com

ISBN 978-1-5290-6248-9

Title page photograph: (Temple of Dendur) Dustin Pittman/Fairchild Archives
Book 1 photograph: (brothers) *New York Herald Tribune*, May 13, 1950
Book 2 photograph: (Purdue Pharma) Peter Fisher
Book 3 photograph: (Guggenheim Museum) *The New York Times*/Redux

3 5 7 9 8 6 4

A CIP catalogue record for this book is available from the British Library.

Printed and bound by CPI Group (UK) Ltd, Croydon, CR0 4YY

Visit **www.picador.com** to read more about all our books
and to buy them. You will also find features, author interviews and
news of any author events, and you can sign up for e-newsletters
so that you're always first to hear about our new releases.

FOR BEATRICE AND TRISTRAM

AND FOR ALL THOSE WHO HAVE LOST
SOMEONE TO THE CRISIS

We have often sneered at the superstition and cowardice of the mediaeval barons who thought that giving lands to the Church would wipe out the memory of their raids or robberies; but modern capitalists seem to have exactly the same notion; with this not unimportant addition, that in the case of the capitalists the memory of the robberies is really wiped out.

—G. K. Chesterton (1909)

CONTENTS

EMPIRE OF PAIN

THE TAPROOT

THE NEW YORK HEADQUARTERS of the international law firm Debevoise & Plimpton occupy ten floors of a sleek black office tower that stands in a grove of skyscrapers in midtown Manhattan. Founded in 1931 by a pair of blue-blooded attorneys who defected from a venerable Wall Street firm, Debevoise became venerable itself, expanding, over the decades, into a global juggernaut with eight hundred lawyers, a roster of blue-chip clients, and nearly $1 billion in annual revenue. The midtown offices bear no trace of the oak-and-leather origins of the firm. Instead, they are decorated in the banal tones of any contemporary corporate office, with carpeted hallways, fishbowl conference rooms, and standing desks. In the twentieth century, power *announced* itself. In the twenty-first, the surest way to spot real power is by its understatement.

One bright, cold morning in the spring of 2019, as reflected clouds slid across the black glass of the facade, Mary Jo White entered the building, ascended in an elevator to the Debevoise offices, and took up position in a conference room that was buzzing with subdued energy. At seventy-one years old, White epitomized, in her very physicality, the principle of power as understatement. She was tiny—barely five feet tall, with close-cropped brown hair and wizened eyes—and her manner of speech was blunt and unpretentious. But she was a fearsome litigator. White sometimes joked that her specialty was the "big mess" business: she wasn't cheap, but if you found yourself in a lot of trouble, and you happened to have a lot of money, she was the lawyer you called.

Earlier in her career, White had spent nearly a decade as the U.S. Attorney for the Southern District of New York, where she prosecuted the perpetrators of the 1993 World Trade Center bombing. Barack Obama appointed her chair of the Securities and Exchange Commission. But between these stints in government, she always returned to Debevoise. She had joined the firm as a young associate, becoming the second woman ever to make partner. She represented the big dogs: Verizon, JP Morgan, General Electric, the NFL.

The conference room was teeming with lawyers, not just from Debevoise but from other firms, too, more than twenty of them, with notebooks and laptops and mammoth three-ring binders bristling with Post-it notes. There was a speakerphone on the table, and another twenty lawyers from across the country had dialed in. The occasion for which this small army of attorneys had assembled was the deposition of a reclusive billionaire, a longtime client of Mary Jo White's who was now at the center of a blizzard of lawsuits alleging that the accumulation of those billions had led to the deaths of hundreds of thousands of people.

White once observed that when she was a prosecutor, her job was simple: "Do the right thing. You're going after bad guys. You're doing something good for society every day." These days, her situation was more complicated. High-end corporate attorneys like White are skilled professionals who enjoy a certain social respectability, but at the end of the day it's a client-driven business. This is a familiar dynamic for a lot of prosecutors with a mortgage and tuitions to think about. You spend the first half of your career going after the bad guys and then the second half representing them.

The lawyer who would be posing the questions that morning was a man in his late sixties named Paul Hanly. He did not look like the other attorneys. Hanly was a class-action plaintiffs' lawyer. He favored custom-made suits in bold colors and tailored shirts with stiff, contrasting collars. His steel-gray hair was slicked straight back, his piercing eyes accentuated by horn-rimmed glasses. If White was a master of muted power, Hanly was the opposite: he looked like a lawyer in a *Dick Tracy* cartoon. But he had a competitive edge to match White's and a visceral contempt for the veneer of propriety that people like White brought to this sort of undertaking. Let's not kid ourselves, Hanly thought. In his view, White's clients were "arrogant assholes."

The billionaire being deposed that morning was a woman in her early seventies, a medical doctor, though she had never actually practiced medicine. She had blond hair and a broad face, with a high forehead and wide-set eyes. Her manner was gruff. Her lawyers had fought to prevent this deposition, and she did not want to be there. She projected the casual impatience, one of the lawyers in attendance thought, of someone who never waits in line to board an airplane.

"You are Kathe Sackler?" Hanly asked.

"I am," she replied.

Kathe was a member of the Sackler family, a prominent New York philanthropic dynasty. A few years earlier, *Forbes* magazine had listed the Sacklers as one of the twenty wealthiest families in the United States, with an estimated fortune of some $14 billion, "edging out storied families like the Busches, Mellons and Rockefellers." The Sackler name adorned art museums, universities, and medical facilities around the world. From the conference room, Kathe could have walked twenty blocks downtown, to the Sackler Institute of Graduate Biomedical Sciences, at NYU Medical School, or ten blocks uptown to the Sackler Center for Biomedicine and Nutrition Research, at Rockefeller University, then farther uptown to the Sackler Center for Arts Education at the Guggenheim Museum, and along Fifth Avenue to the Sackler Wing at the Metropolitan Museum of Art.

Over the previous six decades, Kathe Sackler's family had left its mark on New York City, in a manner that the Vanderbilts or the Carnegies once did. But the Sacklers were wealthier now than either of those families that traced their fortunes to the Gilded Age. And their gifts extended well beyond New York, to the Sackler Museum at Harvard and the Sackler School of Graduate Biomedical Sciences at Tufts, the Sackler Library at Oxford and the Sackler Wing at the Louvre, the Sackler School of Medicine in Tel Aviv and the Sackler Museum of Art and Archaeology in Beijing. "I grew up," Kathe told Hanly, "with my parents having foundations." They contributed, she said, to "social causes."

The Sacklers had given away hundreds of millions of dollars, and for decades the Sackler name had been associated in the public mind with philanthropy. One museum director likened the family to the Medicis, the noble clan in fifteenth-century Florence whose patronage of the arts helped give rise to the Renaissance. But whereas the Medicis made their fortune in banking, the precise origins of the Sacklers' wealth had, for a long time, been more mysterious. Members of the family bestowed their name on arts and education institutions with a sort of mania. It was etched into marble, emblazoned on brass plaques, even spelled out in stained glass. There were Sackler professorships and Sackler scholarships and Sackler lecture series and Sackler prizes. Yet, to the casual observer, it could be difficult to connect the family name with any sort of business that might have generated all this wealth. Social acquaintances would see members of the family out, at gala dinners and Hamptons fund-raisers, on a yacht in the Caribbean or skiing in the Swiss Alps, and wonder, or whisper, about how they made their money. And this was strange, because the bulk of the Sacklers' wealth had been accumulated not in the era of the robber barons but in recent decades.

"You graduated from NYU undergraduate in 1980," Hanly said. "True?"

"Correct," Kathe Sackler replied.

"And from NYU Medical School in 1984?"

"Yes."

And was it true, Hanly asked, that after a two-year surgical residency she had gone to work for the Purdue Frederick Company?

Purdue Frederick was a drug manufacturer, which subsequently became known as Purdue Pharma. Based in Connecticut, it was the source of the vast majority of the Sackler fortune. Whereas the Sacklers tended to insist, through elaborate "naming rights" contracts, that any gallery or research center that received their generosity must prominently feature the family name, the family *business* was not named after the Sacklers. In fact, you could scour Purdue Pharma's website and find no mention of the Sacklers whatsoever. But Purdue was a privately held company entirely owned by Kathe Sackler and other members of her family. In 1996, Purdue had introduced a groundbreaking drug, a powerful opioid painkiller called OxyContin, which was heralded as a revolutionary way to treat chronic pain. The drug became one of the biggest blockbusters in pharmaceutical history, generating some $35 billion in revenue.

But it also led to a rash of addiction and abuse. By the time Kathe Sackler sat for her deposition, the United States was seized by an opioid epidemic in which Americans from every corner of the country found themselves addicted to these powerful drugs. Many people who started abusing OxyContin ended up transitioning to street drugs, like heroin or fentanyl. The numbers were staggering. According to the Centers for Disease Control and Prevention, in the quarter century following the introduction of OxyContin, some 450,000 Americans had died of opioid-related overdoses. Such overdoses were now the leading cause of accidental death in America, accounting for more deaths than car accidents—more deaths, even, than that most quintessentially American of metrics, gunshot wounds. In fact, more Americans had lost their lives from opioid overdoses than had died in all of the wars the country had fought since World War II.

✢ ✢ ✢

Mary Jo White sometimes observed that one thing she loved about the law is the way it forces you "to distill things down to their essence." The opioid epidemic was an enormously complex public health crisis. But, as Paul Hanly questioned Kathe Sackler, he was trying to distill this epic human tragedy down to its root causes. Prior to the introduction of OxyContin, America did not have an opioid crisis. After the introduction of OxyContin, it did. The Sacklers and their company were now defendants in more than twenty-five hundred lawsuits that were being brought by cities, states, counties, Native American tribes, hospitals, school districts, and a host of other litigants. They had been swept up in a huge civil litigation effort in which public and private attorneys sought to hold pharmaceutical companies accountable for their role in marketing these powerful drugs and misleading the public about their addictive properties. Something like this had happened once before, when tobacco companies were made to answer for their decision to knowingly downplay the health risks of cigarettes. Company executives were hauled before Congress, and the industry ended up agreeing to a landmark $206 billion settlement in 1998.

White's job was to prevent that sort of reckoning from happening to the Sacklers and Purdue. The attorney general of New York, who was suing Purdue and had named Kathe and seven other members of the Sackler family as defendants, argued in a legal complaint that OxyContin was "the taproot of the opioid epidemic." It was the pioneer, the painkiller that changed the way American doctors prescribed pain medication, with devastating consequences. The attorney general of Massachusetts, who was also suing the Sacklers, maintained that "a single family made the choices that caused much of the opioid epidemic."

White had other ideas. Those bringing cases against the Sacklers were twisting the facts to scapegoat her clients, she argued. What was their crime? All they had done was sell a drug that was perfectly legal—a product that had been approved by the Food and Drug Administration. This whole charade was "a litigation blame game," White contended, insisting that the opioid epidemic "is not a crisis of my clients' or Purdue's creation."

But in the deposition that day, she said nothing. After introducing herself ("Mary Jo White, Debevoise & Plimpton, for Dr. Sackler"), she simply sat and listened, allowing other colleagues to jump in and interrupt Hanly with objections. Her function was not to make noise but to serve as a holstered gun, silent but visible, by Kathe's side. And White and her team had coached their client well. Whatever White might say about the law getting to "the essence" of things, when your client is in the hot seat in a deposition, the whole point is to avoid the essence.

"Dr. Sackler, does Purdue bear any responsibility for the opioid crisis?" Hanly asked.

"Objection!" one of the lawyers interjected. "Objection!" another chimed in.

"I don't believe Purdue has a legal responsibility," Kathe replied.

That's not what I asked, Hanly pointed out. What I want to know "is whether Purdue's conduct was a *cause* of the opioid epidemic."

"Objection!"

"I think it's a very complex set of factors and confluence of different circumstances and societal issues and problems and medical issues and regulatory gaps in different states across the country," she replied. "I mean, it's very, very, very complex."

But then Kathe Sackler did something surprising. One might suppose, given the dark legacy of OxyContin, that she would distance herself from the drug. As Hanly questioned her, however, she refused to accept the very premise of his inquiry. The Sacklers have nothing to be ashamed of or to apologize for, she maintained—because there's nothing wrong with OxyContin. "It's a very good medicine, and it's a very effective and safe medicine," she said. Some measure of defensiveness was to be expected from a corporate official being deposed in a multibillion-dollar lawsuit. But this was something else. This was *pride*. The truth is, she said, that she, Kathe, deserved credit for coming up with "the idea" for OxyContin. Her accusers were suggesting that OxyContin was the taproot of one of the most deadly public health crises in modern history, and Kathe Sackler was outing herself, proudly, as the taproot of OxyContin.

"Do you recognize that hundreds of thousands of Americans have become addicted to OxyContin?" Hanly asked.

"Objection!" a pair of lawyers blurted. Kathe hesitated.

"Simple question," Hanly said. "Yes or no."

"I don't know the answer to that," she said.

✢ ✢ ✢

At one point in his questioning, Hanly inquired about a particular building on East Sixty-Second Street, just a few blocks from the conference room where they were sitting. There are actually two buildings, Kathe corrected him. From the outside, they look like two discrete addresses, but inside "they're connected," she explained. "They function as one." They were handsome limestone town houses, in a rarefied neighborhood alongside Central Park, the sorts of timeless New York buildings that prompt real estate envy and conjure reveries of an earlier era. "That's an office which is"—she caught herself—"*was*...my father and my uncle's offices originally."

Originally, there had been three Sackler brothers, she explained. Arthur, Mortimer, and Raymond. Mortimer was Kathe's father. All three of them were doctors, but the Sackler brothers were "very entrepreneurial," she continued. The saga of their lives and the dynasty they would establish was also the story of a century of American capitalism. The three brothers had purchased Purdue Frederick back in the 1950s. "It was a much smaller company, originally," Kathe said. "It was a small family business."

BOOK I

PATRIARCH

Chapter 1

A GOOD NAME

ARTHUR SACKLER WAS BORN in Brooklyn, in the summer of 1913, at a moment when Brooklyn was burgeoning with wave upon wave of immigrants from the Old World, new faces every day, the unfamiliar music of new tongues on the street corners, new buildings going up left and right to house and employ these new arrivals, and everywhere this giddy, bounding sense of *becoming*. As the firstborn child of immigrants himself, Arthur came to share the dreams and ambitions of that generation of new Americans, to understand their energy and their hunger. He vibrated with it, practically from the cradle. He was born Abraham but would cast off that old-world name in favor of the more squarely American-sounding Arthur. There's a photo, taken in 1915 or 1916, of Arthur as a toddler, sitting upright in a patch of grass while his mother, Sophie, reclines behind him like a lioness. Sophie is dark-haired, dark-eyed, and formidable. Arthur stares straight at the camera, a cherub in short pants, his ears sticking out, his eyes steady and preternaturally serious, as though he already knows the score.

Sophie Greenberg had emigrated from Poland just a few years earlier. She was a teenager when she arrived in Brooklyn in 1906 and met a mild-mannered man nearly twenty years her senior named Isaac Sackler. Isaac was an immigrant himself, from Galicia, in what was then still the Austrian Empire; he had come to New York with his parents and siblings, arriving on a ship in 1904. Isaac was a proud man. He was descended from a line of rabbis who had fled Spain for central Europe during the Inquisition, and now he and his young bride would build a new beachhead in New York. Isaac went into business with his brother, operating a small grocery store at 83 Montrose Avenue in Williamsburg. They called it Sackler Bros. The family lived in an apartment in the building. Three years after Arthur was born, Isaac and Sophie had a second boy, Mortimer, and four years after that, a third, Raymond.

Arthur was devoted to his little brothers and fiercely protective of them. For a time, when they were small, all three brothers shared a bed.

Isaac did well enough in the grocery business that the family soon moved to Flatbush. A bustling neighborhood that felt like the heart of the borough, Flatbush was considered middle class, even *upper* middle class, compared with the far reaches of immigrant Brooklyn, like Browns-ville and Canarsie. Real estate was the great benchmark in New York, even then, and the new address signified that Isaac Sackler had made something of himself in the New World, achieving a degree of stability. Flatbush felt like a place you graduated to, with tree-lined streets and solid, spacious apartments. One of Arthur's contemporaries went so far as to remark that to Brooklyn Jews of that era it could seem that other Jews who lived in Flatbush were "practically Gentiles." With his earn-ings from the grocery business, Isaac invested in real estate, purchasing tenement buildings and renting out apartments. But Isaac and Sophie had dreams for Arthur and his brothers, dreams that stretched beyond Flatbush, beyond even Brooklyn. They had a sense of providence. They wanted the Sackler brothers to leave their mark on the world.

✢ ✢ ✢

If Arthur would later seem to have lived more lives than anyone else could possibly squeeze into one lifetime, it helped that he had an early start. He began working when he was still a boy, assisting his father in the grocery store. From an early age, he evinced a set of qualities that would propel and shape his life—a singular vigor, a roving intelligence, an inexhaustible ambition. Sophie was clever, but not educated. At sev-enteen she had gone to work in a garment factory, and she would never fully master written English. Isaac and Sophie spoke Yiddish at home, but they encouraged their sons to assimilate. They kept kosher, but rarely attended synagogue. Sophie's parents lived with the family, and there was a sense, not uncommon in any immigrant enclave, that all the accumulated hopes and aspirations of the older generations would now be invested in these American-born kids. Arthur in particular felt the weight of those expectations: he was the pioneer, the firstborn Ameri-can son, and everyone staked their dreams on him.

The vehicle for achieving those dreams would be education. One fall day in 1925, Artie Sackler (he went by Artie) arrived at Erasmus Hall High School on Flatbush Avenue. He was young for his class—

he had just turned twelve—having tested into a special accelerated program for bright students. Artie was not one to be easily cowed, but Erasmus was an intimidating institution. Built by the Dutch in the eighteenth century, the original structure was a two-story wooden schoolhouse. In the first years of the twentieth century, the school expanded, around that ancient schoolhouse, to include a quadrangle in the style of Oxford University with castle-like neo-Gothic buildings clad in ivy and adorned with gargoyles. This expansion was designed to accommodate the great surge of immigrant children in Brooklyn. The faculty and students at Erasmus saw themselves as occupying the vanguard of the American experiment and took the notion of upward mobility and assimilation seriously, providing a first-class public education. The school had science labs and taught Latin and Greek. Some of the teachers had PhDs.

But Erasmus was also enormous. With some eight thousand students, it was one of the biggest high schools in the country, and most of the students were just like Arthur Sackler—the eager offspring of recent immigrants, children of the Roaring Twenties, their eyes bright, their hair pomaded to a sheen. They surged into the corridors, the boys dressed in suits and red ties, the girls in dresses with red ribbons in their hair. When they met under the great vaulted entrance arch during the lunch hour, it looked, in the words of one of Arthur's classmates, like a "Hollywood cocktail party."

Arthur loved it. In history class, he found that he admired and related to the Founding Fathers, and particularly Thomas Jefferson. Like Jefferson, Artie had eclectic interests—art, science, literature, history, sports, business; he wanted to do *everything*—and Erasmus put a great emphasis on extracurriculars. There must have been a hundred clubs, a club for practically everything. On a late afternoon in winter, when classes had ended for the day and dark had fallen, the whole school was lit up, windows blazing around the quad, and as you walked the corridors, you would hear the sounds of one club or another being convened: "Mr. Chairman! Point of order!"

In later life, when he spoke of these early years at Erasmus, Arthur would talk about "the big dream." Erasmus was a great stone temple to American meritocracy, and most of the time it seemed that the only practical limitation on what he could expect to get out of life would be what he was personally prepared to put into it. Sophie would prod him about school: "Did you ask a good question today?" Arthur had grown up to be gangly and broad-shouldered, with a square face, blond hair, and eyes that were blue and nearsighted. He had tremendous stamina, and he needed it. In addition to his studies, he joined the student newspaper as an editor and found an opening in the school's publishing office, selling advertising for school publications. Rather than accept a standard pay arrangement, Arthur proposed that he receive a small commission on any ad sale he made. The administration agreed, and soon Arthur was making money.

This was a lesson he learned early, one that would inform his later life in important ways: Arthur Sackler liked to bet on himself, going to great lengths in order to devise a scheme in which his own formidable energies might be rewarded. Nor was he content with the one job. He set up a business to handle photography for the school yearbook. After selling advertising space to Drake Business Schools, a chain specializing in postsecondary clerical education, he proposed to the company that they make him—a high school student—their advertising manager. And they did.

His inexhaustible gusto and restless creativity were such that he always seemed to be fizzing with new innovations and ideas. Erasmus issued "program cards" and other pieces of humdrum curricular paperwork to its eight thousand students. Why not sell advertising on the back of them? What if Drake Business Schools paid for rulers branded with the company name and issued them to Erasmus students for free? By the time Arthur was fifteen, he was bringing in enough money from these various hustles to help support his family. He was accumulating new jobs more quickly than he could work them, so he started to hand some of them off to his brother Morty. Initially, Arthur felt that Ray, as the youngest, shouldn't have to work. "Let the kid enjoy himself," he would say. But eventually, Ray took jobs, too. Arthur arranged for his brothers to sell advertising for *The Dutchman,* the student magazine at Erasmus. They persuaded Chesterfield cigarettes to run ads aimed at their fellow students. This generated a nice commission.

For all of its orientation toward the future, Erasmus also had a vivid connection to the past. Some of the Founding Fathers whom Artie Sackler so revered had been supporters of the school he now attended: Alexander Hamilton, Aaron Burr, and John Jay had contributed funds to Erasmus. The school was named after the fifteenth-century Dutch scholar Desiderius Erasmus, and in the library a stained-glass window celebrated scenes from his life. The window had been completed just a few years before Arthur arrived, dedicated to "the great man whose name we have carried for a hundred and twenty-four years." Each day, Arthur and his fellow students were inculcated with the idea that they would eventually take their place in a long line of great Americans, a continuous line that stretched back to the country's founding. It didn't matter that they lived in cramped quarters or wore the same threadbare suit every day, or that their parents spoke a different language. This country was theirs for the taking, and in the span of a single lifetime true greatness could be achieved. They spent their days at Erasmus surrounded by traces of great men who had come before, images and names, legacies etched in stone.

In the center of the quad, the ramshackle old Dutch schoolhouse still stood, a relic of a time when this part of Brooklyn had all been farmland. When the wind blew in the wintertime, the wooden beams of the old building would creak, and Arthur's classmates joked that it was the ghost of Virgil, groaning at the sound of his beautiful Latin verses being recited in a Brooklyn accent.

✦ ✦ ✦

Arthur's hyperactive productivity in these years might have stemmed in part from anxiety: while he was at Erasmus, his father's fortunes began to slip. Some of the real estate investments went bad, and the Sacklers were forced to move in to cheaper lodging. Isaac bought a shoe shop on Grand Street, but it failed and ended up closing. Having sold the grocery in order to finance his real estate investments, Isaac was now reduced to taking a low-paying job behind the counter at someone else's grocery store, just to pay the bills.

Arthur would later recall that during these years, he was often cold but never hungry. Erasmus had an employment agency to help students find work outside school, and Arthur began to take on additional jobs to support the family. He got a newspaper route. He delivered flowers. He didn't have time to date or attend summer camp or go to parties. He worked. It would become a point of pride for him that he never took a holiday until he was twenty-five years old.

Even so, in stray moments, Arthur glimpsed another world—a life beyond his existence in Brooklyn, a different life, which seemed close enough to touch. From time to time, he would take a break from his frenetic schedule and trot up the stone steps of the Brooklyn Museum, through the grove of Ionic columns and into the vast halls, where he would marvel at the artworks on display. Sometimes, his delivery jobs would take him into Manhattan, all the way uptown to the gilded palaces of Park Avenue. At Christmas, he would deliver great bouquets of flowers, and as he walked along the broad avenues, he would peer through brightly lit windows into the apartments and see the twinkle of Christmas lights inside. He loved the sensation, as he entered a big doorman building, his arms full of flowers, of stepping off the frigid sidewalk and getting enveloped in the velvet warmth of the lobby.

When the Great Depression hit in 1929, Isaac Sackler's misfortune intensified. All of his money had been tied up in his tenement properties, and now they were worthless: he lost what little he had. On the streets of Flatbush, forlorn-looking men and women joined breadlines. The employment agency at Erasmus started accepting applications not just from students but from their parents. One day, Isaac called his three sons together. With a defiant flash of the old family pride, he informed them that he would not be going bankrupt. He had marshaled his meager resources responsibly and had at least been able to pay his bills. But he had nothing left. Isaac and Sophie desperately wanted their sons to continue their education—to go to college, to keep climbing the ladder, to do everything that a young man with ambition in America was supposed to do. But Isaac did not have the money to pay for it. If the Sackler boys were going to get an education, they would have to finance it themselves.

It must have been painful for Isaac to say this. But he insisted that he had not given his children nothing. On the contrary, he had bestowed upon them something more valuable than money. "What I have given you is the most important thing a father can give," Isaac told Arthur, Mortimer, and Raymond. What he had given them, he said, was "a good name."

✤   ✤   ✤

When Arthur and his brothers were children, Sophie Sackler would check to see if they were sick by kissing them on the forehead to take their temperature with her lips. Sophie had a more dynamic and assertive personality than her husband and a very clear sense, from the time that her children were little, of what she wanted for them in life: she wanted them to be doctors.

"By the time I was four, I knew that I was going to be a physician," Arthur later said. "My parents brainwashed me about being a doctor." Both Sophie and Isaac regarded medicine as a noble profession. During the nineteenth century, many doctors had been perceived as snake oil salesmen or quacks. But Arthur and his brothers were born into what has been described as the golden age of American medicine, a period during the early twentieth century when the efficacy of medicine— and the credibility of the medical profession—were greatly enhanced by new scientific discoveries about the sources of various illnesses and the best means of treating them. As a consequence, it was not unusual for Jewish immigrant families to aspire to have their children pursue medicine. There was a sense that doctors were morally upright, and it was a vocation that served the public good and promised prestige and financial stability.

The year of the stock market crash, Arthur graduated from Erasmus and enrolled as a premed student at New York University. He loved college. He had no money. His books were used or borrowed and often falling apart. But he held them together with rubber bands and studied hard, poring over the lives of the ancient medical thinkers like Alcmaeon of Croton, who identified the brain as the organ of the mind, and Hippocrates, the so-called father of medicine, in whose famous admonition, "First, do no harm," the very idea of the integrity of doctors was enshrined.

Despite the rigors of his course load, Arthur somehow managed to continue his interest in extracurriculars, working on the college newspaper, the humor magazine, *and* the yearbook. At night, he found time to take art classes at Cooper Union and tried his hand at figurative drawing and sculpture. In an editorial from around this time, Arthur wrote that an eclectic approach to extracurricular activities "arms the student with an outlook on life and its problems which will enhance manyfold the effectiveness and usefulness of the techniques and facts which he has acquired from the formal curriculum." At lunchtime, he waited tables in the student café on campus. In the spare hours between classes, he found a job as a soda jerk in a candy store.

Arthur sent money back to Sophie and Isaac in Brooklyn and coached his brothers on how to maintain the jobs that he had passed along to them. To Arthur, Morty and Ray would always be his "kid brothers." It might simply have been the crisis of the Depression, in which Arthur was forced to provide for his own parents, or his exalted status as the firstborn son, or just his naturally domineering personality, but there was a sense in which he functioned less as an older brother to Mortimer and Raymond and more as a parent.

In those days, the NYU campus was all the way uptown in the Bronx. But Arthur ventured out into the great metropolis with excitement. He visited the museums, his footfalls echoing through marble galleries named after great industrialists. He took dates to the theater, though he could afford only standing-room tickets, so they would watch the whole show on their feet. But his favorite shoestring evening out was to take a date for a cruise around lower Manhattan—on the Staten Island Ferry.

By the time Arthur graduated from college in 1933, he had made enough money (in an era of record unemployment) to purchase another store for his parents, with living quarters in the back. He was accepted to medical school at NYU and enrolled immediately, taking a full course load and editing the student magazine. There's a photo of Arthur from this period. He's wearing a smart suit, poised, self-serious, a pen in his hand. It looks as though he's just been interrupted mid-thought, though the picture is clearly staged. He loved medicine—loved the riddle of it and the sense of possibility, the way that it could "reveal its secrets" to the diligent investigator. "A physician can do anything," he would observe. Medicine is "a fusion of technology and human experience."

Yet he was also aware that medicine is a profound responsibility, a vocation in which the difference between a good decision and a bad one could be a matter of life or death. When Arthur was a senior on surgical service, the chief of the department was an esteemed older surgeon who was aging rapidly and who seemed, to Arthur, to be showing signs of senility. The man failed to recognize the standard protocols of hygiene, scrubbing up for an operation, then bending to tie his shoelace. More worryingly, his skills with the scalpel had deteriorated to a point where patients were dying in his care. This was happening with sufficient frequency that some of the staff had taken to referring to the surgeon, behind his back, as "the Angel of Death."

One Tuesday, Arthur was accompanying the surgeon on his rounds when they arrived at the bed of a young woman in her thirties who was suffering from a perforated peptic ulcer. The ulcer had been walled off in an abscess, and when Arthur examined the patient, he saw that she was in no immediate danger. But the surgical chief announced, "I'll do that case Thursday."

Alarmed that the woman might be risking her life in an unnecessary procedure, Arthur appealed to her directly, suggesting that she was all right and should check herself out of the hospital. He told her that her children needed her, that her husband did, too. But Arthur did not feel that he could divulge to her the real source of his concern; to do so would be regarded as a deeply insubordinate breach of protocol. The woman was disinclined to leave. So Arthur appealed to her husband. But he could not be persuaded to check her out of the hospital, either. Many people who are unschooled in medicine themselves have a natural impulse to trust the expertise and good judgment of doctors, to put their lives, and the lives of their loved ones, into a physician's hands. "The professor is going to operate," the husband told Arthur.

On the appointed day, the Angel of Death operated on the woman. He tore through the walled-off abscess and she died. Had Arthur allowed his own career ambition to blind him to the stakes at play? If he had broken rank and confronted the Angel of Death directly, he might have saved the woman's life. He would forever regret having permitted the operation to go forward. And yet, as he would later reflect, "medicine is a hierarchy, and perhaps it must be."

In addition to the grave responsibility associated with a career in medicine, Arthur had other lingering concerns. Would the life of a practicing physician be enough, on its own, to satisfy him? Being a doctor had always seemed to entail financial stability. But then, during the Depression, there were doctors in Brooklyn who were reduced to selling apples on the street. And leaving aside material wealth, there was also the matter of mental and intellectual stimulation. It wasn't that Arthur ever thought he would be an artist; that would be far too impractical. But he had always possessed an entrepreneurial sensibility, a keen interest in business, and any vow he made to medicine could not change that. Besides, he had landed an interesting part-time job during medical school, yet another side gig, this time as a copywriter for a German pharmaceutical company called Schering. Arthur had discovered that of all his many talents one thing he was particularly good at was selling things to people.

Chapter 2

THE ASYLUM

WHEN MARIETTA LUTZE ARRIVED in New York from Germany in 1945, she felt as if the odds were stacked against her. It was, to put it mildly, not a hospitable moment for German nationals in the United States. A few months earlier, Hitler had shot himself in his bunker as Russian troops streamed into Berlin. Marietta was twenty-six when she arrived in America, tall, slender, and aristocratic, with curly blond hair and bright, mirthful eyes. She was already a doctor, having received her degree in Germany during the war, but she discovered upon arriving that she would need to do two internships before she could sit for the New York State medical boards. So she found a job at a hospital in Far Rockaway, Queens. The transition wasn't easy. People tended to be skeptical of this new arrival with her thick German accent. They were even more dubious when it came to the spectacle of a female doctor. When Marietta started her internship in Far Rockaway, nobody—not her patients, not the emergency personnel who brought the patients in, not even her own colleagues—seemed to take her seriously. Instead, as she made her rounds of the hospital, she was trailed by catcalls.

But she worked hard. She found the work exhausting but stimulating. And she did manage to make a couple of friends—a pair of young interns from Brooklyn who happened to be brothers, named Raymond and Mortimer Sackler. Mortimer, the older of the two, was garrulous and jovial, with a conspiratorial smile, curly hair, and piercing dark eyes. Raymond, the younger brother, had lighter hair, which was already thinning on top, green eyes, soft features, and a milder manner.

Like Marietta, the brothers had commenced their medical training outside the United States. After completing their undergraduate degrees at NYU, both Mortimer and Raymond had applied to med school. But during the 1930s, many American medical programs had established quotas on the number of Jewish students who could be enrolled. By the mid-1930s, more than 60 percent of applicants to American medical schools were Jewish, and this perceived imbalance prompted sharp restrictions. At some schools, such as Yale, applications from prospective students who happened to be Jewish were marked with an *H*, for "Hebrew." Mortimer, who applied to medical school first, found that he was effectively blacklisted on the basis of his ethnicity. He couldn't find a medical school in the United States that would take him. So, in 1937, he boarded a ship, sailing steerage, to Scotland, to study at Anderson College of Medicine in Glasgow. Raymond followed him a year later.

Many American Jews, excluded from universities in their own country, were pursuing their medical education abroad. But there was a perverse irony in the notion that the Sackler family, having left Europe just a few decades earlier in search of opportunity in the United States, would be forced, within one generation, to return to Europe in search of equal access to education. Raymond and Mortimer's sojourn in Scotland, Marietta would come to understand, had been financed by their older brother. Their lodging was cold, because there was a coal shortage, and they subsisted on baked beans. But both brothers grew to love the warmth and wit of the Scottish people. In any event, they did not stay long: after Germany invaded Poland in 1939, the brothers were forced to discontinue their studies in Scotland and ended up finding places at Middlesex University in Waltham, Massachusetts—a nonaccredited medical school that refused to impose Jewish quotas and would eventually become part of Brandeis.

That was how, after the war, Morty and Ray ended up interning together at the hospital in Far Rockaway. The brothers were intelligent and ambitious. Marietta liked them. The internship might have been overwhelming, but the Sacklers had a joie de vivre that she appreciated. Their dispositions were quite different: Morty was hot-blooded and hot-tempered, with an acerbic wit, whereas Ray was more even-keeled and cerebral. "Raymond was a peacemaker," one person who knew them both recalled. "Mortimer was a grenade thrower." Despite their different coloring, the brothers had similar features, so occasionally they would swap places at the hospital, and one would pretend to be the other for a shift.

One night, after a particularly grueling stint, the interns decided to throw a little party in a spare room at the hospital. They brought drinks and, abandoning their white coats, got dressed up for the occasion. Marietta wore a black knit dress that showed flashes of her pale skin underneath. The medical residents were all drinking and talking, and at a certain point in the evening people started to sing songs. Marietta was normally quite shy, but she liked to sing. So she stood up before the revelers, summoned her confidence, and launched into a song that she used to sing back in Berlin. It was a French song, "Parlez-moi d'amour"—"Speak to Me of Love"—and before she knew it, Marietta found herself leaning into the performance, crooning in a deep, sexy, cabaret-style voice.

As she sang, she noticed an unfamiliar man in the crowd who was sitting very still and watching her intently. He had ash-blond hair and rimless spectacles, which gave him a professorial air, and he stared right at her. The moment Marietta finished the number, the man made his way over to her and told her how much he had enjoyed her singing. He had clear blue eyes and a soft voice and a very confident way about him. He was a doctor, too, he said. His name was Arthur Sackler. He was Morty and Ray's older brother. All three of them were physicians; their parents, Arthur liked to joke, "got three out of three."

The next day, Marietta received a phone call from Arthur, asking her on a date. But she declined. Her internship was overwhelming; she didn't have time to date.

Marietta didn't see or hear from Arthur Sackler again for a year. Instead, she focused on her work. But as her first internship was coming to an end, she set out to find a second one. She was interested in Creedmoor Hospital, a state psychiatric facility in Queens, and when she asked Ray Sackler if he might have any contacts there, Ray said that as a matter of fact he did: his big brother Arthur, whom she had met at the party, worked at Creedmoor. So Marietta called Arthur Sackler and made an appointment to see him.

✢ ✢ ✢

Founded in 1912 as a farm colony of Brooklyn State Hospital, the Creedmoor Psychiatric Center had grown, by the 1940s, into a sprawling asylum that consisted of seventy buildings spread across three hundred acres. Throughout history, human societies have struggled with the question of what to do with people who are mentally ill. In some cultures, such people were cast out, or burned to death, as witches. Other cultures turned to those with psychological afflictions for inspi-

EMPIRE OF PAIN 23

ration, assuming them to possess some special wisdom. But in America, dating back to the nineteenth century, what the medical establishment tended to do was confine these people in an ever-expanding network of asylums. By the mid-twentieth century, some half a million Americans were held in such facilities. And these were not temporary inpatient visits: people who checked in to places like Creedmoor generally did not leave. They stayed for decades, living out their days in confinement. As a result, the facility was terribly overcrowded: a hospital certified to hold just over four thousand people now housed six thousand. It was a bleak and spooky institution. Some patients were simply comatose: mute, incontinent, unreachable. Others were prone to wild fits. Visitors would see patients roaming the grounds, confined in white straitjackets, like a vision from an etching by Goya.

Arthur Sackler had first arrived at Creedmoor in 1944, having completed his medical degree at NYU and spent a couple of years interning at a hospital in the Bronx. In that internship, he had worked thirty-six-hour shifts, delivering babies, riding around in ambulances, and always learning, always stimulated, enjoying the constant exposure to new illnesses and treatments. Along the way, Arthur developed a special fascination with psychiatry. He trained with Johan van Ophuijsen, a white-haired Dutch psychoanalyst who, as Arthur liked to boast, had been "Freud's favorite disciple." Arthur called him "Van O," and he was Arthur's kind of guy: a Renaissance man who saw patients, did research, wrote papers, spoke multiple languages, and, in his spare time, boxed and played the organ. Arthur revered Van O, describing the older man as his "mentor, friend, and father."

In those days, psychiatry was not considered a premier field of medicine. On the contrary, in the words of one of Arthur's contemporaries, it was "a rather derelict career." Psychiatrists made less money than surgeons and general practitioners did, and they enjoyed less social and scientific cachet. After he completed his residency, Arthur wanted to continue his research into psychiatry, but he had no desire to open a practice in which he saw patients, and he still felt the need to make money to support his family; after all, he had his brothers' medical education to pay for. So Arthur found a job in the pharmaceutical industry, at Schering, the drug company where he had freelanced as a copywriter in his student days. For a salary of $8,000 a year, Arthur worked on Schering's medical research staff and in the firm's advertising department. After the United States joined the war, Arthur's poor eyesight kept him out of combat. But in lieu of military service, he started a new residency—at Creedmoor.

For millennia, doctors had sought to understand the mystery of mental illness. They had run through any number of theories, many of them crude and grotesque: in the ancient world, many believed madness was a result of an imbalance of bodily "humors," like black bile; in the Middle Ages, doctors thought that some forms of mental illness were the result of demonic possession. But whereas the first half of the twentieth century marked a period of enormous progress in other areas of medicine, by the time Arthur arrived at Creedmoor, American physicians were still largely mystified by the function and dysfunction of the human mind. They could recognize a condition like schizophrenia, but they could only guess at what might cause it, much less how to treat it. As the novelist Virginia Woolf (who suffered from mental illness herself) once observed, there is "a poverty of the language" when it comes to certain infirmities. "The merest schoolgirl, when she falls in love, has Shakespeare, Donne, Keats to speak her mind for her; but let a sufferer try to describe a pain in his head to a doctor and language at once runs dry."

When Arthur came of age as a physician, there were, broadly speaking, two opposing theories about the origins of mental illness. Many doctors believed that schizophrenia—and other conditions, like epilepsy, or intellectual disabilities—was hereditary. Patients were born with these conditions, and as such they were innate, immutable, and uncurable. The best that the medical community could do was to segregate such sorry cases from the rest of society—and, often, to sterilize these patients in order to prevent them from passing their afflictions on.

On the other end of the spectrum were the Freudians, who believed that mental conditions were *not* intrinsic and present at birth, but instead sprang from the patient's early lived experience. Freudians like Van O believed that many pathologies could be treated through therapy and analysis. But talk therapy was an expensive and bespoke solution and not practical for an industrial facility like Creedmoor to pursue.

Historically, the diagnosis of mental illness has often betrayed a notable gender imbalance: at Creedmoor, female patients outnumbered male patients by nearly two to one. When Arthur arrived, he was assigned to R Building, a special ward for "violent women." It could be a terrifying place. Sometimes, Arthur had to tackle his patients in order to restrain them. On other occasions, they attacked him. One woman assaulted him with a metal spoon that she had filed into a dagger. Even so, Arthur felt great compassion for his patients. What did it say about American society, he wondered, that these sensitive, suffering people had been isolated in walled communities, relegated to what he came to think of as "the limbo of the living dead"? It was folly to believe that locking these people up should be enough—that institutionalizing such patients somehow discharged the obligation of the community in general (and of doctors in particular) to relieve their suffering. "It almost seems as though society has anesthetized itself or deluded itself with the belief that such intense individual suffering and such mass destruction of human talents and capacities does not exist—because we have put it behind hospital walls," Arthur reflected at the time. Van O shared his distaste for public asylums. The United States was suffering from an epidemic of mental illness, Van O believed. To address it by imprisoning patients—to "bury" them in a mental hospital—was to consign them to a kind of death.

Arthur had a relentlessly analytical mind, and as he evaluated this dilemma, he concluded that the practical problem was that mental disorders appeared to be growing at a faster rate than the ability of the authorities to build asylums. A stroll through the overcrowded wards of Creedmoor would tell you that. What Arthur wanted to do was come up with a *solution*. Something that worked. The challenge, when it came to mental illness, was efficacy: perform a surgery, and you'll generally be able to judge, before too long, whether the procedure was a success. But tinkering with the brain was more difficult to measure. And the fact that it was hard to evaluate results in this manner had led to some truly outlandish experiments. Just a few decades earlier, the superintendent of a state hospital in New Jersey had become convinced that the way to cure insanity was to remove a patient's teeth. When some of his patients did not appear to respond to this course of treatment, the superintendent kept going, removing tonsils, colons, gallbladders, appendixes, fallopian tubes, uteruses, ovaries, cervixes. In the end, he cured no patients with these experiments, but he did kill more than a hundred of them.

The favored treatment at Creedmoor during this period was a procedure that was not as invasive but that Arthur nevertheless disdained:

electroshock therapy. The treatment had been invented some years earlier by an Italian psychiatrist who arrived at the idea after a visit to a slaughterhouse. Observing how pigs were stunned with a jolt of electricity just before they were killed, he devised a procedure in which electrodes were placed on the temples of a human patient so that a current of electricity could be administered to the temporal lobe and other regions of the brain where memory is processed. The shock caused the patient to convulse, then lapse into unconsciousness. When she came to, she was often disoriented and nauseous. Some patients experienced memory loss. Others felt profoundly shaken after the procedure and did not know who they were. But for all of its blunt force, electroshock therapy did seem to offer relief to many patients. It appeared to alleviate intense depression and to soothe people who were experiencing psychotic episodes; it might not have been a cure for schizophrenia, but it could often mitigate the symptoms.

Nobody understood *why* exactly this treatment might work. They just knew that it did. And at a place like Creedmoor, that was enough. The therapy was first used in the hospital in 1942 and was eventually administered to thousands of patients. To be sure, there were side effects. The convulsions that patients experienced as the electric charge pulsed through their heads were painful and deeply frightening. The poet Sylvia Plath, who was administered electroshock treatment at a hospital in Massachusetts during this period, described how it felt as if "a great jolt drubbed me till I thought my bones would break and the sap fly out of me like a split plant." The singer Lou Reed, who received electroshock treatment at Creedmoor in 1959, was temporarily debilitated by the ordeal, which left him, in the words of his sister, "stuporlike" and unable to walk.

Electroshock had its defenders, and even today it remains a widely used treatment for major depression. But Arthur Sackler hated it. Before long, at Creedmoor, every patient building was outfitted with an electroshock machine. Arthur was forced to perform the procedure again and again. Sometimes patients got better. Sometimes they didn't. But the treatment seemed so brutal—tying patients down so that they didn't hurt anyone when they flailed, adjusting the electrical current like the mad scientist in a Hollywood film—and it often left patients deeply traumatized.

Arthur had always urged his younger brothers to follow in his footsteps—at Erasmus, into the various part-time jobs he had secured for them, and ultimately into medicine. Now he recruited Mortimer and Raymond to join him at Creedmoor, and soon they too were administering shock therapy. Among them, the brothers conducted the procedure thousands of times, an experience they came to find demoralizing. They were disgusted at the limitations of their own medical knowledge—at the idea that there was no more humane therapy that they could offer.

As if electroshock therapy weren't bad enough, a far more severe technique was also coming into vogue: the lobotomy. This procedure, which involved severing nerves in the brain of a patient, appeared to alleviate psychological unrest. But it did so by, in effect, turning a light off in the brain. In overcrowded state hospitals like Creedmoor, it was an attractive procedure, because it was quick and efficient. "Nothing to it," one doctor explained, demonstrating how the procedure worked in 1952. "I take a sort of medical ice pick, hold it like this, bop it through the bones just above the eyeball, push it into the brain, swiggle it around, cut the brain fibers like this, and that's it. The patient doesn't feel a thing." The procedure really was that quick. The patients were often on their way home a few hours later. You could spot them leaving the hospital, because they had black eyes. Some patients—many of them women—were lobotomized not for schizophrenia or psychosis but for depression. The procedure was irreversible, rendering people pliable by turning them into zombies.

Confronted with this array of grisly techniques, Arthur Sackler and his brothers became convinced that there had to be a better solution to mental illness. Arthur did not believe that madness was immutable and untreatable, as the eugenicists suggested. But he also felt, even though he had trained as a Freudian, that one's lived experience could not fully account for mental illness—that there was a biochemical component—and there must be a more robust course of treatment than Freudian analysis. Arthur set to work finding an answer, some key that might unlock the mystery of mental illness and set these people free.

The head of Creedmoor was a doctor named Harry LaBurt who was not a man you would describe as particularly welcome to new ideas. LaBurt enjoyed the power that was conferred to him as head of the asylum. He lived in a grand home on the grounds of the hospital, known as the director's mansion. His office in the Administration Building was always locked: if you wanted to see him, you had to be buzzed in. LaBurt could sometimes seem not so much a physician as a prison warden. One of Arthur's contemporaries at Creedmoor described the place as "a six thousand bed jail." LaBurt liked the status quo and did not seem all that intent on conjuring new and creative solutions that might release these people from the walled kingdom over which he presided. "The board has observed, with a great deal of satisfaction, the beneficial effects of television on patients," one of Creedmoor's annual reports declared. To a restless and ambitious personality like Arthur Sackler, such complacency could only have rankled, and Arthur and LaBurt did not have a good relationship.

But in conversation with his brothers, Arthur started to think through the problem of mental illness. What if the eugenicists and the Freudians were both wrong? What if the answer lay not in the genes of the patient or in life experience but in derangements of brain chemistry?

✢ ✢ ✢

As it turned out, Marietta Lutze did not end up needing a job at Creedmoor: she found an internship at a different hospital in Queens. But when she went to visit Arthur Sackler to inquire about Creedmoor, he took advantage of the opportunity to ask her out again. This time, Marietta consented. As it happened, Arthur was due to attend a medical conference in Chicago, and he asked if she might like to accompany him. Marietta had been so focused on work since arriving in New York that she had not traveled anywhere else in the country. So she agreed. One day, she put on a black suit and a broad-brimmed hat and made her way to midtown Manhattan. They had agreed to meet at Grand Central Terminal. But they would not be taking a train. Instead, Marietta found Arthur waiting for her on the street outside the station by a massive, beautiful midnight-blue Buick Roadmaster convertible.

On the long drive to Chicago, Marietta told Arthur about her background. She had grown up in a comfortable family; they owned a well-known German pharmaceutical company, called Dr. Kade. Marietta recounted her experiences during the war. Even though she had been a medical student in Berlin, she maintained, she had little idea of the horrors unfolding around her. Many Americans, upon learning that she had recently emigrated from Germany, became hostile, challenging her about her personal history. But not Arthur. If he was skeptical of her account of the war, he did not express it. Instead, he listened intently.

Marietta had not been completely disconnected from the fighting. In fact, she had been married—to a German naval officer. His name was Kurt. He was a surgeon who was quite a bit older than she was; they met and married during the war but lived together for only a month before Kurt deployed. He was captured by American forces in Brest and sent to a prisoner of war camp. For a time, Kurt wrote her letters, little notes that he scribbled on cigarette paper and managed to smuggle out of the prison. But he was held captive for such a long period that eventually the marriage dissolved.

It could only have been strange for Arthur—an American Jew who had experienced anti-Semitism firsthand, who, as a student, had protested against the rise of Hitler, whose family loathed the Germans just as ardently, and probably more so, than other Americans did—to listen to Marietta's story. But then, until recently, Arthur himself had worked for a German-owned company, Schering. There might also have been something exotic about Marietta, this Teutonic bombshell who looked like Ingrid Bergman in *Casablanca* and was a medical doctor to boot. Xenophobia was on the rise in postwar America, but one abiding trait of Arthur Sackler's was an intense curiosity about people and cultures that were radically different from his own. Arthur said little about himself on the drive to Chicago, Marietta noticed, preferring to ask questions in his soothing voice. This made for a nice contrast to her previous experience with American men; so few of them seemed to take her seriously as an adult, much less a physician. But Arthur just absorbed her stories. At the time, this imbalance struck Marietta as a simple matter of unaffected curiosity. Only later would she come to recognize in Arthur's reserve a certain penchant for secrecy.

When they got back from Chicago and Marietta returned to Queens General Hospital, flowers started arriving at her ward by the bushel. It was an abundance of flowers, an *embarrassment* of flowers, with new bouquets appearing each day. Arthur, the onetime flower delivery boy, sent her elaborate corsages, the sort of thing Marietta could not possibly wear on her rounds. And he started to telephone her at the hospital, interrupting her work, at all hours, to express his ardor.

"I have to see you—now," he would say, in the middle of the night.

"I can't," Marietta would protest. "I'm exhausted."

"I have to see you," he pressed. "When?"

His sheer focus felt overwhelming. And yet there was something about Arthur Sackler—his life force, his won't-take-no-for-an-answer tenacity, his vision. When you were with Arthur, Marietta came to feel, it seemed as if anything were possible. There was no such thing as an insurmountable obstacle. In fact, by the time Marietta learned that Arthur Sackler, the man she had been seeing, already had a wife and two children, Arthur treated it as a mere detail, a minor technicality that should not slow the two of them down.

❖   ❖   ❖

One day at Creedmoor, the Sackler brothers chipped in a few dollars each to purchase a rabbit. If electroshock treatment worked, at least some of the time, the brothers wanted to understand why. What was it about zapping a patient's brain that brought him some measure of relief? They hooked the bunny up to an electroshock machine at Creedmoor, attaching electrodes to one of its floppy ears. Then they administered the shock. Observing the rabbit, the brothers noticed that the blood vessels in the ear immediately swelled full of blood. Seconds later, they noticed that the blood vessels in the bunny's *other* ear—the one that didn't receive the shock—were swelling, too. The electrical current appeared to have liberated some chemical that, once it circulated in the bloodstream to the opposite ear, dilated the vessels. At this point, the brothers remembered a body hormone called histamine, a chemical that they knew was released when tissues are injured, causing the vessels to dilate. What if the reason electrical shock treatment worked was that it was releasing histamine into the bloodstream, causing blood vessels to dilate and bring more oxygen to the brain? And if that was the case, couldn't it be possible to just administer histamine directly and cut out the shock altogether?

The Sacklers started conducting experiments on patients at Creedmoor. From a clinical point of view, the industrial scale of Creedmoor had always been a disadvantage; there were too many patients, too few staff, and always some emergency to attend to. But if you were studying mental illness, rather than just treating it, the size of the patient population became an advantage. It was a *data set*. Arthur was so excited by the prospect of this research that he lured his old mentor, Van O, to join the brothers at Creedmoor.

When they injected forty patients who had been diagnosed as schizophrenic with histamine, nearly a third of them improved to a degree where they could be sent home. Some patients who had not responded to any other course of treatment *did* respond to histamine. Drawing on this research, the Sackler brothers proceeded to publish more than a hundred medical papers. Their aim was, as they put it, to trace "the chemical causes of insanity." With his unusual experience as an editor, a marketing director, and an adman, Arthur knew how to attract breathless press coverage. "The doctors think they have found a means of treating mental ailments without hospitalization," *The Philadelphia Inquirer* announced. The brothers predicted that their discovery might double the number of patients who could be released. An article in *Better Homes and Gardens* suggested, with ample hyperbole, that "the chemical activity theory of the Sacklers is as revolutionary, and almost as complicated, as Einstein's relativity."

There was a sense, in their press clippings, that this trio of brothers at a mental hospital in Queens might have stumbled upon a solution to a medical riddle that had bedeviled societies for thousands of years. If the problem of mental illness originated in brain chemistry, then perhaps chemistry could provide the solution. What if, in the future, the cure for insanity was as simple as taking a pill? The *Brooklyn Eagle* celebrated the Sacklers as neighborhood boys made good. "It was just a case of the three Erasmus Hall High School students—brothers—following the same trail," the paper stated, adding, "They all have offices in Manhattan now."

These press accounts seldom differentiated among the brothers, referring to them simply as "the Sacklers," but Arthur remained the leading man—a position of authority that was only reinforced when Isaac Sackler died. The brothers were at Creedmoor when they learned that he'd had a heart attack, and they rushed to his bedside. In his final hours, Isaac's mind was still clear, and he took fond leave of his family. He told Sophie that he still remembered the blue dress she was wearing the first time he laid eyes on her. And he told his sons that he regretted not being able to leave them with any inheritance, apart from their good name. This had become a mantra for Isaac. If you lose a fortune, you can always earn another, he pointed out. But if you lose your good name, you can never get it back.

After his father's death Arthur started using his own money to subsidize his research with Raymond and Mortimer, and in many of the papers they published, a line of attribution would mention that the work was made possible "by grants made in the memory of Isaac Sackler." Arthur was generally the first credited author, the prime mover. A photo in the *New York Herald Tribune* captured the brothers accepting a prize: there was Raymond, with a slightly goofy smile and the soft skin of the baby brother; Mortimer, with thick black-framed glasses, his dark hair slicked back, his full lips pursed, a cigarette between his fingers; and Arthur, in profile, wearing a suit with peaked lapels and gazing benevolently at his brothers. The Sacklers looked as if they were on the cusp of something. They told people that their research might ultimately "prevent insanity."

✣   ✣   ✣

Arthur had been married since 1934, when he was still in medical school. His wife, Else Jorgensen, was an émigré, the daughter of a Danish ship's captain. They had been introduced by a college friend of Arthur's. Marrying was against academic policy at the medical school, so initially Arthur kept it a secret. Else had done two years at NYU but dropped out because she needed to make money. They moved in to a furnished unit on St. Mary's Place, near Lincoln Hospital in the Bronx, and then to an apartment on West Twenty-Fifth Street in Manhattan. In 1941, their first daughter, Carol, was born, followed by another daughter, Elizabeth, in 1943.

Nevertheless, when Marietta learned that Arthur had a family—had this whole other life—she couldn't help but feel that his focus remained, unwaveringly, on her. One night not long after they returned from Chicago, he took her to an Italian restaurant on Mulberry Street in Little Italy, the Grotta Azzurra. It was a romantic spot, and Arthur told Marietta that he wanted to see her more often.

"I'm too exhausted," she protested. "The hospital is taking everything out of me."

Arthur didn't want to hear it. After all, he, too, was working hard—at *several* jobs—and he had a family at home to boot. Yet he managed to make time for Marietta, and he wanted to find more.

"I want to be with you. All the time," he told her.

"You know, Arthur, you're the kind of man I could marry," Marietta said. "But I don't want to break up your marriage."

Arthur was undeterred. He wrote love letters, suggesting, in the summer of 1949, that they "start a new life," a life "full of hope, of joy and of passion." What Arthur proposed to Marietta was a partnership, and one with a distinctly public spirit. "We will join and work as one to help people, to pioneer new fields and make our contribution…to mankind." Eventually, his letters became more insistent. "Life has literally become impossible without you," he wrote. "I love you and you alone…I belong to you and you alone."

Still, they both felt some ambivalence. Marietta was focused on her career in medicine and had her family back in Germany to think about. Her grandmother had recently died, and Marietta had inherited the family drug company. She was also starting to realize that Arthur was prone to indecision and had a tendency to let things drift along. He had always done everything, taken every class, worked every job. He tended to respond to any either-or type of choice by simply opting for both. He was not someone who took well to limitation. Arthur had a wife, children, and a number of budding careers. There might have been some sense in which he could have been comfortable just adding Marietta to the mix. "It was always very difficult for him to make clear-cut choices," she would reflect much later, adding, "The fact that I was pregnant forced a decision."

Chapter 3

MED MAN

IN 1949, AN UNUSUAL advertisement started to appear in a number of medical journals. "Terra bona," it said, in bold brown letters against a green backdrop. It wasn't clear what "Terra bona" meant, exactly— or, for that matter, if there was any specific product the advertisement was supposed to be selling. "The great earth has given man more than bread alone," a caption read, noting that new antibiotics discovered in the soil had succeeded in extending human life. "In the isolation, screening and production of such vital agents, a notable role has been played by ... *Pfizer.*"

For nearly a century, the Brooklyn firm Chas. Pfizer & Company had been a modest supplier of chemicals. Until World War II, outfits like Pfizer sold chemicals in bulk, without brand names, whether to other companies or to pharmacists (who would mix the chemicals them- selves). Then, in the early 1940s, the introduction of penicillin ushered in a new era of antibiotics—powerful medications that can stop infec- tions caused by bacteria. When the war broke out, the U.S. military needed great quantities of penicillin to administer to the troops, and companies like Pfizer were enlisted to produce the drug. By the time the war ended, the business model of these chemical companies had forever changed: now they were mass-producing not just chemicals but finished drugs, which were ready for sale. Penicillin was a revolution- ary medicine, but it wasn't patented, which meant that anyone could produce it. Because no company held a monopoly, it remained cheap and, thus, not particularly lucrative. So Pfizer, emboldened, began to hunt for other remedies that it *could* patent and sell at a higher price.

This was the era of the "miracle drug": the postwar years were a boom time for the pharmaceutical industry, and there was a wide- spread optimism about the potential of scientific innovation to devise unheard-of chemical solutions that would curb death and disease and generate untold profits for drugmakers. The same utopian promise that the Sacklers had been evangelizing for at Creedmoor—the idea that any human malady might one day be cured with a pill—was beginning to take hold in the culture at large. By the 1950s, the American pharmaceutical industry was introducing a new drug of one sort or another almost every week.

These new treatments were known as "ethical drugs," a comforting designation meant to signify that they weren't the sort of witch's brew you might buy off the back of a wagon; they were medications that were only marketed to—and prescribed by—a doctor. But because there were so many new products, the pharma companies turned to advertisers in order to come up with creative ways to make patients and doctors aware of their innovations. The president of Pfizer was a dynamic young executive named John McKeen. His company had recently developed a new antibiotic called Terramycin, which took its name from the city of Terre Haute, Indiana, where Pfizer scientists had supposedly isolated the chemical in a clump of soil. McKeen thought that if the drug was marketed right, it might really take off. He wanted to pitch it aggressively to wholesalers and hospitals, so he turned to a boutique agency in New York that specialized in pharmaceutical advertising. The agency was called William Douglas McAdams. But the man who owned it—and handled the Pfizer account—was Arthur Sackler.

"You give me the money," Arthur told McKeen and his colleagues, "and I'm going to make Terramycin and the name of your company household words."

William Douglas McAdams was a former newspaperman from Winnetka, Illinois, who had written for the *St. Louis Post-Dispatch* before quitting journalism in 1917 to get into advertising. Initially, he ran a traditional agency, advertising a range of products, from Mother's Oats to Van Camp's Beans. But one of his accounts was cod liver oil, which was manufactured by a pharmaceutical company, E. R. Squibb. McAdams had an idea: Squibb might sell more cod liver oil if the product was marketed directly to doctors. So he placed an ad in a medical journal. It worked. Sales went up, and by the late 1930s McAdams decided to focus exclusively on the pharmaceutical sector. In 1942, he hired Arthur Sackler.

Arthur was not yet thirty at the time, but because he had vaulted directly into adulthood during the Depression, and worked his way through high school, college, and medical school by selling and writing ads, when McAdams hired him, he'd already been working in the industry for half his life. In addition to his medical training, Arthur had a strong visual sensibility and a nimble way with language. He also had a knack for cultivating mentors. Just as he had apprenticed himself to Van O in psychiatry, he now did the same with McAdams (or "Mac," as Arthur called him) in advertising. Arthur might have been an exemplary candidate for the job, but he was grateful to Mac for hiring him, because he regarded the ad industry on Madison Avenue as "largely a closed club" when it came to Jews. With his light eyes and fair hair, Arthur could pass for a gentile, and occasionally did. But he was sensitive to anti-Semitism, which was pervasive, even in New York.

Officially, the McAdams job was a part-time gig, because Arthur already *had* a full-time job at Creedmoor. So on nights and weekends, he would spend long hours in the ad firm's midtown offices. But the opportunity to combine his interests in medicine, marketing, and pharmaceuticals proved irresistible, and Arthur thrived at McAdams. The marketing of ethical drugs had traditionally been a staid business, compared with other types of consumer advertising. While ad execs devised snappy campaigns for cigarettes, cars, and cosmetics, historically most prescription drugs had been generic, with no brand names and little product differentiation. Besides, drugs weren't sexy. How do you sell a pill?

Arthur's answer was to adopt the seductive pizzazz of more traditional advertising—catchy copy, splashy graphics—and to market directly to an influential constituency: the prescribers. Arthur had inherited from his parents a reverence for the medical profession. "I would rather place myself and my family at the judgment and mercy of a fellow physician than that of the state," he liked to say. So, in selling new drugs, he devised campaigns that would appeal directly to clinicians, placing eye-catching ads in medical journals and distributing literature to doctors' offices. Seeing that physicians were most heavily influenced by their own peers, he enlisted prominent doctors to endorse his products. It was the equivalent, for physicians, of putting Mickey Mantle on a box of Wheaties. At Arthur's direction, drug companies cited scientific studies (which had often been underwritten by the companies themselves) as evidence of the efficacy and safety of each new drug. John Kallir, who worked under Arthur for ten years at

McAdams, recalled, "Sackler's ads had a very serious, clinical look—a physician talking to a physician. But it was advertising."

Arthur could be self-important, particularly when it came to the nobility of medicine. But he had a quick wit, and he imbued his work with a winking sense of play. One Terramycin ad was designed to look like a vision test at an optometrist's office:

O

CU

LAR

INFEC

TIONS

RESPOND

TO BROAD

SPECTRUM

TERRAMYCIN

Two years after Arthur started working at McAdams, Mac made him president of the company. Pfizer was a big client, and Arthur handled the account directly, making his way to the company's headquarters at 11 Bartlett Street, in Brooklyn, to see John McKeen himself. (Privately, Arthur referred to these excursions as visits to "the lion's den.") Arthur was, in the words of one of his contemporaries, "an unparalleled idea man." And Terramycin was a new kind of antibiotic—a "broad spectrum" drug. The first antibiotics were so-called narrow spectrum, meaning that they were designed to address specific ailments. But new drugs were now being developed to treat an ever-wider range of maladies. For a drug company, this was a profitable strategy: you don't want to niche a product; you want to sell it to as great a range of patients as possible. The term "broad spectrum" sounds clinical, but the truth is, it was coined by advertisers: it first entered the medical literature with Arthur's campaign for Terramycin.

That initial green-and-brown "Terra bona" advertisement didn't even mention Terramycin. What Arthur was really selling was the *promise* of some new product and the fact that it would be brought to you by Pfizer. Arthur knew, intuitively, that the brand name of the company was as important as the name of the drug, and he had promised to make Pfizer, with its exotic silent *P*, a household name. The "teaser"—

in which an advertisement hints, with great fanfare, at the impending arrival of some new product—had been employed in other areas of consumer marketing before. But until Arthur Sackler used it for Terramycin, it had never been done in pharma advertising.

Next, Arthur worked with McKeen to launch an unprecedented marketing blitz. The shock troops in this campaign were the so-called detail men—young, polished sales representatives who could visit doctors in their offices, armed with promotional literature, and talk about the values of a drug. Initially, there were only eight detail men working on Terramycin. But they promoted the new drug so aggressively that, in the words of one press account at the time, they set "something of a speed record...for the trip from laboratory to wide clinical use." Within eighteen months, Pfizer had increased its sales force from those eight men to three hundred. By 1957, they would have two thousand. Terramycin wasn't a particularly groundbreaking product, but it became a huge success because it was marketed in a way that no drug ever had been. It was Arthur Sackler who would be credited not just with this campaign but with revolutionizing the whole field of medical advertising. In the words of one of his longtime employees at McAdams, when it came to the marketing of pharmaceuticals, "Arthur invented the wheel."

Henceforth, medicine would be pitched to doctors on more or less the same terms as swimwear or auto insurance was marketed to average consumers. To sell broad-spectrum antibiotics, Arthur would employ a broad-spectrum advertising strategy. In addition to the lavish spreads in medical journals, detail men would drop by doctors' offices, maybe volunteer to buy them a meal, and leave behind some official-looking medical literature. An avalanche of direct mail also went to physicians, informing them about new products. "The doctor is feted and courted by drug companies with the ardor of a spring love affair," one commentator observed. "The industry covets his soul and his prescription pad because he is in a unique economic position; he tells the consumer what to buy."

The seduction was intense, and it started early. Just as Arthur had distributed free rulers stamped with the name of his business school clients to students at Erasmus High, the drug company Eli Lilly started offering free stethoscopes to students in medical schools. Another company, Roche, provided free textbooks, on sleeping problems, alcoholism, anxiety—all afflictions that Roche happened to have ideas about how to fix. Pfizer eventually started organizing golf tournaments in which the company name was stamped on all the balls. This paradigm shift toward promotion and brand differentiation was an instant success. Just a few years after Arthur initiated the Terramycin campaign, *The New York Times* remarked that "more and more physicians are specifying by brand or manufacturer's name" the products to be used in filling prescriptions.

Not everyone was thrilled about this new synergy between medicine and commerce. "Is the public likely to benefit if practicing physicians and medical educators must perform their duties amidst the clamor and striving of merchants seeking to increase the sales of drugs?" Charles May, a prominent professor at the Columbia Medical School, wondered. He worried about what he described as "an unwholesome entanglement" between the people who prescribe our medicines and the people who make and market them.

But Arthur brushed off such critiques on the grounds that what he was doing wasn't advertising at all. It was education. There were so many new drugs coming onto the market that doctors needed help knowing what was out there. Arthur was merely a facilitator in a benevolent cycle whereby drug companies developed new lifesaving remedies, admen informed physicians about them, and physicians prescribed the remedies to their patients, saving lives. Nobody was looking to exploit or deceive anybody else, Arthur argued. After all, in his view, doctors were unimpeachable. It was laughable, he asserted, to suggest that a physician might be seduced by a glossy layout in a medical journal in the same manner that a housewife might be swayed by a slick ad in a magazine. The doctor's job is to look out for the patient, Arthur argued in one unpublished polemic, and neither doctors nor patients need any advocate or referee to protect them against misleading advertising, because they are not "so obtuse as to be deceived for long."

Arthur felt as if he had seen the future, and it was a future in which drug companies and drug advertisers would bring fantastic innovations to the public—and make a lot of money at the same time. These naysayers seemed to want to put the brakes on the tremendously exciting medical progress that was happening all around them. What they really wanted, Arthur believed, was to "turn back the hands of the clock."

By the time he launched the Terramycin campaign, Arthur had

bought the agency from McAdams. Mac was "old and tired," as one agency employee who knew both men put it, and Arthur was brilliant and full of energy. When Arthur was inducted into the Medical Advertising Hall of Fame, half a century later, the citation would say, "No single individual did more to shape the character of medical advertising than the multi-talented Dr. Arthur Sackler." It was Arthur, the citation continued, who brought "the full power of advertising and promotion to pharmaceutical marketing."

✦ ✦ ✦

One day in February 1950, with the Terramycin campaign in full swing, Arthur, Mortimer, and Raymond joined their mentor Van O for the opening of their own research center—the Creedmoor Institute for Psychobiologic Studies. The new institute would be housed on the grounds of the asylum, in H Building, where sixty-two rooms would be devoted to the treatment of patients and studies in histamine and other alternatives to shock therapy. It was a triumph for Arthur. But while he was indisputably the driving force behind the institute, he chose to install Van O as the director and public face. Arthur would assume a lesser title: "director of research." This might simply have been a gesture of deference to his mentor. But with the exigencies of juggling two full-time jobs, at the advertising agency he was running in midtown and at the state asylum in Queens, Arthur was also finding that for someone with a range of potentially conflicting commitments, it can occasionally be most prudent to operate behind the scenes.

Even so, he liked a little fanfare and knew how to mark an occasion. Four hundred people came out for the opening. The dedication was performed by the president of the United Nations General Assembly. Even Harry LaBurt, the imperious and unimaginative director of Creedmoor, with whom Arthur had tangled in the past, had no choice but to make an appearance and salute the achievement of his precocious subordinate. Van O gave a speech announcing the grand designs that he and the Sackler brothers had for the center. They would figure out how to diagnose mental disease earlier and how to use biochemistry to treat it. With the opening of this institute, Van O promised, they would usher in "a golden era in psychiatry."

Several miles away, in a room in New York Hospital, in lower Manhattan, Marietta Lutze was in labor. Arthur had a lot going on in his life, and by unfortunate coincidence he had been forced to choose between being present for the birth of his institute and the birth of his child. He chose the institute. Upon learning that Marietta was pregnant, Arthur had decided to leave his wife, Else. They took a family vacation to Mexico, where they obtained a quickie divorce. (A privately published account drawn from Arthur's own recollections and published by a family foundation would paint the separation as not just amicable but inevitable and suggest that Else "accepted that Sackler was an extraordinary achiever and she could simply not keep up with him.")

When Arthur returned from Mexico, he and Marietta were hastily and quietly married, in December 1949. They moved to suburban Long Island, buying a house on Searingtown Road in Albertson. It took them a while to find their new home, because Arthur would not settle for anything too conventional: he wanted a residence that was unique and remarkable, and because he was prospering in the advertising business now, money was not a concern. They found an old Dutch farmhouse that had originally been constructed around 1700, in Flushing, and subsequently transplanted to Albertson. It was surrounded by boxwood trees and had exposed beams, double Dutch doors, and hand-pegged, wide-planked floors. Marietta found the place a bit dark, but it must have appealed to Arthur's romance with the past. The house dated to the same era as the old Dutch schoolhouse in the center of Erasmus Hall High School.

Marietta was very happy to be with Arthur, but the transition had not been easy. His mother, Sophie, fiercely disapproved of the marriage, because it had ended Arthur's first marriage and because Marietta was a German gentile. Much later, a friend of Arthur's would describe Marietta as having "fled the Nazis in Germany," a fiction that made her sound like some sort of resister or a persecuted Jew. But at the time, this fantasy was more difficult to sustain. For the first few years of the marriage, Sophie refused to speak to Marietta or acknowledge her existence. Marietta enjoyed a friendly relationship with Mortimer and Raymond, whom she had met on her own terms, before she was with Arthur, but she still felt like an interloper in the close-knit Sackler family. "I was seen as the intruder who forced him into a marriage," she wrote later, "compounded by the fact that I came from a country so hated and despised."

On the day Marietta went into labor, Arthur had driven her to the hospital. But as the hour of the Creedmoor dedication approached, he took his leave and hastened to Queens. She let him go; she knew how much the institute meant to him. She gave birth that day to a baby boy. He was slight, long-legged, and wrinkly. It is not typical in Jewish families to name sons after their fathers, but Marietta chose the name Arthur Felix. She wanted to identify the baby with his father—to pass on the good name. There might have also been, in the choice of name, a bid for legitimacy, a hedge against any suggestion that the offspring of the second wife was anything less than a full-blooded Sackler. Marietta felt, after the birth, as though she had taken on a new relevance, having played a part in the dynastic process, as if giving birth to the firstborn son had elevated her status within the family. After the Creedmoor dedication, Arthur raced back to the hospital to greet his child. Ray and Morty came, too. They brought flowers.

When she got pregnant, Marietta had elected to give up work, a decision Arthur welcomed but about which she felt some misgivings. So she went home to take care of the baby, and Arthur would drive into the city for long days at Creedmoor followed by long nights at McAdams. In the evening, with the baby asleep, Marietta would prepare dinner for her husband, change—he liked it when she dressed for dinner—light candles, and wait for him to come home.

Rather than cutting back on his professional commitments in order to accommodate his new family, Arthur now took on more projects than ever. He became editor of the *Journal of Clinical and Experimental Psychobiology*. He started a medical publishing company. He launched a news service for physicians, became the president of the Medical Radio and Television Institute, and started a round-the-clock radio service, which was sponsored by pharmaceutical companies. He opened a laboratory for therapeutic research at the Brooklyn College of Pharmacy, on Long Island. There was a frenzy to this activity; he seemed to file articles of incorporation for some new entity every week. His rationale for setting up these outlets was that he and his brothers were doing such terrific research at Creedmoor but people didn't *know* about it. Arthur was aiming, with his new publishing ventures, to fill that gap. He would tell people, with his customary grandiosity, that he was working in the tradition of Hippocrates, who not only saw patients but was an educator as well. Marietta thought of her new husband as Atlas, the great bronze statue that stood outside Rockefeller Center, holding the world on his muscular shoulders.

The metamorphosis of the outer-borough child of the Depression seemed complete. Arthur Sackler was an accomplished researcher and adman, with a commensurate sense of his own importance. Some of the old-timers at McAdams, people who had known him since his school days, still called him "Artie," but most of the world knew him now as "Dr. Sackler." He wore elegant suits and carried himself with an air of authority. He thrived on power and adulation and seemed to derive new energy from it, as if he had found a way to metabolize other people's admiration. He had mostly shed his Brooklyn accent, and in its place he cultivated a sophisticated mid-Atlantic diction. He still spoke softly, but with a silken, cultured assuredness.

One day just over a month after the birth of his son, Arthur joined Van O on a trip to Washington to testify in a congressional hearing. In a hall on Capitol Hill, the two doctors appeared before a Senate subcommittee to request funds for their institute at Creedmoor. "The approach to mental disease as a biochemical disorder will do more than increase the discharge rate of patients from mental hospitals," Arthur promised the senators. "Biochemical therapy can help to keep more patients *out* of mental hospitals." Why not address these problems in the doctor's office? he argued. "Certainly prevention is a better way than just limiting our efforts to building more and more institutions."

The subcommittee chairman, a senator from New Mexico named Dennis Chavez, was not convinced. What if the federal government were to allocate funds for this type of research, and the doctors at Creedmoor, having gotten the benefit of this valuable, government-subsidized training, then turn around and go into private practice? he wondered. "Should this work be done for the benefit of the people as a whole? Or should it be done for the benefit of psychiatrists?"

Arthur, with his abiding belief in the bedrock integrity of the medical profession, took issue with the premise of the question. "The basic function of the physician *is* the interest of the people as a whole," he said.

"That is right," Chavez replied. "But I have known some that are regular Merchants of Venice."

For an instant, Arthur reeled. Coded anti-Semitism was a routine feature of American life in 1950, even in the U.S. Senate. But *Merchant of Venice*? The reference was so obvious it was hardly a code at all. Did the committee take Arthur for some Shylock, looking to hoodwink them out of their precious appropriations?

"I have been fortunate ...," Arthur began.

But Chavez, mishearing him, interrupted. "It is *un*-fortunate," he barked.

"I have been fortunate," Arthur continued, with as much dignity as he could muster, "that I have not met them."

✣   ✣   ✣

Whatever prejudice Arthur might encounter in the outside world, at the McAdams agency he was king. Word had spread in advertising circles that exciting things were happening under Sackler's leadership, and, in the words of one former employee, the firm became a "magnet" for talent. Arthur had an eye for good people, and he started hiring copywriters and artists, luring them away from other agencies. He was an unusually open-minded employer by the standards of the day. If you had talent and drive, he didn't much care about other prerequisites. He hired many Jews, at a time when they couldn't find work at other agencies. "Sackler had a soft spot for hiring refugees from Europe," Rudi Wolff, an artist and designer who worked for McAdams in the 1950s, recalled. There were Holocaust survivors and people who had fled poverty and upheaval. "There were people who were physicians," Wolff continued. "PhDs who would never be working for an ad agency, but he sniffed them out. People who couldn't find work easily, because they had accents. We had Blacks. Some of the writers he hired had suffered under the McCarthy hearings and could not get work. But Arthur hired them." On one occasion, a Swedish designer, who was a communist, made a scene by starting a small fire in the office and burning some of McAdams's own advertisements, to indicate his distaste for such "capitalist trash." "The art director scolded him," Wolff recalled. "We all thought it was hilarious. But he kept coming in."

Arthur had flirted with communism himself during the 1930s, getting involved with labor organizing during his medical school years and joining an anti-Fascist organization. This was not at all unusual for young people who had come of age in Brooklyn during the Great Depression: there was a widespread sentiment, during those years, that capitalism had failed. Mortimer appears to have shared these views, and according to the declassified files of an FBI investigation, Raymond became a card-carrying member of the Communist Party, along with his wife, a young woman named Beverly Feldman, whom he married in 1944. "McAdams had many politically dubious people," John Kallir, who went to work for Arthur during this period, recalled, before adding, wryly, "Which appealed to me."

The firm occupied several floors of a building at 25 West Forty-Third Street, and the place had a freewheeling, bohemian vibe. One of their downstairs neighbors was *The New Yorker*, and Kallir and his colleagues were delighted to discover, one day, that the famous cartoonist Charles Addams, creator of the macabre series *The Addams Family*, worked at a desk several floors below. As a joke, a few of the artists used the Photostat to print a picture of a baby, then attached it to a piece of string and lowered it out the window, like a fishing lure, so that it would float into Addams's line of sight. After a few minutes, they felt a slight tug on the line and reeled it back in, to discover that Addams had punched a little bullet hole into the baby's forehead.

"We had oodles of money to spend on artwork, and artists would come in with their portfolios," Rudi Wolff recalled. One young artist who visited the office was Andy Warhol. "Being art director and having all this money, I would say, 'Andy, do ten heads of children, nice drawings,'" Wolff continued. "He drew beautifully." Warhol liked to draw cats. McAdams used one of his cat pictures for an Upjohn ad.

Arthur might have cultivated a loose, creative atmosphere, but that didn't mean he was easy to work for. In the words of Tony D'Onofrio, another former employee, he was "controversial, unsettling, and difficult." Arthur was hard driving, and he drove those around him hard. Because he had experience as a copywriter, he felt no compunction about micromanaging. Even Arthur's benevolence had an edge to it. When Jewish employees came to him and insisted on a raise, Arthur would refuse, citing the prevailing anti-Semitism in the industry and saying, "Where else are you going to go?" When a copywriter got a job offer from Eli Lilly, Arthur scoffed, "Lilly? They don't like Jews. They're going to get rid of you in a month."

"We weren't paid terribly well," Rudi Wolff recalled. "But nobody left."

Wolff was Jewish himself and kept strictly kosher. When he got engaged, Arthur surprised him by throwing a party to celebrate at the house on Searingtown Road. Arthur and Marietta had the party catered, and Arthur was careful to arrange for kosher offerings, which were marked with little flags bearing the Star of David. Wolff was touched, yet at the same time he saw some artifice in the gesture. "It sort of helped his image," he recalled; it enabled Arthur to play the part of sensitive, humane employer. "I wasn't stupid," Wolff said. "He was doing it for me, but he was also doing it for himself." As another colleague from those years, Harry Zelenko, recalled, "Artie could be quite charming. But he was also, basically, a selfish man."

When Arthur arrived at McAdams, he had one obvious rival: a young woman named Helen Haberman, who was another protégée of McAdams's and who some thought would go on to take over the firm when Mac retired. Haberman wrote a novel, a roman à clef about the life of a young woman working at a Manhattan ad agency, in which one character is an ambitious young New Yorker who speaks with great excitement about the experiments he is doing with hormones and biochemistry and who would "keep right on working at it three hundred and sixty-five days a year until there wouldn't be many other men around who had worked as long or with that intensity." But it was difficult enough for a woman to advance as an advertising executive in the 1940s, much less take over the agency. "Artie outsmarted her and took over," Harry Zelenko recalled. "He was a tough customer."

"He wasn't a backslapper," another former McAdams employee, Phil Keusch, said. "You felt like if you were involved with him at all, you'd kind of earned it." But everyone in the advertising world seemed to recognize that they were witnessing a once-in-a-generation talent. "If you asked me to define the term 'genius,' I would attribute it to him," Keusch continued. "I would see him in meetings with the clients. Upjohn. Roche. He would take over. It all boiled down, ultimately, to him. You'd have all these people around the table, all these titles. But he was the one who made the most sense. I thought he was the most brilliant person I'd ever met. In essence, he created the business."

✣ ✣ ✣

Arthur did appear to have one major rival in the industry. McAdams was not the only advertising firm to devote itself exclusively to pharmaceuticals. It jockeyed for dominance with another firm called

L. W. Frohlich. Named after its enigmatic president, Ludwig Wolf-gang Frohlich, who went by Bill, the agency seemed to handle every big account that McAdams didn't. Bill Frohlich was a debonair German émigré who lived in a brownstone on East Sixty-Third Street. His firm occupied a nine-story brick office building on Fifty-First. Frohlich boasted that his was "probably the largest agency" focusing on pharmaceuticals, but he shared with Arthur Sackler a penchant for secrecy and refused to divulge his billing, so it was impossible to know for sure. Frohlich was a smooth-talking evangelist for pharmaceutical advertising who liked to highlight the swashbuckling glamour of his line of work. "We are living in the midst of a pharmacological revolution," he would say. "The concept of conscious, directed effort to develop specific drugs to combat specific diseases…has captured the imagination of all."

As it happened, Frohlich had once worked for Sackler. In his early days at Schering, Arthur had hired Frohlich to do type design. Arthur's first wife, Else Sackler, would later say, recalling how she first met Frohlich around 1937, "He started out being an art director doing work for others. Art work for other agencies. That was really his gift." At the time, Frohlich had arrived only recently from Germany. He was not a doctor, like Arthur, but he had a good eye. In 1943, he opened his own agency. Before long, the Frohlich agency and McAdams found themselves in a zero-sum relationship: if a big account was not at one firm, it was at the other.

Frohlich had a reputation as a bon vivant: he was a fixture at the opera and threw parties at his beach house on Long Island. But he was very controlled and disciplined. He once remarked that the pharmaceutical industry was characterized by "a competitive zeal" that would "have warmed Adam Smith's heart." In "the pharmaceutical art," as Frohlich rather grandly put it, you have to make your money "in the interval between marketing and obsolescence."

Arthur Sackler acknowledged this competitive reality. "We operate in an area of incredibly intense competition," he once observed, noting that to secure and hold each account, he had to fend off "twenty rival agencies." But the biggest competitor appeared to be Frohlich. *Advertising Age* described the rivalry, calling them "the two top ones in the field." John Kallir put it bluntly: "Frohlich and McAdams dominated."

Some people who knew Frohlich thought that there must be more to him than met the eye. With his German accent and punctilious manner, some wondered if he might be concealing a secret Nazi past. In fact, the FBI had investigated Frohlich during the war, to determine whether he had links to Hitler's regime. But he didn't. On the contrary: Frohlich was Jewish. Arthur might have occasionally passed for a gentile, but Frohlich had fully inhabited the role, obscuring and denying, from his earliest days in the United States, this aspect of his identity. Many of his closest friends and associates did not know, until long after his death, that he was Jewish. Nor did they know that he was gay and living a scrupulously closeted life. But this was not entirely unusual in the mid-century circles in which Frohlich moved, in which certain men led multiple lives, some public, others cloaked in secrecy.

✣ ✣ ✣

"The momentum of the business does not reflect its billing, but continues to accelerate at a giddy rate," Arthur wrote to a friend in 1954, noting that his responsibilities seemed to be multiplying: "A million and one things are happening." It must have seemed to all three Sackler brothers that the hypotheses they had been dreaming up at Creedmoor were now being borne out. Smith, Kline & French had recently introduced a new drug, Thorazine, which was precisely the sort of antipsychotic silver bullet that the brothers had envisaged. Patients who had formerly been aggressive were rendered docile. Asylums were able to reintroduce matches so that psychotic patients could light their own cigarettes, without fear that they might set the hospital on fire. Arthur didn't handle the advertising for the drug, but he might have: Smith, Kline's slogan was that Thorazine keeps "patients out of mental hospitals." In 1955, the annual intake of patients to American psychiatric facilities declined for the first time in a quarter of a century. The coming decades would witness the great deinstitutionalization of the mentally ill in America, as the wards at asylums like Creedmoor began to empty out. The success of Thorazine was hardly the only factor driving this seismic change, but it did seem to substantiate the theory to which Arthur subscribed—that mental illness was caused by brain chemistry, rather than immutable genetic tendency or a traumatic upbringing or flawed character. In fact, Thorazine created a whole new research agenda for scientists: if you could address mental illness by tinkering with chemical deficiencies in the brain, surely there were other afflictions that could be cured in a similar fashion. As one historian put it, "Helping schizophrenics would be only the beginning." A new era was now under way in which a pill might be devised for practically any ailment.

Arthur felt this excitement, and he seemed forever to be dreaming up new synergies between pharmaceutical science and commerce. Working with Pfizer, he helped introduce one of the first forms of "native advertising"—as paid promotion that is camouflaged to resemble editorial content is known—when the company included a sixteen-page color supplement in the Sunday *New York Times*. (The *Times* later maintained that the supplement was "plainly labeled" as advertising but acknowledged that it was "intended to be taken as editorial matter by the casual reader.") For someone who portrayed himself as a champion of open communication, Arthur was demonstrating a persistent tendency to inflect the truth when it was advantageous to him (or to his clients) to do so. And it often was.

He revealed a preference, during this period, for concealing his own hand in things as frequently as he could. After taking over McAdams, he gave half of the stock to his first wife, Else. This was a gift, which he bestowed in lieu of a divorce settlement. But it was also a fig leaf. Else played no meaningful role in the management of the company, but her formal ownership created a zone of plausible deniability in which Arthur could claim that his personal stake was smaller than it was. He was happy to defer credit if it meant he could remain behind the scenes.

As it happened, Arthur was also nursing a more serious secret—a secret that he would take to his grave but that he shared, during his lifetime, with Bill Frohlich: one of the entities in which Arthur possessed a clandestine stake was his ostensible rival, the L. W. Frohlich agency. To the outside world, Sackler and Frohlich were competitors. But the truth was, Arthur had helped Frohlich set up his business, staking him money, sending him clients, and, ultimately, colluding with him in secret to divvy up the pharmaceutical business. "It was very, very important at that time to . . . make sure you could get as much business as possible," Arthur's longtime attorney, Michael Sonnenreich, would explain, decades later. The challenge was that because of conflict of interest rules no single agency could handle two accounts for competing products. "So what they did was, they set up two agencies," Sonnenreich said. This arrangement was "not illegal," he insisted. But he acknowledged that it was deliberately constructed in order to mask a clear conflict of interest.

Arthur Sackler and Bill Frohlich were lifelong friends. A number of executives at L. W. Frohlich developed a suspicion that Sackler might have a financial stake in the agency. But Arthur himself always denied it. The truth was, he did have a stake, and not just a minority interest. According to Sonnenreich, Arthur was the controlling force behind the agency: "Frohlich's firm, basically, was Arthur's."

But the bond between the two ran deeper still. It wasn't just Arthur who was close with Bill Frohlich: Mortimer and Raymond Sackler also became friends and confidants of the German adman. They might have seen in him a kindred spirit: a mid-century hustler who had reinvented himself and now stood poised to conquer the world. The four of them—the Sackler brothers and Frohlich—referred to themselves as the "musketeers," like the three musketeers and d'Artagnan, in Alexandre Dumas's novel. To Marietta, it seemed that the closeness of the brothers and Bill Frohlich was "unusual"—a club from which everyone else, even wives, was excluded. The men would sit up late into the night, discussing and debating their work and their plans for the future. The motto of Dumas's musketeers was "One for all and all for one," and on a snowy evening in the late 1940s the brothers and Bill Frohlich had stood on a street corner in Manhattan and made a similar pact. According to Richard Leather, an attorney who represented all four men and subsequently formalized the agreement, they pledged to pool their combined business holdings. They would help one another in business and agree to share all of their corporate assets. When one died, the remaining three would inherit control of the businesses. When the second died, the remaining two would inherit. When the third died, the last musketeer would assume control of all of the businesses. And when the last man died, all of those businesses would pass into a charitable trust.

This was a significant commitment. Bill Frohlich had no children, but the Sackler brothers were all married, with kids. Mortimer had married a Scottish-born woman named Muriel Lazarus and moved to Great Neck, on Long Island, and they had two daughters, Kathe and Ilene, and a son named Robert. Raymond and Beverly had moved to East Hills, also on Long Island, and had two sons, Richard and Jonathan. At the time of the agreement, Arthur had his daughters, Carol and

Elizabeth, with Else, and would soon have a son, and then a daughter, with Marietta. What the musketeers were saying when they made their pact was that their own children would not inherit their business interests. Instead, each man would be entitled to leave a reasonable sum to his heirs, and the rest would pass, eventually, to the charitable trust. "I'd made enough by 1950 for my children and grandchildren," Arthur later said. "The rest is going to the public trust." This civic-minded commitment might have been a function of the socialist philosophy that the brothers shared: they would generate wealth, but they wouldn't hoard it.

✢   ✢   ✢

That ideology was not something the brothers took lightly. Indeed, it was an affiliation for which they would soon be forced to pay. When the Korean War broke out, the U.S. Atomic Energy Commission turned to Creedmoor Hospital for help in researching the effects of burns caused by radioactive substances. It might have been this entanglement with the federal government that threw a spotlight on Creedmoor, but suspicions arose about a "communist cell" at the hospital. The country was in the throes of a red scare, and as it turned out, the FBI had been quietly investigating the Sackler brothers and had discovered evidence of communist ties. In 1953, Mortimer and Raymond were fired from Creedmoor after refusing to sign a "loyalty pledge" to the United States, because it required them to report on people involved in "subversive matters."

Arthur ended up resigning from Creedmoor himself. For the rest of his life, he would speak of the harm that came to those close to him during the McCarthy era. But in truth, the brothers had already been looking to further expand their portfolio beyond advertising and psychiatric research. A *New York Times* article about the dismissal of Raymond and Mortimer noted that the brothers had set up offices in a building at 15 East Sixty-Second Street, just off Central Park, on Manhattan's Upper East Side.

"Arthur was a wonderful buffer for Mortimer and Raymond," Richard Leather, the attorney, said. "He wasn't just an older brother; he was really the paterfamilias." Even before Mortimer and Raymond had been pushed out of Creedmoor, Arthur was devising another plan for the Sacklers. In 1952, he purchased a small pharmaceutical company for his brothers. Officially, it would be a partnership; each brother would own a third. But the money was Arthur's, and he would effectively be a silent partner: Mortimer and Raymond would run the business, with Arthur behind the scenes. They bought the company for $50,000. It wasn't much: a patent medicine business with a few run-of-the-mill products, $20,000 in annual billing, and a narrow redbrick building on Christopher Street in Greenwich Village. But it had a sturdy, blue-blooded name, which the brothers decided to keep: Purdue Frederick.

Chapter 4

PENICILLIN FOR THE BLUES

ONE DAY IN 1957, a chemist named Leo Sternbach made a startling discovery. Sternbach was in his late forties and worked in a lab in Nutley, New Jersey, at the sprawling campus of the Swiss-owned pharmaceutical firm Roche. For the last few years, Roche had been trying to devise a minor tranquilizer. Thorazine, the drug that had proved to be such a success when it was administered in asylums like Creedmoor, was known as a "major" tranquilizer, because it was powerful enough to treat psychotics. But ambitious pharma executives recognized that there are only so many patients who suffer from the kinds of severe conditions that necessitate a major tranquilizer. So they set out to concoct a *minor* tranquilizer: a less powerful medication that could treat more quotidian (and widespread) afflictions, like anxiety.

One of Roche's competitors, Wallace Laboratories, was first to market, with a minor tranquilizer called Miltown, which became a galloping success. Prior to Miltown, people who were nervous or neurotic could soothe themselves with barbiturates or sedatives or alcohol, but these remedies had unwelcome side effects: they made you sleepy, or inebriated, and they could be addictive. Miltown was said to have no side effects whatsoever, and it became a blockbuster. Suddenly *everyone* seemed to be taking Miltown. And there wasn't any stigma associated with using the drug. You might think twice before confessing to a colleague that your doctor had put you on a course of Thorazine, but Miltown was nothing to be ashamed of. On the contrary, it became fashionable—a party drug in Hollywood. People boasted about having a prescription.

The pharmaceutical industry was notoriously herdlike, so other companies now set out to develop minor tranquilizers of their own. At Roche, Leo Sternbach's orders were simple: invent a drug that can outsell Miltown. "Change the molecules a little," his superiors told him.

Make something different enough that we can patent it and charge a premium to sell a competing product, but not so different that we won't be able to muscle in on Miltown's market.

Sternbach, who thought of himself as a chemist's chemist, found this guidance somewhat irritating. When he was growing up in Krakow, Poland, his father had been a chemist, and Leo would pirate chemicals from his dad's shop and experiment, combining different elements to see what might spark an explosion. He felt a deep sense of loyalty to Roche, because the company allowed him to do what he loved but also because the company might have saved his life. When World War II broke out, Sternbach had been working in Zurich, at the headquarters of Roche's parent company, Hoffmann-LaRoche. Switzerland was officially neutral, but many Swiss chemical companies decided to "Aryanize" their workforces, purging Jews. Hoffmann-LaRoche did not. As circumstances for European Jews grew more dire, the company, recognizing that Sternbach was, as he put it, an "endangered species," took the precaution of relocating him to the United States.

Sternbach felt a debt to Roche because of that history. But he had now spent two years trying to dream up a drug that could compete with Miltown, without success, and his bosses were growing impatient. He had produced more than a dozen new compounds, but none did precisely what he wanted. Sternbach was frustrated. Good chemistry takes time, and he did not like to be rushed. Then, just as management was poised to pull the plug on the project and get him working on something else, he had a breakthrough. He'd been experimenting with an unlikely compound, which up to that point had been used mainly in synthetic dyes, when he realized that he might have stumbled upon the very answer he'd been looking for.

He called this new concoction Roche compound No. 0609. Testing it on mice, he found that the compound did not make them groggy, the way that Miltown (notwithstanding its reputation for having no side effects) did. Instead, it relaxed them but left them alert. Before applying for a patent, Sternbach took a big dose of the new drug himself, carefully recording in his notebook the sensations that it made him feel. "Cheerful," he wrote. This was what Roche had been looking for. They named the new drug Librium, a portmanteau of "liberation" and "equilibrium." To market it, they turned to Arthur Sackler.

✦ ✦ ✦

"No one at Roche, no one at the agency, none of us knew how big Librium would become," John Kallir recalled. Arthur assigned Kallir to work on the new account, but "it was not easy, because we had no product to illustrate." It was important, moreover, that Roche and McAdams reach a wide audience with this campaign. Just a few years earlier, it might have seemed that marketing directly to doctors was enough, but post-Miltown such an approach seemed quaint. Patients had started going to their doctors and requesting each new wonder drug by name. When Roche conducted clinical trials on Librium, the company enthusiastically concluded that the drug could treat an astonishing range of afflictions. Anxiety. Depression. Phobias. Obsessive thoughts. Even alcoholism. With each new "indication," the potential market for the drug expanded. But if Librium was going to be a pharmaceutical for the masses, how could Arthur Sackler and his team at McAdams devise a campaign that would reach them?

There was one immediate obstacle confronting them: at the time, FDA regulations forbade pharmaceutical companies to advertise directly to consumers. But, as Arthur knew, there are many ways to reach the public. In April 1960, *Life* magazine carried a story with the headline "New Way to Calm a Cat." The article featured two photos of a lynx at the San Diego Zoo. In one picture, the lynx was ferocious, baring its fangs. In the other, it looked serene and benign. In fact, it appeared to be smelling a flower. The article explained that this miraculous transformation in the animal's mood had occurred after doctors administered "a new tranquilizer called Librium." A veterinarian weighed in, with the assuredness of a pitchman, pointing out that "unlike previous tranquilizers, which made beasts groggy and repressed, Librium leaves them active but turns them genuinely gentle and friendly." The article mentioned, in passing—as if this were not the whole point of the story—that Librium "may eventually have important human uses."

This feature, appearing in one of the largest-circulation magazines in the country just a month before Librium went on the market, was hardly a coincidence. The piece had been planted by Roche, and one of Arthur Sackler's public relations whizzes was dispatched to "help" the journalist who wrote the story. "The PR guy was with us every inch of the way, every lunch we had, every drink we drank," the reporter said later. "He was a very smooth fellow . . . who wouldn't let us alone."

And the article was just the opening salvo. Roche would spend $2 million marketing Librium in its inaugural year. The company sent vinyl records to doctors' offices with audio recordings of physicians talking about the benefits of Librium. McAdams inundated physicians with dozens of mailings and placed extravagant advertising spreads in medical journals. As one critique published in a medical newsletter in 1960 observed, many of the claims about Librium's effectiveness were not "backed by convincing evidence." But the assertions seemed incontrovertible: after all, they were being made by doctors to doctors, often in the pages of prestigious journals. You might think that the journals would have an interest in vetting the advertisements that people like Arthur Sackler and Bill Frohlich placed, but many of these publications were heavily dependent on advertising revenue. (*The New England Journal of Medicine,* where many of Arthur's ads appeared, was making more than $2 million a year in this manner by the end of the 1960s, most of it from drug companies.)

Arthur had become a unique figure in the pharma business, his longtime deputy, Win Gerson, reflected. He had an almost clairvoyant grasp of "what pharmaceuticals could do." And his timing could not have been better. One Librium ad, which ran in a medical journal, promoted the pill as a cure-all for "The Age of Anxiety," and it turned out that the Cold War was a perfect moment to usher in a tranquilizer for the masses. The arms race was on. The nightly news carried regular updates on the Soviet menace. A nuclear conflagration seemed not just possible but likely. Who *wouldn't* be a little high-strung? One study found that in New York City as much as half of the population might suffer from "clinical" anxiety.

When it was introduced in 1960, Librium did $20,000 in sales its first month. Then it really took off. Within a year, doctors were writing 1.5 million new prescriptions for the drug every month. Within five years, fifteen million Americans had tried it. McAdams had marketed Librium as a category killer, not just another tranquilizer, but the "*successor* to the Tranquilizers." In doing so, Arthur and his colleagues helped turn Leo Sternbach's compound into what was, at that point, the greatest commercial success in the history of drugs. But Roche wasn't finished.

Sternbach had played no role in the marketing of Librium. Of course, he was gratified by the astonishing success of the product, but he was already back in the laboratory, doing what he loved to do. He was searching for other members of the same chemical family as Librium to see if there might be different compounds that would also make effective tranquilizers. By the end of 1959, before Librium had even been released, Sternbach had developed a different compound, which seemed as if it might potentially be more effective even than Librium, because it worked at smaller doses. Deciding what names to bestow upon new drugs was more of an art than a science, and, in any case, not Sternbach's specialty. So it was someone else at Roche who came up with a name for the compound, a play on the Latin word *valere,* which means to be in good health. They called it Valium.

Before it could launch Valium in 1963, however, Roche faced an unusual challenge: they had just introduced this groundbreaking tranquilizer, Librium, which was still doing gangbusters business. If the company now rolled out a second tranquilizer that performed even better, wouldn't they just cannibalize their own market? What if Valium rendered Librium obsolete?

The answer to this conundrum lay in advertising—in the province of Arthur Sackler. With Librium's success, Roche had become Arthur's most important client. The McAdams agency had moved in to new offices at 130 East Fifty-Ninth Street and now had roughly three hundred employees. An entire floor in the new space was devoted to the Roche account. "Arthur was in pretty heavy with management at Roche," the McAdams art director Rudi Wolff recalled. "There were always rumors that Arthur was *running* Roche."

Librium and Valium were both minor tranquilizers. They both did pretty much the same thing. What Arthur's team at McAdams had to do was convince the world—both doctors *and* patients—that actually the drugs were different. The way to do this was to pitch them for different ailments. If Librium was the cure for "anxiety," Valium should be prescribed for "psychic tension." If Librium could help alcoholics stay off the bottle, then Valium could prevent muscle spasms. Why not use it in sports medicine? Soon, doctors were prescribing Roche's tranquilizers for such a comical range of conditions that one physician, writing about Valium in a medical journal, asked, "When do we *not* use this drug?" To Arthur and his colleagues, this was what made

Valium such an easy product to sell. As Win Gerson remarked, "One of the great attributes of Valium is that it could be used by almost every specialty."

Just as women had outnumbered men in the wards of Creedmoor, it now emerged that doctors were prescribing Roche's tranquilizers to women much more often than to men, and Arthur and his colleagues seized on this phenomenon and started to aggressively market Librium and Valium to women. In describing an ideal patient, a typical ad for Valium read, "35, single and psychoneurotic." An early ad for Librium showed a young woman with an armful of books and suggested that even the routine stress of heading off to college might be best addressed with Librium. But the truth was, Librium and Valium were marketed using such a variety of gendered mid-century tropes—the neurotic singleton, the frazzled housewife, the joyless career woman, the meno-pausal shrew—that as the historian Andrea Tone noted in her book *The Age of Anxiety*, what Roche's tranquilizers really seemed to offer was a quick fix for the problem of "being female."

Roche was hardly the only company to employ this sort of over-the-top disingenuous advertising. Pfizer had a tranquilizer that it recom-mended for use by children with an illustration of a young girl with a tearstained face and a suggestion that the drug could alleviate fears of "school, the dark, separation, dental visits, 'monsters.'" But once Roche and Arthur Sackler unleashed Librium and Valium, no other company could compete. At Roche's plant in Nutley, mammoth pill-stamping machines struggled to keep up with demand, churning out tens of mil-lions of tablets a day. Initially, Librium was the most prescribed drug in America, until it was overtaken by Valium in 1968. But even then, Librium held on, remaining in the top five. In 1964, some twenty-two million prescriptions were written for Valium. By 1975, that figure reached sixty million. Valium was the first $100 million drug in history, and Roche became not just the leading drug company in the world but one of the most profitable companies of any kind. Money was pouring in, and when it did, the company turned around and reinvested that money in the promotion campaign devised by Arthur Sackler.

As a boy, at Erasmus, Arthur had negotiated to make a commission on the ads he sold so that he could be rewarded in success, and he had favored this model ever since. Before he agreed to promote Librium and Valium, he had struck a deal with Roche in which he would receive

EMPIRE OF PAIN   59

an escalating series of bonuses in proportion with the volume of drugs sold. And year after year, the volume kept rising. For an adman, the new tranquilizers were the perfect product, a chemical requisite for anxious modern life—or, as some people called them, "penicillin for the blues."

On February 28, 1955, Marietta gave birth to a second child, a daughter, Denise. This time, Arthur was present for the birth. She was born with straight black hair, and her father examined her and pronounced her healthy. When Arthur's son, Arthur Felix, had been born five years earlier, the only visitors who came to celebrate at the hospital were Raymond and Mortimer. But Arthur's star had risen in the interim, and this time the hospital room was filled with bouquets sent by friends and colleagues and associates and admirers of Arthur, and there seemed to be a constant stream of well-wishers, coming to pay their respects. How their life had changed, Marietta thought. She was delighted.

✢ ✢ ✢

During these years, Arthur carried a big briefcase with him everywhere he went. In it, he had papers associated with the different careers and lives he was maintaining so that he could flit from one milieu to the next, materializing suddenly, like a superhero who flies in to save the day. As if his medical research and his thriving advertising firm weren't enough, he began to publish a weekly newspaper geared to doctors. Arthur had always liked convergences and synergies—ways in which the different parts of his life could work in harmony—and the *Medical Tribune* featured articles that tended to be favorable to Arthur and his clients. It also featured lots of advertising. "The *Medical Tribune* was his baby," the former McAdams employee Phil Keusch recalled, saying that Arthur would "force" McAdams clients to take out ads in the paper. The whole purpose was to reach physicians and to influence them ("educate" them, Arthur would insist), so the *Medical Tribune* was subsidized by pharma ads and distributed for free. It soon reached millions of doctors in the United States and (in foreign editions) around the world. One of the biggest advertisers in the *Medical Tribune* was Roche, and for decades virtually every issue featured elaborate multi-page spreads for both Librium and Valium.

Arthur seems to have been aware that some might perceive a potential conflict between his roles as head of both a medical newspaper and a pharmaceutical advertising firm. He once explained that his tendency to remain obscure and anonymous as much as possible sprang from a sense that this would enable him to "do things the way I want to do them." Initially, his name could not be found anywhere on the masthead of the newspaper—nor could any acknowledgment to readers that the guiding editorial hand behind the publication happened to be heavily invested in the drug business. But Arthur was untroubled by these conflicts. For many years, the *Medical Tribune* and the McAdams agency occupied the same office space. In some instances, they shared employees. It was all part of the family.

As he built a life with Marietta and their two children on Long Island, Arthur continued to enjoy a close relationship with his first wife, Else Sackler, who, after the divorce, continued to use his name. "Dr. Sackler and I remained close friends and business associates," Else remarked later. (Even in his own family, Arthur was "Dr. Sackler.") Because he had put half of McAdams in Else's name, for many years Arthur and his ex-wife were the firm's only shareholders. He also spent a great deal of time with Else at the apartment he had installed her in, following the divorce, on Central Park West. His ostensible reason for these visits was that he wanted to be present in the lives of his two older daughters, Carol and Elizabeth. But he also enjoyed an ongoing relationship with Else. They were not just friends but confidants. "We talked on a daily basis," Else recalled, saying that she and Arthur were "in constant touch." Arthur was, in the words of one of his own attorneys, "a very private person," a secretive man who, with every passing year and each new benchmark of success, became more careful about pruning his own public persona. Perhaps because Else had known him before he was the august Dr. Sackler, had known him back when he was just Artie from Brooklyn, he could open up to her in a way that seemed too risky with other people. When Arthur had exciting news—when he had completed a big business deal or achieved some new laurel—he would race to tell Else first. Once, she was with friends at a performance at Carnegie Hall, and when the show broke up, they found Arthur pacing outside the venue, waiting for her. He knew she was there that night, and had some bit of news to share.

In the old Dutch farmhouse out on Long Island, Marietta Sackler's initial satisfaction that her husband had worked out an amicable situation with his ex-wife morphed into something more anxious. Of course, she knew that Arthur felt guilt about having abandoned his wife and children to marry her, and she thought that Arthur should be commended for trying to maintain a relationship with Carol and Elizabeth. But the reality was that he was already so invested in his work that he was not devoting huge amounts of time to Marietta and *her* children. The house on Searingtown Road was beautiful, but it was isolated, all on its own, surrounded by woods, and with Arthur gone in the city from morning to late at night, Marietta felt quite alone.

Their family life assumed a predictable rhythm. Arthur would work in the city all week, taking on more and more, often with meetings late into the night. Marietta still prepared a nice meal, late at night, and got gussied up for his arrival. But when he did come home, Arthur wouldn't want to talk about his work, and this seemed particularly unfair to Marietta, because unlike some other housewife on Long Island she could understand it all—she had a medical degree! But Arthur was simply exhausted. In theory, weekends were reserved for family, but when he did come home on weekends, he mostly slept, to recover from the exertions of the previous week. They compensated for this estrangement with an ardent sex life. But before long Marietta was starting to feel as though she were living in a gilded cage.

She got a little dog for company, a wire fox terrier she called Bottoms, because he had a black spot on his rear end. And her son, little Arthur, ended up spending a lot of time with a kindly gardener, George, who helped out around the place and taught him the sorts of things the man whose name he carried did not. For all his devotion to the idea of family, Arthur was largely absent as a parent. Once, when Denise was about six, she was jumping rope in the house and Arthur admonished her, warning that she might break something. "Play with me, Daddy," she pleaded.

"I'm going to wait until you're an adult," Arthur said. "Then I'll have a conversation with you."

Arthur came home later and later at night, and eventually he started calling some nights to say that he wouldn't be home at all. Marietta knew he was consumed by work. But it bothered her that in the time he did have, he ate dinner a couple of nights a week with Else and her children in Manhattan. On Saturday mornings, he would go back into the city to eat brunch with his other family before spending the rest of the day at the office.

At McAdams, where Arthur already seemed to be living a double life, because he came in and out and was also servicing his other
careers, it did not go unnoticed that he appeared to be living a double
life at home. John Kallir sometimes gave Arthur a ride into the office,
and on at least one occasion Arthur instructed Kallir to pick him up in
the morning at the apartment on Central Park West.

✛ ✛ ✛

Librium and Valium made Arthur Sackler very rich. But even as
they were doing so, troubling signs were starting to emerge that the
miracle drugs devised by Leo Sternbach at Roche might not be quite
so miraculously free from side effects as the advertising campaigns had
suggested. Roche had informed doctors and regulators that the drugs
could be prescribed without fears of abuse, because unlike barbiturates
these tranquilizers were not addictive. As it turned out, this assurance
was based more on wishful thinking than on science. In fact, when the
company was doing all those clinical trials in order to establish the
myriad different medical conditions for which Librium and Valium
might provide the solution, they never conducted a single study into
the question of potential abuse.

Roche hadn't just blithely assumed that the powerful drugs it was
about to introduce to the public would be safe: the company had deliberately obfuscated evidence to the contrary. In 1960, Roche had enlisted
a Stanford professor and physician named Leo Hollister to consult on
Librium. Hollister worried that if Librium was as great as Roche was
saying, it would be abused. So he decided to conduct a test. He administered high doses of Librium to thirty-six patients for several months,
then switched eleven of them to a placebo. Ten of the patients who were
abruptly taken off the drug suffered unpleasant withdrawal symptoms;
two of them had seizures. When Hollister informed Roche, executives
at the company were not happy. "I wasn't trying to kill their drug," he
later recalled. He just thought that patients should know that the image
Roche and McAdams were projecting—of a happiness pill completely
free from downsides—wasn't accurate.

Roche was anything but chastened by Hollister's findings. In fact,
when he published his research, the company's medical director shot
back that Hollister was misreading his own study. The withdrawal was
not a sign of any dangerous physical dependence on Librium, but an

intensification of the underlying condition that the Librium was meant to address in the first place. All the patient needed, in other words, was *more Librium.*

Even so, there were actual cases, increasingly, of real consumers becoming hopelessly dependent on tranquilizers. Confronted with this sort of evidence, Roche offered a different interpretation: while it might be true that some patients appeared to be abusing Librium and Valium, these were people who were using the drug in a nontherapeutic manner. Some individuals just have addictive personalities and are prone to abuse any substance you make available to them. This attitude was typical in the pharmaceutical industry: it's not the drugs that are bad; it's the people who abuse them. "There are some people who just get addicted to things—almost anything. I read the other day about a man who died from drinking too many cola drinks," Frank Berger, who was president of Wallace Laboratories, the maker of Miltown, told *Vogue.* "In spite of all the horror stories you read in the media, addiction to tranquilizers occurs very rarely." In 1957, a syndicated ask-the-doctor column that appeared in a Pittsburgh newspaper wondered whether "patients become addicted to tranquilizers." The answer assured readers that contrary to any fears they might harbor, "the use of tranquilizers is not making us a nation of drug addicts." The newspaper identified the author of this particular piece of advice as "Dr. Mortimer D. Sackler."

In 1965, the federal government started to investigate Librium and Valium. An advisory committee of the Food and Drug Administration recommended that the tranquilizers be treated as controlled substances—a move that would make it much harder for consumers to get them. Both Roche and Arthur Sackler perceived this prospect as a major threat. As a general rule, Arthur was skeptical of government regulation when it came to medicine, and he recognized that new controls on the minor tranquilizers could be devastating for his bottom line. For nearly a decade, the company resisted efforts by the FDA to control Librium and Valium, a period in which Roche sold hundreds of millions of dollars of the drugs. It was only in 1973 that Roche agreed to "voluntarily" submit to the controls. But one FDA adviser would speculate that the timing of this reversal was no accident: at the point when Roche conceded defeat, its patents on the drugs were set to expire, meaning that Roche would no longer enjoy the exclusive right to manufacture them and would be forced to lower its prices in the face of generic competition. As Arthur's friend and secret business partner Bill Frohlich had observed, the commercial life span of a branded drug is the short interval between the point when you start marketing it and the point when you lose patent exclusivity. Roche and Arthur didn't need to fight off regulation forever; they just needed to hold it off until the patents had run out.

By the time Roche allowed its tranquilizers to be controlled, Valium had become part of the lives of some twenty million Americans, the most widely consumed—and most widely abused—prescription drug in the world. It had taken time for the country to wake up to the negative impact of Valium, in part because there was some novelty, for average consumers, in the idea of a drug that could be dangerous even though it was prescribed by a doctor. Moral panics over drugs in America had tended to focus on street drugs and to play on fears about minority groups, immigrants, and illicit influences; the idea that you could get hooked on a pill that was prescribed to you by a physician in a white coat with a stethoscope around his neck and a diploma on the wall was somewhat new. But, eventually, establishment figures like the former first lady Betty Ford would acknowledge having struggled with Valium, and Senator Edward Kennedy would blame tranquilizers for producing "a nightmare of dependence and addiction." Roche stood accused of "overpromoting" the drug. The Rolling Stones even wrote a song about Valium, "Mother's Little Helper," whose lyrics evoked the McAdams campaign aimed at women.

"Valium changed the way we communicated with physicians," Arthur's deputy, Win Gerson, later said. He remained proud of the drug. "It kind of made junkies of some people," he allowed, "but that drug worked." For Arthur, however, there was a paradox. In polishing his own public image, he relied heavily on an appearance of propriety and the idea that he was a righteous and judicious man of medicine. Yet his fortune could be traced directly to the rampant sales of two highly addictive tranquilizers. To be sure, Arthur had many business interests: he started companies left and right and invested widely in a range of industries. But the original House of Sackler was built on Valium, and it seems significant, and revealing, that for the rest of his life Arthur would downplay his association with the drug, emphasizing his achievements in other areas and deliberately obscuring (or leaving out altogether) the fact that his first fortune was made in medical advertising. Eventually, he started to acknowledge his role as publisher of the *Medical Tribune*, adding his name to the masthead and writing his own column, called "One Man & Medicine," in which he held forth on medical issues of the day. In these columns, Arthur often railed against the dangers of cigarettes, pointing out not just the health risks associated with smoking but the perils of addiction. Yet he seemed incapable of applying that same scrutiny to his own role as a lavishly compensated shill for an addictive and dangerous product. And because Arthur was so effective in marketing not just his products but his own persona of unimpeachability, he was seldom asked to account for this dissonance. On the rare occasion when he did address the ravages of Valium, he would echo the sentiment of his clients at Roche and the makers of other tranquilizers: it wasn't the pills that were getting people addicted; it was the addictive personalities of the patients who were abusing them. Valium was a safe drug, he would insist, and news reports to the contrary made him feel no self-doubt or regret. People who encountered problems with the drug must have "mixed it with alcohol or cocaine," he would say.

Another person who shared this view was Leo Sternbach. While Arthur had cannily negotiated to profit from Librium and Valium in proportion to their sales, Sternbach did not make a fortune. Instead, he was paid $1 for each of the patents, as was standard practice for a staff chemist at Roche. When his creations became the best-selling pharmaceutical products in the history of the world, Roche gave Sternbach a $10,000 bonus for each drug. Yet he was not bitter. He had no desire for villas or yachts, no expensive hobbies he wanted to indulge. Instead, he lived out his days doing chemistry, without complaint. Like Arthur Sackler, Sternbach resisted any sense of accountability for the downsides of the minor tranquilizers. He had merely invented the compounds, ushering them into the world. He felt no moral responsibility for their subsequent misuse by the public. "I mean, everything can be abused," Sternbach said.

Chapter 5

CHINA FEVER

WHEN ARTHUR AND MARIETTA moved into the Dutch farmhouse on Long Island, they realized that they did not own enough furniture. Arthur had arranged to purchase a rectory table and a bedroom set from the people who sold them the house, and Marietta brought an antique chest of drawers, which was a family heirloom from Germany. But that was hardly enough to fill the big space, and when the couple invited people over for dinner, they had to improvise, carrying dining room chairs into the living room so that everyone could have a seat.

As long as Marietta was going to be stuck at home, she decided that she would install bookshelves and cabinets. As it happened, there was a cabinetmaker who lived nearby, and he was German, too, from Bavaria. One Saturday, after some cajoling, Marietta persuaded Arthur to join her on a visit to the cabinetmaker's shop. While they were browsing the furniture on display, Arthur's eye fell on a distinctive rosewood table. When he inquired about it, the cabinetmaker explained that the table belonged to a local man who collected old Chinese furniture and sometimes brought items in to be restored. Intrigued, Arthur asked, "Do you know if he'd be willing to sell any of his pieces?"

When Arthur Sackler saw something he wanted, he tended to pursue it with unstinting zeal; this was how he had pursued Marietta. So, the next day, he arranged to visit the owner of the table. His name was Bill Drummond, and he lived nearby, in a ranch house in Roslyn Heights. Drummond was originally from Chicago, but for thirty years he had lived, on and off, in China, where he had an antiques business. His brother still lived there, though he had been forced to relocate to Hong Kong after the communists took over in 1949. Drummond's home was full of beautiful Chinese furniture: teak tables, lacquered desks with gold hardware, reproductions of pieces that once adorned the emperor's Summer Palace in Beijing. Chinese furniture has "a double face," Drummond liked to say—"a respect for what's left unsaid." Drummond had a double face himself: initially, his furniture business was merely a cover for his actual job as an American spy in China, working for the Office of Strategic Services, the precursor to the CIA. But that notion of leaving things unsaid could only have resonated with Arthur Sackler. Many of the pieces were actually more recent reproductions of designs that were hundreds of years old. But they were built to last and had a sturdy, timeless quality that Arthur admired. It was as if they had always existed, and always would.

Antique Chinese furniture was not exactly in vogue on suburban Long Island in the 1950s. And following the communist takeover in China, the United States had imposed an embargo on all goods from the country, so supplies were limited. But, as one longtime friend, Harry Henderson, would observe, Arthur was "proud of his 'eye' for what had been overlooked, whether it was in art, proofreading, or logic." And the items that Drummond had for sale—particularly the furniture from the Ming period—captured Arthur's imagination. He decided, on an impulse, to buy them: not one or two choice items, but enough of Drummond's collection that Marietta worried about whether they could actually afford it.

In addition to the furniture, Arthur bought some Han-era pottery and other antiques from Drummond. This discovery of Chinese aesthetics seemed to awaken something inside him. Marietta shared her husband's appreciation for the beauty of Chinese art and design, but Arthur plunged into this newfound interest with a passion that bordered on obsession. He had never had hobbies per se; as a child of the Depression, he tended to focus every last iota of energy on professional advancement. But Arthur did have money now, and there was something in the hunt for these precious relics of an ancient society that he found transfixing. "It was at that time that Arthur caught the China fever," Henderson said, "and never got over it."

On some level, Arthur had always appreciated art. There were the childhood visits to the Brooklyn Museum and the night classes in sculpture at Cooper Union. To Marietta, it seemed that he was fundamentally a creative person who might have pursued a career in the arts, were it not for the Depression and the need to provide for his parents and his brothers. But it is also true that people who achieve a certain level of wealth and professional renown often tend, at a certain point, to start buying art. Perhaps this mode of acquisition is an effort to silence some inner doubt about their own place in the culture, or perhaps it merely represents a new realm to be conquered. But long before Arthur Sackler, rich men of accomplishment had a predictable habit of seeking pleasure and meaning in paintings, sculpture, and antiques. J. P. Morgan, who died the year that Arthur was born, had a second career as a collector. He ended up spending half his fortune on art.

Soon, Arthur was haunting the auction houses and studying museum catalogs and volumes on Chinese history and archaeology. He approached collecting with the rigor of a scientist, endeavoring, as he put it, to assemble a large "corpus of material" and then study it. When he got back to Long Island late at night after a marathon day in the city, he would crawl into bed with Marietta, then pull out a stack of scholarly literature and stay up reading. The family started visiting museums in a more systematic manner, seeking out the Chinese galleries, moving through collections quickly, with Arthur picking out specific objects for close scrutiny and delivering disquisitions to his embarrassed children, comparing the works on display to pieces that he owned. He took great care to pronounce all of the Chinese names correctly.

As he immersed himself in this new world, Arthur was inducted into a small fraternity of equally obsessive collectors. On one occasion, in 1957, he purchased thirty bronzes at Parke-Bernet, an auction house in Manhattan. Afterward, he discovered that they had all been consigned by the same man, a New Jersey doctor named Paul Singer. When he looked Singer up, Arthur discovered that the doctor was his kind of person—a psychiatrist, and an émigré, who had fled Austria in 1938. Singer was a self-taught expert, a connoisseur with an impeccable eye who had purchased his first piece of Asian art, a bronze image of the bodhisattva Manjushri, when he was just seventeen.

"I've bought all the things you've consigned," Arthur told Singer, when he reached him on the telephone. "Next time you want to sell anything, let's eliminate the middleman."

Arthur discovered that Singer lived in a modest two-bedroom apartment in Summit, New Jersey, that was cluttered, floor to ceiling, with precious Chinese artifacts. Here was a man who shared his fixation but had enjoyed a considerable head start. When Arthur started spending time with him, Singer later recalled, "I met a very eager pupil." Arthur barraged him with pointed questions about the history of Chinese art and the mechanics of collecting, and Singer was pleased to witness the intense pleasure that the artworks elicited from this new initiate. He showed Arthur a collection of beautiful Chinese jades, and when Arthur picked up the first piece and held it in his hands, "it was like an electric charge," Singer recalled. Really serious collecting, in Singer's view, was driven by a pattern of arousal and release that was downright erotic: "The pulse beats faster, the beholder sees beauty that he wants to own. He is willing to give of his substance to possess it."

Marietta, too, saw this in her husband. She recognized that the "hunt" was what excited Arthur, that identifying some precious artifact and then figuring out how to claim it was a "secretive, sensual" process. Once Arthur had established his bona fides as no mere dilettante but a serious collector, people started showing him their rarest treasures. One of the dealers he got to know, a man named Dai Fubao, who went by the name Mr. Tai, had a shop on Madison Avenue, with a staircase that led to a special room in the basement in which the buyer could commune with an object before agreeing to pay for it. One day, Singer telephoned Arthur and told him that Mr. Tai had come into possession of a document, written on silk, that was known as the Ch'u Manuscript, and dated to 600 B.C.E. "If you were to dump your whole present collection into the Hudson, it would not matter as long as you were the owner of this piece of silk," Singer said.

When Arthur arrived at Mr. Tai's shop, the dealer acknowledged having the manuscript but said that he had no wish to sell it.

Arthur refused to take no for an answer. "Either you are a dealer or you are a collector," he said. "If you are a collector, I wouldn't be able to do business with you, because you're in competition with me. If you are a dealer, you should set a price and sell this priceless manuscript." Mr. Tai's price was half a million dollars. Arthur paid it.

The sub-rosa, backroom quality of these transactions appealed to Arthur's natural sense of secrecy. "I have one of those things about the importance of privacy," he would say. He was most comfortable operating out of the headlines and off the books. His son Arthur would later recall witnessing his father do business in this manner, noting, "They were handshake deals." To his new associates in the art world, Arthur was a figure of mystery. He was imperious, single-minded, determined, and eager, whenever possible, to maintain his anonymity. Sometimes, he would arrange to meet auction house representatives at a hotel, where he was registered under a false name. Nobody seemed to be able to say with any certainty quite how Arthur Sackler had made his money—people did not appear to know about the Valium connection—but what they did know was that Arthur had money, and lots of it. Sometimes, he would telephone an auction house with instructions to call off an auction, because he intended to purchase every item. He acquired a reputation for spending lavishly, and, some thought, indiscriminately: in the words of one museum director, Arthur purchased "whole collections seemingly with one glance."

But if he was profligate, he was also a zealous negotiator. "After the deal had been struck," the same museum director recalled, "Sackler would invariably start bargaining." To Marietta, it seemed that Arthur's broad knowledge—of everything from the tax code to the psychology of the people he was dealing with—made him a tough negotiator. He had a habit, she recalled, "of maximizing each deal, contract or agreement for just that last extra bit in his favor."

New boxes would arrive at the Long Island house, full of exquisite objects. The children helped open them. Sometimes other connoisseurs came over for the occasion. The unboxing took on the spiritual aspect of a séance, as Arthur lifted out ritual bronzes and ancient weapons, mirrors and ceramics, inscribed bones and archaic jades. The bystanders would let out whistles of awe as Arthur and his family handled these mystical objects, communing with ghosts, touching history.

Of course, with all these priceless artifacts in the house, it could be difficult for the children to run around uninhibited. At a dinner party once, one of the guests asked Arthur's daughter Denise what she most desired. "A big dog!" she replied, before catching herself, and pointing out that big dogs have big tails, which can knock over ancient bronzes. (They ended up getting a Yorkshire terrier, with a short tail. They called it Jade.)

Arthur had accomplished a great deal by the time he started to collect in his forties. But it was art that "put him on the world stage," Marietta observed. Within a decade, he had amassed one of the greatest collections of Chinese art ever assembled. His inventory of bronzes was as good as that of any museum. His lacquers were the best in private hands. Whatever it was that drove this passion for collecting, it had an important civic function, Marietta thought. After all, without the largesse of the Medici family, would the Renaissance have happened?

Would Florence possess the eternal collection of architecture, painting, and sculpture that it does today? Arthur's acquisitions brought him public recognition in a way that advertising and medicine had not. But, more important, Marietta thought, the notion of assembling a collection of ancient masterpieces, a collection that would bear his name and be so significant that it would live on, past his lifetime, offered Arthur something else: "the possibility of immortality."

✦ ✦ ✦

With this notion in mind, perhaps, Arthur was insistent that he was not merely some plutocrat collecting baubles: he was creating a durable public good. This was a scholarly enterprise, he maintained, so the works he was collecting should not just adorn his home or sit in storage. They should be displayed and studied by art historians and debated in public symposia. In the late 1950s, Arthur started dabbling in a new realm, one that mingled nicely with his passion for collecting: philanthropy. He began to give money to Columbia University—not his own alma mater, NYU, but the more prestigious Ivy League school, which nobody in his family had attended, uptown. In 1959, he arranged for what he called "the Sackler Gift," to support Far Eastern studies at the university. He also expressed an interest in setting up what he called "the Sackler Fund," an account that could subsidize both academic research and the purchase of objects, which would become part of "the Sackler Collection."

Arthur Sackler would eventually be celebrated for his extraordinary generosity, but from the start his philanthropy was also an exercise in family branding. He had come of age in a city that had been enriched and transformed by the contributions of wealthy men who erected civic monuments that bore their own names. He was in medical school in 1935 when the former mansion of the industrialist Henry Clay Frick was converted into the Frick Collection. J. P. Morgan and Andrew Carnegie and the Rockefellers and the Mellons had left not just their mark on the city but their family names. So why would the Sacklers operate any differently?

This did create one challenge for Arthur, however. How could he reconcile this ardent desire for recognition of the Sackler name with his equally strong preference for personal anonymity? Arthur was not shy about attaching stipulations to his gifts: he would soon become notorious for sending long, binding, legalistic agreements governing his various benefactions. And his own ambivalence over publicity is captured in his missives to the administration at Columbia. In one letter, he mandated that "no personal publicity in respect to general press releases, photos or other forms be associated with this grant." As one university administrator explained to another, "Dr. Sackler is quite particular about the use of his name" and preferred that he personally not be mentioned in any promotional announcements. At the same time, however, he wanted all the materials purchased with the fund to be identified as part of "the Sackler Collection at Columbia University." He desired posterity, but not publicity. The last thing Arthur wanted to do was call attention to his own wealth and holdings, and do so in a manner that might raise questions about his overlapping careers. He resolved this dilemma by positing a family fortune that had simply appeared, fully formed, as if the Sacklers were not three upstart brothers from Brooklyn but scions of some long-established dynasty, as timeworn and venerable as Ming furniture. Arthur was the quintessential self-made man, but he hated that expression, "self-made man." So, the Sackler Collection at Columbia just appeared in the world, as if by virgin birth, with few discernible links to the man who made it.

This would be a family enterprise in more ways than one: Arthur indicated to Columbia that once the fund was established, it would be not just he who contributed but "members of my family." Arthur had always enlisted his brothers and his wives in his pursuits, though it was sometimes hard to know whether he did so in order to give them an actual stake or merely to use them as fronts for his personal ownership. The Sackler Fund would be no different. It started with approximately $70,000. But the funds came not from Arthur but from Raymond, Marietta, and Arthur's first wife, Else Sackler. These contributions arrived at Columbia within four days of one another, raising the question of whether the funds really did come from Raymond, Marietta, and Else or whether it was money that Arthur had given them to donate to the school. It was difficult to tell where one bank account ended and another began. And to make matters simpler (or more complicated, depending on your point of view), everyone seemed to be represented by the same accountant, a close friend and confidant of the Sackler brothers' named Louis Goldburt.

In 1962, Columbia launched the first exhibit of the Sackler Collection. Because Arthur had never done anything like this before, he was anxious about the show and hoping it would be a smashing success. Columbia had agreed to make available the rotunda of Low Memorial Library, a beautiful columned building, designed by the famous architect Charles Follen McKim, which was meant to evoke an ancient temple, and patterned after the Pantheon in Rome. But Arthur worried about how the objects would appear in the rotunda's dim, windowless interior. So he telephoned Tiffany, because he admired the way the company displayed jewelry in the windows of its Fifth Avenue store. It was a classic Arthur innovation, importing the latest techniques from the glossy world of commerce to bring some luster to the fusty atmosphere of Columbia University. Someone at Tiffany referred Arthur to one of their expert window dressers, who set and lit each object so beautifully that Arthur and Marietta prevailed upon the man, later, to help decorate their home. The show opened on November 20, 1962, and Arthur wrote an introduction for the catalog, saying that he hoped the exhibit would provide visitors with "the thrill of discovery" and enhance "our regard and respect for man—his skills, artistry, ingenuity, and genius."

Even so, administrators at Columbia remained a bit skeptical of the Sackler brothers, suspicious that their benevolence might be underpinned by some ulterior motive. At one point, Louis Goldburt informed the university that Mortimer and Raymond were interested in donating "some property in Saratoga Springs." This turned out to be a small parcel of land that was unconnected to the university or any other ostensibly academic purpose but had at one stage been home to a factory that belonged to a pharmaceutical company the brothers had bought. "This seems to be a tax gimmick," one administrator noted in the file.

But the awkward reality was that when it came to benefactors, Columbia could not afford to be choosy. It was a cash-strapped university, and a clear dynamic had already been established with the wealthy brothers—namely, that Columbia would take what it could get. Writing to Arthur in 1960, one university official mentioned that he had read in the newspaper about the grand new headquarters of Pfizer, which was then nearing completion on Forty-Second Street. "I hope you can make an inquiry about their old furniture," the administrator wrote, suggesting, pathetically, that Arthur might solicit for the university some hand-me-down tables and chairs.

Over time, Arthur became more adamant about the use of his family's name. In the blunt assessment of his personal attorney, Michael Sonnenreich, "if you put your name on something it is not charity, it's philanthropy. You get something for it. If you want your name on it, it's a business deal." Arthur proposed to Columbia a plaque for Low Library, recognizing the Sackler Collections "in Memory" of his father, Isaac Sackler. He suggested, in a letter to the university, that "all photographs of Sackler objects must at all times bear the attribution of either Sackler Collection, Sackler Gallery or Sackler Institute." Internally, people who worked at Columbia regarded Arthur as difficult and weird. "Dr. Sackler is a most unusual person," one official noted in a memo, adding that the university's position was " 'as long as the money keeps coming in, don't worry about it.' "

But Arthur had a vision for Columbia, what he described, in one letter to the university's president, as a "dream": he wanted to build a Sackler museum. This was, on the one hand, a welcome suggestion for the university: a new facility devoted to art history and East Asian studies, paid for by a wealthy donor and coming with its own world-class art collection. But, confusingly, Raymond and Mortimer Sackler had initiated a separate conversation with the university about funding the construction of a science center that would bear the family name. Well into adulthood, Arthur referred to his younger siblings as his "kid brothers." He so often spoke for them—telling them what to do professionally, telling them to whom they should donate money—that it could be easy to think of the family as a monolith, all consulting the same accountant, and drawing on the same big bank account, for all anyone knew. Yet here was an indication, however subtle, of discord.

Arthur took care of it. "I have no doubt my brothers' interest in endowing a Life Sciences Institute must inevitably raise a measure of intellectual conflict," he wrote to Columbia's president. "The historic perspective, however, suggests that the unique opportunity that currently exists in the arts probably will not recur again and this important aspect differs from the situation as regards the sciences." And that was that. There was no further serious talk of any life sciences building to be financed by Raymond and Mortimer.

✢   ✢   ✢

The Dutch house on Long Island had a beautiful pond on the property, and Arthur had it planted with bamboo, hoping to create the effect, in his own backyard, of a Chinese landscape. But bamboo is a notoriously invasive species, and once planted, it can be difficult to control. The shoots kept spreading, upward and outward, until they threatened to consume the whole backyard. "They had to keep cutting it back," a family friend, who was a frequent visitor, recalled. "The bamboo took over."

Inside the house, the boxes were piling up. Arthur was now purchasing Chinese art at such a clip that new acquisitions were arriving more quickly than the family could open them. Upstairs, downstairs, in the attic: there were boxes everywhere. Without losing stride, Arthur arranged to have new purchases sent to various private storage spaces. Before long, the sheer volume of material that he owned had reached a point where it could not really be understood or kept track of by the human eye; instead, it became the province of packing lists, inventories, endless reams of paper with line after line of minute markings, dates, prices, lot numbers, catalog notations. And still, Arthur didn't stop. He collected relentlessly, insatiably. Soon, bills were piling up, too, because he was spending a fortune. As quickly as all that tranquilizer money sloshed into his accounts, it seemed to slosh back out again, leaving Arthur feeling as though he needed to work harder in order to keep up with his own collecting. Even his friend Paul Singer, who shared his passion if not the resources that Arthur had to indulge it, remarked that the "spark" he'd seen in Arthur's eyes when he held that first piece of jade had now grown into "a conflagration."

"Each purchase overshadowed the last," Marietta recalled. The moment a deal was consummated, any allure that the object might have seemed to possess was overtaken by his hunger for the next conquest. She thought she detected, in his increasingly manic collecting, a fear of aging, of disillusionment, of death. "In this realm, he could be master, he could have the control he could not have in medicine or in his business and personal life," she wrote. "Arthur found safety and comfort in objects; they could not hurt him, they could not make demands on him."

Chapter 6

THE OCTOPUS

AS DR. HENRY WELCH took the stage, a hush fell over the crowd. Hundreds of doctors, chemists, pharmaceutical executives, and admen had convened in Washington, D.C., for the Fourth Annual Symposium on Antibiotics. They had gathered at the Willard, an opulent hotel overlooking the National Mall, just a few blocks from the White House, for a series of presentations about the latest developments in antibiotics, with guest speakers from across the country and around the world. It was the first day of the conference, a mid-autumn morning in 1956, and Welch, who was one of the impresarios behind the event, extended a warm welcome to the participants.

This would not be one of those perfunctory early morning speeches that the crowd, more focused on settling in and finding coffee, half ignores. Welch was an important figure in pharmaceutical circles: the chief of antibiotics at the Food and Drug Administration, a man with the power to make or break a drug. People in the room wanted to hear what he had to say. He was not actually an MD, but he had a PhD in medical bacteriology, and he was regarded as an authority in the field. Square-faced and jowly, with horn-rimmed glasses and the meaty physique of an ex-athlete, Welch was also the drug-industry equivalent of a war hero: during the war, he had developed a system for testing and approving all of the lifesaving penicillin that was distributed to U.S. forces abroad, a contribution for which he had been awarded a Distinguished Service Gold Medal from the federal government.

The people assembled in the room that day had a sense that they were engaged in an important mission that was inextricable from the American national interest. Before the conference, Welch had received a telegram from the White House in which President Eisenhower welcomed the attendees, noting that the nascent antibiotics industry, "developed through the cooperative efforts of scientists and business executives," had "been instrumental in saving the lives of thousands of citizens."

Launching into his upbeat welcome, Welch invoked the "worldwide interest" in the research that they were all doing and "the tremendous dollar expansion of this young industry." Together, they were fighting an epic battle against germs, he said. They had made great progress, but the war was not yet won, because the widespread use of antibiotics had given rise to new, battle-hardened bacteria that were *resistant* to these drugs.

As Welch spoke, a thin man with an olive complexion and a pencil mustache looked on with muted excitement. His name was Félix Martí-Ibáñez, and he was a charming, if slightly unctuous, physician and Welch's partner in organizing the event. Martí-Ibáñez was a psychiatrist by training who had practiced in Barcelona and been wounded in the Spanish Civil War before immigrating to the United States. In New York, he had held positions at a number of pharmaceutical companies, including Roche, and done research in the asylum at Creedmoor, where he worked closely with the Sackler brothers. In a letter he wrote in 1956, Arthur Sackler described Martí-Ibáñez as his "dearest friend," remarking, "There is no man in medicine, in fact, no man I know, for whom I have greater affection than Félix."

Like Arthur, Martí-Ibáñez fashioned himself as a Renaissance man. He discoursed on a wide range of subjects in his mellifluous Spanish accent and liked to claim that his father, who had been a professor in Spain, was the author of "some five hundred books." In addition to publishing medical papers with the Sacklers, Martí-Ibáñez wrote novels and short stories and volumes of medical history and columns in popular magazines (*Cosmopolitan*, 1963: "It is no longer 'fashionable' to be ill").

In recent years, Martí-Ibáñez had been working for Arthur at his advertising agency, William Douglas McAdams. But he had also been focusing on a publishing company that he'd established a few years earlier, called MD Publications. MD put out a glossy magazine about medicine, featuring lots of sumptuous advertising from pharmaceutical companies. It also published a pair of technical journals, *Antibiotics and Chemotherapy* and *Antibiotic Medicine and Clinical Therapy*, which Henry Welch co-edited with Martí-Ibáñez. The journals were sponsors of this conference. It was Martí-Ibáñez who had proposed to Welch that they work together. The two men were very different: whereas Martí-Ibáñez was a flamboyantly cultured European, with a habit of speaking in flowering mixed metaphors, Welch was a plainspoken, meat-and-potatoes mid-century American man. But they forged a close friendship, with Martí-Ibáñez tending to business in New York while Welch continued to run his division at the FDA in Washington. Martí-Ibáñez liked to send Welch letters with comical doodles in the margins, like a tiny cartoon man reaching for a big bottle of the tranquilizer Miltown.

If the notion of an FDA regulator serving as editor of a private sector journal that covered the very industry that he happened to be regulating seemed a bit strange, neither Welch nor Martí-Ibáñez dwelled on it. And if anyone at the FDA had issues, they knew better than to raise them. "Welch had strong opinions and did not brook contradiction," one former associate recalled. Welch had *created* the antibiotics division at the FDA, and he was not averse to throwing his weight around in the bureaucracy or exercising his available prerogatives. When he wanted to build a swimming pool at his home in suburban Maryland, he ordered a bunch of his FDA underlings to leave the agency for an afternoon and come dig it themselves. (They "felt obliged," another former FDA colleague recalled. "In order to keep their job.")

The conference at the Willard was co-sponsored by the FDA, but all the expenses were paid for by the journals that Martí-Ibáñez and Welch published. In a letter to Welch, Martí-Ibáñez described the "unique opportunity" the two men had to "slant" the symposium in a direction that would "be most useful to the audience of our publications." From the beginning of their relationship, Welch had known, or at least suspected, that there was some other silent partner who had a stake in the journals: some unnamed backer who helped bankroll the whole enterprise. But when he pressed Martí-Ibáñez about who this person might be, the Spaniard was evasive, saying that the "private and confidential aspects of our work" should not be "open to anyone." Not even Welch.

"We are now in the third era of antibiotic therapy," Welch announced, triumphantly, at the Willard. The first era had involved "narrow spectrum" antibiotics, like penicillin. The second era came with the introduction of broad-spectrum therapies, like the Pfizer drug Terramycin, which were effective against a range of disease-causing bacteria. The *third* era, Welch explained, would be characterized by "synergistic" combinations of different therapies, which could attack even illnesses that resisted traditional antibiotics.

A few of the foreign visitors in the ballroom that morning expressed unease at the spectacle of America's antibiotics czar sounding so much like an industry booster. But such skeptics were in the minority. "Deadliest Ills Defeated by Antibiotics," *The Washington Post* declared, describing the conference in excited tones and extolling the "conquest" of stubborn infections and the power of "the so-called wonder drugs." Scarcely an hour had passed after Welch's remarks before Pfizer put out a press release hailing "the third era in antibiotic treatment" and introducing a new drug of its own, Sigmamycin, which the company billed as the first "synergistic combination," which could attack "germs that have learned to live with older antibiotics." The release pointed out that no less an authority than Henry Welch of the FDA had cited synergistic combinations as "comprising a new and powerful trend."

For Welch and Martí-Ibáñez, the conference was a resounding success. But the symposium—and in particular Welch's opening speech about the "third era" in antibiotics—would soon embroil both men in a scandal and a federal investigation that would end one of their careers and ensnare Arthur Sackler and his brothers.

✦ ✦ ✦

One day in 1960, Arthur Sackler bought a house in Manhattan. It was an impulse buy. He didn't even consult Marietta. It was a small town house, four stories and a basement, on East Fifty-Seventh Street. After he surprised Marietta with the news that he had purchased a new home, she joked that it was "too small for all of us but just right for him!" The building *would* be helpful for Arthur's business, she acknowledged, and, anyway, she had been feeling cooped up in the house on Long Island. After Denise was born, Marietta had briefly gone back to work, passing her medical exams. But Arthur did not see why she insisted on working, and she felt guilty being away from the children, so she ended up abandoning her career after a year. If the family moved into the city, perhaps it would be an opportunity for them to spend more time with Arthur. So, while Arthur supervised the decorating of the new home, Marietta oversaw the relocation of herself, her kids, the dog, the ham-

ster, and a litter of white mice. They would hold on to the Long Island
house, as a weekend retreat. And, not long after moving in, Marietta
began negotiating with the woman who owned an identical town house
next door, with an eye to buying it and combining the two, which the
Sacklers ultimately did.

Marietta liked the idea of her children living in the city, where
they might encounter a diversity of experience and stimulation beyond
the narrow idyll of their suburban life on Long Island. In the city, she
mused, they might cross paths with "a poor man, a blind person, a beg-
gar." She treated the whole experience as if it were an urban safari, rife
with danger, but also with wonder and beauty. When little Arthur was
ready to go off to his new school in the big city, she gave him a compass,
in case he got lost.

The town house on Fifty-Seventh Street was just a short walk from
the building at 15 East Sixty-Second Street where the Sackler brothers
had recently set up shop. The warren of offices, in a narrow limestone
building just a few steps off Central Park, had become home to the
brothers' psychiatric research activities, to the new foundations that
they established to administer their charitable giving, to their publishing interests, and to a range of other, smaller concerns. From here, the
brothers could shuttle to the McAdams agency on Fifty-Ninth Street
or down to their pharmaceutical company, Purdue Frederick, in Greenwich Village.

As the youngest son, Raymond Sackler was spending a lot of time
tending to their mother, Sophie. After several years of the silent treatment, Sophie had finally started talking to Marietta, and eventually the
two women developed a warm relationship. But Arthur had conflicted
feelings about his mother and spent as little time as possible with her.
He felt great respect for her and gratitude for all that she had invested
in him. But Sophie was overbearing and always had been. She made
sure that her secular sons celebrated Passover and other high holidays,
but otherwise Arthur kept his distance. Eventually, Sophie was diagnosed with lung cancer. Mortimer kept her in his home and arranged
her medical care. When the younger Arthur Sackler turned thirteen,
the family decided to throw him a Bar Mitzvah, on the grounds that
it would bring Sophie comfort to see the firstborn son of her firstborn
son initiated into the faith. There was no service at the synagogue, just
a party at the Waldorf Astoria, but the whole family came. The older

Arthur wore a bow tie. Sophie beamed with pride, a rope of pearls around her neck.

Purdue Frederick had enjoyed success, earlier in the century, with Gray's Glycerine Tonic, a sherry-based "elixir" that, the company suggested, stimulated the appetite, promoted nutrition, and should be taken "whenever a general tonic is needed or desired." It became a winking joke at the company that this pick-me-up had done "extremely well during Prohibition." In more recent years, Purdue had specialized in a range of unglamorous products, like an earwax remover and a laxative called Senokot, for "care of the delinquent colon." ("Have you considered the possibility for one of your Senokot mailings of a world map showing the geography of constipation?" Félix Martí-Ibáñez asked Raymond and Mortimer in 1955. Constipation, he noted, was a "world problem.") But the company was now looking to leverage this somewhat embarrassing success by branching into other markets. While Raymond focused on the domestic side of Purdue, Mortimer traveled abroad, in an effort to expand the company. Mortimer was the most extroverted of the Sackler brothers, and the most freewheeling. He took well to the role of roving international businessman. "I leave for Brussels tomorrow afternoon, then Amsterdam, London and back to Paris by Friday evening," he wrote to Martí-Ibáñez from the Hotel Eden au Lac in Zurich in 1960. "Next weekend either Scandinavia or home, depending on word from New York." If Arthur was consumed by a mania for art collecting, Mortimer was developing his own mania, for travel. "Have finished four days of ski lessons in beautiful St. Moritz and am a confirmed ski bug, looking forward to Vermont, Pittsfield, points West and back to Italy, France, Switzerland and Austria next year," he wrote, adding, as a wistful aside, "But there is still no substitute for the Riviera."

The dawn of the 1960s was a grand moment for the Sacklers. So many of their aspirations seemed to be coming to fruition, and there was so much yet to come. In a letter to Martí-Ibáñez, Arthur wrote that in "the occasional moment or two that I can get my head above water," he had been thinking about "what the future holds" for the Sackler brothers. But what Arthur did not know was that on the busy sidewalks at the corner of Fifth Avenue and Sixty-Second Street, mingling with the crowd walking to and from Central Park, were federal investigators, who had placed the Sackler headquarters under surveillance.

✢ ✢ ✢

The trouble started when Arthur Sackler attracted the scrutiny of a nettlesome investigative reporter, a man named John Lear. A science editor at the *Saturday Review,* Lear had come from *Collier's* magazine, where he had acquired a reputation as a dogged muckraker with a theatrical flair. In August 1950, five years to the week after the U.S. nuclear attack on Japan, Lear had published a cover story in *Collier's* called "Hiroshima, U.S.A.," which explored in gruesome, if conjectural, detail what a Soviet nuclear attack on New York City might look like. The cover featured an apocalyptic full-color illustration of lower Manhattan engulfed in flame, with bridges collapsing into rivers and a mushroom cloud darkening the sky. Like Arthur Sackler, Lear knew how to get people's attention.

One night in the late 1950s, Lear had dinner with a research physician he knew. When they had finished their meal, the man invited Lear to visit the hospital laboratory where he worked. There was something the doctor had grown concerned about, which he wanted to discuss with Lear. "Take a look at this stuff," he said, opening a drawer filled with pharmaceutical advertisements and free samples of new drugs. The ads were often fraudulent, the doctor said, with indignation. They made unsupportable claims about what the drugs could do. This was a big story, he insisted, as he showed Lear a series of ads for Sigmamycin, the "third era" combination antibiotic that Pfizer had unveiled at the conference at the Willard back in 1956.

One of the ads, a brochure that had been sent to doctors in the mail, said,

More and More Physicians Find Sigmamycin
the Antibiotic Therapy of Choice

It featured an array of business cards with the names, addresses, and office hours of eight doctors, who appeared to be endorsing the product. There was a doctor in Miami, another in Tucson, a third in Lowell, Massachusetts. Sigmamycin was not just "highly effective," the ad suggested, but "clinically proved." As Lear inspected the brochure, the doctor explained that he had written to each of the named physicians, to inquire about the results of the clinical tests that they had presumably conducted. He handed Lear a stack of envelopes. It was the letters he had written. They were all stamped RETURN TO WRITER—UNCLAIMED.

Intrigued, Lear wrote to the doctors himself. His letters came back unopened. He sent telegrams, only to be informed that no such addresses existed. Finally, he tried calling the telephone numbers on the business cards in the ad, but without success: the numbers were made up, too. Pfizer had blasted this advertisement, with its fake endorsements, to physicians across the country. And it looked so plausible, so real, with the special patina of authority conferred by eight MDs. The ad was polished, impressive, and fundamentally deceptive. It had been produced by Arthur Sackler's agency.

In January 1959, Lear published the initial results of his investigation in a *Saturday Review* article called "Taking the Miracle Out of the Miracle Drugs." In stark contrast to the euphoria that generally accompanied public discussion of antibiotics, Lear suggested that these drugs were being wildly overprescribed, often without any firm medical basis for doing so, and that the ubiquity and sophistication of pharmaceutical advertising shared some of the blame.

After the article was published, Lear was deluged with mail. A number of the medical professionals who got in touch suggested that if Lear was pursuing this particular theme of the corruption of medicine by business interests, he might want to look into the fellow who ran the Division of Antibiotics at the FDA, a guy named Henry Welch. So Lear put in a call to Welch, to request an interview.

What a coincidence, Welch said, when Lear got him on the phone. He had just been sitting down at that very moment to write Lear a letter about all the "mistakes you made in your article."

Lear traveled to Washington to see Welch, and they spoke for two hours. Welch seemed at ease. He assured Lear that any fears about the marketing of new drugs were misplaced. Surely, he scoffed, America's doctors "are not naive enough to be fooled by ads." The dangers of antibiotics had likewise been exaggerated, Welch continued, and to the extent that Lear had sources in the medical community who were telling him otherwise, they were people who "spoke from ignorance." In a textbook Washington power move, Welch had invited an aide from the FDA to join him for the interview, and the function of this apparatchik, it seemed to Lear, was mostly to express profound agreement with everything that Welch was saying. But now Lear turned the tables, saying he would like to speak with Welch in private and asking, politely, if the subordinate could leave. When they were alone, Lear said that he had spoken to sources who suggested that Welch derived significant income from the two journals that he ran with Félix Martí-Ibáñez.

"Where my income comes from is my own business," Welch snapped, dropping the pretense of affability.

This struck Lear as a peculiar position for a public official to stake out. Welch explained that the two journals were run by an outfit called MD Publications and that he had no financial stake in that company. "My only connection is as an editor, for which I receive an honorarium," he said, adding that he enjoyed editing the journals, "and I don't intend to give them up." Lear had hoped to ask a few more questions. There was that business about the "third era" of antibiotics, for instance. But Welch had turned brittle, and the interview was over.

Welch might have thought, when he got Lear out of his office, that he had seen the end of this matter. But if he did, then he badly underestimated John Lear, because Welch was not the only official in Washington whom Lear was talking to. In fact, Lear had recently met with a couple of staffers of a U.S. senator—a senator who happened to share Lear's penchant for investigation.

✦ ✦ ✦

Senator Estes Kefauver was a ruddy, rawboned public servant who stood six feet three and had grown up in the mountains of Tennessee. A Yale-trained lawyer, he was a southern liberal and the sort of earnest do-gooder who can occasionally strike even his supporters as being a bit in love with his own virtue. Kefauver was a trustbuster, chairman of the powerful antitrust and monopoly subcommittee. This was a time when congressional committees enjoyed enormous power and resources. When Kefauver started looking into the pharmaceutical industry in the late 1950s, his subcommittee had a full-time staff of thirty-eight.

Kefauver liked to investigate things. A decade earlier, he had leaped to national prominence when he launched a groundbreaking investigation of the Mafia. He traveled around the country holding hearings in Chicago, Detroit, Miami, and other cities, summoning underworld capos with names like Jake "Greasy Thumb" Guzik and Tony

"Big Tuna" Accardo to testify. The hearings were televised, at a time when television was still a relatively young medium, and they garnered unprecedented ratings. The press anointed Kefauver's hearings "the greatest TV show television has ever aired." *Time* magazine put the senator on the cover—three times. Kefauver ran for president in 1952, beating Harry Truman in the New Hampshire primary but ultimately losing the Democratic nomination to Adlai Stevenson. Four years later, he made another unsuccessful run for the White House, this time as Stevenson's vice presidential candidate. By 1958, Kefauver appeared to have resigned himself to his role as a powerful senator, and it was at this point that the famous TV crime fighter turned his attention to the drug industry.

As Kefauver's staff commenced their investigation, they fanned out across the country and interviewed some three hundred people. The investigators were in close touch with John Lear, and behind the scenes he fed them tips and valuable contacts. When Kefauver was investigating the mob, he had noticed that racketeers insulated themselves with a cadre of putatively legitimate lawyers, politicians, and fixers. The steel industry did the same thing, paying top dollar to professional influence peddlers in pin-striped suits. As this new investigation got under way, Kefauver noticed that executives in the pharmaceutical industry had elevated this form of combat by well-paid proxy to an art. "These drug fellows pay for a lobby that makes the steel boys look like popcorn vendors," one of his staffers remarked. Kefauver had noticed the way the mob could corrupt government—how they bought off sheriffs and threw around so much money that the very public agencies that should have been policing their activities were co-opted instead. Again, there seemed to be a parallel with the pharmaceutical business. Kefauver believed that regulatory agencies can be hoodwinked, all too easily, into doing the bidding of the industry they are regulating. But when he started convening hearings, at the end of 1959, he might not have been prepared for what they would reveal.

One of the witnesses summoned before the subcommittee was a woman named Barbara Moulton who had spent five years as a drug examiner at the FDA before resigning in protest. The agency had "failed utterly" in its task of policing the way prescription drugs were marketed and sold, she testified. Moulton described an environment at the FDA of unrelenting pressure from the drug companies and a culture in which regulators, rather than regulate the drug companies and their products, showed slavish deference to the private sector. Moulton's insistence on actually doing her job had stalled her advancement at the agency, she said. She had been reprimanded by a supervisor for not being "sufficiently polite to members of the pharmaceutical industry." Moulton singled out the Pfizer antibiotic Sigmamycin as a typical case in which the agency had subjected a new drug to scant review. "I found it impossible to believe that anyone with a knowledge of clinical anti- biotic medicine could honestly reach the conclusion that it substanti- ated the claims made for these products," she said. The drug industry "misleads" physicians, Moulton concluded. The notion that the FDA actually protects American consumers was nothing but a comforting myth.

The initial purpose of the hearings had been to focus on monopo- listic pricing in the pharma industry. But once Kefauver and his staff started calling witnesses and asking them questions, the inquiry reori- ented to the more profound and widespread problems of deceptive drug marketing. Kefauver was a patient but persistent interlocutor. His affect was mild-mannered and almost melancholy, and he was unfail- ingly polite, letting a witness finish, then taking a deep drag on his cigarette, before prodding, gently, with a pointed question. When the president of Pfizer, John McKeen, came from Brooklyn to defend his company, Kefauver pointed out that Pfizer's own medical director had found that 27 percent of people experienced side effects from a drug that the company promoted as having no side effects. "You have blitzed the medical profession with your advertising," Kefauver drawled. "In my opinion, you have withheld the most important fact from physicians of the United States."

At one point in the hearings, several PR men appeared before the committee, and Kefauver started to ask questions, in his plodding, methodical manner, about the Fourth Annual Antibiotics Symposium at the Willard Hotel several years earlier, and, in particular, about the speech that had been delivered at that symposium by Henry Welch. This was the speech in which Welch had talked about the "third era in antibiotics," a line Pfizer executives liked so much that they immedi- ately incorporated it into their advertising for Sigmamycin. Kefauver called a young man named Gideon Nachumi to testify, and Nachumi explained that when he was in medical school, some years earlier, he had taken time off to make money in the advertising business. Initially, he worked on the Pfizer account at William Douglas McAdams, before moving to Pfizer itself, where he served as an in-house copywriter. Of course, it was McAdams that had produced the fraudulent ad with the business cards. But Kefauver was more interested in an experience that Nachumi had at Pfizer. At some point in the early fall of 1956, Nachumi testified, he had been given an assignment, to "revise a speech by Dr. Welch." The remarks, he was told, would be presented at the Fourth Annual Antibiotics Symposium. Prior to the conference, Nachumi revealed, Henry Welch had delivered to Pfizer a copy of his proposed remarks, "for approval." The company had then instructed Nachumi to give the speech a quick once-over, to "jazz" it up. The subcommittee staff had obtained, by subpoena, a copy of the original draft of Welch's speech, and when Kefauver presented it to Nachumi, the young doctor acknowledged that the one big change he had made was to add to the speech the passage about the "third era of antibiotics." Someone at Pfizer had dreamed up the line, he explained, as a marketing "theme" for Sigmamycin. It wasn't that Pfizer admired the FDA man's sound bite so much that they borrowed it for their ad copy. The company had insinuated its own ad copy directly into the speech.

"You definitely have a recollection that it was *your* suggestion that this sentence be included?" one of Kefauver's aides asked Nachumi.

"Yes, sir," Nachumi replied. After all, he explained, having such a quotation come from a "respected authority" like the chief of antibiotics at the FDA positioned the company to build a whole promotional campaign. The dawn of the third era was signified, in Pfizer's ads, by an image of a glowing sun rising over the sea, he said. "I think one can see its pictorial value," Nachumi mused. "It kind of implies that the development of Sigmamycin is of comparable importance to the discovery of the broad spectrum antibiotics, and perhaps even of penicillin."

As it turned out, Welch's final remarks had been published in one of the journals that he edited with Félix Martí-Ibáñez. And, under the terms of his deal with Martí-Ibáñez, Welch was entitled to half of any income generated by the sale of those reprints. And Pfizer, following the symposium, had ordered reprints. Lots of reprints. To be precise, Pfizer had ordered 238,000 copies of the speech.

"It was a standing joke in the office," another Pfizer PR man, Warren Kiefer, testified. Of course, the ostensible purpose of ordering the

reprints was that the company could give them away, as part of its promotional effort. But how many copies of Dr. Henry Welch's welcome
remarks from the Fourth Annual Antibiotics Symposium could you
realistically give away? Through the course of the whole promotional
campaign, they managed to get rid of only a few hundred.

"Were they piled up around your office?" Kefauver wondered.

"They tended to clutter the storeroom," Kiefer replied.

"Were they . . . thrown out eventually?"

"I would assume so," Kiefer said.

And now Kefauver moved in for the kill. "What was the reason for
buying so many, do you know? If you had no use for them?"

The PR man dissembled. But to anyone who was paying attention,
the answer was clear: by buying all those reprints, Pfizer was bribing
Henry Welch.

✛ ✛ ✛

As the hearings played out over several months in Washington,
Kefauver's staff was investigating the Sacklers. Arthur might not have
been personally implicated in the various improprieties the committee was uncovering, but he kept popping up at one degree of remove.
McAdams was his agency. Pfizer was his client. Sigmamycin was his
campaign. Félix Martí-Ibáñez was his friend and had been his employee
at McAdams. "During the course of the drug investigation, I have from
time to time heard rumors of the 'Sackler Brothers,'" one of Kefauver's trusted deputies, John Blair, wrote in a memo on March 16, 1960.
At first, Blair had assumed that the Sacklers were a "fringe" operation.
But the more he looked into it, the more frequently that name kept
appearing. Blair had learned that Martí-Ibáñez had a silent partner in
his publishing venture, MD Publications. He was convinced that it was
the Sacklers.

"Any outfit which has been able to establish such close ties with the
most powerful man in government with respect to antibiotics is hardly
a fringe operation," Blair wrote, adding that the "clandestine manner"
in which the brothers operated "suggests that there may be more here
than meets the eye." As Kefauver's staff attempted to tally the many
interests of the Sacklers, it emerged that they were enormously prolific.
But the brothers had been so effective in concealing their activities that

they remained mysterious, even to government investigators. "There are three Sackler brothers—Arthur, Raymond and Mortimer," Blair wrote. "[They] are said to be psychiatrists." He mentioned a woman named Marietta who "may be Arthur's wife."

The investigators had discovered the family headquarters on Sixty-Second Street, "an unostentatious building" that, upon examination, turned out to house "a bee-hive of activity." Some of the mail that went to the building was addressed to the McAdams agency, some to MD Publications. The investigators identified no fewer than twenty separate corporate entities that were linked to the building. But it was difficult to tell where one ended and the next began, because "the whole operation is cloaked in secrecy."

On several oversized pieces of paper, the staff tried to diagram the sprawling web of the Sacklers' interests, with little boxes containing the names of corporations and individuals and a tangle of lines connecting them. "The Sackler empire is a completely integrated operation," Blair wrote. They could develop a drug, have it clinically tested, secure favorable reports from the doctors and hospitals with which they had connections, devise an advertising campaign in their agency, publish the clinical articles and the advertisements in their own medical journals, and use their public relations muscle to place articles in newspapers and magazines.

Working in tandem with the investigators, John Lear, the journalist, wrote an article in the *Saturday Review* in which he identified Arthur as the "guiding genius of McAdams" and wondered what role he might play in relation to the unfolding scandal involving Martí-Ibáñez and Welch. Kefauver had discovered, when he investigated the mob, that they all tended to use the same accountants, and Lear now pointed out that the Sacklers' trusty accountant, Louis Goldburt, seemed to represent everyone involved. In a letter to Kefauver's staff, Lear wrote that Goldburt was "the first real link I've been able to establish between Martí-Ibáñez and Sackler." He found a document in which Martí-Ibáñez referred to Goldburt as "our chief accountant." He also said that, according to one of his informants, "Arthur Sackler is a silent partner in Frohlich"—Arthur's ostensible rival, the L. W. Frohlich agency. At one point, Lear clipped a cartoon he had come across in a medical journal that depicted an octopus with tentacles that extended to "drug manufacturing," "medical advertising," and "medical journals." Lear sent the clipping to John Blair, with a note that said, "The owner of this particular octopus is a family of three."

What the investigators were most interested in establishing was a firm connection between the Sackler brothers and Henry Welch. They had concluded, at a certain point, that Martí-Ibáñez was "simply a 'front' man" for the Sacklers, but that was the thing about front men: as long as it was Martí-Ibáñez who was doing the dirty work, it would be difficult to assign any responsibility for his conduct—or awareness of it, even—to the Sacklers. That would change if the investigators could uncover some direct link between the brothers and the FDA man.

As for Welch himself, his circumstances were looking dire. The more the subcommittee dug, the more shocking impropriety they unearthed, and Welch was right in the middle of it. In March 1960, as the investigators were issuing subpoenas and taking testimony, he suffered a minor heart attack. On May 5, Kefauver informed Welch and Martí-Ibáñez that they would both need to appear on Capitol Hill to testify in two weeks. Welch vowed to defend his integrity, saying that he would come and fight the allegations "if you have to carry me in on a stretcher."

But he never showed. Martí-Ibáñez refused to appear as well, citing his own health. "Dr. Welch was said to be in danger of a heart attack if placed on the witness stand," the newspapers said. "Dr. Martí-Ibáñez was reported to have such a severe case of glaucoma as to be in danger of blindness."

Martí-Ibáñez had been endeavoring, quietly, to find his friend a soft landing. In March, he had written a letter marked "Personal and confidential" to Bill Frohlich. "Henry Welch was up here last week," Martí-Ibáñez wrote, "and we discussed many things, including his future." Welch was thinking that it might be time for him to leave government, Martí-Ibáñez told Frohlich. He wanted to enter the private sector, which would give him a chance to leverage his "unique connections with the leaders of the pharmaceutical industry." Perhaps Frohlich might have a job for him, Martí-Ibáñez suggested, adding, "I know you are always looking for good people."

But it was too late, by that point, to save the career of Henry Welch. When Kefauver's staff issued subpoenas for bank records, they made a jaw-dropping discovery. Henry Welch had told John Lear that he earned only an "honorarium" for his services editing the two journals with Martí-Ibáñez. But that had been a lie. In fact, he earned 7.5 percent of all the advertising revenue that came into MD Publications, and 50 percent of the revenue generated by any reprints of articles in the two journals he edited. At the FDA, Welch earned a salary of $17,500 a year, a figure that was commensurate with his level as one of the most senior officials at the agency. In addition, the investigators learned, between 1953 and 1960, Welch had made $287,142 from his publishing ventures. "Once those figures get out, they'll murder these fellows," one senator exclaimed, referring to Welch and Martí-Ibáñez.

When the figures did come out, Welch resigned from the FDA in disgrace. He continued to maintain his innocence, blaming "politics" for his ouster and saying, "I challenge anyone to search the journals and come up with any article, paragraph or sentence which reflects a lack of editorial or scientific integrity." But Welch was done. He avoided criminal prosecution, got to keep his full pension, and retired to Florida. The FDA, meanwhile, announced a review of every drug Welch had approved.

This amounted to a significant trophy for the investigation. But Kefauver wasn't finished. He wanted to interview Bill Frohlich and sent him a subpoena. The senator was discovering, however, that one minor public health crisis afflicting the nation appeared to derive from his own issuance of subpoenas, and like Welch and Martí-Ibáñez, Frohlich declined to testify, supplying a letter from his doctor that described "an eye disorder which might be aggravated by his appearance." Just in case anyone doubted this excuse, Frohlich left nothing to chance, making an impromptu trip out of the country. The committee was informed that he was indisposed, "somewhere in Germany."

In December 1961, a press report announced that Kefauver would soon wrap up his hearings, explaining that he hoped the evidence he had gathered would generate support for legislation to correct "abuses in the drug industry." But the article noted that before he concluded the investigation, there was one final witness he wanted to summon: "Dr. Arthur M. Sackler, chairman of McAdams."

❖ ❖ ❖

One thing that Marietta had always noticed about her husband was his peculiar ability to "shut himself off from all but the single area of his focus." As the investigation and muckraking articles and hearings swirled around him, Arthur was busy managing his businesses, his collecting, and his families. He despised Kefauver, whom he regarded as a demagogue out to get the pharmaceutical industry. Arthur had never had much faith in government regulators and tended to regard them, contemptuously, as bumbling bureaucrats, the kinds of people who probably went into public service because they couldn't get into med school. Kefauver's theory, Arthur complained, was that "practicing physicians were either fools or knaves," and medical researchers and scientific publications "could not be trusted." Arthur was particularly sensitive to any implication that he personally might be mired in conflicts of interests. But he dismissed any such suggestion as "innuendoes" and "loose talk" and insisted that all he ever did was try to help people.

He had always shunned publicity, and now that it came, courtesy of investigations by the *Saturday Review* and the U.S. Senate, publicity turned out to be every bit as dangerous as he had long supposed it could be. A number of notable doctors on the editorial boards of journals that Martí-Ibáñez published had started making noises of protest, sending huffy inquiries about whether "the three Doctors Sackler" might secretly own the journals. (Martí-Ibáñez wrote that the Sacklers were "dear and admired friends," while pointedly refusing to answer the question.) "I used to be pleased to have my name on the board" of one of the publications, a prominent physician told *Newsweek*. "Now I'm disgusted. I've resigned."

When he was subpoenaed to come to Washington, Arthur did not claim an eye injury or flee to Europe. In later years, his decision to stand and fight would become a mythic chapter in his biography. "This was the era of McCarthyite witch-hunts so every one in the pharmaceutical business was terrified of ruination," the account published by a Sackler family foundation recalled. "Sackler offered to take the brunt of the scrutiny for the entire industry." He hired Clark Clifford, a legendary Washington power lawyer and fixer who had been a close adviser to President Truman. And on January 30, 1962, Arthur strode into the Senate chamber.

"The committee will come to order," Kefauver said. One theme of the hearings, he pointed out, had been advertising and promotion. "Claims of a drug's efficacy are frequently excessive," Kefauver said, and warnings about side effects are "often wholly absent." So, today, they would hear from the man who ran one of the two leading firms in drug advertising. "Do you solemnly swear the testimony you will give will be the whole truth and nothing but the truth?" Kefauver asked.

"I do," Arthur replied.

This was a big moment for Kefauver's staff: the octopus himself. They had been war-gaming this interrogation for weeks, drawing up a series of scripts, with questions that Kefauver should ask and plausible answers Sackler might offer.

"I am a doctor of medicine and the chairman of the board of William Douglas McAdams," Arthur said. "I am currently the Director of the Laboratories for Therapeutic Research and professor of therapeutic research at the Brooklyn College of Pharmacy, Long Island University." He continued, "I have published, presented, or reported approximately sixty papers in medical periodicals, at international conferences on psychiatry and physiology." For the committee's reference, he had brought along a bibliography: "I would appreciate its incorporation in the record." Arthur noted that his psychiatric research "has been recognized here and abroad." He had two careers, he said, one in medicine and the other in business. He pursued them "concurrently in time but independently of each other."

When he had last appeared on Capitol Hill, a decade earlier, Arthur had been less sure of himself. He had come hat in hand, begging for funding, and been put in his place by an anti-Semitic senator. But the Arthur Sackler in the chamber today was a different person: a man of culture, refinement, and tremendous medical authority. He had a patrician accent, which he wielded on his interlocutors like a switchblade. "He seemed to parade his voice as a clear sign of his achievements," one person who knew him recalled. As Kefauver and his associates asked questions about the ways in which drugs are made and marketed, Arthur was unflappable and accommodating, occasionally exhibiting a gentle impatience with the ignorance of these nonmedical types. The McAdams agency wasn't just a bunch of admen, he pointed out. There were *doctors* who worked there, many of them. Under the firm's "predominantly medical management," McAdams adhered to a credo that "good ethical pharmaceutical advertising plays a positive role in advancing the health of the community." Arthur had long ago come to appreciate that it always helps to underplay the size of one's influence and assets, and now he insisted that McAdams was not one of the two biggest medical advertising agencies at all. In fact, it was a pretty tiny operation. "We at McAdams would naturally be *flattered* to think that we are important," he purred. "But the cold figures show our relatively small size in the economic sphere."

Kefauver's preferred mode of interrogation was to use his own politeness to lull a witness into a false feeling of security and let him talk until he'd talked himself into a corner. But this deferential approach was backfiring, badly, with Arthur Sackler. Medical advertising *saves lives,* Arthur proclaimed, in full filibuster, because it cuts down the time between the discovery of a new drug and its use by medical practitioners. "Each week, each month, or year that rapid, reliable pharmaceutical communications reduce the discovery-use time gap saves patients' lives, comfort, morale, and money," he continued, adding that he would be happy to supply the senators with "the background material for that."

All those detailed battle plans Kefauver's staff had drawn up had officially gone out the window. Arthur was lecturing the committee as if they were a bunch of first-year medical students. Doctors would never be seduced into believing false advertising, Arthur proclaimed, and, anyway, *what* false advertising? Most of the advertising he saw, and certainly all of the advertising he produced, was more than reasonable. He interrupted his own soliloquy long enough to say, "I hope I am not going too rapidly," before barreling on. At one point, Kefauver asked, almost apologetically, if Sackler might "yield to a question."

"Senator Kefauver, could I proceed simply because I believe that my testimony will clarify things so that there may be no need for further questions," Arthur replied.

That shut the senator up, but not for long. Eventually, he just went ahead and interrupted Arthur, blurting out a question, and Arthur said, "We are coming to that in a moment, Senator," without breaking stride.

It was an extraordinary performance. At a certain point, one of the staffers barked, "Doctor, are you *through?*" But he wasn't. He challenged the committee's facts and its interpretation of the facts. "Senator Kefauver, I would like to make this point very clearly," Arthur said, as he corrected some elementary misimpression. "If you personally had taken the training that a physician requires to get a degree, you would never have made this mistake."

He danced and danced, and none of them could land a blow. Of course, there is no therapy that is completely without side effects, Arthur conceded. But when Kefauver questioned him about a specific side effect—hair loss—associated with a heart medication, Arthur deadpanned, "I would prefer to have thin hair to thick coronaries."

So overwhelming was the rout that day that the investigators failed to question Arthur about a series of letters that they had obtained in response to their subpoenas. The letters were never raised in the hearing, or made public in any way, but the subcommittee had them: for decades, the letters would remain tucked away, in a great stack of folders, in a cardboard box, in a collection of forty similar cardboard boxes that contain the complete files of Kefauver's drug investigation. They are letters between Henry Welch and Arthur Sackler. "Dear Dr. Sackler," Welch wrote on February 23, 1956, "I was very glad to have the opportunity to talk with you by phone and sorry that we could not get together on my recent trip to New York." Welch proceeds to ask Sackler for "a little outside help" in funding a new journal.

"I would very much like to meet you and get to know you better," Sackler wrote back, five days later. Three years after that, when Welch's troubles started, Arthur wrote to him again. "I would like to tell you at a time of trial that you have many friends, who...stand shoulder to shoulder with you. The unjustified persecution to which you have been exposed through the headline seeking sensational efforts of a petty individual"—a reference to the journalist John Lear—"is heartbreaking." To the compromised head of antibiotics at the FDA, a man whose compromise Arthur, as silent partner in MD Publications, had helped to underwrite, a man Arthur's client Pfizer had bribed with the purchase of hundreds of thousands of useless reprints, Arthur wrote, "To you and your family, our warmest wishes for everything good."

But the investigators never had a chance to ask Arthur about Welch. They had a set amount of time for questioning, which had presumably been negotiated in advance by Clifford, Arthur's powerful attorney, and during the time they had, they hardly got a word in edgewise. As he and his lawyers stood and prepared to leave the chamber, Arthur could only have felt victorious. Before he walked out the door, he took a final look at Kefauver and thanked him for the opportunity to state his case. Then he said, with a flourish, "The record speaks for itself," and walked out.

Chapter 7

THE DENDUR DERBY

A SMALL TEMPLE STOOD on the banks of the Nile. It had originally been erected by the local Roman governor, a decade or two before the birth of Christ, to commemorate a pair of brothers who were said to have drowned in the river. The temple was made of sandstone, and its walls were decorated with carved depictions of the brothers, Pedesi and Pihor, worshipping the god Osiris, and his consort, Isis. Jesus Christ was born and died, and eventually the temple was converted into a Christian church. Over the centuries, new religions flourished, new languages were born, great empires rose and fell. And all the while, the temple stood. Of course, there was plunder: among the great temples of Egypt, any treasure that could be removed was eventually looted by ragged grave robbers, or, later, by more elegant grave robbers who wore linen suits that sagged in the sun and called themselves Egyptologists. For centuries, people came to study the temple and to ponder the vanished universe of which it was a relic. Alongside the original carvings, the temple bore graffiti, which had been carved into the wall in demotic script, and the graffiti lived on, long after the demotic language died and there was nobody left, apart from scholars, who could read it. In 1821, an American lawyer and war veteran named Luther Bradish visited the temple and carved his name into the wall: L. BRADISH OF NY US 1821. A French photographer named Félix Bonfils visited in the late nineteenth century and scrawled his name in paint on the building. In photographs taken forty years later, after the Frenchman himself had died, you could still see his tag, BONFILS. But eventually the paint faded, and Bonfils was forgotten.

The impulse to defile an ancient temple by writing one's name on it could be seen as vandalism. But it was also an act of defiance—defiance of mortality, defiance of time itself. Today we know the names of those brothers, two thousand years after they drowned in the Nile. But we know the names of the vandals, too, because we can still read them on the temple wall. The man is dead. His name lives on.

By the 1960s, Egypt was a rapidly modernizing nation, and in order to control the annual flooding of the Nile, the country set out to build a dam. The dam would make it possible to manage the irrigation of the region. It would convert millions of acres of desert into arable land, and turbine units buried underground would generate hydroelectricity. The dam was hailed as a technical wonder, a "new pyramid." There was only one problem: by redistributing a huge body of water, the dam would create a three-hundred-mile lake, flooding the surrounding areas and engulfing five ancient temples that lay scattered in its path. For thousands of years, these architectural wonders had withstood the ravages of time. But now Egypt would be forced to choose between its future and its past. The Temple of Dendur, as it had become known, after the name of the place where it stood, was one of the vulnerable structures. It would be swept away.

An international campaign was launched to save "the Nubian monuments." The United Nations agreed to assist Egypt in relocating each ancient temple that would be affected by the dam. This would cost money, however, money that Egypt didn't have. So, the United States committed to pay $16 million to assist the effort. An Egyptian official, Abdel el Sawy, was moved by this act of generosity, and in 1965 he offered to give the Temple of Dendur to the United States, as a token of thanks. A nice gesture. But how do you give an eight-hundred-ton temple? And where in such a young country could such an old artifact live?

✧ ✧ ✧

The Metropolitan Museum of Art, which occupied a grand location on Fifth Avenue, jutting into Central Park, had originally been conceived in the immediate aftermath of the Civil War, when a group of prominent New Yorkers decided that the United States needed a great art museum to rival those of Europe. The museum was incorporated in 1870 and moved into the Fifth Avenue site a decade later. It started with a private art collection, consisting mostly of European paintings, which was a gift from John Taylor Johnston, a railroad tycoon, along with donations from some of his fellow robber barons. But from the very beginning, the museum exhibited a fascinating tension between the

interests and indulgences of its coterie of wealthy backers and a more
public-minded, egalitarian mission. The Met would be free, and open
to the public, but subsidized by gifts from the rich. At the dedication
of the museum, in 1880, one of its trustees, the lawyer Joseph Choate,
gave a speech to the Gilded Age industrialists who had assembled and,
in a bid for their support, offered the sly observation that what philanthropy really buys is immortality: "Think of it, ye millionaires of many
markets, what glory may yet be yours, if you only listen to our advice,
to convert pork into porcelain, grain and produce into priceless pottery,
the rude ores of commerce into sculptured marble." Railroad shares
and mining stocks—which in the next financial panic "shall surely
perish, like parched scrolls"—could be turned into a durable legacy,
Choate suggested, into "glorified canvases of the world's masters, which
shall adorn these walls for centuries." Through such transubstantia-
tion, he proposed, great fortunes could pass into enduring civic institutions. Over time, the crude origins of any given clan's largesse might
be forgotten, and instead future generations would remember only the
philanthropic legacy, prompted to do so by the family's name on some
gallery, some wing, perhaps even on the building itself.

By the early 1960s, the Met had become one of the biggest art museums in the world. But it was struggling. On the one hand, the museum
was aggressive in acquiring great art. In 1961, the Met paid a record
$2.3 million for the Rembrandt painting *Aristotle Contemplating a Bust of
Homer.* But at the same time, the museum could hardly afford to keep its
doors open and to pay its staff and was relying on allocations from the
already strained New York City budget to make ends meet. Attendance
wasn't a problem: after the Rembrandt acquisition, eighty-six thousand
visitors paraded past the painting in a few hours (to judge for themselves, one press account suggested, whether "a painting is worth the
price of a missile"). Three million people visited the museum every
year. The difficulty was, none of them were paying.

The sheer volume of visitors also compounded another problem:
the building had no air-conditioning. In high summer—peak tourist
season—the galleries were sweltering. So the museum needed funds
for a renovation that would include the installation of cooling units.
The Met's director at the time was a stocky, pipe-smoking connoisseur named James Rorimer. He announced a goal, in 1961, to have air-
conditioning installed at the Met by the time the New York World's

Fair opened three years later. He just needed to find a way to pay for it. So he turned for help to Arthur Sackler.

Rorimer chose his moment well. The Sackler brothers had just started dabbling in philanthropy, and Arthur's passion for art collecting was in full bloom. The brothers had emerged from the Kefauver investigations completely unscathed, which left them feeling energized and bullish. According to Richard Leather, who served as a lawyer for all three brothers during this period, "They were proud that they had escaped." And Rorimer had something that the brothers wanted. Dating back to Joseph Choate and his fellow grandees in 1880, the Met had been the ultimate insiders' club in New York City. The Sackler brothers were giving money to a wide range of institutions, but notably their contributions were often directed to places where they did not have any prior personal connections. Arthur hadn't gone to Columbia; he went to NYU. Mortimer and Raymond couldn't even get into NYU for medical school, on account of anti-Semitic quotas. Yet the brothers donated to Columbia, and eventually to NYU, and to the most elite university of them all, Harvard. Their generosity had a conspicuously aspirational quality.

But the Met was in a class by itself. The institution's credo of free access to the public was offset by its reputation for tremendous exclusivity when it came to the wealthy donors who supported the place and won a coveted seat on the museum's board. It was a charity with unparalleled cachet. It was also, unmistakably, Arthur Sackler's kind of place. Every marble corridor and vestibule and gallery was positively stuffed with treasures. The Rembrandt might have represented a big purchase, but the truth was, the museum already *had* Rembrandts. Thirty of them. The Met was the art museum equivalent of the kid with the most toys. When he was approached by Rorimer, Arthur agreed to make a substantial gift, pledging $150,000 for a renovation on the second floor of the museum, on the condition that the space be renamed the Sackler Gallery.

This was a standard ask. When donors gave money, they liked to see their name on the wall. But Arthur also proposed a more exotic arrangement. He suggested that he would purchase from the Met all of the artworks that would fill the new space—a series of Asian masterpieces that the Met had acquired back in the 1920s. He offered to pay the price that the Met had originally paid—the 1920s price—and then donate the works back to the museum, with the understanding that each piece would henceforth be described as a "gift of Arthur Sackler," even though they had belonged to the museum all along. This would be a convenient way for the museum to generate some additional revenue and for Arthur to attach the Sackler name to more objects. Arthur had also become attuned to the advantages of gaming the tax code, so for tax purposes he declared each donation not at the price he paid for it but at the present market value. It was a classic Arthur Sackler play: innovative, showy, a little bit shady; a charitable gesture in which, considering the tax advantages, he would actually *make* money. But the museum needed cash, so it agreed.

Rorimer was a peculiar character. During the war, he had worked to recover artworks stolen by the Nazis, and as director of the Met he would prowl the museum, like a cop on the beat, his flannel suit accented by combat boots. His sense of custodial responsibility for the treasures in his collection was such that he would stop to wipe dust off displays. A thousand schoolchildren visited the museum each day, and when he spied an errant young visitor pawing a statue, Rorimer would bark, "That's four thousand years old." Even so, he had a deep commitment to the concept of the museum as a humanizing force in society. "Familiarity with beauty can only breed more beauty," he liked to say.

This credo resonated strongly with Arthur, who still nurtured vivid memories of his own childhood visits to the Brooklyn Museum. Arthur liked Rorimer, seeing in him not just a man he could do business with but a fellow aesthete. He would later recall the "marvelous" times he spent with Rorimer at the Met: "We'd talk for hours, of pure scholarship and connoisseurship, like two ancient Chinese gentlemen-scholars." As his relations with the Met matured, Arthur also discovered the benefits of a situation he had learned to enjoy in his dealings with Columbia. Think of it as the *dangle:* a wealthy patron can often enjoy favor and influence with a hard-up institution that are far out of proportion to any gifts that have actually been made, because the canny donor learns to dangle the possibility of future gifts, and that is a possibility that the museum or university cannot afford to overlook. When the dangle is executed correctly, there is almost nothing that the institution will not do to keep the donor (or even the *prospective* donor) happy.

Arthur wanted things. For instance, he wanted a space of his own inside the Metropolitan Museum where he could store his rapidly expanding personal art collection. Both the Dutch house on Long Island and the town house in New York were filling up with furniture, ancient pots, paintings, and sculptures. Arthur's art collection was literally displacing his family. So he needed space. Why rent a mere storage locker when you could have your own dedicated enclosure at the Met? Such an arrangement would be more prestigious, and matters like climate control and security were just part of the package. So the museum arranged for Arthur to have what he referred to, with his customary grandiloquence, as a private "enclave" in the museum. Arthur then proceeded to move several thousand objects from his collection into the space, along with his own personal curator, who would work there. He also arranged for his friend Paul Singer, the Viennese psychiatrist and connoisseur who had been his mentor in Asian art, to be given an office inside the enclave. Arthur installed a new lock on the door so that he and his associates would have access to the space but the staff of the Met would not. Rorimer signed off on this arrangement, hoping that if he did so, Arthur might someday donate the great treasure trove he was assembling to the museum.

In accordance with Arthur's wishes, the whole arrangement was kept secret. The museum's own staff did not understand what was happening in this mysterious space. Much later, Arthur would suggest that the enclave hadn't been his idea, that Rorimer had proposed this accommodation, because having the collection under his roof would make it "harder for me to go elsewhere." But this is difficult to believe, not least because Arthur had, simultaneously, arranged to have *another* enclave at a different institution, the Museum of the American Indian.

One Wednesday in the spring of 1966, James Rorimer put in a full day at the Met, then went home to his apartment on Park Avenue, got into bed, and had a heart attack. His abrupt death marked a great loss for Arthur and for the Met, but he was soon replaced by an even more colorful successor. Thomas Hoving was a young and ferociously ambitious dynamo of a man, a political animal, who had been the director of the Cloisters, in Washington Heights, and also parks commissioner for New York City, a job that had previously been held, for decades, by Robert Moses. Hoving was a publicity hound and an unabashed populist who pranced around the city's green spaces in a pith helmet, organizing "happenings" to lure New Yorkers into the parks. He was an impresario who believed that the Met should be a big, splashy, popular institution, a venue not just for scholars and intellectuals but for the mass public. Hoving had a particular fascination with the ancient Egyptians, and he decided he would make it his mission to get the Temple of Dendur.

✦ ✦ ✦

The temple now consisted of a rubble of 642 sandstone bricks: it had been dismantled by the Egyptian government, one stone at a time, and was awaiting a new home. After Egypt announced its intention to donate the structure to the United States, Hoving expressed his avid conviction that the only appropriate permanent home for the temple was at the Metropolitan Museum, in New York. But as it turned out, the Smithsonian, in Washington, wanted it, too. If Hoving was an eager salesman, all New York hustle and moxy, S. Dillon Ripley, the head of the Smithsonian, opted for a patrician air of entitlement. "We have not been campaigning for it," Ripley announced, before adding, almost as an afterthought, "We would want it."

The Met and the Smithsonian were not the only contenders, however. Twenty cities put together bids. Memphis! Phoenix! Philadelphia! Miami! U.S. senators appealed to the State Department. Civic organizations weighed in. And what about Cairo, Illinois? What better home for an Egyptian temple in America than a tiny midwestern city called Cairo? The contest for this magisterial prize grew intense and bitter. The press called it "the Dendur Derby."

The future location of the temple was regarded as a matter of sufficient national importance that the ultimate decision would fall to no less an authority than the former president of the United States Dwight Eisenhower. Eisenhower appointed a panel of experts to help him deliberate. The Smithsonian and the Met quickly emerged from the pack as the two leading contenders. But they had markedly different proposals for what to do with the temple. The Smithsonian suggested it should be placed outdoors, surrounded by nature, as it had been for two millennia. Ripley explained that he would prefer to see the temple exhibited "in as naturalistic a way as possible." But at the Met, Hoving had bigger ideas: he wanted to build a new wing of the museum to hold the temple. It was, frankly, ludicrous, in his view, for the Smithsonian to propose keeping the temple outdoors, and in *Washington* of all places. It might have withstood the Egyptian elements for two thousand years, but in the frigid winters and swampy summers of the nation's capital it wouldn't stand a chance. "We have evidence," one Met official proclaimed, ominously, that if the temple were placed outdoors in the District of Columbia it would soon be reduced to "a pile of sand."

This proved to be the winning argument, and in April 1967, Eisenhower announced that the Temple of Dendur would go to the Met. Thomas Hoving was the victor. "I'm really so happy you have the temple now," his friend the former first lady Jackie Kennedy cooed, adding that "John John," her son, loved to run around the Egyptian section of the Met. Hoving planned to erect his new wing for the temple at Eighty-Fourth Street, just off Fifth Avenue, which happened to be right across from Kennedy's apartment. "I'll light the temple up," he promised, "so that you'll have a good view of it from your window."

But this was easier said than done. Hoving's plan involved an ambitious expansion and modernization of the museum. There would be a series of new spaces: a Rockefeller wing, which would hold the collection of Nelson A. Rockefeller, the governor of New York and grandson of the billionaire John D. Rockefeller, and a Lehman gallery, which would house the collection of Robert Lehman, the grandson of the co-founder of Lehman Brothers, who now ran the bank himself. The plan was to station the Temple of Dendur in its own wing, with a reflecting pool and a great glass wall, so that passersby could see it. But because Hoving's intention was to push the museum structure farther into the green space of Central Park, the former parks commissioner now met with a storm of resistance from conservationists. Critics decried Hoving's proposal as "the rape of Central Park." Lawsuits were filed. Cantankerous rallies were convened outside the Met.

And besides, who would pay for all this? A month or so after Eisenhower awarded the prize of this ancient Egyptian temple to the Met, modern-day Egypt went to war with Israel. Hoving had always intended to raise money from wealthy New Yorkers, but Egypt and all things Egyptian were suddenly out of fashion. The temple itself had been shipped in pieces, arriving at a dock in Brooklyn, and it now sat in a parking lot, cocooned in a protective plastic bubble, while Hoving tried to raise the money to build its new home. But no donor wanted his name on a temple from Egypt. Hoving was feeling increasingly fatalistic. He joked, darkly, that he'd been doomed by "the mummy's curse." But he was indefatigable, and one day it dawned on him that there was one person he hadn't yet asked: Arthur Sackler.

When Hoving took over at the Met, he had learned about the Sackler enclave and found the whole arrangement somewhat bizarre. Had Sackler ever *explicitly* said that the Met would end up getting the artworks he was storing there? Hoving wondered. Nobody could say that he had. Hoving didn't even really understand the source of Arthur's wealth. He knew only that Arthur was rich, that he had given money to the Met, and that he seemed to want to give more. So Hoving telephoned the doctor to inquire if there was any chance he might consider making a contribution. Arthur Sackler was not an easy man to reach: because he was so busy, and constantly moving from one job to another, even those who were close to him found that he could be difficult to track down. But within thirty minutes of Hoving's picking up the phone, Arthur appeared, in person and slightly breathless, at his office at the Met.

Hoving launched right into his pitch. Arthur was the only person in the city with "the guts" to make this donation, he said. It was at this point, generally, that other donors could be expected to raise objections, just on principle, to the notion of underwriting a new home for an adopted Egyptian temple. But Arthur was still listening. So Hoving took the plunge. What I need, he said, is $3.5 million.

This was an epic sum in 1967, a huge multiple of anything that Arthur had ever given before.

"I'll do it," Arthur said.

Of course, there would be conditions. Arthur stipulated that the money would be paid out by himself and his brothers, Mortimer and Raymond, and that it would be paid not up front in one lump sum but slowly. The new wing, which would take its place alongside the Rockefeller Wing and the Lehman Collection, would be called the Sackler Wing. The temple enclosure would be the Sackler Gallery for Egyptian Art. A set of new exhibit spaces would be the Sackler Galleries for Asian Art. In any signage related to these new spaces, Arthur, Mortimer, and Raymond would each be named individually, each with his middle initial, each with the letters "M.D." following his name. All of this was spelled out explicitly, as binding contractual provisions. One Met administrator joked that the only thing missing from the carefully negotiated signage was "their office hours."

In the spring of 1974, after Hoving had finally secured the necessary approvals, a clamor of drills and jackhammers rang out across Central

Park as construction got under way. *The New York Times* announced that the new wing was made possible "thanks largely to a recent gift of $3.5 million from Drs. Arthur M. Sackler, Mortimer D. Sackler and Raymond R. Sackler." But the truth was that, because the Sacklers had negotiated to pay their donation out over twenty years, when it came time to actually build the wing, the Met did not have enough cash on hand to finance construction and was forced to raise more funds. (The city ended up chipping in $1.4 million.)

On the north side of the Met, a team of craftspeople unwrapped the great sandstone blocks and began arranging them on a vast concrete platform. The stones had been sitting, disassembled, for eleven years. Each one had been numbered, and the team at the Met consulted a scale plan and photographs to assist in putting them back together. It was like a giant Lego project. As the temple rose, the workers could still make out not just the ancient carvings that had lined the walls since it was built but the subsequent graffiti, the demotic tags, and the name of that nineteenth-century New York lawyer, L. BRADISH, who had gone to Egypt and carved his name in the side of a building, only to have the building wind up in New York.

This had all the makings of a triumphant moment for the Sackler brothers, but if Arthur believed that all it took to be accepted in New York high society was a wing with his name on it at the Met, he was mistaken. He threw himself into the life of the museum, joining a Met-sponsored trip to India. (When another participant in this junket, the philanthropist Edward Warburg, fell ill, Arthur opened the suitcase he always carried, and it turned out to be so brimming with medications that Warburg joked it resembled "an apothecary shop.") And Hoving genuinely liked Arthur, inasmuch as a professional seducer can like his conquest. "He was touchy, eccentric, arbitrary—and vulnerable," Hoving would later remark, "which made the game much more fascinating."

But other officials at the Met chafed at the many restrictive conditions that Arthur placed on his gifts. And when it came to the old-line burghers of the art world, they were dismissive if not openly contemptuous of this deep-pocketed, overeager arriviste. Arthur Sackler had all the charm "of a dollar sign," one auction house executive told *Vanity Fair*. A visitor to the art-stuffed Xanadu where he resided likened the home to "a mortician's annex." Arthur badly wanted a seat on the museum's prestigious board of trustees, and he felt, not unreasonably, that he had earned one. "I gave the Met exactly what the Rockefellers paid for their wing," he complained.

But the museum would not appoint him to the board. There was a feeling, among the leadership, that there was something unseemly about Arthur Sackler. He could tell: he was sufficiently sensitive to the subtle dynamics of social gatekeeping in elite circles to register that something was up, and it felt, to him, like something familiar. The Met, Arthur concluded, was simply "an anti-Semitic place."

But the truth might have been more complicated. For one thing, there were other Jews on the board of the museum. One senior Met official, Arthur Rosenblatt, joked that the administrators had no choice but to start taking money from Jewish donors, because at a certain point they ran out of old rich WASPs. But some people also nursed suspicions that there was something legitimately dubious about Arthur and his brothers. One Met official noted that because the brothers negotiated to pay their $3.5 million donation over twenty years, with tax write-offs along the way, "the Sackler wing is a generous gift, but also a marvelous deal for the Sacklers." Another official, Joseph Noble, described Arthur as "slippery" and whispered that the enclave that Rorimer had made available to him was "the biggest giveaway" in the museum's history. "Throw him out," Noble warned Tom Hoving. "Before there's a scandal."

✣ ✣ ✣

By the end of 1978, construction was complete, and Hoving unveiled the Sackler Wing with the launch of a new exhibit: *The Treasures of King Tut*. It was a masterstroke. The exhibit included fifty-five dazzling funerary objects discovered in the tomb of the boy emperor Tutankhamun. One evening, before the show was open to the public, the Met threw a black-tie gala in the new wing to celebrate. There was the temple, standing again, beautifully restored and dramatically lit, with the names of those two brothers who once drowned in the Nile still etched in the sandstone, along with the names of other visitors through the centuries, and now the names Arthur, Mortimer, and Raymond Sackler carved into the great edifice of the Met itself.

The Sacklers had commissioned a new work, to mark the occasion, from the famed choreographer Martha Graham, whom Arthur regarded as "the goddess of modern dance." Like a flock of maenads,

Graham's dancers performed in the temple itself. The mayor of the city, Ed Koch, was there. He had become friends with Arthur. By extraordinary coincidence, President Jimmy Carter had just presided over the Camp David Accords, ending the conflict between Israel and Egypt. Koch, who was Jewish himself, pointed to the symbolism of three Jewish doctors sponsoring the relocation of an Egyptian temple to New York and the manner in which it seemed to echo the geopolitics at play. "And what greater way to mark it," he said, "than the opening of the Sackler Wing of the Temple of Dendur."

Later in the evening, there were cocktails and a dance band. The Sackler brothers were there, beaming, for what felt, undeniably, like a major benchmark in the story of their family. They had arrived. If Arthur looked at all distracted that evening, nobody made mention of it. But Met officials had not been wrong to worry about a scandal. Even as the brothers celebrated, the attorney general of New York had gotten wind of the Sackler enclave and had launched an investigation. For Arthur, there was also a more proximate and personal scandal brewing. On his arm that evening was an elegant, long-limbed young woman. She was almost three decades younger than he was, British, and not his wife.

Chapter 8

ESTRANGEMENT

MORTIMER SACKLER'S FIRST MARRIAGE, to Muriel Lazarus, had ended in divorce. Muriel was an impressive woman: born in Glasgow, she had come to New York in her youth, gone to Brooklyn College, and earned a master's in science from MIT in 1945 and a PhD from Columbia. She and Mortimer had three children: Ilene was born in 1946, Kathe in 1948, and Robert in 1951. But in the mid-1960s, at around the time he marked his fiftieth birthday, Mortimer had fallen in love with a young woman named Gertraud Wimmer. Geri, as she was known, was Austrian and statuesque. She had managed an art gallery in Munich. At barely twenty, she was the same age as Mortimer's daughter Ilene, but despite the age difference she and Mortimer started a relationship. If some people might have looked askance at this development, others celebrated Geri as a fitting trophy for an accomplished man. Purdue Frederick, the little pharmaceutical outfit that Arthur had purchased for his brothers back in 1952, had turned out to be quite successful, and Mortimer was now a wealthy man. Félix Martí-Ibáñez, the Spanish doctor whose dealings had been a focus of the Kefauver hearings, remained close to the Sackler brothers after the scandal. He referred to Mortimer's new wife, unfailingly, as "the *bellissima* Geri."

Over the course of the 1960s, Mortimer had started to spend more and more time abroad. For a period, he was anchored, somewhat, by the obligation to care for his aging mother, Sophie. Arthur, who was devoted to Sophie in theory, found that in practice he did not want to spend much time with her, even when she was ill. Sophie resented this, joking sourly that if only she were a piece of jade, Arthur might pay her some attention. In any case, her care fell to the younger brothers. Mortimer set Sophie up with a round-the-clock nurse. But she died, of cancer, in 1965, with her sons by her side.

After Sophie's death, Mortimer started spending more time in Europe. "The Cote D'Azur this year is not as mobbed," he wrote to Martí-Ibáñez in the summer of 1966. "There has been, as usual, a change in the places that are in and those not in. There has been a new crop of bikini girls, and the leftovers of the last few crops." Mortimer was officially working, expanding the brothers' interests in the pharmaceutical industry. That year, he oversaw the purchase of a moribund British drug company called Napp, which would work in tandem with Purdue Frederick back in New York. But Mortimer had always been more of a sensualist than either of his brothers, and now he settled into the life of a European playboy. His days were spent at the Hôtel du Cap-Eden-Roc, a storied resort on a promontory overlooking the Mediterranean in Cap d'Antibes, where F. Scott and Zelda Fitzgerald used to drink and the Kennedys had once vacationed. There was a soothing, dreamy lethargy to the place, with languid gardens, fresh seafood, and poolside cocktails served by starched attendants. Mortimer played tennis almost every day. (He was competitive. But if other people appeared to get worked up over a match, he would scoff, "Calm down. Take a tranquilizer.") He mingled with a cohort of jet-set expatriates like the novelist and screenwriter Paul Gallico, who was married to a baroness (his fourth wife) and lived in a nearby villa, where he composed his books by dictating, with long pauses, to an American secretary. Mortimer liked to swap gossip about the hot restaurants and to go out dancing at night. He developed the Mediterranean tendency to devote a great deal of conversational energy to the subject of the weather. "The sun is with us daily," he wrote to Martí-Ibáñez, "and we are all happy to be here."

Like Arthur, Mortimer was not a particularly attentive parent. His daughters, Ilene and Kathe, were old enough to be independent by the time their father took up with Geri Wimmer. But Bobby, the youngest, continued to live with his mother, Muriel, in Manhattan. "I was expecting Bobby to join me this week," Mortimer wrote in 1966. But, as it turned out, Bobby had come down with mono and could not make the trip. "Will have to make it up later in the year," Mortimer resolved. Two summers later, in 1968, he wrote to Martí-Ibáñez with exciting news. "Geri and I are expecting . . . a child!" Privately, he noted that this was "her decision." But both he and Geri were very happy, living for the summer with the Gallicos and planning to return to New York City in the fall. In September, they had a daughter, Samantha. The following year, they were married.

Mortimer wanted his own place in Cap d'Antibes, so he purchased a beautiful villa, which had been designed by the American architect Barry Dierks, who had also created homes for the novelist Somerset Maugham and the film producer Jack Warner. Built in 1938, the home was surrounded by elaborate gardens and conveniently located just up the road from the Hôtel du Cap. "The house is far from finished and we have much to buy," Mortimer wrote in July 1969. "Though I refer to this summer as 'camping,' it is really comfortable."

It might have been his upbringing in polyglot Brooklyn, or his sojourn in Glasgow during the 1930s, but Mortimer increasingly felt like a roaming cosmopolite, a citizen of the world. He purchased an enormous town house at 10 East Sixty-Fourth Street, just two blocks from the Sackler headquarters on Sixty-Second, which he occupied when he was back home. But he also maintained a grand apartment on Rue Saint-Honoré, not far from the Tuileries, in Paris. He frequented the opera when he was in Paris, and the theater when he was in London, where he also bought a home. Describing the social life in late-1960s London, he joked that he had become a "swinger." Mortimer had an ego and a competitive streak. But he was not obsessed with work in the way that his brother Arthur was. He wanted to live what he described as "a full and vigorous life dedicated to life and love and the struggle to fulfill both." In one letter, he needled Martí-Ibáñez about his passion for reading and recommended more corporeal delights: "While books and the written word give much pleasure, I am sure you will agree with me that we must explore all avenues of pleasure, relaxation and contentment."

In 1971, Geri gave birth to a second child, a boy, whom they named Mortimer David Alfons Sackler. Like Arthur, Mortimer chose to name the first son from his second marriage after himself. He referred to his children with Geri as "the new family," which, along with his departure for Europe, might have created the impression that the three children from his first marriage were the *old* family—a skin he had shed. In a further sign that he was taking leave, in some emotional sense, from the United States, Mortimer renounced his American citizenship in 1974, electing to become a citizen of Austria, like Geri. (He did so, Geri later explained, for tax reasons, a curious move for a onetime communist. But people change.) That spring, Martí-Ibáñez wrote to Mortimer that in all the years they had been friends, since first meeting in 1946, he had never seen Mortimer so happy.

When Mortimer D. A. Sackler was still a baby, there was already talk about his someday becoming a doctor. As it happened, Mortimer's older son, from his first marriage, Bobby, also carried his father's name: he was Robert Mortimer Sackler. But by the time Bobby was a teenager, he did not seem to be a likely candidate for medical practice. He had grown up rich, a child of divorce, splitting his time between his stern Scottish-born mother, who lived in an apartment on the Upper East Side, and his gallivanting hedonist father, whose new wife was just a few years older than Bobby was. Eventually, the relationship between father and son grew tempestuous. Mortimer complained that Bobby was unhelpful and inconsiderate. But then they would reunite for a vacation and things would appear to improve: Bobby would play tennis with his father, or they would swim together in the Mediterranean, and he would seem as though he might be pulling out of his postadolescent funk and becoming the well-adjusted young man that Mortimer expected him to be.

✧   ✧   ✧

"My sense is that Arthur was a little jealous of Mortimer," Michael Rich recalled. Rich started dating Denise Sackler, Arthur's daughter with Marietta, at Pomona College in the mid-1970s, and eventually married into the family. "Mortimer was a better philanderer than he was, with topless young ladies in Cap d'Antibes." According to Rich, Arthur would occasionally refer, with "no small amount of envy," to his brother's exploits in the South of France. "I think he felt that Mortimer had more time to play than he did, because Arthur was a workaholic." But the resentment had a deeper dimension as well, Rich said. Arthur seemed to feel that "the reason Mortimer *had* that time was that Arthur had made it possible."

To Arthur, Rich said, Mortimer and Raymond had always been "the little brothers, following in his wake." He didn't think of them "as equal to him. He felt he had to carry them." He still intervened from time to time when they needed him at Purdue Frederick, but for the most part they were running the business on their own, making their own investments, launching their own philanthropic initiatives, bringing in their own money, and plenty of it. The various business interests of the three brothers were still very much intermingled: the *Medical Tribune* ran ads for Purdue Frederick products in nearly every issue, and McAdams handled some of the advertising for the firm. But, occasionally, Arthur would embarrass his brothers, intervening in the ad campaigns at McAdams and condescending to Raymond in front of junior staff.

The two younger brothers remained very close. Raymond, who was responsible for minding the fort in New York while Mortimer oversaw their international ventures, had a more retiring personality than either of his brothers. As his business interests expanded, he and Beverly shrugged off their earlier commitment to communism. But they remained very committed to each other. "Ray was quiet, reasonably honest, always married to the same woman," the former McAdams adman John Kallir recalled. "The least interesting of the three brothers." Raymond continued to live in the suburbs, in Roslyn, on Long Island, and he and Beverly raised two sons, Richard and Jonathan. Richard was even planning on becoming a doctor.

Mortimer and Raymond might have had very different personalities, but having grown up together in Arthur's shadow, they shared a deep bond. Arthur sometimes fretted that he could not even guess the whereabouts of the peripatetic Mortimer. "I have never been so 'out of contact,'" he wrote one summer. "To this day I have never received from Mortie an itinerary." But whereas Mortimer wrote letters to others while he was in Europe, he kept in close touch with Raymond by phone. Raymond and Beverly liked to visit Mortimer in France, though they were less adventurous when it came to travel. Raymond was content, as he put it, to "let Morty be our guide." And Mortimer and Geri would come back to New York for Purdue Frederick budget meetings, which were held on the roof of the Pierre hotel, just around the corner from the family's office building on Sixty-Second. While they were in town, Geri would throw extravagant black-tie dinners for friends and family at their town house. The brothers would still occasionally sign a letter "Arthur, Mortimer and Raymond," as if they were a single, undifferentiated being, and it could be difficult to figure out which of them had actually written it. Martí-Ibáñez praised Mortimer for his efforts to hold the "'family' together." But the inescapable reality was

that what had once seemed to be an inviolable fraternal unit was beginning to fracture, and the younger brothers were growing increasingly
estranged from Arthur.

Marietta believed that Sophie Sackler had been the last thing that
held the three of them together. "It seemed to me that her strong,
matriarchal force had maintained the vision of family togetherness,"
she wrote. "When she was gone, that vision began to dissolve."

It might have also been the case that Arthur had simply reached
some absolute limit on the number of close relationships that he could
juggle. Arthur maintained close ties with his two daughters from his
first marriage, but he had a strained relationship with his namesake,
Arthur Felix. "I tried to interest my son in medicine," he would sigh,
but it "was futile." The younger Arthur was dyslexic and ended up
drifting into the counterculture. He moved around, studying at a small
college in Wisconsin, spending a year on a commune in Vermont, buying a farm in Maine. Marietta began to fear that she might get a phone
call one night, with news that something terrible had happened to him.
Denise went to Pomona for college, where she majored in studio art
and met Michael Rich. When Arthur visited for her senior show, he was
enormously proud. "This is the way the name Sackler should be on the
wall of an art gallery," he told her. "Not just as a donor, but as an artist."

Arthur was still seeing his first wife, Else, which Marietta increasingly resented. In addition to his weekly visits to the apartment on
Central Park West, he and Else would frequent museums together and
attend lectures on art. Sometimes, he would take holidays with Else,
from which Marietta was excluded, like a vacation to Cannes in 1957.
On that trip, they popped in to an art gallery, and Arthur bought Else a
Renoir lithograph. In 1962, he surprised her with a beautiful painting,
by Monet, of a stand of poplar trees. Else had special lighting installed
in her apartment to highlight the gentle nuances in the painter's use of
color. Arthur liked to linger before it, in Else's living room, admiring
the painting and relating the story of how he had managed to acquire
it for a reasonable sum, because it had been owned for a long time by
the same family in Switzerland, so the price had not been run up by
frequent sales. He would express his great satisfaction at having been
able "to find a Monet for Else."

None of this made Marietta particularly happy, and she didn't know

the half of it, because even as Arthur maintained such an overtly intimate relationship with his first wife, he was also secretly seeing a third
woman, named Jillian Tully.

"I met Dr. Sackler in 1967," Jillian said, years later. She was twenty-
eight at the time, working at an advertising agency in London. Arthur
was in his mid-fifties. His hair had receded and gone gray, and he had
developed a bit of a paunch. But he was still physically and intellectually vigorous, and Jillian was immediately taken by this brilliant,
charming, wealthy older man. "He was incredibly clever," she recalled.
"He was at the top of the art world and the science world."

Arthur told Jillian that he was estranged from his second wife, and
they began to see each other, mostly when he was in London. As they
grew closer, Arthur told Jillian that he would like to marry her but
that he was unable to divorce Marietta until he resolved "a complex
property settlement." Jillian understood. Within a couple of years, she
had moved to New York to be closer to him. When Arthur was with Jillian, he simply behaved as though he were no longer married to Marietta. Arthur "treated me as his wife, introduced me as his wife," Jillian
would later recount. Arthur had always had a thing about his name, and
having bestowed it on a museum wing, he now wanted Jillian to carry
his name as well. So she started to refer to herself as "Mrs. Arthur M.
Sackler," which, along with Else and Marietta, meant that there were
now three Mrs. Arthur Sacklers, all living in Manhattan. "It troubled
him that this was not literally accurate," Jillian explained—that she was
merely borrowing the name, like an actor assuming the guise of a character in a play. So, eventually, Arthur "insisted that I change my name
legally from Tully to Sackler." On March 4, 1976, she officially changed
her name, in London, to Jillian Sackler, though she and Arthur were not
actually married, and Arthur was still married to Marietta.

✢ ✢ ✢

The Sackler family now seemed to have split into two discrete factions, with Arthur in one corner and Raymond and Mortimer in the
other. Jillian never grew close with his brothers, and indeed, as time
passed, Arthur spoke to them less and less. "This was not a family that
got together for Fourth of July barbecues," Michael Rich said. The
branches of the Sackler clan had become "very compartmentalized."

To those outside the family, this appeared to be a gradual drift, occasioned by time, geography, and busy lives. But to the brothers themselves, there was one obvious incident that became a source of tremendous acrimony and distrust—a definable moment when the relationship between Arthur and his kid brothers soured. In 1954, their friend Bill Frohlich, the German adman and fourth musketeer, had founded a company in New York called IMS. The idea behind IMS was to aggregate pharmaceutical sales data, gathering information about what drugs doctors were prescribing, and furnishing that data to pharma companies, which would pay a premium for it, in order to hone their marketing. As an official matter, it was Frohlich who started IMS. But, just as Arthur had been the hidden hand behind the L. W. Frohlich advertising agency, he also, secretly, played a role in establishing IMS. In fact, it appears that the company had originally been his idea. Reluctant to create another obvious conflict of interest, Arthur allowed Frohlich to be his designated front man and kept his own role in the company secret.

Frohlich's ad agency continued to prosper. By 1970, it had offices in London, Paris, Frankfurt, Milan, Madrid, and Tokyo and nearly $40 million in revenue. Frohlich acquired a Mediterranean refuge to match Mortimer's, on the island of Elba, in Italy. When Mortimer visited him there, he swooned over this "most beautiful villa high on this hill in Elba overlooking the sea." One day in 1971, Frohlich returned from a Caribbean vacation and assembled his staff for a meeting, only to start babbling incoherently, then pass out. When Arthur heard that his old friend was ill, he immediately took charge, setting Frohlich up with the best doctors. But it was too late. Frohlich was diagnosed with a brain tumor and died in September 1971, at the age of fifty-eight.

Frohlich had played such a central role in the L. W. Frohlich agency that the firm did not survive his death, going out of business not long afterward. But IMS was still a going concern, and a year after Frohlich's death executives at IMS made an astonishing discovery. Frohlich, they learned, had entered into a secret agreement with the Sackler family whereby Raymond and Mortimer Sackler would inherit a majority ownership stake in the company following his death. The agreement was known as a tontine, an antique investment instrument, with origins in seventeenth-century Europe, in which a number of participants band together in what is effectively a mortality lottery, pooling their funds with an understanding that the last investor to die will win everything.

But what the IMS executives had actually stumbled upon was the residue of the four-way musketeers agreement that the brothers had made with Bill Frohlich on a snowy night in New York City back in the 1940s. During the 1960s, the four participants had engaged the attorney Richard Leather, who was a partner at the law firm Chadbourne & Parke, to formalize the pact. According to Leather, there were two written agreements, one governing domestic businesses, and another governing international businesses. All four men were party to the domestic pact, which became known as the "four-way agreement." But Arthur, for some reason, opted not to join the international arrangement, so that became known as the "three-way agreement," between Raymond, Mortimer, and Frohlich. The intention was that when the first man died, his businesses would pass not to his heirs but to the other members of the pact. And now, much sooner than any of them had expected, Bill Frohlich was dead.

Technically, under the agreement, Arthur should have inherited IMS, along with his brothers. But as his personal attorney Michael Sonnenreich subsequently acknowledged, he "couldn't possibly" have been one of Frohlich's beneficiaries, "because he was running McAdams and it would have been a conflict. So he put his brothers into it." Raymond and Mortimer had "nothing to do with" IMS, according to Sonnenreich, but they were parties to the agreement and, not for the first time, they served the purpose of obscuring their brother's involvement. When IMS subsequently went public, Frohlich's family—his sister and her two daughters—received $6.25 million in total. The musketeers agreement had always held that each man could set aside a reasonable amount of money to care for his heirs. Raymond and Mortimer, together, made nearly $37 million.

Arthur's expectation, at this point, was that they would honor the agreement they had made and cut him in on this considerable haul. After all, it was he who had dreamed up IMS in the first place: the brothers played no actual role in the company. "Four people founded IMS," Raymond's son Richard Sackler would later say, suggesting that Raymond and Mortimer had played a role and Arthur was simply "one of the four." But Raymond himself told a journalist, Adam Tanner, that his involvement with IMS was negligible, saying, "I knew very little if anything about that business." According to Sonnenreich, under the four-way agreement, Arthur "gave away his rights to IMS, but his understanding with Frohlich was that if he ever sold it, he was entitled to one fourth."

When the company went public, however, Raymond and Mortimer had other ideas. They claimed that because IMS had offices around the world, it was, in effect, an international business, and should therefore not fall under the domestic "four-way" agreement, but the international one, to which Arthur was not a party. "They moved the company out of the country," Arthur's son, Arthur Felix, would later explain, saying that his father was "pissed off" because he "didn't get any participation."

"Dad came up with the idea for IMS and on a handshake with Bill Frohlich, Bill was given the go-ahead," Arthur's daughter Elizabeth Sackler recalled. "When Frohlich died, Raymond and Morty made out like bandits when the stock went public."

Arthur, jilted, perceived this as a great betrayal. According to his children Elizabeth and Arthur, this was "the beginning of the whole rift." In later years, Arthur would seldom speak of the incident, but when he did, he could only mutter, in bitter wonderment, "When IMS went public, I got nothing."

✢ ✢ ✢

There was another, darker secret that came to haunt the Sackler family during this period. When Mortimer's son Bobby had his Bar Mitzvah in 1964, Félix Martí-Ibáñez, who was never one to allow such an occasion to pass unmarked, had written Bobby a letter. "You are entering life with the greatest assets any young man may have: loving and devoted parents," Martí-Ibáñez wrote. But the other thing that Bobby had inherited, the Spaniard pointed out, was "a very famous name." What a tremendous advantage, to enter adulthood as a Sackler. What a privilege. What a leg up. To be sure, Martí-Ibáñez allowed, "nothing in life is easy, but that is part of the fun." The important thing is to work hard, he told Bobby, and to excel. "I believe that a man should strive for only one thing in life, and that is to have a touch of greatness."

For Bobby, however, the Sackler name would not prove to be the sort of amulet that Martí-Ibáñez believed it could be. He struggled, emotionally and mentally. He maintained an apartment in a building that the family owned on Sixty-Fourth Street. But, according to Elizabeth Bernard, who worked as a housekeeper for Mortimer Sackler for three decades, Bobby also spent time, in his twenties, at a psychiatric facility. When he was away, Bernard would take care of his cats. At times, he stayed with his mother, Muriel, in her book-lined apartment on the ninth floor of a grand old building on East Eighty-Sixth Street, just off the park. "Robert was very distraught. He was off the charts," Dolores Welber, a friend of Muriel Sackler's, recalled. "He was crazy," she continued. "She had a son who was totally uncontrollable." On one occasion, Welber said, Bobby was found wandering in Central Park with no clothes on. "Probably, it was drugs," Welber said.

Others who knew the family came to believe that Bobby struggled with addiction. Decades later, when she was deposed by the lawyer Paul Hanly in the offices of Debevoise & Plimpton in New York City, Bobby's older sister Kathe would make a stray remark about the heroin crisis in the 1970s. "I have friends. Relatives. I mean, I know people, individual people who have suffered," she said. "It touches everyone's life. It's horrible." If Bobby had a problem with heroin, it was not the only drug he was using. According to Elizabeth Bernard, Bobby started using PCP, or angel dust. Originally developed as a tranquilizer in the 1950s, PCP was rejected for human use after it was discovered to cause hallucinations, convulsions, and violent behavior. But it became a popular street drug in the 1970s. When Bobby took it, Bernard recalled, "he freaked out."

The doormen at Muriel Sackler's building on Eighty-Sixth Street were well aware that her son had a drug problem. "She was complaining, 'He's using drugs,'" Ceferino Perez, who served as a doorman in the building for forty-seven years, recalled. "He was a little cuckoo. He was the kind of guy that nobody was going to hire." Sometimes, Bobby would come in "wired"—either high or in withdrawal—to see his mother, Perez recalled. "He would fight with her."

One Saturday morning in the summer of 1975, Perez was working the door. Bobby showed up at the building, irritable and angry. He shouted at the elevator operator, then disappeared into Muriel's apartment. But there was a commotion and sounds of an argument. "He wanted money," Perez recalled. "Maybe to buy drugs. But she wouldn't give it to him." Perez and the elevator operator consulted with the building's superintendent. But he told them not to get involved.

So Perez went back to his post under the awning at the front door. It was a hot July morning. Tourists strolled by on their way to the Metropolitan Museum, and dog walkers and weekend joggers passed as they headed into Central Park. Then Perez heard a noise from above, the sound of breaking glass, then a much louder, closer sound as something heavy landed on the sidewalk. The impact was so intense that it sounded like a car crash. But when Perez looked over, he saw that there was a body on the sidewalk. It was Bobby Sackler. He had fallen nine stories. His head had cracked open on the pavement.

For an instant, everything stood still. Then Perez heard a telephone ring. It was the front door phone. When he answered, he heard the voice of Muriel Sackler.

"My son jumped out the window," she said. "He broke the window with a chair." She was distraught. She asked Perez, "Do you think he's dead?"

Perez looked at the body. There was no question. "I'm sorry to tell you," he stammered. "He's dead."

Perez hung up the phone. A crowd had gathered. People were stopped in their tracks, staring. The police were on the way. Somebody found a blanket and Ceferino Perez placed it, like a shroud, over Bobby Sackler.

Chapter 9

GHOST MARKS

THE MORE ARTHUR SACKLER took on, the more he traveled, the more he collected, the more esteem he achieved, the further he seemed to drift from Marietta. She didn't understand why it was that he took on as much as he did: he had already accomplished and acquired so much. Why not stop and appreciate it? But Marietta had come to realize that for Arthur there was always some new mountain to scale. His collecting must be driven not just by a desire for public recognition, she concluded, but by a deeper need for "his name not to be forgotten by the world."

Her children had grown up. Arthur Felix had drifted away from his parents, then drifted back: he worked for his father at McAdams, and then at the *Medical Tribune,* and became involved in the management of Marietta's family drug company back in Germany, Dr. Kade. Denise had a more remote relationship with her father. She stayed out west and eventually married Michael Rich.

Arthur was traveling more. Rather than slow down as he grew older, he seemed to be accelerating, as though he were in a race with time. Marietta felt adrift and depressed. Eventually she enrolled in psychotherapy. Arthur opposed this decision: sticking, obstinately, to the theories of his early research at Creedmoor, he insisted that if she had a psychological problem, it must have some metabolic, physiological origin and should be addressed with an appropriate pharmaceutical rather than through therapy. But Marietta found the analysis helpful, so much so that she decided to retrain as a psychotherapist herself. For a long time, her chief remaining connection with her husband was sex. Arthur had always been voracious in that department. But for Marietta, it felt as though there was no emotion in the act anymore, no tenderness. Like so much else with Arthur, she thought, it had come to feel like "conquest." Eventually, Arthur lost interest even in sex. He seemed entirely inaccessible to her now, and one night in the early 1970s she pleaded with him that if it was business that was causing him so much stress, they could just sell the businesses and live a simpler life. *Please*, she implored him. But he seemed uninterested.

Then Marietta asked, "Do you still love me?"

And Arthur said, "I love somebody else."

Finally, he told her about Jillian, the younger woman with whom he had been romantically involved for years. If Marietta was shocked, she was also forced to confess, now, that there had been signs. Long absences. Unexplained disappearances. A night not long ago when Arthur was supposedly staying in the city, and on a whim Marietta drove in from Long Island to see him, only to arrive at an empty town house. She sat up all night, worried, and when he walked in the next morning, he was surprised to find her there and told a story (which was frankly ludicrous in retrospect) about how his car had broken down and he was unable to find his way home in the dark.

Even so, in confessing his affair to Marietta, Arthur did not appear to be asking to end their marriage. Rather, he was informing her, in simple terms, about this new situation. What Arthur wanted, she realized, was a more "open" arrangement, one in keeping with the liberal mores of the 1970s. According to Marietta, what he proposed was that they maintain the outward appearance of their marriage but that he be free to continue his relationship with Jillian.

By an excruciatingly awkward coincidence of timing, in the aftermath of this devastating revelation, Arthur was set to turn sixty on August 22, 1973, and Marietta had been planning to throw him a party. The couple elected to go ahead with the festivities, at the house on Long Island. Everyone kept up appearances. Family and friends gathered, though not Jillian, obviously. Marietta was supposed to give a speech, and you might suppose that she would back out, unable to swallow the humiliation—or, alternatively, that she would let it rip, telling the assembled Sacklers and their assorted hangers-on what she *really* thought about her situation. But instead, in a flourish of self-abnegation, Marietta delivered the speech that she had been planning, a fawning retrospective about Arthur's career. She presented him with a series of carefully compiled scrapbooks chronicling his many accomplishments in medicine and in the arts. The title of her speech was "Sixty Years of Underachievement."

Arthur had broken through to a new social strata. There he was at the Goya show, avoiding the flashbulbs of the paparazzi. Or feting a visiting French marquise at a party in Los Angeles. He still refused to give press interviews, for the most part, but he no longer feared seeing his own name in print. In his *Medical Tribune* column, "One Man & Medicine," he served up an idiosyncratic miscellany of righteous polemics against things that he hated (cigarettes, FDA regulation, "lay" journalism written by nondoctors) and name-droppy journal entries about his life and travels. He devoted three columns to an extended conversation with the opera singer Luciano Pavarotti. Stories on a range of subjects somehow returned to his close personal friendship with the king of Sweden. Arthur boasted about having been an early booster of Ralph Nader's consumer safety work, though the head of an organization Nader started, Public Citizen's Health Research Group, once declared, "What passes for news in the *Medical Tribune* is highly filtered editorial comment irrationally favorable to the drug industry."

If Arthur was getting used to the idea of publicity, he insisted that it was publicity on his own terms. "He wanted to be the editor in chief," the art collector Edward Warburg, who served as an official at the Met, remarked. "He didn't want anyone else to have the last word." In 1975, Arthur was honored at the Philbrook Art Center in Tulsa, which was going to show a traveling exhibit of his Piranesi prints and drawings. He got to talking to a nice young man, only to realize, belatedly, that he was a reporter for the *Tulsa World*. "Good heavens," Arthur said, as it dawned on him that he had just inadvertently granted an interview. "I hope the New York and London papers don't read the *Tulsa World*."

Those who worked with him still saw traces of the boy from Depression-era Brooklyn. "I am one of the few men born in New York City who stayed," Arthur liked to say. He might have been profligate when it came to purchasing art or making named donations, but he was still thrifty about other things. He loved air travel and would rhapsodize about the miracle of the 747: "Man now flies through the skies with a speed and comfort unmatched by the fabulous golden chariots of the gods of Greece." But he had a famous preference for flying economy and always requested a seat in the back of the plane near the emergency exit, where there was room for his legs and his briefcase.

He had become a companion to the good and the great. He grew close with Anwar Sadat, the president of Egypt, and got to honor Sadat

in the Sackler Wing at the Met. To mark the occasion, Arthur presented him with a piece of jade that was five hundred years old. "I knew
a lot of geniuses," Arthur's daughter Elizabeth, from his first marriage,
later recalled, because in her father's social circle "they were hanging
around." Arthur became friends with the painter Marc Chagall and
with the novelist Bernard Malamud. Malamud had grown up in Brooklyn; he and Arthur had overlapped at Erasmus, only to reconnect in
later life. Reflecting on the friendship, Malamud's daughter, Janna Malamud Smith, noted that both men had started out with "fathers who
were running grocery stores." It made sense that they found each other,
she thought, because they both had big egos, and men with big egos
who become venerable tend to recast their dinner parties so that they
include others of similar stature. To Malamud Smith, it seemed that
"they both probably took a lot of pleasure in being seen through each
other's eyes for their accomplishments." Any memory of the unpleas-
antness of the Kefauver hearings was long gone. In fact, these days, it
was practically a rite of passage for each new head of the FDA to sit for
a lengthy interview with the publisher of the *Medical Tribune,* Arthur
Sackler.

✤ ✤ ✤

In his weekly column, Arthur sometimes wrote about mental illness, addiction, and suicide. But the death of his brother Mortimer's
son Bobby in the summer of 1975 passed without mention. The story
was kept out of the press. The family issued a small paid death notice
to the *Times,* which said simply that Robert Mortimer Sackler had died
"suddenly in the 24th year of his life." There was a service at River-
side Chapel. The men cut off the ends of their neckties, a traditional
Jewish custom of mourning that symbolized the rending of garments.
A memorial scholarship fund was established at Tel Aviv University,
but there was never any explanation associated with this endowment of
who Robert Sackler had been in life. It was a strange paradox: the Sacklers had put their name everywhere. But when a member of the family died young, they did not commemorate him in any public fashion.
They did not speak of him, for the most part. He was erased.

His mother, Muriel, stayed in the apartment on Eighty-Sixth Street.
Someone repaired the window, and she continued to live there for the
rest of her life. Like Marietta, she retrained in psychoanalysis, becom-

ing involved in a close-knit circle of fellow New York psychoanalysts. But she never seemed to speak of her son. She worked from home and saw her patients in the apartment where Bobby had killed himself. Eventually, she met a kind international lawyer named Oscar Schachter and fell in love. But even Schachter found that with Muriel the subject of Bobby's death was off limits. On one occasion, one of Schachter's adult daughters from a previous marriage spent an afternoon with Muriel, going through a shoebox of old photographs. Every time they came across a picture of a boy, Muriel would push it away, burying it in the pile. She could not look at him.

Mortimer Sackler had been in France when Bobby died. He returned to New York for the funeral, devastated. Not long afterward, his second marriage, to Geri Wimmer, fell apart. By the summer of 1977, they had separated, and Geri, according to an account in the tabloids, "couldn't wait to tell everyone she's getting a divorce." Three years later, Mortimer married for a third time. He might have grown estranged from his older brother, but he followed Arthur's lead once more by taking up with a much younger Englishwoman. Theresa Rowling was from Staffordshire and had been working as a schoolteacher in London's Notting Hill. At thirty, she was younger than Mortimer's daughters from his first marriage, Ilene and Kathe. Mortimer continued to spend time at the villa in the South of France, and in Gstaad, in the Swiss Alps; those lessons he took in St. Moritz as a young man had ignited a lifelong passion for skiing. But he and his new bride established their primary residence in a colossal white stucco mansion on Chester Square, perhaps the most exclusive block in Belgravia, which was perhaps the most exclusive neighborhood in London.

Though Mortimer was now in his sixties, Theresa proceeded to have three children, Michael, Marissa, and Sophie. They would be raised British, far from the streets of Flatbush, where their father had grown up, or Connecticut, where their uncle Raymond still presided over the family business, or the Upper East Side, where their older half brother Bobby had killed himself.

✤ ✤ ✤

One night in September 1982, a thousand people arrived at the Metropolitan Museum of Art for the fall/winter couture show of the Italian designer Valentino. Inside, models paraded through one of the great halls in sleeveless jackets, petal skirts, and extravagant gowns of silk and velvet. It was an over-the-top production, one that fully embraced the new decadence of the 1980s. One of the dresses featured in the collection was rumored to sell for $100,000. After the show, three hundred guests were invited to stay for a dinner in the Sackler Wing. The actress Raquel Welch bantered with the novelist Norman Mailer. The dancer Mikhail Baryshnikov chatted with the seventeen-year-old model Brooke Shields. Muhammad Ali performed magic tricks as Valentino himself circulated, bronzed and grinning, in a tuxedo. The tables were adorned with white flowers and hundreds of votive candles, which cast flickering shadows on the walls of the Egyptian temple.

When he learned about the party, Arthur Sackler was disgusted. In a bid to bring in extra revenue, the Met had started to rent out the Sackler Wing as an event space, and Arthur was incensed at what he thought of as the "cheapening" of the Temple of Dendur. He had been maintaining a private tally of "breaches" by the Met of its contract with the Sackler family over use of the temple. Arthur liked the idea of the venue being utilized for official functions—State Department ceremonies, for example. But a fashion show?

For more than a decade, Arthur had been subjecting the Met to the dangle, giving every impression that he would eventually bestow his priceless art collection on the museum. But, to his dismay, he found that he did not get along particularly well with the latest director of the Met, Philippe de Montebello, a cultured curator with an aristocratic mien. Arthur had become accustomed to a certain level of solicitous flattery and accommodation from museum directors, but he did not feel that he got it from de Montebello.

For years, he had kept his private enclave at the museum. "It was kind of like that last scene in *Citizen Kane*," Arthur's son-in-law Michael Rich recalled. "It was like a storeroom. It wasn't a place that celebrated the art. I flashed on Rosebud when I saw that place." But, eventually, the existence of the secret arrangement granting Arthur the use of this space had been exposed. A sociologist and occasional journalist named Sol Chaneles, who chaired the Department of Criminal Justice at Rutgers, had gotten wind of the enclave and requested an interview with Arthur. At first, Arthur had refused to speak with him, but eventually, when it became clear that Chaneles was going to publish one way or another, Arthur got on the phone.

"He offered me several gifts—including a Piranesi—in order not
to have the story published," Chaneles later claimed. The arrangement did end up getting exposed, though not by Chaneles. *ARTnews*
published a story about the Sackler enclave in 1978, asking "whether a
museum can properly devote space to an individual's private collection
and staff... without betraying its public purpose." The article reported
that New York's attorney general had opened an investigation into the
propriety of this accommodation. Arthur was forced to submit to a
deposition ("He considered it a waste of his time," one of the investigators recalled), but he was not ultimately charged with any wrongdoing.

Administrators at the Met were embarrassed by the scandal, but
they wondered if it might not have a certain upside. Could it force
Arthur to make them honest, as it were—by giving them the collection
that they had been housing rent-free all these years? And Arthur had
been very open about his intention to donate the vast bulk of his holdings. "Great art doesn't belong to anybody," he would say, as though
he were just a temporary custodian of these treasures he had paid so
dearly for. "The more successful your collections are, the more they
cease to be your property." Philippe de Montebello might not have flattered and cultivated Arthur to the same degree that his predecessors
had, but he was candid about his ambitions. He hoped that "at least
some part—needless to say, the best—of his collection would come to
the Met in due course."

The museum never did put Arthur on the board, though. There
might have been a disdainful sense, in some uptown circles, that he
simply wanted it too badly. He had always fiercely resented being made
to feel like an upstart or an outsider, and he fumed that in denying
him a seat on the board, the Met was seeking to punish him for "taking advantage" of the museum with his enclave. Hadn't Brooke Astor
served beyond her regulation term on the board? Why couldn't he take
that seat? He complained that the Met had violated its contract with
him over the Sackler Exhibition Hall, where the museum had installed
an espresso bar and a gift shop for its new Vatican show. And speaking
of the Vatican show, he exclaimed, that whole exhibit had been his idea!
Yet the Met had denied him any credit. (De Montebello countered,
acidly, that it doesn't take "any particular genius to think it might be a
good thing to show works of art from the Vatican.")

Arthur still enjoyed some aspects of his association with the Met.

It was fun to be able to send one of his new friends, the scientist and Nobel laureate Linus Pauling, a formal invitation to spend an afternoon at the museum that would begin in "the Arthur M. Sackler Stone Sculpture Gallery," then proceed to a tour of "the bronze exhibition in the Sackler Wing." But he was transparent about his expectation that a philanthropist should be entitled, in exchange for his generosity, to a broad range of prerogatives. Philanthropy wasn't charity, as his lawyer Michael Sonnenreich insisted. It was a business deal. After Arthur donated money for the restoration of the Palace Theatre, a historic vaudeville house in Stamford, Connecticut, Jillian wrote a letter to Pauling in which she described the theater as "Arthur's new toy."

Part of what Arthur came to loathe about Philippe de Montebello was that he appeared to resist this premise. "If you're a director and you have a donor, you spend time," Sonnenreich said. "Philippe decided he didn't have time for Arthur." Indignant at being treated so dismissively, Arthur fixated on de Montebello. He sought out Thomas Hoving, the former director, with whom he had enjoyed a better relationship, and aired his grievances, expressing effrontery that de Montebello had appeared in a photo spread for *Harper's Bazaar*, like some sort of "male model." Going so far as to compare de Montebello to Adolf Hitler, Arthur appealed to Hoving for help in forcing "the man out of the museum."

But de Montebello wasn't going anywhere. So, eventually, Arthur did. "Dear Doctor Sackler," S. Dillon Ripley, the head of the Smithsonian in Washington, wrote to Arthur in 1980. Ripley might have lost out to the Met in his bid for the Temple of Dendur, but now he would take his revenge. He mentioned to Arthur that he had heard about "your desire to make arrangements in the near future for the disposition of some of your great collections." Such collections, he continued, "deserve a place on the Mall in Washington." He had a plan for Arthur Sackler, a vision of a "single magnificent gift."

Ripley had chosen his moment well. Arthur had been thinking lately, he said, about making "a major gift to the nation." And so the dance began. Ripley reeled Arthur in slowly. But it would not be an easy negotiation; with Arthur, it never was. In an internal memo, Ripley wrote, "Sackler very much wants his name over the door." Those were his terms: he would not be donating his collection unless he got a whole museum with his name on it. The proposal was "a mixed bless-

ing," Ripley pointed out. An "extremely handsome gift, both in cash
and in kind, but not really large enough to justify 'Sacklerizing' the
new museum."

Arthur's suggestion was that he would give $4 million to the Smith-
sonian, along with the best works from his collection. But the museum
would require more funds to build the new facility, which created a
dilemma. "Your very generous offer of a major gift from your magnificent collections, and four million dollars toward construction of the
Sackler museum, is very deeply appreciated," Ripley wrote to Arthur.
"Our problem continues to be that we must find ten million dollars for
the construction of that gallery, and that we must do so in a manner
consistent with its bearing your name. This of course limits the possible
funding sources to which we might turn." How could he persuade other
donors to supply millions of dollars to help finance the construction of a
museum that was already named after Arthur Sackler? In a subsequent
phone call, Arthur indicated that this might be Ripley's problem, but it
wasn't his. He reiterated his original offer and said it was his "unshakeable" position.

Arthur prevailed. The two men forged a deal in which Arthur
would agree to donate a thousand objects from his collection, which
Ripley estimated to have a value of roughly $75 million. The museum
would open to the public in 1987.

When the deal was announced, Philippe de Montebello tried to
mask his annoyance. "Disappointed? The disinherited always have
that view," he said to *The Washington Post*. He pointed out that for years
museum officials had allowed Arthur to store his collection at the Met,
saying, "Obviously, the reason it was housed here was so that we would
ingratiate ourselves to Dr. Sackler." One day, a squad of curators from
the Smithsonian arrived in New York and filed into the Met. They
made their way to the Sackler enclave, then set to work picking through
it, selecting the very best of the masterpieces that had been stored there
so that they could be carted off to Washington.

✢   ✢   ✢

For a time, Arthur managed to juggle the women in his life. He
kept coming home to Marietta, but then he would also be gone for long
stretches, with Jillian. It seemed to Marietta that what he wanted was
not to choose—to have it all, just as he had with Marietta and Else.

But ultimately, Marietta decided that she could not accept this situation. She had movers come and clear Arthur's belongings out of the old Dutch house on Searingtown Road. She informed Arthur that she had no desire to be just another romantic partner in his "collection."

Arthur requested that Marietta spell out, in a letter, what she would hope to see in a divorce settlement. So she sat down and wrote it. She wanted the house in Long Island and also an apartment that the couple had purchased across from the United Nations. According to Marietta, she didn't ask for any of the art, which she felt was a significant concession, given how much of it the two of them had collected together.

Marietta waited for an answer, but none came. Months passed. Occasionally, she would ask Arthur when she could expect a response, and he would always say that he had more pressing business to attend to and would get to it "next week." After a while, it began to seem as if Arthur were not so much busy as in denial. Marietta was coming apart. She felt as though she were trapped in limbo, and the crazy thing was that Arthur *liked* limbo. He thrived on it. He'd built a life around fuzzy boundaries, overlapping identities, conflicts of interest. Limbo was his element. But it was driving her mad. One day, Marietta called him, feeling frantic, and demanded an answer. Arthur, in a controlled rage, told her that she had better find a good lawyer.

Distraught, Marietta hung up the phone. Then, on an impulse, she grabbed a handful of sleeping pills and stuffed them into her jacket pocket. She felt singed by Arthur's hatred, and she found herself on the street, walking in a daze along the sidewalk, then running, making her way to Arthur's office in the adjoined town houses that he had bought for her, back in 1960. When she stormed into the office, she found Arthur huddled with a few of his business associates, and they all looked up, startled. "You have to listen to me now," Marietta told him. "I need an answer."

Arthur, furious, reprimanded her for bursting into his office with her demands and for making a spectacle. Marietta had brought with her a copy of the letter outlining what she wanted in the divorce and now she thrust it at him, demanding an answer. Arthur took the letter and read it. But this only made him more angry. He threw the letter on the floor, with contempt.

So Marietta reached into her pocket, grabbed the sleeping pills, and before Arthur could stop her, she swallowed them. All she wanted in that moment was to escape, to disappear into sleep. She felt some dark part of herself rising up, some primitive, malignant force taking over. The pills tasted bitter, and suddenly her senses were confused. She found herself on the carpet, where Arthur had thrown the letter. She was aware of a commotion around her. Voices. Someone shouting. Then lights. Hands on her body. Pressure. Somebody calling her name.

✛   ✛   ✛

When Marietta woke up, she was in a hospital bed. Her throat was sore and dry. Her memory of what had happened was confused. But Arthur was there, by her bedside, waiting for her to wake up.

What he said to her, when she came to, was, "How could you do this to me?"

Marietta recovered, and eventually the divorce was finalized. Arthur married Jillian the next day. He got the house on Long Island, in the end. Marietta got the apartment at UN Plaza. She was there at nine o'clock one morning when a team of movers arrived. Arthur had sent them, and they proceeded to pack up the art in the house and take it away. They removed bronzes, statues, vases, hundreds of items, objects that she didn't care about and objects that were instilled with tremendous meaning. The wishing well. The granary jar. The jade horse that used to sit on the piano. It took the movers ten hours, but eventually they had crated everything up and carted it away. And Marietta was left there, feeling very alone in the big apartment, and she cried, surrounded by bare shelves and what she thought of as "ghost marks" on the walls, the discolored rectangles where paintings used to hang.

Chapter 10

TO THWART THE INEVITABILITY OF DEATH

SANDERS THEATRE IS A cavernous Gothic Revival building on the campus of Harvard University, with beautiful woodwork, a vaulted ceiling, and marvelous acoustics. One evening in the fall of 1985, Arthur Sackler strode onto the same stage where Teddy Roosevelt, Winston Churchill, and Dr. Martin Luther King Jr. had all spoken in the past. Arthur gazed out at twelve hundred people, gathered in their finery, and he beamed. "President Bok," he said, looking over at Harvard's president, Derek Bok. "Excellencies. Lords and Ladies. Distinguished faculties and fellow students. Beloved friends and honored guests." This was the court of Arthur Sackler, a great room full of dignitaries, all there to listen to what he had to say. To honor him. He had come to Cambridge for three days of parties and receptions to celebrate the opening of the Arthur M. Sackler Museum at Harvard.

The museum would be housed in a new brick-and-glass facility, designed by the British architect James Stirling, which would function as an extension of the university's art museum, the Fogg. Harvard had been struggling to finance the extension, going so far as to entertain the idea of selling off some of its collection in order to pay for the construction. At one point Derek Bok had actually canceled the project altogether. But Arthur came to the rescue, with the understanding that the new building would have to bear his name. By the time he took the stage at Sanders Theatre, he had given Harvard more than $10 million.

"A new millennium begins in but a decade and a half," Arthur announced, invoking one of his favorite themes: the ability of the human species to control nature. "After billions of years and myriads of species, a newcomer, *homo sapiens,* in just two score years has traversed a range of global watersheds, completely reversing realities that ruled throughout the existence of our earth," he said. Arthur's friend Linus Pauling, who had been awarded Nobel Prizes in both Chemistry and Peace, was in the audience, having come to town for the occasion. The violinist Itzhak Perlman was there as well, and the actress Glenn Close, and the artist Frank Stella. *The Boston Globe*, apparently unaware of Arthur's interest in all things Asian, noted that the opening ceremonies would include "music, dance, tours and (for some reason) martial arts demonstrations."

For billions of years, Arthur continued, "all species were at the mercy of the environment." But now, the environment is "at the mercy of one species." Humans put a man on the moon, he pointed out, and devised ingenious methods with which to influence "heredity and evolution." Advances in medical science meant that what was previously inconceivable had become "routine" and that humans, alone among species, had learned to "thwart the inevitability of death." The new millennium would only accelerate this progress. It was time to think deeply about the questions that would govern the quality of life in the twenty-first century, Arthur said, and to build bridges between the arts, the sciences, and the humanities. "Toward these ends, I have dedicated a lifetime," he concluded, "and now dedicate this institution."

Not long after the Harvard celebration, the Smithsonian announced its own plan to open the Arthur M. Sackler museum on the Mall in Washington, pointing out, in a press release, that the Sackler name "is associated with a wide range of scientific institutions," such as the Sackler School of Medicine in Tel Aviv, the Arthur M. Sackler Sciences Center at Clark University, and the Arthur M. Sackler Center for Health Communications at Tufts. Yet in telling the world about the man for whom this new gallery would be named, the Smithsonian relied upon a biography, supplied by Arthur, that was oddly selective. Arthur once told his colleagues at McAdams that he had "spent the greatest part of my adult life" at the advertising agency. It had been, in many ways, his most formative professional home. But the biography that he put together for the Smithsonian made no mention of McAdams at all. It covered other parts of his life in gratuitous detail, noting that in high school he had been "editor on all the student publications." But it completely left out the advertising agency that Arthur still owned, or any mention of Librium and Valium, the drugs that had generated a large part of the very fortune that had put him in a position to be so generous.

The Smithsonian plan entailed building a new underground art center that would house the National Museum of African Art as well as the Sackler Gallery. Arthur and Jillian traveled to Washington for the groundbreaking, and he looked jovial, in a dark business suit and a bow tie. It had been raining for a week, so the area was a sea of mud. The Smithsonian erected a special tent for the dignitaries who had assembled for the event. Security was tight: Warren Burger, the chief justice of the Supreme Court, was there, along with Vice President George H. W. Bush. This was "a very privileged moment," Arthur announced. The plan was for Arthur to deliver a check for the second installment of his donation. He had expressed an interest in handing it directly to Vice President Bush. But before he could do so, a young woman from the Secret Service intervened. Arthur explained that he had something to give to the vice president. The Secret Service agent said that she would need to examine it first. So Arthur pulled out his checkbook and, with impish satisfaction, wrote the words "Two Million."

It might have seemed, now that Arthur was entering the valedictory phase of his career, that he could finally relax. He made the Forbes 400 list in 1986; the magazine estimated that he was worth "$175 million plus." And he did have a pronounced personal tendency to take stock of his own achievements. On the twentieth anniversary of the *Medical Tribune,* he compiled a long list of "firsts"—areas in which, in Arthur's view, his newspaper had broken new ground. Readers might "want to add to it," he suggested, as if he alone could hardly tally the feats. In 1986, Jillian organized a three-day "Festschrift" in Woods Hole, Massachusetts, in which friends and colleagues of Arthur's gathered to praise him and share stories of his many contributions to the arts and the sciences. Just as Marietta had done, Jillian found herself scrapbooking for her illustrious husband, endlessly updating a document that she described as his "list of achievements."

But for all the retrospective celebration he was engaged in, Arthur did not regard his career as over. He still had so many things that he wanted to do. In the words of one longtime friend, Louis Lasagna, "His agenda would have required three lifetimes for completion." Arthur might talk about the ability of humankind to bend nature to its devices, but the truth was that he couldn't bend time, and he knew it. Time "is my greatest enemy," he complained. "*Time* is a vicious dictator, inflexible, inexorable—and ultimately always the victor." He liked to tell people that in marrying Jillian, he had "got it right the third time." But he also spoke about the decision as a sort of gambit to outwit the clock. "One thing about her being younger," he told a friend, "is that it will lead to a hundred years of philanthropy and great works. My fifty years—and the fifty years after she outlives me."

In the meantime, he would continue to push himself. He still maintained a punishing schedule, working seven days a week, with frequent travel. In bed at night, he still read medical journals, to keep up with the latest research. But his age, and the pace that he maintained, was starting to catch up with him. In the fall of 1986, Arthur fell ill and was confined to bed for several weeks with shingles.

A few months later, Mortimer celebrated his own seventieth birthday with a lavish party in the Sackler Wing of the Met. It could scarcely have escaped Arthur's attention that his own brother might now be accused of engaging in precisely the sort of crass defilement of the Sackler temple that Arthur himself so disdained. The party, which was orchestrated by Mortimer's third wife, Theresa, featured hundreds of guests and a giant cake that had been custom made to resemble an Egyptian sarcophagus, but with the bespectacled visage of Mortimer himself. Theresa engaged an interior designer and had ambitious plans, initially, to augment the Temple of Dendur with two additional pillars. But the Met rejected the plans, protesting that to make "architectural changes" to the ancient temple, even for the purposes of a very important birthday party, seemed a bit unnecessary. Mortimer, offended, snapped, "They can irritate the gift giver."

Whatever distaste he might have felt, Arthur put in an appearance at Mortimer's party. Marietta attended as well. She and Arthur had not seen each other for some time. The fallout from their divorce had not been pleasant. Their daughter, Denise, took Marietta's side and effectively cut her father off. She ended up legally changing her last name to Marika, a portmanteau of the first names of her mother and grandmother, Marietta and Frederika. To someone who did not know the family, this might have seemed like a fanciful, new age affectation. But for the daughter of Arthur Sackler, it was a gesture freighted with meaning. To cast off the Sackler name was the ultimate act of renunciation. "She stripped that name off her body with a steel brush," one friend of Denise's said. Just the same, Arthur was cordial when he saw Marietta and suggested that they have lunch together someday.

They met at a little French restaurant that they used to frequent, near the apartment at the United Nations. When they had been seated and started to talk, Arthur asked if they could switch tables, because he had grown hard of hearing and wanted to sit in such a way that Marietta could speak into his good ear. She did most of the talking, catching him up on her life. After a period of devastation and anger, she was beginning to find some happiness, writing poetry, traveling to Europe. She left New York for good, settling in Vermont, and eventually found a kind man who was different, in many ways, from Arthur—a lesser man, perhaps, in his achievements, but one who made her happy. Arthur mostly listened, just as he had on that long car ride to the medical conference in Chicago four decades earlier. But Marietta noticed that he seemed distracted and agitated, only half there.

For such a wealthy man, Arthur still worried about money. He continued to acquire art and make philanthropic commitments at a frantic pace, and he feared that he was overextending. As a consequence, perhaps, his relations with Jillian had suffered. A few months after the lunch with Marietta, he sent Jillian a terse memo, which he dictated to an aide in the car on his way to the airport. He had resolved "to take over responsibility of all finances I deploy," he informed Jillian, demanding that she produce a "budget for household expenses," with itemized entries for each of their four homes, detailing costs of "food, maintenance, Christmas and other tips, insurance, telephones, gas and electricity, furnishings." He appeared to be seized by a manic anxiety. "Upon my return on Thursday afternoon, I want whatever above data you can provide me with together with an agenda and schedule of how you will supply the rest." Arthur reprimanded his wife for her "repeated complaints" about "the unavailability of funding and support for your interests." It was only because he was in a hurry that he was sending her a memo, he explained: "In the future I will dictate my instructions directly to you." He felt enormous strain, he told her. People were spending his money too loosely. But he was determined "to take command."

One of Jillian's interests that required "funding and support" was a passion for collecting old jewelry—not antique jewelry, which lots of people collect, but *ancient* jewelry. Arthur had encouraged this newfound hobby, welcoming the notion that his spouse would build a collection of her own, and that spring the Royal Academy of Arts in London was planning an exhibition, *Jewels of the Ancients: Selections from the Jill Sackler Collection*. The exhibit would feature more than two hundred pieces, which the museum billed as "the most comprehensive private collection of ancient Near Eastern jewelry in private hands." In an essay to promote the show, Jillian wrote that her "determination to collect jewelry began with gifts from my husband, who is himself a passionate collector as well as an eminent scientist and psychiatrist and a major benefactor of museums and institutions in the arts, sciences and humanities."

The exhibit opened that May. The treasures on display were stunning: wreaths and chains of filigreed gold and amulets of lapis lazuli. Some of the pieces were believed to be older even than the Temple of Dendur, dating as far back as the third millennium B.C. Jillian made it clear that she was not merely hoarding bling. On the contrary, like her husband, she was seeking to promote academic study. As her collection expanded, she observed, she was "pleased to find myself almost alone in a field virtually devoid of prior scholarship." The curators insisted on maintaining dim lighting for the show, so as not to damage the ancient artifacts. But the jewelry glittered brilliantly. It was extraordinary to think, as one visitor subsequently wrote, that "jewels so delicate as the wreaths or an exquisite gold flower had survived intact for several thousand years—shimmering as if they had been made yesterday."

But the exhibit was not the triumph Jillian had hoped. After it launched, *The Sunday Times* published a shocking story that raised doubts about the authenticity of some of the items. "I believe a large proportion of the flashier objects are fake," Jack Ogden, a museum consultant with a specialty in identifying forgeries, told the paper. "Yet showing them at the Academy gives them credence. It will set back the study of jewelry twenty years." Jillian insisted that this could not be the case, saying, "I would be very, very surprised if any pieces are wrong." But the Royal Academy convened twenty-four experts from around the world to spend two days studying the collection, and they issued a statement saying that "there was a unanimous opinion that some of these pieces, including some major items, were not ancient."

The scandal was devastating for Jillian—and for Arthur. The Arthur M. Sackler Gallery at the Smithsonian was set to open in the fall, and the plan had been for the Jill Sackler Collection of Ancient Jewelry to tour, showing at the National Gallery in Washington. But after the revelation that some of the most flamboyant pieces might be counterfeit, preparations for that exhibit were quietly abandoned.

On the subject of best-laid plans, Arthur liked to use an expression: "Man proposes, but God disposes." As the controversy was playing out in London that May, he flew to Boston for a meeting at State Street Bank, where he had become a major shareholder. While he was in Boston, he experienced a strange pain in his chest. He flew back to New York early, went to his office, and announced that he might have had a heart attack.

Arthur was seventy-three. He had always hated being sick. It put him in the position of being dependent on others, which he did not like. And he might have had a fear that people would take advantage of him when he was impaired. Whatever the precise rationale, when he was admitted to the hospital, he chose not to inform his family. As an added precaution, and in a nod to his old preference for anonymity, he checked in under a pseudonym. As a consequence of all this secrecy, none of his family, apart from Jillian, knew that Arthur was in the hospital. By the time his children arrived to see him, he was already dead. When Denise called her mother to relay the news, Marietta could not believe it. There was a part of her that had assumed Arthur Sackler might live forever.

✢ ✢ ✢

Arthur had always enjoyed being feted for his accomplishments in life, so it was a pity that he couldn't witness the events that followed his death; they would have pleased him. There were elaborate, star-studded ceremonies at Harvard, at Tufts, at the Smithsonian. There was a memorial concert at the Kennedy Center in Washington, which two thousand people attended. And one afternoon that June, four hundred people filed into the Sackler Wing at the Met, to pay their respects. "Jews are not usually eulogized in a synagogue," Ed Koch, the New York mayor, observed. But Arthur "built his own synagogue," Koch continued. "It is a tribute to him that the very place he built, glorious as it is, is the place in which we are engaging in this eulogy." Koch looked out at the crowd. "I am sure he liked the fact that you are in his temple."

"How can I find words to do him justice?" Jillian said, when it was her turn to speak. "He was supreme." Arthur "did his best for his family," she noted, putting his "brothers through school and medical school, and setting up all the family businesses." Yet the dozens of speeches by high-profile friends and associates of Arthur's in all the various public memorials did not feature any remarks from either Raymond or Mortimer. In fact, by the time Arthur died, they were barely speaking.

"What is so ironic is that this person should have died *in media res*," J. Carter Brown, the director of the National Gallery in Washington, pointed out in the ceremony at the Met. This was a recurring theme in the remarks, the idea that Arthur was, in Brown's phrase, "only halfway through." Just as Isaac Sackler had repeated to his sons that sentiment about the importance of a "good name," Arthur Sackler had a precept that he had often intoned to his own children. "When we leave," he told them, "we have to leave the world a better place than when we arrived." There was a keen sense, in the Sackler Wing that afternoon in 1987, that though Arthur Sackler's life had ended, it was too soon yet to take the full measure of his legacy.

BOOK II

DYNASTY

Chapter 11

APOLLO

RICHARD KAPIT FIRST ENCOUNTERED the Sackler family in the spring of 1964 as he was finishing his freshman year at Columbia. Kapit was a smart kid on a partial scholarship, from an inauspicious town dead in the center of Long Island. He was physically unassuming, and somewhat shy, and he didn't have a huge cohort of friends. But in the evenings, at his dorm, a bunch of guys would gather to hang out while ostensibly studying, and when Kapit mentioned that he still needed to find a roommate for the following year, one of them suggested "Sackler." So Richard Kapit sought out Richard Sackler and learned that he, too, was looking for a roommate. The son of Raymond Sackler and his wife, Beverly, Richard Sackler had also grown up on Long Island, though in rather different circumstances, and he turned out to be a brainy kid, like Kapit, so they became fast friends.

Rather than live in one of the dormitories, Sackler and Kapit went looking for an apartment off campus and found one a few subway stops away, in a modern complex on Columbus Avenue called Park West Village. It was a two-bedroom apartment on the ground floor, right across the street from a fire station, and after they moved in, they discovered that they would have to get used to the nightly shriek of sirens as fire trucks careened in and out. It was only when they set out to furnish the place that Kapit got his first indication that his new friend Sackler might come from an unusual family. Sackler took him across Central Park, to a town house on East Sixty-Second Street, just around the corner from the Pierre hotel. It belonged to his family, he explained. The place struck Kapit as a small palace, something out of a storybook fantasy of New York. It was a bit ambiguous whether the building belonged to Sackler's parents or to others in his extended family, but he ushered Kapit down to a room in the basement that was full of spare furniture—not the rickety chairs and bric-a-brac shelving of the standard college apartment, but sturdy, adult furniture. They took what they needed, and that was how they furnished the place.

Kapit was captivated by his new roommate: Richard was smart, and quirky, and *fun*. He was stocky, with a wide forehead, a straight nose, a husky voice, and a goofy grin. Richard's most distinctive trait, Kapit discovered, was a headlong enthusiasm for life. He was only intermittently engaged by his classwork and preferred to devote himself to more epicurean pursuits. He liked smoking cigars and pipes, and sought out the finest tobacco, and he loved to sit around the apartment in the evening, smoking and talking. The two of them would fill pipes with a special variety of Syrian tobacco that Richard favored, which had allegedly been cured over fires of camel dung. It had a rich, intense aroma, and Richard would sit back in his chair, wreathed in pipe smoke, and cogitate, like Sherlock Holmes. He kept one closet in the apartment stocked with a collection of fine wine, buying cases at a time, and pulling out different bottles to sample. The two of them would sip deeply and discourse, drunkenly, about the subtle distinctions among varietals.

For Kapit, this was a "mind-bending" experience, an education of the senses. Richard regarded himself, proudly, as a sensualist— someone who wanted to see and taste and touch the finest, most exotic bounty. And he was marvelously unselfish, happy to foot the bill, wealthy enough not to care, eager to induct his less worldly roommate into these mysteries. "Sharing with me was a big part of it," Kapit later recalled. "He needed someone to share these things with in order to complete his pleasure of them." Richard's devotion to his own passions was "absolute," Kapit was finding. "For him, what made life really worthwhile was these wonderful things that you could buy."

Kapit paid his share of the rent, but on almost every other account he found that he soon came to rely on Richard's generosity. It made him uncomfortable. His own background was modest: his mother was a dietitian, and his father was a schoolteacher. But Richard Sackler was not just incrementally better off. He was rich. He was generally a pretty carefree guy, and he seemed to live in a stratosphere where he wouldn't even resent always picking up the check, because these gestures that were so significant to Richard Kapit were, for Richard Sackler, ultimately trivial. It seemed to Kapit that money wasn't something he worried about, because he didn't need to worry about it; it had always been there, in abundant supply, to invest or save or waste as he pleased. Like air.

But Kapit also couldn't help but notice that he seemed to be Richard Sackler's only real friend in college. Or, rather, his only male friend. Sackler had a serious girlfriend, Margie Yospin, who was a student at Barnard, the women's college just across Broadway from Columbia. Richard and Margie had been dating since high school, in Roslyn, on Long Island. They had both been part of a coterie of brainy social outliers who called themselves the "un-group." Richard was in the geometry club. He was one of the few kids in his cohort who had his own car, and he and his friends would buy a bottle of whiskey and drive around in search of a place to drink it.

Margie was smart and worldly; as a high school student, she had spent nine months on a student exchange in Argentina, so she spoke fluent Spanish. Richard Kapit liked her, and the three of them started spending all their spare time together. Kapit couldn't understand why exactly Sackler did not have more friends. But, over time, he noticed that his roommate had some unusual qualities. Though he was tremendously generous, he seemed to lack empathy—the ability to reflect on the experience or emotions of others, or on how his own behavior might affect other people. Once, Richard suggested that Kapit take one of his cousins out on a date. Kapit met up with the young woman, and had an evening planned, but as the city bus pulled up and he indicated that this would be their mode of transportation, she blanched and backed away. Kapit was humiliated. He didn't have the money to convey her around town in taxis, and he felt as if Richard Sackler should have known that and should have known that for this cousin the bus would be a nonstarter. But it simply never occurred to him. When Kapit indicated, afterward, that the experience had upset him, Sackler did not seem to understand why. "It was as though his parents had raised him specifically not to have a lot of hang-ups," Kapit recalled.

Another reason that Sackler might not have had friends was that he didn't seem particularly interested in going to class. That's not to say that he wasn't smart and curious. Initially, he was impressed by the intensity of the course load. "The rigor is stupefying," he wrote in a letter to one Roslyn friend, before signing off, as only a college student can, "I have Sophocles to read." He complained about the work and grumbled that Raymond and Beverly Sackler would be watching his grades. "I have been doing more work than ever before," he wrote in the spring of his first year. "That does not mean that I have metamorphosed into a grub: simply, I must work or face the Wrath of Home."

Richard had a sense of humor. He liked telling jokes, and hearing them, and he developed his own brand of scabrous, Shakespearean vulgarity: "gaping ass-hole. Who in Hell does he think he is?" he wrote in one letter, of some peer who had apparently given offense. "I hope you ram his overblown membrum virile down his beshitted throat."

By the time he was a sophomore, according to Kapit, Richard Sackler had become more interested in his own course of study. One subject that he found very interesting was sex. Richard Kapit was a virgin, a shy kid who had what he privately feared was a debilitating inhibition around women. Richard Sackler had long since lost his virginity, and Kapit felt that he flaunted his sex life with Margie. Proud sensualist that he was, Richard made it clear to Kapit that he didn't know what he was missing, and suggested that he just get over whatever issue he had and find someone to have sex with. But Richard also just liked to talk about sex, and one subject that the two of them would discuss, in a fog of Syrian pipe smoke, was the orgasm. Sackler was very interested in the physiology of the orgasm—what caused it, how to understand it. This was an important matter, it seemed to him, one that science had neglected for too long. So the Richards decided to make a project of this inquiry, a kind of independent study.

Kapit had been intending to find a summer job when the term ended. But Richard had other ideas. Don't get a job, he proposed. Instead, let's devote this summer to solving the scientific riddle of the orgasm. Richard would cover all the necessary expenses. So, why not? "His enthusiasm was infectious," Kapit remembered. "He viewed life as a playground, and almost anything was possible and worth trying, if it might generate something of interest or reward." It was bewitching, even empowering, for Kapit to spend time in the company of someone who had never been denied much. Richard marched through life emboldened, convinced that absolutely anything was possible, that no practical limit should constrain an idle fancy from becoming a reality.

So they spent the summer studying orgasms. They visited medical libraries, consulting scientific treatises and obscure journals. At one point, Richard identified a scientist at the Woods Hole Oceanographic

Institution, on Cape Cod, who did work on the nervous system and might be able to shed some light on their inquiry. We should go see him, he announced. So Richard borrowed his mother's car, a Pontiac Grand Prix, and they picked up Margie; then the three of them drove to Massachusetts. And this eminent neurophysiologist at Woods Hole, when he grasped why precisely it was that these three very earnest college sophomores had driven all the way from New York City and were now sitting in his office, just laughed. "What a chuckle he had," Kapit recalled. "It was a gas."

The three of them shared a motel room in Cape Cod, which Richard paid for, and occupying a room with Richard and Margie, Kapit once again experienced some tension over the issue of sex. Richard had been pressuring him to find a woman with whom he could lose his virginity. Kapit had met several of Richard's older relatives—his father, Raymond, and his uncle Arthur—and it seemed to him that these men shared a macho expectation that a vigorous sex life was part of what made a young man a young man. Once, Richard invited Kapit to lunch with Arthur Sackler. They met at an elegant, high-end Chinese restaurant in midtown. Kapit was dazzled by Arthur: his air of authority, his rapacious intellect, the cut of his suit. Their waitress was a young Chinese woman. At one point in the meal, to Kapit's alarm, Arthur Sackler started hitting on her. The woman became visibly uncomfortable, and Kapit flushed with embarrassment. But Richard Sackler seemed unfazed.

Richard admired his uncle Arthur. He proudly showed off to Kapit a copy of *MD,* the magazine that Félix Martí-Ibáñez published and Arthur secretly owned. Their time at Columbia happened to coincide with the period when Arthur was beginning to give generously to the university. When Columbia launched the first big exhibit of Arthur's Asian art, in Low Library—the one that was staged by the window designer from Tiffany—Richard brought his roommate along to the show. "It was a big deal for Richard," Kapit said. "He was so excited to see those beautiful objects." The "whole family," Kapit realized, "had a thing about Asian art and Asian beauty."

✤ ✤ ✤

On July 24, 1969, the Apollo 11 space capsule hurtled through earth's atmosphere at twenty-five thousand miles per hour, shedding flaming shards of protective casing so that it resembled a giant fireball. Inside were the astronauts Neil Armstrong, Buzz Aldrin, and Michael Collins, who had just made history by walking on the moon. In the sky over the South Pacific, three parachutes deployed, and the capsule glided into a smooth splashdown, rolling and bobbing in the rough waves like a cork. Soon, a helicopter approached, and several navy frogmen dropped into the ocean to stabilize the capsule with an inflatable collar. The divers inflated a raft, and as the astronauts emerged from the capsule, the frogmen washed them down with a brown antiseptic solution, in case they had inadvertently brought any "moon germs" back to this planet. The astronauts climbed into the raft and, one by one, they submitted to what looked like the sort of sponge bath you might give a baby, as the frogmen scrubbed their arms and legs. It was a comical first step in NASA's postflight procedure, but an essential one. The solution that the frogmen used to anoint each astronaut was called Betadine.

Purdue Frederick had acquired Physicians Products, the Virginia company that made Betadine, three years earlier. Betadine was used as a surgical scrub and would have important battlefield applications during the Vietnam War. But the space program was a great coup and priceless publicity for the company. "Splashdown!" a Purdue Frederick advertisement clamored, noting that while NASA might use Betadine for space germs, it was also available, here on earth, as a "mouthwash/ gargle."

One thing that struck Richard Kapit, from early on, about his friend Richard Sackler was his devotion to the family business. So far as Kapit could tell, Purdue Frederick's biggest product seemed to be the laxative Senokot. The company's advertisements for Senokot were ubiquitous, and cringe-inducing, with copy about the virtues of "a softer stool" and photos of grimacing men in the throes of constipation. But Richard was in no way self-conscious: he was proud of the company and its products. And say what you will about Senokot, but people bought it, because it worked. On a few occasions, Richard brought Kapit on trips to Purdue Frederick's headquarters, which had moved to a big building in Yonkers. Kapit knew, also, that the family had some connection to Valium, which was an enormously successful drug. As it happened, Kapit's father had worked as a pharmacist before becoming a schoolteacher, and his family shared the Sacklers' faith that such wonder drugs were a symbol of human progress and a glimpse of the future.

They certainly seemed to represent Richard Sackler's future. It was taken for granted that he would go to medical school and then join the family business. In fact, the family was so evangelical about the excitement and nobility and financial rewards of the medical profession that after a conversation with Raymond Sackler, Richard Kapit decided he, too, should be premed. He ended up applying to medical school and getting into NYU; Richard's girlfriend, Margie, would eventually become a doctor, too.

But by that point, the two Richards were no longer speaking. After the summer studying orgasms, they had returned to school for their junior year. But Richard Kapit found himself increasingly uncomfortable in the friendship. Later, he would be unable to put his finger on precisely what it was that unsettled him. Perhaps it had something to do with sex and the strange pressure that Richard exerted on him in that regard. Or perhaps the natural tension in the triangular friendship with Margie was simply unsustainable. But he was certain that one element was a gradually increasing discomfort with his perpetual status as Sackler's guest and a nagging worry that he had become a freeloader. One night, Kapit and Sackler were having dinner in the apartment. They had been drinking wine, and the sink was full of dirty dishes. A question arose about who would wash up, and suddenly Kapit snapped. He didn't know why he got upset, exactly. The dishes were clearly just a pretext. But he exploded, shouting at Richard. It was as if, he later said, "a lid had popped off." Richard stared at him, blindsided, as though he'd lost his mind. "He felt he had always treated me very well, and he had. In his own terms, he had," Kapit said. "So, for him, this was out of the blue."

Not long afterward, Kapit found a room in a dorm on campus and moved out. "Richard seemed very hurt by it," he recalled. Sackler's blindness to the emotions of others might have left him unable to see that his benevolent relationship with his less-well-off best friend was not as uncomplicated as it had seemed. The Richards stopped seeing each other. At one point, when some time had passed, Kapit called the house in Roslyn just to check in and see how Richard was doing. His mother, Beverly, answered the phone, but she refused to put Richard on. "I think you've hurt him enough," she said.

With his casual approach to his own studies, Richard Sackler did not get into a premier medical school like Harvard or NYU, even with the connections that his family was spending so much money to cultivate. Instead, he went to SUNY Buffalo for two years and eventually managed to transfer to NYU. It didn't ultimately matter, in any case. Wherever he went to med school, and however well or poorly he did, there was little doubt about where Richard Sackler would end up.

"My dearest nephew and colleague Richard," Félix Martí-Ibáñez wrote to him on June 7, 1971. "Only a few years ago I had the joy of attending your bar mitzvah and today I am privileged to attend this celebration of your graduation as a physician. On the first occasion you became a man; today you have become more than a man." To be a physician, Martí-Ibáñez told Richard, is to be "the chosen of the Gods." He was joining an elite priesthood, and doing so with every conceivable advantage, Martí-Ibáñez pointed out. After all, he was a Sackler: "I know that throughout your life you will honor the illustrious name you bear."

Chapter 12

HEIR APPARENT

ONE DAY IN AUGUST 1972, a Connecticut millionaire named W. T. Grant died, at the age of ninety-six. Grant had started from nothing and built a great fortune by opening variety stores. He left behind a vast private estate in the affluent suburb of Greenwich. It was an enormous property: twelve acres on a peninsula jutting into the Long Island Sound, with a rambling main house, a separate, Tudor-style complex with living quarters for staff, a greenhouse, a tennis court, and a seven-car garage. The main home came equipped with peculiarly mid-century amenities, such as a closet with its own climate control system that was specifically designed for fur coats.

Grant had no heirs. So, having erected this lavish estate for himself, he chose to leave it, upon his death, to Greenwich Hospital. The hospital sought to convert the property into a medical facility, but as it turned out, local zoning restrictions prevented it. So Greenwich Hospital, stuck with a gift it couldn't use, decided to sell. But when they put the home on the market, nobody wanted to buy it, on account of the exorbitant price. The problem, in the tart summation of *The New York Times,* was that "there are not many buyers looking for a $1,850,000 house on the water." Even in wealthy Greenwich, the Grant estate represented luxury on a scale that the merely rich could not afford. Without a buyer, Greenwich Hospital was finding that what had started out as a generous donation had turned into an albatross: between taxes, maintenance, and other expenses, just carrying the property was costing the hospital thousands of dollars every month.

Finally, in the summer of 1973, the Grant estate sold, for $1.3 million—a steep discount on the asking price, but still the highest figure ever paid for a single-family home in Greenwich. The purchaser did not wish to be identified, but when an enterprising reporter from the *Times* telephoned the attorney who handled the deal, he learned that the buyer intended to use the home as a private residence. According to the deed, an entity called Rock Point Ltd. had put up $325,000 in cash for the purchase, while another entity, Mundi-Inter Ltd., supplied a mortgage of $1 million. Mundi-Inter had an address in Norwalk, Connecticut. When the *Times* reporter called a phone number associated with the address, an operator picked up and informed him that he had reached the offices of the Purdue Frederick Company. The *Times* never got any further than that in its reporting and did not publish the name of the actual buyer of the Grant estate. But it was Raymond Sackler.

Raymond's move from Long Island to Connecticut was prompted by the fact that his company was moving there, too. Having originated in Greenwich Village, and eventually moved to Yonkers, Purdue Frederick would now consolidate in a brand-new twelve-story office building in downtown Norwalk. Two hundred employees would make the move. One of them, who had only recently joined the company, was Raymond's son Richard Sackler.

After transferring to NYU, Richard had received his degree, the coveted MD. But his intention was never to practice: the only clinical work he ever did was an internship in internal medicine, at Hartford Hospital. In 1971, Richard joined Purdue Frederick. His title was assistant to the president. The president was his father.

The company that Richard joined had been very profitable for the Sacklers over the decades, profitable enough that Raymond could purchase the most expensive home in Greenwich. But it still specialized in bread-and-butter, over-the-counter products, rather than sophisticated prescription pharmaceuticals. Senokot remained a mainstay: the production facility in Yonkers gave off the aroma of senna, an herb with special laxative properties that was its central ingredient. "All of Yonkers smelled of Senna," one former employee recalled. It became a joke among the staff: "If sales get any bigger, they'll have to build bigger sewers." The disinfectant Betadine was also a big success, and the company offered a range of other humdrum remedies, from Cerumenex (an earwax remover) to Paremycin Elixir (for the treatment of diarrhea).

When Purdue was in Yonkers, Raymond had continued to run day-to-day operations mostly from the Sackler town house in Manhattan. He worked there, surrounded by a coterie of close advisers, and the atmosphere, in the words of one employee, was "old world." Raymond was a genteel presence. He opened doors for women and pulled out chairs so that they could sit. Twice a day, a maid would come through the office and serve coffee on elegant china.

When Purdue Frederick moved to Norwalk, Raymond sought to instill this same ethos in the new, more corporate surroundings. In the 1970s, it was a "conservative" company, in the words of Danielle Nelson, who spent thirty-four years working for Purdue. "It felt very small and intimate," recalled Charles Olech, who joined Purdue as a salesman at around this time. "They couldn't compare with the Mercks and other big pharmaceutical companies, but they gave you the feeling that they were a close-knit family organization." Unlike Arthur, with his passion for acquisition and achievement, or Mortimer, with his restless travel and splashy nightlife, Raymond was more plodding and predictable, a creature of habit. He and Beverly were happily married. They liked to go to the opera in the city. On weekends, they had guests over to the Greenwich mansion for tennis (Raymond was competitive, if not a great talent) followed by lunch served by their domestic staff. And each weekday, Raymond would make the short drive to the new office in Norwalk, arriving at ten o'clock. At lunchtime, he presided in a private dining room, often inviting senior executives to join him. At 5:00 p.m., he would make his rounds, walking the corridors of the building, poking his head into people's offices and saying, "What's going on, kiddo?"

"An integral part of our philosophy is our concern for all employees," Raymond and Mortimer wrote in a brochure for the company, and Raymond was regarded by his staff as a benevolent figure. He was a fiercely private man, as the layers of obfuscation concealing his real estate purchase would indicate. It was often said that Arthur Sackler made a fetish of privacy, but compared with Raymond, Arthur was an exhibitionist, with his keynote speeches and his column in the *Medical Tribune*. Just prior to purchasing the Greenwich property, Raymond had made a donation, along with his brothers, of $3 million to establish the Sackler School of Medicine at Tel Aviv University. Raymond made a visit to Israel, his first. This must have been a deeply emotional pilgrimage; a few years before Raymond was born, in 1917, his parents had sold Sophie's jewelry to donate funds toward the foundation of a Jewish homeland in Palestine. But when a reporter from *The Jerusalem Post* buttonholed the visiting American benefactor for an interview, he declined to answer even basic questions about himself. The paradoxical impression that Raymond managed to convey was of a man who was as self-effacing as it was possible to be while simultaneously contributing large sums of money to build a school with his name on it.

Sometimes, when Raymond and Beverly were out of the country, Richard would move in to their house in Greenwich, slipping into the baronial life of Jay Gatsby, as if he owned the place. Richard continued to nurture his passions. He still chased scientific hunches with the same boundless enthusiasm he had once devoted to the physiology of orgasm. He was an avid skier. But he was not engaged with the world—with art, with politics—in the manner that his father and uncles were. Having been born into privilege, he seemed unencumbered by the ambition that the older Sacklers nursed to win the acceptance of high society. By the time Richard finished medical school, he and Margie Yospin had broken up. But he eventually met a young woman named Beth Bressman. She had grown up in suburban New Jersey, a bright, sociable young woman whose every achievement was chronicled in the local newspaper. She went to college at the University of Pennsylvania, where she protested the war in Vietnam. She was smart, like Richard: she went on to pursue her PhD in clinical psychology at George Washington. They married in 1979.

But what Richard Sackler seemed to love above all else was the business. From his early days at Purdue, he would rotate from one department to the next, which supplied him with a broad range of experience. If there was a management track, he was on it. Richard took courses at Harvard Business School, though he never obtained a degree. Purdue Frederick was still owned three ways, by Arthur, Mortimer, and Raymond. But Arthur had no day-to-day involvement in the company, and Mortimer was busy running the family's international ventures. That left Raymond in Norwalk, and Raymond was clearly grooming his son to take over.

"I had a lot of ideas," Richard would later recall. "A lot of them were product development ideas." He was passionate about scientific research. "He's very into throwing a lot of science at you, if he thinks something is interesting," one person who worked with him at Purdue observed. Richard was a budding inventor; his name would eventually end up on more than a dozen patents. When some far-flung notion for a new product occurred to him, he would pick up the phone and call someone who worked for the company, to see what they could do. It didn't matter that he was still a kid, barely out of medical school, or that the people he was calling were older and more experienced, or even that they might outrank him on the company org chart. Purdue Frederick was Richard's inheritance, and he acted like it. In the Norwalk offices, he was regarded as a bit of a princeling, an entitled dilettante, who cycled through departments—R&D, medical, marketing, sales— and presented himself to more seasoned colleagues not as someone who was there to learn but as someone who was there to teach. His enthusiastic interventions were almost never welcome. And he lacked his father's gentility: whereas Raymond ruled with a silken authority, Richard was brusque, all rough edges.

"Richard was a young man in a hurry," Bart Cobert, a doctor who joined Purdue in 1983, recalled. "He was very bright—clearly bright— but he was born with a silver spoon in his mouth." Cobert did not come from money. "I was a poor kid from the Bronx," he said. The Sacklers had always had a practice of hiring immigrants and refugees, Jews who had been excluded from other jobs, or hungry strivers from the wrong side of the tracks. So the offices could feel quite cosmopolitan, with a conspicuous diversity of accents and religious observances. But the second-generation Sacklers showed no trace of humble origins.

Cobert was hired to work with a doctor whom Richard had recruited to Purdue named Bill Pollack. A recipient of the prestigious Lasker Award for his work on an important vaccine back in the 1960s, Pollack seemed to be a notable scientist, and Cobert was excited at the prospect of working with him. When he first stepped into the Norwalk building, Cobert was impressed. It was ultramodern, by the standards of the day, with its own helicopter and rooftop heliport. The offices had magnificent views of the Long Island Sound and, in the autumn, miles of radiant foliage. The company offered Cobert a very competitive salary; Purdue might have been small, but it attracted talent by paying well and taking care of them. As an assistant director, Cobert was entitled to a company car.

But when he started work, he quickly realized that Purdue Frederick was not what it seemed. Bill Pollack might have looked, on paper, like a renowned scientist and a great hire by Richard Sackler. But, as Cobert discovered almost immediately, Pollack was "on a downward swing in his career." Richard's enthusiasms extended to the people he hired: he would meet someone on an airplane, or on the ski slopes, fall into conversation with them, and then decide spontaneously that they should really come and work at Purdue. It might have been the important work Pollack had done two decades earlier that led Richard to hire him, but the science at Purdue was not cutting edge. As a new hire, Cobert learned that he would be working on a fiber cookie that could be marketed as a laxative. He was nonplussed. "I have double boards in medicine," Cobert said. "I didn't want to work with cookies."

But he went into the office each day, gamely, hoping to make the best of a suboptimal situation. As it turned out, Richard Sackler was a difficult taskmaster. One of his frustrations was that Senokot seemed to function too slowly. "Get it to work more quickly," he instructed Cobert.

This directive was baffling to Cobert. The drug worked in the colon. In order to function, it had to pass from the mouth, when you swallowed it, through the digestive tract, a process that took hours. This wasn't a design flaw. This was human biology. "There's no way," Cobert protested.

"*Do it*," Richard barked, and stormed off.

That was typical of Richard, Cobert recalled. "He expected the folks beneath him to do exactly what he said." He had a personal assistant, a slim young Korean-American man, and Richard would deputize this adjutant to deliver his impossible assignments. Cobert and his colleagues came to fear the man's visits: "He would come in with some absurd idea or request that made no sense and I would say, 'I don't know what that *means*.'"

"Richard was a character," another former employee who worked with him during this period reflected. "I wondered about his mental stability sometimes. There was something a little weird. 'Thoughtlessness' is the word that comes to mind."

Still, there was a sense that Richard was protected. After all, this was a family business. Inside Purdue Frederick, power was determined entirely by one's relationship to the family. There were certain old hands in the Norwalk office who were known as "Sackler connections," meaning that they were personal friends of the family, and thus untouchable. Some of them were, in truth, pretty incompetent, just riding a desk and collecting a check. Nobody could say for certain how they contributed or what they did all day. But they had shown loyalty to the Sacklers, and it was a key feature of the company that such loyalty would be rewarded. In the politics of the organization, if you did not have a direct line to the Sacklers, it was useful to find an ally who did.

If loyalty determined influence, the chief loyalist and premier Sackler connection was a shambling, overweight attorney named Howard Udell. Udell had grown up in Brooklyn and still had a trace of an accent. Fresh out of NYU Law School in 1966, he had taken a job at a tiny firm with three attorneys that did legal work for the Sacklers, and he eventually joined Purdue as vice president and general counsel. Udell showed unwavering loyalty to the Sacklers. "Corporate attorneys can do one of two things," Bart Cobert said. "They can go to management and tell them, 'You can't do that.' Or they can go to management and say, 'Tell me what you want, and I'll figure out a way to do it.' Howard was in the second category." Udell described his own professional philosophy in very similar terms. It's not the job of a lawyer to tell management that "the company can't do what it needs to do," he would say. Udell "was like Tom Hagen in *The Godfather*," one attorney who dealt with him recalled. "*Very* loyal to the family."

It might have been useful for the Sacklers to have people like Udell around who could serve as guardrails for young Richard. There was a story about Richard that circulated in the company, and might or might not have been true, but that was told and retold because it captured his peculiar liabilities. At one point in the 1970s, Raymond had gone on vacation, leaving Richard alone for a couple of weeks with the keys to the family company. Always eager to innovate, Richard decided that there might be ways in which the company could save money by producing Betadine more cheaply. After some close study, he determined that by substituting a different, cheaper iodine, they could save a certain number of dollars on every batch. So, without consulting Raymond, Richard ordered a run of the new formula, and according to the story the company started selling this version, only to learn that it caused minor burns when applied to human skin. When Raymond realized what had happened, he ordered an immediate recall. "They put the bottles in a warehouse," one former employee said, chuckling. "Every now and then, one of them would pop."

Was the story true? Nobody could say for certain. But the moral of the fable was clear: Richard was a smart guy, with lousy judgment. "He wanted to become the next Merck or Lilly," Bart Cobert said. "But he didn't know how to do it, and he probably didn't *know* he didn't know how to do it." What was clear to everyone was that whatever limitations he might have, Richard had great ambitions for himself and for his family's company. "He was always looking for new opportunities, new drugs," another employee who worked there during this period recalled.

Tired of making cookies, Cobert ended up leaving Purdue after less than a year. But during his time there, he befriended an older scientist named Eddie Takesue. Takesue had joined Purdue as director of clinical research in 1975. He had been around, seen everything. Just be careful with Richard Sackler, he warned Cobert. "Watch out."

❖ ❖ ❖

Richard's uncle Mortimer was an intermittent presence at the company during these years. At the headquarters in Norwalk, he was regarded as a slightly mysterious figure. "Mortimer was in Europe. He had girlfriends and a castle," said one former employee, summing up the prevailing caricature of the company's playboy co-owner among the rank and file in the 1980s. Mortimer "waltzed in and out," Bart Cobert remembered. He would occasionally come and visit company headquarters, but never for long: "He was distant and removed and elegant."

"My legal residence is Switzerland," Mortimer would say. But the truth of his domestic arrangements was a bit more complicated. He had renounced his U.S. citizenship in 1974, to become a citizen of Austria. But he didn't actually live in Austria. Instead, he divided his time between his residences in London, Paris, New York, Gstaad, and Cap d'Antibes. Richard had been working at Purdue for four years when his cousin Bobby, Mortimer's son, took his own life. People knew about the tragedy in the office at Norwalk, but it was never addressed directly, only whispered about. At first, it was said that Mortimer had lost a son in a tragic accident: that the young man had fallen out a window. But eventually, a rumor began to circulate that Bobby had jumped. It was difficult to verify, though, because the incident received no press coverage at all, and the Sacklers did not speak of it.

After Mortimer separated from his second wife, Geri, in 1977, he had purchased a fifteen-room apartment for her on East End Avenue and given her a budget of $140,000 for "decorations and furnishings." Geri would raise their two young children, Samantha and Mortimer, in this apartment, while the older Mortimer retained his own apartment facing the park on Fifth Avenue. But in practice, Mortimer was abroad so often that Geri ended up occupying both places. At one point, Mortimer got a call from his housekeeper in New York, Elizabeth Bernard, informing him that Geri had moved in and fired Bernard. Relations had been strained to begin with, but now Mortimer was indignant: this felt like an invasion. He raced back to New York, only to discover, upon entering his apartment, that it was occupied by a commune of photographers and models who were camping out there. Geri herself was nowhere to be found, but these louche interlopers informed Mortimer that his ex-wife had granted them permission to stay. When Mortimer opened his bedroom closet, he flew into a rage at the sight of another man's clothing hanging inside. He kicked the squatters out, changed the locks, and posted a security guard to prevent Geri from reentering the apartment. Then he took her to court, accusing her of "boundless" greed and suggesting that her aim was "to create as unpleasant a ruckus as possible so that I will pay her off." (The case ended up settling out of court.)

But even in the face of such personal turmoil, Mortimer was carefully expanding the family's pharmaceutical empire. Arthur Sackler liked to opine that the problem with midsized pharma companies was that they often had no research and development capacity with which to discover new drugs. But in England, Mortimer now oversaw Napp Laboratories, a company that had ambitious designs. Napp had been acquired by the Sacklers in 1966, but its origins dated back to the 1920s. It was in the business not just of licensing products to sell, as Purdue Frederick traditionally had, but of developing new drugs of its own. Mortimer encouraged patient investment in this process. "Only one in ten products will succeed," he cautioned. But if they could just devise the right drug, it might transform the fortunes of the company.

In the late 1970s, Napp produced a new product that was genuinely innovative: a morphine pill. The company had been prompted to do so by a hospice in London called St. Christopher's, which was run by Cicely Saunders, a crusading physician who had written a book called *Care of the Dying* and pioneered a new palliative care movement, arguing that the medical establishment should provide a more compassionate environment for terminally ill patients to die in. At St. Christopher's, Saunders had appointed a doctor named Robert Twycross to research the use of narcotics in palliative care, and eventually Twycross met with Napp's medical director and urged him to develop a morphine pill.

Until that point, morphine had often been administered intravenously, either on a drip or as a regimen of shots. This meant that patients who were suffering from late-stage cancer or other very painful afflictions had little choice but to spend their final days in the hospital so that their pain medication could be administered. But Napp had recently developed a special coating system for pills that allowed the diffusion of a drug into the bloodstream of a patient to be carefully regulated over time. They called the system Continus, and they had already used it for an asthma drug. But what if you applied it to morphine? It would mean that a patient could swallow a pill and the morphine would slowly release into the body, in the same manner that it would on a drip. The new drug, which would become known as MS Contin, was released in the U.K. in 1980, and it was a breakthrough.

"MS Contin really was an incredible medicine because it allowed cancer patients, particularly, not to have to be hospitalized to have their pain treated," Mortimer's daughter Kathe reflected later. "Before that, patients were in and out of hospital to be treated for their pain." MS Contin "changed that," she said. In three decades under Sackler ownership, Purdue Frederick had made smart and lucrative business decisions, like licensing Senokot and Betadine, but the company had shown no penchant for innovation. So MS Contin marked a big departure: a genuinely groundbreaking product. In 1983, the London *Times* quoted one physician describing the new drug as among "the most important advances in narcotics this century," and another saying it represented the "most important step forward in drug control of pain since morphine itself." The Sacklers were hugely proud of this achievement, boasting that the Continus delivery system had "revolutionized" the administration not just of morphine but of drugs in general. In an advertisement, Napp quoted the *Times* article, and heralded the company's growth and ambition, saying, "We have no intention of stopping."

Having developed this drug in England, under Mortimer, the Sacklers' next step would be to market it in Raymond's domain, the United States. But this raised an interesting dilemma. The Sacklers were committed to the narrative that MS Contin was new, even revolutionary. But the FDA's procedures for securing approval of any new drug required a lengthy and cumbersome regulatory application process. What if the company asserted that this wasn't *actually* a new drug at all? The only active ingredient was morphine, an old and familiar drug that had long since been approved. Really, it was just the distribution mechanism that had changed. As it happened, a new federal regulation was in the works that would forbid the grandfathering in of new twists on old drugs without the FDA's standard New Drug Application. When Howard Udell learned that this regulation was coming, he decided that Purdue should try to beat it. "Before this goes into effect, let's *make* MS Contin—and put it on the market," he said, according to a former executive who worked with him during this period. So without alerting the FDA, much less asking for permission, Purdue started manufacturing MS Contin at a plant in New Jersey and offered it for sale in October 1984.

When a pharmaceutical company releases a new drug, they have a big launch meeting, which can seem like some unholy combination of a bachelor party, a marketing convention, and a revival meeting. "They're phenomenal, drug launch meetings," the former Purdue executive who worked with Udell said. "You bring in all the sales reps from all over the country. Wine and dine. You get some dynamic speaker to exhort these people to start selling this drug." This executive attended the launch meeting for MS Contin. Hundreds of people assembled in a ballroom. And there were speeches. A British sales manager rolled up his sleeves and bellowed about the virtues of this game-changing drug and how the sales force was going to go out and make it a huge success. According to the executive who witnessed the speech, the sales manager was rallying people to sell the drug, "not just for you, not just for the company, but for Richard." There was a sense that Richard Sackler was personally invested in MS Contin and in the future of Purdue, that he was a great man with a bold vision, and the sales force would be his shock troops. "I was picturing Nuremberg in 1934," the executive recalled. "People were on their feet. It scared the shit out of me."

So the sales force went out and started to pitch MS Contin to doctors across the United States as a bold new tool for treating cancer pain, even though the drug did not actually have FDA approval. It was Purdue's position that the company didn't *need* anybody's approval to market its morphine pills. MS Contin had been on sale for three months when the FDA sent a letter to Norwalk informing Purdue that it had no right to market a new drug for which it had never filed a New Drug Application.

Upon receiving the letter, Howard Udell and a squadron of Purdue attorneys descended on Washington for a series of urgent meetings with the agency. In theory, Purdue was in trouble and would have to recall the drug and start all over again, following the rules this time, with a New Drug Application, an extensive back-and-forth with the agency, approval (if they were lucky) and *then* a launch meeting. But by blithely upending this process and selling their painkiller without approval, Purdue had created new facts on the ground. There were cancer doctors now—and cancer patients, lots of them—who had come to depend on MS Contin for relieving pain. The FDA's commissioner, Frank Young, worried that with so many patients already taking the drug, it might be damaging to abruptly yank this course of therapy.

Udell and his colleagues argued that this was all just a misunderstanding and they were never obliged to secure approval for MS Contin, because really it was only morphine. But the FDA responded that pills in such large doses represented a new product. According to the former executive, Purdue eventually went over the agency's head, appealing to the political leadership in the Reagan administration. "They were putting pressure on the White House," the executive said.

This strategy succeeded. The FDA ultimately told Purdue that the company could continue to sell the drug, so long as they now submitted the application they were supposed to have prepared before doing so. Purdue would keep marketing MS Contin, Udell announced triumphantly: "FDA will not interfere."

MS Contin would go on to generate $170 million a year in sales, dwarfing anything that Purdue Frederick had sold in the past. The Sacklers had already been rich, by any measure. But with the introduction of their first painkiller, they suddenly became a lot richer. From the beginning, Richard Sackler had entertained dreams for the company that exceeded his father's grandest ambitions. It seemed, now, that they were starting to become a reality.

Chapter 13

MATTER OF SACKLER

ONE DAY IN THE summer of 1987, a few months after Arthur Sackler's death, his first wife, Else, approached the pair of linked town houses on East Fifty-Seventh Street that Arthur had purchased for his second wife, Marietta. The properties had remained in the family; Arthur and his third wife, Jillian, used the buildings for storage and office space and occasionally entertained there. Else was seventy-three years old now, slowing down but still active, somewhat more reclusive, since Arthur's death, but as flinty and sharp as she had ever been. In accordance with her ex-husband's wishes, she was serving as one of the executors of his estate.

At the town house, Else encountered Jillian Sackler. Jillian was still in her forties. The two women had little in common, but they had maintained cordial relations during Arthur's life, notwithstanding the general assessment, among the Sacklers, that Jillian was a trophy wife and a floozy. At his memorial, Jillian had described Else as Arthur's "dearest friend—and mine." But then, the force of Arthur's personality, and the tendency of both of these women to want to keep him happy, made it difficult to judge whether their mutual accommodation was a feature of genuine sentiment or simply a reflexive propensity to give Arthur what he wanted.

A meeting had been convened to discuss Arthur's estate. Marietta was not invited, because she did not feature in the will: after the fraught divorce negotiation and her suicide attempt, Arthur had cut her out of his estate planning altogether. But her son, Arthur Felix, was there. Else's two daughters, Carol (now a doctor in Boston) and Elizabeth (still in New York, and involved in the arts), showed up, along with Arthur's longtime assistant, Miriam Kent, and three lawyers.

"We know we have a net worth in nine figures," one of the lawyers, Stanley Bergman, announced. But because of Arthur's many interests, and his taste for secrecy, it was going to be difficult to work out the precise dimensions of the fortune he left behind. It wasn't just assets, either: Arthur had debts. In order to finance his art acquisitions and his philanthropy, he had borrowed. He borrowed from his own companies. He bought art on credit. He made charitable commitments that he promised to pay with company stock. He had the art world equivalent of a runaway bar tab. And for years, he borrowed from his most trusted friend and confidante, his first wife. To Arthur, it might have seemed that even though they had been divorced for decades, Else's money was still effectively his money: she hadn't held a job since the 1930s, and her income was chiefly generated by her 49 percent ownership stake in William Douglas McAdams, which Arthur had given her as part of their divorce. McAdams was still very successful; one family attorney described it as a "cash cow." So Else had done quite well. But Arthur felt no compunction about asking her for funds. And Else would always oblige. "Don't worry," she would tell him. "Just do good things with it."

The problem, as the younger Arthur pointed out to the others, was that when his father borrowed things, and when he lent things, even when he *bought* things, there was often no paper trail. His specialty was the handshake deal. As a consequence, when Arthur died, it emerged that he had outstanding commitments—promises to pay for art he had already acquired, charitable pledges that remained unfulfilled. Jillian, as his widow, scarcely had a moment to grieve before she was inundated with bills and IOUs. Now it was incumbent upon Arthur's heirs, Jillian insisted, to find and allocate enough funds to satisfy the many promises he had made. She was anxious, she maintained, "that the Sackler name not be tarnished in any way through the breach of charitable commitments."

"Each of you ... know something about Arthur's past and history," Bergman told the assembled Sacklers. Bergman had represented Arthur during his lifetime, and now he wanted the family to think about what assets Arthur had that might not yet be accounted for, and what obligations. Arthur had always compartmentalized his life, to a point where, quite by design, there was nobody who saw the whole. What the executors needed to do, Bergman said, was assemble "all of the pieces of the puzzle." It would be an education process, for all of them. But they needed to sort out the estate, and to do so "without Uncle Sam taking a clip." The money should go where Arthur intended it to go and not to "the United States government," Bergman said.

Though Arthur had first become romantically involved with Jillian in the late 1960s, he didn't marry her until his divorce was final, in 1981. Jillian was roughly the same age as Elizabeth and Carol. When he was alive, Arthur had kept her apart from his adult children, citing the slightly nonsensical rationale that because Jillian had no offspring of her own, it might be upsetting for her to spend time with his. It seems more likely that this was yet another instance of Arthur's trying to keep the separate spheres in his life from touching. He might also have simply detected the hostility and derision of his children, who regarded Jillian as a usurper ("the secretary," as they called her) who had hoodwinked their father into an ill-considered marriage. In any event, Jillian never developed a warm relationship with the younger Sacklers. And it could not have helped matters that Arthur's last will and testament contained a bombshell: he left each of his four children $600,000, along with the *Medical Tribune* newspaper business, which was valued at approximately $30 million. But the balance of his $100 million estate would go to Jillian.

The resentment that Arthur's children felt was subtle—until it wasn't. The children took over the town house on Fifty-Seventh Street, claiming it as their own, and changed the locks so that Jillian could not enter. And this was not the only fault line that seemed in danger of cracking open. In the wake of Arthur's death, Mortimer and Raymond had been outwardly supportive of his family. But it was no secret that Arthur had become estranged from "the brothers," as his children called them, by the time of his death. Many of Arthur's most lucrative business assets had started out as ventures that were jointly owned with Raymond and Mortimer, and the respective wings of the Sackler family would now need to settle accounts. At the meeting on Fifty-Seventh Street, Arthur Felix announced that Uncle Morty had already inquired with him about whom precisely the brothers should be negotiating with.

This would be a delicate process, Bergman cautioned. Mortimer and Raymond might be family, but that did not mean they could be trusted. Because the brothers had been so close during the period when they built their empire, and had subsequently grown apart, they had developed a tendency to deceive one another about the actual value of their various businesses. Some of this was probably just an impulse, learned from Arthur: going back to his testimony before the Kefauver committee, when he insisted to the senators that his ad agency was just a trifling concern with meager billings, it had always been his practice to understate the size and value of his holdings. "Dad said he purposely undervalued them," Elizabeth pointed out, "because he didn't want Morty and Ray to think they were more valuable."

Maybe, Bergman said, but that didn't mean the ruse worked. "I wouldn't underestimate the intelligence of your uncles."

One immediate question facing Arthur's heirs was whether they should sell their stake in Purdue Frederick. Two weeks before the meeting, Arthur's longtime attorney, Michael Sonnenreich, had flown to London to meet with Mortimer. The brothers were interested in buying out Arthur's share of the company. The question was, what was it worth? Sonnenreich had been working up an estimate of what might be a reasonable selling price, and Bergman pointed out that selling would "provide us with another area of capital" with which to pay off Arthur's debts. Sonnenreich had complained, privately, to the other lawyers that he was in a no-win situation, because whatever deal he cut for the company, Jillian would complain that he should have gotten the brothers to pay more.

It was taken for granted that Mortimer and Raymond would drive a hard bargain and deceive their nieces and nephew about what Purdue was really worth. "Your father did the same thing," Bergman told the children. "So there were no absolutely white lilies here on either side." In the end, he said, "They're your uncles, but I'm your lawyer. And I have to presume that everyone might act like a businessman and try to get the upper hand."

Else Sackler had been a quiet presence at the meeting. But she seemed crestfallen to find herself at this juncture. Arthur had wanted to pass along a coherent family legacy, but his estate was proving to be a poisoned chalice. Rather than bring the family together, the wealth and possessions that he had accumulated over a lifetime seemed to be pitting them against one another. Else had known Morty and Ray for half a century. She'd grown up with them, thinking of them as Arthur's little brothers, and known them through triumph and tragedy. Perhaps, she said, when the negotiation happens, some member of Arthur's family can attend. Not to negotiate, just to be there. "There's something about looking someone in the eye," she said.

✧ ✧ ✧

If Arthur's heirs thought they could present a unified front in this fight, they were sorely mistaken. The tensions with Jillian, which they managed to keep at a simmer during that July meeting, would soon boil over in a sensationally ugly fashion. Arthur's life had been a long exercise in carefully orchestrated ambiguity. He had spent so many years spinning so many plates. Now they were starting to shatter.

"There were promises, verbal promises," Elizabeth told her fellow executors at one point. In Arthur's vast art collection, she said, there were "a certain number of pieces that I could select." Now she wanted what was rightly hers. "I'm not making a formal thing," she said, with a healthy dose of passive aggression. "I'm just letting you know." But what was the appropriate status of objects that belonged to Arthur and Jillian at the end of Arthur's life but that he might have promised, without any sort of formal promissory note, to his children?

The Ming bed, for instance. That should go to Elizabeth, Else asserted, even if she didn't actually have possession of it at the time Arthur died. "It was impractical for you to own a Ming bed where you were living," Else pointed out.

That's true, Elizabeth agreed. And she had always felt entitled to that bed. In fact, she said, at the age of fourteen, "I had the pleasure of taking my boyfriend and showing him the bed."

A similar dispute arose over *Poplars*, the Monet painting that Arthur had purchased for Else. Several months after Arthur's death, Else approached Jillian about the painting, which had been hanging in the Park Avenue triplex that Jillian and Arthur shared. The Monet was actually on loan, Else informed Jillian: Arthur had bought it for her as a gift, back in 1962. Jillian grudgingly permitted Else to remove the painting. But as soon as it was out the door, she had second thoughts. After all, there was no piece of paper saying that the painting belonged to Else, or that Arthur had given it to her. Had it not hung for years in Jillian's apartment? "She offered no proof," Jillian complained. "She simply came and took the Monet away."

Jillian had come to feel that she was being viewed with suspicion by Arthur's heirs. As they attempted to survey and account for Arthur's endless holdings, one of Else's attorneys insinuated that Jillian might actually be *stealing* paintings from the collection and smuggling them out of the United States. Before long, the whole pretense of amicable cooperation had evaporated. Everyone lawyered up—and not with your average estate attorneys, either, but with high-end white-shoe gunslingers. The meetings got bigger, the tone more vexatious, the paperwork more formal and elaborate. Marietta had thought of Arthur as a sun around which all these planets seemed to orbit, in tenuous harmony. Now that he was gone, they went to war. Jillian found herself barred from the enclave where Arthur had stored his art. (No longer housed in the Met, for obvious reasons, it now occupied a storage space in a warehouse on the Upper East Side.) She complained that the children were engaged in a "smear" campaign to depict her as "an avaricious, unprincipled, grasping widow," trying to "enrich myself at the expense of others." She confided to a friend that the fracas with Arthur's family had threatened not just his charitable projects but "my income," which had been "very much held up."

For their part, Arthur's kids claimed in legal papers that Jillian was "inspired variously by greed, malice or vindictiveness." There were lawsuits and countersuits, affidavits and depositions, dozens of lawyers, thousands of billable hours, endless vituperation. No stock share or hunk of sculpture went uncontested. The fight took on a life of its own, unspooling into a Dickensian saga that would drag on for years, *Matter of Sackler*, as the case was known. In 1993, Christie's prepared a major auction of Arthur's collection of Renaissance pottery, only to be forced to cancel at the last minute, after Jillian secured an injunction to stop it. By one estimate, the litigation over the estate cost the Sacklers more than $7 million. But the real figure was likely much higher.

For the last fifteen years of his life, Arthur had worked closely with a personal curator, a woman he had hired away from the Brooklyn Museum, named Lois Katz. But as the battle lines were drawn, Arthur's children came to regard Katz as loyal to Jillian. On one visit to the enclave, Katz was affronted when she was instructed, by Elizabeth and Carol, to leave her bag outside, lest she pilfer any of the Sackler treasures.

One day, Elizabeth informed Katz that her services at the Arthur M. Sackler Foundation would no longer be needed. Elizabeth would be taking over the management of the foundation. Among Arthur's children, it was Elizabeth who emerged as the principal custodian of the great man's legacy. She was a formidable presence herself, quick-witted and domineering, with a certain regal hauteur. She had trained at the School of American Ballet to be a dancer, and in 1968, while she was a college student, she entered the Miss America contest and was named Miss Vermont. Elizabeth went to the final competition in Atlantic City and performed a dance routine that she choreographed herself, to protest the Vietnam War. She won "Best Talent," and Arthur was enormously proud. He bragged about his beauty queen daughter and hung a framed photo of Elizabeth performing her routine on the wall of his office.

Arthur had been, at best, an indifferent father. When Denise, his daughter with Marietta, was in high school, she had to "make an appointment" with his secretary if she wanted to speak to him, according to one family friend. But he had always been devoted to Elizabeth. Once, when she was twenty-four, he took her as his plus-one to a party in SoHo hosted by the artist Robert Rauschenberg. When Arthur introduced Elizabeth as his daughter, Rauschenberg chuckled and said, "A likely story," assuming that she must actually be his date. Arthur did not seem to mind this misapprehension. In fact, he wrote a column in the *Medical Tribune* afterward, boasting that others had made the same mistake that evening and making the icky confession that at a certain point, "I gave up explanations and just enjoyed their fantasy."

"My father loved his passions," Elizabeth recalled not long after his death. "He loved the opera, ballet, Peking duck, and matzo-ball soup. He was a great ballroom dancer." When he decided that he wanted to learn how to dance, he had a professional instructor come to his office to teach him so that he wouldn't waste time, she explained. "We traveled by boat to Europe in those days," she recalled. "And he and I would dance together at night."

Elizabeth loved to rhapsodize about her father's "genius." If he had cemented the Sackler name as an enduring symbol of achievement and prestige, then she would buff and tend to that legacy. This could occasionally mean that she clashed with people, like Lois Katz, whom Arthur had been close to in his life. After Arthur's death, the Viennese psychiatrist Paul Singer, who had been his mentor in collecting Asian art, wanted to donate some of the objects from his own collection to the Smithsonian. But Elizabeth objected, pointing to an agreement that

Singer had made with Arthur decades earlier, in which Arthur committed to subsidize Singer's purchases, but on the understanding that they would ultimately end up in the *Sackler* collection. It was not that Elizabeth had any problem with the Smithsonian's receiving these works: it was that she wanted them to be described not as part of the "Singer Collection" but of "The Dr. Paul Singer Collection of Chinese Art of the Arthur M. Sackler Gallery." She had inherited from her father a devotion to the talismanic significance of names. Singer, who was now in his nineties, had grown exasperated with the Sacklers. He fired off an angry letter to Elizabeth's attorney, saying, "If the bunch of Arthur's heirs does not get off my back, they can jump in the lake."

✤ ✤ ✤

Threading through the legal proceedings over Arthur's estate, like a subtle recurring stitch, was the musketeers agreement that Arthur had forged with Raymond, Mortimer, and Bill Frohlich back in the 1940s and formalized in a pair of legal agreements in the 1960s. According to Richard Leather, the attorney who drafted those agreements, the intention of the four men had always been that as each one died, the remaining musketeers would inherit his business interests, and the last man would put all of those combined remaining assets into a charitable trust. And in the minutes of the meetings of the executors and the litigation over Arthur's estate, there are plenty of references to Frohlich, and "the four-way agreement," and even to Arthur's aspiration to establish charitable trusts.

In a deposition, one attorney asked Else if Arthur ever entered into "a business relationship with Mr. Frohlich."

"I don't recall that he ever did," she replied.

This was either a fortuitous moment of senility or an outright lie. Else's memory was still relatively sharp in her seventies, and she had been more intimately acquainted than any other family member with Arthur's business dealings and circle of confidants. Arthur had multiple, intense, overlapping business relationships with Frohlich; there was no way Else did not know that.

"Do you know whether they were in a partnership or whether they had formed a joint venture?" the lawyer asked.

"I don't know," Else replied. "I don't think I quite understand your question."

"Can you tell me," she was asked, "what stockholdings, rights or properties were jointly built between Dr. Sackler and his brothers and Mr. Frohlich?"

"I don't know anything about Mr. Frohlich," she insisted, before conceding, "I mean they mutually built things... companies."

The lawyer asked if Else had known about "a proposal during Dr. Sackler's lifetime" whereby stock in companies he created "would be sold and the proceeds would be contributed to charity."

"Absolutely not," she said.

The lawyer was getting at a significant threshold question underlying the whole proceeding: under the terms of the original musketeers agreement, Jillian and Else and the children should have inherited much less. Instead, the shared businesses should have passed along to Mortimer and Raymond and then ultimately, upon their deaths, to charity. "Nobody had a *right* in any of these assets," Richard Leather said. "The assets were to flow to the end. Subject to a reasonable taking care of family, they were to follow to the last survivor." When the last of the musketeers died, he continued, "Those assets were to go to a charitable trust." The very premise of the whole estate proceeding was, in Leather's judgment, "a fraud."

It appears, however, that by the time Arthur Sackler died, he and his brothers had, through some mutual agreement, quietly jettisoned their arrangement. The pact that the four had made as young men might have simply been the product of youthful idealism—a nice sentiment, but doomed, from the beginning, by its impracticality. What really undermined the arrangement, though, was the decision to have Richard Leather draft *two* agreements in the 1960s, one governing domestic businesses, which would be shared by all four men, and another governing interests abroad, which would bind Raymond, Mortimer, and Frohlich, but not Arthur. Arthur's children agreed that what they called "the rift" had begun after Frohlich's death, when Raymond and Mortimer inherited tens of millions of dollars in IMS stock but Arthur got nothing.

Soon, the brothers started to shift business from the United States abroad, in order to deceive one another about what would and would not be covered by the four-way agreement. This was part of the reason that Mortimer's role as international CEO was so important: by transferring as much of their pharmaceutical interests as they could abroad,

Raymond and Mortimer were depriving Arthur of his share. And, as his children acknowledged in one estate meeting, Arthur did the same thing, establishing the *Medical Tribune International* and focusing assets and energies and capital there, because his brothers did not have a stake in it.

What this meant is that by the time Arthur died, the spirit of the deal had long since been abandoned, and the letter mostly forgotten. There was no talk of Raymond and Mortimer inheriting all of Arthur's domestic business interests, or of the combined interests of the family eventually going to charity. Instead, it would be a no-holds-barred fight to see who would inherit which assets and how they might be priced. Purdue Frederick was a domestic concern, and Arthur's heirs controlled a third of it. Mortimer and Raymond now wanted to buy them out.

This was a particularly interesting juncture for the company: Napp Laboratories in England had enjoyed phenomenal success with the sustained-release morphine treatment MS Contin. But in 1987, the drug had only recently gone on the market in the United States. Bergman, the lawyer, was concerned that the musketeers agreement had created an atmosphere of deception. "The main thing I'm worried about," he told the children, "is how much legitimate business of Purdue Frederick was transferred to the overseas operation because the two brothers own the overseas operation and we have interest in the domestic." None of Arthur's heirs seemed particularly attuned to the precise nature of Purdue's business. Napp had just pioneered a revolutionary and very profitable painkiller that Purdue was already marketing in the United States. But Else, at one point in the discussions, said, "I don't really know what Napp is, to tell you the truth."

Even so, Michael Sonnenreich, Arthur's attorney, who handled the negotiations with Mortimer, said that Purdue Frederick was simply not that valuable. "Is the price right? Yes," he announced, adding, "I know what the value of companies are. This is a small company." Arthur's heirs ended up selling their one-third stock interest in Purdue Frederick to Mortimer and Raymond for $22 million. In light of what the company was about to become, this was, for Arthur's heirs, a spectacularly foolish transaction.

Chapter 14

THE TICKING CLOCK

IMAGINE YOU INVENT A new drug. To sell the drug in the United States, you will generally need to get it approved by the FDA. But before you even apply for that approval, you're going to want to get a patent. What a patent grants you is a temporary monopoly on the right to produce your invention. The system was created in order to encourage innovation, by, as Abraham Lincoln once put it, adding "the fuel of interest to the fire of genius, in the discovery and production of new and useful things." But a patent is a tricky thing. In order to receive it, you need to *publish* your invention, taking the project you have been working on in secret and exposing it to the world. Patents are published on the website of the U.S. Patent and Trademark Office, and here again the idea is to spur innovation: sharing knowledge, rather than hoarding it, might encourage others to develop new ideas of their own. The patent holder is protected, at least in theory, from someone else just stealing her idea when she publishes, because she has a monopoly on the right to produce it. And it is this monopoly that accounts for the outsized profits in the pharmaceutical business. Research and development to produce new drugs takes time and costs a great deal of money. Mortimer Sackler suggested that only one bet in ten might pay off, and by the standards of the industry those odds are better than average. So when a drug does work, and gets approved, and addresses a medical need in a way that no previously available product has been able to, pharmaceutical companies will often charge exorbitant prices for it. The consumer is paying not just for the costs of producing a bottle of pills but for all of the trial and error that went into creating the drug in the first place.

But there's another reason that drug companies charge such high prices: the monopoly granted by the patent is only temporary. Once you have received a patent, you generally have twenty years in which to market the product exclusively, though in practice it is often less time, because the patents tend to be issued before FDA approval. After the patent expires, any other company can make its own generic version and sell the drug at a cheaper price. You've made it easy for them to do so—by publishing the formula in exchange for your patent.

The Sackler brothers hated generic drugs. Under Arthur's stewardship, the *Medical Tribune* maintained what one account described as a "nonstop news and editorial campaign" against cheaper, non-branded versions of popular drugs. Arthur criticized generics not for threatening his profits, or those of the pharmaceutical firms that were his clients, but for inadequate quality control. But his campaign was also clearly self-interested and given to hysterical exaggeration. In 1985, the *Medical Tribune* published a story, "Schizophrenics 'Wild' on Weak Generic," describing how "all hell broke loose" at a Veterans Administration hospital in Georgia after the psychiatric unit switched patients from Thorazine, the brand-name antipsychotic, to a cheaper generic substitute. Eleven patients who had previously been stable ran amok, according to the article, only to revert back to normal ("as if a switch had been flipped") when they were given Thorazine again. According to a subsequent investigation by *The New York Times,* the FDA examined this incident and found the story in the *Medical Tribune* to be completely bogus. The hospital had actually started administering the generic medication, without incident, "six months before the purported problems began."

Arthur's campaign notwithstanding, generic competition was a reality that any drug company would be forced to contend with: a horde of competitors just watching the calendar and waiting for the moment when the patent exclusivity is set to expire. As Bill Frohlich had declared back in 1960, there is a limited window in which a maker of branded drugs can reap outsized profits. Even when a drug is tremendously lucrative—in fact, *especially* when a drug is tremendously lucrative—the drugmaker is always selling on borrowed time, conscious that at some fixed point in the future the patent will expire and the generics will come rushing in to decimate profits. There's a phrase used in the pharmaceutical business to describe this inevitable but terrifying stage in the process. They call it "the patent cliff," because that's what a graph of revenue resembles at the moment when the patent expires: a drop so steep it's like plummeting off a cliff.

✛ ✛ ✛

Richard Sackler was a key proponent of Purdue Frederick's transition into pain management. In 1984, he helped to organize a conference in Toronto, the International Symposium on Pain Control. The event, which was held in the auditorium at the University of Toronto's medical school, was sponsored by Purdue. Richard personally wrote to pain specialists, inviting them to participate. "This is truly an international forum and will provide for an interesting exchange of worldwide concepts of pain theory and management, including that of cancer pain," he wrote in his invitation to one speaker. The event had all the appearances of an academic colloquium. But, in truth, there was a corporate agenda at play. Many of the physicians who spoke at the conference offered testimonials about their experience administering the painkiller MS Contin. One of the featured speakers was Robert Kaiko, a specialist in the use of analgesic medicine (as pain medicine is known) who had been at Memorial Sloan Kettering before taking a job at Purdue Frederick. Kaiko had a PhD in pharmacology from Cornell. He was also an inventor who had been instrumental in the clinical development, by Napp, of MS Contin.

There was a movement under way in American medicine to reexamine the treatment of pain. An emerging cohort of doctors was arguing that for too long the medical profession had overlooked pain, thinking of it merely as a symptom of underlying conditions and not as an affliction that merited serious clinical attention itself. Doctors like Cicely Saunders, the hospice care advocate in London, argued that patients had been forced to suffer unnecessarily, because clinicians did not take pain seriously. "Pain is the most common symptom that patients have," Richard would say. The challenge is that it is so subjective. "No doctor can look at you and say, 'Oh, you've got a pain level of three,'" Richard explained. "You have to depend on the patient's report."

Richard had been corresponding with a doctor named John J. Bonica, whom many credited with initiating this new movement around the treatment of pain in the United States. Bonica was a colorful figure: born on a tiny island off the coast of Sicily, he had immigrated to America in 1927, at the age of ten, and worked as a shoeshine boy, a newspaper hawker, a fruit and vegetable vendor, and eventually a professional wrestler. Competing under the stage name the Masked Marvel, Bonica became the light-heavyweight wrestling champion of the world. But along the way, he also developed an interest in medicine and ended

176 PATRICK RADDEN KEEFE

up wrestling his way through med school and working on the side as a strong man at the circus. Prompted, in part, by the agonizing toll of injuries he had sustained in wrestling, Bonica began to focus on the study, such as it was, of pain. He published a seminal book, *The Management of Pain*, in 1953. After his own wife nearly died in childbirth, Bonica was instrumental in the development of epidural anesthesia. Over the years, he came to believe that as much as one-third of the U.S. population could be suffering from undiagnosed chronic pain—not just cancer pain and sports injuries, but back pain, postoperative pain, injuries suffered on the job. Yet physicians simply took this suffering for granted, he complained, pointing out that "no medical school has a pain curriculum." Even cancer doctors had no clue about how to address the physical agony caused by the disease, he said. "They don't know how to treat it because they haven't been taught how to treat it." As a result of this inattention, Bonica believed, America was in the throes of a silent plague of undiagnosed suffering, an "epidemic of pain."

Part of the problem, Bonica and Richard agreed, was that physicians had been far too reluctant to administer morphine to people suffering from pain. Morphine could be a very effective drug when it came to relieving pain. The trouble, in Richard's view, was that it had been stigmatized. It had acquired this stigma, Richard said, "because of a popular understanding shared by both professionals and by laymen that morphine was an end-of-life drug." Because morphine had long been perceived as a drug with a high risk of addiction, physicians reserved it for particularly severe cases. Consequently, patients and their families were often reluctant to have doctors prescribe morphine, because in the popular imagination it was seen, as Richard put it, to be "a death sentence."

MS Contin was meant to address this therapeutic gap, by offering a more approachable delivery mechanism for morphine, in pill form. The participants at the conference in Toronto held a collective view that morphine was an excellent treatment that was not being used nearly enough. Yes, there might be a perception that morphine was potentially addictive, but, according to the doctors in Toronto, such fears were misplaced. "Addiction does *not* occur in patients requiring morphine for pain control," one of the speakers, a doctor from Austria named Eckhard Beubler, asserted in his remarks.

That message was repeated many times throughout the event—that when morphine was used to treat pain, it was not actually addictive. In the words of another participant, a retired radiation oncologist from Louisiana named Jerome Romagosa, it was important "to counteract numerous myths" surrounding morphine and other opioids, as drugs that are derived from the opium poppy are known. "Many of these myths have become a part of the folklore of the medical and nursing professions," Romagosa lamented. Richard had personally invited Romagosa to attend the conference. Sounding a bit like Arthur Sackler when he dismissed the dangers of Valium, Romagosa asserted that fears of people becoming hooked on morphine had been overblown, because addiction "is a psychological malady" and only occurred when morphine was misused by "those who do not need it."

For the Sacklers, this was a helpful message. And the conference had the sort of reassuringly clinical patina that Arthur would have admired: it was a bunch of doctors, talking medicine, at a medical school. At the same time, however, everyone in attendance realized that Purdue Frederick was poised to release its own morphine product, MS Contin, in the United States. The president of the medical school, in his welcoming remarks, pointed out that MS Contin was already "revolutionizing the Canadian narcotic analgesic market." And Purdue was underwriting this whole event. The closing speaker, a British professor of pharmacological science named John W. Thompson, made a pun on the patented continuous-release mechanism of MS Contin, thanking Purdue Frederick for their "generous and sustained release of hospitality."

Back in the 1950s, Arthur Sackler had realized that a canny pharmaceutical executive could enlist ostensibly independent medical practitioners to validate his product, and this event was precisely the sort of carefully orchestrated exercise in validation that he had envisioned. Following the conference, some of the doctors in attendance issued a joint statement on their findings. It said, "Morphine is the safest and best drug for the control of severe chronic pain."

✢ ✢ ✢

When Purdue Frederick released MS Contin in the United States, it became an enormous success, changing the fortunes of the company. Here was an opportunity for Purdue to become what Richard Sackler had hoped it could be: a major player. The company had caught a perfect wave in this incipient reconsideration of pain medicine. Profits were soaring in a way that they never had with Senokot or Betadine. Yet all the while, in the background, a clock was ticking, as the day approached, inexorably, when the Sacklers would lose their exclusive patent on the very controlled-release morphine tablets that they had introduced to the world. Richard had always been a stickler for details, and now he obsessively followed the latest figures on how many pills the company was selling. "I hope sales weren't off last week," Bob Kaiko would joke. "When things get bad, Richard comes in and blows out the pilot light to save gas."

In 1990, Kaiko sent Richard a memo. "MS Contin may eventually face such serious generic competition that other controlled-release opioids must be considered," he wrote. If Purdue was going to lose the monopoly on its flagship painkiller, perhaps it would be possible to use the Contin time-release system as a delivery mechanism for *other* opioids, in order to secure new patents.

Decades later, Richard's cousin Kathe Sackler would claim that it was she who first suggested oxycodone. Kathe was also a medical doctor who had received her degree from NYU in 1984. She was in some respects very similar to Richard: brainy, brusque, entitled, socially awkward. She would end up marrying a woman named Susan Shack and having two children. Kathe was named after Käthe Kollwitz, a leftist artist from Germany whose work had focused on the proletariat; the name might have been some relic of Mortimer's early flirtation with communism. But Kathe was comfortable with her wealth. She liked to wear a big Hermès belt buckle in the shape of an H. Kathe's involvement with the company would wax and wane over time, with some employees recalling her as a regular presence in the building and others seeing her as not very involved at all. Her level of engagement at Purdue appeared, as much as anything else, to be a function of whim.

When Arthur Sackler was alive, Mortimer and Raymond had come together to form a unified front and oppose him. But after he died, significant divisions emerged between the two younger brothers themselves. During board meetings, the brothers would sit on opposite sides of the table and argue, viciously, swearing at each other, in full view of the board. Mortimer had a voluble temperament, and for all his surface gentility Raymond was very stubborn. On one occasion, the brothers fought with such rancor at a board meeting that they physically came to blows, throwing punches at each other. (One of them missed and hit a lawyer.)

With Mortimer away in Europe much of the time, Kathe had become his eyes and ears at Purdue. She was there, in Norwalk, to advocate for his interests and the interests of his branch of the family. Mortimer and his heirs were known, within the company, as the A side, after the designation of the shares they owned in Purdue. Raymond and his heirs were the B side. As Mortimer's proxy, Kathe would routinely check in with people, requesting an update "for Dr. Mortimer." She and her father had similar handwriting, which meant that it could occasionally be difficult to tell which of them was represented on a piece of paperwork. Richard, meanwhile, was increasingly a proxy for his own father, though Raymond was still in the building and in full control of the firm. The tension between the two poles of the family, Mortimer and Raymond, was now echoed by a new polarity between their children, Kathe and Richard. And whereas the older generation could seem regal and out of touch at times, their children were less benign. "Raymond and Mortimer were thought of as kind and benevolent," one former employee recalled. "Kathe and Richard were very self-important."

For her part, Kathe would complain that she felt excluded in the Norwalk office. "There was a kind of informal way of meeting where they met over lunch every day," she later said. In the executive dining room, Raymond Sackler would hold court with Richard, the lawyer Howard Udell, and other trusted advisers. "I was not invited to those lunches," Kathe noted. "So, to the extent that they had to include me because we're fifty-fifty partners and I was there, they did. But not beyond that." It "wasn't easy" for her at the company, Kathe said. Richard clearly had designs on the leadership, but Kathe was able to question his decisions in a way that would have been too dangerous for non-Sackler employees to do. She could be cutting. "I don't think Richard's the last word on what the company is doing, necessarily," Kathe declared. "Or the first."

As Purdue stared down the approaching patent cliff for MS Contin, Kathe and Richard had dinner together one night in Connecticut. Richard had been working in R&D and focusing on pain. The challenge was to find a successor to MS Contin. The real innovation in MS Contin was not the morphine but the Contin system, so they had been talking about other drugs that could be used with that system. At meetings, they would constantly discuss the possibilities, and Richard would throw out various ideas. Over dinner that night, Kathe suggested using oxycodone, an opioid that had been synthesized in Germany in 1917.

According to Kathe, Richard did not know what oxycodone was. So she told him: it was another opioid, a chemical cousin of morphine—and also of heroin. But oxycodone was much more potent than morphine. The drug was already widely available as a painkiller, in mild treatments like Percodan and Percocet. But there was only a small amount of oxycodone in those pills, because in Percodan it was mixed with aspirin and in Percocet it was mixed with acetaminophen, both of which can be toxic if a person takes too much of them. If you deployed pure oxycodone using the Contin system, however, it might be possible to administer a larger dose that would filter slowly into the bloodstream, allowing the patient to take a more formidable quantity.

Richard would have a different recollection of this pivotal moment in the company's history. "The project started in the late eighties," he said. According to Richard, it was Bob Kaiko's idea, not Kathe's. Indeed, in the 1990 memo, Kaiko had suggested oxycodone, saying that it was "less likely to initially have generic competition."

Though the company had moved to Norwalk, it continued to have a presence in Yonkers, at the Purdue Frederick Research Center, on Saw Mill River Road. Whereas Norwalk was slick and corporate, this facility was anything but: the operation was housed in a converted carpet factory and surrounded by high fences fringed in razor wire. The neighborhood was sketchy; at one point in the late 1980s, a dead body was found in a nearby culvert. "We would have the occasional people come for an interview who would drive into the parking lot, look around, and leave without ever coming in," one former employee who worked there recalled. "It was not glamorous, by any means."

Larry Wilson was a chemist who took a job at the research center in 1992 and spent the next fifteen years working at the company. He ended up assigned to "the oxycodone project," as it was then known. The initial efforts at creating a formulation had not been successful, and by the time Wilson arrived, the team was working day and night on the new drug. "As the patent began to come up for MS Contin, more and more effort went into it," Wilson recalled. Bob Kaiko was running the project day to day. Wilson liked him: Kaiko had a great deal of experience treating people with narcotics, and he believed passionately in the therapeutic potential of a controlled-release oxycodone product.

Richard Sackler was also a frequent presence, and Wilson liked him, too. Richard could be imperious, but to Wilson it seemed that he had no "class consciousness," in that he would speak to anyone, at any level of the company, remembering people's names and asking them, in detail, about their work. This was not some remote executive who wanted to be kept in the loop but took no specific interest in the work going on in the trenches: when it came to the oxycodone project, Richard was in the trenches himself. "He worked hard. I think he never slept," Wilson said. "I wasn't the only one who got the emails from him at three in the morning. He just had all kinds of ideas."

Not everyone found Richard's style of micromanagement so congenial. He was an early adopter of email, and at meetings he could be a discomfiting presence, focusing on his huge laptop computer, as if he weren't listening to what anyone in the room was saying, only to look up, suddenly, and ask a pointed question. Periodically, he would stand, walk over to the wall where there was a phone jack, and plug his laptop in. Then everyone would be forced to listen to the rings and dings of Richard's noisy dial-up connection so that he could send an email. Richard's work ethic could be taxing for those who worked under him. If you emailed him at midnight after a long evening of work, he would email you back, immediately, with questions. If you didn't get him what he wanted, he would call you at home. He knew that many of his employees thought he was a pain in the ass, but there was a compulsion in this behavior, a single-minded devotion to making the new oxycodone product a worthy successor to MS Contin.

The younger generation of Sacklers were becoming increasingly involved in the company. Richard officially joined the board in 1990, along with his brother, Jonathan, and Kathe and her sister, Ilene. The following year, the family created a new company, Purdue Pharma. Purdue Frederick would continue to exist, handling the traditional over-the-counter remedies. But the creation of this new corporate entity signaled the ambition of Richard and his generation of Sacklers. "Purdue Frederick was the original company that my father and uncle acquired in 1952," Richard would explain. Purdue Pharma was established to "take on the risk of new products."

It was a subtle distinction: yet another Sackler company. But it was emblematic of the direction in which Richard wanted to push the business. His aim, he said, was "more innovative products, more frequently launched, with more skills and resources applied." Gone were the days when Purdue was content to be a sleepy manufacturer of laxatives and earwax remover. What was required now, Richard believed, was "a new aggressiveness." In 1993, Richard ascended to the position of senior vice president. The family had what looked as if it could be a very successful new drug in the works. They had decided to call it OxyContin. An OxyContin Project Team memo in December 1993 noted that the new pills would be marketed "against Percocet" and might ultimately "replace our MS Contin line" if the generic competition became unsustainable. It had the potential to be a very effective drug for cancer pain.

But a more tantalizing idea had also presented itself. Richard had always been interested in marketing, and in 1984 he had hired a new head of marketing, Michael Friedman, a tall, ruddy Brooklyn-born executive who had worked as a high school teacher on Long Island, then got his start in sales, hawking power tools, before going back to school for his MBA. In a characteristically idiosyncratic recruiting move, Richard had hired Friedman after sitting next to him on an airplane. Friedman was the son of Holocaust survivors who had met in a refugee camp after the war. When his parents married, they had no money for a wedding dress, so his father traded two pounds of coffee for a parachute and his mother traded two packs of cigarettes to have someone sew it into a frock. (The garment would end up on display at the Holocaust Museum in Washington, D.C.) Friedman was garrulous and glad-handing. "Dr. Richard would listen to Michael Friedman, and Michael Friedman would listen to everybody else," one former Purdue executive who worked with both men recalled. On account of Friedman's height and his ginger coloring, Richard referred to him, jokingly, as "Big Red."

In 1994, Friedman wrote a memo marked "Very Confidential" to Raymond, Mortimer, and Richard Sackler. The market for cancer pain was significant, Friedman pointed out: four million prescriptions a year. In fact, there were three-quarters of a million prescriptions just for MS Contin. "We believe that the FDA will restrict our initial launch of OxyContin to the Cancer pain market," Friedman wrote. But what if, over time, the drug extended beyond that? There was a much greater market for *other* types of pain: back pain, neck pain, arthritis, fibromyalgia. According to the wrestler turned pain doctor John Bonica, one in three Americans was suffering from untreated chronic pain. If that was even somewhat true, it represented an enormous untapped market. What if you could figure out a way to market this new drug, OxyContin, to *all* those patients? The plan would have to remain secret for the time being, but in his memo to the Sacklers, Friedman confirmed that the intention was "to expand the use of OxyContin beyond Cancer patients to chronic non-malignant pain."

This was a hugely audacious scheme. In the 1940s, Arthur Sackler had watched the introduction of Thorazine. It was a "major" tranquilizer that worked wonders on patients who were psychotic. But the way the Sackler family made its first great fortune was with Arthur's involvement in marketing the "minor" tranquilizers Librium and Valium. Thorazine was perceived as a heavy-duty solution for a heavy-duty problem, but the market for the drug was naturally limited to people suffering from severe enough conditions to warrant a major tranquilizer. The beauty of the minor tranquilizers was that they were for everyone. The reason those drugs were such a success was that they were pills that you could pop to relieve an extraordinary range of common psychological and emotional ailments. Now Arthur's brothers and his nephew Richard would make the same pivot with a painkiller: they had enjoyed great success with MS Contin, but it was perceived as a heavy-duty drug for cancer. And cancer was a limited market. If you could figure out a way to market OxyContin not just for cancer but for any sort of pain, the profits would be astronomical. It was "imperative," Friedman told the Sacklers, "that we establish a literature" to support this kind of positioning. They would suggest OxyContin for "the broadest range of use."

Still, they faced one significant hurdle. Oxycodone is roughly twice as potent as morphine, and as a consequence OxyContin would be a much stronger drug than MS Contin. American doctors still tended to take great care in administering strong opioids because of long-established concerns about the addictiveness of these drugs. For years, proponents of MS Contin had argued that in an end-of-life situation, when someone is in a mortal fight with cancer, it was a bit silly to worry about the patient's getting hooked on morphine. But if Purdue wanted to market a powerful opioid like OxyContin for less acute, more persistent types of pain, one challenge would be the perception, among physicians, that opioids could be very addictive. If OxyContin was going to achieve its full commercial potential, the Sacklers and Purdue would have to undo that perception.

Chapter 15

GOD OF DREAMS

THE OPIUM POPPY IS a slender, seductive plant, a small bud atop a long stem, swaying gently in the breeze. It flowers beautifully, deep red or pale pink, and looks mellow and maddeningly indifferent, almost vain. Poppies are naturally occurring. They spread their own seeds, scattering them as they swing in the wind, like a saltshaker. Thousands of years ago, at the dawn of human history, someone figured out that if you slice into the head of a poppy, it will ooze a milky paste, and this substance has medicinal properties. The Mesopotamians harvested poppies. The Sumerians did, too. The nectar of the poppy is referenced in Assyrian medical tablets dating back to the seventh century B.C. In ancient Greece, Hippocrates himself suggested drinking white poppy juice mixed with nettle seeds as a remedy for a range of afflictions. Ingesting this substance could stimulate sleep, calm the nerves, and induce a distinctive sensation of cocoon-like comfort and euphoria. Most remarkably, the opium poppy could make pain go away.

If the plant seemed to possess magical properties, it was also understood, even in the ancient world, that it carried certain dangers. So overwhelming were its powers that the user could become possessed by them, slipping into dependence or succumbing to permanent sleep. The plant could kill you. It could create a state of relaxation so profound that at a certain point you just stopped breathing. The opium poppy might have been used as a medicine, but it was also used as a poison and as an instrument of suicide. In the symbolic vocabulary of the Romans, the poppy stood for sleep, but also death.

The potency of this slim flower was such that it could take hostage not just individuals but whole societies. In the nineteenth century, the poppy became an implement of empire: the lucrative opium trade led the British to wage bloody war on China, twice. In parts of Europe, it became fashionable to use the drug recreationally, inspiring the

Romantic poetry of Samuel Taylor Coleridge and Percy Bysshe Shelley. And doctors and chemists administered opium for a broad range of maladies, from fever to diarrhea. At the turn of the nineteenth century, an apothecary's assistant in Prussia had conducted a series of experiments in which he managed to isolate the chemical alkaloids in opium and synthesize the drug. He named this new substance morphine, after Morpheus, from Greek mythology—the god of dreams.

In his book *Opium: A History*, Martin Booth observes that when it comes to products derived from the opium poppy, "history repeats itself." During the American Civil War, morphine was widely embraced as a salve for terrible battlefield injuries, but it produced a generation of veterans who came home after the war addicted to the drug. By one estimate, in 1898, a quarter of a million Americans were addicted to morphine. A decade later, President Theodore Roosevelt appointed an opium commissioner, Dr. Hamilton Wright, to combat the scourge of abuse. Opium, Wright warned, was "the most pernicious drug known to humanity."

But as it happened, a team of chemists in Germany had recently managed to refine morphine into a new drug, heroin, which the German pharmaceutical company Bayer began to mass market as a wonder drug—a safer alternative to morphine. Heroin was created by the same research team that invented aspirin. Bayer proceeded to sell the drug in little boxes with a lion printed on the label, and suggested that differences in the molecular structure of heroin meant that it did not possess the dangerous addictive qualities of morphine. It was an appealing proposition: throughout human history, opium's upsides and its downsides had appeared to be inextricable, like the twined strands of a double helix. But now, Bayer claimed, they had been decoupled, by science, and with heroin, humans could enjoy all the therapeutic benefits of the opium poppy, with none of the drawbacks. In fact, some people advocated using heroin as a *cure* for morphine addiction.

None of this had any basis in fact. In reality, heroin was roughly six times more powerful than morphine and just as habit forming. Within a few years, the medical establishment had discovered that, as it turned out, heroin was addictive after all. People who took heroin often developed a craving for it, and because the body develops a tolerance for the drug, over time, the user tended to require ever stronger doses in order to feel a sense of equilibrium. This is true of all the opioids. As the body grows accustomed to the drug, it becomes necessary to administer more of it in order to relieve pain, deliver euphoria, or just stave off withdrawal. The contours of this experience are sometimes described, by doctors, as resembling "peaks and troughs," a sensation of unparalleled bliss at the moment the drug hits your system, followed, as it dissipates in your bloodstream, by despondence and an overpowering, almost animal sense of need. Physical dependence can often lead to bouts of debilitating withdrawal. Deprived of opium or morphine or heroin, the addicted individual will writhe and sweat and retch, his whole body shivering, or convulse violently, flopping like a fish on the floor.

By 1910, the very doctors and chemists who had been counseling heroin as a medical cure were recognizing that this might have been a terrible mistake, and the medical use of heroin declined. Bayer stopped making the drug in 1913. But there were still many for whom the essential transaction associated with consuming heroin seemed, ultimately, to be worth it. Heinrich Dreser, one of the German chemists at Bayer who is credited with inventing heroin, is rumored to have become addicted to the drug himself and died of a stroke in 1924. The risks may be formidable, but the high is sublime. Opioids can deliver you, if only for a few minutes, from physical or emotional pain, from discomfort, from anxiety, from need. It is like no other human experience. "I'll die young," the comedian Lenny Bruce once said of his own addiction. "But it's like kissing God." (He did die young, naked on his bathroom floor, from a morphine overdose, at forty.)

✢   ✢   ✢

Throughout Richard Sackler's life, he had pursued his passions with impetuous fervor. Once the idea had been hatched to position Purdue's new controlled-release opioid, OxyContin, as the successor to MS Contin, Richard devoted himself to this new project with a feverish energy. "You won't believe how committed I am to make OxyContin a huge success," he wrote to a friend. "It is almost that I dedicated my life to it."

Richard worked hard and drove his subordinates hard. "You need a vacation, and I need a vacation from your email," Michael Friedman, his vice president in charge of marketing, wrote to him at one point. Friedman was one of the few people at Purdue who could actually talk to Richard that way. But he had a certain license, because Richard had brought him into the company.

Friedman might have also held particular sway with Richard when it came to OxyContin because he was responsible for marketing and Richard had bold plans for the marketing and promotion of this new drug. Purdue would fight the ticking clock on the MS Contin patent with a radical strategy: the company would unveil this new, more powerful painkiller, OxyContin, and market it against MS Contin—*against its own drug*—in order to completely upend the current paradigm in pain treatment. This, Richard proclaimed, would be "the first time that we have chosen to obsolete our own product."

But Richard was not looking merely to supplant MS Contin. When it came to OxyContin, he had a grander vision. Morphine was still widely regarded as an extreme drug. If a doctor informed you that your grandmother was going onto morphine, that meant your grandmother was dying. "What we kept hearing over and over again was that health-care professionals were not telling patients that MS Contin was morphine because morphine had a stigma to it," one former Purdue executive who worked with Richard and Friedman recalled. "Family members, or even pharmacists, would tell patients, 'You can't take that. That's morphine!'" A company market research memo in 1992 pointed out that orthopedic surgeons, for instance, seemed "scared" or "intimidated" to administer morphine because it signaled "serious drug/dying patient/ addiction." At the same time, the memo noted, these surgeons would welcome the idea of a long-acting pain pill that was *not* morphine. Oxycodone, the former executive pointed out, "didn't have the stigma."

Different drugs have different "personalities," Michael Friedman liked to say. When he and Richard were trying to decide how to position OxyContin in the marketplace, they made a surprising discovery. The personality of morphine was, clearly, that of a powerful drug of last resort. The very name could conjure up the whiff of death. But, as Friedman pointed out to Richard in an email, oxycodone had a very different personality. In their market research, the team at Purdue had realized that many physicians regarded oxycodone as "weaker than morphine," Friedman said. Oxycodone was less well known, and less well understood, and it had a personality that seemed less threatening and more approachable.

From a marketing point of view, this represented a major opportunity. Purdue could market OxyContin as a safer, less extreme alternative to morphine. A century earlier, Bayer had marketed heroin as morphine without the unpleasant side effects, even though heroin was actually more powerful than morphine and every bit as addictive. Now, in internal discussions at Purdue headquarters in Norwalk, Richard and his colleagues entertained the notion of a similar marketing strategy. In truth, oxycodone wasn't weaker than morphine, either. In fact it was roughly twice as potent. The marketing specialists at Purdue didn't know why, exactly, doctors had this misapprehension about its being weaker, but it might have been because for most physicians their chief exposure to oxycodone involved the drugs Percocet and Percodan, in which a small dose of oxycodone was combined with acetaminophen or aspirin. Whatever the reason, Richard and his senior executives now devised a cunning strategy, which they outlined in a series of emails. If the true personality of oxycodone was misunderstood by America's doctors, the company would not correct that misunderstanding. Instead, they would exploit it.

Like MS Contin, OxyContin could be useful to cancer patients suffering from severe pain. But, as Friedman pointed out to Richard, the company should be very careful about marketing OxyContin too explicitly for cancer pain, because that might complicate the non-threatening "personality" of the drug. "While we might wish to see more of this product sold for cancer pain," Friedman wrote, "it would be extremely dangerous at this early stage in the life of the product to tamper with this 'personality' to make physicians think the drug is stronger or equal to morphine." Of course, OxyContin *was* stronger than morphine. That was a simple fact of chemistry—but one that the company would need to carefully obscure. After all, there are only so many cancer patients. "We are better off expanding use of OxyContin," Friedman wrote. The real jackpot was "non-malignant pain." OxyContin would not be a "niche" drug just for cancer pain, the minutes of an early Purdue team meeting confirm. By the company's estimates, fifty million Americans suffered from some form of chronic pain. *That* was the market they wanted to reach. OxyContin would be a drug for everyone.

✧   ✧   ✧

It would prove very helpful that by the time the Sacklers started to develop OxyContin, a major reconsideration was already well under way regarding the manner in which doctors thought about the treatment of pain. Dating back to the 1984 conference that Richard had helped to organize in Toronto, Purdue had been assiduously cultivating this community of revisionist physicians. One breakout star of this new movement was an intense young doctor with a clipped beard and a confident manner named Russell Portenoy. Portenoy was in his thirties and had worked as a professor of neurology and neuroscience at Cornell before he was recruited to Beth Israel Medical Center in New York to create the new Department of Pain Medicine and Palliative Care. Smart, telegenic, and very persuasive, Portenoy was an excellent spokesman, an avatar of the new orthodoxy when it came to the treatment of pain. For too long, he argued, the medical establishment had not taken pain seriously. In conferences and articles and appearances on the nightly news, Portenoy argued that the suffering of millions of Americans had been ignored by mainstream medicine. In his office, he prominently displayed a magazine mock-up that referred to him as "the King of Pain."

To Portenoy, opioids were a "gift from nature." He once joked that his method of treating patients could be summarized with the phrase "Here. Six months of drugs. See you later." Portenoy developed an early and enduring relationship with Purdue Pharma, as well as other pharmaceutical companies. Two years after Richard's conference in Toronto, Portenoy co-authored an influential article with another physician who was at the forefront of this push for a reconsideration of pain, Dr. Kathleen Foley, in which they explored the sustained use of opioids for pain relief. They wrote the paper, Portenoy would later explain, to highlight "the possibility of long-term pain relief from opioid therapy, without the development of... serious adverse effects, including drug abuse." It was not a rigorous study; the evidence was mostly anecdotal. But this sort of article would prove to be exceedingly useful for a company like Purdue.

Portenoy shared Richard's view that opioids bore an unfair taint because of concerns about their addictive properties and this had discouraged generations of doctors from employing what might be the best and most effective therapy for the treatment of pain. In Portenoy's opinion, American physicians had sharply underestimated the benefits of opioids and sharply overestimated the risks. Of course, some people who took these drugs developed a problem, he acknowledged. But people who became addicted tended not to be genuine pain patients who took the medication as prescribed by their doctors. Rather, Portenoy suggested, in these cases there were often "predisposing psychological, social and physiological factors." Some people simply have addictive personalities. They can't help themselves. Give an individual like that morphine and she may very well abuse it. But that's a reflection of her proclivities, rather than any inherently addictive properties of the drug. Portenoy described the fear of opioids as a kind of hysteria. He gave it a name, "opiophobia."

With encouragement from Portenoy and his fellow pain crusaders, by the late 1980s medical opinion was beginning to swing. In the first four years of the 1990s, morphine consumption in the United States rose by 75 percent. Richard Sackler knew Portenoy and Kathleen Foley and followed their work closely. In an impressively credentialed, apparently independent clinical setting, these pain specialists were validating the commercial research and development that Richard and his colleagues were doing at Purdue. "Until last week, our belief that oxycodone in high dose might be a satisfactory alternate to high-dose morphine was supposition," Richard informed colleagues, excitedly, one day in 1991, when the company was in the early phases of developing OxyContin. "As recent as this past July, Dr. Kathleen Foley told me that 'The idea is very promising, but whether one can use oxycodone in high doses for cancer pain is not known because nobody has ever used it.'" But Foley had been working with oxycodone liquid, administering it in large doses to patients, Richard explained, and "it has performed excellently," with "no unexpected side effects." She was giving patients mammoth doses, Richard added, as high as "1,000 milligrams per day." (Presented with this figure, decades later, Richard's cousin Kathe Sackler would say, "That's pretty shocking, a thousand milligrams. My God, that's an enormous dosage.") But at the time, Richard saw nothing but boundless commercial promise. According to Foley's research, he marveled, even that sort of gargantuan dose did not represent "a practical limit."

✦ ✦ ✦

Like Arthur Sackler, Mortimer and Raymond had always made a fetish of secrecy, and even as their profiles in the world of philanthropy grew, they remained staunchly averse to publicity. As he took control of the family company, Richard Sackler was no different. So it was surprising, in the summer of 1992, when Purdue Frederick took the unusual step of agreeing to cooperate with an extensive article in the local newspaper, the *Hartford Courant*. "Norwalk Firm Finds Niche Among Pharmaceutical Giants," the headline announced. The Sacklers had always invoked their medical degrees as a badge not just of achievement but of propriety, and the article noted that the drugmaker was "physician-owned," though apart from mentioning that the Sacklers "still take an active role in running the company," it said almost nothing about the family. This might have seemed like an opportune moment for Richard, having assumed a measure of control from his father and uncle and eclipsed his cousin and putative rival, Kathe, to step into the spotlight. But his name appeared nowhere in the article. Instead, the Sacklers put forward, as the face of Purdue, the family's consigliere and company lawyer, Howard Udell.

Purdue had grown "successful in a field of giants," Udell boasted, posing in a photo with an array of the company's over-the-counter products. The firm still retained some trace of its bread-and-butter origins (the article mentioned the triumph, decades earlier, of Betadine being used by NASA and noted, brightly, that Purdue "recently began marketing a treatment for genital warts"). But with help from MS Contin, annual sales were now approaching $400 million, and Udell said that Purdue was focused on the future.

The article was published at what was, in fact, a crucial juncture for the company. Purdue was in the process of trying to secure FDA approval for OxyContin. With MS Contin, the company had simply rushed the drug onto the market without even bothering to ask for approval—a risky gamble that Howard Udell had encouraged. This time would be different. MS Contin might have been a groundbreaking product, but OxyContin would represent an even more radical departure. And the company would need the FDA: the agency would have to approve the drug for sale, but also approve many aspects of how it could be sold and marketed. If Richard and his executives were going to carry out their plan to market the drug not just for cancer pain but for virtually any chronic pain, they would have to keep the agency happy. The whole process of securing FDA approval for a new drug had evolved into a heavily choreographed years-long bureaucratic gauntlet. It was cumbersome, more cumbersome than the drug approval process in other countries. The modern system of FDA approval had taken shape in the aftermath of the Kefauver hearings back in the 1960s, with elaborate requirements for establishing the efficacy and safety of a new drug. The agency had a small army of examiners who wielded the kind of regulatory authority that could make or break a billion-dollar product.

Richard Sackler was not a patient human being. He had big ambitions, and he was in a hurry. "Things are changing faster, and we must develop products faster than previously in order to grow as we want to grow," he told employees. "Developing products faster means getting our product portfolio approved faster." Enough with the sleepy dependability of yore, Richard was saying. It was time for Purdue to pick up the competitive momentum. But the fact remained that he needed FDA approval for OxyContin, and in particular he needed the approval of a man named Curtis Wright who oversaw pain medication at the agency and would be the medical reviewer and chief inquisitor in charge of approving OxyContin.

Wright had earned his medical degree at night while working as a chemist at the National Institute of Mental Health, then joined the navy, where he served as a general medical officer. He left to do a post-doctoral fellowship in the behavioral pharmacology of opioids, before his wife told him that he had better get a real job or they would be moving out of their home and into a public park. So, in 1989, he took a position at the FDA. Wright had worked on the approvals of several other opioid painkillers prior to OxyContin, and he was the main regulator whom the company would need to satisfy. They had to prove to him that OxyContin was safe and that it worked.

OxyContin would be sold as a "scheduled narcotic," under the Controlled Substances Act of 1970. As with any strong opioid, there would be the matter of possible addictive potential to contend with. You might suppose that Purdue would conduct tests of the addictive properties of its new drug. But the company didn't. Instead, Purdue argued that the patented Contin coating on a dose of OxyContin would obviate the risk of addiction. The whole principle of addiction to opioids was premised on the idea of peaks and troughs—of dose and withdrawal, euphoric high followed by the onset of craving. But because the controlled-release coating caused the drug to filter slowly into the bloodstream, over the course of twelve hours, the patient would not experience the immediate rush of an instant-release drug and, as a result, would not be whipsawed between high and withdrawal.

In fact, Purdue argued, it wasn't just that OxyContin carried little risk of addiction. The drug's unique qualities made it *safer* than other opioids on the market. The chemists at Bayer might have thought that they solved the essential therapeutic paradox of opium when they introduced heroin, and been mistaken. But this time, Purdue argued, they actually *had* cracked the code, uncoupling, once and for all, the medical power of the poppy from the attendant perils of addiction. They'd hacked it.

Not everyone at the FDA was convinced. Curtis Wright cautioned that it might be a bridge too far for Purdue to claim that OxyContin was actually safer than other available painkillers, warning the company that "care should be taken to limit competitive promotion." He also told officials at Purdue that some of his colleagues at the FDA had "very strong opinions" that opioids "should not be used for non-malignant pain."

But of course, that was Purdue's whole plan for OxyContin. So the company continued to press its case. The FDA would most likely restrict the initial launch of OxyContin to the cancer pain market, Michael Friedman wrote in a memo to Richard, Raymond, and Mortimer Sackler in 1994. "However, we also believe that physicians will perceive OxyContin as controlled-release Percocet (without acetaminophen) and expand its use."

"The original indication was for chronic cancer pain," Larry Wilson, the chemist who worked on the development of OxyContin at the Purdue Research Center in Yonkers, recalled. When Wilson and his colleagues were initially developing the drug, as a successor to MS Contin, he "never heard anyone say anything except about cancer." But, as Wilson pointed out, "once a company gets approval for a drug, a doctor can prescribe it for anything they want."

In order to succeed with OxyContin, Purdue officials needed the agency to approve the so-called package insert, the little booklet of fine-print information that would accompany each bottle. The package insert was "the Bible for the product," Richard Sackler liked to say, and each word had to be carefully negotiated with the FDA. The insert was revised more than thirty times, with Purdue's experts haggling with the government and poring over each word or phrase. The goal, according to Richard, was not merely to inform the consumer about the risks, benefits, and proper use of the drug but to create "a more potent selling instrument."

Gradually, Richard's team cultivated Curtis Wright. Early on, when Wright saw Purdue's first draft of the OxyContin package insert, he had remarked that he'd never seen an insert that contained so much promotional and marketing material. Wright told the company that all of this obviously promotional language would have to go. But, in the end, it stayed.

Under normal circumstances, interactions between an FDA official and a company whose drug he is evaluating would be tightly controlled, for the sake of transparency, and in order to guard against any undue influence or corruption. This sort of institutional precaution grew out of the scandal in which Henry Welch had been corrupted by the Sacklers and Félix Martí-Ibáñez back in the 1950s. But one Purdue official, Robert Reder, who played a key role in overseeing the application process for OxyContin, happened to attend a medical conference in Washington in 1992 and bump into Curtis Wright. They got to talking about OxyContin, and in an internal Purdue memo about the interaction he wrote that Wright "agreed to more such informal contacts in the near future." Richard could not help but gloat about "how far we have come in building a positive relationship" with Wright and the agency.

Sometimes, Wright would instruct Purdue to send him certain materials at his home office, rather than at the FDA. According to a confidential memo that was subsequently prepared by federal prosecutors, at one point a small delegation of Purdue officials traveled to Maryland and rented a room near Wright's office. Then, in a highly unusual step, the team from Purdue spent several days helping Wright compose the reviews of clinical study reports and the integrated summaries of the efficacy and safety of their own drug.

At times, it could seem that Wright had given up his role as impartial federal regulator and become a sort of in-house advocate for Purdue. The package insert went through endless drafts and iterations, and at some point a new line of text crept into it: "Delayed absorption, as provided by OxyContin tablets, is believed to reduce the abuse liability of the drug." This was a peculiar bit of rhetoric. Is *believed*? Believed by whom? It seemed more aspirational than scientific. Much later, when a question arose about who had actually written this line for inclusion, nobody would take responsibility. Curtis Wright would maintain that he had not inserted the passage, implying that Purdue must have written it. Robert Reder suggested that, on the contrary, it was Wright who added the line. In a sworn deposition, Wright allowed that he *might* have. It was possible. But he had no specific memory of doing so. It was a parentless fragment of text.

Even at the time, though, this language prompted immediate skepticism inside the FDA. "Sounds like B.S. to me," one of Wright's colleagues, Diane Schnitzler, told him, in an email.

"Actually, Diane, this is literally true," Wright wrote back. "One important factor in abuse liability determination is how fast the 'hit' is from a drug."

The assurance about how OxyContin's coating was "believed" to reduce abuse liability ended up staying in the package insert, and on December 28, 1995, the FDA approved OxyContin. "This didn't just 'happen.' It was a deftly coordinated, planned event," Richard Sackler told his staff. "Unlike the years that other filings linger at FDA, this product was approved in eleven months, fourteen days." Richard admitted to feeling some satisfaction in having personally "had a lot to do with" the quality of the package insert. But he also credited the "unparalleled teamwork" between Purdue Pharma and the FDA.

As for Curtis Wright, he had been giving some thought, lately, to leaving the federal government. After the approval for OxyContin went through, he resigned from the FDA. Initially, he joined a small pharmaceutical firm in Pennsylvania called Adolor. But he did not stay long. Barely a year later, he moved on, to a new position at Purdue Pharma, in Norwalk, with a first-year compensation package of nearly $400,000.

In subsequent testimony, Wright denied making any overtures to Purdue before he ultimately took the job, insisting that he was approached by a headhunter only after he had left the FDA. It made sense that the company would want to hire him, he argued, not because of any favors he might have done for Purdue, but because he was "a particularly fair and effective FDA reviewer."

But the truth is that one of Wright's first calls in his new job at Adolor had been to Purdue, to seek out areas where they might collaborate. And Richard Sackler, in his own subsequent sworn deposition, maintained that it was Wright who first approached the company about the possibility of a job—and that he did so before he had even left government. "He spoke to somebody at Purdue when he was planning on leaving the FDA," Richard recalled. But at the time, Richard felt that this might not be a good look for the company. He discussed it with a colleague, and they "agreed that we should not hire somebody who had reviewed our product." Instead, Wright "went to another company" for a year, Richard concluded. That was sufficient as a cooling-off period, apparently, to allay any concerns that Richard Sackler might have had about the appearance of a conflict of interest.

Chapter 16

H-BOMB

CALIXTO RIVERA WOKE BEFORE dawn. Outside, it was cold and raining, a sodden April morning in 1995. Calixto lived in Newark, New Jersey, in an apartment with his wife and children. The couple had a three-month-old son, which could be exhausting, and when Calixto opened his eyes that morning and registered just how unpleasant it was outside, he thought about calling in sick and skipping work. He was worn out. Like everyone else at the Napp chemical plant in Lodi, he had been putting in extra shifts in order to finish off several big projects before the plant closed that weekend for several weeks of renovations. Still toying with the idea of going back to bed, Calixto telephoned a woman he worked with, as if looking for some tacit permission. But she urged him to power through. "It's only an eight-hour shift, Papo," she said, using a nickname he'd had since childhood. "Just get through the next eight hours and you'll have two weeks to stay in bed." So Calixto murmured a quiet goodbye to his family and headed out into the rain for work.

Lodi is a working-class borough near Hackensack where a series of chemical plants lie scattered among quiet residential neighborhoods. The chemical and pharmaceutical industries had long dominated the state of New Jersey: in 1995, the chemical business was the state's biggest industry, generating some $24 billion in revenue every year. New Jersey had nearly fifteen thousand chemical plants. There were fourteen just in Lodi. The Napp facility occupied a sprawling, two-story complex on the banks of the Saddle River. It had originally been a turn-of-the-century dye works, and the plant was still surrounded by the vestigial shells of abandoned industrial buildings. Napp had purchased the Lodi property in 1970, in order to manufacture the chemicals for its pharmaceuticals. Lately, the mayor of Lodi had been trying to shut the plant down, looking to find a commercial developer so that he could launch condemnation proceedings against Napp. Local residents didn't like having an aging chemical facility in their backyard. It made them nervous.

Calixto Rivera had been working at Napp for nine years. His family was originally from Puerto Rico and had relocated to New Jersey. He was a hard worker, strong and handsome, a fastidious dresser, with a mustache and dark eyebrows, which accented his facial expressions, like punctuation marks. He trudged through the cold rain to the plant. It was going to be an interesting day. The company had restructured a couple of years earlier and started mixing chemicals not just for Napp and its parent company, Purdue Frederick, but for other firms that needed batches of chemicals mixed on a contract basis. This meant that, rather than processing the same raw chemicals for the same Napp products week in and week out, Calixto and his colleagues were now working with new and unfamiliar chemicals each day.

This week, they had been hired by a Rhode Island company to mix a series of particularly volatile chemicals that would be used to create the gold plating on consumer electronics. Twenty steel drums had arrived at the plant a few days earlier, with warnings on the side that indicated that the contents were hazardous. For a few days, the chemicals just sat there in a corner, because nobody was particularly eager to handle them.

When Calixto reached the gates of Napp, something was clearly off. The plant operated around the clock, on three eight-hour shifts, and it was time for the morning shift change. The night shift had been mixing the chemicals that had arrived in those drums. But, as Calixto learned when he got to the plant, something had gone wrong.

The truth was, the Napp facility was not the safest workplace. The plant had been cited for numerous violations. Napp paid its employees at the facility less than the going rate offered by other chemical companies in the area, and it was known to hire people who had been fired from other jobs. It was an open secret around Lodi: if you were desperate, and willing to work for less, Napp was happy to take you on. As one employee put it, "If your body was warm, they hired you." There was one guy at the plant who was an alcoholic and occasionally came to work and handled dangerous chemicals while drunk. The staff didn't have much training, and their inexperience became only more pronounced when the plant started taking on outside contract work to generate extra revenue for the owners, which meant that employees were dealing with new chemicals all the time. Safety training did not appear to be a major company priority. A further issue was the diversity of the workforce: employees at the plant came from numerous different countries. Not all of them spoke English, but there was also no other single shared language, like Spanish. As a consequence, there could occasionally be misunderstandings about quantities and proportions, which, when it comes to mixing chemicals, was a hazardous scenario.

To do the mixing, the plant workers used a ten-foot-tall, double-lobed Patterson Kelley blender, which was constructed of stainless steel and shaped like a giant heart. They had started mixing the Rhode Island chemicals the previous day, adding eight thousand pounds of sodium hydrosulfite to the blender, along with a thousand pounds of aluminum powder, a substance so explosive that it is sometimes used in rocket fuel. A supervisor stood watch on a catwalk above as the silvery-white powder settled in the mixer. Next, the staff was supposed to add benzaldehyde, a colorless liquid that would be sprayed into the mixer through a nozzle. But there was some kind of blockage in the valve, which meant that they had to troubleshoot and clean it. By the time the graveyard shift commenced the previous evening, a terrible smell had started to emanate from the mixer. Some of the employees were so inexperienced that when it came to chemicals, they couldn't tell a good smell from a bad one. But others recognized the telltale eggy stench of decomposing sodium hydrosulfite.

As a general rule, you're not supposed to get water on chemicals. There were signs in the mixing room: DO NOT USE WATER INSIDE OR NEAR THE ROOM. Even a single drop can be deadly. Sodium hydrosulfite in particular reacts violently when wet. It wasn't clear how it happened, exactly, but somewhere in the process of trying to clear the old feeding valve on the mixer, some water must have gotten inside. The maintenance workers who had been brought in to clean the valve were not trained in the handling of chemicals, and it might have been the case that they did not fully appreciate the danger. In high concentrations, wet sulfur can be more poisonous than cyanide gas. So, when the smell started, the managers on duty told staff to leave the vat alone and work on other projects. They opened a valve on the top of the mixer to allow any gas to escape. Everything was fine, they said. Then they left the mixer alone, for hours.

Gradually, the temperature and pressure gauges on the mixer began to climb. The chemicals were smoldering and bubbling, like the contents of some infernal cauldron, and emitting this sickening, noxious smell. Some of the workers thought it smelled like a dead animal. While Calixto had been sleeping through the rainy night in his apartment in Newark, the pressure gauge on the tank kept rising. There was a fire station a hundred yards away from the plant, but staff did not alert them. The Napp pharmaceutical company liked to keep things private and to deal with any problems discreetly.

By the time Calixto arrived at shift change that morning, the whole plant was being evacuated. At the gates, Calixto met up with a friend of his, Jose Millan, who was also about to start the next shift. Jose was a veteran of the plant, like Calixto; he had been working there for eight years. Everybody was standing around, shivering in the frigid drizzle, and grumbling; people hadn't had time to grab coats from their lockers when they evacuated, so they were cold. They were also apprehensive. The malodorous smell from the mixer was so intense now that it was drifting out of the vents on the roof of the plant, and the men could smell it outside. It smelled dangerous. As Calixto and Jose congregated in the rain with the other evacuated workers, a shift supervisor announced that someone had spoken to a chemical engineer at Napp who had advised that the men go back into the plant and try to empty out some of the material in the mixer. A team of seven men was selected. It didn't include Calixto or Jose, so Jose proposed that they walk to a nearby deli and grab a coffee. But as Calixto watched the managers designate this impromptu cleanup crew to go in and remove the chemicals, he noticed that one of the people chosen was an older guy, a man he knew who was nearly seventy.

Don't go, Calixto told him. I'll go in your place.

The company would later maintain that managers did not order the men to reenter the plant, but a dozen workers who were there that day said that they did. Calixto asked Jose to pick up an extra coffee and bring it back for him. Then he and the other six men put on face masks with carbon filters and walked back into the plant.

❖ ❖ ❖

Inside, the Napp plant was eerily quiet. The smell was overpowering. But the men moved through it—*toward* it—and into the blending room. What they could not see, or know, was that when water crept into the vat, it caused the sodium hydrosulfite to break down, which generated heat. The heat produced steam, which reacted with the aluminum powder to create hydrogen gas. Inside the great hull of the mixer, a chain reaction had initiated, and the pressure had been building, hour upon hour. As one chemist would subsequently observe, the contents of the steel drum had the makings of a hydrogen bomb.

None of the men who went back into the plant was a chemist. When they reached the mixing room, they opened the vat, and started to empty the smoldering chemicals into smaller barrels. Then, suddenly, there was a loud hissing noise—the sound of gas rapidly escaping. Then a moment of silence. Six of the men, including Calixto, stood there, frozen. A seventh man started sprinting away. Then—

Boom.

The steel mixer popped like a balloon, and scraps of metal and white-hot chemicals exploded in every direction. The blast was so strong that it lifted the ten-ton block of concrete that supported the mixer clear off the ground and hurled it fifty feet across the plant as if it were a Frisbee. A firestorm engulfed the space, with ferocious tendrils of flame rushing down corridors and bursting straight through fire doors. A roaring orange column tore through the roof. The windows in storefronts up and down Main Street shattered. Flaming debris rained down on the houses of Lodi. Jose Millan was walking back to the plant with a coffee for Calixto when the blast threw him clear off his feet. The sundered roof of the plant belched acrid chemical smoke into the air. Jose watched the conflagration, knowing his friend was inside. He didn't know what to do. He felt helpless.

Calixto was killed instantly, his skull crushed by the force of the blast. He was burned so badly that, later, his corpse could be identified only by dental records. Three other men were killed alongside him in the explosion. Another was covered in burns over 90 percent of his body and would die in the hospital several days later. Forty people were injured. One man who had been inside the plant and seen the fireball, but survived, said that it was like staring into the sun.

For days, the plant smoked. Homes were damaged. A toxic green runoff oozed out of the devastated facility. It trickled down Main Street and drained into the Saddle River. The pollution fed into the Passaic River, sickening waterfowl. Thousands of fish went belly up and drifted to shore, lining the riverbank, pale and dead. A federal investigation would eventually cite Napp for a bevy of safety violations and issue a conspicuously modest fine of $127,000. Prosecutors considered bringing manslaughter charges but opted not to in the end. One longtime Purdue Frederick employee, Winthrop Lange, said at the time that Napp should not have made the transition to manufacturing chemicals for other companies on a contract basis, because it didn't have "the facilities or the technical people to do custom blending." Another former Napp official, a Polish-born chemist named Richard Boncza, concluded that the company had been reckless in assigning dangerous jobs to inexperienced workers. "They never asked questions to decide whether someone had an aptitude for chemical work," he said. Facing a storm of emotion and acrimony from its own employees and from the people of Lodi, Napp announced that it would not rebuild the plant, meaning that everyone who managed to survive the blast would now lose their jobs. A spokesman quoted the company's owners as saying, "We will not go where we are not wanted."

✤ ✤ ✤

The spokesman was at pains not to mention any names, but the owners he was referring to were the Sacklers. If this were a different company, or a different family, there might have been some lip service to prevailing notions of where the buck stops or the finer points of corporate social responsibility, or even just an expression of sympathy for the dead. But the Sacklers assiduously distanced themselves not just from any sense of responsibility for the tragedy but from any connection to it whatsoever. The family issued no apologies or condolences. They appeared at no funerals. They made no public statements whatsoever. Howard Udell, the company lawyer, oversaw the legal response for the Sacklers, and as a rule he tended to counsel against issuing apologies or making any admissions of personal accountability. Richard Boncza, the Polish chemist, who had originally been hired by Richard Sackler himself, said that the company had issued strict orders that nobody discuss what had gone wrong. What it felt like, Boncza said, was "a coverup."

Just the same, it didn't take long for journalists from the local Bergen County paper, *The Record*, to discover the real identity of Napp's owners. "They're a family of American tycoons and philanthropists," the paper reported. "Their international spectrum of friends includes Britain's Princess Diana, Nobel Prize winners, influential entrepreneurs—in general, the upper crust of society... They're not the Rockefellers. They're the Sacklers."

For months, reporters from *The Record* tried to solicit a comment from Raymond or Richard Sackler. But neither father nor son would say a word. They were implacable, apparently indifferent. Finally, one day in the fall of 1995, seven months after the explosion, one of the reporters ventured into Manhattan and managed to buttonhole Raymond Sackler outside the British consulate on Sixty-Eighth Street. This was Raymond's territory, the Upper East Side, just a few blocks from the Sackler town house on Sixty-Second. It was another rainy day, and Raymond was dressed for a special occasion and on his way into the consulate when the reporter stopped him and asked about the blast.

"We've been in the field for forty-odd years," Raymond said. "We know what safety is. And we're very concerned with people's lives—all people's lives."

But do you feel any sense of personal responsibility for this tragedy? the reporter asked.

"Absolutely not," Raymond replied.

Then he turned and headed into the building. It was an exciting day for Raymond, one that he was not going to allow some pushy reporter from New Jersey to mar. In recognition of his record of philanthropic gifts in the arts and the sciences, he was being granted an honorary knighthood by Queen Elizabeth, and the British consul general was to present him with a special medal in a formal ceremony. On the subject of this distinction, Raymond was more forthcoming, declaring himself deeply moved to be recognized by the queen in this manner.

"It's an honor," he said. "It has a great impact on me."

Chapter 17

SELL, SELL, SELL

IN THE FIRST WEEK of 1996, the East Coast of the United States was engulfed by a great blizzard. An avalanche of snow descended on the region, inundating small towns and big cities, paralyzing commerce, and blanketing everything in a dense, muffled carpet of white. Thousands of travelers were stranded in airports and in bus terminals and at rest stops along highways as blinding gusts created white-out conditions, making transportation impossible. In New York City, the homeless sought refuge wherever they could find it, rather than freeze to death on the street. In Greenwich, Connecticut, frost laced the windows of elegant homes, and when the snow finally ceased, brightly bundled children ventured outside to throw snowballs. Carloads of Latino men materialized, as if by magic, and these impromptu work crews went door-to-door, shoveling driveways and front walks.

On the other side of the country, twenty-four hundred miles away, the sun was shining. A party was under way at the Wigwam, a luxury resort and country club in the high desert outside Phoenix that was known for its three golf courses and kitschy Native American theme. It might have been snowing in New York, but here it was seventy-five degrees. The mood was festive, the alcohol was flowing, and the sales force of Purdue Pharma had assembled for the official launch of OxyContin.

The FDA had formally approved the drug a few weeks earlier, so this was a celebration and a fun opportunity for team building: a few days of training sessions and pep talks in beautiful, 5-star surroundings. Company employees took part in contests to see who could take home various prizes (in keeping with the Native American motif, the prizes were referred to as "the Wampum"). And now, after a celebratory dinner in the main lodge, hundreds of sales representatives applauded as Richard Sackler stepped up to the podium.

"For millennia, humans knew that great changes in the fortunes of civilizations and enterprises are heralded by cataclysms in geology and weather," Richard began. He had never been a naturally charismatic leader, and he had no particular facility for public speaking. But he was visibly excited, reading from a prepared speech that he had clearly put real effort into. Richard had been delayed getting out of Connecticut, he explained; a few senior executives were still stuck on the East Coast. But this blizzard, he announced, was "an omen of change." He proceeded to launch into a rambling, aphoristic joke about how he and a few other senior members of the company had traveled to the Himalayas to consult a soothsayer. "Oh, Wise One," they said, by way of introduction. "We are salesmen." The story went on a bit long, but Richard had a captive audience (he owned the company, after all) and he really committed to it. He even managed to work in a few of the antique exclamations he had been throwing around since college. "Balderdash! Poppycock! Twaddle!"

A generation earlier, when Arthur Sackler helped Pfizer turn Librium into a blockbuster, the company had made it happen by recruiting an army of aggressive salespeople. Now Purdue would do the same for OxyContin, and, Richard proclaimed, the snowstorm back in Connecticut would be remembered as a mystical portent of their success. "The launch of OxyContin tablets will be followed by a blizzard of prescriptions that will bury the competition," he predicted. "The prescription blizzard will be so deep, dense and white that you will never see their White Flag." He continued, leaning further into the metaphor, "Commerce in competitive products will come to a halt." OxyContin would be a "revolutionary" drug, Richard told the reps. "You will revolutionize the treatment both of chronic cancer pain, and of non-malignant painful conditions, as well."

This was Richard Sackler's moment, the culmination of his grandest designs. He had sought to remake the family company in his own image, to transform it from a reliably profitable purveyor of unglamorous staples into something more aggressive, more imaginative, more competitive, and less orthodox. He had patiently cultivated the community of pain specialists and advocates, cajoled the regulators at the FDA, and devised strategies for how to persuade American physicians who might be reluctant to prescribe strong opioids that they should reconsider. Now he stood poised, with the introduction of this new painkiller, not just to catapult the firm into a new stratosphere of profitability but to eclipse his own father and uncles.

"OxyContin tablets is the most important product launch in the company's history," Richard said. "In the years to come, we will look back on this week as the beginning of a new era for our business, and for ourselves." He spoke of "the expanding commitment of the Sackler family" to the business and praised the OxyContin product team, which had secured FDA approval in record time, and the sales force, which he recognized would now be essential in determining the fortunes of the drug: "There is absolutely nothing that is ethical and legal that we won't do to make the greatest sales force on earth even more successful!"

Richard stood there, basking in the reflected glow of his people, his empire, his prospects. Then he blurted, "I love this business!"

✛ ✛ ✛

Sales reps aren't doctors. They're salespeople: bright, often quite young (sometimes just out of college), capable, personable, easy to talk to. Pharmaceutical reps are also, famously, often physically attractive. These qualities might not be essential prerequisites, but they're helpful in a job that is in some ways pretty challenging. The pharmaceutical rep spends her days dropping in on doctors, surgeons, pharmacists, anyone who can influence the prescribing of a drug. As a rule, the people she is calling on are busy and overworked, so they may not welcome this unsolicited intrusion in an already hectic day. They're also professionals, with specialized training. The pharma rep has no medical training, no pharmacy degree, yet her job is to coax the prescriber into prescribing differently. Reps are door-to-door missionaries. The good ones are naturally persuasive. Their *job* is to persuade.

In Richard Sackler's view, the most valuable resource at Purdue Pharma was not the medical staff or the chemists or even the Sackler brain trust but the sales force. "We had a product that had tremendous potential," he would later recall. "Our principal means of getting it used was to convince physicians...to use it." Some of Purdue's sales reps had been with the company for years, even decades, and welcomed the transition into analgesics. Pain medicine seemed cutting edge and important: a sustained-release opioid painkiller was a hot product to be selling, and for longtime Purdue reps this marked a refreshing change of pace. "I sold Betadine antiseptics, Senokot laxatives, a product called Cerumenex, for the removal of ear wax, X-Prep, which was a bowel evacuant," one veteran rep recalled. "Needless to say, I was not the person who was a hit at a cocktail party."

But OxyContin felt like a seminal product, and the sales push would be a huge undertaking, so Purdue augmented its existing sales force with a phalanx of new recruits. Each sales rep was prepared: drilled by instructors, coached on talking points, armed with serious-looking medical literature that spoke to the revolutionary properties of Oxy-Contin. They were on a mission, one Purdue official told them: "Your priority is to *sell, sell, sell* OxyContin."

If a doctor was already treating a patient with another painkiller, the sales reps would persuade the doctor to switch to OxyContin. Even in cases where the painkiller the doctor was already prescribing was Purdue's own drug MS Contin, the reps would counsel switching to Oxy: the Sacklers' commitment to the new product was so absolute that they were prepared to phase out the old one.

OxyContin was the painkiller "to start with and to stay with," the reps said. This was a carefully scripted phrase that they intoned like a mantra. What it meant was that OxyContin should not be regarded as some extreme nuclear solution to which a pain patient might graduate only after lesser remedies had failed. For "moderate to severe pain," OxyContin should be the first line of defense. And it was good for acute, short-term pain, as well as for chronic, long-term pain; this was a drug you could use for months, years, a lifetime, a drug "to stay with." From a sales perspective, it was an enticing formula: start early, and never stop.

Of course, Richard and his executives knew that many physicians might have reservations. Prior to the launch of the drug, they had conducted focus groups in which doctors expressed concerns about the potentially addictive properties of strong opioids. But the sales reps were issued explicit instructions to challenge such concerns. In training sessions, they did role-playing exercises in "overcoming objections." If clinicians expressed concerns about the danger of abuse and addiction, the reps would parrot the language from the package insert, which Curtis Wright, of the FDA, had approved: "The delivery system is believed to reduce the abuse liability of the drug." They memorized the line and recited it like a catechism.

And the reps went well beyond the dry assurances of the label. They were instructed by Purdue to inform doctors that "fewer than 1 percent" of patients who took OxyContin became addicted. What causes addiction, they explained, is the "peak and trough" phenomenon. Because OxyContin released its narcotic payload into the bloodstream gradually, the peaks and valleys were less pronounced, which made addiction less likely. Richard Sackler was adamant on this point. At Purdue headquarters in Norwalk, a story circulated about the time he supposedly popped an OxyContin pill himself, in a meeting, to demonstrate that it would not make him high or in any way impair his functioning.

When the sales reps made their visits, they wrote up each encounter in notes, which were reviewed by supervisors at Purdue. These field notes were little haikus, dashed off quickly in the car between calls, full of cryptic shorthand and utilitarian abbreviations. But they were littered with references to the promises that Purdue made about the safety of OxyContin:

> Discussed side effects of abuse and that Oxy is less
> likely to be abused than Percocet and Vicodin.

> Worried re addiction w/ Oxy... Oxy is long-lasting,
> has fewer peaks... less addictive.

> Seemed to hear the Oxy message better on no buzz potential.

> Emily [the pharmacy director at a Walmart in Kentucky] told
> me that Dr. Kennedy is writing Oxy with both hands. She
> rolled her eyes and told me it is doing very very well.

In urging doctors to write more OxyContin prescriptions, the sales reps often referred to medical literature, and to one study in particular. "In fact, a survey of more than 11,000 opioid-using patients, taken over several years, found only four cases of documented addiction," they would say. The study had been published in the prestigious *New England Journal of Medicine*, they would explain, with a title that spoke for itself: "Addiction Rare in Patients Treated with Narcotics." In truth, the item in the journal was not a peer-reviewed study at all, but a five-sentence letter to the editor by two doctors at Boston University Medical Center. The research it described was anything but comprehensive: it was based on a group of patients who were monitored on a short-term basis during brief stays in a hospital setting. Much later, one of the authors of the letter, Hershel Jick, would say that he was "amazed" by the degree to which Purdue and other companies used this minor academic offering to justify the mass marketing of strong opioids. The industry had co-opted his work, he suggested, using it "as an ad."

But for the reps, the study was irresistible, because it conveyed such a useful message: opioids might be associated in the public mind with addiction, but really it was exceedingly rare for a patient to become hooked on narcotic painkillers, so long as the drugs were being administered in a doctor's care. And Purdue created the impression that this new perception of opioids was an increasingly mainstream view. The sales team had what the company described as "non-branded" literature: material generated by ostensibly independent groups, which had actually been produced or funded by Purdue. The company established a speakers bureau, through which it paid several thousand doctors to attend medical conferences and deliver presentations about the merits of strong opioids. Doctors were offered all-expenses-paid trips to "pain management seminars" in places like Scottsdale, Arizona, and Boca Raton, Florida. In the initial five years after OxyContin's release, the company sponsored seven thousand of these seminars.

The marketing of OxyContin relied on an empirical circularity: the company convinced doctors of the drug's safety with literature that had been produced by doctors who were paid, or funded, by the company. Russell Portenoy, the so-called King of Pain, was emblematic of this conflict of interest. He was chairman of the Department of Pain Medicine and Palliative Care at Beth Israel in New York but also had a financial relationship with Purdue. He was president of the American Pain Society and part of the American Pain Foundation, both ostensibly independent groups that in fact were subsidized by Purdue and other pharma companies. And everywhere he went, he argued that opioids had been unfairly stigmatized. The issue was not that Portenoy and other pain specialists were taking money to express views that they did not believe. Portenoy *did* believe, adamantly, that opioids were safe and should be more widely prescribed. It was more of a coincidence of interests: he and Purdue helped each other amplify the same message. Portenoy himself would later acknowledge that until Oxy-

Contin "no other company had previously promoted an opioid drug as aggressively."

Purdue advertised OxyContin in medical journals, sponsored websites about chronic pain, and distributed a dizzying variety of OxyContin swag: fishing hats, plush toys, luggage tags. The sales reps left a trail of these giveaways wherever they went so that anywhere a doctor turned, she would be greeted by reminders of the product. Often, reps would devise wily strategies for cadging a few minutes of a busy doctor's time, like showing up at midday with a take-out lunch, compliments of Purdue.

Physicians often scoff at the suggestion that their prescribing habits might be swayed by the blandishments of pharmaceutical companies. This had been a cornerstone of Arthur Sackler's worldview: the notion that doctors are priest-like figures, immune to flattery or temptation or greed, focused exclusively on the narrow dictates of appropriate medical care. In Arthur's view, it was laughable—even insulting—to insinuate that a colorful ad or a steak dinner might be enough to sway the clinical judgment of an MD. Doctors, he argued, simply can't be bought.

But, of course, this is no more true today than it was when Arthur Sackler said it. Doctors are human, and the notion that donning a white coat might somehow shield them from temptation is a fantasy. A 2016 study found that purchasing even a single meal with a value of $20 for a physician can be enough to change the way that he prescribes. And for all their lip service to the contrary, the Sacklers didn't need studies to tell them this. Some years, Purdue would allocate as much as $9 million just to buy food for doctors. Richard Sackler was enough of a stickler for detail that he would never countenance such an outlay of funds unless he was assured a good return on investment. In a 1996 email to Michael Friedman, he pointed out that according to Purdue's own data, "physicians who attended the dinner programs or the weekend meetings wrote more than double the number of new Rxs for OxyContin compared to the control group." ("Rx" is an abbreviation for prescription.) He noted that "weekend meetings had the greatest impact."

Even physicians who took no hand-outs from the company proved to be highly susceptible to the message Purdue was promoting. "The primary goal of medical practice is the relief of suffering, and one of the most common types of suffering that doctors see is pain," David Juur-link, who runs the Division of Clinical Pharmacology and Toxicology at the University of Toronto, pointed out. "You've got a patient in pain, you've got a doctor who genuinely wants to help, and now suddenly you have an intervention that—we are told—is safe and effective." What the company was really selling, some of Purdue's marketing materials suggested, was "hope in a bottle."

✣ ✣ ✣

"All indications are that we have a potential blockbuster product on our hands!" a Purdue manager, Mike Innaurato, told the sales force. For the reps, this could be a lucrative opportunity, Innaurato pointed out: "Now is the time to cash in on the bonus earnings that OxyContin will provide." Purdue was still a midsized company, smaller than the big publicly traded pharmaceutical giants. But it was known as a great place to work. The Sacklers paid well and took care of their own, and they encouraged salespeople to bet on themselves. "The Sacklers really believed that the people who worked for them were part of their fam-ily," one former executive recalled. "The way they compensated was unique. Long before OxyContin, they were using the same compensa-tion program. Most pharma companies capped what kind of additional bonus you could make as a rep. Purdue didn't." It was, in essence, the deal that Arthur Sackler had worked out for himself when he was mar-keting Valium. If sales grew, you'd get a bigger bonus. There was no cap. "Purdue never capped," the executive said, "because they wanted their people to be incentivized."

Steven May was an ex-cop who lived in Roanoke, Virginia, and had worked as a sales rep for a rival pharmaceutical company before he joined Purdue in 1999. May knew about the company by reputation. It was known to pay better than other places, and OxyContin was a hot product. There was a sense, in the industry, that Purdue was doing right and doing well—providing an innovative product that was help-ing people and making money hand over fist. "We felt like we were doing a righteous thing," May recalled. "There's millions of people in pain, and we have the solution." May traveled to Norwalk for three weeks of classroom training in the home office. At a celebratory outing to a steak house one night, he posed for a photo with Raymond Sackler in front of an ice sculpture that said "Purdue." At dinner, he happened to be seated at the same table as Richard Sackler. "I was blown away," May recalled. "My first impression of him was, 'This is the dude that made it happen. He has a company that his family owns. I want to *be* him one day.'"

May was one of seven hundred or so Purdue sales reps who fanned out across the country with instructions to get doctors to prescribe OxyContin to as wide a range of patients as possible. In total, they called on nearly a hundred thousand physicians. As May put it, "What Purdue did really well was target physicians, like general practitioners, who were *not* pain specialists." In doing this, the sales reps had access to a powerful tool. Back in the 1950s, Arthur Sackler and his friend Bill Frohlich had founded the market research firm IMS—the very firm that would become the source of the rift between the Sackler brothers after Frohlich's death, when Raymond and Mortimer refused to give Arthur his share of the company. But IMS stayed in business and grew, over the decades, into a big data company with extraordinarily fine-grained information about the prescribing habits of physicians. Using data supplied by IMS, Steven May and other sales reps could look into which doctors to call on. They targeted certain regions in particular—places where there were a lot of family physicians, where people had workers' comp, injuries they had sustained on the job, disabilities. "We focused our salesmen's attention," Richard Sackler explained, "to physicians who...write a lot of prescriptions for opioids." A doctor who wrote a lot of painkiller prescriptions was a priceless commodity. Like casino employees talking about an especially profligate gambler, the sales reps referred to these doctors as "whales."

Purdue also explicitly instructed sales reps to target family physicians who were, in the company's language, "opioid naive"—doctors who had little experience prescribing this kind of medication. To May, it seemed that for some of these doctors the primary source of knowledge about the use of opioids in pain management was Purdue itself. Headquarters advised the sales force to avoid "words such as 'powerful,'" which "may make some people think the drug is dangerous and should be reserved for more severe pain." In one 1997 exchange with Richard Sackler, a company official pointed out that many physicians believed, erroneously, that oxycodone was weaker than morphine, when in fact it was twice as strong, and said, "It is important that we be careful not to change the perception of physicians."

May's region comprised parts of western Virginia and southern West Virginia, and he went out to sell. Purdue had discovered that in some places there was an almost inexhaustible demand for the product. "There was growth instantly, from the beginning," May recalled. "Phenomenal growth." As soon as a given sales territory hit a certain volume, the company would split the territory and add another rep. "The belief was you could grow the product," May explained. "So if *those* two territories do well, you split them again. Put *more* reps. Grow it even more."

Part of the reason that the drug did so well, it seemed to May and his colleagues, was that it worked. It worked miraculously. At headquarters in Norwalk, the company started receiving letters—the most extraordinary letters—talking about the ways in which this drug had helped patients. People who had been suffering with debilitating chronic pain testified to how OxyContin had transformed their lives: for the first time in memory, they could sleep through the night, or go back to work, or pick up their grandchildren.

Richard Sackler was emboldened by these reports. "We may need to start a campaign," he suggested in 1997, "to focus attention on the untreated patient in severe pain who is mobilized and given his life back by our products." Following Richard's instructions to the letter, the company produced a promotional video called *I Got My Life Back,* which featured testimonials from patients with rheumatoid arthritis, fibromyalgia, and other conditions, recounting the private horrors of living with untreated pain. "It felt like somebody had a ice pick all the time, gouging right down in my backbone," Johnny Sullivan, a heavy-set construction worker, drawled. The video had been put together with assistance from one of Purdue's paid speakers, a doctor who ran a pair of pain clinics in North Carolina named Alan Spanos. Spanos, the video announced, had received his medical training "from Oxford University in the United Kingdom." He was a thin man with a comb-over, dressed in a green tie and a pale green shirt. In the video, Spanos addressed the camera, flanked by a series of medical textbooks and a framed diploma, and said, "There's no question that our best, strongest pain medicines are the opioids." They might "have a reputation for causing addiction and other terrible things," he said, but this was a misconception. "In fact, the rate of addiction amongst pain patients who are treated by doctors is much less than 1 percent." Opioids were nothing short of miraculous, according to Spanos. "They don't wear out, they go on working, they do not have serious medical side effects."

At headquarters, Michael Friedman was delighted when he saw the testimonials, calling the material "very powerful" and instructing his subordinates to finish the video in time for the national sales meeting that January. The Sacklers took a personal interest in the *I Got My Life Back* video; Richard's brother, Jonathan, discussed it with Michael Friedman and other senior executives. When it was finished, the company distributed more than twenty thousand copies of the video in 1998.

It was occasionally said, at Purdue, that OxyContin was so good it would "sell itself." This was just a turn of phrase, rather than a formal marketing strategy, but the Sacklers took the notion seriously enough that Purdue initiated a costly program to issue free samples of Oxy-Contin to pain patients. This was an old technique in the pharma business. When Bayer marketed heroin at the turn of the twentieth century, it offered free samples of the drug to potential customers. When Roche was seeking a foothold for Valium in Canada during the 1970s, the company gave away eighty-two million Valium pills as free samples in a single year. If you are selling a product that makes people feel good (and may also be highly addictive), that first free hit will generally pay for itself many times over.

For OxyContin, Purdue developed a "card program" in which the company issued coupon cards that patients could use to receive a free thirty-day prescription of the drug. Michael Friedman explained that the free samples were used to "acquaint" patients with OxyContin. If OxyContin really was the one to start with and the one to stay with, enough people who took the drug the first time would probably want to stay with it. By the time the program was suspended in 2001, Purdue had subsidized thirty-four thousand free prescriptions.

OxyContin was sold in a range of dose sizes: 10 milligrams, 20 milligrams, 40 milligrams, and 80 milligrams. In 2000, a colossal 160-milligram pill was introduced. According to the company, there was "no maximum daily dose—or 'ceiling' dose," though Larry Wilson, the Purdue chemist who worked on OxyContin, felt that "160 was a bit too much." In the first year, Purdue sold $44 million of OxyContin. The following year, sales more than doubled. The year after that, they doubled again.

"I am pleased to report sales, through September 1999 year-to-date, of $601 million," Michael Friedman wrote to Richard, Raymond, and Mortimer Sackler, noting that "OxyContin prescription trends continue to accelerate." The company attributed this astonishing growth to "the continued existence of a substantial unsatisfied market." There were millions of Americans living with untreated chronic pain who had been poorly served by lesser medications. As the company spread the word about OxyContin, and issued free samples to people who were experiencing pain, it was little wonder sales were taking off. "There is no sign of it slowing down!" Richard Sackler told a team of company representatives in 2000.

Richard was relentlessly focused on the drug. He and Beth had three children now, David, Marianna, and Rebecca. He was a demanding father, and his brusque manner and blunt conversational style meant that he could occasionally appear to be less than nurturing. "He just cannot understand how his words are going to land on somebody," David Sackler would later observe. David played hockey, and when Richard attended a game and was dissatisfied with his son's performance, he let it be known. David would later acknowledge that his father's sharp tongue, and the thoughtless way that he wielded it, could be deeply hurtful.

But Richard was not particularly focused on family during these years. "After the initial launch phase, I will have to catch up with my private life again," he wrote in an email to a friend, three years after the launch of the drug. As profits from OxyContin spiked, Richard obsessed over sales figures. OxyContin was now being rolled out in other countries, and at one point Richard wondered whether it might be possible to sell the pills as an "un-controlled" medication in Germany—that is, as an over-the-counter remedy that would not require a prescription from a doctor. This was, to put it mildly, a bold idea. Bold enough that Robert Kaiko, the Purdue employee who was credited with inventing OxyContin, responded that it would be a terrible move. "I'm very concerned," Kaiko wrote in an email, recommending "against" the proposal. Purdue's sales reps might be promising doctors across America that OxyContin posed little danger of abuse, but privately Kaiko cautioned Richard that the company did not have "a sufficiently strong case to argue that OxyContin has minimal or no abuse liability."

Undeterred, Richard asked, "How substantially would it improve your sales?"

Kaiko had worked with Richard for years and understood his boss's obstinate tendencies. So, rather than rely on a public safety argument, he made the case in terms that Richard would be more likely to appreciate, outlining the full implications of what such a move might mean for *sales*. "If OxyContin is uncontrolled in Germany, it is highly likely that it will eventually be abused there and then controlled," Kaiko wrote. "This may be more damaging to OxyContin internationally than any temporarily higher sales that could be gleaned from an uncontrolled status."

Ultimately, Kaiko prevailed and the notion was abandoned. But Richard let it be known that he was not happy about it, grumbling, "I thought it was a good idea."

OxyContin was priced in such a way that greater dose strength meant greater profits for Purdue. As a consequence, perhaps, another fixation for Richard was the idea of a ceiling effect. Steven May and his fellow reps were under constant pressure, from headquarters, to urge doctors to "titrate" up, or increase the prescribed dose. Since Oxy-Contin was an opioid, this was particularly relevant, because the body develops a tolerance for opioids: a patient who starts with 10 milligrams of OxyContin twice a day may find that this dose is enough to stop the pain at first, but over time 10 milligrams won't do the trick. In theory, the range of OxyContin pills would address this problem, and the patient could simply graduate from 10 milligrams to 20, and so on, all the way up to 160. But some doctors seemed to be skeptical about prescribing such vast quantities of OxyContin, suggesting that the drug might have a ceiling—a practical therapeutic limit on the size of the dose. This incensed Richard Sackler. He complained to Michael Friedman that some oncologists appeared to believe there was a dose beyond which OxyContin would not be effective, and asked, "What materials could we pull together that would smash this critical misconception?"

✢ ✢ ✢

"This was a pretty special company," Steven May reflected. When he started working for Purdue, he felt as though he had joined "the elite of the elite." It was "a classy corporate environment that just spoke to success." The astronomical sales of OxyContin lifted the spirits, and the fortunes, of the whole company.

"There was a feeling of being kings of the world," one executive who worked closely with the Sacklers during this period recalled. "There was money to spend. There were hundreds of millions sloshing around. We would go out to dinner in Darien, Connecticut. Dinner was $19,000. People were spending. Flights were bumped up." Arthur Sackler had been famously stingy when it came to travel, flying economy even as a rich man. Now some Purdue executives took the Concorde—the sleek, supersonic luxury aircraft that could cross the Atlantic in under four hours. "You are part of a legend in the making," Richard told the sales force at the annual meeting in January 2000. In an email, he took stock of OxyContin's early success, observing that the drug's launch "has outperformed our expectations, market research, and fondest dreams."

For the sales force, it was an intoxicating time. "$$$$$$$$$$$$$ It's Bonus Time in the Neighborhood!" a sales manager in Tennessee wrote in a memo. Purdue had a program called Toppers, in which it recognized the leading sales reps from across the country. As a reward for their efforts, the company sent the Toppers on all-expenses-paid vacations to places like Bermuda. There was fierce competition among sales districts, which Purdue encouraged. "Now is the time to cash in on the bonus earnings," a manager told the reps. "You have the knowledge. You have the tools. All you need is the hunger to make it to Toppers."

Among the dispersed national sales force, fantastical stories began to circulate about how much OxyContin some were selling, and bonuses of mythical proportions. There were stories about reps making six figures in a quarter. There was a tale about one rep in Myrtle Beach, South Carolina, who supposedly made $170,000 in three months. Within four years of the launch celebration at the Wigwam in Arizona, OxyContin hit $1 billion in sales, surpassing the quintessential blockbuster drug of that era, Viagra. Within five years of OxyContin's introduction, Purdue had more than doubled its sales force. In 2001, the company paid $40 million just in bonuses. Average annual bonuses for sales reps would climb to nearly a quarter of a million dollars, and the top reps earned much more. Eventually, Michael Friedman informed the Sacklers that the principal barrier to higher sales at this point was just "product supply." The company literally could not make OxyContin fast enough to sell it.

For Steven May, being an OxyContin rep felt like a dream come true. He was working hard and making a lot of money. He had a big Veterans Administration hospital in his region, and he marketed aggressively there, as well as in smaller communities around Virginia and West Virginia. He had been trained to urge doctors, relentlessly, to titrate up the dose of OxyContin, and he was incentivized to do so, because his bonus was based not on number of prescriptions but on dollar volume—so the higher the volume of OxyContin prescribed, the more he was paid. His sales were so brisk that one year the company sent him on an all-expenses-paid vacation to Hawaii.

One day in 2000, May drove to Lewisburg, a small city in West Virginia. There was a doctor there who had become one of his top prescribers, and he wanted to pay her a visit. But when he arrived, the doctor was ashen. A relative had just died, she explained. The girl had overdosed on OxyContin.

ANN HEDONIA

BARRY MEIER, AN INVESTIGATIVE reporter at *The New York Times*, got an intriguing tip one day in early 2001. At fifty, Meier was slight and balding, with rimless spectacles and restless eyes. He had about him a jittery energy that is not uncommon among big-league muck-rakers, his nose always twitching at the whiff of a story. Meier had grown up in and around New York City, the son of German Jews who fled to the United States in the 1930s. He was an old-school newspaper-man who spoke in a salty idiom that was rich in "fucks." But his route to the highest rungs of journalism was not a conventional one by the standards of the *Times*. Meier had dropped out of college at Syracuse just shy of graduating, at the height of the Vietnam War. He ended up drifting around the country, working odd jobs, and eventually stumbled into a position at an industry publication with the glamorous title *Floor Covering Weekly*. Meier liked this new gig. He found that writing came easily to him; in his beatnik phase, he had entertained the idea of becoming a novelist. He distinguished himself covering the floor-covering business, and before long he hopped to a bigger, better trade publication, *Chemical Week*.

It was at *Chemical Week* that Barry Meier began to nurture his im-pulse to investigate. As it turned out, he had a real talent for reporting. *Chemical Week* was an industry publication, which was read mostly by people in the industry. Yet here was Meier, not content to write boost-erish pablum, delving into the dirty secrets of the business as if he were Woodward and Bernstein. "I kept writing stories that drove the com-panies that were reading *Chemical Week* crazy," he recalled. But he had a supportive editor, a man named John Campbell who thought that their publication should aspire to be something more than a house organ. "I always enjoyed going through documents and old files and shit like that," Meier said. At one point, he was doing some reporting related to Dow Chemical, in the National Archives in Washington, when he came across old records indicating that during the Vietnam War, when Dow was producing the defoliant Agent Orange, in Midland, Michigan, chemicals had leached into the local groundwater. Meier started preparing a story, but Dow Chemical "hit the fucking roof," he said. A posse of executives flew to New York and met with John Campbell. They did everything they could to stop the article. But Campbell supported his writer and would not back down. After Meier's exposé ran in *Chemical Week, The Wall Street Journal* picked it up. Then the *Journal* offered him a job.

After several years of writing big investigative stories on environmental disasters and consumer safety scandals, Meier ended up taking a job at the *Times.* In the late 1990s, he was assigned to cover the litigation against big tobacco companies over the adverse health consequences of smoking. Generations of Americans had suffered and died from cancer and related illnesses caused by smoking, and it was now emerging that the tobacco companies had been aware of the risks associated with their products and had systematically downplayed the danger. In 1998, the companies agreed to a massive settlement with states that had brought lawsuits against them, for $206 billion. It was an epic story and an exhausting one to cover. But Meier always felt as if he had come onto it too late. "It was the kind of story where the glory was gone," he recalled. "The only thing left to do was not fuck up. I wasn't going to break this story. It was broken."

When the tobacco litigation was finally behind him, Meier was sitting at his desk in the *Times* newsroom on Forty-Third Street one day when an editor came by with a tip. He had gotten a call from a source in the Midwest who said there was a "hot new drug" on the street. It was the most popular drug going, but the crazy thing about it was that it was actually a prescription pharmaceutical that was being promoted as impossible to abuse.

"It's called OxyContin," the editor said.

Meier knew very little about the pharmaceutical industry. He looked up the name of the company that made the drug, Purdue Pharma. He'd never heard of them. Working with a colleague, he started making phone calls. What Meier discovered was that a lot of people seemed to be abusing OxyContin. The drug had been a big success with patients, easing terrible pain, but it was also being used recreationally and was said to deliver an intense and very pure high. In theory, the Contin coating on each pill was supposed to prevent users from experiencing the full force of the drug's narcotic payload right away. But people had figured out that if you crushed the pills—even if you just chewed them with your teeth—you could override the controlled-release mechanism and unleash a mammoth hit of pure oxycodone. It did not take much trial and error to make this discovery. In fact, each bottle came with a warning that, in retrospect, doubled as an inadvertent how-to: "Taking broken, chewed, or crushed OxyContin tablets could lead to the rapid release and absorption of a potentially toxic dose of oxycodone."

Meier spoke to law enforcement sources who described an active black market in OxyContin. He talked to pharmacists and doctors who testified to the aggressive marketing tactics of Purdue Pharma's sales force. "They're coming in and promoting this as non-abusable," one pharmacist told him. "But that's not tracking with what I'm seeing."

In November 2000, Michael Friedman warned colleagues that a reporter was "sniffing around the OxyContin abuse story." Mortimer Sackler added the matter of this apparent threat to the agenda for the company's next board meeting. In devising a plan for addressing any potential controversy, Michael Friedman suggested a strategy that "deflects attention away from the company owners."

On February 9, 2001, Meier and a colleague, Francis X. Clines, published a front-page story in the *Times,* "Cancer Painkillers Pose New Abuse Threat." It made no mention of the Sacklers, but it did paint an alarming picture: "Harried police detectives in dozens of rural areas in Eastern states are combating what they say is a growing wave of drug abuse involving a potent painkiller prescribed for terminal cancer patients and other people with severe pain." OxyContin, it turned out, was a hit not just in the licit marketplace but on the black market as well. "Once crushed, the drug can be snorted by addicts or dissolved for injection," Meier and Clines reported. They identified instances of abuse, overdoses, and illegal trafficking of OxyContin in Maine, Kentucky, Ohio, Pennsylvania, Virginia, West Virginia, and Maryland.

✢ ✢ ✢

By the time Barry Meier started writing about Purdue, the company had moved into new office space. Having outgrown the Norwalk headquarters, the Sacklers purchased a modern building in Stamford,

Connecticut, which overlooked Route 95. The design consisted of wide floors of varying sizes, clad in dark glass and stacked on top of one another in a shape that was reminiscent of a ziggurat—an ancient temple.

The atmosphere inside the company was giddy. "None of us, I think, thought it would become what it did," one former executive recalled, explaining that the company's sales pitch to doctors had gone over far better than anyone could have hoped. "We had to ramp up manufacturing," the executive continued. At Purdue's plant in Totowa, New Jersey, crews worked around the clock, cranking out pills. "We priced the drug hefty," the executive said, with satisfaction. "And it still sold."

If the initial success of OxyContin, and the boundless riches that it brought, had exceeded Richard Sackler's wildest dreams, he recalibrated those dreams pretty quickly. One day in 1999, Michael Friedman emailed Richard to inform him that the drug was now generating $20 million a week. Richard wrote back immediately, at midnight, that this was "not so great." They could do better. "Blah, humbug," he wrote. "Yawn."

Richard was appointed president of the company that year. His brother, Jonathan, and his cousins Kathe and the younger Mortimer were now vice presidents. The elder Mortimer and Raymond ("Dr. Mortimer" and "Dr. Raymond," as they were known inside the company, because there were so many "Dr. Sacklers" that it was necessary to use first names) were still involved as well, copied on emails and generally revered. "They are so spry and with it," one Purdue official marveled at the time. But, increasingly, the younger generation of Sacklers was now running the company. In the new building at One Stamford Forum, the family installed itself in the executive suite on the ninth floor. The rest of the building looked like a regular office complex, and only certain employees could even access the ninth floor. But it was its own special domain. The carpet was royal purple, and the atmosphere was clubby. "The lighting was different," one former Purdue employee who spent time on the ninth floor recalled. "There was art. It was all female assistants. It was like stepping back in time."

Richard's office was on the ninth floor, and Kathe, Jonathan, and Raymond had offices there, too. Raymond turned eighty in 2000 but still drove to work in his Jaguar every day. He still had lunch brought up to the executive dining room. Jonathan would occasionally eat an impromptu lunch with his father. But Richard, who was busier and less easygoing, would have his administrative assistant telephone Raymond's administrative assistant so the two of them could schedule lunch. Even though Richard was now the boss of the company, he could still behave, occasionally, like the little rich boy family scion, and he was not particularly well liked by the administrative staff. When he came to work, he would leave his car with one of the company's parking attendants, with instructions to fill it up with gas.

The company lawyer, Howard Udell, also had an office on the ninth floor. At this point, Udell had been working for the Sackler family for nearly four decades, and he was considered, in the words of one of his colleagues, "the heart and soul of the organization." Udell had grown very overweight, and at one point after the launch of OxyContin he had a heart attack. But he was as committed as ever to the family and the company, and he *believed* in OxyContin; for a time, when he was unwell, he took the drug himself. When this extraordinary product that had so changed the fortunes of the company came under assault, Udell assumed responsibility for orchestrating the damage control.

In the corridor outside Udell's office sat a woman I am going to call Martha West. She was a longtime legal secretary who had been working at Purdue since 1979. One day in 1999, Udell asked her to do some research into the abuse of OxyContin. "He asked me to go on the internet and go into the news groups," West would later recall. There were discussion boards online that were devoted to recreational drug use, and Udell wanted West to peruse them and "find out how they are misusing the product." When prompted to log in with a username, West employed a pseudonym, Ann Hedonia, a pun based on the word "anhedonia," which means the inability to feel pleasure. Lurking in the discussion groups, West found people talking about crushing OxyContin tablets, sucking the time-release coating off, snorting the drug, cooking it, shooting it with a hypodermic needle. She wrote a memo outlining her findings. According to subsequent testimony by Martha West, the memo was then circulated to numerous senior Purdue officials and to "all the Sacklers" who were then actively involved in the company.

Within Purdue, Howard Udell was regarded by many not just as a loyal stalwart bent on protecting the Sacklers but as a paragon of ethical conduct. "I loved Howard Udell," the senior executive who was involved in the OxyContin launch recalled. "Howard Udell was one of the most ethical people I knew." One of Udell's own sons, who was a federal prosecutor in New York, said that for his father being a lawyer wasn't so much a job as "a way of life." But as OxyContin's profits soared and the press began to cover stories about abuse of the drug, Martha West noticed that her boss was becoming increasingly secretive. It appeared that Udell had begun to worry about the prospects of litigation involving OxyContin. The company had already fought off a number of nettlesome lawsuits attempting to challenge its exclusive patent on the drug, and Richard Sackler and Udell shared a certain macho swagger when it came to this kind of legal scrap. They both proudly self-identified as counterpunchers. In 1996, Richard had proposed hiring a public relations firm to spread the word about their litigation successes "so that we are feared as a tiger with claws, teeth and balls."

In a message to a colleague, Udell acknowledged that the company had "picked up references to abuse of our opioid products on the internet." But he appears to have made efforts to limit any written record of concern within Purdue that the company's wonder drug was being misused. When sales reps from across the country started including in their call notes the conversations they were having with doctors and pharmacists about stories of addiction and abuse, Udell issued instructions that call notes were to be short and to the point: if people encountered issues, they should not put them in writing. Around this time, he also mentioned to West that he was developing a new email program that would automatically destroy all emails after three months. He called it "Disappearing Ink." The idea sounded a bit fantastical, even paranoid. Udell was an attorney, not an inventor. But sure enough, he ended up applying for a patent for a "self-destructing document and email messaging system." (According to Kathe Sackler, "It didn't really work.")

Udell shared with the Sacklers an abiding faith in the chemical wizardry of OxyContin. He simply could not bring himself to believe that the drug might actually be dangerous. In fact, his faith in the painkiller was so sincere that when he noticed Martha West limping in the office one day, and learned that she had been struggling with back pain related to an injury she had sustained in a car accident, Udell said, "We got to get you on OxyContin." He set her up with a referral from someone in the medical department at Purdue, and she went to see a local pain specialist in Connecticut. The doctor wrote Martha West a prescription for a bottle of OxyContin, and she started taking it.

✢　✢　✢

The truth was that well before Martha West wrote her memo, something was happening. Nobody could say precisely where or how it started, but the first hints of it cropped up in rural Maine, in the rust belt of western Pennsylvania and eastern Ohio, in the Appalachian areas of Virginia, West Virginia, and Kentucky. The abuse spread, quickly, like some airborne virus, from one small community to the next. The regions where the problem began often had large numbers of people who were out of work, or who worked hard, manual-labor jobs, people who were disabled or chronically ill, people who were suffering from pain. As it happened, these were also precisely the kinds of regions that Steven May and other Purdue sales reps had targeted—regions that the IMS data told them would be fertile terrain for OxyContin. In some cases, these communities also happened to have long-standing problems with prescription drug abuse. In some parts of Appalachia, people would pair an OxyContin with a Valium—one of Richard Sackler's pills and one of his uncle Arthur's. They called this "the Cadillac high."

Soon, pain patients were "doctor shopping," seeking appointments with multiple different physicians and stockpiling prescriptions, selling pills or sharing them with friends, sometimes dealing to feed their own habit. Black-market pills sold for a dollar a milligram, and suddenly everyone was a dealer, a shadow OxyContin sales force that would come to dwarf Purdue's own. Some communities began to resemble a zombie movie, as the phenomenon claimed one citizen after another, sending previously well-adjusted, functioning adults into a spiral of dependence and addiction. You could spot them out and about, pillheads, fiending outside the mini-mall, or nodding off in a parked car, a toddler bawling in the backseat. For all Purdue's instructions to the sales team to avoid using words like "powerful" when describing OxyContin, it was a fiercely potent narcotic, and that was part of the appeal, for the user, but also part of the danger. An overdose could induce respiratory failure: you fall into a sleep so deep and blissful that you stop breathing. At small hospitals, patients were being admitted close to death. In trailers and dingy apartments and remote farmhouses, police and paramedics would arrive to a familiar scene—the OxyContin overdose—and set about trying to revive the user.

In February 2000, the top federal prosecutor in Maine, Jay McCloskey, sent a letter to thousands of doctors across the state, warning them about the increasing dangers of abuse and "diversion" of OxyContin. Howard Udell, when he learned of McCloskey's letter, was dismissive. He derided McCloskey as "some overly zealous prosecutor with political ambition" who was just "trying to grab a headline." But this was a federal official, raising the alarm about a drug that was now generating $1 billion a year. So, several months later, Udell flew to Maine, along with Michael Friedman, to meet with McCloskey personally. The prosecutor was concerned about increasingly rampant abuse of Oxy-Contin. Kids were taking the drug, he said. Bright kids. It was ruining their lives. He found it a little strange that his small state had now become one of the highest consumers of OxyContin, per capita, in the nation. McCloskey mentioned the jumbo 160-milligram pills. "One of the doctors up here told me that one of these tablets could kill a kid if swallowed," he said. "Is that so?"

"Probably," Udell and Friedman acknowledged.

The meeting was frosty. When it was over, Udell said to Friedman, "We've got to figure out how to deal with this."

One way that the company chose to deal with McCloskey was to claim that it was only after he wrote his letter in 2000 that anyone at Purdue became aware of abuse problems related to OxyContin. Richard Sackler himself would later testify under oath that the first time he ever heard of OxyContin being diverted or abused was "early in the year 2000." This was not true. In fact, Purdue had been receiving notes from its own sales force, dating as far back as 1997, not long after the initial launch of OxyContin, informing the company that abuse was happening. Because they were dispersed throughout the country, in pain clinics and family practices and pharmacies and hospitals, the sales reps were like an early warning system, the eyes and ears of the Sacklers. Like Steven May learning about the girl who overdosed in West Virginia, the reps heard about these incidents. Years later, when investigators searched through field reports filed by Purdue reps between 1997 and 1999, they would find hundreds of references to words like "street value," "snort," and "crush." In November 1999, one Florida rep wrote to an official at Purdue, "I feel like we have a credibility issue with our product. Many physicians now think 'OxyContin' is obviously the street drug all the drug addicts are seeking." That same year, a Purdue official forwarded Richard an email describing the ways in which people were abusing the drug: "The best ones for snorting are the 40-milligram ones cuz you're not snorting lots of filler."

To Richard, stories about abuse and addiction were initially easy to dismiss. "I was trained as a physician," he would later explain. "In my statistics, an 'N of 1' is called the index case, and it might alert you to look for more, or be responsive to more. But I was trained not to chase what could be random events." This was a characteristic Richard response, ostentatiously clinical and cerebral on the surface while also masking a deeper emotional reaction. Richard was so closely invested in OxyContin that he could not abide any suggestion that the drug might be addictive. As early as 1997, he had been sensitive to concerns about the addictive properties of the painkiller, warning that health insurance providers might cite concerns over addiction "to 'just say no'" to OxyContin and that such objections must be "obliterated."

So, McCloskey's letter in 2000 did not, by any stretch, represent the first time that Richard or other senior officials at Purdue became aware of a problem. Rather, McCloskey's intervention marked the point at which the problem had become so widespread that it was no longer possible to feign ignorance. In the spring of 2000, Michael Friedman emailed Richard about an "OxyContin Thief" who was hitting pharmacies in Ohio. "We had the story out of Maine and the one from Florida, but they are isolated," Friedman wrote. "The Ohio situation is almost every month."

"I hate this," Richard replied. "This will feed on itself." Why does the guy just want OxyContin? Richard wondered. Does he not steal "other opioids"?

Having marketed its drug as superior to other painkillers, in an effort to "bury" the competition, Purdue was now facing the consequences. "Eventually, these stories will appear in every state," a Purdue sales official pointed out in an internal email a few weeks later. In January 2001, a sales executive named Russell Gasdia attended a meeting at a high school in Gadsden, Alabama, that was put together by mothers who had lost children to overdoses of OxyContin. "Statements were made that OxyContin sales were at the expense of dead children," he reported to Richard afterward. Some participants had said that "the only difference between heroin and OxyContin is that you can get OxyContin from a doctor."

The following month, the younger Mortimer shared a press article with Richard which noted that there had been fifty-nine deaths related to OxyContin in a single state. Richard Sackler responded to the article in an email, "This is not too bad. It could have been far worse."

In the initial months and years after OxyContin's release, Purdue had received so many letters from patients who thanked the company for doing a noble thing, for restoring comfort and mobility and agency to lives that had been decimated by pain. The Sacklers and their executives had been understandably proud of these letters. But now a very different kind of letter was arriving on the ninth floor of Purdue headquarters in Stamford. "My son was only 28 years old when he died from OxyContin on New Year's Day," a bereaved mother wrote to the company. "We all miss him very much, his wife especially on Valentine's Day. Why would a company make a product that strong (80 and 160 mg) when they know they will kill young people? My son had a bad back and could have taken Motrin but his Dr. started him on Vicodin, then OxyContin... Now he is dead!"

At a certain point, even Richard Sackler was forced to concede that each isolated tale of grief was no mere N of 1. "[We] need a strategy to contain this," one company PR executive declared. And Richard had one.

✢   ✢   ✢

Arthur Sackler rarely spoke about the toll of addiction and abuse associated with the tranquilizers that made him rich. But when he did, he made a telling distinction. People did abuse these drugs, Arthur conceded. But the real explanation for this phenomenon was not any intrinsically addictive properties of the drugs themselves. Rather, it was a reflection of the addictive personalities of the users. As evidence emerged that OxyContin was being abused, Richard Sackler adopted a similar view. He had birthed into the world an unprecedented pharmaceutical product, a pill that could restore some form of normalcy to millions of lives while delivering untold billions to the Sackler family. It had now become undeniable that the drug was causing some people to overdose and die. But the *drug* wasn't the problem, Richard contended. The problem was the abusers. What Purdue should do, he decreed, was "hammer on the abusers in every way possible." They are "the culprits," he declared. "They are reckless criminals."

Following Richard's lead, this became the official message that the company promoted to the outside world, and also to its own workforce. As news coverage of the scourge of OxyContin intensified, Purdue told its staff that this was nothing but a misguided media narrative. "Most employees felt that we were doing the correct thing, the best thing for people that were seeking relief from pain," Gary Ritchie, who worked at Purdue as a scientist from 1993 to 2003, recalled. "The abuse problem came from users who believed that it was a substitute for other illegal drugs."

According to this thesis, the real victim of the emerging crisis wasn't some addict who, of her own free will, chose to crush and snort an FDA-approved drug. The real victim was Purdue Pharma. "We are losing sales because physicians have become scared or intimidated from press reports," Michael Friedman complained to the *Hartford Courant* in 2001. In truth, the company's sales were soaring. When Purdue officials spoke about "diversion" of their product, they meant diversion from the realm of doctor-prescribed licit commerce to the underground pill market. But there was no illicit *manufacturing* of OxyContin. Every single Oxy 40 or Oxy 80 that was floating around in the secondary market had initially been produced and sold by Purdue Pharma.

In some ways, Richard's argument about OxyContin mirrored the libertarian position of a firearms manufacturer who insists that he bears no responsibility for gun deaths. Guns don't kill people; people kill people. It is a peculiar hallmark of the American economy that you can produce a dangerous product and effectively off-load any legal liability for whatever destruction that product may cause by pointing to the individual responsibility of the consumer. "Abusers aren't victims," Richard said. "They are the victimizers."

There were a number of problems with this hypothesis, but the most significant flaw was that not everyone who developed a problem with OxyContin started out as a recreational abuser. In fact, many people who were prescribed the drug for legitimate pain conditions and took it precisely as the doctor ordered found that they, too, had become hopelessly addicted. In 2002, a twenty-nine-year-old New Jersey woman named Jill Skolek was prescribed OxyContin for a back injury. One night, after four months on the drug, she died in her sleep from respiratory arrest, leaving behind a six-year-old son. Her mother, Marianne Skolek, was a nurse. Distraught and bewildered, she became convinced that OxyContin was dangerous. Skolek wrote to FDA officials, demanding that they do something about Purdue's aggressive marketing of the drug. At one point, she attended a conference on addiction at Columbia University, where Robin Hogen, a Purdue public relations man, was one of the presenters. Hogen had sandy hair and an Ivy League affect; he wore a pin-striped suit and a bow tie. With a breezy confidence, he informed Skolek that she seemed to have misunderstood the circumstances of her own daughter's death. The drug wasn't the problem, Hogen said. The problem was Jill, her daughter. "We think she abused drugs," he said. (Hogen subsequently apologized.)

One reason that some patients were becoming hooked on OxyContin might have been Purdue's own claims about how the drug would provide twelve-hour relief. The truth was that the dangers of OxyContin were intrinsic to the drug—and Purdue knew it. The time-release formula meant that, in principle, patients could safely ingest one giant dose every twelve hours. But internal Purdue documents tell a different story: even before the company received FDA approval, it was aware that not all patients who took OxyContin were achieving twelve-hour relief. In fact, the first patients to use OxyContin, in a study overseen and paid for by Purdue, were ninety women recovering from surgery in Puerto Rico. Roughly half of the women ended up requiring more medication before the twelve-hour mark.

For Purdue, the business reason for obscuring such results was clear. The claim of twelve-hour relief was an invaluable marketing tool. The company built a whole advertising campaign around an image of two little paper dosage cups—suggesting, to people suffering from pain, that with OxyContin they would not need to be dosing every four hours, as they did with other painkillers, and could sleep through the night without interruption. But prescribing a pill on a twelve-hour schedule when, for many patients, it works for only eight is a recipe for withdrawal and precisely the sorts of "peaks and troughs" that Purdue's sales reps claimed OxyContin avoided. It is a recipe, in other words, for addiction.

Many people who were prescribed OxyContin found themselves experiencing withdrawal symptoms between doses. In fact, if anybody at the company had looked closely at those appreciative letters they received from grateful patients, they might have noticed that in many instances the letter writers described taking OxyContin more than twice a day, because, as one letter suggested, the drug seems "to level off for me after 8 hours." When reps called on physicians, they would hear about patients who were on prescriptions for three pills a day. "As a salesperson, you're saying, holy shit, it's supposed to be every twelve hours," a Louisiana rep named Dodd Davis, who worked for Purdue from 1999 to 2002, recalled. "But that's another dose in the middle of the day, so that's more pills, more money for me. So you'd say, 'You know, Doc, I can't speak to off-label prescribing. But I can tell you, you're not the first person that's had to do it.'"

✤   ✤   ✤

By 2001, the company knew that 20 percent of all OxyContin prescriptions were being written on a more frequent dosing schedule than twelve hours. An internal document, highlighting this phenomenon, noted, "These numbers are very scary." In March that year, a Purdue employee emailed a supervisor, describing some data on the issue of withdrawal and wondering whether to write up the results, because doing so might "add to the current negative press." The supervisor responded, "I would not write it up at this point." In July, the FDA announced that it had directed Purdue to amend the packaging of Oxy-Contin with a so-called black box—the agency's most severe warning to indicate the life-threatening risks of a drug.

One patient who was struggling with OxyContin was Howard Udell's own legal secretary, Martha West. In a 2004 deposition, West explained that after she started taking the drug for her back pain, "I found that it didn't work for the length of period that it was supposed to." She was only meant to take one pill every twelve hours, but she found that the pain would return hours before it was time for her next dose. "If I wanted enough relief, you know, instant relief, enough to go to work so I could go to work and function through the day, I had to make it immediate release," she said. And having done her research, as Ann Hedonia, in those internet forums, she knew precisely how to do this. Before heading in to work at her desk outside Howard Udell's office on the ninth floor at Purdue, with its regal purple carpet, Martha West would crush one of her OxyContin pills and snort it.

✤   ✤   ✤

After publishing his first big piece on OxyContin, Barry Meier stayed on the story. Smaller newspapers around the country had already been covering the fallout from OxyContin, particularly in the regions that had been hardest hit. But Meier brought a level of national attention to the issue that it had not received before. He might have come to the tobacco story too late to break it, but he got onto the OxyContin story very early, and he was shocked by what he learned. "Unlike many drug companies that are publicly traded, Purdue Pharma is privately held and part of a network of concerns founded by three brothers, Arthur, Mortimer and Raymond Sackler," Meier wrote in a follow-up story in March 2001. "The company is now run by the son of Dr. Raymond Sackler, Dr. Richard Sackler." He asked to speak to the Sacklers about the unfolding crisis involving their drug. They refused.

Instead, the company put forth its PR representative Robin Hogen, along with a pain specialist who worked for Purdue named David Haddox. A former dentist who had retrained as a pain doctor, Haddox was a curious spokesman, an intense, caustic, arrogant man, with spectacles and a salt-and-pepper beard. He liked to inform people, as if to establish his bona fides, that he came from Appalachia himself. "I grew up among the mining communities of West Virginia," he would say. "I did not have to go to medical school to learn about pain. I've seen the effects of pain on injured miners and their families since I was a young boy."

Like Richard Sackler and Howard Udell, Haddox was a true believer. OxyContin was, in his view, entirely beyond reproach—a magnificent gift that the Sacklers had bestowed upon humanity that was now being sullied by a nihilistic breed of hillbilly pill poppers. Haddox once likened OxyContin to a vegetable, saying, "If I gave you a stalk of celery and you ate that, it would be healthy. But if you put it in a blender and tried to shoot it into your veins, it would not be good." To Barry Meier, he said that any overdose deaths attributed to OxyContin "typically involved multiple factors, like alcohol," and warned that any "exaggeration" of the abuse problem might create undue obstacles for legitimate pain patients who were seeking the drug. If any pain patients happened to find themselves becoming addicted, Haddox offered no apologies. "A lot of these people say, 'Well, I was taking my medicine like my doctor told me to,' and then they start taking more and more and more," he told the Associated Press in 2001. "I don't see where that's my problem."

Haddox had an answer for everything. It was true, he allowed, that patients who were prescribed the drug tended to build up a tolerance to it, and it was not unusual for some patients who had been using Oxy-Contin to find that they were experiencing symptoms of withdrawal—such as itching, nausea, or the shakes—before the twelve-hour dosing cycle was over. This was not actually addiction, Haddox argued, but mere physical dependence, which is different. In fact, he coined a term, "pseudo-addiction," which Purdue started to incorporate into its promotional literature. As one pamphlet distributed by the company explained, pseudo-addiction "seems similar to addiction, but is due to unrelieved pain." A misunderstanding of this subtle phenomenon might lead doctors to "inappropriately stigmatize the patient with the label 'addict.'" But pseudo-addiction generally stops once the pain is relieved, the pamphlet continued, "often through an increase in opioid dose." If you're experiencing withdrawal between doses, the company suggested, the answer is to *increase the dose*. Haddox's clinical solution just happened to dovetail with the marketing imperative that Purdue had issued to its sales force: urge doctors to titrate up.

If this distinction between addiction and pseudo-addiction could be construed as self-serving, it was also, clearly, more semantic than clinical. If you are going into bouts of agonizing withdrawal between doses of a drug, what you choose to call the aching dependence that takes hold of you is somewhat beside the point. "There's no difference," Martha West said of her own blossoming addiction to OxyContin. "You get sick when you stop taking it... 'Addicted' or 'dependent.' Whatever you want to call it. Same problem. You can't stop taking it."

After Meier's initial story, he received a message one day from a company insider who wanted to talk. They arranged to meet at a diner in the city of White Plains, a short drive north of Manhattan. The insider, a sales rep, was nervous about speaking to Meier, even on deep background, but also very upset about what was happening at the company. The rep would not give Meier a name, and to this day, decades later, Meier will not divulge even the gender of his source. The insider took something out of a bag. It was a piece of ruled notebook paper, and on it was a handwritten list of names. There were ten of them, all salespeople for Purdue. At the top of the sheet, the insider had written "Toppers." It was the top ten sales reps in the country. Next to the name of each rep was the name of a place—his or her sales region. Look up those regions, the source told Meier: every district that is represented on that list is a "hot spot" for OxyContin abuse.

Meier was astonished. It was an obvious idea, once you stopped to think about it, but he hadn't stopped to think about it until that moment: Purdue knew, down to the last pill, where its drug was selling the most. The whole "Toppers" compensation scheme, with the jumbo bonuses and the tropical vacations, was premised on a detailed map of where in the country the company was moving product. But what if you superimposed that map onto the map that law enforcement and public health officials were beginning to draw of the townships and counties with the most emergency room visits, the most pharmacy break-ins, the most overdoses and deaths?

Meier decided to write a story about the sales region of the number one rep on the list, a man named Eric K. Wilson, whose territory was Myrtle Beach, South Carolina. As it turned out, Myrtle Beach was home to a number of "pill mills." These pain clinics, which were run by physicians who were either unscrupulous or impossibly naive, had cropped up across the country to satisfy the demand for OxyContin and other painkillers by issuing prescriptions to almost anyone who asked for one. At Comprehensive Care, a strip-mall clinic in Eric Wilson's territory, there was often a line out the door, with fifteen or twenty people waiting for prescriptions, and cars with out-of-state license plates jammed in the parking lot from morning until night.

On a reporting trip to Myrtle Beach, Meier learned that local pharmacists and law enforcement officials had warned Purdue Pharma about the clinic but the company had done nothing about it. On the contrary, Purdue's sales in the district had surged by more than $1 million in a single quarter, the highest increase of any district in the country. In response to Meier's inquiries, the company issued a statement saying, "It is not unusual for the volume of prescriptions for OxyContin and other pain medications to change significantly from quarter to quarter." When Meier reached Robin Hogen, the company spokesman, to ask about the huge volume of pills that were being sold in the area, Hogen was dismissive. "Oh, there are a lot of old people living in Myrtle Beach, and they have pain," he told Meier. "They have arthritis. So it's only natural." Purdue saw no particular cause for concern when it came to Comprehensive Care. But the Drug Enforcement Administration did and shut the clinic down, suspending the narcotics licenses of six doctors who worked there, because they posed an "immediate danger to public health and safety." To Meier, an awful irony was beginning to emerge. Officially, Purdue might be "hammering the abusers," as Richard Sackler had ordered. But the only way to understand what was happening in a place like Myrtle Beach was that the sales figures were so high *because* of the abuse.

✢ ✢ ✢

After the terrorist attacks of September 11, 2001, a Purdue sales executive recorded a voice mail to send to the entire national sales force in which he acknowledged that it had been a tragic day but pointed out that, on the upside, at least this would knock OxyContin out of the headlines for a while. Barry Meier lived five blocks from the World Trade Center and witnessed the moment when the first plane hit the North Tower. He was traumatized. But, as the rest of the paper geared up to cover the aftermath of the attacks, Meier wanted to continue writing about OxyContin. What interested him about the story, he found, was not the illicit side: the dealers and the pillheads and the police stings were important, to be sure, but only up to a point. What fascinated Meier was that people were now dying in considerable numbers, and it seemed to be a function not just of the underground drug market but of this putatively legitimate business, which was raking in billions of dollars and operated out of a sleek office building in Stamford. He started to look into the Sackler family and was startled to learn about the position that they occupied in philanthropic circles and the ways in which the Sackler name had become a byword for generosity in the arts and the sciences. When he wrote to Purdue with some pointed questions about the family, the company responded with a threatening legal letter.

As the negative publicity continued to swirl around OxyContin, Richard Sackler was privately seething. "The whole thing is a sham," a sympathetic friend reassured him. If people die because they abuse the drug, "then good riddance."

"Unfortunately, when I'm ambushed by *60 Minutes,* I can't easily get this concept across," Richard replied. He had no doubts about what exactly was going on, but that didn't mean he could just come out and say it. "Calling drug addicts 'scum of the earth' will guarantee that I become the poster child for liberals" who want to "distribute the blame to someone else," he complained.

Richard never made any connection, at least not publicly, between the sort of hateful rhetoric he employed to describe people who suffered from addiction and the secret drug-related tragedy of his own cousin Bobby Sackler. But as it happened, one of those drug addicts that he so vilified worked just a few feet away from Richard, outside Howard Udell's office on the ninth floor.

"At some point, I became addicted to OxyContin," Martha West later testified. "I was starting to unravel." She had quit drinking eight years earlier, but now she started again. "Once the Oxy is out of your system, you start going into narcotics withdrawal," she continued, and one symptom of the withdrawal was back pain. "I didn't know that's what was causing it," she said, so she just took more pills. "I thought my condition was getting worse, and it—it turns out it wasn't. It was the medication that was making it seem that way."

Gradually, her judgment started to slip. She did stupid things. Dangerous things. She started trying other drugs. At one point, she found herself in Bridgeport, buying cocaine. Eventually, she was fired by Purdue. After twenty-one years at the company, she was let go for "poor work performance" and escorted out of the building by security. When she asked one of the lawyers at the company if she could come back to retrieve some personal files from her computer, the lawyer said that her hard drive had been erased, so there was nothing left to retrieve.

Martha West eventually sued Purdue, though the suit never went anywhere. When she was deposed in a separate lawsuit against the company, in 2004, she told the story of how Howard Udell had asked her to prepare the memo on the ways in which OxyContin was being abused. She had a very distinct memory of having written the memo, but in discovery attorneys were not able to find it in Purdue's files. The existence of the memo was subsequently confirmed, however, by a Justice Department investigation, and by Purdue Pharma itself. West's memo had been dated June 1, 1999, and described "numerous discussions of misuse and abuse of Purdue products, in particular, OC." In the deposition, she also recalled the moment when she learned that Purdue was planning to produce a 160-milligram OxyContin pill. "They are killing themselves with the 80s," West wrote to Udell. "Why would we come out with a 160?"

According to West, as soon as Udell received her email, he stormed out of his office and said, "What are you doing? If this ever comes out in discovery we are screwed." So she deleted the email, and presumably so did he. (Purdue ended up pulling the 160-milligram pill from the market in the spring of 2001.)

The company's handling of Martha West closely mirrored Richard Sackler's general attitude toward the abuse of OxyContin. While Purdue did not deny that she had become addicted to the drug, company lawyers suggested that she was an individual with a problem. Purdue obtained her health records, and a lawyer questioned her about her history of addiction. Was OxyContin not just the latest entry in a litany of substances she had abused? The company got hold of hospital records and confronted her with them during the deposition, reading aloud notes that were made after she was admitted: "Patient is completely focused on revenge concerning her termination from work . . . obsessive screaming on how to get back at them, plans millions of ways to humiliate this company, including her suing them, buying them out, and firing everyone she knows."

West was, by her own admission, a damaged, unstable person, and Purdue now painted her as an irresponsible, vengeful fabulist—precisely the sort of person that Richard Sackler would describe as the "scum of the earth."

"I was angry at the time," West acknowledged, stunned and embarrassed to hear her private medical records read back to her. "People say stupid things when they are angry." It was ludicrous, obviously, for her to have thought that she, a lowly legal secretary with a drug problem, would ever stand a chance against the Sacklers and Purdue. "*Yeah*. I am going to buy the company," she said wryly. "I don't think so."

Chapter 19

THE PABLO ESCOBAR OF THE NEW MILLENNIUM

ON THE LAST TUESDAY in August 2001, a subcommittee of the U.S. House of Representatives gathered for an unusual hearing in a municipal building in Bensalem, a small township in Bucks County, Pennsylvania. The hearing had been convened by a Pennsylvania congressman, James Greenwood, who chaired the subcommittee on oversight and investigations of the House Energy and Commerce Committee. He had asked his colleagues to make the trip from Washington just before Labor Day weekend to hold a discussion about the impact of OxyContin in a community where that impact had been felt. A local osteopath named Richard Paolino had recently been arrested after it was revealed that he was running a massive pill mill out of his practice. Michael Friedman from Purdue Pharma had been asked to testify and had arrived, along with Howard Udell and a thin man with a mustache and a professorial air named Paul Goldenheim, the company's chief medical officer.

This had become a familiar ritual for the trio. Richard Sackler might have been running Purdue, and he might have felt great personal pride and satisfaction in having made OxyContin such a success, but he had no desire to be the public face of his company. He gave no interviews, issued no statements, made no public appearances. Instead, he deputized Friedman, Udell, and Goldenheim to hit the road, speaking to worried officials, addled police chiefs, and bereaved parents. The men could avail themselves of a well-rehearsed roster of talking points, from which they almost never deviated. In fact, it didn't matter who was speaking; their public statements were interchangeable, because they often read from the same text. "We are more distressed than anyone at hearing that our product, which is providing so much relief to so many people, is being abused," Friedman told the panel of lawmakers that day. "While all of the voices in this debate are important, we must be especially careful to listen to the voices of patients who, without drugs like OxyContin, would be left suffering from their untreated or inadequately treated pain." Some fifty million Americans suffer from chronic pain, Friedman continued. "They are not addicts. They are not criminals," he said. "They are people who, because of cancer, sickle cell anemia, severe back injuries, or some other physical insult or disease, have had their lives taken away from them by unrelenting pain."

During the seventeen years that Friedman had worked with Howard Udell, the two men had become close friends. They often vacationed together with their wives. During workdays, they were constantly connected, emailing back and forth on their BlackBerrys. Since late 2000, they had been traveling together in a road show to defend their drug and persuade public officials to not do anything to jeopardize the availability of OxyContin. Goldenheim rounded out the team. He was impressively credentialed, having been educated at Harvard Medical School and served as clinical director of the Pulmonary Unit at Massachusetts General Hospital. (Richard Sackler had personally hired him; according to his former colleague Bart Cobert, Richard was "enamored of Harvard.") Goldenheim's medical credentials were useful to the company in projecting an image of Hippocratic virtue. In one advertisement that Purdue placed in newspapers as the addiction crisis blossomed, he appeared in a photograph dressed in a white coat, like a man playing a doctor at a costume party.

This was Richard Sackler's brain trust. Privately, the three men shared a swashbuckling, macho banter. Goldenheim would say things to Friedman like "We have a tiger by the tail and I wonder if we should add more muscle. Let's discuss over live sushi!" But when they went out to talk about OxyContin in public, their posture was different: they were serious and ashen, projecting an air of sober earnestness. Purdue understood the problem, they insisted. In fact, nobody was doing more to *address* the problem than the good people at Purdue Pharma. This was a crisis, no question. But, as the Purdue executives explained, it was really a law enforcement problem. Criminal drug abusers were diverting and misusing their product, and Purdue was cooperating closely with law enforcement. The company had produced new "tamperproof" prescription pads and issued them, free of charge, to health-care providers, which in theory might stop people from making fraudulent edits to legitimate prescriptions in order to obtain irresponsible quantities of the drug. Friedman, Goldenheim, and Udell also suggested that Oxy-Contin should not be singled out, that to the degree people were dying from OxyContin overdoses, that was just a symptom of a much broader national trend involving the abuse of prescription drugs. The company sponsored an advertising campaign to tell teens not to raid their parents' medicine cabinets.

In his testimony before the committee, Friedman maintained that Purdue was completely blameless and that the sudden spike in abuse, crime, and death could in no way be attributed to the company's campaign to "de-stigmatize" opioids and push OxyContin. "Purdue's marketing efforts for OxyContin have been conservative by any standard," Friedman insisted. The company did not accept the premise that "aggressive marketing played any role whatsoever in the abuse and diversion of OxyContin."

This was a central feature of Purdue's effort to defend itself: just as there was no link between the intrinsic properties of the pill and the fact that people became addicted to it, there was also no connection between the marketing juggernaut that Richard Sackler had unleashed to sell OxyContin and the range of social ills that followed. The company had no way of predicting in advance that abuse might be a problem with OxyContin, Friedman testified. In seventeen years of marketing its predecessor drug, MS Contin, he said, "Purdue was aware of no unusual experience of abuse or diversion." And even after OxyContin was released in 1996, the company saw no indications of any problems whatsoever for the first four years. "It was early in April of 2000 that Purdue was first alerted to reports of abuse and diversion of OxyContin by accounts in Maine newspapers," Friedman said.

This, too, had become a standard talking point in Purdue's defense. It was also, quite simply, a lie. It was true that in early 2000 it had become unsustainable for Purdue to pretend that it was not aware of a problem, after Jay McCloskey, the U.S. Attorney in Maine, issued his letter warning doctors about OxyContin. But the company had known prior to that letter, for *years*, that the pill was being widely abused. There was the 1999 memo about abuse that Martha West had written for Howard Udell, who sat alongside Michael Friedman now as he testified. That memo had also gone to Friedman. But long before that, a chorus of Purdue's own sales reps had been informing the company of the horror stories they were hearing about addiction and abuse, and they had memorialized these alarm signals in their call notes. The company clearly knew that there was a problem, virtually from the beginning. As early as October 1997, one senior Purdue executive had emailed another, cc'ing Michael Friedman, to report that the number of mentions of OxyContin on internet sites and chat rooms was "enough to keep a person busy all day," adding that the company had "three people" monitoring the traffic.

But none of the members of Congress who had come to Pennsylvania for the hearing that day knew any of this. It would seem that a decision must have been made, internally, at Purdue headquarters in Stamford, to rewrite the timeline and assert that the company had no inkling of any problems before 2000. Indeed, in an email to Richard Sackler on February 16, 2001, Friedman had written, "I think that it is imperative that we get our story absolutely straight and consistent." The lawmakers didn't realize it, but in making his statement about the timing under oath, Friedman appeared to be perjuring himself. Goldenheim, in separate testimony before a U.S. Senate committee chaired by Ted Kennedy, told the same lie, also under oath.

Nor was it merely the timing that they lied about. One recurring theme in the company's defense was the suggestion that Purdue had never encountered any problems with MS Contin, either. But this, too, was far from true. In May 1996, an employee sent Richard Sackler and Howard Udell a press report describing the abuse potential associated with users extracting the morphine from MS Contin tablets. In March 1997, Robert Kaiko emailed Mortimer Sackler, Richard Sackler, Friedman, Goldenheim, and Udell to inform them that in New Zealand, MS Contin had become "the most common source of parenterally abused morphine/heroin." In March 1998, Udell sent a memo to Friedman, as well as Mortimer, Raymond, Richard, and a handful of other Sacklers, attaching an article from *The Ottawa Citizen* that described how MS Contin had become a street drug in Canada with enough prevalence to have earned a nickname—"purple peelers." (According to *another* press account, which also circulated among the Purdue executives, the pills were known as peelers "because addicts peel off the coating designed for the medication's slow release," and the pills are "crushed, mixed with water, heated on a spoon and then injected.") In an internal memo from January 1999, Udell acknowledged to Friedman and others that the company had been tracking references to abuse of both MS Contin and OxyContin online.

But for the moment, Representative Greenwood knew none of this. He had no reason to believe that the delegation from Purdue would be anything less than straightforward with him, and he was cordial and gracious, at pains not to make Friedman or his colleagues feel as though the committee were treating them like criminals. "Look, we stipulate— *I* stipulate—yours is a good company with a long and exemplary record," Greenwood said. "And I believe that your product and your company has done, by orders of magnitude, more to relieve pain in this country than to cause it." He reassured Friedman, "You are not on trial here."

Then Greenwood asked an apparently simple question: "What does your company know about how many prescriptions each physician writes for your OxyContin?"

"We do acquire data very much along the lines that you describe," Friedman said. "IMS Health captures this data through the computers at pharmacies," he explained.

"Okay. Now when you have that data, I would guess that one of the things that you would do with that data is arrange it so that you can rank these physicians. You have some indication as to who is writing the most, who is writing the least, and in between," Greenwood said. "Do you look at that information in that way?"

"Yes," Friedman replied.

Then Greenwood mentioned Richard Paolino, the rural osteopath who had just been busted for writing thousands of OxyContin prescriptions. Paolino must have been an "outlier," Greenwood pointed out, a man with a small practice who "without any regard whatsoever for the medical condition of the patients, wrote these prescriptions as fast as he could, purely for profit-making purposes." But wouldn't Purdue have known? Wouldn't they have seen that unusual volume of prescriptions in the IMS data? "I would hope that he would have stuck out like a sore thumb and that there must be *other* Dr. Paolinos in this country who do the same," Greenwood said, adding that "your company would be aware of that kind of information." What Greenwood wanted to know, he said to Friedman, is how does your company respond to that, when you see a doctor who "is just a little osteopath here in Bensalem, doing this vast number? What do you *do* with that information?"

"We don't measure or assess how well a physician practices medicine," Friedman said, evasively. "We are not in the office with a physician and a patient observing the examination or involved in that process. We know, for example—"

"Well, why do you want that information then?" Greenwood interrupted. Then he answered his own question. "You want to see how successful your marketing techniques are."

"Sure," Friedman replied.

But if Purdue was using the data to calibrate its marketing, Greenwood pointed out, then it should also have been able to use that data to track abuse. "Why wouldn't you have been using this data to make sure that the Dr. Paolinos of the world weren't wrecking the reputation of your product?"

Friedman was floundering, so Howard Udell intervened. He was not a physically graceful man, but now he pulled his chair up to the microphone and took over. "You can't look at prescriptions alone," Udell said. The raw number of prescriptions is not an indication of whether the doctor is practicing medicine appropriately, he insisted. "You have to look at what the doctor is actually doing in the office."

Not true, Greenwood responded. A local pharmacist in Pennsylvania had taken one look at the rough data, "and he saw, from his perspective—he looked at that data and he said, 'Holy God, there is some guy in Bensalem called Paolino, and he is writing prescriptions out the wazoo!'"

"Yes," Udell said.

"Now, he had that data. And he blew the whistle."

"Correct."

"And you had that data. What did you do?"

✢ ✢ ✢

There was probably a moment, early on, when the Sackler family could have chosen to respond differently to the unfolding crisis surrounding OxyContin. The family could have paused the aggressive marketing of the drug, halting the quest to secure new customers. They could have acknowledged that there was a major problem brewing and that the company's own marketing efforts might have played a role in sparking it. There was a strange disconnect: the family and the company had been very explicit, in the initial planning phases for the launch of OxyContin, about the degree to which success would be contingent on an ability to change the mind of the American medical establishment about the dangers of prescribing strong opioids. This effort was successful. To a degree that must have surprised even the Sacklers, their company had initiated a sea change. Suddenly family physicians—the very people the company had described as "opioid naive"—were prescribing the drug. The effort was so successful that other pharmaceutical firms rushed to develop and promote their *own* long-acting opioid painkillers. And this might have been part of the reason the Sacklers felt that they had done nothing wrong: the fact that other companies soon joined them.

But the Sacklers and Purdue were the first. "It was more potent," one former Purdue chemist who worked on OxyContin recalled. "There are other molecules that could have come out. It's just that *that* one was the first that did what it did the way it did and got approved. Other molecules could have been the tip of the spear, but this is the one that changed the game." For a time, the family and the company were happy to take credit for this revolution in pain management. It is in the very nature of the pharma business that there are serious rewards for changing the game, for being first.

But when people started dying, the company shrank from any suggestion that it was the pioneer. And rather than make any allowances, the Sacklers elected to fight. This was, almost certainly, an expression of Richard Sackler's personality—his stubbornness, his all-in devotion to his own ideas, his icy sense of intellectual superiority. But the company had a board, and the board voted; Richard was not making decisions alone. Purdue had always been a family enterprise, and there were no major outliers or dissenters within the family.

The unapologetic posture that the company now adopted was also a reflection of the personal style of Howard Udell, who, having staked his career on unstinting loyalty to the Sackler clan, had now become a wartime consigliere. Udell's philosophy of combat was to give no quarter, and with billions of dollars still flowing into the company, and billions more on the line, he proceeded to assemble a battalion of high-end lawyers and prepared to go on the offensive. In the Bensalem hearing, Representative Greenwood asked Udell whether Purdue might consider dedicating "some percentage of your profits to rehabilitation of those who have become addicted to your product." It was not an unreasonable question, particularly in light of the Sacklers' carefully cultivated reputation for extravagant philanthropic giving.

But Udell didn't like the idea. "The people who end up in treatment centers, they need the help," he acknowledged. But that has nothing to do with Purdue Pharma, he insisted, and the company has no obligation to those people. They were screwed up long before they ever took OxyContin, he suggested. "The system has failed them earlier on."

This was a consistent refrain. "Virtually all of these reports involve people who are abusing the medication, not patients with legitimate medical needs," Paul Goldenheim would say, in his own testimony, before the Senate. "While all the voices in this debate are important, we must be especially careful to listen to the patients who, without medicines like OxyContin, would be left in pain." The mantra never wavered. "They are not addicts," Goldenheim intoned. "They are not criminals."

Earlier that summer, Richard Blumenthal, the attorney general of Purdue's home state, Connecticut, had written a letter to Richard Sackler in which he expressed concern about addiction and abuse connected to OxyContin and suggested that Purdue's efforts—tamperproof prescription pads and education for young people—"fail to address the fundamental and serious risks inherent in the drug itself." It was true that there were other prescription drugs being abused, Blumenthal conceded. "But OxyContin is different." It is "more powerful, more addictive, more widely sold, more illicitly available, and more publicized."

Around the country, prosecutors and plaintiffs' attorneys were beginning to look at the destruction wrought by OxyContin and the profits still flowing to the company. They started to initiate investigations and lawsuits. But Howard Udell and his team at Purdue vowed to battle all comers. "While we have the highest regard for your leadership in law enforcement, we would ask that you give some recognition to our experience," Udell wrote to Blumenthal, in a response that was shimmering with condescension. "We have a lot of experience in what tactics will—and will not—work to address this problem," he asserted, dismissively, before going on to blame the controversy on the media, plaintiffs' lawyers, and people "who claim to have become addicted to OxyContin."

Purdue's spokesman Robin Hogen adopted a different approach when it came to wrangling the Connecticut attorney general. After

Blumenthal initially questioned Purdue's marketing techniques, Hogen telephoned his office and left a menacing voice mail in which he pointed out that Purdue was "a significant supporter of the Democratic party" and said that it was "very unfortunate that this had to happen to one of your major benefactors." Hogen was a man with the sort of brash confidence to threaten a state attorney general *in a voice mail*. There was an election coming up, he reminded Blumenthal, before adding, ominously, "I can assure you that this has not helped."

In 2002, Udell announced that Purdue had already spent $45 million fighting off lawsuits. The company let it be known that Udell had "no budget" for this effort; he had carte blanche to spend whatever it might take to prevail. Everyone was working around the clock, nights and weekends. Udell's strategy was to win at all costs. "I read all this bullshit, this stuff about 'deliberately this' and 'carelessly that,'" he would sputter. "We have not paid a penny in any of these cases, and we have no intention of doing so."

Numerous lawsuits had been filed and withdrawn in the face of Udell's hardball tactics. But one fear was that this controversy might follow the model of the Big Tobacco litigation, in which states and counties partnered with private plaintiff's attorneys to bring cases against the industry. The Sacklers had always taken pride in paying for top-shelf legal assistance, and Udell had built a formidable legal department, with eighteen attorneys in-house at the office in Stamford. He also hired several outside law firms, some of which were veterans of the tobacco litigation. And he sought out expert local counsel, hiring the best lawyers in town anytime a case popped up in a new jurisdiction. Before long, Udell was spending $3 million a month on litigation. But it was worth it.

Lawyers, not unlike physicians, like to tell themselves that they swear an oath and answer to a code, that they are members of a professional tribe that is undiluted by improper influence. Udell himself liked to give little homilies about the importance of integrity. But he also recognized that, realistically, the practice of law can be heavily influenced by the subtle pressures of coterie politics, and if a client has the finances to buy that kind of influence, it can be enough to tip a case in his favor. In Washington, Udell hired Eric Holder, the former deputy attorney general, who was a partner at the law firm Covington & Burling. In New York, he hired the former U.S. Attorney Mary Jo White.

If you were appealing to current prosecutors, it could be very helpful to send someone they recognized, someone who had worked the same sort of job, someone they knew, perhaps, someone they might admire. As Robin Hogen put it, at the time, "We have to be politically Machiavellian, often, to win the day."

Shortly after Rudolph Giuliani stepped down from his position as mayor of New York City, he went into business as a consultant, and one of his first clients was Purdue. When he entered the private sector, Giuliani was looking to make a lot of money quickly. In 2001, he had a net worth of $1 million; five years later, he would report $17 million in income and some $50 million in assets. For Purdue, which was working hard to frame OxyContin abuse as a law enforcement problem, rather than an issue that might implicate the drug itself or the way it was marketed, the former prosecutor who had led New York City after the 9/11 attacks would make an ideal fixer. In Michael Friedman's view, Giuliani was "uniquely qualified" to help the company.

"Government officials are more comfortable knowing that Giuliani is advising Purdue," Udell pointed out. Giuliani, he maintained, "would not take an assignment with a company that he felt was acting in an improper way."

Sometimes, Purdue employed its resources not just to put well-connected former prosecutors on the payroll but to enlist the very prosecutors who had been investigating the company. Early in 2001, the U.S. Attorney for eastern Kentucky, Joe Famularo, had characterized OxyContin as a "locust plague" that was rolling through his state. Later that year, he started working as an unpaid "consultant" for Purdue, though the company paid his expenses associated with speaking at conferences. Upon reflection, Famularo announced, he didn't think OxyContin was a locust plague at all, but rather, "a fine product." That same year, Jay McCloskey, the Maine prosecutor who had been the first federal official to raise the alarm about OxyContin, stepped down from his position. He started working as a paid consultant for Purdue. It was, in some ways, the same pattern that had played out with Curtis Wright, the former FDA examiner: the very government officials whose job it was to regulate the company and hold it to account ended up seduced by a new job at the company itself. McCloskey said later that when he came to "understand the company's corporate culture," he was "deeply impressed by the unmistakable interest in the public welfare" that "emanated" from Purdue's executives.

The Sacklers prided themselves on their ability to cultivate political connections. "We can get virtually every senator and congressman we want to talk to on the phone in the next 72 hours," Richard boasted in 2001. But one compelling aspect of the argument that Purdue made for itself was that it was not some solitary corporate behemoth motivated by a selfish desire to continue reaping billions from a dangerous drug. On the contrary, Purdue was driven solely by a sincere—and, really, selfless—duty to help patients who were suffering from chronic pain. Dating as far back as Richard's involvement in the Toronto pain conference nearly two decades earlier, the company had fostered a sense that pain care was a *movement*. And it was true that there were hundreds of thousands, perhaps millions, of patients who had indeed found relief from OxyContin and other opioids and were now concerned that they might lose access to such relief if any sorts of controls were imposed on these drugs. At every turn, Udell, Friedman, and Goldenheim insisted that the "voice" of the pain patients should be at the forefront of discussions and should not be upstaged by a bunch of reckless drug addicts.

But if the community of pain patients seemed to express the organic medical concerns of a broad national constituency, it was also true that Purdue stood ready to enlist this demographic in a decidedly cynical manner. In 2001, Kathleen Foley, the doctor who collaborated with Russell Portenoy, the King of Pain, and had served as an early evangelist for broader use of opioids, wrote to Richard Sackler to reassure him that the criticism Purdue was receiving was "garbage." She advised him not to "waste much time on it." Foley had been thinking, she told Richard, "of an alternative strategy of bringing together all of the members of the pharmaceutical industry," or, anyway, all the companies that had painkillers on the market. What they needed to do, Foley suggested, was "come together as a sort of cohesive voice." But there was "a tightrope that you need to walk," she cautioned Richard, "because you are a drug company and it would be much better if the advocacy came from outside the drug company."

New groups started to assert themselves, nominally independent advocacy groups, representing the rights of patients in what Foley called "the pain community." There was the American Pain Foun-

dation, the American Academy of Pain Medicine, and the Pain Care
Forum, which was a loose coalition of pharma companies, trade groups,
and dozens of nonprofit advocacy organizations. The Pain Care Forum
was founded and run by a man named Burt Rosen, who was based in
Washington, D.C., and happened to work as a full-time lobbyist and
government relations executive for Purdue. This was a tactic that had
been pioneered by the fossil fuel industry, to very successful effect—
funding groups that appeared to be grassroots organizations but that
actually were awash in corporate money; "astroturf" groups, as they
are sometimes called. These organizations produced studies and lobbied agencies and lawmakers. What this meant in practice was that
when the authorities entertained the possibility of taking any concrete
steps to control the ever-widening distribution of OxyContin, Purdue
could frame such a prospect not just as a potential setback to the company but as an assault on this long-suffering community. "We are in
the middle of a real fight," Richard Sackler declared when the DEA
discussed the possibility of tightening the quotas on legal oxycodone
that Purdue would have access to. "This is a clear attack on the pain
movement. There can be no other interpretation."

Richard's strategy, he told Paul Goldenheim, was "to bind these
organizations more closely to us," to a point where Purdue's products
"are inextricably bound up with the trajectory of the pain movement."
Publicly, the company might pay lip service to the notion that such
groups were independent, but internally that pretense was abandoned,
and Purdue executives were candid about the degree to which these
organizations should take their board members and their general direction from their corporate sponsors. "If they want our bucks (and they
honestly cannot survive without industry support) they are going to
have to live with 'industry' reps on their board," Robin Hogen pointed
out in an internal email. "I don't think they can expect huge grants
without some say in governance." The U.S. Senate would eventually
publish a report about the origins and influence of these pain groups,
detailing the manner in which they served as a "front" for the pharma
industry. The report concluded that though numerous companies
manufactured opioid painkillers, Purdue Pharma was the single largest
funder of these "third party advocacy groups."

✣ ✣ ✣

In an effort to tilt the media narrative, Udell also hired an outside public relations specialist named Eric Dezenhall. A political operative turned "crisis management" mercenary, Dezenhall had developed a specialty in the dark arts of killing unfavorable media stories and "placing" favorable ones. Dezenhall was famously discreet about his clients, preferring to work behind the scenes and leave no fingerprints. But according to a report in *BusinessWeek*, one of his other clients during this period was ExxonMobil, and his services included orchestrating a pro-Exxon demonstration on Capitol Hill in which several dozen protesters waved signs reading STOP GLOBAL WHINING and CAPITALISM ROCKS.

"Our first month of work for Purdue was quite busy," Dezenhall wrote to Howard Udell in late 2001. He was particularly proud of an opinion column he had managed to arrange in the *New York Post* that blamed "rural-area drug abusers" and "the liberals" for cooking up a fake controversy over OxyContin. When the article ran, Dezenhall sent it to Udell, Hogen, and Friedman with a promise that he could turn around the negative narrative. "The anti-story begins," he wrote.

Dezenhall worked closely with a psychiatrist named Sally Satel who was a fellow at a conservative think tank, the American Enterprise Institute. Satel published an essay in the Health section of *The New York Times* in which she argued that hysteria over opioids had made American physicians fearful of prescribing much-needed pain medication. "When you scratch the surface of someone who is addicted to painkillers," Satel wrote, "you usually find a seasoned drug abuser with a previous habit involving pills, alcohol, heroin or cocaine." In the article, she cited an unnamed colleague, and a study in the *Journal of Analytical Toxicology*, but did not mention that the colleague actually worked for Purdue. Or that the study had been funded by Purdue and written by Purdue employees. Or that she had shown a copy of her essay, in advance, to a Purdue official (he liked it). Or that Purdue was donating $50,000 a year to her institute at AEI.

In his progress report to Udell, Dezenhall also mentioned that he had been working with "investigative resources," and specifically a company called Kroll, on "litigation aspects of the program." Kroll was a private investigations firm that had been established in the 1970s and had since morphed into a shadowy international company that conducted "corporate intelligence" for high-end clients. At this point, there were a dozen new lawsuits being filed against Purdue every month, and Udell was convinced that the only way to forestall these cases was to bring the hammer down on anyone who had the nerve to sue. He warned enterprising attorneys who might be looking to file suit that he would come after them "in every case, in every jurisdiction." Normally, when plaintiffs' lawyers sue a publicly traded company, they have a "lever," Udell would explain, which was that they could "keep the pressure up," stoking media outrage to a point where it might begin to hurt the company's stock price. That often meant it was cheaper for a public company to resolve a lawsuit than it would be to fight it—creating a powerful incentive to settle. But Purdue wasn't a public company, Udell gloated. It was owned by the Sacklers, who were apparently unswayed by the bad publicity about their product. So "that's a lever they don't have over me."

The company was sufficiently proud of its gladiatorial posture that in 2003, Udell put out a press release under the headline "65–0," touting Purdue's litigation stats in cases involving opioid deaths and addiction as though they were the record of a high school basketball team. "These dismissals strengthen our resolve to defend these cases vigorously and to the hilt," he said.

It was useful, for a counterpuncher like Udell, to have the help of private spies from Kroll. Just as Purdue had sought out the hospital records of Martha West to discredit her, the company went to great lengths to dig up dirt on anyone endeavoring to hold the business to account. In 2002, a former sales rep named Karen White filed suit against the company in Florida, alleging that she had been wrongfully terminated after she declined to participate in legally questionable marketing practices associated with OxyContin. Purdue fiercely denied her allegations and countered that White had actually been let go because she failed to meet "sales quotas."

As it happened, sales quotas were at the heart of White's lawsuit. When the case went to trial, White's attorney told the jury that Purdue had retaliated against her after she refused to call on two doctors who she believed were operating pill mills. One of the doctors had given up his federal certificate to prescribe narcotics because a nurse had been illegally writing prescriptions out of his office. The other lost his license after he was accused of exchanging drugs for sex. But according to White, when she complained to her supervisor at Purdue about the doctors, the supervisor said that she should continue to call on them, because they had the potential to prescribe high doses of OxyContin. In her lawsuit, White maintained that she balked at orders to pressure doctors to prescribe "megadoses" of Oxy. "It behooved us to call on... doctors who are inappropriately prescribing narcotics," she explained in a deposition, because those were the very doctors who could put a sales rep on the Toppers list. "If a Purdue representative knew... that a doctor was inappropriately prescribing and was a pill mill, a lot of times they didn't turn them in to Purdue because they were making tons of money off of these doctors."

According to White, the whole enterprise at Purdue Pharma was driven by a single-minded focus on sales. "The company was all about the bottom dollar," she said. "Sell OxyContin. Period."

At one point during her deposition, White was talking about the parameters of her job as a saleswoman when one of Purdue's attorneys abruptly changed the subject. "Ma'am, have you ever taken illegal drugs?"

White was caught off guard by the question. "Have I ever what?" she said.

"Taken illegal drugs."

"No," White said.

"Never in your life?"

"No," she repeated.

"Ever taken speed?"

"No."

"Ever taken anything referred to as crank?"

"No," she said. Then, "Not that I can recall."

"So it's your testimony today that you've never done that," the lawyer said. "Correct?"

White's tone had changed. "I don't recall whether I did or not," she said. Then she clarified: "I may have in college."

Purdue had been investigating Karen White's past. "Do you recall taking speed, what's also known as crank, in college?" the lawyer asked.

"I do," White said.

"Speed is illegal, correct?"

"That is correct."

"Can you describe it to me?" the lawyer pressed. "Was it in pill form?"

"I believe it was in pill form," White said.

When the case went to trial, White's attorney made a motion to exclude evidence of this youthful indiscretion, which Purdue might have used to try to discredit her as a witness. But this was typical of Howard Udell's tactics. Just as it had with Martha West, Purdue took an individual who had raised legitimate questions about the company's conduct and sought to smear her as unstable, unreliable, a drug abuser.

Karen White had not been seeking any sort of big payday from Purdue. She was asking for $138,000 in lost pay and benefits, a figure that was a tiny fraction of the money the company was now paying its lawyers and investigators to fight the case. In the courtroom, a fleet of high-end attorneys sat behind Purdue's table. At the opposite table, it was just White and one solitary lawyer. "This marketing system was corrupt," the lawyer told the court. "It was corrupted by money, corrupted by greed, and this lady refused to go along." But, in the end, the jury sided with Purdue.

"I was definitely the underdog going in," White said afterward. But she hadn't been wrong. In the lawsuit, she ended up naming thirteen specific doctors whom she had developed concerns about during her time at Purdue. Eleven of them were ultimately arrested or lost their licenses for irresponsible prescribing.

✦ ✦ ✦

The Sacklers and Purdue adopted a similar gloves-off approach when it came to scrutiny from the press. Robin Hogen, who was in charge of managing the company's PR response to the crisis, assumed an overtly hostile posture to the journalists he was dealing with, warning reporters to be careful about their coverage, because "we're going to be watching them." In October 2003, *The Orlando Sentinel* published a major series about OxyContin and its discontents: "OxyContin Under Fire: Pain Pill Leaves Death Trail." The *Sentinel* investigative reporter who wrote the series, Doris Bloodsworth, suggested that not everyone who overdosed from OxyContin was a ritual "abuser," as Purdue had been claiming. On the contrary, she reported that there were instances of "accidental addiction," in which pain patients took the medication exactly as prescribed, but nevertheless got hooked.

The series had taken Bloodsworth nine months to report. When she sought to obtain Purdue's marketing plans from state investigators who had subpoenaed them, the company went to court to block their release, claiming that they contained "trade secrets." When the series appeared, it looked like the sort of account that could be a major blow to Purdue. Bloodsworth had homed in on the central claim of the company's defense—that patients who are prescribed OxyContin by a doctor and take it only as directed will not become addicted—and found it dubious.

But Purdue put its crisis counselor Eric Dezenhall on the case. One service that Dezenhall offered his clients was a close examination of any hostile media stories, because, as he pointed out, even established journalists occasionally get "sloppy." When Dezenhall and his associates began to investigate, they found cracks in Bloodsworth's reporting. Two of the people she wrote about and described as having "accidentally" become addicted turned out to have abused drugs in the past. A close study of Bloodsworth's data on overdose deaths demonstrated that while OxyContin might have been in the systems of many of those who died, there were often other drugs present as well. So why single out OxyContin? Udell discussed bringing a libel action against the *Sentinel*, suggesting that he had a "virtually ironclad case for actual malice." Instead, Purdue pushed for, and ultimately received, a major retraction from the paper.

Of course, the central thrust of the *Sentinel* series was true: pain patients did become addicted to OxyContin, and in some cases they overdosed and died. But Bloodsworth's flawed execution provided the company's PR apparatchiks with the ammunition they needed, and they went after her, hard. One journalist, who was sympathetic to Purdue's cause, wrote an article in *Slate* on the "myth" of the accidental addict, accusing Bloodsworth of spreading hysteria and disinformation and suggesting that, in reality, people who died from OxyContin were "just plain druggies." Bloodsworth ended up resigning from the newspaper and eventually left journalism altogether. A spokesman for Purdue acknowledged the company's satisfaction in having the opportunity to "set the record straight."

Another target of Purdue was Barry Meier. He had continued to write articles for the *Times* about the company, and his stories were devastating. By the end of 2001, he had decided that he would expand his reporting into a book. At one point, he took the train out to Stamford for a meeting in Purdue's offices with Friedman, Goldenheim, and

Udell. All three men were cordial, offering a stiff impression of infor-mality. "We, until early 2000, didn't really know there was a problem," Friedman told him. On the subject of MS Contin, Goldenheim said, "I didn't hear anything about addicts seeking out this drug to use it." Meier was very interested in Purdue's program, which was then still active, to issue patients with "starter" coupons for a free month's supply of OxyContin.

"We're now in a sort of different era," Meier said. "Any innocence this country may have had about how OxyContin could be abused, we're already long beyond that." Knowing this, he wondered, "why would you want to continue giving out free samples?"

"What we're involved in is the business of teaching doctors how to treat pain and use our products," Friedman said. "And we feel we should be able to do that."

As Meier got to work on his book, Udell wrote him a stern letter, suggesting that he submit the manuscript, prior to publication, to Pur-due so that Udell could review it. When Meier declined to take him up on this offer, Udell wrote to the president of Rodale, Meier's publisher, expressing his "grave concerns" about the author's bias and demand-ing, again, to review the text. "Both of our companies—and the fami-lies which founded them—have worked very hard for a long time to achieve deservedly excellent reputations," Udell wrote, with just a hint of menace. "Both companies will be seriously harmed if this book is published without careful review to assure its accuracy."

✢ ✢ ✢

The coverage of OxyContin, by Meier and other journalists, almost never mentioned the Sackler family. But that did not mean that the family was not worried by it. The public might have failed to link the Sackler name with OxyContin, but when friends and acquaintances of the Sacklers' read the negative press, they understood who owned the company in question. "Hang in there Richard," a friend named Jay Wettlaufer emailed, after reading a negative press account in 2001. "Just remember you are a great person with good intentions. No reporter or lawyer can take that away from you."

"Thanks for your support," Richard wrote back, after midnight on a Saturday night. "This vilification is shit."

The next day, Richard followed up, saying, "I'd like to try an argument on you. I believe the media has nefariously cast the drug abuser as a victim instead of a victimizer." For people who knew Richard, this refrain had probably grown a bit tiresome by now. But Wettlaufer had put himself forward as a sympathetic ear. "These are criminals," Richard continued. "Why should they be entitled to our sympathies?"

"I do not believe most drug abusers are nefarious criminals," Wettlaufer replied, "and I'm sure when you aren't so pissed, you don't either." Such people have lives that "are far more difficult to cope with than ours," Wettlaufer pointed out. "They deserve pity." Just the same, he assured Richard, "You are doing NOTHING WRONG. That's what counts...Deep breaths Richard. You will get through this with your humanity intact. In the final hour, it's all you have anyway."

Never one to shrink from an argument, least of all this one, Richard wanted to go another round. "I understand what you are saying. But we don't agree," he wrote. "The abusers are misbehaving in a way that they know is a serious crime. They are doing it in complete disregard of their duties to society, their family and themselves."

At this point, Wettlaufer was starting to lose patience with his friend. "Poor people in the inner city and in the backwoods of Kentucky almost never have the luxury of thinking about their 'duty to society.' They are surviving day to day," he wrote. Their "criminal intent" is "driven not by greed or hatred, but by a powerful addiction. I'd bet any sum of money the vast majority of abusers don't want to be addicts."

"Don't make that bet," Richard replied. Addicts *want* to be addicted, he proclaimed. "They get themselves addicted over and over again."

For such a brainy guy, Richard was able to sustain an impressive degree of emotional and cognitive detachment from reality. In 2002, another friend, an anesthesiologist, got in touch. The man informed Richard that at his daughter's tony private school, OxyContin was now considered "a designer drug, sort of like heroin." The anesthesiologist said, "I hate to say this but you could become the Pablo Escobar of the new millennium."

Richard was not alone among the Sacklers in feeling that the family had nothing to apologize for and no amends to make. The different wings of the family, the A side and the B side, often struggled to find common ground. But on this much, they were in agreement. It was a collective denial, one that came to pervade not just the family but the ranks of their company. At one point, Robert Reder, the Purdue executive who had overseen the FDA application for OxyContin, sent an email to some members of senior management, telling them about Silver Hill Hospital, a Connecticut psychiatric facility that was close to Purdue's headquarters and specialized in the treatment of substance abuse disorders. Perhaps someone from Purdue should join the hospital's board, Reder suggested. This would be a deft public relations move—a signal that while the company might bash people who had struggled with addiction, that did not mean that the Sacklers or Purdue were entirely incapable of compassion. Any interest? Reder inquired.

"While I think it is a wonderful institution, I have a pretty full plate right now," Michael Friedman responded.

Then Howard Udell replied with the exact same phrase: "While I think it's a wonderful institution, I have a pretty full plate right now."

"Ditto," wrote Paul Goldenheim.

Finding no takers, Reder appealed directly to Kathe Sackler. "Kathe, do you want someone from Purdue on the board at Silver Hill?"

"Robert," she replied, "only if it would be helpful to our business."

✣ ✣ ✣

In the fall of 2003, Barry Meier published his book, *Pain Killer: A "Wonder" Drug's Trail of Addiction and Death*. It was a groundbreaking work of journalism and a brutal assessment of the impact of OxyContin and of the culpability of Purdue. "In terms of narcotic firepower, OxyContin was a nuclear weapon," Meier wrote. Purdue executives "seemed unable or unwilling to take dramatic action until long after circumstances or adverse publicity had forced their hand." But by that time, it was "too late," he wrote. The drug had already unleashed "a catastrophe."

As it happened, by the time Meier's book came out, his newspaper was dealing with one of the greatest challenges in its 152-year history. The *Times* had discovered that a young reporter named Jayson Blair had secretly been breaking all the rules of the profession: Blair had fabricated characters and quotations, he had lied about being places where he hadn't been, he had plagiarized the work of others. It was a tremendous scandal for the newspaper, one that occasioned a great deal of institutional soul-searching. This was an interesting study in contrasting corporate cultures. Purdue Pharma would never admit a mistake, much less don the hair shirt and ask for forgiveness. But instead of glossing over Blair's transgressions, or writing them off as the isolated crimes of a single bad apple, the *Times* was seized by a fit of existential angst and shaken to its very core. The paper's two top editors resigned. One likened the whole experience to "stepping on a land mine."

Suddenly the venerable *New York Times* had become a caricature of unreliability, the butt of jokes on late-night television. In the period of introspection that followed, the *Times* assembled a committee of twenty-five journalists to compile a list of recommendations for how the paper could assure that no such thing could ever happen again. One of the suggestions was that the publisher appoint an ombudsman who could serve as a sort of in-house referee, a check on the zealous impulses of reporters and editors. In October 2003, the paper appointed its first "public editor," a veteran journalist named Daniel Okrent.

Okrent was not a newspaperman. He came from the world of magazines. But his job would be, as he put it, to take a hard look at the reporting of the *Times* and figure out "if the reader has been dealt with straight."

During the months he spent working on *Pain Killer,* Barry Meier had not been publishing articles about OxyContin in the newspaper. But after the radio host Rush Limbaugh confessed, in the fall of 2003, that he had developed an addiction to OxyContin and other painkillers that had been prescribed to him for back pain, Meier wrote an article about the episode. With the book done and out, it appeared that he was back on the beat.

For the leadership at Purdue, this was alarming. They had been complaining about Meier and his coverage of OxyContin for years now, asserting that he had smeared the company with a "sensationalized and skewed account." Back in 2001, Udell had tried to go over Meier's head, arriving at the *Times* newsroom with a small posse of Purdue officials, to appeal directly to Meier's bosses. But to Udell's great frustration, the editors stood by their reporter. The newspaper "blew us off," as one of Udell's colleagues complained. And Meier didn't budge from the story.

Now, with the *Times* weakened and Okrent looking for fodder in his new role, Udell and his war council saw an opportunity. They appealed directly to Okrent, making an appointment to see him and crowding into his little office on the fifteenth floor at the *Times.* Barry Meier should not be permitted to write about Purdue or OxyContin for the newspaper anymore, they argued, because now he had published a book on the same subject and this was a conflict of interest. Anything Meier wrote in the paper was effectively just advertising for the book, Udell contended.

This was a specious argument—the sort of argument you make when you have no other arguments to make. But there was reason to believe that if Purdue could remove Meier from the story, things might get a lot more comfortable for the company. It wasn't as though there were some big enterprise team at the *Times* working the OxyContin beat. Meier *was* the team. If they could just knock him out, it would give the company a much freer hand.

Udell asserted that the publication of *Pain Killer* represented an egregious conflict. He cited the newspaper's written policy that "staff members must never give an impression that they might benefit financially from the outcome of news events," and demanded that Meier be taken off the story. After the meeting, Okrent sent Meier a list of questions about his reporting. Meier was livid. It seemed transparent to him that in the aftermath of the Blair scandal the *Times* had grown scared of its own shadow and Purdue was cynically making the most of this opportunity.

Not long after he received Okrent's questions, Meier was summoned into the office of Al Siegal, one of the top editors at the *Times,* to discuss whether it was appropriate for him to write an article about painkillers when he had a book to sell on the same subject. *Of course* it was appropriate, Meier exclaimed. He was an expert on the subject! He knew the story inside out! He had the technical knowledge! He had the sources! And it's not as though he had gratuitously mentioned his book in the Rush Limbaugh piece. He hadn't even mentioned *Purdue* until the eleventh paragraph. "It was hugely frustrating," Meier recalled years later. "I felt it was unfair."

Okrent published a column titled "You Can Stand on Principle and Still Stub a Toe," in which he said that he found Meier's reporting to be "generally accurate and fair," but argued that there was indeed a conflict of interest. Some might contend that Purdue was "making a mountain out of a molehill," Okrent allowed. But the paper's "reputation" would be best served, he concluded, "by removing even the slightest hint of a conflict."

"You're not going to write about opioids," Al Siegal told Meier. The *Times* was taking him off the story. Much later, Okrent would point to the fact that he was still new to his position at the *Times* when he wrote the column about Purdue, and acknowledge that he has often wondered, in the years since, "whether I made a mistake." Meier was furious—"batshit," Okrent said. In Meier's view, Okrent had been "played for a chump," and the leadership at the *Times,* paralyzed by fears about the besieged integrity of the paper, had allowed themselves to be strong-armed by corporate thugs. Purdue Pharma had engaged in egregious misconduct, misconduct that Meier believed was almost certainly criminal. For two years, Udell and other Sackler henchmen had been trying to neutralize him, to stop him from reporting the truth about what their company had been doing. Now, it seemed, they had finally succeeded.

Chapter 20

TAKE THE FALL

JOHN BROWNLEE WAS A young prosecutor with political ambitions. He had grown up in Virginia, the son of an infantry officer who served in Vietnam. Brownlee attended law school at William & Mary and spent four years on active duty in the army. A few weeks before September 11, 2001, George W. Bush appointed him to serve as U.S. Attorney for the Western District of Virginia. This was a plum job, but people who knew Brownlee at the time say that he regarded it as a stepping-stone. What he really wanted to do was climb the ranks of the Republican Party and run for state attorney general. And beyond that, who knows? Governor? Senator?

By the time Brownlee took the position, his state was awash in OxyContin. He'd been on the job less than a month when his office announced guilty pleas from a ring of individuals who had been trafficking the drug. The crisis had been keeping prosecutors busy: every other week, it seemed, they were bringing charges against doctors, dealers, pharmacists, thieves who robbed pharmacies. And as more and more of these cases cropped up, there was a common denominator—this pill that seemed to be exerting such a powerful hold on the community. Who was *making* it? Brownlee wondered. This storm of trouble had descended, practically overnight, on his state. But where did it come from?

The answer, his staff told him, was Connecticut. After Brownlee's first few months as U.S. Attorney, his office indicted a local physician, Cecil Knox, for illegally dispensing OxyContin. This was, in some ways, a standard scenario: a clinic that asked few questions and became a prolific distributor of opioid painkillers. But when Brownlee's office looked into Knox, they discovered he had a sideline as a paid speaker. "We know he gave some promotional speeches," Brownlee said in a press conference. "For Purdue."

Brownlee liked holding press conferences. In fact, he was precisely the sort of lawyer that Howard Udell liked to deride as an "overly zealous prosecutor with political ambition." He clearly relished the publicity that came with announcing indictments and guilty pleas. It was a bit comical: when Brownlee traveled around the state, he brought a portable lectern with folding legs in the trunk of his car for impromptu statements to the media.

As it happened, a couple of prosecutors who worked for Brownlee, Randy Ramseyer and Rick Mountcastle, had already opened an investigation into Purdue. Ramseyer and Mountcastle worked out of a field office in Abingdon, a small town in the Blue Ridge Mountains. It was a lean operation: their office was housed in a tiny storefront next to a dentist's office in a strip mall. But they were both tough, experienced career federal prosecutors, and they had seen firsthand the misery that OxyContin had inflicted on their community.

Any prosecutor is motivated by a complex brew of principle and desire. For some, the imperatives of justice are paramount; for others, the spotlight. But either impulse is satisfied by the prospect of big game. "We were sitting around talking about where the biggest bang would be," Rick Mountcastle recalled. "We decided, let's take a look at Purdue." This family-owned drug company a world away in Stamford, Connecticut, was suddenly making billions of dollars selling Oxy-Contin and seemed like a big player. Sure, there were other bad drug companies, other firms marketing opioids. But Purdue seemed like the chief culprit at the time. Prescription drug abuse had always been an issue in Appalachia. The advent of OxyContin had changed the whole game, however, and Mountcastle and Ramseyer kept hearing stories about the aggressiveness of Purdue's sales reps and how they would strong-arm local pharmacists into filling prescriptions. A small-town pharmacist tended to know his patients on a first-name basis and know who might have a legitimate need for a large volume of opioid painkillers and who clearly didn't. What kind of business model would drive Purdue reps to pressure a local pharmacist to continue issuing pills to people the pharmacist knew were not legitimate patients?

When the prosecutors mentioned their idea of targeting Purdue to Brownlee, he was immediately supportive and told them to move "full speed ahead." This would not be a civil matter, of the sort that the company had already been facing from many quarters and fighting off with great success. This would be a criminal investigation. The prosecutors would begin by gathering evidence, interviewing people, and requesting internal documents from the company.

"What if we don't find anything?" Ramseyer wondered out loud.

"At least we looked," Mountcastle said.

On December 3, 2002, the prosecutors in Abingdon sent a subpoena to Connecticut, demanding corporate records on the manufacturing, marketing, and distribution of OxyContin. Mountcastle had been a lawyer for twenty years at that point. He had worked at the Department of Justice in Washington and tried cases all over the country. He didn't see any reason why a couple of lawyers working out of a strip-mall annex in a backwoods district of Virginia couldn't bring a novel criminal case against a mighty corporation.

But if they were going to do it, they were going to need more office space. About a mile away from the strip mall, on the other side of the highway, someone had built a modern office complex that was completely out of proportion to its surroundings and, by Abingdon standards, pretty deluxe. Mountcastle called it the Taj Mahal. The prosecutors set up a suite of offices there where they could work on the case. Because they were so leanly staffed themselves, they cobbled together a pickup team of borrowed hands from other agencies: a Medicaid fraud specialist from the state attorney general's office, a pair of criminal investigators from the FDA, a special agent from the IRS.

If Purdue was going to be compelled to turn over documents, Mountcastle figured that the company would probably resort to an old litigation trick: bury the prosecutors in paper. Purdue's lawyers would respond to the subpoenas by turning over so many documents that the prosecutors could never hope to go through them all. If there *were* incriminating files, the company was going to make them as difficult as possible to find. Sure enough, boxes full of files began arriving at the Taj Mahal. They came in FedEx trucks, one banker's box after the next, tens of thousands of pages, then hundreds of thousands, and eventually *millions* of pages. It was an ocean of paper. More than any one person— any team of people—could read in a lifetime. At one point, someone took a photo of the evidence room, showing a thousand or so file boxes stacked neatly, nine up and twenty across, on a network of steel shelves.

But the investigators had anticipated this challenge, and they confronted it in a systematic fashion. As each new document arrived, they scanned it and entered it into a database. And as they consulted Purdue's internal files and started to develop a picture of the inner workings of the company, the investigators issued new, more detailed subpoenas. Eventually, the prosecutors in Abingdon would send the company nearly six hundred different subpoenas as they scoured Purdue's confidential records, homing in on particular areas of interest.

To fight the case, Howard Udell retained a powerful Washington lawyer named Howard Shapiro, who had previously served as general counsel of the FBI and was now a partner at the law firm Wilmer Cutler Pickering Hale and Dorr. Having worked in Washington himself earlier in his career, Rick Mountcastle had grown skeptical of a phenomenon that is sometimes described as the "revolving door." At a firm like Wilmer, many of the partners had worked in high positions in the Department of Justice, and at Justice many of the senior political officials had worked in the past (and might hope to someday work again) at firms like Wilmer. As a result, there was an inescapable familiarity between the top partners at such private law firms and the political appointees at Justice. Walk into a fancy restaurant near the White House on a weekday and you could occasionally spot Justice officials fraternizing with the enemy over lunch. Mountcastle might have had a chip on his shoulder; he liked to joke, drily, that he was just "an attorney from this small Podunk office." But if Purdue was using a lawyer like Howard Shapiro, Mountcastle worried that the company might try to beat the case not by prevailing on the merits but by getting its high-priced lawyers to go over Mountcastle's head—and over the head of his boss, John Brownlee—to persuade the political leadership at Justice to kill it.

Which is precisely what the company did. As the prosecutors issued their subpoenas, the defense team appealed directly to one of the most powerful officials at Justice, the deputy attorney general, James Comey. The message to Comey was simple: these prosecutors out in Abingdon had strayed, and the department needed to, as Howard Shapiro would put it, "rein in the Western District of Virginia." So, Comey instructed John Brownlee to come to Washington for a meeting. In advance of the meeting, Mountcastle and Randy Ramseyer briefed Brownlee extensively, spelling out the evidence they had found so far and the reasons that this was a legitimate investigation. Then Brownlee drove to Washington. But when he got into the grand office of the deputy attorney

general, Comey didn't even want to see the evidence. He asked Brownlee to summarize the broad parameters of the investigation. There
was a moment of confusion, when Brownlee had to explain to Comey
that this was a case against Purdue Pharma, the maker of OxyContin,
and not Perdue Farms, the chicken processing concern. When he had
cleared that up, Comey said, "Go back to Virginia and do your case."
He didn't need to hear the full briefing.

This was a great relief. The prosecutors in Virginia had Comey's
confidence and support—his "top cover," as they say in Washington.
So they got back to work. Rick Mountcastle knew that they were up
against a brigade of lawyers—Shapiro probably had twenty associates
at his law firm working on the case, for all Mountcastle knew—so he
would devise little tricks to keep his adversaries on their toes. Sometimes, Mountcastle would set his alarm for 4:00 a.m. on a Sunday, then
wake up, get dressed, go into the office, and send a fax to Purdue's lawyers. This way, when they saw the time stamp on the fax, they would
think that the attorneys in Abingdon must have an army of associates,
too, and that they were working around the clock.

In addition to the millions of pages of documents they received,
the investigators conducted some three hundred interviews. What
they discovered was staggering. The leadership at Purdue had been
peddling a narrative about their company to the authorities and to the
public just as effectively as they had peddled OxyContin to physicians.
Before she was fired, Howard Udell's legal secretary, Martha West, had
noticed that Udell seemed to have grown paranoid about the retention
of documents at Purdue and the types of statements that employees put
into writing. As it would turn out, Udell had good reason to be nervous.
With their subpoenas, Brownlee's investigators collected emails and
memos and meeting minutes and marketing plans from the company.
In addition, they got field notes written by sales reps like Steven May,
documenting every interaction they had with a physician or a pharmacist. What the investigators discovered, as they pored over this material, was that nearly every major element of the story that Purdue had
been telling about its own conduct was untrue.

✣ ✣ ✣

The assertion by Purdue officials that the company had no reason
to predict, in advance, that OxyContin might be abused was under-

mined by their own documents. The very executives who had testified about having no indication of significant MS Contin abuse had emailed about the subject on numerous occasions. "When I was a manager in the Midwest...I received this type of news on MS Contin all the time, and from everywhere," one company official, Mark Alfonso, wrote in a June 2000 email. "Some pharmacies would not even stock MS Contin for fear that they would be robbed." (Michael Friedman, forwarding the email to Howard Udell, asked, "Do you want all this chat on email?")

But another reason that Purdue should have anticipated that the drug might be abused was that its own internal studies showed that the therapeutic effects of OxyContin often did not work as advertised. In one of Purdue's clinical studies, of osteoarthritis patients, two out of seven subjects reported undergoing withdrawal when they stopped taking even low doses of the drug. Yet the final package insert for Oxy-Contin claimed that patients on doses of 60 milligrams or less could stop "abruptly without incident," and Brownlee's prosecutors discovered that the sales force was instructed to distribute an article asserting that there was no withdrawal when people stopped taking low doses.

When Barry Meier interviewed Friedman, Goldenheim, and Udell in 2001, they told him they had been completely surprised to learn that people might dissolve OxyContin in water and then shoot the drug intravenously and that they had never entertained such a possibility. But as the prosecutors discovered, the company had studied just that, conducting a so-called spoon and shoot study to determine how much oxycodone someone could get by dissolving one of the pills in liquid. The study found that most of the narcotic payload of OxyContin could be accessed in this manner. (According to the prosecutors' findings, Purdue nevertheless trained sales reps to tell doctors that the drug could not be injected.)

One might hope that the FDA would have been alert to these dangers. But the investigators in Abingdon uncovered troubling clues about the relationship between Purdue and the FDA examiner Curtis Wright. Wright's contacts with Purdue executives had been "largely informal in nature," the prosecutors concluded. Brownlee's team found a March 1995 email in which Robert Reder, the Purdue executive who oversaw the FDA application, advised Howard Udell, nine months prior to the actual approval, that Wright had "confirmed" that OxyContin would be approved. Rick Mountcastle began to suspect that Wright must have come to an understanding with Purdue about the possibility of a future job even before he left the agency. "I think there was a secret deal cut," Mountcastle reflected. "I can never prove it, so that's just my personal opinion. But if you look at the whole circumstances, nothing else makes sense."

Purdue had no evidence to suggest that OxyContin was less prone to abuse than other painkillers, yet the FDA allowed the company to make the claim. Then the sales reps proceeded to engineer a great con. Field notes from the sales force documented reps telling doctors and pharmacists, again and again, that there was no buzz with OxyContin, there were fewer peaks and troughs, and less than 1 percent of users became addicted. What the prosecutors concluded, when they analyzed these notes, was that this had been a coordinated—and heavily scripted—campaign. "The defense in a case like this is always, 'We had a few bad eggs,'" Brownlee pointed out. "But when you see the call notes, you begin to get a sense that this is corporate policy." The investigators had a map of the United States, and every time they found evidence of fraudulent marketing claims in the call notes, they would color the state where the call took place in red. "All of a sudden *all* of the states are red," Brownlee recalled.

"These folks were trained," he concluded. The reps weren't dreaming up these exaggerated claims about the drug's safety on their own. And there was proof of that, too. Purdue turned over videotapes showing their own instructional sessions for the sales force, in which company supervisors explicitly encouraged them to make claims that Purdue officials knew were not true. Brownlee was agog. "They literally were *training* people to lie about the product."

The investigators found evidence of sales reps continuing to call on doctors even when they knew that their licenses had been temporarily suspended. They found notes from a rep in Ohio who reported to the company in 1999 about a visit to a physician who wanted to talk only about the "street value of OC." They found a transcript of a call that Michael Friedman had done with a public relations specialist in 1999 in which Friedman said, "I mean, we have an OC pill that's 80 milligrams per pill. Now, that is as much oxycodone as in 16 Percocet tablets... That's why the addicts want to go after our pills."

Even Purdue's claims about its own noble contributions in alleviating pain turned out, in many instances, to be bogus. Back in the 1950s,

Arthur had produced the advertisement for Sigmamycin with the real-looking business cards of physicians who had supposedly endorsed the product, and John Lear, the *Saturday Review* journalist, discovered that the doctors did not exist. After Richard Sackler suggested producing a collection of testimonials, the company had turned to Alan Spanos, the North Carolina pain specialist, to put together the *I Got My Life Back* video. But it emerged that these testimonials were not as compelling as they seemed. Johnny Sullivan, the construction worker who talked about how much better things were for him now that he was taking OxyContin, had eventually stopped taking the drug. "He now takes methadone instead of OC to reduce the cost," Spanos acknowledged, in an email that the investigators uncovered. But, even so, Spanos hoped that Johnny could feature in a follow-up Purdue video, *I Got My Life Back, Part II.* "Johnny comes across so well on film," Spanos enthused. "I hope this won't debar him from a repeat appearance!" Johnny did appear in the second video, even though he was no longer taking Oxy-Contin. He spoke about how he could "ride a motorcycle" now and "move heavy equipment." He praised OxyContin for having no side effects, saying, "Never a drowsy moment around here."

The legacy of the *I Got My Life Back* videos turned out to be more dire even than the prosecutors in Abingdon could have imagined. For the Sacklers, the suggestion had always been that there is a simple taxonomy—patients on the one hand, abusers on the other—and that legitimate pain patients do not become addicted to OxyContin. But some patients did become addicted, even patients who appeared in Purdue's own promotional videos. According to a report in the *Milwaukee Journal Sentinel,* three of the seven patients in the original *I Got My Life Back* video benefited greatly from OxyContin, using it to manage long-term pain. But others had more difficulty. One of the patients, Lauren, spoke in the video about her severe back pain. But eventually, her OxyContin dose was doubled, then doubled again. She lost her job and could no longer afford the $600 a month that she now needed for Oxy-Contin. When she tried to cut back, she experienced acute withdrawal. Lauren couldn't afford to pay her mortgage, and spent her money on OxyContin instead, so she lost her car, then her home, and eventually filed for bankruptcy. Later, she finally managed to wean herself off the drug. She had concluded, she said, that "if I didn't get off this medicine, I'd probably end up dead."

Another patient in the video, Ira, had fibromyalgia and said that OxyContin had enabled him to get exercise and do physical therapy. A few years later, he was found dead in his apartment, at the age of sixty-two. The cause of death was high blood pressure and cardiovascular disease. But he had two opioids in his bloodstream, according to a toxicology report, one of which was oxycodone. Ira had recently been released from a detox center. He had pills in his pocket when he died.

Johnny, the construction worker, also struggled with his pain medication, becoming addicted to OxyContin. At one point, his wife, Mary Lou, told their sons, "That medicine is going to kill him." He had been hospitalized on more than one occasion after overdosing accidentally. Over time, he grew so incapacitated by his dependence on OxyContin and morphine that Mary Lou was forced to tend to him like an invalid, putting on his socks and shoes, shaving him, washing his hair. Johnny had a pouch of pills that he kept under the seat of his pickup truck. One day he was driving home from a hunting trip when the truck flipped, killing him instantly. He was fifty-two.

✣   ✣   ✣

As the investigators in Virginia launched their case, the Sackler family was planning a big celebration, in Connecticut, to commemorate the fiftieth anniversary of Sackler ownership of Purdue. The year 2002 marked half a century since Arthur Sackler had purchased the small Greenwich Village patent medicine business for his brothers. The corporation that Mortimer and Raymond went on to build—and that Richard had subsequently modernized—was now an enormously lucrative enterprise that was generating well over $1 billion a year. Mortimer and Raymond had increasingly stepped back from the company to focus on their various philanthropic endeavors. Mortimer had recently been awarded the Legion of Honor, the highest distinction bestowed by the government of France, in recognition of his generosity. He was also knighted by the British queen, in 1999, as Raymond had been several years earlier. (According to one person who knew them both, Mortimer was annoyed that his younger brother, who didn't even *live* in England, should have received this particular laurel before he did.) One British commentator, in the magazine *Harpers & Queen*, suggested that the sort of big-ticket giving to cultural and educational institutions in which the brothers were now principally engaged was a way to "buy immortality."

In 2003, as the Virginia investigators were sorting through subpoenaed records in the file room at the Taj Mahal, Richard Sackler stepped down from his position as president of Purdue. "I was an active executive until 2003," he later testified. "After that, I was just a board member." In truth, this was a change in his formal title rather than in his practical role, and Richard remained intimately involved in the day-to-day operations of the company. He continued to feel an enormous sense of personal investment when it came to OxyContin, and he would obsessively monitor the performance of the drug, demanding regular updates. "Dr. Richard has to back off," one executive complained in an internal email years after Richard had supposedly "stepped away" from the company. "He is pulling people in all directions, creating a lot of extra work and increasing pressure and stress." To take Richard's place as titular head of Purdue, the Sacklers appointed Michael Friedman— the very man who had overseen the marketing push for OxyContin that was now inviting such scrutiny. Richard had hired Friedman. "He and Michael were very close," Robin Hogen recalled. "Dr. Richard was with him every step of the way, as an adviser, a critic, a coach, a cheerleader." But Richard had never been one to hand over the steering wheel. At one point, Friedman complained to Richard about his "frequent interactions with my subordinates," saying, "You influence priorities with your communications and undermine the direction I give people. This undermines my effectiveness. You will not stop, but that does not make it right."

Richard's brother, Jonathan, and his cousins Kathe and Mortimer would eventually step down as vice presidents as well. But, as one prosecutor later explained, "those moves were for show. The Sacklers kept control of the company." The family's pride in OxyContin was undiminished by the tide of death or the wave of civil lawsuits or the federal investigation in Virginia. In fact, as the fiftieth anniversary celebration approached, one of Kathe Sackler's main worries was that Richard, her rival in the family, would steal credit for being the one who dreamed up the idea of the drug in the first place—credit she felt should rightly be hers. The Sacklers were planning to produce a special booklet to commemorate the anniversary, and Kathe was concerned about the way in which the booklet would present this important chapter in the family's history. After reviewing the draft text, she fired off an intemperate email to her father: "I will strenuously protest approval of any document that suggests or implies, as this draft does, that Richard Sackler was responsible for the idea of developing a controlled-release oxycodone product. As you know, when I told Richard of my idea in the mid-80s, he asked me what oxycodone was."

✦   ✦   ✦

The initial appeal by Purdue's legal team to James Comey might have been unsuccessful, but that was no reason for the Sacklers to feel alarmed. They had Howard Udell to protect them, and Howard Shapiro, in Washington, as well as Mary Jo White. And as if this team were not sufficiently formidable, they had a ringer—the former New York City mayor Rudy Giuliani. The reason Purdue had hired Giuliani to begin with was that he was, at that time, regarded as an impressive figure of national renown. His name was often floated as a prospective candidate for the 2008 presidential election; many saw him as the presumptive Republican nominee. Giuliani enjoyed the sort of profile and name recognition in Washington that a political aspirant like the prosecutor John Brownlee could only dream of. Eventually, Giuliani expressed an interest in meeting with Brownlee to talk about the case. Before the two men sat down, Brownlee bought and read a copy of Giuliani's book, which had just been published; it was called *Leadership*.

"Giuliani was good at this," Brownlee observed: the former mayor didn't seem particularly well versed on the minutiae of the case, but that wasn't what Purdue had hired him for. "He was very personable, political, easygoing," Rick Mountcastle, who also met with him, recalled. "They wanted this thing to go away and Giuliani's portfolio was to go in and close the deal."

Brownlee was courteous. But he didn't back down. "He's not a magician," he recalled. "He couldn't change the facts." His prosecutors had assembled evidence of conduct so egregious that they thought it warranted felony charges not just against the company itself but against the three executives whom the Sacklers had thrust forward as the public face of OxyContin: Michael Friedman, Paul Goldenheim, and Howard Udell.

In Abingdon, Rick Mountcastle put together a secret document known as a prosecution memo in which he drew together all the incriminating evidence that the prosecutors had assembled and laid out the case. The document was dated September 28, 2006. It was more than a hundred pages long, the product of five years of investigation, with meticulous footnotes. The memo was an incendiary catalog of corporate malfeasance. It wasn't just that it spelled out a litany of prosecutable misdeeds: it substantiated, in forensic detail, the knowledge and direction of those misdeeds at the highest levels of Purdue. "The conspirators trained Purdue's sales force, and provided them with training and marketing materials" to make fraudulent claims, the memo asserted. The sworn testimony of Friedman, Goldenheim, and Udell was flatly contradicted by the company's own documents, the report noted. The prosecutors did not mince words: the Purdue executives had testified "falsely and fraudulently" to Congress.

According to five former Justice Department officials who were familiar with these discussions, Brownlee wanted to bring multiple felony charges against the three executives, including "misbranding" (a fraud charge involving the mislabeling of pharmaceutical products), and wire fraud, mail fraud, and money laundering. Prosecutors are often reluctant to file criminal charges against publicly traded companies because of a fear that if the stock price plummets, it could create punishing financial losses for shareholders who might have had no knowledge of the criminal conduct in question. But in the case of Purdue, there *were* no mom-and-pop stockholders. There was only the Sacklers. The prosecution memo told the story of an intricate, years-long, extraordinarily profitable criminal conspiracy. The company's records indicated that Purdue had already sold more than $9 billion of OxyContin. So, in addition to felony charges against the business and its senior executives, the prosecutors would demand a fine. They debated what a reasonable number would be, and any demand would be subject to intense negotiation with the defendants. But it was decided that the number they would put on the table was $1.6 billion.

The Sacklers might have derived some comfort from knowing that they personally did not appear to be immediate targets of the criminal case. This was precisely the kind of situation in which the decades-long Sackler ruse of obscuring the connection between the family and its various enterprises could really come in handy. But when federal prosecutors bring a criminal case against a corporation, they rarely start by indicting the CEO or the chairman of the board. Instead, they tend to begin by targeting members of senior management who are a rung or two below the top. One rationale for this approach is that it is often easier to assemble evidence against this lower level, because these executives play a more hands-on operational role and leave behind a more extensive paper trail. But, in white-collar criminal cases, such defendants also make for notably soft targets. These are generally pampered men in middle age with soft hands and unblemished reputations. If you indict them on criminal charges, and they are suddenly looking at the prospect of actual jail time, the very thought of incarceration is enough to flood them with terror. As a consequence, they can often be persuaded to flip—implicating the CEO or board chairman in exchange for more lenient treatment.

Richard Sackler's name came up repeatedly in the prosecution memo. Having served as president of the company himself, and maintained near constant contact with Friedman and the other executives, it was only natural that he would find his way into the crosshairs of the investigation. In the prosecution memo, Mountcastle referred to the Sacklers as "The Family" and noted that Friedman, Goldenheim, and Udell all "reported directly to The Family." If the prosecutors could bring felony charges against the executives, with the threat of an actual prison sentence, there seemed to be a good chance that they could induce at least one of the men—or all three of them, for that matter— to betray the Sacklers and serve as a prosecution witness.

Before the criminal charges against the executives could be approved, however, the case was sent for review to the Department of Justice in Washington. In the department's criminal division, the file landed on the desk of a young attorney named Kirk Ogrosky. He spoke with the prosecutors in Virginia and spent ten days going through the memo. Then he prepared a memo of his own about the case. It was rock solid, he concluded. "Perhaps no case in our history rivals the burden placed on public health and safety as that articulated by our line prosecutors in the Western District of Virginia," he wrote, noting that "OxyContin abuse has significantly impacted the lives of millions of Americans." This was a "righteous case," in the lingo of the department, and Ogrosky recommended that his colleagues proceed with multiple felony charges against the executives and the company. He stressed that this should happen without further delay, pointing out that Purdue had "a direct financial incentive for seeking an extension," given that its "fraudulent sales and marketing" of OxyContin continued to generate another $100 million every month.

If the case actually went to trial, with this bounty of evidence, in a courthouse in the Western District of Virginia, where so many prospective jurors would know someone whose life had been upended by OxyContin, it would not be difficult to convict. In fact, if the three executives were so much as indicted, they would likely take one look at their odds and then race to sign a cooperation agreement. As one attorney who played a role in the case observed, "My gut was that if one of the three did that, the Sacklers go down."

✣   ✣   ✣

They didn't. One day in October 2006, John Brownlee got a phone call informing him that a meeting had been scheduled for the defense team to come in and do a briefing in the office of the assistant attorney general. Brownlee and his team were alarmed. Not every defendant in a criminal case is afforded the opportunity to go over the heads of the people prosecuting him and bring an informal appeal directly to senior officials at the Department of Justice, but such prerogatives are available to Americans with enough wealth and wherewithal to exercise them. Even in a justice system rigged in favor of the rich and powerful, however, it is customary for the prosecutors to at least be given an opportunity to brief their own bosses on the particulars of the case before the bosses meet with the defense.

Brownlee, Mountcastle, and Ramseyer traveled to Washington. The meeting took place in a large conference room attached to the office of the assistant attorney general, a woman named Alice Fisher. There was a long oak table surrounded by leather chairs. Law books lined the walls, creating an atmosphere of solemn probity. Howard Shapiro filed in, along with Mary Jo White and other attorneys for Purdue and the three executives. The meeting was run by Fisher, along with several more junior officials who were political appointees in the Bush administration, including Fisher's deputy chief of staff, Rob Coughlin. Coughlin would subsequently plead guilty himself, in an unrelated case, to a felony charge that in exchange for meals at expensive restaurants, tickets to sporting events, and other inducements, he did favors, at Justice, for clients of the criminal lobbyist Jack Abramoff. But for now, he appeared to be a credible official of the U.S. government, and he and Fisher gave the Purdue lawyers plenty of time to make their case. The attorneys delivered a robust presentation about how Brownlee and his prosecutors were being overzealous in their pursuit of Purdue. In particular, they argued that it would be highly inappropriate to bring felony charges against Friedman, Goldenheim, and Udell. These men bore no real personal criminal culpability. To the degree that Purdue could be said to have done anything untoward when it came to the marketing of OxyContin, it was a matter of a few rogue sales reps—conduct that these executives would not have tolerated (much less condoned), had they known about it (which they hadn't).

After the meeting concluded, Brownlee was informed that notwithstanding the evidence he and his prosecutors had spent five years assembling, the department would not support them seeking felony charges against the three executives. Instead, the company could be indicted for felony misbranding, and Friedman, Goldenheim, and Udell could each be charged with a single misdemeanor. "Brownlee was rip-shit pissed," one former Justice official who spoke with him at the time recalled. Rick Mountcastle and Randy Ramseyer were "apoplectic."

Years later, this decision, which was made behind closed doors at the Justice Department, would become an enduring mystery, because none of the officials involved wanted to own it. The choice to drop felony charges against Friedman, Goldenheim, and Udell appears to have been made by the assistant attorney general, Alice Fisher. But several attorneys who worked with Fisher at the time stressed that she would not have had the authority to overrule a U.S. Attorney like Brownlee, and that, as such, she must have been carrying out the orders of her boss, the deputy attorney general, Paul McNulty. Fisher, who rarely speaks about internal deliberations during her time at Justice, made an exception, to insist that "I did not make or overrule any charging decisions in this case," which would seem to indicate that it must have ultimately been McNulty's call. John Brownlee recalled meeting with McNulty personally, to talk about the case. But in an interview, McNulty claimed that he *didn't* make the decision to downgrade the charges against the executives, and indeed, that he was not consulted on it in any way. It was an orphan directive: a backroom deal for which none of these former public servants would take responsibility.

This was "a political outcome that Purdue bought," one former Justice official who was involved in the case said. Paul Pelletier, another former official who reviewed the prosecution memo at Justice, reflected, "This is the reason we *have* the Department of Justice, to prosecute these kinds of cases. When I saw the evidence, there was no doubt in my mind that if we had indicted these people, if these guys had gone to jail, it would have changed the way that people did business."

But Purdue had other ideas. To Rick Mountcastle, this was the very scenario he had feared: the prosecutors in a little satellite office in Abingdon devoted a substantial chunk of their careers to putting together an airtight case against Purdue, only to have a handful of white-shoe influence peddlers in Washington go straight over their heads and short-circuit the whole endeavor. According to a subsequent deposition by Howard Shapiro, Purdue paid his firm more than $50 million for its work on the case.

✤ ✤ ✤

Even after the prosecution had been successfully defanged, Purdue's lawyers kept pushing for advantage. Brownlee wanted, at the very least, a guilty plea by the company, acknowledging its own felonious conduct as a corporation even if no individuals were going to do time. He wanted a fine, a big one, and those misdemeanor pleas from the three executives. But Mary Jo White and the other attorneys, having established that Brownlee's authority was ultimately pretty limited, kept working, quietly, to further undermine the case. The prosecutors were *still* asking for too much, Purdue's lawyers argued; the company was in no hurry to sign a guilty plea, and they continued to fight the idea that Friedman, Goldenheim, and Udell would plead even to misdemeanors.

Finally, Brownlee issued an ultimatum. Purdue and the executives could sign the guilty plea or face criminal charges. The company had five days to decide. On the night that the offer was set to expire, Brownlee still didn't have an answer. He was at home in Virginia that evening when his phone rang. It was a young man named Michael Elston who was chief of staff to Paul McNulty, the deputy attorney general. Elston told Brownlee that Purdue's attorneys were complaining that the prosecution was being pushed too fast. His sympathy with Purdue was so self-evident that Brownlee felt he was "inquiring almost on their behalf." The message was unmistakable: Call this off. Slow this down. The company does not want to sign this guilty plea. Don't force them.

Elston didn't say so to Brownlee at the time, but he was intervening on behalf of his boss. Paul McNulty had received a personal phone call from Mary Jo White. "It's Mary Jo White," McNulty said. "It's somebody who thought of herself as having access" to the deputy attorney general. For a lawyer of White's stature, he noted, "the boldness of the presumption isn't necessarily out of character." So McNulty told his chief of staff "Mary Jo had called" and instructed him to speak to John Brownlee and "find out if he could accommodate her."

John Brownlee was perceived even by his own prosecutors as a political guy: a good and honest man, but one who happened to have transparent ambitions for higher office. He was a Republican, and the administration of George W. Bush was known to prize loyalty. This cohort of well-connected political appointees who had quietly arrayed themselves in Purdue's corner were the very sorts of power brokers that a person like John Brownlee would need to cultivate. Richard Sackler had once boasted about being able to get any senator on the telephone, and for Purdue this was an elegant, and devilishly efficient, play: one phone call from Mary Jo White to McNulty, at Justice, then a second phone call from Elston to Brownlee—the man who was overseeing the prosecution but who also, given his personality and career plans, might be uniquely susceptible to this sort of eleventh-hour bid, from a politically influential figure, for a stay of execution.

But Brownlee refused to roll over. He told Elston that as U.S. Attorney, he had the authority to bring these charges, so Elston had better "back out of the way," because the case was moving forward. Some people who knew Brownlee thought that he had simply reached the limits of his own willingness to be pushed around. Others thought that he might have felt compelled to stand on principle by the sheer toll of human devastation that OxyContin had visited upon his state. One way or another, Rick Mountcastle said, "I gained a lot of respect for him that day."

After making it clear to Elston that he was not going to back down, Brownlee hung up. Later that evening, he got word that Purdue and the three executives would sign the plea. But Brownlee's refusal to play the Washington game would not be forgotten. Less than two weeks after their phone call that evening, Michael Elston prepared a list of U.S. Attorneys to be fired, by the Bush administration, for political reasons. Because federal prosecutors were supposed to be nonpolitical by definition, this was a highly unusual move, one that would cause an uproar in Washington, spurring a congressional investigation and ultimately costing Elston his job. The hit list that he prepared was characterized as hinging on political "loyalty," and the U.S. Attorneys who were on it had apparently shown insufficient allegiance to the Bush administration. Elston added Brownlee's name to the list. The scandal came to light before Brownlee could actually be dismissed. But Brownlee later testified that he was certain his name ended up on that list because of his refusal to scuttle the case against Purdue Pharma.

✢ ✢ ✢

One day the following spring, Barry Meier was in New York when he got a message from someone who worked in Brownlee's office: Purdue would soon be pleading guilty in federal court. The company had asked that no reporters be present in the courtroom during the hearing. Of course, the final outcome could have been significantly worse for Purdue, but just the same this would be an embarrassing day for the company—and particularly for Friedman, Goldenheim, and Udell.

"Brownlee wants you to be there," Meier's contact told him. When they were putting together the case, the prosecutors had relied on his book, *Pain Killer,* and on his reporting for the *Times.* So, as a courtesy, they tipped him off.

Meier had not published any articles about Purdue since the *Times* management took him off the story, at Udell's request, three years earlier. But he had a new editor these days, and he explained that he would like to go to Virginia and do a piece about the guilty plea.

"All is forgiven," the editor said. "Write about it."

On the day before the court hearing, Meier took the train to Washington, then rented a car and drove as far as Roanoke, where he had dinner with John Brownlee. The outcome of the case might not have been what the prosecutors had hoped, but Brownlee was philosophical. In the end, the company had agreed to make a guilty plea to a criminal charge of felony misbranding. Friedman, Goldenheim, and Udell would each plead guilty to a misdemeanor count of misbranding as well and be barred for a period of twenty years from doing business with any taxpayer-financed health-care program, like Medicare. (That exclusion period was subsequently reduced to twelve years.) The men would accept a sentence of three years of probation and four hundred hours of community service. And Purdue would pay a $600 million fine. That was nothing to sniff at.

The following morning, Meier woke early and drove to Abingdon, where he met up with a freelance photographer. He knew that Friedman, Goldenheim, and Udell had flown in the night before and spent the night at a hotel that was adjacent to the courthouse, the Martha Washington Inn. The executives would be spared the indignity of handcuffs, but they would be doing the white-collar equivalent of a perp walk from the hotel into the courthouse, and Meier wanted a photo. Together with the photographer, he crouched in a row of cars lining the street. Then they saw the men coming. They all wore dark suits and somber expressions. Friedman seemed to have lost some of his swagger. Udell still struggled with his weight. The executives were startled, and visibly displeased, to see Barry Meier pop out from between the cars as his photographer snapped pictures. They hadn't seen Meier since the meeting they all had at Purdue headquarters in Stamford five years earlier, at which they had told him one brazen lie after another. Now the three men said nothing to him and scurried into the courthouse. "Purdue Pharma acknowledged in the court proceeding today that 'with the intent to defraud or mislead,' it marketed and promoted OxyContin as a drug that was less addictive, less subject to abuse and less likely to cause other narcotic side effects than other pain medications," Meier wrote in the *Times*. But the subtext of his dispatch was clear: *I told you so. Fuck you.*

On a rainy day later that summer, Friedman, Goldenheim, and Udell were forced to return to Abingdon for the sentencing. This would be a more public proceeding. A large number of spectators had come from across the country to witness this event. Many of them had lost loved ones to OxyContin, and the judge in the case, James Jones, who was in his sixties, with a kind smile and a full head of white hair, had granted these victims the opportunity to speak.

"Gentlemen," a woman named Lynn Locascio said, turning to Friedman, Goldenheim, and Udell. "You are responsible for a modern-day plague." The courtroom was packed to capacity. Locascio had come all the way from Palm Harbor, Florida. She recounted how her son had become addicted to OxyContin after it was prescribed to him following a car accident. One by one, other parents stood to offer brief, heartrending stories of pain. "Please do not allow this plea bargain to proceed," a man named Ed Bisch, who lost his eighteen-year-old son, Eddie, implored the judge. "These criminals deserve jail time." One mother had brought with her to the courtroom an urn holding the ashes of her child.

Some of the parents spoke candidly about how their children first took OxyContin recreationally, at parties, before becoming addicted and dying. But others described a habit that formed under a doctor's care. A man named Kenny Keith recounted his own addiction, after the drug was prescribed to him for chronic pain. "I am one of the patients who got addicted to OxyContin who lived through it," he said. "Whenever I tried to stop it, the withdrawals were worse than the pain that I was having." He lost his house. He lost his family. "I was an animal, out of control," he said.

Marianne Skolek, the nurse whose daughter, Jill, had overdosed and died, made the trip to Virginia. Since Jill's death, she had become an active member of a grassroots campaign to hold Purdue accountable. Skolek spoke about how her daughter had been prescribed OxyContin in January 2002 and died four months later. "She left behind her son, who was six years old at the time of her death," Skolek said. "Brian is here in the courtroom with me today because he needed to see that bad things do happen to bad people." Turning to Friedman, Goldenheim, and Udell, Skolek told the men that they were "sheer evil."

One person who was not there to testify that day was Howard Udell's former legal secretary, Martha West. She had been interviewed by Brownlee's investigators, and they included an account of her 1999 research into the abuse of OxyContin in their prosecution memo. They had even arranged for her to appear before the grand jury in Abingdon. But it never happened, because the evening before her testimony Martha West had vanished. Her lawyer found her the next morning, in the emergency room of a local hospital, where she had shown up to beg the staff for painkillers.

✦ ✦ ✦

In pleading guilty, Purdue accepted responsibility for a pattern of fraudulent misconduct. The prosecutors and defense lawyers had collaborated to hammer out an "Agreed Statement of Facts" to which Purdue was pleading and that it would not contest. In addition to the $600 million fine, Friedman, Goldenheim, and Udell had agreed to pay $34 million in fines (though, in practice, they wouldn't pay this money, the company would).

Even so, in the sentencing phase Purdue's attorneys argued that the defendants really weren't pleading guilty to all that much in the way of improper conduct and that this whole scandal was the work of a few unidentified bad actors. "Certain employees made or told others to make statements about OxyContin to some health care professionals," Howard Shapiro told the court. But, he insisted, "these misstatements were far from pervasive."

In advance of the hearing, Judge Jones had received a bevy of letters from friends and colleagues of the executives, pleading for lenience and expressing great effrontery that such pillars of society should be subjected to the stigma of a misdemeanor charge. Michael Friedman's brother, Ira, suggested, in effect, that these were trumped-up charges and that Michael had done nothing wrong, saying, "The media have done him a terrible injustice." Goldenheim's wife, Anne, recalled the "intense commitment" that Paul had felt when he raised his hand and swore the Hippocratic oath at his medical school graduation back in 1976.

"Simply put (and with apologies to my parents), Howard Udell is the finest person I have ever known," Richard Silbert, an attorney in the legal department at Purdue, wrote. Executives at the company had shown an occasional tendency to imply that the real victims in the opioid crisis were not those struggling with addiction but the company itself, and these letters of support echoed that refrain. Howard Udell had "endured the slings and arrows of the press," his son Jeffrey wrote, complaining that his father had been portrayed as "no better than a drug pusher." This was, in his view, "a horrible mischaracterization."

The statute under which the executives had been charged held that they need not have personally done anything wrong themselves: if the company broke the law, they, as senior corporate officers, were responsible. This was a convenient distinction for those who defended the three men, because it was possible to assert that they had pleaded guilty despite being entirely innocent. To Rick Mountcastle and others who worked on the case, however, the preening sense of righteousness on display was galling. After all, they had gathered ample evidence of specific criminal activity by these men. They'd been fully prepared to charge each of the three with multiple felonies.

But there was an underlying theme in the letters that insinuated, without ever saying so explicitly, that wealthy white executives—men with families and impressive educational pedigrees, men who give to charity and play an important role in their local communities— were temperamentally incapable of committing the kinds of crimes that should land a person in prison. They weren't the types of people who *belonged* in prison, one letter after another suggested. Jay McCloskey, the former Maine U.S. Attorney who had first sounded the alarm about the opioid crisis in Maine, before leaving government to work for Purdue, chided his fellow prosecutors, saying that "this is a case of unusual, if not unprecedented, prosecutorial discretion" and lamenting the "stigma" that Howard Udell would now bear, after such a long and "unblemished" career.

"There is no evidence at all of any personal wrongdoing by Mr. Udell," Mary Jo White announced during the sentencing hearing, describing her client as a "high minded" and "thoroughly ethical" person. "What has happened here," she said to the courtroom full of families who had lost loved ones in the opioid crisis, "is a personal tragedy for Mr. Udell."

Making the most of the hand he'd been dealt, John Brownlee announced that "Purdue and its executives have been brought to justice." He ended up stepping down as U.S. Attorney in 2008 and announced almost immediately that he would run for state attorney general. (He didn't win, and instead returned to private practice.)

On one level, the case could be described as a setback for Purdue. In actuality, though, it was anything but. Decades earlier, when the Sackler brothers created a multitude of business entities with different names, they became wizards at the shell game of corporate nomenclature. Now the company was able to play this name game to its decisive advantage. If Purdue Pharma pleaded guilty, as a corporation, to a criminal conviction, it would have a devastating effect on the business, because government-funded programs like Medicare would be barred from doing business with the company. So it was agreed that Purdue Pharma would not plead guilty to any charges at all, even though it was Purdue Pharma that was guilty. Instead, Purdue *Frederick*—the legacy corporation, the purveyor of earwax remover and laxatives—would enter the guilty plea. Purdue Frederick would take the charge, and die, so that Purdue Pharma could live on and continue to prosper.

As for the Sacklers, none of them made the journey to Virginia for the guilty plea or the sentencing, and their name appeared nowhere in the Agreed Statement of Facts. Brownlee didn't mention the Sacklers in his press conference about the case, and none of the press coverage of the sentencing or the fine mentioned them either. The nine Sacklers who were board members of the company had voted that Friedman, Goldenheim, and Udell should plead guilty as individuals, thereby protecting the family and the company. In his letter to the judge about the great moral rectitude of Howard Udell, the Purdue attorney Richard Silbert suggested that Udell had no choice but to "accept responsibility for the misconduct of others." But nowhere in the court record, or in any of the press coverage, did anyone suggest that what the executives were doing, by pleading guilty, was protecting the Sacklers.

Inside the company, however, this was very much the impression. Friedman, Goldenheim, and Udell "took responsibility on themselves and pleaded guilty," Kathe Sackler would later say. In doing so, they were ensuring that the family would not be implicated. "Those three guys basically took the hit for the family, because the family was going to take care of them," Gary Ritchie, who spent eleven years at Purdue as a chemist, recalled. "'Keep yourself out of prison; we'll take care of you off the books.' That's just how they did business," he said. Not long after the guilty plea, the Sacklers voted to pay Michael Friedman $3 million. Howard Udell got $5 million. The dynamics in play resembled nothing so much as a Mafia film. As one friend of Goldenheim's put it, the three men had been designated to "take the fall."

✢ ✢ ✢

The same month that they paid Udell his $5 million, the Sacklers voted to pay themselves $325 million. One of the grieving parents at the sentencing, a Florida man who had lost his son less than a year earlier, had likened the whole pas de deux between the government and the company to a game. The penalty was "just another move," he said. "They haven't changed a thing. They're working it just as hard as ever. They're going to take money out of the checkbook. Pay it. Keep going."

In theory, this conviction was supposed to represent a major step in reforming Purdue. But inside the company, it was regarded as little more than a speeding ticket. In a subsequent congressional hearing at which John Brownlee testified about the case, Arlen Specter, the Republican senator from Pennsylvania, remarked that when the government fines corporations, rather than sending executives to jail, it amounts to "expensive licenses for criminal misconduct." And this appears to be the way that the sanction against Purdue was perceived by the Sacklers and their executives. Not long after the guilty plea, a new administrative assistant, Nancy Camp, overheard Purdue's chief financial officer, Ed Mahony, talking about the $600 million fine. "That's been in the bank for years," he said. "That's nothing to us."

Shortly after the settlement in Virginia, the Sacklers voted to expand Purdue's sales force by hiring a hundred additional reps. It was time to get back to selling OxyContin. As for the Agreed Statement of Facts—the recitation of Purdue's misdeeds, which had been negotiated with such care by all of the attorneys for the company and the Department of Justice and was meant to form the basis for Purdue's good behavior moving forward—on the ninth floor of headquarters in Stamford, it was not taken very seriously.

When Richard Sackler was later asked, under oath, whether there had been anything in the document, in the way of corporate misconduct, that surprised him, he seemed curiously unprepared to answer.

"I can't say," Richard replied.

"As we sit here today, have you ever read the entire document?" an attorney asked.

"No," said Richard Sackler.

LEGACY

LEGACY

Chapter 21

TURKS

THE TINY BRITISH OVERSEAS territory of Turks and Caicos is an archipelago of coral islands that lie scattered, like a handful of bread crumbs, across the opalescent waters between the Bahamas and the Dominican Republic. Most of the islands remain uninhabited, and with clear water and beaches of powdery sand Turks retains an aura of Robinson Crusoe seclusion that is a rarity among the more built-up corners of the Caribbean. As a consequence, it has become popular as a holiday refuge for the superrich. Movie stars like Brad Pitt and athletes like David Beckham vacation in Turks. Until his death, from an opioid overdose in 2016, the musician Prince had a private compound on the main island of Providenciales. During the high season, between Christmas and New Year's, the little airport on Providenciales is busy, with sleek private jets taking off and landing.

In 2007, on a stretch of windswept coastline, a new resort was being built. It was called Amanyara and was part of a small chain of discreet, superluxury properties that originated in Southeast Asia. Guesthouses at the resort would rent for as much as $10,000 a night, and a series of sumptuous private residences were also available for sale, at prices ranging from $11 to $20 million. One investor in the property, who bought a residence for himself and his family, was the oldest surviving son of Mortimer Sackler, Mortimer junior.

The younger Mortimer had grown up in Manhattan, one of two children from his father's brief, tempestuous second marriage to the Austrian Geri Wimmer. After the divorce, the children were raised mostly by Geri, who started her own short-lived business, a company that developed herbal skin creams and toners that, she proclaimed, would be "the highest-priced beauty product on the market." (The creams were derived from skin treatments that had been used, in

Geri's dubious description, by monks "in eighteenth-century Italian monasteries.")

Mortimer attended Dalton, the ritzy private school on the Upper East Side. He was a delicate child, with big eyes and a mop of dark curls, and some of his classmates made fun of him, because even by the standards of the 1980s the name Mortimer had a cartoonishly old-rich-guy ring to it. In the recollection of one student who overlapped with him at Dalton, "He just seemed innocent and mocked and friendless and rich." And Dalton was a *school* for rich kids, "so to be ostracized on that basis, you had to be pretty fucking rich." Mortimer ended up finishing high school at Exeter, the elite New Hampshire prep school, then attending Harvard (where a museum was named after his uncle) for college and NYU (where an institute was named after his father) for a business degree.

At NYU, he met a slender society girl named Jacqueline Pugh. She, too, had grown up in Manhattan, and they married in 2002, settling in a loft in Chelsea that had been designed by the architect Peter Marino. "Mortimer and his family are involved with several organizations in the city," Jacqueline told *Vogue*, with considerable understatement, in an interview about a nonprofit she had started for "young philanthropists." "But it's exhausting to be as social as we could be and then come to the office every day," she said. "We work ourselves to death."

Mortimer's father had always distinguished himself, among the original three Sackler brothers, with his wanderlust and his tendency to accumulate glamorous homes. For the first few years of their marriage, Mortimer and Jacqueline liked to vacation at the family retreat in Cap d'Antibes, but eventually they purchased a sprawling estate in Amagansett, in the Hamptons, which had once been the village lawn tennis club before it was converted into a mansion. They also upsized their Manhattan home, paying $15 million for a five-story beaux arts town house on Seventy-Fifth Street, just off the park, a short walk from the Sackler Wing at the Met.

The Turks and Caicos refuge was finally ready for move in at around the time Purdue finalized its guilty plea in Virginia. If that unfortunate episode had caused Mortimer any undue anxiety, Amanyara offered an excellent balm. He and Jacqueline had two sons by now. After a few short hours on a plane from New York, a Range Rover, stocked with scented moist towels to refresh them after their flight, would pick the

family up and ferry them to the resort, which was full of Zen vistas and
overgrown vegetation and abutted an expansive nature preserve. The
name Amanyara is meant to evoke a place of peace and nirvana, and
the architecture was soothing, consisting of Asian-inspired, pagoda-
style pavilions. There was no loud music, no Jet Skis, no cruise ships.
None of the louche, unsightly package tourists who had besmirched
the more consumer-accessible parts of the Caribbean. Instead, Amanyara offered pure solitude and tranquillity. The Sackler villa was really
more of a compound, consisting of a series of buildings and a private
swimming pool. The design was spare but elegant, with hand-carved
stone from Indonesia, silk from Thailand, and lots of teak (each villa
featured materials that had been shipped to Turks and Caicos from
thirty-nine different countries). The Sacklers had their own personal
chef, who was on call twenty-four hours a day, and a coterie of "butlers"
and other attendants, who hovered and swooped, catering and scrubbing, like courtiers at Versailles. The ratio of staff to visitors at Amanyara was approximately five to one.

There were facilities dedicated to health and wellness, with spa
treatments and high-end yoga and Pilates instructors who were flown
in from the United States. Such amenities were helpful for Mortimer,
who, as he got older, developed back pain. Unlike the disgraced lawyer
Howard Udell, who took OxyContin, Mortimer did not avail himself
of the family product. Instead, he relied on a regimen of massage, acu-
puncture, and other alternative remedies. According to a yoga instructor whom the family brought to Amanyara on a number of occasions, on
one visit to the villa Mortimer's back pain was so severe that Jacqueline
(who, when it came to staff, had a reputation as a fearsome taskmaster)
ordered a couple of the butlers to accompany Mortimer as he hobbled
about, propping him up as "human crutches."

At another resort, this might have seemed beyond the call of duty.
But Amanyara was dedicated to the idea that for the wealthy client
customer service should be a concept without any practical limitation.
In keeping with the Asian theme at the resort, the staff was, for the
most part, not drawn from the local population, or from surrounding
islands, for that matter. Instead, nearly half of the employees were Fili-
pino. If the sand on the beach got too hot in the noonday sun, staffers
would spray it with water so that guests could stroll where they wanted
without fear of burning their feet. Haiti was just a couple of hundred

miles across the water, and occasionally migrants who were desperate to flee that country would board flimsy vessels and navigate in the general direction of Turks. From time to time, a dead body would wash ashore, some poor soul who hadn't survived the voyage, her dreams extinguished, her lungs full of seawater. But employees had been specifically instructed to be alert for this type of eventuality, and when a corpse washed in overnight, the whole staff would mobilize to make sure any trace of it had been removed from the beach before the guests arose the next morning.

It is a cliché to observe that in any family dynasty in which great wealth is created, the second generation is often less impressive than the first. But it was precisely this thought that often struck those who had occasion, in a social or professional milieu, to interact with the younger Mortimer Sackler. As Mortimer grew older, his hairline receded and his chin softened. His eyes had a somewhat nervous cast to them, and when he and Jacqueline were out on the town for a charity auction or some other society function, which they often were, he would arrange his features into an awkward smile, like a third grader who has been prompted to pose for a class photo. He donated generously, in the family tradition, joining the board of the Guggenheim Museum and making gifts to other blue-chip cultural institutions. Jacqueline became a budding society hostess, a "patron" of the American Museum of Natural History's winter dance, alongside other young socialites such as Ivanka Trump.

There she was, striding past the flashbulbs in a strapless, harlequin-print Yves Saint Laurent gown into the Young Collectors Council gala at the Guggenheim, where the main hall had been festooned with a thousand long-stemmed roses and tricked out with half a dozen life-sized mechanical bulls. ("The mechanical bulls are fantastic," Jacqueline enthused.) And there was Mortimer, by her side at one catered function after another, looking coddled and vacant-eyed, like the kind of well-upholstered young man who seems untroubled by the possibility that his only real distinction in life might be his money.

"Mortimer is like the TV character version of himself," one former Purdue employee who dealt with him observed. "He's the billionaire's son." He had joined the family business and served as a vice president, alongside Kathe ("Even though we have different mothers," Kathe once said, "he's my brother"), and the two of them advocated for the

A side, as the Mortimer Sackler wing was known, while Richard and his brother, Jonathan (who had also served as a vice president), advocated for the Raymond wing, the B side. Mortimer was more than two decades younger than his cousin Richard, however, and not a medical doctor. He was very involved in the company, but Purdue might not have been quite so fundamental to his sense of identity as it had always been for Richard. Mortimer had other investments, other projects, and he was much more active than Richard was on the philanthropic circuit. He also seemed to recognize that the negative headlines associated with OxyContin might impart a certain subtle taint in the stuffy social ecosystem that he and Jacqueline inhabited, so he tended not to dwell on Purdue in conversation. On the Upper East Side, friends of his would whisper, among themselves, about the sordid origins of the family wealth. As one person who knew Mortimer socially put it, "I think for him, most of the time, he's just saying, 'Wow, we're really rich. It's fucking cool. I don't really want to think that much about the other side of things.'"

At times, Mortimer would express an interest in getting out of the drug business altogether. "The pharmaceutical industry has become far too volatile and risky for a family to hold 95% of its wealth in," he wrote to Richard and Jonathan not long after the guilty plea, in 2008. "It simply is not prudent for us to stay in the business given the future risks we are sure to face." The Sacklers had discussed selling the company in the past. But whenever the idea was raised, people would say, "That's never going to happen while Dr. Raymond is alive." The old man did not want to see the company that he and his brother had built simply sold. So the family chose to stay in the business, though, according to Mortimer, it had "not been a pleasant experience (to say the least)."

Even so, after the guilty plea, he allowed that "things are looking better again now." And they were. The truth was, there was no way that the Sacklers were going to get out of the opioid trade. It was simply too profitable. Annual revenues for OxyContin continued to soar, and in the aftermath of the criminal case in Virginia, they reached a new high, of $3 billion. Having faced down a potentially mortal threat to its existence, OxyContin was booming. And it wasn't just that Purdue kept selling the drug. The company continued to engage in the very same aggressive marketing tactics that it had vowed to put an end to.

✢ ✢ ✢

After the guilty plea, Purdue had signed an agreement committing to improve its conduct and to subject itself to independent monitoring. Publicly, the company boasted about the steps it took to redress any issues it might have had in the past: hiring new compliance people, stressing to sales representatives that they should not make unfounded assertions about the drug. But, in practice, the Sacklers and the company leadership very quickly revived the old manner of selling OxyContin. Sales reps continued to market the drug as a safe opioid that would not cause addiction. The company continued to distribute literature that made false claims about the safety of opioids and suggested that those who showed signs of dependence and withdrawal were merely suffering from "pseudo-addiction." In Tennessee, the company trained its sales representatives to "ABC," or "Always Be Closing," citing a line delivered by Alec Baldwin in the 1992 film *Glengarry Glen Ross*, which is about salesmen using deceptive tactics to con unsuspecting buyers into investing in worthless real estate. In their notebooks, the new reps dutifully wrote down, *Always...Be...Closing.*

The Sacklers did not appear to be chastened by having to pay a $600 million fine. Instead, the family and their adjutants continued to abide by Richard's philosophy that it was not the drug that was the problem. A year after the guilty plea, in May 2008, staff sent the Sacklers a series of "key messages that work" in promoting strong opioids. "It's not addiction, it's abuse," one of the messages read. "It's about personal responsibility." That same year, the company distributed a pamphlet to doctors that suggested addiction "is not caused by drugs." Rather, "it is triggered in a susceptible individual by exposure to drugs, most commonly through abuse." In a separate campaign, Purdue advised pain patients to "overcome" any concerns they might have about addiction. At a board meeting that fall, the Sacklers were informed that Purdue's own sales data showed abuse and diversion of OxyContin "throughout the United States" and that availability of the product and "prescribing practices" were helping to drive this phenomenon. At the same meeting, staff announced to the Sacklers that a new Toppers contest had been established—to incentivize the very sales reps who were pushing the availability and prolific prescribing of the drug.

By 2008, the United States was in the throes of a full-blown opioid emergency, and people had started to talk about it as a public health crisis. The plague of addiction was no longer confined to rural areas. The death of the actor Heath Ledger that January, from an overdose involving a long list of painkillers, including oxycodone, brought a new level of national attention to the problem. Fatality numbers were on the rise, and on Capitol Hill, Senator Joe Biden called a hearing on this "trend that has crept into our households and communities across the country."

OxyContin had been on the market for twelve years. For Purdue's sales reps, out in the field, the red flags associated with improper prescribing were often laughably easy to spot. In 2008, a crime ring in Los Angeles recruited an elderly physician named Eleanor Santiago, who was in poor health and struggling with debt, to set up a phony clinic near MacArthur Park, called Lake Medical. Santiago began prescribing a great deal of OxyContin. One week in September, she prescribed fifteen hundred pills—more than many pharmacies might sell in a whole month. The next month, the number jumped to eleven thousand pills. A disproportionate number of Santiago's prescriptions were for 80-milligram OxyContin pills, the largest available dose, which, as it happened, was also the most popular dose on the black market, where they were known as 80s and sold for $80 apiece. By the end of 2008, Santiago had prescribed seventy-three thousand pills.

A shady operation this might have been, but it was characterized by an industrial efficiency that was hard not to admire. Members of the crime ring would descend upon Skid Row, in downtown L.A., and recruit homeless people, shuttling them off in vans and paying them $25 each to come to Lake Medical for a bogus examination. Next, they would escort these phony patients to a pharmacy, present the prescription that Dr. Santiago had just written, and collect a bottle of Oxy-Contin 80s, which the ring would then proceed to sell, in bulk, to drug traffickers, who distributed them on the black market up and down the West Coast and as far away as Chicago.

In Stamford, Purdue was tracking these orders, using the fine-grained data supplied by IMS. Company officials saw these extraordinary prescription volumes being generated by Lake Medical but took no steps to intervene. In September, a Purdue district manager named Michele Ringler visited the clinic with one of her sales reps. From the outside, the building looked abandoned. But inside, they found a little office that was packed full of people. Ringler later reported that she thought some of the individuals standing around looked as if "they just got out of L.A. county jail." Growing nervous for their own safety, she and her sales rep decided to leave before they even had a chance to speak with Dr. Santiago.

"I feel very certain that this is an organized drug ring," Ringler wrote to a compliance official at Purdue. "Shouldn't the DEA be contacted about this?"

"As far as reporting to DEA—this is under serious consideration," Jack Crowley, the compliance official back in Stamford, replied. But the company did not report Lake Medical to the authorities, even as complaints—nearly a dozen of them—started coming in from Los Angeles pharmacists expressing their own suspicions about the operation. Purdue concluded that at least one of the pharmacies filling orders for Lake Medical was *itself* corrupt and part of the crime ring. But the company took no steps to cut off the supply of pills. Crowley would later acknowledge that in the five years he spent investigating suspicious pharmacies at Purdue, the company did not suspend the flow of pills to a single one.

Purdue did maintain its own secret list of potentially problematic prescribers. It was known, within the company, as "Region Zero." Officials at Purdue flagged Santiago and placed her name on this list. But the company did nothing to alert law enforcement about its suspicions. In fact, it was only in 2010 that Purdue reported to the authorities any concerns regarding Lake Medical. By that time, the clinic had been shut down, and Dr. Santiago and other members of the ring had been indicted. (She pleaded guilty to health-care fraud and was sentenced to twenty months in prison.) Investigators had finally caught on to Lake Medical with no help from Purdue, having been alerted to the problem by tips from the community. Jack Crowley mused, in an email, that it had taken the government "a long time to catch up with these jokers."

A Purdue lawyer defended the company's conduct, saying that reports about inappropriate prescribing are often "anecdotal" and "unconfirmed," and if Purdue were to act too quickly to cut off supply, it might jeopardize the availability of the drug for legitimate pain patients. But Purdue's reticence when it came to doing anything about the problem was also quite lucrative, as a corporate policy. According to an investigation by the *Los Angeles Times,* during the two years between when Michele Ringler, the Purdue district manager, sounded the alarm internally and when Lake Medical was shut down, the company supplied more than a million OxyContin pills to this criminal enterprise.

✢   ✢   ✢

To the degree that the Sacklers were forced to address this rising tide of misery and death, they tended to treat it as a business problem, one of a number of "pressures" that their company was facing. In 2008, Kathe Sackler sent an email to staff instructing them to enumerate these various pressures and provide "quantification of their negative impact on projected sales." Purdue was still contending with a host of private lawsuits related to OxyContin and spending a great deal of money in order to fight them off. For a period of time following the guilty plea in Virginia, Howard Udell had continued to work for the company. But having agreed, along with his fellow defendants, Paul Goldenheim and Michael Friedman, to a guilty plea in which the men could no longer work for any company that did business with the federal government, Udell eventually had no choice but to exit Purdue for good. (He complained mightily about this exclusion, as did Goldenheim and Friedman. The three executives went so far as to challenge the penalty in court, but without success.)

In lieu of prison time, the executives had been given probation and ordered to perform several hundred hours of community service. Udell chose to work with veterans and ended up establishing a legal services organization in Connecticut that provided much-needed assistance to the veteran community. Purdue Pharma was also doing work with veterans during this period, organizing special events with doctors to encourage them to prescribe opioids to American servicemen and servicewomen who were returning from the wars in Iraq and Afghanistan. The company sponsored the publication of a book, *Exit Wounds: A Survival Guide to Pain Management for Returning Veterans and Their Families.* The author, Derek McGinnis, was a former navy corpsman who had lost a leg in the Battle of Fallujah in 2004. The book was published by the putatively independent American Pain Foundation ("A United Voice of Hope and Power over Pain"). Only in the fine print, on the copyright page, did it acknowledge the "generous support" of Purdue Pharma.

"Many veterans of Operation Enduring Freedom have probably seen the flowers of the opium poppy," McGinnis wrote, noting that the plant is widely cultivated in Afghanistan. "The pain-relieving properties of opioids are unsurpassed," he continued, asserting that these drugs are "considered the 'gold standard'" when it comes to pain management. Yet despite their great benefits, he marveled, opioids are still "underused." As for any fears that wounded veterans might have about addiction, *Exit Wounds* was reassuring. "Long experience with opioids shows that people who are not predisposed to addiction are unlikely to become addicted," the book asserted.

Howard Udell eventually died of a stroke, at the age of seventy-two, in 2013. The woman who founded the veterans legal center with him, Margaret Middleton, described his charitable work as "the most amazing redemption." But in truth, Udell never felt that he needed to be redeemed, because he, personally, hadn't done anything wrong. After his death, a sympathetic article in the *Hartford Courant* suggested that Udell had no knowledge of any misrepresentations by Purdue, "which amounted to remarks made by a few representatives in the field to some physicians."

The Sacklers shared this benign view of the man who had represented them for four decades and had ultimately chosen to fall on his sword for the family. On the eighth floor of Purdue headquarters at One Stamford Forum, the family rechristened the small legal library the Howard Udell Memorial Library and hung a photograph of Udell in his prime, as a tribute. For some employees, the continued presence of a shrine to the former general counsel who had been forced to retire after the company pleaded guilty to a federal crime tended to undercut, in a subtle way, any platitudes that the Sacklers or their current retinue of senior executives might offer about their commitment to fighting the opioid crisis. "I mean this is a guy who pled guilty. What does that tell you?" one former Purdue executive pointed out. In terms of institutional culture and unspoken signals to employees about what types of behavior might and might not be acceptable, the continued reverence for Howard Udell spoke volumes.

Udell's retirement and subsequent death might have appeared to leave a vacuum at Purdue, but the Sacklers had a stable of capable attorneys who stood more than ready to take his place. Foremost among them was a man named Stuart Baker. A classic corporate gray man, Baker was almost invisible to the outside world. But behind the scenes, he was a steady and calculating advocate for the Sacklers. Nominally, Baker was a partner at Chadbourne & Parke (which was subsequently renamed Norton Rose Fulbright), the New York law firm that had represented the family for decades, where the attorney Richard Leather had been a partner when he drew up the musketeers agreement between the Sackler brothers and Bill Frohlich. The firm had a long history as a fierce advocate for the tobacco industry. But Baker seemed to devote nearly all of his time to the representation of one particular client. In fact, he had his own office on the ninth floor of Purdue headquarters and his own full-time administrative assistant at the company. Kathe Sackler once described Baker as serving as a "liaison" between the board and senior management at Purdue. But he often served as a liaison between the two wings of the family as well. At board meetings, which could occasionally descend into name-calling, on account of the frequent and acrimonious disagreements between the A side and the B side, Baker tried to maintain the peace, physically positioning himself between the quarreling wings of the family. Occasionally, Kathe would be railing on about some subject at a board meeting, and her cousin Jonathan would interrupt to tell her that she was being difficult and should stop talking. Baker would quietly attempt to get the meeting back on track, but Kathe would say, "No, Stuart. I don't think this should continue until Jonathan gives me an apology."

"I'm not going to apologize for *your* behavior," Jonathan would say, leaving Baker to try his best to smooth things over as the twenty or so people attending the board meeting avoided eye contact and tried to hide their embarrassment. "He had a number of roles," Kathe said, of Stuart Baker. Some executives in the company referred to him as "the concierge."

"Stuart had more power than anyone in the company, including the CEO," one former Purdue employee recalled. Because he served as liaison between the Sacklers on the board and the company leadership, he was "the choke point." He sat on the boards of multiple different Sackler-owned business interests around the world. "He was sort of the glue that held everything together," the former employee concluded. Once, in a meeting at the company, Baker mentioned the guilty pleas by Udell, Goldenheim, and Friedman. "Those people had to take the fall to protect the family," Baker acknowledged. The company's strategy, he said, was "to protect the family at all costs." (Two former employees recall witnessing this exchange. Afterward, one of them said, "I remember going home and saying, 'Where the fuck am I *working*?'")

Richard Sackler might not have wanted to sell Purdue, but he agreed with his cousin Mortimer's concern about how heavily the family had invested in the company and the resulting concentration of risk. So, he proposed an alternative. In a memo to his relatives in 2008, Richard suggested that they install a CEO at Purdue who would be "loyal" to the family. Then, rather than sell the company, they could simply "distribute more free cash flow" to themselves. What this would mean, in practice, was frequent distributions of cash to the various heirs of Raymond and Mortimer Sackler. Apart from the brothers themselves, there were ultimately eight family members, from three generations, who served on the board: Mortimer's British wife, Theresa, and his children Ilene, Kathe, and Mortimer, as well as Raymond's wife, Beverly, along with her children, Richard and Jonathan, and, eventually, Richard's son David. The board met frequently and often in luxurious foreign locales: Bermuda, Portugal, Switzerland, Ireland.

Richard Sackler was an unpredictable presence in board meetings. Often, he would ignore whoever was delivering a presentation and become so focused on his laptop that Jonathan would snap, "Richard, get off your computer. Put that away." Whereas the younger Mortimer was most engaged by the financial particulars of any given agenda item, Richard was more interested in the science. "He'll ask a question," one executive who sometimes presented to the board recalled. "And if you answer it, he'll ask another. And if you answer that one, he'll ask another. And he'll keep going until he gets to a question that you *can't* answer, and then he's won. Because he's the smartest guy in the room. And he'll ask a hundred questions, if that's what it takes to get to the one you have no answer to." Then, the executive continued, "if Richard gets his gotcha question, Kathe has to get hers in." Kathe always seemed to want to one-up Richard, according to the executive. But Richard showed her nothing but disdain. "It almost felt like the board meetings were mostly about each side of the family trying to prove to the other that they were smarter."

The problem, in Jonathan Sackler's view, was that there was a "Mortimer camp" and a "Raymond camp," and these factions had come to mirror the "dysfunctional relationship" between the brothers themselves. "We've inherited it, and to some extent embodied it in our own routines," he thought.

Board meetings generally ended with a family-only session, from which all the other executives, apart from Stuart Baker, were excluded. And at each meeting, the Sacklers would vote to pay themselves. A hundred million here, a hundred million there. If the younger Mortimer felt that he was not being paid promptly and in the amount that he had anticipated, he would complain. "Why are you BOTH reducing the amount of the distribution and delaying it and splitting it in two?" he fumed in 2010, upon learning that the company would need to reduce the family's quarterly disbursement from $320 million to $260 million and pay the money out in two tranches. Because the older Mortimer had seven children from his three marriages, whereas Raymond, who was still married to Beverly, had only two, a dynamic took hold in which members of the A side were always pressing for greater distributions, because they had more mouths to feed. Fortunately, there was no shortage of cash flow. In June 2010, Purdue presented the Sacklers with a ten-year plan that was projected to generate $700 million each year for the family, for the next ten years.

One downside of this strategy was that it didn't leave much of a war chest for Purdue to reinvest in the business. In a publicly traded company, this might have been identified as a potentially existential risk. But the Sacklers owned Purdue and could do what they wanted with it. Mortimer personally directed the company to slash spending on research and development. For scientists who worked at Purdue, this was frustrating: OxyContin was still generating a tremendous amount of revenue, but the Sacklers seemed more intent on pulling money out of Purdue than on growing or diversifying the company. The family might have assumed an undue concentration of risk by betting all its chips on the pharma business. But Purdue itself now had an undue concentration of risk, because all of its chips were on OxyContin. Jonathan Sackler characterized the company's strategy as more of a "milking program than a growth program."

This was a particularly imprudent game plan because the inescapable reality of the pharma business is that any drug's moment of peak profitability will eventually pass, when the patent lapses, giving way to generic competition. The Sacklers had discovered this, in a frightening way, just a few years earlier. One of Purdue's competitors, Endo, had filed a patent application in 2000 to make a generic version of OxyContin. Purdue's patent had not yet run out, so the company sued Endo to prevent it from selling this cheaper substitute. It was critical that Purdue kill off this challenge: two other companies were watching the case and preparing their *own* generic versions of OxyContin. But in 2004, a judge in Manhattan ruled that the original patent for OxyContin was invalid, because Purdue had misled the Patent and Trademark Office in its application. The company had secured its patents by asserting that OxyContin was unique, because 90 percent of patients supposedly got relief by taking relatively small doses. But Paul Goldenheim admitted, under oath, that at the point when Purdue made these claims to the PTO, the company's researchers "weren't anywhere close" to proving that. These bold assertions, Goldenheim said, had been an expression of Robert Kaiko's "vision," rather than scientific fact. Suddenly Purdue faced the prospect of generic competition, and it looked as though sales would plummet. The company made a round of painful layoffs. It appeared that OxyContin's run might be over, a turn of events that would cost Purdue and the Sacklers billions of dollars. But Howard Udell had invested in very good patent lawyers, and they persuaded an appeals court to vacate the 2004 judgment, so Purdue was able to restore its monopoly on the drug. They were back in business, but more mindful than ever that they had to maximize the windfall from Oxy-Contin before they lost exclusivity for good.

After the guilty plea in 2007, the Sacklers engaged with the consulting firm McKinsey, which began to advise the company on how to keep growing the market for OxyContin. A team of McKinsey analysts went in-house, camping out in a conference room at Purdue headquarters. Sales of OxyContin were at an all-time high, but the amount of oxycodone prescribed by American doctors was beginning to flatten. Ed Mahony, Purdue's chief financial officer, warned the Sacklers that projections now indicated sales of OxyContin could plateau. If that was the case, the promised decade of annual $700 million disbursements would almost certainly not materialize, and this worried the family. Richard convened a meeting in the summer of 2009, in order to strategize about how to "reverse the decline." He demanded weekly status updates on OxyContin sales. (This caused consternation among staffers, who didn't customarily generate the types of reports Richard was looking for. They deliberated over whether they should tell him that no such reports existed, but ultimately opted to create a new kind of weekly sales report, just for Richard.) McKinsey made a series of recommendations to the Sacklers about how Purdue could "turbocharge" the sales of OxyContin. It was important, the consultants suggested, to convince physicians that opioids provide "freedom" for patients and "the best possible chance to live a full and active life."

For these outside advisers, the assignment was a bizarre crash course in the curious corporate anthropology of Purdue. When the McKinsey consultants interviewed staff members at the company, they learned that while the Sacklers were officially just board members at this point, in practice they still maniacally directed day-to-day operations. The board "gets involved in too many decisions that it shouldn't," staff told the consultants. In the assessment of one McKinsey executive, "The brothers who started the company viewed all employees like the guys who 'trim the hedges'—employees should do exactly what's asked of them and not say too much."

✧ ✧ ✧

The original Mortimer Sackler was now in his nineties and still living a full and active life. In board meetings, he was a curmudgeonly presence, scowling behind his rectangular glasses. Employees at Purdue found him much less warm and avuncular than Raymond. But he had always enjoyed his leisure time more than work. He still jetted between his various grand residences. He loved to play backgammon and had continued to play tennis well into his eighties. On the last night of 2009, Mortimer welcomed his sprawling family and hundreds of guests to his vast country manse in Berkshire, outside London, which was known as Rooksnest and set in ten acres of manicured gardens and rolling woodlands. A huge tent had been erected for the wedding of his daughter Sophie. The bride was twenty-seven and beautiful. She had grown up in London and attended Oxford University, where a library was named after her father. There, she met a young cricket player named Jamie Dalrymple, who would go on to play for England's national team. For music at the wedding, the Sacklers had arranged for seventy members of a choir to come all the way from Swansea, in Wales. They sang the hymn "Guide Me, O Thou Great Redeemer":

Open now the crystal fountain
Whence the healing streams do flow.

Mortimer had always liked parties. He stayed up reveling until well past midnight. Three months later, he was dead. He had outlived his big brother, Artie, by nearly a quarter of a century and had eclipsed him in business and, arguably, in his impact on the world. Mortimer's death was mourned on both sides of the Atlantic, and in the many reminiscences from those who knew him, his life was recognized chiefly for his philanthropic contributions. "Mortimer D. Sackler, Arts Patron," was the headline of his obituary in *The New York Times,* which noted that he had been a "major donor to Oxford University, Edinburgh University, Glasgow University, the Tate Gallery in London, the Royal College of Art, the Louvre, the Jewish Museum in Berlin and Salzburg University, among other institutions." It was not until the ninth paragraph that the article made reference to OxyContin, "a widely abused street drug responsible for a number of overdose deaths," before adding, "None of the Sacklers were ever accused of any wrongdoing." Another extensive obituary, in the London *Times,* made much of Mortimer's benefactions not just to universities and art museums but in "the horticultural world." There was the Sackler Crossing, a lovely, curving bridge of black granite over a lake in London's Kew Gardens, for instance. And the time that Theresa Sackler (who was "Dame" Theresa by now and still a member of Purdue's board) made the winning bid at a charity auction to name a new species of rose. Dame Theresa, who had a passion for gardening, chose to name the flower after her husband. She was quoted, in the obituary, drawing an analogy between the Mortimer Sackler rose and its namesake. "The blooms give the impression of delicacy and softness," she said, "but are, in fact, very tough, and little affected by bad weather." The obituary made no mention at all of OxyContin.

Chapter 22

TAMPERPROOF

ONE DAY IN THE summer of 2010, without fanfare or warning, Purdue Pharma stopped shipping the OxyContin pills it had been churning out and distributing across the United States for nearly fifteen years and replaced them with a new kind of OxyContin that had been subtly reformulated. At a glance, the pills that started shipping that August looked almost identical to those that had come before. The only visible difference was that the new pills were slightly thicker and each one was stamped not with the "OC" that had traditionally adorned each pill but with "OP" instead. The payload in these new pills was precisely the same: pure oxycodone. It was the coating that had been reinvented.

As far back as 2001, people at Purdue had been talking about the possibility of a silver bullet solution to the problems bedeviling Oxy-Contin. What if they could develop a version of the pill that couldn't be crushed? If abusers broke the pill down in order to override the time-release mechanism and unleash the drug's full narcotic force, then perhaps Purdue's scientists could devise a pill that would thwart the "criminal addicts" Richard Sackler so despised—a pill that could not be abused.

This was a delicate project for the business to pursue, because part of the ethos of the Sackler family (and, as a consequence, part of the culture of the family company) was a reluctance to concede, even hypothetically, the possibility of error or wrongdoing. If Purdue made too much noise about how it was developing an abuse-resistant version of OxyContin, that could be interpreted as a rhetorical concession that the drug they had been selling all these years actually was, as critics had long maintained, dangerously susceptible to abuse.

But the idea that Purdue might invent an OxyContin pill that could only be swallowed, defying those in search of an immediate high, was irresistible, and some people at the company came to think of this project as the ultimate moon shot. The research took years and a great deal of trial and error. According to one of the key executives involved, Purdue devoted "a very large proportion" of its already limited R&D budget to the effort. Part of the motivation was no doubt an earnest desire to protect Purdue's marquee product from abuse. But another element might have been the fact that some of Purdue's competitors were also racing to devise a crushproof oxycodone pill. If one of these other companies beat Purdue to market, they could promote their pill as a safer alternative to OxyContin. "Purdue should be leading the charge on this type of research," the younger Mortimer Sackler told Richard in 2008. "Why are we playing catch up?"

Richard had long since stepped down from his role as titular head of the company, but he was still extremely active in the business. He continued to come into the office every day. He had a bulldog, which he often brought with him. The dog was named UNCH, after the stock market abbreviation for "Unchanged," which indicates that a company's share price ended the trading day at the same level where it started. Sometimes, an employee would get dressed up in his best suit for a meeting with Richard, only to arrive in the boss's book-lined office and notice, under the glass-topped desk, that UNCH was slobbering all over the freshly pressed leg of his trousers. UNCH had a tendency to shit in the hallways, and Richard had a tendency to not pick it up. So visitors to the ninth floor learned to weave around the occasional deposit left by the dog on the royal purple carpet.

Richard had conducted his own research into tamperproof formulations, obtaining several patents in which he was the named inventor, and he stayed in close touch with the Purdue team handling submissions to the FDA about this new product. He even weighed in on potential names for the pill. (It was ultimately just called OxyContin OP.) The company applied for FDA approval in late 2007, but it was only in 2010 that the agency granted Purdue permission to market this new "abuse-resistant" OxyContin.

The new pills were a scientific marvel. If you crushed them, they wouldn't fragment or break down into a fine powder that could be snorted or dissolved in liquid and injected intravenously. Instead, they squashed, like a piece of candy. You could slam one of the pills with a hammer, and it would crack but not shatter. With some effort, you could pry it into pieces, but if you tried to snort the bits that broke off,

they'd get stuck in your nostril. This was a small miracle, more innovative, in its way, than OxyContin had been in the first place. As one
former Purdue executive put it, when you tampered with the reformulated OxyContin, it turned "into a Gummy Bear."

Purdue Pharma had never been shy about making bold claims to
the FDA, and the company touted this new pill for its unprecedented
safety. Having exhibited in the past a remarkable tendency to accommodate Purdue by approving exaggerated marketing claims, the FDA
eventually bestowed upon the company another gift: for the first time
in its history, the agency permitted a claim, in the package insert for
reformulated OxyContin, about the "abuse deterrent" properties of the
pill. Richard Sackler had bragged, back when OxyContin was originally released, about how the company got the agency to approve a
label with more marketing claims than it ever had before, and now once
again the agency was permitting Purdue to claim that its new product
was safer than the competition. In another echo of the original launch
of OxyContin, the assertion about these abuse-deterrent advantages
was, for the moment, largely aspirational. A press release from the FDA
noted that Purdue would be required to conduct a "postmarket" study
to collect data on "the extent to which the new formulation reduces
abuse and misuse of this opioid"—that is, the extent to which the claim
that the FDA was already approving for the label might turn out to
actually be true. But in the meantime, Purdue was authorized to suggest to anyone who cared to listen that reformulated OxyContin was
less liable to be abused than other opioids on the market.

To the casual observer, the reformulation of OxyContin might
have appeared to be an instance in which the Sacklers, after years of
obstructing efforts to curb the disastrous impacts of their painkiller,
had finally seen the error of their ways. But the timing of the reformulation was interesting—and indicated that the company might have
been motivated by other considerations. Purdue originally secured its
patents conferring the exclusive right to market OxyContin back in
the 1990s. The continued exclusivity granted by the patents meant that
the company could prevent rival pharmaceutical firms from producing
a generic version of OxyContin. But all the while, in the background,
during these years of epic profitability, the patent clock was ticking.
The prospect of a branded drug going "off patent" is a terrifying one for
the drugmaker, but there are certain maneuvers that the cunning cor-

poration can employ to extend the life of a patent. There is a name for such tactics: "evergreening." Often, companies will wait until the original patent has nearly run its course and then introduce some minor tweak to the product, thereby obtaining a new patent and effectively restarting the clock. Nearly a decade earlier, in January 2001, Michael Friedman had conferred with another Purdue executive, Mark Alfonso, about the company's plans for developing abuse-resistant OxyContin, which they described as a "line extension." Rolling out this new version, Alfonso wrote, would be a way to "close the door to the competition." Prior to the introduction of OxyContin OP, the patent for the original formulation had been set to expire in 2013.

"It was *all* about the intellectual property around Oxy," one executive who joined the company during this period recalled. Purdue sold other products, but nobody was under any illusions. "It was 100 percent an OxyContin story. That's where the money was coming from," the executive continued. "Because they didn't have the skill sets that an integrated pharma company has, it was 'Protect the patents at all costs.' So the investment part of it, the talent within the company, it was all highly skewed toward protecting and preserving OxyContin." Purdue's leadership was so single-minded in extending the life of OxyContin, in fact, that it sometimes seemed to this executive as if the company wasn't a pharmaceutical business at all but "an intellectual property law firm that happened to have some R&D and a marketing arm."

For more than a decade, in the face of an ever-expanding public health crisis, the Sacklers and Purdue had maintained, defiantly, that the original formulation of OxyContin was safe and effective. Howard Udell had gone to his grave insisting as much. But after Purdue released the reformulated version of OxyContin in 2010, as the patent on the original formulation was set to expire, the company made an audacious about-face. Purdue filed papers with the FDA, asking the agency to refuse to accept generic versions of the *original* formulation of OxyContin—the version the company had been selling all these years—on grounds that it was unsafe. The company said that it was voluntarily withdrawing the original formulation from the market for reasons "of safety." On the very day that the patent for the original formulation was set to expire, the FDA, ever obliging, declared that the benefits of the old version of OxyContin "no longer outweigh" the risks. "Purdue is gratified that the FDA has determined that OxyContin extended release tablets were withdrawn from sale for reasons of safety," the company said in a press release, noting that the FDA would "not accept or approve" any applications for a generic version of the drug.

✢ ✢ ✢

It was not entirely fair to suggest that Purdue had no other products in the pipeline. In fact, not long after releasing OxyContin OP, the company introduced another opioid painkiller, a transdermal patch called Butrans. The Sacklers might have responded to the widespread criticism of Purdue and the criminal indictment and the multitude of lawsuits by taking steps to diversify their company away from opioids. Instead, they had opted to double down, positioning Purdue as an "integrated pain management company."

Richard Sackler had drifted apart from his wife, Beth, over the years. They would ultimately divorce in 2013, and Richard moved to Austin, Texas, where he bought a modern hilltop mansion on the outskirts of the city, in an area favored by tech billionaires. But he was still prone to meddling, fanatically, in the most minute operational details of his company. Pining, perhaps, for the glory days of the Blizzard of '96, when he oversaw the gangbusters launch of the original OxyContin, Richard now scrutinized every particular of the rollout of Butrans. He demanded "intelligence" on the drug's performance from the Purdue executive Russell Gasdia. He wanted to know whether the sales team was "encountering the resistance that we expected and how well are we overcoming it, and are the responses similar to, better, or worse than when we marketed OxyContin® tablets?" (Even in emails, Richard took the trouble of appending the registered trademark symbol to OxyContin, an indication, perhaps, of his high esteem for the law of intellectual property.)

It wasn't just that Richard wanted updates, practically in real time, about sales figures. He would also ask staff to furnish him with spreadsheets of raw sales data so that he could perform exotic calculations of his own. He had a lot of thoughts about how Butrans should be marketed and which types of doctors it should be promoted to. "Who have you chosen for me to go to the field with the week after the budget meetings?" he wrote to Gasdia in 2011. In order to get a truly vivid understanding of how the sales force was functioning, Richard had asked to personally accompany individual sales reps while they made their rounds. "Can we conveniently do two reps each day?" he wondered.

Fearful, perhaps, that Dr. Richard, unable to restrain himself, might start hand-selling opioids to random physicians, Gasdia sounded a quiet alarm, raising the issue with Purdue's chief of compliance, Bert Weinstein.

"LOL," Weinstein replied, with a levity that might seem cavalier for the internal watchdog of a firm that had pleaded guilty to federal charges of fraudulent marketing. Richard was going to be Richard: it was an inflexible law of life at Purdue, which everyone in the company had been forced to accept. Weinstein made it clear to Gasdia that he, for one, would not be putting his foot down to try to prevent the boss from going. But he did suggest that on these sales visits "Richard needs to be mum and be anonymous," as though this were some cameo on a reality show in which chief executives don wigs and fake mustaches before making incognito visits to the company warehouse. (In the end, Richard opted not to make the trip, though he did ride along with a Connecticut sales rep on another occasion that year.)

"Anything you can do to reduce the direct contact of Richard into the organization is appreciated," Gasdia wrote to John Stewart, the company's new CEO, who had taken over after Michael Friedman was forced to step down. "I realize he has a right to know and is highly analytical, but diving into the organization isn't always productive."

"I work on this virtually every day," Stewart wrote back, "some with more success than others."

Butrans was a scheduled narcotic—a powerful opioid, like OxyContin, with a corresponding risk of addiction. But Richard was frustrated by the degree to which a perception that the drug was potentially risky might be impacting sales. He complained about what he perceived as unnecessarily alarmist cautionary language about the downsides of the drug. The warning "implies a danger of untoward reactions and hazards that simply aren't there," Richard protested, suggesting that the company find "less threatening" ways to describe its opioids.

The launch of Butrans was moderately successful. If there was one thing, apart from donating money, that the Sacklers knew how to do, it was sell opioids. But compared with OxyContin, Butrans was no great triumph, and this bothered Richard and the other members of the board. "Do you share my disappointment?" he asked his staff in the spring of 2011. "What else more can we do to energize the sales and grow at a faster rate?" Mortimer joined his cousin in expressing concern, requesting more information on sales figures. But that June, staff reported to the Sacklers that earnings were hundreds of millions of dollars shy of their earlier projections. In Richard's view, the company had erred by failing to target "high potential" prescribers. He demanded to know how "our managers have allowed this to happen."

Privately, Gasdia complained about the family's "myopic focus" on opioids. "It's been hard to convince colleagues and the board that our success in this market is over," he wrote to a friend. Four months later, the Sacklers fired him.

✤ ✤ ✤

OxyContin continued to sell well in its new formulation. It was the best-selling painkiller in America, with more than $3 billion in annual sales, almost double the number of its nearest competitor drug. But did this new version actually deter abuse? That was a different question. Inside the company, there was an acknowledgment that Purdue's claims about abuse deterrence were, at best, theoretical. The Sacklers knew, because their staff informed them, that the leading method for abusing OxyContin was not snorting or shooting the pills at all but swallowing them whole, which the reformulation would not prevent. John Stewart told Richard Sackler explicitly at one point that reformulating Oxy-Contin "will not stop patients from the simple act of taking too many pills." At a meeting in early 2011, staff showed the board data indicating that 83 percent of patients who were admitted to substance abuse treatment centers had started using opioids by swallowing them.

At the same time, there were indications that for many people who were already hooked on OxyContin, the reformulation *was* making the drug more difficult to abuse. In online forums, longtime OxyContin users swapped stories about the great lengths to which they had gone to extract their fix from these new pills. People microwaved the pills, baked them in the oven, stuck them in the freezer, soaked them in all manner of solvents. But if Purdue's narrow objective was to prevent people from breaking down the pills, then this new coating seemed to work. In fact, there were telling indications, almost immediately, in Purdue's own sales data, which suggested that some habitual Oxy-Contin users were frustrated by the tamperproof pills. Despite what the company would tell the FDA about how the original formulation should now be considered unsafe, Purdue continued to sell the old version of OxyContin in Canada for a year after the new version was released in the United States. According to a subsequent study, during the months following the 2010 reformulation, sales of the traditional OxyContin in Windsor, Ontario, suddenly quadrupled. Windsor sits just across the border from Detroit. This was a clear indication that the pills were being purchased in Canada and then smuggled back into the United States—to be sold on the black market, because they were preferable to the new pills. Through IMS data, Purdue would have been able to monitor this abrupt surge in Canadian sales and to deduce the reason for it. (The company eventually acknowledged that it was aware of the spike and maintains that it alerted authorities, but declined to say when, exactly, it did so.)

Before long, the rate of deaths in the United States associated with overdoses involving OxyContin started to diminish. It was still too soon to say whether the reformulated drug could actually be described as "abuse deterrent," because many people who abused OxyContin swallowed the pills and did not necessarily turn up dead. The Centers for Disease Control would ultimately conclude that there are no studies suggesting that "abuse-deterrent technologies" are actually an effective strategy for "deterring or preventing abuse." The FDA would agree, in findings that were not released until 2020, saying that while the reformulation might have decreased the number of people who snorted or injected the drug, "evidence was not robust that the reformulation caused a meaningful reduction in *overall* OxyContin abuse."

Even so, if the reformulation was driving any number of people away from snorting or injecting OxyContin, that would appear to be a step in the right direction. And Purdue didn't really need to conduct complex research studies to develop a sense of the impact of the new pills. The company could just look at its bottom line. According to a research abstract by a team of scientists at Purdue, after the reformulation, sales of 80-milligram OxyContin pills dropped 25 percent nationwide.

On the one hand, this was an impressive metric of Purdue's success in curbing abuse of OxyContin by developing the new crushproof pills, and the company would tout the investment it made in the reformulation as evidence of its efforts to address the opioid crisis. On the other hand, that drop in sales offered a stark indication that for years

Purdue had been deriving a quarter of its revenue on the highest dose of OxyContin from the black market. The company studied the phenomenon; Richard complained about the "sudden decline" and wanted to know what "corrective actions" could be taken. According to court documents, Purdue concluded, internally, that the lost profit could be attributed in significant measure to a "reduction in medically unnecessary prescriptions."

Critics maintained that Purdue should not be celebrated for the new pills, because this was too little, too late. "It should not clear their conscience," Steven Tolman, a state senator from Massachusetts who led a commission to investigate OxyContin abuse, declared shortly after the reformulation. "Why didn't they do this years ago?"

And, as it turned out, this question of timing would prove to be deeply significant, because Purdue's reformulation had one momentous unintended consequence. If the Sacklers had replaced the original OxyContin with a tamper-resistant alternative a decade earlier, it might have had the potential to really curb abuse, because fewer people would have come to discover the intoxicating powers of the drug. But by 2010, the nation looked markedly different than it had in 2000. It was now in the grip of a full-blown opioid epidemic. Millions of Americans had become addicted to OxyContin and other opioids, whether they had done so through recreational abuse or under a doctor's care. Indeed, whatever the Sacklers might have wanted to tell themselves about their own intentions and the nature of the business they were in, this large population of addicted people was part of the reason that Purdue's sales were still so strong. The numbers didn't lie. The company's old marketing slogan had turned out to be more apt than anyone might have predicted: OxyContin really was the one to start with and the one to stay with, and now there was a huge captive market that was already dependent on the drug.

By the time OxyContin OP was rolled out, it had already become more difficult for some habitual users to access the drug. Authorities had shut down pill mills and prosecuted doctors, and many physicians had started to ask more questions before writing a prescription for OxyContin or other strong opioids. Now, on top of these other challenges, the pills stubbornly refused to deliver the full rush of oxycodone right away. As a consequence, many people simply gave up on OxyContin. In an ideal world, they would have just quit cold turkey, braving the torture of withdrawal, or sought treatment and carefully tapered their use of the drug. But the reality was that a lot of these people were already addicted. Many had been for years. They had passed a point of no return. And as it happened, there was an inexpensive substitute for OxyContin that was cheaper and stronger and widely available: heroin.

For some users, the reformulation of OxyContin triggered a transition to other, more readily abusable prescription opioids. But many graduated to heroin instead. Chemically speaking, the two drugs were closely related. In some ways, heroin had always been the benchmark for OxyContin. The tremendous potency of Oxy led to its reputation as "heroin in a pill." When it first became popular as a recreational high in Appalachia, OxyContin acquired the nickname hillbilly heroin. So, it might have been only logical that when they could no longer count on OxyContin, people who already had an opioid use disorder would make the short segue to heroin itself.

In the book *Dreamland,* the journalist Sam Quinones describes the manner in which, at around this time, drug syndicates in Mexico, sensing an emerging market in the United States, began smuggling unprecedented volumes of cheap heroin into the country. Almost overnight, crews of clean-cut, unarmed, highly professional heroin dealers began popping up in communities across the United States, offering baggies of heroin that had been harvested from poppies in the mountains of Nayarit, along Mexico's Pacific coast. Just as Purdue had once identified a giant potential market of people suffering from undertreated chronic pain, these young entrepreneurs from Mexico now spotted another huge population that might be induced to try a new drug. They had not had the opportunity to study at Harvard Business School, like Richard Sackler, or at NYU, like Mortimer. Instead, they were largely self-taught. But in trying to build a robust market for Mexican heroin, these traffickers from Nayarit employed a set of sales tactics that were, in some instances, eerily reminiscent of Purdue's original marketing playbook for OxyContin. The Sacklers had targeted populations that seemed particularly susceptible to their drug, focusing the initial marketing effort on communities where many people suffered from work-related injuries or disabilities and chronic pain. The heroin crews often scouted new clients in the vicinity of methadone clinics, where people who were already struggling with an opioid use disorder might be found. Purdue had offered patients coupons for a free one-month prescription of OxyContin. The heroin dealers offered free samples to their customers as well.

There was also the matter of what Purdue had referred to as "overcoming objections." The Sacklers had known, dating back to their earliest days in the opioid trade, that one challenge to be managed was consumer inhibition. There was a stigma associated with these products, the irrational hobgoblin of opiophobia. Back when the Sacklers' English company Napp first developed MS Contin, part of the rationale for the drug had been that a morphine pill felt safer and more approachable than anything administered by a needle. This same aversion to intravenous drug use—to shooting up—had also served as a natural cap on the size of the market for heroin in the United States. But when somebody who is already addicted to opioids starts to feel the first pangs of withdrawal, a lifetime's worth of inhibitions can be swiftly cast aside. This is the logic of addiction. Maybe needles make you queasy. But if your body is acting as if you might die if you don't get a hit, you'll start doing all sorts of things you might have sworn, in the past, that you would never do.

That was how what had been a national, decade-long prescription drug epidemic morphed, right around 2010, into a heroin epidemic. In later years, certain members of the Sackler family would call attention to precisely this transition, casting the shift to heroin (and, eventually, to another, even more lethal substitute, fentanyl) as an exculpatory trump card for the family. Here was the proof that people who became addicted to OxyContin were not legitimate pain patients but omnivorous drug abusers. And heroin was a street drug, sold out of the back of a car by anonymous young Mexicans of uncertain immigration status, whereas OxyContin had been approved by no less an authority than the Food and Drug Administration. The Sacklers were legitimate businesspeople, pillars of American society. Even after the felony conviction for Purdue, as controversy continued to swirl around OxyContin, Richard Sackler served on the advisory board of the Yale Cancer Center. Just prior to the reformulation, he and Beth, along with Jonathan and his wife, Mary Corson, had donated $3 million to establish the Richard Sackler and Jonathan Sackler Professorship in Internal Medicine at Yale. "My father raised Jon and me to believe that philanthropy is an important part of how we should fill our days," Richard said, in a rare public statement, at the time. Before moving down to Texas, Richard had also been appointed adjunct professor of genetics at Rockefeller University in Manhattan, another institution to which he donated generously. He and his family were still routinely celebrated for exemplifying the highest tradition of American values and of American medicine. He was not some south-of-the-border heroin baron. The fact that these junkies who had previously abused OxyContin were now moving on to heroin only solidified the family's sense that they were beyond reproach.

But Richard had always prided himself on his aptitude for data, and in this instance the data suggested that while the Sacklers certainly weren't dealing heroin, it would be incorrect to suggest that they bore no connection whatsoever to the heroin crisis. In subsequent years, scholars would sift through statistics related to the sudden rise in heroin overdoses beginning in 2010 and conclude that many of the Americans who were taking heroin had started out taking OxyContin and other prescription drugs. According to the American Society of Addiction Medicine, four out of five people who started using heroin during this period did so after initially abusing prescription painkillers. A survey of 244 people who entered treatment for OxyContin abuse after the reformulation in 2010 found that a third of them had switched to other drugs. Seventy percent of those who switched turned to heroin. Dodd Davis, the former Purdue sales rep from Louisiana, is now a drug treatment counselor. Having once sold OxyContin for a living, he now works with people who are addicted to heroin. In his judgment, "The reason heroin *happened* is because the whole OxyContin deal fell apart." In 2019, a team of economists from Notre Dame, Boston University, and the National Bureau of Economic Research published a dense research paper on the timing of the "rapid rise in the heroin death rate" in the years since 2010. The title of the paper was "How the Reformulation of OxyContin Ignited the Heroin Epidemic."

Chapter 23

AMBASSADORS

THE ONLY MEMBER OF the Sackler family to spend any time in prison was Richard Sackler's niece Madeleine. A slight young woman with a narrow face and dark, serious eyes, she was the daughter of Richard's brother, Jonathan, and his wife, Mary Corson. They had three children—Madeleine, Clare, and Miles—and lived in a rambling mansion on Field Point Circle, the same exclusive enclave in Greenwich, Connecticut, where Raymond and Beverly lived in the waterfront estate that Raymond had purchased back in 1973. Jonathan was quite different from his brother, Richard, more naturally social and approachable, and he and Mary cultivated a somewhat bohemian, intellectual sensibility. Jonathan wore a lot of Patagonia and was an amiable conversationalist who played host, in his home, to a roving salon of interesting artists and thinkers. One of his particular passions was the issue of education reform, and he became heavily involved in the charter school movement, donating money and writing op-eds. "I think we can do much better for kids, particularly kids growing up in our cities," he would say, adding, "It's a privilege to be able to support the important causes of our day." He and Mary helped to fund a charter network that built schools across Connecticut.

Madeleine, who was born in 1983, attended public schools in Greenwich. She was thirteen when OxyContin was released, and she came of age as a teenager during the years when many American teens, even in places like Greenwich, had started to abuse the drug. Smart and studious, she went to Duke, where she studied biopsychology (a subject that could only have appealed to her grandfather). Madeleine assumed that she would follow in the footsteps of Raymond, or of her uncle, Richard, and go on to medical school. But she found, in college, that she loved photography. She ended up pursuing filmmaking rather than medicine and made her first feature documentary at the age of twenty-eight. It was called *The Lottery*, and it was about a charter school in Harlem. (Madeleine shared her father's enthusiasm for charter education.) The film, which was released in 2010, the same year that Purdue released the reformulated OxyContin, follows four working-class families in Harlem and the Bronx who are seeking better educational opportunities for their children. It's "morally wrong" that underprivileged Americans do not have reliable access to a strong education, Madeleine opined in an interview on C-SPAN. The film was shown at the Tribeca Film Festival and short-listed for an Academy Award.

While Madeleine was making *The Lottery,* she started to think about the role of prison in American society. "It's kind of the flip side," she observed. "It's what happens when people don't get a good education. I knew we had more people in prison than anywhere in the world." Madeleine decided that she would explore the vexing problem of mass incarceration by making a fictional feature film about an older prisoner on the eve of his release. As a documentarian, however, she wanted the film to feel grounded in the real world. So she decided she would try to make the movie inside an actual functioning prison—"with prisoners acting."

To another young filmmaker, this might have seemed like an artistically ambitious but logistically impossible notion. But Madeleine Sackler was exhibiting, in the arts, a family trait that her great-uncle Arthur had manifested in medical advertising and her uncle, Richard, had applied to pharmaceuticals—the sense that any dream can be yours, no matter how outlandish it might seem, and that sometimes you just have to plunge forward and ask, "Why not?" In 2015, after much negotiation, Madeleine was admitted to the Pendleton Correctional Facility, a maximum-security state prison in Indiana, along with a small crew and a handful of professional actors, among them the award-winning stage and film actor Jeffrey Wright. Wright had visited Pendleton, along with Madeleine, on a couple of research trips, which he found "incredibly moving." He connected with the incarcerated men he met on these visits, and committed to the project. The prison had been built in the 1920s, mostly by inmates. It was a grim place, "the hardest environment I have ever worked in," Wright said. For several weeks, Madeleine shot scenes inside the imposing cellblocks.

Another major part in the film was played by a man named Theothus Carter, who was actually an inmate in the prison. Carter had been in and out of confinement for much of his life, often on drug-related charges, and was now serving a sixty-five-year sentence for armed burglary and attempted murder. But with tutoring from a friend of Madeleine's, the actor Boyd Holbrook, who starred in the Netflix show *Narcos* and was helping to produce the film, Carter delivered a stirring performance. ("Prison—it's like a character actor convention," Madeleine joked.) Eventually, the actor George Clooney, an outspoken proponent of progressive social issues, signed on to the project as a producer. The completed film, called *O.G.*, was acquired by HBO.

As if making the film had not been difficult enough, Madeleine also put together, simultaneously, a feature-length documentary about life inside Pendleton called *It's a Hard Truth, Ain't It*, which would eventually be nominated for an Emmy Award. In recognition of her work on both films, she would receive the Bill Webber Award for Community Service, for using her platform (as she put it on her personal website) "to elevate the voices of those incarcerated."

When Madeleine's films were released, HBO arranged for invitation-only screenings and invited journalists who work on civil rights and racial justice issues, community activists, and groups like the American Civil Liberties Union. Madeleine was an effective booster for her own work, understated but articulate and immensely confident. It helped that when she was promoting her films, and putting herself forward as someone who thought deeply about the consequences of certain types of systemic societal dysfunction in the lives of ordinary people, she was almost never asked to account for her own priors.

Madeleine lived a relatively unostentatious life by the standards of her family; she resided in Los Angeles, where she paid $3 million in cash for a home in the hipster enclave of Los Feliz. But the fact remained that she was an OxyContin heiress. Her father, Jonathan, might have been a genial intellectual, but he was also a longtime director at Purdue, a onetime vice president, and an extremely active board member who presided over the huge success of OxyContin and still hounded company executives for profit projections and sales updates. Madeleine gave no indication of any sort of public break with her family or even any evident discomfort when it came to the legacy of the drug that had made them all so wealthy. Among her social and professional acquaintances, she was known to disdain any conversation about Purdue. When the family business came up at all, she tended to scoff at the suggestion that she might be perceived as having any connection whatsoever to the company, pointing out that she herself played no role in the business.

In Indiana, where Madeleine made her prison films, deaths arising from opioid overdoses had been steadily increasing since 2010. Doctors in the state wrote opioid prescriptions at well above the national average. In the year she made the film, in Madison County, where the prison is located, there were 116 opioid prescriptions for every 100 residents, an off-the-charts figure, even for the state. In the very prison where Madeleine arranged to shoot, 1,000 inmates received addiction treatment for drugs or alcohol every year, out of a population of 1,800. According to the prison's own statistics, nearly 80 percent of the people incarcerated there had a history of "problematic substance use."

African Americans had been spared the full brunt of the opioid epidemic: doctors were less likely to prescribe opioid painkillers to Black patients, either because they did not trust them to take the drugs responsibly or because they were less likely to feel empathy for these patients and want to treat their pain aggressively. As a result, levels of addiction and death were statistically low among African Americans. It appeared to be a rare instance in which systemic racism could be said to have protected the community. But people of color were disproportionately affected by the war on drugs. Purdue executives might have evaded jail time for their role in a scheme that generated billions of dollars for Madeleine's family, but in 2016, Indiana's governor, Mike Pence, signed a law reinstating a mandatory minimum sentence for any street-level dealer who was caught selling heroin and had a prior conviction: ten years. Nationwide, 82 percent of those charged with heroin trafficking were Black or Latino.

It is impossible to speak honestly about mass incarceration without also speaking of the war on drugs. And it's impossible to speak honestly about the war on drugs without addressing the opioid crisis. Yet this was the rhetorical needle that Madeleine Sackler somehow managed to thread. It was a deft performance. For the most part, she was able to weigh in, sagely, on the plight of America's prison population without being asked to account for her own familial connection to one of the underlying drivers of that crisis. Were her films financed, to any great or small extent, by OxyContin money? The subject almost never came up, but when it did, she would state vaguely that she hadn't spent her own money to make the films, but not offer any further detail. During the years she spent developing *O.G.*, before the production was financed, Jeffrey Wright was under the distinct impression that she was funding the development herself.

Jonathan Sackler had always scrupulously followed press coverage of the OxyContin problem, poring over press clippings and bristling at any characterizations that he perceived to be unfair. He had expressed concerns inside the company about how public health campaigns to prevent opioid addiction might end up hurting sales of OxyContin. The whole family was sensitive to negative press. Even as an old man, Raymond would still inquire about whether anything could be done to induce the *Times* to be "less focused on OxyContin." But Jonathan was also particularly keen to make sure that if journalists were going to refer to the opioid epidemic and potentially mention OxyContin and Purdue, they at least not mention the connection to the Sackler family. The company hired numerous public relations specialists to help with this delicate campaign to keep the family name *in* any positive stories about philanthropy and movie premieres but *out* of any negative coverage relating to the prescription opioids they sold. This effort had been remarkably successful. The family was, for the most part, not mentioned in negative media stories about Purdue. The source of the Sacklers' wealth continued to seem obscure and distant, as though the fortune had been acquired long ago.

On the rare occasions when Madeleine was asked directly about the apparent disconnect between the social justice message of her films and the specific provenance of her own personal fortune, she was dismissive. In a generous profile of Madeleine that was published in *The New Yorker,* Jeffrey Wright pointed out that a lot of the men inside Pendleton prison had little personal agency in ending up where they did. "All the negligence, abuse, addiction," he said, "a lot of these guys never had a chance." Yet when the author of the piece, Nick Paumgarten, mused aloud to Madeleine that the film might represent some form of expiation—a subtle acknowledgment of her family's sins and an effort, through art, to atone—she challenged the premise of the question. There was nothing to expiate, she responded, asserting that when it came to the opioid crisis, she felt no sense of moral responsibility or, really, even personal connection. Her family background was a mere distraction, she insisted. Was she not entitled, as a filmmaker, to have her work simply judged on its own merits? "It pains her," Paumgarten wrote, "to think that the perception of her project... would be tainted in some way by her pedigree."

Jeffrey Wright had learned about Madeleine's family while he was working on the project. At one point, he asked her about her background, but she deflected, clearly preferring not to talk about it. When Wright saw her documentary, he was struck by a moment when one of the inmates, a goateed man named Cliff, talks about his difficult childhood—and how his mother "had a prescription drug problem." It troubled Wright that Madeleine could include such a scene with no disclosure of her own connection to the story. "It becomes polluted when you don't acknowledge who you are, when you're hiding your place in it all," he thought. The stories of the men in the film were important, he believed, and the impulse to tell those stories was worthy, even urgent. "But when you take that element of transparency out of the equation, when doing that hides the significance of *your* story as it relates to *their* stories, then there's something rotten that can't be expunged," he said. As a consequence, the film is "fundamentally flawed," Wright concluded, "because there is something incredibly fraudulent about that, and deceptive."

When *O.G.* premiered, Madeleine made an appearance on the red carpet in an elegant all-black ensemble and was celebrated at parties. She posed for photographs with the former Obama administration official and CNN personality Van Jones and with the Black Lives Matter activist Shaun King. Before the premiere, Wright had sent Madeleine an email, praising the "honesty and openness" of the men in her documentary. But there is an "elephant" in the room, he wrote. "You've provided a tremendous gift to those men. Something the likes of which they've rarely, if ever, been given." But they know "nothing of your story," he pointed out. "You never spoke to me about any of that. I was aware and only once tried to broach the subject with you. You didn't open up about it. I went on with my work." Wright wanted to address it now, though. "Do you think you should take into consideration that this will become part of the dialogue around these films?" he asked.

Madeleine never responded.

✣   ✣   ✣

Madeleine was, in some ways, typical of the third generation of Sacklers. Many of them had done summer internships at Purdue, but the only member of this generation who went on to have any direct involvement in the family company was Madeleine's cousin David, Richard Sackler's son. As a high school student, David had interned at Purdue. He studied business at Princeton and became an investor. He had some of his father's off-putting interpersonal tendencies; he could be brusque and domineering, and he would sit in meetings with his eyes glued to his phone, appearing to be preoccupied, only to look up suddenly and interject with a difficult question. He set up his own investment group, which listed, as its offices, 15 East Sixty-Second Street, the old limestone town house where his father and Richard Kapit had scored furniture for their college apartment back in the 1960s. The family still owned the building.

David took a seat on Purdue's board in 2012. "I think my dad's vision was that I would replace him at some point," he said later, suggesting that Richard saw a direct line of succession in which he would hand to his own son the business that his father handed him. David was loyal to Richard and seemed to share some of his combative partisanship on behalf of the company. He derided critics of Purdue as "cynics." The 2007 guilty plea had been, in his telling, a small matter of a "number of sales reps" who made a few misstatements before the company could weed them out.

In joining the board, David took his place in a self-selecting subset of the family that continued to manage Purdue. "Raymond and Mortimer had worked so hard to build this company," one longtime Purdue executive pointed out. "They had seen failures and setbacks." But the younger generations "grew up thinking that they were the smartest people in the room, because they'd been told that their whole lives." They drove cars that were provided by the company and used cell phones paid for by the company. (According to a subsequent court filing, Purdue ended up paying $477,000 for the personal phone bills of a handful of Sacklers.) When Kathe was having computer trouble at her mansion in Westport, she would telephone Purdue headquarters to have them send a company tech. "Richard would say, 'I'm going to Europe in two weeks and I have my flight ready, but I just saw that gas prices are lower and Delta's having a special, and can you look into what would be cheaper?'" Nancy Camp, the former administrative assistant, recalled. "All of this to save $200. And after I did the research, he would end up keeping his original flight."

"They would just *inflict* themselves on us," a former Purdue executive who dealt with the family recalled. "What Kathe liked to do was
call you to her office late in the day and just lecture you for hours," he
said. "Nobody on the business side would ever pull her into any kind of
business discussion because she wasn't helpful in any sense of the word.
Everybody called her 'Dr. Kathe,' but I don't know that anyone was
really impressed with her doctoring credentials."

To some employees, this air of self-importance could seem comical. "They liked that sense that they were serious businesspeople," one
former staffer who dealt with the family pointed out. "They confused
being good at something with stepping in shit and getting lucky. The
thing I found specifically with the family was that the next generation, they struck gold in the backyard, basically. It's like you moved to
Odessa, Texas, and said, 'What is this black stuff coming out of the
ground?' Outside of OxyContin, the company has never been that successful. Without OxyContin it would be this sleepy $50 million pharma
company you'd never heard of." But the success of the one drug had
given rise to a self-regarding aura of superhuman business prowess,
the staffer continued. The Sacklers had come to think of themselves as
"the smart billionaires who knew better." More than one person who
worked at Purdue during this era likened the experience to the acidly
humorous HBO show *Succession,* in which a trio of overindulged adult
children vie, haplessly, to seize control of a conglomerate built by their
hard-driving father.

Mortimer sought the counsel of a psychiatrist and psychoanalyst
named Kerry Sulkowicz, a sought-after "leadership confidant" who
served as a guru for business executives. Though he was wealthy by
any standard, Mortimer nevertheless found that he could occasionally
overextend himself. When his father was alive, Mortimer could turn to
him for a "bridge" loan, but now, when he found himself in a pinch, he
had to request an emergency cash infusion from one of the family trusts.
At one point, he shared with Dr. Sulkowicz a set of talking points he
had drafted for the awkward conversation with the trustees. "Start off
with saying I am not happy," he wrote. "I am falling significantly behind
financially." He was prepared to sell "artworks, jewelry, stock positions,"
but even so, he needed assistance with a "shorter term cash flow problem." What Mortimer needed, he said, was "$10 million near term and
a possible additional $10 million." That, he promised, was "the MAX."

Part of the problem, he complained, was that he was so busy working on behalf of the family business and having to "play hardball with Richard and Jon," which was stressful, and perhaps not the most productive use of his energies. "I have been working for years on Purdue at what I consider to be a considerably discounted value relative to what MY TIME IS WORTH," he wrote. "I am LOSING money by working in the pharma business." He suggested that the loan could be "reported in the trust accounts as loan/cash flow assistance to family members but not be specific." He didn't want everyone in the family to realize he was having issues. "I don't want to hear my siblings' opinions on this, and I don't need more stress for this. I need to have this resolved," he wrote. "This needs to happen, the question is only how much DRAMA will be needed for this to happen." He noted that "historically," his father had been "more than willing to help me."

David Sackler was disdainful of his cousin Mortimer. His wing of the family had been more careful about money. It was a point of pride. His uncle Jonathan boasted about how little money he spent; David joked that Jonathan's "wardrobe hasn't seen a dollar invested in it for a decade." When David got married and wanted to buy a bigger apartment, Richard signaled his disapproval, and David sent his father and mother an emotional email. "I realize dad isn't great with email, so he may not read this," he wrote, but he wanted to "voice some thoughts." He had been working hard to "manage the family fortune," and it hadn't been easy. "Beyond pushing myself to excel, I work for a boss (Dad) with little understanding of what I do." Rather than being supportive of his efforts, Richard characterized his work as "'terrible, bad, shitty, crappy, broken, in the doldrums' or any other derisive term you'd like to lob at me." Part of his job, David acknowledged, was "managing dad." He was Richard's "right hand for everything," and he worked tirelessly to "make the family richer." This might look easy, David said. But it is "quite literally the hardest job in the world."

There were certain pathologies that had passed down within the Sackler family, David observed. His grandfather, Raymond, had "started a pattern of behavior that is very hurtful. By holding money over people's heads while getting them to work for family enterprises, he was able to exert a huge amount of control." Richard himself had said numerous times that he hated this dynamic, David pointed out. Yet here was Richard expecting total devotion to the family business while trying to manage David's spending. It wasn't like David wanted "to live like Mortimer Jr. or his siblings," he groused. "I don't have life goals of a plane, yacht or anything crazy like that." He just wanted a bigger home! Besides, even Richard flew private, and nobody gave him a hard time about that.

"I'm like Dad," David wrote. "I stuck it out for the family and took the stress that comes with it. I accepted the manipulation to work towards my goals and help the family." Most of the Sacklers, he noted, did not do so. In fact, most of the Sacklers were more like Madeleine: they pursued their own interests outside the pharmaceutical industry and lived lives that bore no apparent connection to opioids, apart from being subsidized by them. Madeleine's brother, Miles, was a computer programmer in California; her sister, Clare, was also a filmmaker. Richard's daughter Rebecca was a veterinarian. His other daughter, Marianna, had spent several years as an employee of Purdue and Mundipharma, but ultimately stopped working ("she's got no career, and likely will never have one," David remarked) and now lived in a $12 million home in the Pacific Heights neighborhood of San Francisco. One of Mortimer's grandchildren, Jeffrey—whose mother, Ilene, still served on Purdue's board—started a popular chain of restaurants in New York called the Smith.

But Mortimer's heirs were mostly concentrated in London. There was Samantha, his daughter from the marriage to Geri Wimmer, who had married an entrepreneur in the coffee business and purchased a £26 million home in Chelsea that had previously belonged to the actor Hugh Grant and the film producer Jemima Khan. Samantha was very taken with art deco design and set out to restore the house, which featured a big secluded garden, in pristine 1930s detail. There was Mortimer's son from his third marriage, Michael Sackler, who like Madeleine and Clare had gone into the film business, starting a financing company called Rooks Nest Ventures, after the family estate in Berkshire. They had offices just off Soho Square. Michael's sister Marissa founded what she described as a "non-profit incubator," called Beespace, which supported the Malala Fund and other causes. Marissa did not like the term "philanthropist," she told the magazine *W.* She preferred to think of herself as a "social entrepreneur." She made "social investments" and delivered keynote speeches and spoke in an impenetrable patois of corporate buzzwords.

When Richard Sackler graduated from medical school, Félix Martí-Ibáñez had tried to impress upon him the sort of esteem he would enjoy in life because he bore the Sackler name. This was only more true now, and perhaps nowhere more so than in London. The name was *everywhere* in the United Kingdom. There was the Sackler Building at the Royal College of Art, the Sackler Education Centre at the Victoria and Albert Museum, the Sackler Room at the National Gallery, Sackler Hall at the Museum of London, the Sackler Pavilion at the National Theatre, the Sackler Studios at the Globe Theatre. In 2013, the Serpentine Gallery was renamed the Serpentine Sackler, with a gala opening co-hosted by *Vanity Fair* and the New York mayor, Mike Bloomberg (who was a friend of the family). One of the stained-glass windows in Westminster Abbey was dedicated to Mortimer and Theresa. It was decorated in lovely reds and blues depicting the seals of Harvard, Columbia, NYU, and other recipients of the family's largesse. "M&T Sackler Family," the window said. "Peace Through Education." The Sacklers' impulse to slap their name on any bequest, no matter how large or small, might have found its surreal culmination at the Tate Modern, the cavernous temple to modern art that occupies an old power station on the south bank of the Thames, in which a silver plaque informs visitors that they happen to be riding on the Sackler Escalator.

Mortimer and Theresa Sackler had donated more than $100 million to the arts and sciences in the U.K. After Mortimer's death, Theresa was awarded the Prince of Wales Medal for Arts Philanthropy. When this distinction was conferred, Ian Dejardin, the Sackler director of the Dulwich Picture Gallery, remarked, "It's going to be difficult not to make her sound utterly saintly."

Most of this charitable giving was administered by the Sackler Trust, based in London, and the heirs of Raymond and Mortimer benefited from a series of other trusts in which the proceeds from OxyContin—those regular disbursements of hundreds of millions of dollars—were kept. Since its release nearly two decades earlier, OxyContin had generated some $35 billion. A sizable amount of this revenue was channeled not through London or New York but through the tax haven of Bermuda, where, for decades, an anonymous-looking modern office building on a narrow street lined with palm trees had served as a clearinghouse for the family's wealth. The building was known as Mundipharma House.

By routing money through Bermuda, the Sacklers had avoided paying hundreds of millions of dollars in taxes, according to one former
financial adviser to the family. This was not illegal, and it wasn't as
though the family had not bestowed ample gifts upon the countries in
which its members happened to reside. They just preferred that the
gifts be on their own terms—to the arts and sciences, with naming
rights—rather than be left to the discretion of the state.

✣   ✣   ✣

Mundipharma House was named for the network of international
companies that the Sacklers controlled, which were known as Mundipharma and which sold the company's various products abroad. As
sales of OxyContin began to plateau in the United States, the Sacklers
had been turning their attention to new markets in other parts of the
world. In board meetings, the family was frequently informed by staff
that further growth in the United States might be unrealistic, particularly because doctors and patients appeared to be growing more mindful of the potential hazards of strong opioids. But for Mundipharma,
the future looked more promising. In Latin America and in Asia, hundreds of millions of people were joining the middle class. These people
suddenly had access to better health care and more money to spend
on health and wellness. So, even as Purdue contended with a host of
lawsuits in the United States, Mundipharma set out to cultivate a new
market for painkillers abroad. To succeed in this effort, the company
employed a familiar playbook. Eyeing a new market, Mundipharma
would begin by producing statistics that suggested the region was suffering from a crisis of untreated pain. When Mundipharma moved into
Mexico in 2014, company representatives announced that twenty-eight
million people in the country were living with chronic pain. And that
was nothing compared with Brazil, where the number was eighty million. In Colombia, the company suggested that twenty-two million
people—47 percent of the population—were suffering from this "silent
epidemic."

Two decades earlier, Purdue had engaged physicians to serve as
paid speakers, delivering lectures at conferences, spreading the gospel
of pain management, arguing that the best and safest means for treating chronic nonmalignant pain was opioids. Now the company did the

same thing abroad, turning, in some instances, to the very doctors who had been so obliging the first time. They called these paid representatives "pain ambassadors," and the company flew them to emerging markets to promote opioids and warn about the dangers of opiophobia. "You show up, do a presentation and then you get back on the plane," Dr. Barry Cole, a pain specialist from Reno, Nevada, told the *Los Angeles Times.* Cole had helped the company promote OxyContin in the United States back in the 1990s, but now he had a new sideline as a pain ambassador and traveled the world, educating other doctors about the benefits of strong opioids in places like Colombia, Brazil, South Korea, and the Philippines.

Some of the physicians the company dispatched were not, perhaps, the most esteemed representatives of their field. There was a Florida doctor, for instance, Joseph Pergolizzi Jr., who hawked a pain-relieving cream of his own invention on cable TV and flew to Brazil for Mundipharma to advise medical practitioners about "the tools you need to properly address pain." In making this pitch, Mundipharma often relied upon the same discredited literature that Purdue had employed decades earlier, citing the letter to the editor in *The New England Journal of Medicine* that suggested less than 1 percent of patients develop a problem with opioids and telling physicians that it was "almost impossible for those with chronic or severe pain to become addicted."

In 2014, Richard Sackler enthused that the company's growth in emerging markets "is exceptional and ahead of forecast." Jonathan Sackler was similarly bullish, saying, in an email that year, that if the family was "smart and diligent around emerging markets," they could continue to make money on opioids "for decades to come." The Sacklers appointed an executive named Raman Singh to serve as CEO of the company's Asian operations, based in Singapore. With long black hair, shiny suits, and an impish smile, Singh exemplified a certain hustle. "This is where the growth is coming from," Singh announced. Between 2011 and 2016, annual revenues for Mundipharma Emerging Markets, which he oversaw, grew 800 percent, to $600 million. In India, Mundipharma pushed its own expensive opioids as an alternative to cheap, Indian-made morphine. But the real prize, as Singh pointed out, was China. "China is so critical to our trajectory," he said, explaining that the company sells five different opioids, including OxyContin, in China. "We have been very, very successful in commercializing for pain," Singh said. By 2025, he hoped, China might overtake the United States as the number one market for the Sacklers' products.

Given China's fraught history with opioids—the country fought the Opium Wars in the nineteenth century to stop Britain from dumping the drug there, which had given rise to a scourge of addiction—one might assume that there would be formidable barriers to entry when it came to an effort by Mundipharma to change the culture of prescribing. But the company was ravenous for new customers and prepared to engage in marketing tactics that were extreme even by the standards of Purdue. Mundipharma China had been established back in 1993, the same year that the Arthur M. Sackler Museum of Art and Archaeology opened in Beijing. The *China Medical Tribune,* which Arthur had founded, now boasted a readership of more than a million Chinese doctors. In seeking to convince physicians and patients in China that opioids were not, in fact, dangerously addictive, Mundipharma assembled a huge sales force. They were under a great deal of pressure from the company to perform, and they were encouraged with the type of aggressive incentive structure that the Sacklers had always favored. Come in over the company's quarterly sales targets and you could double your salary. Come in under and you could lose your job. Mundipharma supplied the reps with marketing materials that included assertions about the safety and effectiveness of OxyContin that had long since been debunked. The company claimed that OxyContin was the World Health Organization's preferred treatment for cancer pain (it isn't). According to an investigation by the Associated Press, Mundipharma reps in hospitals actually donned white coats and pretended to be doctors themselves. They consulted directly with patients about their health concerns and made copies of people's confidential medical records.

Mundipharma released a series of flashy promotional videos about its products and its global ambitions, featuring images of smiling patients from a range of different ethnicities. "We're only just getting started," one of the videos said.

✤ ✤ ✤

In 2013, Purdue staff informed the Sackler board members that overdose deaths had more than tripled since 1990 and that these deaths were only the "tip of the iceberg," because for every individual who died of an overdose, there were a hundred others suffering from prescription opioid dependence or abuse. When Sam Quinones published his book about the crisis, *Dreamland,* in 2015, he pointed directly to the complicity of the Sackler family, just as Barry Meier had in his book, *Pain Killer,* twelve years earlier. But this criticism did not seem to stick. The Sacklers continued to move through the world largely unencumbered by any association with the opioid crisis. At Tufts University, where the Sacklers had donated generously for decades and the School of Graduate Biomedical Sciences was named after the family, a committee voted against assigning *Dreamland* to incoming medical students, because the school felt it should show "deference" to its donors and not endorse a book that might undermine the family name. When *Forbes* magazine added the Sacklers to its tally of the wealthiest families in the United States and acknowledged the source of their wealth by describing them as "the OxyContin Clan," no universities or art museums expressed any discomfort about accepting Sackler money. "I'm glad they picked a really nice picture," Richard said, of the accompanying photograph, which featured his mother and father, beaming, at an awards ceremony in Europe. The article pegged the family's wealth at $14 billion, but Richard couldn't say if this was accurate. Nobody ever "sat down and . . . did an inventory," he said.

This sort of press coverage—the rich list in *Forbes*—might be faintly embarrassing. But the Sacklers could live with it. And staff at Purdue were working hard to make sure that the family name remained unsullied by the more incendiary coverage that occasionally cropped up about OxyContin. "I'm quite pleased with where we ended up," Raul Damas, an executive in charge of public affairs, concluded in an internal email after a press story about a lawsuit involving OxyContin. "There's almost nothing on the Sacklers and what is there is minimal and buried in the back." This was the status quo that the company had become accustomed to. Dame Theresa Sackler could still appear at champagne ribbon cuttings to say a few words and flash a magnanimous smile. Madeleine Sackler could still show up at film festivals and offer trenchant observations about rehabilitation for ex-convicts and the dilemma of the urban poor. The family could weather negative coverage of the company, even coverage in which the Sackler name might appear, provided it did so only on the margins. But all of that was about to change.

Chapter 24

IT'S A HARD TRUTH, AIN'T IT

ONE DAY IN AUGUST 2015, a plane landed in Louisville, Kentucky, and Richard Sackler stepped out, surrounded by attorneys. The State of Kentucky had sued Purdue, in a case that originally started eight years earlier, charging the company with deceptive marketing. Greg Stumbo, the state attorney general who initiated the lawsuit, had lost a relative to a fatal overdose of OxyContin. The whole region had been decimated by the drug.

Purdue fought the case with its customary rigor, pushing to move the proceedings elsewhere, on the ground that the company could not get a fair trial in Pike County, Kentucky—the rural stretch of coal country where the state intended to try the case. In support of this motion, Purdue commissioned a demographic study of Pike County and submitted it to the court as an illustration of potential bias in the jury pool. The report was revealing in ways that Purdue might not have intended. According to the filing, 29 percent of the county's residents said that they or their family members knew someone who had died from using OxyContin. Seven out of ten respondents described Oxy-Contin's effect on their community as "devastating."

A judge ruled that Purdue could not shift the venue for the trial, and it looked as though the company might actually be forced to fight this case in a Pike County courtroom. The lawyers bringing the case wanted Richard Sackler to sit for a deposition. This had never happened in any of the hundreds of cases that had been filed relating to OxyContin abuse, even though Richard's family owned Purdue and he had been president and chairman of the board. Attorneys for the company fiercely resisted the idea that Richard might be forced to fly to a place like Kentucky and answer questions, under oath, about Oxy-Contin. But eventually, the defense team had no further recourse, and the judge ordered the deposition to happen.

Richard had been living in Austin. In a town with a conspicuous overrepresentation of brainy rich eccentrics, he almost fit in. He had developed a friendship with a courtly law professor named Philip Bobbitt who was about Richard's age and had also grown up in great privilege. Bobbitt was over-credentialed in a way that could only appeal to Richard: he had advised numerous presidents on foreign affairs and now taught at the University of Texas Law School, Columbia, *and* Oxford, jetting from one institute of higher learning to the next to deliver lectures, and he was the author of ten turgid volumes on military strategy and constitutional law. Bobbitt had a fondness for seersucker suits and fat cigars, and he liked to blow smoke rings and relate wistful anecdotes about his "celebrated uncle," Lyndon Johnson, and discourse grandly on important subjects. He was Richard Sackler's kind of guy.

"Richard is an odd duck," one former Purdue employee said, describing a man who seemed, increasingly, to inhabit an alternate reality of his own fussy design. "His life's falling apart and he's recommending a book you should read." In theory, his physical exile, nearly two thousand miles away in Texas, might have bought the leadership at Purdue some respite from his obsessive interventions. They had hired a new CEO named Mark Timney in early 2014. Timney came from Merck, and this was the first time that an outsider—someone who was not a member of the family or a longtime loyalist—had been brought in to run Purdue. One of Timney's goals, which he announced upon arrival, was to change the corporate culture at Purdue. He recognized that some things had gone wrong in the past, and he believed that some of the dysfunction in the firm stemmed from its origins as a family business. He wanted, in the words of someone who worked closely with him, to "make it a company you would recognize"—to make it look more like Merck. To that end, he wanted less direct intervention in the company by the Sackler family. But this was, to say the least, a challenging mandate, because Purdue had always done things a certain way. Disentangling the family from the family business would prove, very quickly, to be impossible.

In Texas, Richard was perpetually on email, and even from afar he continued to exercise tremendous influence over the company. "Our major problem has been our failure to diversify the US product line and ameliorate the squeeze on OxyContin," he wrote in a 2014 email to other family members. "However, in the years when the business was producing massive amounts of cash, the shareholders departed from the practice of our industry peers and took this money out of the business. Now, unfortunately, the decline in the US sales of OxyContin has reduced our income and free cashflow." Even so, Richard remained hopeful and determined. "The companies have provided the family for over 60 years," he wrote. The "Raymond family is optimistic about the prospects for the overall business," and he felt certain that "persistence will be rewarded."

The challenge Richard faced when it came to Purdue was to persuade the Mortimer side of the family to stay the course and reinvest in the business. Because there were so *many* Mortimer heirs, there had been a pronounced tendency, on that side of the family, to focus on the periodic distributions of cash. Privately, Richard's son, David, who was becoming an increasingly influential voice on the board, complained to his father, and to his uncle, Jonathan, about attempts by the A side to "pillage" cash from the company. He mocked the bizarrely "bureaucratic" manner in which they carried on, likening their decision-making process to "the DMV."

Raymond Sackler was now ninety-five years old. But well into his twilight years he continued to drive his Jaguar from the Greenwich estate at Field Point Circle to the office in Stamford. The prospect of this ancient potentate, hands on the wheel, weaving through traffic on I-95 was sufficiently disconcerting to Purdue Pharma's security team that sometimes they would dispatch two escort cars to accompany Raymond—one in front, one behind—to make sure that he didn't hit anyone. Some people in the company assumed that Raymond was on the brink of senility, stationed behind his desk, dressed in a suit and tie, a wax museum smile on his face. He would offer the occasional visitor a cookie, but he didn't appear to be doing much of anything. It was also whispered, by some who had known the Sackler family for decades and held the older generation in high esteem, that Purdue's reckless devotion to opioids was a predilection of Richard and the younger cohort, whereas Raymond—*had he only known*—would never have stood for it.

But the truth was that Raymond knew precisely what was going on at the company. A year before Richard flew to Kentucky for the deposition, his father forwarded him a memo about Purdue's strategy, which addressed the company's plans to bolster profits by pushing for patients to be placed on higher doses of opioids for longer periods of time, and acknowledged that such a strategy was predicated on over-coming objections from physicians who believed that this might not be the best thing for the patients themselves. "We should discuss it when you have time," Raymond wrote. When McKinsey made a presentation to the board about how the Sacklers could reverse the decline in Oxy-Contin profits by increasing sales calls on the most prolific high-volume prescribers, Raymond presided over the meeting. "The room was filled with only family, including the elder statesman Dr. Raymond," one of the McKinsey executives wrote in an email afterward, noting that the family was "extremely supportive" of the consultants' recommenda-tions. In the words of another member of the McKinsey team, the Sack-lers "gave a ringing endorsement of 'moving forward fast.'"

Just after nine o'clock that morning in Louisville, Richard settled into a chair at a conference table in the law offices of Dolt, Thompson, Shepherd & Kinney on the outskirts of town. He wore a nondescript blue suit and a pressed white shirt, with a lapel microphone affixed to his tie. Richard had recently turned seventy, but he still looked healthy and vigorous. He shifted in his chair, his small eyes remote and quiz-zical. Ready for battle. To one of the attorneys representing the State of Kentucky, a young prosecutor named Mitchel Denham, this show-down, which had been such a long time coming, felt ripe with meaning. "We were face-to-face with the guy whose company had helped to *cre-ate* the opioid epidemic," he recalled.

The questioning would be led by Tyler Thompson, a seasoned per-sonal injury lawyer who was based in Louisville and had an affable self-assurance and a rich Kentucky drawl. Richard stared at Thompson, his eyes lidded, his face a mask of exquisite condescension. He was not going to make this easy.

"On July 30th of 2014, were you a director of Purdue Pharma?" Thompson asked.

"Not that I'm aware," Richard replied.

Thompson produced a document and handed it to Richard. "Does that appear to be your name?"

"That does."

"And it's dated July 30th, 2014. It says, 'Declaration of Dr. Richard Sackler. I am a director of Purdue Pharma.'"

"If that's what it says," Richard said, with a shrug, "then that's what it says."

"I've seen upwards of sixty-nine different corporations, perhaps, that the Sackler family owns," Thompson continued. "Is that correct?"

"If you've counted them," Richard said. "I don't know."

Thompson had entertained no illusions about this pharma baron being an accommodating witness. But even so, he was startled by Richard's tone. There wasn't any lip service to the suffering that the Sacklers' drug had visited upon Kentucky. Richard couldn't even *feign* compassion. It seemed to Thompson that the general impression Richard was trying to convey, not just with his answers but with the tone of his voice and his body language, was that he was above all this. "A smirk and a so-what attitude, an absolute lack of remorse," Thompson marveled later. "It reminded me of these mining companies that come in here and do mountaintop removal and leave a mess and just move on. 'It's not in my backyard, so I don't care.'"

"Have you ever gone back and studied the history of addiction?" Thompson asked Richard.

"I'm not a student of that literature," Richard replied.

"Did you ever do any studies on abuse liability for OxyContin before you all put it on the market?"

"I'm not aware of any."

Richard's voice was deep and gruff. His demeanor was surly and brimming with disdain. He tried to minimize his role in the company, saying that he was involved "at a supervisory level, not an active level." He "didn't do any of the work," he claimed. "I was not a salesperson." But through discovery, the Kentucky lawyers had obtained a raft of internal company documents that told a different story. Thompson started asking Richard about his own emails, highlighting the decisive role that he had played in the marketing blitz for OxyContin, even quoting the "Blizzard of '96" speech that Richard delivered at the Wigwam resort in Arizona for the launch of the drug nearly twenty years earlier. Looking through his old memos and statements, Richard was confronted—in a way that he never had been during the federal case in Virginia or in any of the countless other lawsuits that had been brought against the company—with evidence that he himself had been the architect and ringleader of the OxyContin campaign. At one point, he seemed almost to concede as much, reflecting, with a kind of wry bemusement, that "this whole experience" of being forced to go back and review all the details of the launch of OxyContin was "like reliving a third of my life."

"I don't regret trying to energize our sales force," he told Thompson defiantly. "I think that was my mission." He was not "embarrassed" by the tone he had adopted, he continued. "I think it was very reasonable." Asked about the OxyContin promotional campaign that suggested this was a drug "to start with and to stay with," Richard said that it was not a phrase he had coined himself, but added, "I wish I could lay claim to it."

"Do you believe Purdue's marketing was overly aggressive?"

"No."

"Do you think putting these three thousand doctors on your speakers bureau caused them to write more prescriptions for OxyContin?"

"I don't think it would have had an effect."

As the deposition dragged on, Richard was cryptic and evasive. "I don't know," he murmured, again and again, in response to Thompson's questions. "I don't recall."

"You ever do any follow up to find out whether the participants in the 'I Got My Life Back' video actually got their life back or wound up having problems with dependency on OxyContin?" Thompson asked.

Richard said that he hadn't. But OxyContin was a highly effective painkiller, he insisted.

"But whether it's effective or not also depends on other factors, such as abuse," Thompson pointed out. "I mean, you can kill somebody and take away their pain. But that wouldn't be effective, would it?"

No, Richard allowed, with a flash of dry amusement. "I don't think that death would be considered a sign of efficacy."

In preparing for the trial, Mitchel Denham had discovered an old photograph of the 1997 Pikeville High School football team. Nearly half of the young men in the picture either had died of overdoses or were addicted. "It was going to be a pretty good visual," he said. But Denham never got the opportunity to present the photo to a jury, because before the case could go to trial, Purdue paid $24 million to settle it.

This was a coup for the Sacklers. The settlement was more than Purdue's original offer—the company had initially proposed that it pay the state just half a million dollars—but it was still totally incommensurate with Pike County's needs. In settling the case, Purdue admitted no wrongdoing. And one of the key conditions of this resolution, which Purdue insisted upon, was that all of the millions of pages of evidence that the Kentucky attorneys had amassed through discovery—including Tyler Thompson's videotaped deposition of

Richard Sackler—would be sealed forever from public view. This was an important element in the company's strategy. A dozen or so judges in different cases around the country would ultimately sign off on similar requests to seal records. In Kentucky, Purdue directed the prosecutors to "completely destroy" all of the files.

"That's the main reason these folks don't go to trial," Mitchel Denham concluded. The Sacklers had always preferred to settle cases rather than litigate the culpability of the company (or, worse, of the family) in open court. If a case ever reached the point where lawyers were actually presenting evidence to a jury, Denham pointed out, "all these documents could end up in the public record." After the settlement, a medical news website, STAT, sued to have Richard's deposition unsealed. A state judge ruled in STAT's favor. But Purdue immediately appealed. That deposition represented the most extensive remarks ever made by a member of the Sackler family about the controversy surrounding OxyContin. The family would go to great lengths to prevent it from becoming public.

✢   ✢   ✢

Inside the reflective-glass ziggurat of Purdue's home office in Stamford, there was an encroaching sense that public scrutiny was becoming impossible to avoid. The *Los Angeles Times* had run a major story in 2013 about the ways in which Purdue tracked the suspicious prescribing habits of dodgy doctors. "Over the last decade, the maker of the potent painkiller OxyContin has compiled a database of hundreds of doctors suspected of recklessly prescribing its pills to addicts and drug dealers, but has done little to alert law enforcement or medical authorities," the paper reported. The so-called Region Zero list, which included more than eighteen hundred names, had been a closely guarded secret. Purdue defended its conduct by pointing out that it maintained this database in order to steer its own sales reps away from such doctors, and told the newspaper that it had reported 8 percent of the doctors on the list to law enforcement. But when it came to the other 92 percent of physicians who appeared to be inappropriately prescribing, the company said that it had no duty to act. "We don't have the ability to take the prescription pad out of their hand," a Purdue attorney, Robin Abrams, said.

Of course, until a pill mill was actually shut down by the medical board or the police, Purdue continued to reap the proceeds from all those fraudulent OxyContin prescriptions, and while company officials might want a pat on the back for steering sales reps away from such establishments, pill mills were, generally speaking, pretty reliable prescribers. "Nobody *needed* to call on the really shady doctors," the former Louisiana rep Dodd Davis pointed out. "That business was going to come, regardless." Those doctors are a "gold mine," Keith Humphreys, a psychology professor at Stanford who had served as a drug policy adviser in the Obama administration, told the *Times*. "And the whole time they're taking the money, knowing that something is wrong," he continued. "That is really disgusting."

As if the Region Zero exposé weren't damaging enough, the public affairs department at Purdue had learned, by the time Richard Sackler traveled to Kentucky, that it wasn't a stand-alone article; the paper was preparing a series. Raul Damas, the Purdue public affairs executive, sent an update to the Sacklers about a "mitigation effort" to thwart the series, "marginalizing the LAT's unbalanced coverage." But there wasn't much that the company could do. One day, one of the reporters, Scott Glover, managed to reach Richard Sackler on his personal phone. Startled, Richard quickly ended the call.

Richard demanded to see all correspondence between the *Times* and the company. But the Sacklers seemed, even to their own staff, to be living in a state of willful disconnection. Richard had set up a Google alert for "OxyContin," to make sure he received all the latest news on the drug. But he complained to Raul Damas at one point, "Why are all the alerts about negatives and not one about the positives of OxyContin?" Damas offered to reconfigure the search terms so that Richard would receive only news items that were flattering.

In 2016, the *Los Angeles Times* released another big story, this one about the fact that OxyContin, which for twenty years had been marketed as a painkiller to be taken on a twelve-hour dosing schedule, might not in fact actually work for twelve hours. Purdue had known about this problem since before the drug was even released, when patients in clinical trials complained that their pain was returning before the twelve-hour mark, the paper revealed. But the company had sought to obfuscate the issue, because the whole marketing premise for

OxyContin was that patients had to take it only twice a day. The article noted that over the years since its release "more than 7 million Americans have abused OxyContin."

Next, the *Times* published a third investigative piece that was, if anything, more incendiary. Under the headline "OxyContin Goes Global," it described how the Sacklers had shifted their attention to promoting opioid use in developing markets, through Mundipharma. "It's right out of the playbook of Big Tobacco," the former FDA commissioner David Kessler told the newspaper. "As the United States takes steps to limit sales here, the company goes abroad."

After the story was published, several members of Congress wrote an open letter to the World Health Organization, urging it to help stop the spread of OxyContin and calling out the Sacklers by name. "The international health community has a rare opportunity to see the future," the lawmakers wrote. "Do not allow Purdue to walk away from the tragedy they have inflicted on countless American families simply to find new markets and new victims elsewhere."

At Purdue, there had been a tendency, over the ups and downs of two decades selling OxyContin, to adopt a bunker mentality. During periodic spikes in negative publicity, senior management would send out company-wide emails, reassuring staff that they had been maligned, once again, by a "biased" media narrative and unscrupulous reporters who always assumed the worst about Purdue while overlooking all of the great things that the company was doing. But the *Los Angeles Times* stories occasioned some internal dissent, prompting what could have been an inflection point for the company. Some employees were dismayed when they read the articles. They had known that Mundipharma was pushing opioids abroad, but not that it was using precisely the techniques that had gotten Purdue into trouble in the United States. Asked by some members of staff to account for these allegations, Stuart Baker, the company lawyer, was dismissive. Mundipharma was not breaking the law in those other countries, he asserted. So he didn't see the problem.

A schism was developing between a younger generation of executives, who had come in with the new CEO, Mark Timney, and believed that Purdue urgently needed to remake itself if it was going to survive, and an old guard who had been with the Sacklers for decades and insisted that the company had nothing to apologize for. To many in the younger camp, Purdue seemed wildly dysfunctional and antique. "You wouldn't come in off the street and say, 'Oh my God! This is exactly how you should run a company! Every *Harvard Business Review* article was wrong!'" one former executive said, with a chuckle. At a publicly traded company, there might have been a genuine reckoning after the 2007 guilty plea, with a bunch of people fired and a real commitment to systemic reform. But at Purdue, even David Haddox, who coined the term "pseudo-addiction," still held a senior position. "To this day I'm just dumbfounded that passed the sniff test for all those years," another new-guard employee said of the concept of pseudo-addiction. "The solution is just 'Give them *more* opioids!' I don't think you need a PhD in pharmacology to know that's wrong."

Some members of the new regime were shocked to discover company old-timers who had held jobs for decades and seemed to possess no discernible talents, apart from loyalty to the Sacklers. Nobody could say with any confidence what these people *did* all day. Yet their job security seemed absolute. They might well be unemployable in the real world, but they stayed on the payroll, and this only solidified the loyalty that many staff members felt toward the family. When Mark Timney came in, he sought to introduce standards-based evaluation procedures, of a sort that you might find at a regular company. "A lot of people are going to leave," Timney announced at a meeting in the ground-floor auditorium. "Some are going to get let go. Others are going to decide that this is no longer the place for them. And that's fine."

But if Timney thought that longtime Purdue employees, many of whom enjoyed direct relationships with the Sacklers, were going to allow him to transform the company without a fight, he was mistaken. "There were two camps," one executive who took part in these discussions recalled. Among the new guard, there was a sense that the opioid crisis had now taken on such catastrophic proportions that it was no longer a viable option (if it ever had been) to keep selling opioids without so much as a gesture of conciliation. At this point, more than 165,000 Americans had lost their lives to prescription opioid abuse since 1999. Overdoses had now surpassed car accidents to become the leading cause of preventable death in America. In a midyear update to the Sacklers in June 2016, staffers told the family that, according to surveys, nearly half of all Americans knew someone who had been addicted to prescription opioids.

"Purdue needs a new approach," some of the new-guard executives proposed. In a meeting, they made a presentation, "A New Narrative: Appropriate Use." That it would represent a sharp departure from precedent for Purdue Pharma to begin advocating the "appropriate" use of opioids might have been an indication of just how out of touch the Sacklers had become. In any case, they rejected the proposal.

One unadvertised hazard in the life of a plutocrat is that the people around you can be prone to yes-man sycophancy. In theory, you should be able to avail yourself of state-of-the-art counsel. But instead, you often get lousy advice, because your courtiers are careful to tell you only what they think you want to hear. The danger, whether you are a billionaire executive or the president of the United States, is that you end up compounding this problem yourself, by marginalizing any dissenting voices and creating a bubble in which loyalty is rewarded above all else. The Sacklers took pride in being loyal to those who showed great loyalty to them. If you stood by the family, they would take care of you. But it was an unwritten corollary in the company that anyone who quit to take another job would be blacklisted from returning, for life. Consequently, the Sacklers remained insulated by a retinue of stalwarts who both shared and reinforced the family's view that the company was being unfairly maligned and had done nothing wrong. Among the members of this faction, one former executive recalled, "Nobody was outraged about what the *L.A. Times* uncovered. The reaction was silence."

Mark Timney advocated making some allowances when it came to the opioid crisis. He brought in a new general counsel, Maria Barton, who was a former federal prosecutor, and she too pushed for a change in the corporate culture. In what amounted to a small heresy by the traditional standards of Purdue, Barton suggested that it might not be the most appropriate thing for a portrait of her predecessor Howard Udell to hang in the company library. Raul Damas, who had served in the White House under George W. Bush, and another public affairs executive, Robert Josephson, who had previously worked for World Wrestling Entertainment, counseled the Sacklers to find a way to address the crisis.

But arrayed against these revisionist voices was a chorus of company old-timers, like Haddox, and the lawyer Stuart Baker, and a pair of lobbyists, Burt Rosen and Alan Must, and an executive named

Craig Landau who had served in a variety of positions at the company, including medical director, and was now running Canadian operations for Purdue. Staff proposed to the Sacklers that they establish a foundation to help address the opioid crisis and devote some of their philanthropic energies to addiction treatment centers and other remedies. The family refused. There was a defensive perception, among the old guard, that *any* sort of charitable gesture related to the fallout from OxyContin might be construed as an admission of wrongdoing. "If you do something for addiction," the old guard loyalists told the family, "you're admitting culpability."

Howard Udell might be dead, but his ghost lived on. "That was the Udell philosophy," one former executive observed. "Concede absolutely nothing." The Sacklers declined even to release a general statement, in their own names, acknowledging that the opioid crisis existed and conveying a modicum of compassion. Staff prepared a dozen different versions of such a statement and urged the family to sign off on one of them and release it. But the Sacklers refused.

This reticence was all the more striking given that in other quarters of what Richard called the "pain community," some allies of the Sacklers were beginning to express second thoughts. "Did I teach about pain management, specifically about opioid therapy, in a way that reflects misinformation? I guess I did," the King of Pain, Dr. Russell Portenoy, said in 2012. As it turned out, the risk of addiction with these drugs was significantly higher than he had thought, Portenoy now acknowledged. In fact, they might *not* be the optimal course of therapy for long-term chronic pain, after all. Portenoy had delivered "innumerable" lectures about addiction over the course of his career that, he now admitted, "weren't true." The reality, he told *The Wall Street Journal*, is that "data about the effectiveness of opioids does not exist." Nor was Portenoy alone in disavowing some of the classic bromides of the big campaign for more painkiller prescribing. "It's obviously crazy to think that only 1% of the population is at risk of opioid addiction," Lynn Webster, of the Purdue-sponsored American Academy of Pain Medicine, acknowledged. "It's just not true."

Richard did not like the negative press coverage. "Did you read any articles about me?" he wrote to a friend in 2016. "If so, is there a reason you didn't ask me about them? It's curious because it wouldn't have been any more quiet on email, SMS or phone if the Globe was publishing my obituary!" But rather than come out swinging in a public manner and make the case for his family and his company, Richard opted for the cultivated obscurity that the Sacklers had always preferred. The family might have raged, privately, about the utter righteousness of their own conduct, but that did not mean that they were prepared to be associated, publicly, in any way with Purdue. A new generation of company lackeys was still playing the old shell game devised by Arthur Sackler and his brothers as far back as the 1950s, though with each new press story it got harder to sustain. "Sackler family members hold no leadership roles in the companies owned by the family trust," one draft press statement suggested. But that seemed too flagrantly, checkably untrue, so staff amended it to the more moderate claim that members of the family "hold no management positions." Even that was misleading—eight members of the family still sat on the board of directors, and some of them were maniacally interventionist when it came to management— so, having prepared the statement themselves, the PR team at Purdue opted to have one of the family's foreign entities release it, because the latest round of questions was about Mundipharma's practices abroad, and, as such, nobody in the United States wanted to be responsible. "The statement will come out of Singapore," they decided.

✤ ✤ ✤

One justification that the Sacklers often repeated, to themselves and to others, about their role in the controversy surrounding OxyContin, was that the drug had been approved by the FDA. There were some inside the FDA who felt that the agency's approval of the drug and Purdue's associated marketing claims had been a major mistake. At a 2001 meeting with Purdue, an FDA official, Cynthia McCormick, told the company that some of the clinical trials it had done were misleading and "should never have gone into the label for OxyContin." She complained that because of Purdue's message about the drug being "good for whatever ails you," OxyContin was "creeping into a whole population of people where it doesn't belong." David Kessler, who was the head of the FDA when OxyContin was approved, characterized the de-stigmatization of opioids that OxyContin helped to initiate as one of the "great mistakes of modern medicine."

Apart from a few dissenting voices, however, the FDA had been a reliable ally for Purdue over the years. Craig Landau, the longtime

Purdue executive who had been a protégé of the Sacklers' and served as medical director, would frequently telephone the official in charge of analgesics at the agency. "He'd call him up," one staffer who worked with Landau recalled. "That's completely unusual. You don't call up the head of the division you have products with just to have a chat." The staffer had the impression that Purdue enjoyed "a very inappropriate relationship with that division at the FDA."

A representative for Purdue strenuously denied this characterization, saying that "all of Dr. Landau's relationships at FDA were formal and appropriate." But dating back to the days of Arthur Sackler and Henry Welch, the pharmaceutical industry had found many ways to compromise personnel at the FDA. The malfeasance didn't always entail bribery or some other obvious quid pro quo. It was sometimes enough for the overeducated staffers earning civil servant salaries at the FDA to know that when they chose to leave government, as Curtis Wright had done after he gave OxyContin its approval, there would be lucrative jobs and consulting opportunities awaiting them.

In fact, when a federal agency finally sought to take on the opioid industry, it wasn't the FDA at all, or any Washington agency, for that matter, but the Centers for Disease Control and Prevention in Atlanta. In 2011, the CDC described the crisis of addiction and death that was sweeping the country as an epidemic. One factor that had contributed to this public health problem, many observers agreed, was that so many American physicians had learned what they knew about opioid prescribing from the drug companies themselves. So the CDC set out to create a set of nonbinding guidelines that could assist doctors in determining when to prescribe opioids and, in the process, hopefully reduce the overprescribing of these drugs. The agency convened a panel of experts and made a point of seeking out specialists who did not receive funding from the pharma industry.

This immediately set off alarms at Purdue. "CDC does not want to hear from pharma companies," Burt Rosen, Purdue's lobbyist in D.C., wrote in an internal email. The experts assembling the guidelines "have to be clear of any pharma funding," he noted, which would make it more difficult for the company to exert its influence. The guidelines "are meant to be restrictive," Rosen warned. Once completed, they could represent "the nation's legal standard for opioid prescribing."

"On it," David Haddox replied. As concerns about opioids had intensified over the years, Purdue had become very active, behind the scenes, in lobbying against any measures, at either a state or a federal level, that might impinge upon its business. According to a study by the Associated Press and the Center for Public Integrity, Purdue and other drug companies that manufacture opioid painkillers spent over $700 million between 2006 and 2015 on lobbying in Washington and in all fifty states. The combined spending of these groups amounted to roughly eight times what the gun lobby spent. (By comparison, during the same period, the small handful of groups pushing for limits on opioid prescribing spent $4 million.) One former DEA official described the influence that this lobby exerted over Congress as a "stranglehold." At the state level, Purdue had also fought measures that were designed to help shut down pill mills, arguing that such steps might limit the availability of opioids to pain patients. Richard Sackler had tracked these developments personally and worked with staff to devise strategies for fighting state initiatives to control the crisis.

In addition to the lobby groups, Purdue could count on its array of industry-funded astroturf organizations. Rosen had created the Pain Care Forum to, as he put it in a 2005 email to Howard Udell, "provide for some unified direction" in the "pain community." The forum brought together many of the patient advocacy groups and their corporate backers. Now they had a new unified directive: go to war on the CDC guidelines.

"We know of no other medication that's routinely used for a nonfatal condition that kills patients so frequently," Tom Frieden, the CDC's director, said of opioids. More Americans were "primed" to start using heroin, he noted, because of their exposure to prescription opioids. The reformulation of OxyContin had actually been quite dangerous, in Frieden's view, because it created a perception (reinforced, once again, by the FDA) that these drugs were safe. "It was no less addictive. People thought it was less addictive, but that was a big distraction," Frieden said. "The company knew damn well what it was peddling, and I think that's the right word—peddling."

The draft guidelines counseled doctors to prescribe these drugs not as the remedy "to start with and to stay with" but instead as a last resort, after trying other drugs or physical therapy. The CDC would also advise doctors to prescribe the smallest amount of the drugs and the shortest course of treatment for acute pain. This might have seemed like a reasonable and relatively modest response to a public health emergency. But it ran directly counter to Purdue's strategy of encouraging doctors to prescribe OxyContin in *stronger* doses for *longer* periods of time. For Purdue and other pharma companies, the CDC guidelines seemed threatening, because even though the advice might be nonbinding, if it were to be adopted by insurers or hospitals, it could have a significant impact on their business. So Purdue found common cause with its competitors in the painkiller industry and launched a full-on blitz.

David Haddox had long sparred with the CDC. There *was* no opioid epidemic, he argued in a position paper that he prepared for the agency. CDC officials might like to throw around "provocative language," but it was unclear to Haddox "why these particular problems are considered to be of epidemic proportions." It was true that there was an epidemic, he allowed, just not the one the CDC kept talking about. The *real* epidemic, Haddox said—in fact the "#1 public health problem in the United States"—was untreated pain. Why is chronic pain not portrayed as an epidemic? Haddox wondered. Back in the 1990s, Purdue had estimated that 50 million people suffered from undiagnosed chronic pain. These days, Haddox suggested, the number might be as high as 116 million. More than a third of the country! How was that not an epidemic? And untreated pain, he added, can be every bit as "devastating and disabling for the individual as can be the consequences of abuse and addiction, up to and including death."

When the draft guidelines were initially released, members of the Pain Care Forum attacked them, saying that they were not based on solid evidence and criticizing the CDC for not releasing the names of the outside experts who had advised the agency. One member group, the Washington Legal Foundation, argued that this failure to disclose the names amounted to a "clear violation" of federal law. Another group, the Academy of Integrative Pain Management, asked Congress to investigate the CDC. It was important to Richard Sackler that these front groups be perceived as independent from Purdue. When Burt Rosen was asked, in a subsequent deposition, whether he had played any role in the intervention by the Washington Legal Foundation, he said, "I don't recall being involved." Asked whether Purdue had played a role, he said flatly, "I don't have any knowledge beyond what I've stated." (In 2016, the year that it rebuked the CDC, the Washington

Legal Foundation received a larger-than-usual contribution from Purdue of $200,000.)

The Pain Care Forum produced its own set of "consensus guidelines," which opposed any sort of measure that might create "new barriers" to medication, and prepared a petition with four thousand signatures warning about the danger of stigmatizing pain patients. The group's argument was that the experts that the CDC had assembled were all biased. But of course, the very groups raising this allegation were all funded by Big Pharma. Under fire, the CDC ended up delaying the guidelines, but they were eventually released in 2016. Opioids should not be treated as a "first-line therapy," the guidelines advised. "As a civilization we somehow managed to survive for 50,000 years without OxyContin," one doctor, Lewis Nelson, who advised the agency on the guidelines, said. "I think we will continue to survive."

But there was also some validity to the concern that in the face of the new guidelines and enhanced scrutiny of prescribers by the authorities, physicians might swing too hard in the other direction, abruptly cutting off patients who had come to depend on these drugs. That, too, could have major negative consequences for public health, driving patients onto the black market, or neglecting the legitimate suffering of people who were living with chronic pain. It was an excruciatingly delicate problem, from both a policy and a medical point of view—and it was compounded by the fact that most physicians were not trained in how to gradually taper a patient off opioids. The industry had taught doctors how to get people on these drugs, but not how to get them off.

✢ ✢ ✢

In 2017, Mark Timney's contract was up as CEO of Purdue Pharma. The Sacklers chose not to renew it. "There were people pushing the family to change," one executive who worked with Timney recalled. "But in the end, they didn't want to change." The old guard celebrated Timney's ouster, and the remaining members of the new guard began to plan their own exits. The message was clear: trying to reform the company was a good way to get sidelined or fired. The loyalists had staked their fortunes on the Sacklers. Some of the very people Timney had pushed out of the company now came back. According to another employee who was there during this period, the corporate ethos, once again, was that loyalty would be rewarded: "This whole group of people looked back at what happened with Udell and Goldenheim and Fried-man and said, 'They took care of them.' "

The Sacklers selected as Timney's replacement the CEO of the Canadian business, Craig Landau. Having spent most of his career at Purdue, Landau was perceived as the ultimate Sackler loyalist. As medical director, he had been instrumental in the reformulation of OxyContin. He was not someone who was going to challenge the Sack-lers, or urge them to make any apologies or charitable contributions that they did not want to make. Nor was Landau going to try, as Tim-ney had, to reduce the family's direct intervention in the company. On the contrary, when he prepared his business plan for the job, Landau seemed to concede that his role as chief executive would be largely cer-emonial. He described Purdue as the "Sackler pharma enterprise." In case there was any uncertainty about who would be calling the shots, he characterized the company's board, which the Sacklers still dominated, as "the de facto CEO." Other companies might be giving up on opioids, Landau acknowledged, because the legal and reputational costs were just not worth it. But that was an *opportunity* for Purdue. Rather than diversify away from the business that had brought them so much wealth and trouble, Landau suggested, the company should pursue an "opioid consolidation strategy" as other firms "abandon the space."

One innovative idea the company discussed was a proposal, devised by McKinsey, to offer rebates each time a patient who had been pre-scribed OxyContin subsequently overdosed or developed an opioid use disorder. These payments of up to $14,000 would not go to the patient who had been harmed, but to big pharmacy chains and insurance com-panies, such as CVS and Anthem, to encourage the pharmacies to con-tinue selling OxyContin and the insurers to continue paying for it, even in the face of such potentially lethal side effects. (The company did not end up going through with this idea.)

The month after Landau was appointed, Raymond Sackler died. He was ninety-seven. "He worked the day before he was stricken ill," Richard said with pride. This was the last link to the original owner-ship of the company. And there seemed to be a strong sense, among the younger Sacklers, that they would push forward, defiant, and beat back those who tried to stop the family or slow it down.

Chapter 25

TEMPLE OF GREED

IN 2016, NAN GOLDIN was dividing her time between apartments in Berlin, Paris, and New York. A small woman in her early sixties, with pale skin, a frizzy crown of red-brown curls, and an ever-present cigarette, Goldin had been taking pictures for half a century and was considered one of the most important American photographers alive. She had been raised in the middle-class suburbs of Washington, D.C., in a family that placed great emphasis on propriety. Both of her parents had grown up poor, but her father had managed to go to Harvard, at a time when few Jewish students were admitted to the university. "Most of all, my father cared about Harvard," she once remarked. The fact that he had managed to earn that unimpeachable distinction was "the biggest thing in his life."

When Nan was eleven years old, her older sister Barbara, who was eighteen, lay down in the path of an oncoming commuter train near Silver Spring, Maryland, and killed herself. Nan had worshipped her older sister, but Barbara was troubled, an unconventional child who was prone to wild outbursts. Their parents had chosen to commit her, against her will, in a series of psychiatric institutions. These were not public hospitals like Creedmoor asylum, but smaller private facilities, and Barbara cycled in and out of their bleak wards for six years before choosing suicide. When police officers visited the home to inform the family, Nan overheard her mother say, "Tell the children it was an accident." Devastated, and brimming with resentment for her parents, Nan left home at the age of fourteen. She lived in foster homes and in a commune for a while. She attended a hippie school in Massachusetts, where somebody gave her a camera, and she started taking pictures. She was good at it. At nineteen, she had her first show, in a little gallery in Cambridge.

Goldin's photography was a defiant rejection of the way in which

her parents saw the world—or, rather, chose not to see it. In the sti-
fling aspirational ecosystem of suburban Maryland, Barbara's suicide,
like her unconventionality in life, had been a source of embarrassment
and shame for the Goldin family. Prompted, in part, by "all the denial
around her suicide," Nan decided to "make a record that nobody can
revise." She would not obfuscate the truth of her life, however atypical
or marginal or vulnerable it might be. She would expose it. She started
taking candid snapshots of herself and her friends and her lovers and
her friends' lovers, in dimly lit bedrooms and skanky bars. She was living a beatnik life on the fringes of society, among drag queens in Prov-
incetown and artists and sex workers in New York City. Her photos
had a luminous palette and captured her subjects in raw, discomfitingly
intimate moments. Above all, her work had a bracing candor. In perhaps
her most famous photo, *Nan One Month After Being Battered*, she stares
directly into the camera, her face made up with cherry-red lipstick and
penciled brows, her left eye bruised and swollen half-shut from a beating administered by her boyfriend.

Goldin was living in a loft on the Bowery, in the East Village, when
the AIDS crisis hit. Many of her closest friends and artistic influences
were gay men, and one by one they started dying. Suddenly she found
herself taking pictures in hospital wards and hospices. She eventually
grew close to the gay artist and activist David Wojnarowicz, who was
close with another friend and mentor of hers, the photographer Peter
Hujar. In 1987, Hujar died. Nan had been reckoning with a demon of
her own during these years. Drugs had been a regular feature of the
worlds she had inhabited since leaving home as a teenager, and during
the 1970s she had started using heroin. Like a lot of people who use
heroin, she found a certain glamour in it, until she didn't. She used the
drug on and off for years, but in the late 1980s, it took over. Wojnarowicz had used heroin, too, but he managed to quit. So in 1988, Goldin
entered rehab.

She emerged, sober, the following year, looking forward to a reunion
with her friends. But when she got back to the city, it had changed. The
pace of death had accelerated. In 1989, she curated a seminal exhibit
at a downtown gallery called *Witnesses: Against Our Vanishing*. The show
featured art by people whose lives had been impacted by AIDS. Wojnarowicz wrote an essay for the catalog in which he singled out the
right-wing political establishment for refusing to fund research into

HIV, allowing the epidemic to proceed unchecked. Part of the reason American political leaders stood by for so long and did nothing to intervene was a moralistic attitude that the gay men and intravenous drug users who were getting sick in such large numbers had nobody to blame but themselves—that AIDS was, in effect, a lifestyle choice. Some of the art in the show was by friends who had already died, like a self-portrait by Hujar. Another one of the artists, Goldin's friend Cookie Mueller, died just a few days before the exhibit opened. It was as if a great plague had swept through Goldin's whole community. Wojnarowicz died three years later.

Nan Goldin lived. But she often felt a kind of survivor's guilt, thinking of the friends, so many of them now gone, who stared back at her from her own photographs. Her work found new admirers. Museums ran retrospectives. Eventually, those pictures of her dead friends would hang on the walls of some of the most illustrious galleries in the world. In 2011, the Louvre opened its palatial halls to Goldin, after hours, so that she could stroll through the broad marble galleries, barefoot, and take pictures of the artworks on display, for an installation in which she juxtaposed images of paintings from the museum's collection with photographs from her own oeuvre. The chronicler of life on the margins had become canonical.

In 2014, Goldin was in Berlin when she developed a severe case of tendinitis in her left wrist, which was causing her a great deal of pain. She went to see a doctor who wrote her a prescription for OxyContin. Goldin knew about the drug, knew its reputation for being dangerously addictive. But her own history of hard drug use, rather than making her more cautious, could sometimes mean that she was cavalier. I can handle it, she figured.

As soon as she took the pills, she could see what the fuss was about. OxyContin didn't just ameliorate the pain in her wrist; it felt like a chemical insulation not just from pain but from anxiety and upset. The drug felt, she would say, like "a padding between you and the world." It wasn't long before she was taking the pills more quickly than she was supposed to. Two pills a day became four, then eight, then sixteen. To keep up with her own needs, she had to enlist other doctors and juggle multiple prescriptions. She had money; she had received a major grant to work on new material and was preparing for a show at the Museum of Modern Art in New York. But her efforts to source pills had come to feel like a full-time job. She started crushing pills and snorting them. She found an obliging dealer in New York who would ship her pills via FedEx.

Three years of her life disappeared. She was working throughout, but she was sequestered in her apartment, entirely isolated from human contact, seeing virtually no one, apart from those she needed to see to get her pills. She would spend days counting and recounting her collection of pills, making resolves and then breaking them. What kept her in this spiral was not the euphoria of the high but just the fear of withdrawal. When it hit, she could summon no words to capture the mental and physical agony. Her whole body raged with searing, incandescent pain. It felt as if the skin had been peeled right off her. She did a painting during this period of a miserable-looking young man in a green tank top, his arms festering with boils and wounds. She titled it *Withdrawal/Quicksand*. At a certain point, her doctors caught on to her and she was struggling to access enough black-market OxyContin, so she lapsed back into using heroin. One night, she bought a batch that, unbeknownst to her, was actually fentanyl, and she overdosed.

She didn't die, but the experience frightened her. So in 2017, at the age of sixty-two, Goldin checked back in to rehab. She did this at an excellent clinic in rural Massachusetts, a facility associated with McLean Hospital. She knew that she was fortunate to have access to treatment; only one in ten people who are addicted to opioids do. And she felt lucky to be able to afford a level of care that most could not; the McLean program cost $2,000 a day. She worked with the same doctor who had gotten her sober back in the 1980s. After two months, Goldin had managed to purge the drug from her system. It felt similar, in some ways, to her experience of coming out of rehab three decades earlier: those first wobbly steps, after a long period of seclusion, back in the direction of the living. But she felt now, just as she had in 1989, that she was coming back to a world that had been decimated by a plague. The death count from prescription-opioid-related overdoses had surged past 200,000. According to the latest figures from the CDC, when you factored in illicit heroin and fentanyl, in addition to prescription opioids, 115 Americans were dying each day. One day while she was still in recovery, in the fall of 2017, she read an article in *The New Yorker* about the drug that had nearly killed her, about the company that made the drug, and about the family that owned the company.

✢   ✢   ✢

It was not as though the Sacklers had not been written about before. Barry Meier and Sam Quinones had detailed the history of the family and the company in their books. But until then, the Sacklers had tended to be presented as one strand in a complex narrative involving OxyContin, Purdue, pain doctors, patients, and the burgeoning opioid crisis. This was no surprise, and no shortcoming on the part of the prior reporting: because the Sacklers were so secretive, and Purdue was a privately held company, it had been difficult, up to that point, to tell a story in which the culpability of the family was front and center.

The *New Yorker* article, which I wrote, took a different approach, focusing squarely on the family and highlighting both the role that they had played in directing the company and the dissonance between the Sacklers' unblemished reputation in philanthropic circles and the sordid reality of their fortune. "I don't know how many rooms in different parts of the world I've given talks in that were named after the Sacklers," Allen Frances, the former chair of psychiatry at Duke University School of Medicine, said in the article. "Their name has been pushed forward as the epitome of good works and of the fruits of the capitalist system. But, when it comes down to it, they've earned this fortune at the expense of millions of people who are addicted. It's shocking how they have gotten away with it."

In a coincidence of timing, the *New Yorker* article came out the same week that *Esquire* published a piece about the Sacklers, by Christopher Glazek, with a remarkably similar premise. "We were directed to lie. Why mince words about it?" a former Purdue sales rep told Glazek. "The Fords, Hewletts, Packards, Johnsons—all those families put their name on their product because they were proud," the Stanford psychiatry professor Keith Humphreys said. "The Sacklers have hidden their connection to their product."

Suddenly the family was facing a level of scrutiny completely out of proportion to anything they had encountered in the past. In the weeks after the articles were published, a fissure emerged, for the first time in public, between the Arthur wing of the family and the Mortimer and Raymond wings. When I was working on my article, I tried to get members of Arthur's family to offer an opinion on the legacy of Purdue, this company that Arthur purchased for his brothers. But they would not make any statements on the record expressing even the slightest criticism of the business decisions of the other branches of the family.

After this new wave of publicity, that changed. Elizabeth Sackler, who had endowed the Elizabeth A. Sackler Center for Feminist Art at the Brooklyn Museum and maintained a Twitter feed full of urgent exclamations about the perfidy of Donald Trump and her allegiance to Black Lives Matter, belatedly made a statement in which she distanced herself from her cousins. In an interview with the website Hyperallergic, she said that Purdue's role in the opioid crisis "is morally abhorrent to me." Her father died in 1987, she pointed out, long before the introduction of OxyContin, and she and her siblings had agreed to sell their one-third stake in Purdue to her uncles soon thereafter. So, none of Arthur's heirs had profited from OxyContin, she insisted.

Jillian Sackler, Arthur's widow, was still alive, living in a full-floor apartment in a neoclassical building on Park Avenue, surrounded by paintings and sculptures. She also spoke up for the first time, saying that Arthur "would not have approved of the widespread sale of Oxy-Contin." The heirs of Arthur's brothers "have a moral duty to help make this right and to atone for any mistakes made," she said. Both Elizabeth and Jillian agreed that Arthur was entirely beyond reproach. He "was an amazing man who did tremendous good, and I am just so proud of him," Jillian said. In a flourish that seemed only appropriate for the widow of Arthur M. Sackler, she handed out to reporters a dense CV with the names of her various board appointments and the foundations to which she had contributed.

The question of whether it was fair for the descendants of Arthur Sackler to be tainted by the controversy over OxyContin was an interesting one. On the one hand, it was indisputable that Arthur had indeed died before the launch of the drug and had hardly been speaking with his brothers by the end of his life. On the other hand, it was Arthur who created the world in which OxyContin could do what it did. He pioneered medical advertising and marketing, the co-opting of the Food and Drug Administration, the mingling of medicine and commerce. So many of the antecedents of the saga of OxyContin could be found in the life of Arthur Sackler. The heirs of Arthur were caught in a delicate bind of their own creation. During his lifetime, and to an even greater extent after his death, people like Jillian and Elizabeth had served as wards of his legacy, burnishing the memory of the man and endlessly enumerating (and often overstating) his accomplishments. Arthur had felt, in life, that he deserved credit for a great deal of what his brothers built, and this sentiment was echoed long after his death by his admirers. "Sackler founded a dynasty," the hagiographic biography that was privately published by Jillian Sackler's foundation declared, explaining that he set his brothers up in business and was personally responsible for much of Purdue's success. A description of Arthur's life on Sackler .org, a website maintained by Jillian, describes how he "initiated fact-based medical advertising," then "purchased the pharmaceutical company Purdue Frederick, and started all the other family businesses."

In January 2018, Nan Goldin published some new work in *Artforum*. It featured a series of her photographs from her time in Berlin. She had chronicled the years of her addiction, taking pictures of pill bottles and prescriptions, the banal paraphernalia of her own abuse, and self-portraits when she was high. She contrasted these images with new photos that she had taken of clean geometric signage bearing the Sackler name in various art galleries around the world. "I survived the opioid crisis," Goldin wrote in an accompanying essay, in which she harked back to her own early activism during the AIDS crisis. "I can't stand by and watch another generation disappear." Instead, she wanted to raise a call to arms. "The Sacklers made their fortune promoting addiction," she declared. "They have washed their blood money through the halls of museums and universities around the world." It was time, she said, to "hold them accountable."

If this was going to be some kind of campaign Goldin was launching, it would put Elizabeth Sackler in a tricky spot. She identified not just as a progressive and a patron of the arts but as an activist. "I admire Nan Goldin's courage to speak about her story and her commitment to take action," Elizabeth wrote in a letter to *Artforum*. "I stand in solidarity with artists and thinkers whose work and voices must be heard."

But Goldin, with her particular allergy to the bullshit stories that families tell, was having none of it. Arthur might have died before Oxy-Contin was introduced, she said, but "he was the architect of the advertising model used so effectively to push the drug." And he made his money on tranquilizers! It was a bit rich, she thought, for the Valium Sacklers to be getting morally huffy about their OxyContin cousins.

"The brothers made billions on the bodies of hundreds of thousands," Goldin said. "The whole Sackler clan is evil."

✢ ✢ ✢

The Sacklers were furious about this new coverage. One particular item in *The New Yorker* had incensed some members of the family. The piece suggested that Purdue, "facing a shrinking market and rising opprobrium," had not given up the search for new users, and pointed out that "in August, 2015, over objections from critics, the company received F.D.A. approval to market OxyContin to children as young as eleven."

This was true. Purdue had received permission from the FDA to sell OxyContin to juveniles, despite the long history of children overdosing and dying from the drug. But the Sacklers objected that Purdue had not *sought* this permission. Rather, the company was simply complying with FDA regulations that required it to perform clinical trials to see whether the drug could be prescribed to kids. In an indignant letter to *The New Yorker,* an attorney for the Raymond Sackler side of the family, Tom Clare, asserted that Purdue did not "voluntarily" run these trials, but "did so *only* to comply with FDA's mandate" (emphasis his). Moreover, he stressed, the company had promised, of its own accord, that it would not actively *market* the drug for children.

You could see why the family might be sensitive to the optics of such an inference. But leaving aside the fact that Purdue, at this stage, was expecting some sort of merit badge for not explicitly marketing an opioid directly for use by kids, it was simply not true that this process had been initiated solely to placate the FDA. In fact, Purdue's own internal documents include numerous instances of company officials describing the "pediatric indication" as something that they were very much pursuing. In January 2011, when Craig Landau drafted his "goals and objectives," as chief medical officer, for the year, one of the items on the list was obtaining FDA approval to sell OxyContin to children.

The real reason that the Sacklers were angry over this passage about the pediatric indication was more complicated. According to people who worked at Purdue at the time, the company had wanted to obtain the pediatric indication for years. But the reason was not that the FDA was requiring them to or that the Sacklers thought there was a huge new market for the painkiller among children. Rather, it was because securing a pediatric indication from the FDA is yet another crafty way of extending the patent for a drug. In a pair of laws, the Best Pharmaceuticals for Children Act and the Pediatric Research Equity Act, Congress had authorized the FDA to offer certain incentives to drug companies if they undertook clinical trials to see how their drugs worked on children. At this point, OxyContin had enjoyed patent exclusivity for twenty years—far longer than most pharmaceuticals. This was a credit to Purdue's fiendishly brilliant attorneys. Now, if they could secure the pediatric indication, it would potentially entitle them to an additional six months of exclusivity. The Sacklers claimed that they were obligated by the law to do the clinical trials, but they weren't compelled so much as incentivized. One former executive pointed out that in 2011 six more months of exclusivity could have "meant more than a billion dollars" in revenue. As such, the executive continued, a determination had been made that "it was worth the bad optics." As early as 2009, a budget presentation discussed the idea of securing a pediatric indication in terms of "impact on exclusivity and value created." An email from the younger Mortimer Sackler that same year raised the specter of the "patent cliff" for OxyContin and wondered about "the extension from doing pediatric trials."

The company did end up getting the pediatric indication. But for technical reasons, they were denied the extension of exclusivity, which left them very unhappy and primed, perhaps, to be sensitive to nasty press reports implying that the family might have wanted to sell opioids to children, when what they were really after was an extra six months of monopoly pricing. And even in the face of an unprecedented tide of bad press, the family was still on the lookout for other ways to sell opioids. A few weeks after the *New Yorker* article came out, even as Jonathan Sackler raged about negative coverage depicting his family as greedy pill profiteers, he proposed to Purdue that the company consider launching yet another opioid. Richard continued to demand information about sales, to a point where staff at the company did not know how to respond. "I think we need to find a balance," one employee wrote to another, "between being clear about what the reality looks like... and just giving so much bad news about the future that it just makes things look hopeless." The family was committed to their strategy of urging patients to take bigger doses for longer periods of time. McKinsey had counseled that this was the way to protect company profits. But this advice defied an emerging medical consensus that such an approach was not the best way to address chronic pain. The CDC had recently announced that there was "insufficient evidence" to indicate that these drugs continued to relieve pain in patients who took them for more than three months, and warned that nearly a quarter of all patients who took opioid painkillers long term could become addicted.

Some executives had urged the board to recognize that the strategy of being an integrated pain management company was not working and that they needed to diversify. In 2014, Kathe Sackler had been involved in discussions on an initiative called Project Tango. The idea was that one natural area into which Purdue could now branch out was selling drugs that treat opioid addiction. Richard Sackler himself had been part of a team of inventors who applied for a patent to treat addiction. (The patent application described people who become addicted to opioids as "junkies" and lamented "the drug-related criminal activities resorted to by such addicts in order to raise enough money to fund their addiction.") According to a PowerPoint presentation for Project Tango, the "Abuse and Addiction market" would be a "good fit and next natural step for Purdue." In some ways, this initiative was a riff on a business model that Purdue had long employed. One side effect of opioid use is constipation, and for years Purdue's sales reps had marketed the company's trusty laxative, Senokot, as a useful chaser to OxyContin. With a frankness that even the Sacklers might have found unsettling, the Project Tango presentation declared, "Pain treatment and addiction are naturally linked." The presentation noted that "the opioid addiction space could be an exciting entry point for Purdue."

But in the end, the board voted not to proceed with Project Tango. This was part of a pattern. There seemed to be a recognition at Purdue that the company needed to develop or license other product lines. But anytime the board was presented with potential candidates that weren't opioids, the Sacklers would inquire about how profitable they would be. "There were efforts to make them diversify," one former executive recalled. They looked at products for Parkinson's. For migraines. For insomnia. "But the board wasn't interested. The profit margins weren't the same as with opioids." This was a high bar—few pharmaceutical products are as profitable as OxyContin—so the Sacklers passed on one proposal after another. "They had no interest at all in developing non-opioid products," another former executive recalled. "Their biggest interest was in selling as much OxyContin as possible." Craig Landau, after he was appointed CEO, paid lip service to the idea of exploring other product lines, but the reality, according to this executive, was that "Craig is a businessman. All Craig ever talked about was how much of the business a certain segment of the pain population was. 'This is 10 percent of our business.' 'This is 15 percent of our business.' He never said the word 'patient,' but he talked about the business all the time."

A third former executive recalled the pressure of going before the family to pitch new business ideas: "Going to a Sackler board meeting is like going to a bad Thanksgiving dinner, with two sides of the family that just don't get along. You've got Richard on the Raymond side pulling in one direction and Kathe on the Mortimer side pulling in the other, and they're all fighting and you're standing in the front of the room and asking to go to slide 2." But it was futile. There was "no interest in developing other product lines," the former executive recalled. However novel the proposal, "it wasn't OxyContin."

The good news for the Sacklers was that even after the exposés in *Esquire* and *The New Yorker* it appeared that the negative publicity would do little to unsettle the family's philanthropic relationships or its stature in polite society. After the magazine articles were published, *The New York Times* contacted twenty-one cultural establishments that had received significant sums from the Sacklers, including the Guggenheim, the Brooklyn Museum, and the Met. "But few institutions seem concerned that the money they have received may be tied, in some way, to a family fortune built on the sale of opioids," the paper reported. None of the museums or galleries issued a statement about the Sacklers that was less than supportive or indicated that they would return donations or refuse to accept gifts from the family in the future. Some were openly protective. "The Sackler family continue to be an important and valuable donor," a spokeswoman for the Victoria and Albert Museum told the paper, adding that museum officials were "grateful for their ongoing support." Oxford University was similarly steadfast, announcing that there was "no intention to reconsider the Sackler family and trusts."

✥ ✥ ✥

On a chilly Saturday afternoon in March 2018, Nan Goldin walked into the Metropolitan Museum of Art. She was dressed in black from head to toe and wore a long black muffler around her neck and bright red lipstick, her crimson hair flopping down over her eyes. Once she was inside the museum, she made her way to the Sackler Wing.

She had not come alone. When she reached the hall, with its great wall of banked glass looking out onto the park, she blended into the throng of afternoon museumgoers, but she was quietly coordinating with a group of a hundred or so other people who had arrived, incognito, just as she had. Suddenly, at 4:00 p.m., they started shouting, "Temple of greed! Temple of Oxy!" Someone unfurled a black banner that said, FUND REHAB.

Goldin had started a group, modeled on the 1980s AIDS activists whom she had so admired. They called themselves PAIN, which stood for Prescription Addiction Intervention Now, and they had been meeting in Goldin's Brooklyn apartment and planning a spectacular action. As dozens of protesters chanted, hundreds of people stood around gawking, taking videos with their phones. A number of press photographers, who had been tipped off in advance to be there, snapped photos. Goldin had decided that she wanted to hit the Sacklers where they lived—in the elite milieu of the art museum. The Met had some of Goldin's photos in its permanent collection, and now she would leverage her own standing in that world—and her distinct identity as a revered artist who happened to be recovering from an OxyContin addiction—to call on cultural institutions to refuse Sackler money and to demand that the family use its fortune to fund addiction treatment.

"We are artists, activists, addicts," she announced, taking up position between a pair of imposing black stone statues. A few of her fellow activists had strung up a banner that said SHAME ON SACKLER, and now Goldin stood before it. "We are fed up," she said. The protesters had stationed themselves around the great reflecting pool that had been the centerpiece of so many glittering parties. They reached into their bags and pulled out orange pill bottles; then they hurled the bottles into the pool. "Look at the facts!" they shouted. "Read the stats!"

Met security guards swooped in, trying to get the protesters to settle down and leave, but instead they collapsed onto the floor in a symbolic "die-in." For a few minutes they lay there, arrayed like scattered corpses, to represent the toll of OxyContin. Then they rose and marched out, past the Temple of Dendur, through the cavernous marble halls of the Met, which Arthur, Mortimer, and Raymond had worked so hard to make their own. They waved banners and chanted, their voices ringing through the galleries. "Sacklers lie! Thousands die!" As they marched out of the building and down the steps, Nan Goldin turned and shouted, "We'll be back!"

In the Sackler Wing, nearly a thousand orange pill bottles bobbed in the reflecting pool. They were, in their own modest way, little pieces of art, each carrying a specially designed, very realistic-looking waterproof label. It said,

OxyContin

Prescribed to you by the Sacklers.

Chapter 26

WARPATH

THE ISLAND OF TASMANIA lies 150 miles off the south coast of mainland Australia, in one of the more remote locations on earth. In a place called Westbury, on the northern part of the island, fields of long-stemmed opium poppies quiver in the breeze around the Tasmanian Alkaloids facility. The flowers are mostly pink, with occasional flashes of mauve or white. But these aren't normal poppies. They're a special variety of super poppy that's been genetically engineered to produce a higher proportion of thebaine, an alkaloid that is the key chemical precursor for oxycodone. At the Westbury facility, the poppies are harvested, then processed into a concentrated extract that is flown to the United States, where the raw narcotic material can be processed into oxycodone and other opioids.

This is the breadbasket of the opioid boom. Though it is only about the size of West Virginia, Tasmania grows 85 percent of all the thebaine in the world. During the 1990s, just as Purdue Pharma was developing OxyContin, a company owned by the pharmaceutical giant Johnson & Johnson developed this new strain of opium poppy. Johnson & Johnson started out as a family business like Purdue. People tend to associate the brand with wholesome products like Band-Aids and baby shampoo. But the company has also played a critical role in the opioid crisis. With the launch of OxyContin, Johnson & Johnson's Tasmanian subsidiary, which owned the facility, ramped up production. In a 1998 agreement, it committed to supplying Purdue's "entire worldwide requirements" for the raw narcotic material to produce OxyContin.

This turned out to be quite a commitment. As demand soared, the Tasmanian Alkaloids facility had to encourage local farmers, who had previously grown other crops, like cauliflower or carrots, to switch to poppies. They did this in much the same manner that Purdue sought to stimulate its sales reps, by creating incentive programs and bestow-

ing all-expenses-paid vacations and luxury cars. The weird economics of the poppy rush were such that a weather-beaten Tasmanian
farmer might spend a long workday tending the fields on the back of a
tractor under the blazing sun, then climb into his souped-up climate-
controlled Mercedes for the drive home. At the height of the boom,
in 2013, seventy-four thousand acres in Tasmania were devoted to the
crop. Poppies had become so profitable, one company accountant joked,
that you could up the ante on the incentives and "give them a 747," and
if it got the farmers to grow more opium poppies, it would be worth it.

Historically, the DEA had regulated the quantity of these drugs
that could legally be brought into the United States. But the burgeoning opioid industry pushed to raise these limits, lobbying doggedly, and
over time the DEA accommodated. The opioid crisis is, among other
things, a parable about the awesome capability of private industry to
subvert public institutions. Just as the FDA was compromised and Congress was neutralized or outright co-opted with generous donations
and some federal prosecutors were undermined with a back-channel
appeal in Washington while others were mollified with the promise of
a corporate job, just as state legislators and the CDC were hindered and
sabotaged when they tried to curb opioid prescribing, the DEA was not
immune to these pressures and proceeded to soften its position under
a steady barrage of industry encouragement. Between 1994 and 2015,
the quota of oxycodone that the DEA permitted to be legally manufactured was raised thirty-six times. A subsequent report by the inspector
general of the Justice Department criticized the DEA for being "slow to
respond to the dramatic increase in opioid abuse."

Of course, it wasn't just Purdue applying pressure. This would become a central plank in the Sackler family's defense. In 2016, Johnson & Johnson sold the Tasmanian Alkaloids facility. Physicians were
becoming more cautious about prescribing opioids. And by that point,
many Americans were surveying the carnage that two decades of widespread opioid prescribing had created, and looking around for someone
to blame. Sounding very much like Arthur Sackler in 1961, when he
insisted to the panel of U.S. senators that the McAdams agency was
really just a minor concern, the Sacklers protested that OxyContin's
market share was never more than 4 percent.

There was some truth in this. Janssen, the pharmaceutical branch
of Johnson & Johnson, had its own opioids, a pill called Nucynta and

the fentanyl patch Duragesic, which the company knew was being abused as early as 2001. Then there was Endo (which had Opana), and Mallinckrodt (with Roxicodone), and Teva (with Fentora and the fentanyl lollipop Actiq). And there were others. It was a crowded field. "We are not the only company that marketed opioids," David Sackler would fume. "Johnson & Johnson was massive," he exclaimed, whereas Oxy-Contin was just "this tiny, niche little product with tiny market share."

It was frustrating for the family to feel singled out. In legal papers, lawyers for Purdue complained about "scapegoating." Their biggest competitors were also ensnared in litigation. But nobody was writing unflattering exposés about the CEO of Endo or the board of Mallinckrodt.

While this refrain about the smallness of Purdue always featured prominently in the repertoire of defenses that the Sacklers and their company employed, it was deliberately misleading in several important respects. To begin with, the percentage of total opioid prescriptions was perhaps not the best metric for understanding Purdue's actual role in the marketplace, because that statistic treats every pill the same and does not account for either the size of the dose or the duration of the prescription. The only way that the Sacklers could arrive at their 4 percent market share figure was by including, in the category of opioid prescriptions, even short-term prescriptions for low-dosage medicines like Tylenol-Codeine. OxyContin is an incredibly potent drug. What made it revolutionary—what made the Sacklers so *proud* of it—was the innovative mechanism that enabled Purdue to pack forty or eighty milligrams of oxycodone into a single pill. Moreover, OxyContin was the drug to "start with and to stay with." Purdue's business model was predicated on pain patients who would take the drug month in, month out. For years. For *life* in some cases. Purdue priced its pills aggressively, and sales representatives were incentivized to push patients to "titrate up" their doses, in no small measure because the more massive the dose, the more massive the profits for the company. According to a study by *The Wall Street Journal*, when you take into account the dosage strength of each pill, Purdue actually accounted for a market-leading 27 percent of all oxycodone sold. In a separate analysis, ProPublica found that if you adjust for potency, in some states Purdue's market share of all opioid painkillers—not just oxycodone—was as high as 30 percent.

In making the case that they had only ever been bit players, the

Sacklers and Purdue pointed a finger at their old adversaries, the generic makers. If you want to know where the great bulk of the prescription opioids come from, they suggested, that's where you should look. "OxyContin was introduced in a market dominated by generic opioids," a Purdue spokesman told *The New Yorker* in 2017. The vast majority of prescriptions for opioid pain medications is for generics, he said. But to some who worked at Purdue and were familiar with the convoluted holdings of the Sackler clan, this talking point seemed egregiously insincere, because the Sacklers secretly owned another pharmaceutical company, in addition to Purdue, and it was one of the biggest manufacturers of generic opioids in the United States.

Rhodes Pharmaceuticals was located on a country road in the town of Coventry, Rhode Island, and surrounded by formidable security. The company appeared to be intent on maintaining a low profile; for several years, the website was "under construction." The Sackler family's history with Rhodes, which would eventually be uncovered by the *Financial Times,* dated back to the period following Purdue's guilty plea in the federal case in Virginia. Four months after the plea, the Sacklers established Rhodes. The company was set up as a "landing pad" for the family, according to a former senior manager at Purdue, in case they needed a fresh start following the crisis over OxyContin. Rhodes became the seventh-largest opioid manufacturer in the United States, just behind the generic giant Teva and well ahead of Johnson & Johnson and Endo. Rhodes produced a generic version of MS Contin, but also immediate-release oxycodone, a drug that was widely abused. An article on Purdue's website, "Common Myths About OxyContin," complained about the "misperception that all oxycodone abuse involves OxyContin," suggesting that immediate-release oxycodone was also to blame, without acknowledging the awkward fact that the Sacklers happened to produce both drugs.

Inside Purdue, staff recognized, following the reformulation of OxyContin in 2010, that the company's boasts about the safety of its tamper-resistant opioid might ring hollow if the public understood that a related company, Rhodes, was still busy producing immediate-release oxycodone that was *not* tamper-resistant. In one internal email, a Purdue executive, Todd Baumgartner, discussed the "secretive" manner in which the company sought to obfuscate this contradiction.

Multiple Sacklers played an active role in Rhodes. Dame Theresa and Kathe served on one committee. Mortimer served on another. But according to one longtime Purdue executive who worked closely with the Sacklers, the family member who was most intimately involved was Jonathan. "Jonathan became the champion for Rhodes generic," the executive said. "That was his baby."

The most decisive flaw in the Sacklers' argument about the comparative size of their market share, however, was that when all of these rival pharmaceutical companies began to promote their own powerful opioids, they were following a trail blazed by Purdue. OxyContin was the "tip of the spear," in the words of one Purdue chemist who worked on the drug. Richard Sackler and his team in the 1990s had recognized a significant market barrier—the widespread stigma associated with strong opioids in the medical establishment—and executed a brilliant strategy to remove that barrier and clear the way. Purdue itself acknowledged, in 2001, that the company's promotional efforts helped to bring about a "paradigm shift." Rival drugmakers might have come to supplant Purdue in the marketplace. But they were the followers, not the leader. In a 2002 presentation for Johnson & Johnson, a team of consultants from McKinsey had acknowledged as much. OxyContin "created" a market, they said.

✢ ✢ ✢

In the view of Mike Moore, an attorney, it seemed that Purdue Pharma and the Sackler family were "the main culprit." They "duped the FDA, saying OxyContin lasted twelve hours," Moore said. "They lied about the addictive properties. And they did all this to grow the opioid market, to make it okay to jump in the water. Then some of these other companies, they saw that the water was warm. And they said, 'Okay, we can jump in, too.'"

Moore was in his sixties but looked younger, rail thin, with a bit of a drawl. He came from Mississippi, where he had served as attorney general from 1988 to 2004. During the 1990s, Moore had been regarded as an up-and-coming figure in the Democratic Party, a southern liberal with law-and-order cred who was often compared to Bill Clinton and who, some thought, might one day be a future presidential candidate himself. As attorney general, he excelled at drumming up publicity and at the messy backroom politics associated with putting together coalitions. By his own admission, Moore was a big-picture guy. The fine nuances and endless citations of a legal brief were not his strong suit. But he had passion and energy and charisma in spades, as well as a righteous fervor.

In 1994, Moore decided, along with a coalition of other lawyers, to take on Big Tobacco. Employing an unconventional and risky legal strategy, he became the first state prosecutor to sue cigarette companies in an effort to hold them accountable for the lies that they had told about the health consequences of smoking. He and his allies launched a sequence of lawsuits in which private attorneys collaborated with states to sue the tobacco firms. This was the case that Barry Meier had covered for the *Times*, and it ended in a resounding win for Moore. The defendant companies agreed to the largest corporate legal settlement in U.S. history. Moore and his fellow state prosecutors and plaintiffs' lawyers forced the companies to acknowledge that they had lied about the risks associated with smoking. They got billboards taken down, cigarette vending machines banned, sports promotions canceled. They got rid of Joe Camel, the iconic cartoon mascot, as well as the Marlboro Man. And they forced the companies to pay a landmark fine of more than $200 billion.

In 2004, Moore stepped down as attorney general and opened his own law firm. In the aftermath of the Deepwater Horizon oil spill, he helped secure a $20 billion settlement from BP. He had developed a reputation as a giant slayer, a guy who could bring even the most ferocious corporate behemoth to heal. He'd tangled with the best lawyers on the planet and won. He'd made a considerable fortune of his own, in contingency fees. When the director Michael Mann wanted to make a movie called *The Insider* about the tobacco litigation, most of the real-life characters were played by actors, like Russell Crowe and Al Pacino. Mike Moore played himself. He had a certain swagger.

He also had a nephew who was addicted to opioids. One night in 2006, the nephew had sustained a gunshot wound after an altercation with his wife (his memory of the evening was sufficiently hazy that he couldn't say for sure whether he shot himself or she shot him). A doctor prescribed Percocet. It became an addiction, and by 2010 he was buying fentanyl on the street. Moore did his best to help, but the nephew was in and out of rehab, overdosing and recovering, then overdosing again.

Moore had been involved in a series of civil cases against Purdue back in 2007, culminating in a $75 million settlement in which the

company admitted no wrongdoing and all the internal documents produced in discovery were sealed. But now he got to talking with some of
his old colleagues from the tobacco litigation about trying to apply that
model to the opioid makers. To Moore, the similarities were straightforward. "They're both profiting by killing people," he said.

But this raised an interesting question. The Sacklers had always
espoused a fundamentally libertarian view when it came to the line
of work that they were in. The family produced a product and put it
into commerce. What people did with that product was not the family's responsibility. Purdue's critics argued that this *was* very similar
to the case of Big Tobacco: if you lie about the risks associated with
your product, then you should bear some responsibility when people
rely on those assurances and take it, with fatal consequences. To others, however, the appropriate analogy was not cigarettes but firearms:
it has been next to impossible, in the United States, to hold gun makers
liable for deaths that result from their products. Guns could be said,
to an even greater degree than addictive pharmaceuticals, to lead to
bad outcomes that are not hard to predict. Nevertheless, gun manufacturers (and their lawyers and lobbyists) have argued, successfully, that
they should bear no responsibility for what their customers do with
their product. When someone is injured or killed by a gun, there is
always some irresponsible individual who actually pulls the trigger,
which, gun makers argue, should absolve those who manufactured and
marketed that gun of any liability. The Sacklers took the view that the
same should go for OxyContin. To the degree that people are misusing
the drug and overdosing, the blame lies with any number of potentially
irresponsible parties—the prescribing doctor, the wholesaler, the pharmacist, the trafficker, the abuser, the addicted person—but not with the
manufacturer. Not with Purdue. Much less the Sacklers.

Collaborating with a loose consortium of lawyers, several of whom
were fellow veterans of the tobacco wars, Moore looked at all of the
cases that had been brought in the past against Purdue and other opioid makers. They reviewed the guilty plea in Virginia in 2007 and all
of the other cases in which Purdue had settled to avoid trial (and then
buried the evidence). None of these results seemed particularly satisfy-
ing, especially when considered in light of the pernicious impact that
OxyContin and other opioids had inflicted on communities across the
country and the astronomical profits that the companies enjoyed. So

Moore and his fellow lawyers initiated a new wave of lawsuits. The suits would be brought by state attorneys general but also by cities and counties and Native American tribes. They agreed to pool their resources, sharing information and documents, and pursue not just Purdue but the other major manufacturers, and the wholesalers, and the pharmacies. "The companies might be able to win one case, but they can't win fifty," Moore said. "There's going to be a jury somewhere, someplace that's going to hit them with the largest verdict in the nation's history."

Before long, the sheer number of cases against Purdue and other companies had reached a point where they had to be bundled together into what is known as a multidistrict litigation. There were multiple defendants: Purdue and other manufacturers like Johnson & Johnson and Endo; the big pharmaceutical distributors, like McKesson, which supplied the drugs wholesale to pharmacies; and the pharmacy chains themselves, like Walmart and Walgreens and CVS. The theory of these lawsuits was that Purdue pioneered the deceptive marketing tactics and others followed. According to the CDC, the opioid crisis was costing the U.S. economy nearly $80 billion a year. If American taxpayers were going to shoulder that cost, Moore and his fellow attorneys argued, it seemed only fair that the drug companies should, too. In a court hearing in January 2018, Dan Aaron Polster, a federal judge in Ohio who had been appointed to oversee the multidistrict litigation, noted the great urgency of these proceedings. "We're losing more than fifty thousand of our citizens every year," he said. "One hundred and fifty Americans are going to die today, just today, while we're meeting."

Ohio was an apt forum for this showdown. By 2016, 2.3 million people in the state—approximately 20 percent of the total population—received a prescription for opioids. Half of the children who were in foster care across the state had opioid-addicted parents. People were dying from overdoses at such a rate that local coroners had run out of room in which to store all the bodies and were forced to seek makeshift alternatives. None of the states had enough money or resources to contend with the problem. In light of this urgency, and the sheer complexity of the litigation, Polster urged the parties to arrive at some kind of settlement, rather than fight these cases out one by one. Purdue and the other corporate defendants were also eager to avoid trial.

As the threat of litigation intensified, Purdue officials in Stamford engaged with a small PR firm called the Herald Group, which specialized in digging up opposition research. The group proposed a plan to make state prosecutors "think twice" about joining the litigation, starting with "a deep dive on Mike Moore and his current and past associates." If they could just discredit Moore, one Herald Group executive suggested, it might "give pause" to other attorneys who were thinking of joining the lawsuits. "Moore and his ilk are rich, greedy trial lawyers who make hundreds of millions of dollars suing companies," the group pointed out. One idea that they proposed was to build a website called LearJetLawyers.com. "Learjet Lawyers associates the plaintiff's attorneys with wealth and aligns them with Wall Street, not Main Street," they suggested. "This imagery further damages their credibility and bolsters the narrative that they are not fighting for the common person."

When *The Wall Street Journal* ran an editorial criticizing the lawsuits and arguing that state attorneys general were just seeking to "pad their budgets" at the expense of the pharma industry, Purdue executives celebrated. A Herald Group representative reported that they had "worked with" the writer on the piece.

Mike Moore made no secret about wanting money. He once referred to Johnson & Johnson as "a huge pocket." There is also an entirely reasonable critique to be made of the motivations of personal injury lawyers, who work on contingency and reap outsized fees in success. But it was more difficult to assail the dozens of attorneys general initiating cases, who argued, as Moore did, that the purpose of these suits was to obtain desperately needed funds to build treatment centers, finance research into the science of addiction, and purchase Naloxone, a drug that can be used to reverse the effects of an opioid overdose.

In an interview in February 2018, Moore noted that "the Sacklers have not been named" as defendants in any of the cases. They appeared to remain insulated by the artfully cultivated perception that apart from voting on board resolutions from time to time, they played little role in the family business. But at that very moment, Moore noted, attorneys were trying to find a way "to break through the corporate veil so that they can name the owners."

✤ ✤ ✤

The Sacklers, for their part, were finally starting to freak out. "I received a call today from Mary Woolley," Jonathan informed other members of the family, referring to the head of a group called

Research!America, to which the Sacklers had donated generously. Just seven months earlier, Woolley had eulogized Jonathan's father, Raymond, praising his "keen business insights, personal kindness, extraordinary generosity and determination to advance research." His "legacy," she suggested, "is a model for all those aspiring to serve the public good." But now Woolley informed Jonathan that her organization had experienced a change of heart. "Apparently the bad publicity around Purdue and the family has led their board to decide to rename the Raymond & Beverly Sackler Prize," Jonathan wrote. The decision had come about after some past recipients of the prize ("she would not divulge who") expressed their discomfort at being associated with the Sackler name and inquired about whether they could call the award something else on their CVs.

"Obviously, this will add to the pressure on other boards to take a similar course," Jonathan warned, adding, "We should be prepared." One museum, the South London Gallery, had already backed away from the family, quietly returning a donation. The Academy Award–winning actor Mark Rylance, who had previously served as artistic director of the Globe Theatre in London, publicly urged the Globe to refuse any further donations from the Sacklers. What Jonathan was worried about, he informed a company lawyer, was "a domino effect."

The family convened a weekly conference call, at 8:00 a.m. each Tuesday, to discuss the crisis with their ever-expanding retinue of lawyers and public relations advisers. Everyone seemed to have their own representatives, and the number of participants just kept growing. Mortimer would go to a party and meet someone who recommended a new consultant; then that person would pop up on the call. "All of a sudden you have six different PR firms ringing the cash register, saying, 'For $50,000 a month, I'll do whatever you want,'" one person who advised the family during this period said. Jonathan Sackler would personally wordsmith advertisements that the company put out to defend itself.

"The issue was that the family never wanted to admit guilt," the person who advised the Sacklers recalled. At one point, Maria Barton, Purdue's general counsel, had told them, "Unless the *family* starts saying something, whatever the company does will get drowned out by the family's silence." Some of the Sacklers felt that it was time to issue a statement of some kind, but nobody could come to an agreement about what it should say. When a transcript of Richard Sackler's Kentucky deposition, which the family had fought so hard to keep sealed, leaked to the website STAT, there was a wave of coverage about Richard's heartless comments regarding people who had become addicted to his drug. Mortimer and his wife, Jacqueline, were embarrassed by these revelations and horrified that they had become public. They wanted Richard to express some remorse over his statements.

Richard's mother, Beverly, had stepped down from the board, at the age of ninety-three, at around the time the *Esquire* and *New Yorker* articles were published in 2017. She had never been particularly involved in the business, even when she was on the board. When a journalist reached Beverly at home in Connecticut one day to ask about the controversy engulfing Purdue, she said, "I don't know what I can say about the company except that they've been so careful always to keep from harming anybody." As the scrutiny intensified, the rest of the Sacklers stepped down from the board, one by one. Richard was first. Then David. Then Theresa, and eventually Ilene, Jonathan, Kathe, and Mortimer.

✦ ✦ ✦

Nan Goldin had established a weekly meeting of her own. Her group PAIN met on Wednesday nights in her apartment. It was a friendly and diverse coalition, consisting of artists, activists, longtime friends of Goldin's, people who were in recovery, and people who had lost loved ones to the epidemic. The meetings had a loose, digressive vibe, which belied the fact that the group was planning a series of ever more ambitious demonstrations. Like a paramilitary cell, they communicated on encrypted phone apps and kept their "actions" shrouded in secrecy. They drew up a "hit list" of museums that had taken Sackler funding. Goldin was on the warpath.

In April 2018 she showed up on the National Mall and entered the Arthur M. Sackler Gallery. Trailed by a posse of protesters, she took up position under a lacquer wood sculpture called *Monkeys Grasp for the Moon,* which hung from the ceiling above. Arthur's family still insisted that he should bear no taint of OxyContin, but Nan Goldin begged to differ. "Arthur's skill was marketing pills!" she shouted. "Addiction equals profit!" Her followers produced orange pill bottles, some of them labeled "Valium," and tossed them into a fountain.

One evening in February 2019, the crew filtered into the Guggenheim, where Mortimer Sackler had been a longtime trustee. They climbed the famous walkway that snakes around the central atrium. Then, on a signal, protesters on different levels unfurled bloodred banners, with black text:

SHAME ON SACKLER

200 DEAD EACH DAY

TAKE DOWN THEIR NAME

From the highest reaches of the Guggenheim, members of the group threw thousands of little slips of paper into the air. Like ticker tape at a parade, the paper fluttered and pinwheeled, forming a cloud. Each one was a little "prescription," meant to evoke the blizzard of prescriptions that Richard Sackler had summoned at the launch of OxyContin.

"It's time, Guggenheim!" Goldin bellowed. She was not a naturally charismatic speaker. She was shy by nature, nervous about public speaking; even with a megaphone in her hand, she often looked self-conscious and distracted. And there was something wraithlike about her. Something fragile. She had been sober for barely two years. She felt a deep sense of kinship with the people she encountered who had struggled with addiction or who had lost loved ones to it. The members of PAIN tended to mother Goldin, looking after her. There was a palpable sense within the group that her activism had become an organizing principle through which she was managing her own recovery.

Goldin's most powerful weapon as an activist was her eye. Someone had alerted *The New York Times*, and a photographer showed up at the Guggenheim and took position on the ground floor, then pointed the camera up at the ceiling as the prescriptions floated down into the rotunda. It was an extraordinary image, with the white slips flickering through the museum's white interior, past the bright red protest banners. Goldin and her fellow activists had wanted it to look like an actual snow flurry, so they printed eight thousand prescription slips, to ensure that there were enough to fill the space. The photo ran alongside an article in the paper: "Guggenheim Targeted by Protesters for Accepting Money from Family with OxyContin Ties."

The following month, the Guggenheim announced that after a two-decade relationship in which the Sacklers had donated $9 million, the museum would no longer accept any future donations from the family. The same week, the National Portrait Gallery in London revealed that it had turned down a $1.3 million gift from the Sacklers. Two days after the National Portrait Gallery, the Tate announced that it would not "seek or accept further donations from the Sacklers."

This was the domino effect Jonathan Sackler had worried about. The museums would not "take the name down," as Goldin had demanded: "We do not intend to remove references to this historic philanthropy," the Tate said; the Guggenheim let it be known that there were "contractual" stipulations that meant that the Sackler Center for Arts Education must continue to carry that name. But this unprecedented move by cultural institutions to distance themselves from the Sacklers had clearly happened because of Goldin's influence. In addition to framing each protest as if it were a photograph, she had boldly exercised her own leverage as a prominent figure in the art world. Prior to the National Portrait Gallery's decision, Goldin let it be known that the museum had approached her about doing a retrospective. "I will not do the show," she told *The Observer*, "if they take the Sackler money." When news broke that the museum had declined the gift, Goldin felt vindicated. "I congratulate them on their courage," she said.

The following month, at the London opening of a solo show by the German artist Hito Steyerl at the Serpentine Sackler Gallery, Steyerl delivered a surprising speech. "I would like to address the elephant in the room," she said, and then proceeded to denounce the Sacklers, encouraging other artists to rally behind the cause of disentangling museums from the family. She likened the relationship between the art world and its toxic patrons to being "married to a serial killer." What was needed, she said, was "a divorce." The museum promptly announced that, though it might be named after the Sacklers, the Serpentine had "no future plans" to accept gifts from the family.

✦   ✦   ✦

These protests were not without consequences for the protesters. One night, one of Goldin's close deputies in PAIN, Megan Kapler, was leaving Goldin's Brooklyn apartment when she noticed a middle-aged man sitting behind the wheel of his car, watching her. A few days later, Kapler left her home in another part of Brooklyn to walk her dog and saw the same man. They made eye contact. She kept walking. When she turned back to look at him, the man was taking her picture with his phone.

The members of PAIN assumed that the Sacklers must have arranged for them to be followed, but also that the man was probably a subcontractor of some sort and that it would be very difficult for them to prove definitively whom he was working for. A few days later, he appeared in front of Goldin's home once again. This time, members of the group went outside and filmed him. He wouldn't speak to them, but he didn't hide, either. He stood, leaning on his car, a smirk on his face, and began to clip his fingernails. Had he been sent to monitor them or intimidate them? In a way, it didn't matter. His presence was an affirmation. Their campaign was working. In May, the Metropolitan Museum of Art, home to the original Sackler Wing, announced that it would "step away" from gifts that it determined were "not in the public interest."

At one point, Goldin found out that Madeleine Sackler's prison documentary, *It's a Hard Truth, Ain't It*, would be premiering at the Tribeca Film Festival. She arranged to attend the screening, along with several of her comrades. They brought pill bottles, entered separately, and sat in the audience. There was supposed to be a Q&A after the film, but Madeleine seemed visibly uncomfortable. She must have been alerted to the unwelcome guests. Soon, a security guard approached Goldin and escorted her out of the theater.

"Do you know who made this film?" Goldin said to passersby outside. She handed pill bottles to curious strangers and denounced the documentary as "reputation washing." Of Madeleine, Goldin said, "She presents herself as a social activist but she has been enriched through the addiction of hundreds of thousands of people." In her view, any Sackler heir who "took the money" and made no effort to speak out was "culpable."

When a reporter from *The Guardian* asked Madeleine about her family, she replied that she had been working "more than full-time" on her films and her work was her "sole focus." She did not want to talk about her family. Pressed on the fact that she was tremendously wealthy because of OxyContin, and asked whether she had a problem with that, she said, "With what, exactly?"

Madeleine's argument, insofar as she could be bothered to articulate it, seemed to be that she should be judged solely on her work and not on the basis of any business that her family happened to own. She "never worked at the company or had any influence in it," she said. (After the interview, *The Guardian*'s press invitation to the festivities was revoked.)

"The Sackler name has become synonymous with the opioids crisis," Nan Goldin said. "I want to ask Madeleine, is that the legacy you want? Why not use your name, money and influence to address the crisis, and take responsibility?"

✦ ✦ ✦

Purdue was reeling. In February 2018, the company had announced that it would lay off half its sales force and would no longer promote opioids to physicians. This might have seemed like a considerable concession to the outside world, but internally the company had already calculated that because OxyContin was a "matured" product, the business would still collect hundreds of millions of dollars of profit from so-called carryover sales of the drug, even without a sales force. That summer, the company went further, eliminating its sales force altogether, and saying that Purdue was "taking significant steps to transform and diversify beyond our historic focus of pain medications."

But it was too late now for reinvention. Russell Portenoy, the King of Pain, had signed on to join the multidistrict litigation as a witness against Purdue and other companies, in exchange for being dismissed as a defendant himself. He acknowledged that he personally had become aware of "serious opioid related adverse outcomes" as early as the late 1990s, though he continued to publicly downplay the risks of the drugs. As for Purdue, he said, even among the defendants in the multidistrict case, it deserved a special distinction. No other company "had previously promoted an opioid drug as aggressively, or encouraged the use of an opioid by non-specialists," he said.

But the biggest threat to the Sacklers surfaced in January 2019, when the attorney general of Massachusetts unveiled a legal complaint that did something no other prosecutor had done in twenty years of litigation against Purdue: it named eight members of the Sackler family—Richard, Beverly, Jonathan, David, Theresa, Kathe, Mortimer, and Ilene—as defendants.

Chapter 27

NAMED DEFENDANTS

RICHARD SACKLER'S DAUGHTER-IN-LAW, Joss Sackler, was married to his son, David. She'd been living in Park Slope, in Brooklyn, when she met her future husband on a blind date. Joss thought of David as a "finance guy"—serious, punctual, maybe a bit conventional—whereas she was something more exotic. The daughter of a Canadian diplomat, she had gone to high school in Japan and nurtured a youthful ambition to become a spy. Instead, she went to graduate school in linguistics at the City University of New York. When Raymond Sackler was still alive, Joss and David would spend weekends with him and Beverly at the family compound in Greenwich. Joss found Raymond (or "Poppi," as his grandchildren called him) very impressive. He was this "highly regarded scientist and businessman," she would say. "He was knighted in France and in England." In the mansion overlooking the Long Island Sound, Raymond would receive eminent visitors. He commanded tremendous respect, it seemed to Joss, and just an "outpouring of love." Raymond was such a luminary, in fact, that Joss decided that until she finished graduate school, she should probably keep her maiden name, Jaseleen Ruggles, because she didn't want "preferential treatment." Her dissertation was about the "narco-propaganda" of drug cartels in Mexico and how these criminal drug rings endeavor, as she put it, "to garner public support from local communities."

With her dissertation in hand, Jaseleen Ruggles became Joss Sackler. She might have looked the part of a billionaire's wife—slim and blond and very fit, with lips that puffed and puckered. But she was no mere trophy, she insisted. She started a club for young rich women who drink wine, or, as she referred to it, a "members only, female-led collective celebrating the intersection of art, wine, fashion, and culture." She was a trained sommelier ("Level II") and called the group Les Bouledogues Vigneronnes, the "winemaking bulldogs." LBV for short. "Joss is a threat assessor by training and her research focuses on the risk assessment of violent threats made by the Mexican Cartels," a biography (since removed) on her website declared. She was also "an avid adventurist," "a target shooter, a rock climber, and a mountaineer" who spoke "English, French, Spanish and Farsi."

Like Madeleine Sackler, Joss felt strongly that because she personally did not sit on the board of Purdue, she had no meaningful connection to the pharmaceutical empire and it should certainly not constrain her ability to chase her own dreams. But the association was proving difficult to shake. In an accident of exquisitely awkward timing, it was during the period when the Sacklers were encountering a new level of scrutiny from legal authorities and the press that Joss decided to realize her own long-held ambition to turn LBV into a fashion brand. She produced a series of sporty ensembles in Day-Glo colors that were inspired by her passion for mountain climbing. "I'm committed to make this successful," she vowed, noting that LBV had the potential to become "the next all-American, ready-to-wear, couture-infused brand." She described the venture, in a Facebook post, as "my own women's initiative unrelated to Purdue, aimed at promoting women's empowerment."

But whereas Madeleine had been quite adept at convincing people in her professional circles that her art should be judged on its own merits, without reference to her status as an opioid heiress, Joss would have a rougher time of it. After a fashion reporter from *The New York Times* expressed an interest in her collection, she agreed to an interview, only to be bombarded with impertinent questions about her family. In an indignant web post, Joss framed this contretemps as a gender issue, saying, "Stop talking about who the men in my life are and review the fucking neon hoodies." (The *Times* fashion writer, Matthew Schneier, was privately amused by this, observing to a friend that, had he actually focused on the clothes themselves, the article might have been much harsher.)

Here was Joss's predicament: if you imagine the members of the Sackler clan arrayed across concentric circles of culpability, she lived uncomfortably close to the bull's-eye. Her father-in-law was the father of OxyContin. Her husband was the only third-generation Sackler to serve on the board. And her situation was exacerbated by the fact that unlike the family she married into, Joss Sackler stubbornly refused to remain silent. She threw parties ("$700/Guest, LBV Curated Wines").

She and David paid $22 million in cash for a mansion in Bel Air, then told people that they were angry the sale had been reported in *TMZ* and other media outlets, despite having chosen, to handle the transaction, a celebrity real estate agent from the TV show *Million Dollar Listing*. And she kept giving interviews. "I support my family 500 percent," Joss told *Town & Country*. "I believe they will be completely vindicated. But they have nothing to do with LBV." For that article, Joss met the reporter at a restaurant on Gramercy Park. "They're going to regret fucking with a linguist," she said, of her detractors. "They already do." During the interview, with no encouragement from the reporter, she literally ordered the suckling pig. This Marie Antoinette routine was so over the top (could she possibly be sincere? Or was this some kind of conceptual art performance?) that it seemed custom engineered for the gossip pages, and before long *Page Six* was chronicling Joss's every outré utterance. The paper crowned her "the Lady Macbeth of Opioids." She responded by sending one of the reporters, by text message, an emoji of a middle finger.

✦ ✦ ✦

One major source of Joss's troubles was a woman named Maura Healey, who was serving her second term as the attorney general of Massachusetts. Healey was in her mid-forties. The first openly gay attorney general in the United States, she had grown up in New Hampshire, just over the state line, the oldest of five children who were raised by a single mother. She played basketball at Harvard, then spent a couple of years playing the sport professionally in Europe. She wasn't tall—she was five feet four, with a dimpled smile and an informal manner—but she was tough, and it would become a standard quip in her repertoire of one-liners that as a short woman playing pro basketball, she had learned how to "take on the big guy." Healey always said this in jest. But if it was a laugh line, it was also a warning.

Opioids had hit Massachusetts especially badly. Healey had started investigating in 2015, right after she took office in her first term, because on the campaign trail people from across the state kept telling her about how these pharmaceuticals had devastated their communities. One of Healey's campaign volunteers had a son with an opioid dependency. The woman Healey put in charge of this new investigation, her deputy attorney general, Joanna Lydgate, was close to someone who had overdosed. Along with her staff, Healey began to focus on Purdue. One of her attorneys, Sandy Alexander, started by visiting the medical examiner's office and requesting the death certificates of people in Massachusetts who had died of opioid overdoses since 2009. He cross-checked those names with people who had prescriptions for Purdue's painkillers. The company had always claimed that instances of so-called iatrogenic addiction—people becoming addicted when they were prescribed the drug by a doctor and took it as directed—were practically unheard of. But Alexander was able to confirm that over the last decade, in Massachusetts alone, 671 people filled prescriptions for Purdue painkillers and subsequently died of opioid-related overdoses.

In June 2018, Healey held a press conference in Boston. She invited representatives of a group that assists families who have lost loved ones to opioid-related deaths, and she announced that she was suing not just Purdue Pharma but the eight family members who had served on the company's board. Corporations don't run themselves, she reasoned. They're run by people. And she wanted to name names. "The public deserves answers," Healey said. "That's what this lawsuit is about." A few months later, just before Christmas, Healey announced her intention to file an amended version of her lawsuit, which would supply some of those answers to the public.

Purdue and the Sacklers had employed their usual tactics. As local counsel, they hired a woman named Joan Lukey, who happened to be Healey's friend and mentor and had served as the finance chair on her campaign. This did not strike Healey as a coincidence. Before Healey could formally name the Sacklers in the suit, Mary Jo White traveled to Boston with a team of lawyers, to explain to her why that would be a mistake. But Healey, who earlier in her career had practiced at Wilmer, one of the very white-shoe law firms that represented Purdue, was openly dubious when it came to this sort of backroom overture. Healey knew about White by reputation, and admired her, as someone who had blazed a trail for other women in the law. "It pains me to look at somebody like Mary Jo White, who represented them in 2007 and continues to represent them," she said. "Not that there isn't room to represent corporations, that's worthy work. But this corporation? These people? It's no different from representing a drug cartel, in my mind." When Purdue sent its lawyers, Healey opted not to attend the meeting herself, sending her trial attorneys instead. "I had no interest in meeting with them, particularly because some of them are people I have personal relationships with," she said. "I wanted distance from that. Let them talk to my lawyers."

The multidistrict litigation had created a huge trove of sealed documents that had been secured from Purdue and other pharma companies. Dan Aaron Polster, the Ohio federal judge overseeing the litigation, had ruled that the attorneys who were party to the proceedings could have access to the documents but that otherwise they must remain hidden from public view. "I don't think anyone in this country is interested in a whole lot of finger pointing," Polster had asserted. "People aren't interested in depositions, and discovery, and trials." But now Healey and her prosecutors requested access to the sealed files and received some twelve million documents related to Purdue.

The sealed records told the story of OxyContin as it had played out inside the company, and Healey's team found that while the Sacklers had succeeded for many years in keeping the family name off the opioid crisis, in the private papers of Purdue it was *everywhere*. There were emails from Richard micromanaging the marketing staff and emails from Kathe discussing Project Tango and emails from Mortimer complaining about his disbursements and emails from Jonathan wondering what the company could do to stop their opioid profits from slipping. There were emails from more than one chief executive at Purdue complaining that the constant interference by the family made it impossible for the CEO to do his job. The Sacklers didn't just own Purdue, the Massachusetts prosecutors realized. They ran it. Healey's team updated their complaint, incorporating this explosive new material.

But before they could make the complaint public, Purdue's lawyers intervened, pleading with the state judge overseeing the case in Massachusetts, Janet Sanders, to "impound" the document, preventing it from being released. In a hearing, a Purdue lawyer suggested that Healey had "cherry picked" evidence. But Judge Sanders, invoking the public interest, said, "My antennae go up when there's a request to heavily redact any public filing in a case like this." She issued a ruling saying that Healey's unredacted complaint should be released. In her opinion, Judge Sanders pointed out that Purdue's stated concerns—that the release would "embarrass individuals and spark public outrage"—were not exactly a compelling basis for keeping the complaint suppressed.

She also invoked a dark precedent in Massachusetts: the shameful history of local courts "impounding" information in cases involving allegations of child sexual abuse by Catholic priests.

This decision might have come as a shock to Purdue, which had been so successful, for decades, in persuading judges to keep its compromising internal documents secret. Judge Polster in Ohio had been much more accommodating, so the company's lawyers now made an emergency appeal to him, to see if he might intervene and prevent the complaint about the Sacklers from becoming public. "We did not produce these documents to the Massachusetts AG," a Purdue lawyer, Mark Cheffo, complained in a teleconference with the judge. The company had turned over the documents in the context of the federal litigation, but now they were being used in a different arena, with different rules.

"I'm not very happy with the Massachusetts AG either," Judge Polster grumbled. But his hands were tied, he said. If a state judge in Massachusetts had ordered the full complaint to be released, Polster, as a federal judge in Ohio, had no authority to defy that directive. "I can't control what a state court judge does," he said.

Cheffo was furious. If the complaint is made public, he vowed, then they would all wake up the next morning to "an incredible news cycle."

He was right. Maura Healey believed that in addition to being a mechanism for justice and accountability, the law has another function: truth seeking. For decades, Purdue had obscured the nature and extent of its own culpability by settling cases and sealing records. By contrast, when the Big Tobacco litigation ended, the records weren't sealed or destroyed. Instead, an archive was established, with fourteen million documents from the cigarette companies, and this became an indispensable resource for historians, journalists, and public health specialists. By including a great deal of sensitive, never-before-seen information in her complaint, and then pushing to make the complaint public, Healey was seeking to establish an incontrovertible record of how this historic crisis of addiction had been born.

On January 31, Healey released her 274-page complaint. It alleged that the named Sacklers "made the choices that caused much of the opioid epidemic." The document was studded with meeting minutes and board presentations and internal emails, and it presented a catalog of breathtaking venality. Staff at Purdue had warned the Sacklers in the past that the company's internal documents might one day come back to haunt them, and now that day had come. Healey used the Sacklers' own emails to lay out the chain of command through which the family had managed the company. (The suit also named, as defendants, eight current and former executives and members of Purdue's board who weren't part of the family.) The complaint illustrated, in vivid detail, Richard Sackler's demonization of those who were unfortunate enough to become addicted to Purdue's flagship product. It reproduced the exchange in which Richard had inquired about the possibility of selling OxyContin in Germany as an over-the-counter drug, and the email in which he expressed his disappointment ("Blah, humbug") upon learning that Purdue was selling only $20 million worth of OxyContin a week. It contained numerous instances, many of them quite recent, of the Sacklers expressing an interest in persuading doctors to put patients on higher doses of opioids for longer periods of time, notwithstanding the widespread medical consensus (and guidance from the CDC) that doing so would sharply increase the risk of addiction.

Some of the most shocking details in the complaint concerned the manner in which, years after the guilty plea in Virginia, Purdue sales representatives continued to call on dodgy doctors. One doctor, Fathalla Mashali, who ran a chain of clinics in Massachusetts and Rhode Island, was described by Purdue reps in 2010 as a "very good new target." When the company learned that Mashali was under investigation by authorities in Rhode Island, it instructed reps to continue calling on him in Massachusetts. One Purdue rep described the scene at the doctor's office in 2013 as so crowded that patients had brought "their own 'beach type' folding chairs to sit on because at any given time, he can have 35 or more patients waiting." Mashali eventually lost his medical license, pleaded guilty to twenty-seven counts of healthcare fraud, and was sentenced to seven years in prison.

From 2008 to 2012, the complaint reported, Purdue's top prescriber in all of Massachusetts was a North Andover physician named Walter Jacobs. "He practiced alone," Healey noted. "He often worked only three days a week. Nevertheless, in five years, he prescribed more than 347,000 pills of Purdue opioids." Two hundred thousand of those pills were Oxy 80s. Purdue ended up offering Jacobs a $50,000 contract to give speeches. The doctor was supportive of the Sacklers' mission to keep patients on higher doses over long stretches of time. Before he lost his medical license, the complaint revealed, Jacobs had one patient on OxyContin for two years, with a prescription for twenty-four 80-milligram pills each *day*.

"Purdue took advantage of addiction to make money," Healey wrote. "For patients, it was a massacre." The people who died in Massachusetts "worked as firefighters, homemakers, carpenters, truck drivers, nurses, hairdressers, fishermen, waitresses, students, mechanics, cooks, electricians, ironworkers, social workers, accountants, artists, lab technicians, and bartenders," the complaint read. "The oldest died at age 87. The youngest started taking Purdue's opioids at 16 and died when he was 18 years old."

The Sacklers were furious about the Massachusetts filing. Up to that point, they had been ciphers in the public eye. The family might speak openly about their philanthropy, but they had never given interviews about their business, and Purdue, as a privately held company, had always been a black box. But here was the tawdry reality, laid bare. An attorney for the Raymond side of the family derided Healey's filing as "histrionic." Mary Jo White, who represented the Mortimer side, argued that the claims were "inaccurate and misleading." The Sacklers put together their own filing, which slammed the complaint for "prolixity," ridiculed it as "hundreds of pages of litigational detritus," and urged the judge to dismiss the case. The family hadn't *directed* anyone to do anything, their attorneys contended. And anyway, the court in Massachusetts had no jurisdiction over them. The company might have taken actions that affected Massachusetts, but its business affected *every* state. The argument seemed to be that Purdue was everywhere and yet nowhere. For Massachusetts to exert jurisdiction over the Sacklers, the attorneys argued, would violate their constitutional rights to due process.

The family maintained that their own words had been taken out of context. But when they supplied additional context, it was hardly exculpatory. Taking issue with the complaint's use of the "blizzard of prescriptions" speech, family lawyers pointed out that Richard had used the image as "an allusion to his delayed arrival at that event *due to the well-known Blizzard of 1996*," italics theirs, as if that made some major difference. The lawyers also seized on an email that Healey had used to illustrate Richard's tendency to micromanage. She had quoted an exchange between Richard and a subordinate in which Richard demanded, on a Sunday, that the employee send him some specific data that day. "This is a perfectly appropriate email from a director," Richard's lawyers asserted. When the long-suffering employee ultimately wrote back to Richard, "I have done as much as I can," it was not because Richard had been badgering him but rather because the employee "had family visiting." If anything, this additional detail seemed to compound the impression that Richard was an insensitive taskmaster.

The Sacklers' motion to dismiss the case was denied. In the attorney general's office, on a high floor in a downtown Boston skyscraper, Maura Healey walked from room to room, a big grin on her face, giving hugs to Sandy Alexander, a woman named Gillian Feiner, who was the lead attorney on the case, and other staffers. Healey posted a video of the celebration on Instagram. On the heels of the Massachusetts complaint, the attorney general of New York, Letitia James, had filed her own lawsuit against Purdue, in which she, too, named individual Sackler board members as defendants. James described OxyContin as the "taproot" of the crisis and noted that the Sacklers had paid themselves "hundreds of millions of dollars each year." Her suit highlighted one intriguing factor in particular. According to James, the Sacklers had known by 2014 that the company was being investigated and could eventually face the prospect of damaging judgments. Understanding that this day of reckoning was coming, the Sacklers had assiduously siphoned money out of Purdue, the lawsuit suggested, and transferred it offshore, beyond the reach of U.S. authorities.

This was true. In fact, as far back as 2007, a week after the guilty plea in Virginia, Jonathan Sackler had emailed Richard and David, noting that an investment banker once told him, "Your family is already rich. The one thing you don't want to do is become poor."

"What do you think is going on in all of these courtrooms right now?" David Sackler wrote back. "We're rich? For how long?" It was only a matter of time, David argued, before some lawsuit manages to "get through to the family." What they should do, he suggested, is "lever up where we can, and try to generate some additional income. We may well need it... Even if we have to keep it in cash." So the family started systematically taking more and more money out of the company. From 1997 through the guilty plea in 2007, Purdue had distributed only $126 million in cash to the Sacklers. Beginning in 2008, it started to distribute billions. In a 2014 email to Mortimer, Jonathan acknowledged,

"We've taken a fantastic amount of money out of the business." If the Sacklers took money from Purdue and moved it out of the country because they knew that eventually a lawsuit might "get through to the family," then that might be a form of fraud, James contended, and now she wanted to try to claw back some of those funds.

At McKinsey, the high-priced consultants who had spent so many years helping the Sacklers devise new ways to flog their opioids were starting to worry. It was probably time for the firm to start thinking about "eliminating all our documents and emails," one of the consultants, Martin Elling, wrote to another. "Will do," his colleague Arnab Ghatak replied.

The same month James filed her suit, the Sackler Trust in Britain announced that it would be suspending further philanthropy. In a statement, Dame Theresa blamed the "press attention that these legal cases in the United States is generating." The family name was increasingly regarded as a badge of ill repute. "Five years ago, the Sackler family was considered one of New York City's most esteemed, generous dynasties," the *New York Post* observed. "Now they can't get a museum to take their money."

Nor was it just the museum world that had come to regard the Sacklers as toxic. Achievement First, a charter school network to which Jonathan Sackler had been a major donor, announced that it had "decided not to seek further funding from the Sackler family." A hedge fund, Hildene Capital Management, which had invested some of the family's wealth, said that it was no longer comfortable doing business with the Sacklers. Brett Jefferson, the fund's manager, revealed that someone close to the firm had suffered an "opioid-related tragedy," and said, "My conscience led me to terminate the relationship." Even Purdue's banker, JPMorgan Chase, cut ties with the company.

For most of the Sacklers, who had grown up feeling that their name conferred a certain prestige if not entitlement, the suddenness with which they had become social pariahs must have been unsettling. But this shock does not appear to have occasioned much soul-searching about the company and what it had done. In a private family WhatsApp conversation, the heirs of Mortimer Sackler discussed their tribulations purely in terms of the challenging PR optics. Dame Theresa complained that "trial lawyers have a media campaign against the family." Marissa Sackler derided Nan Goldin's protests as a "stunt." Samantha

Sackler discussed the urgent need to put forward an "alternative narrative." Nowhere, in months of candid text messages, did a single family member express any private misgivings or raise any difficult questions about the conduct of the family.

The Mortimer and Raymond wings might clash over many things, but they shared an embittered conviction that they had done nothing wrong. "The media is eager to distort and portray anything we say or do as grotesque and evil," Jonathan Sackler complained in an email. To Jonathan it seemed that the company had been caught up in a broader culture of "blame" in America. "The 'blame frame' has resulted in massive incarceration and public expenditures," he suggested. Inspired, perhaps, by his daughter Madeleine's films, Jonathan now saw parallels between the plight of Americans who were incarcerated and the scrutiny that his family faced over the billions of dollars they had made selling opioids. "The tort bar, in its genius, figured out how to position the pharmaceutical industry as the latest (and wonderfully deep-pocketed) 'bad guy,'" Jonathan wrote. Why was nobody focusing on fentanyl—which was very deadly, and on the rise? he wondered. Perhaps Purdue should add "a Speakers Bureau program" to help get the word out. It was important, he said, to emphasize that the company is "*trustworthy.*"

David Sackler agreed. The fundamental problem, he thought, wasn't anything that Purdue or the family had done but rather the *narrative*. "We have not done a good job of talking about this," he would say. "That's what I regret the most." The family had a compelling story to tell, David thought. Rather than cowering defensively, they should come out swinging and tell it.

To Mortimer, it seemed that the Sacklers were engaged in a "battle." He shared Jonathan's view that part of the problem was the "tort system." But more fundamentally, he argued in an email to other family members, prescription opioids "are NOT the CAUSE of drug abuse, addiction or the so called 'opioid crisis.'" It was telling that in 2019, Mortimer Sackler was still using scare quotes to describe the epidemic. "I also don't think we should use the term 'opioid crisis' or even 'opioid addiction crisis' in our messaging," he continued. As an alternative, Mortimer suggested, they should talk about "drug abuse and addiction." Privately, the Sacklers were still clinging to their old and cherished notion that it wasn't the drug that was the problem; it was the abusers.

At one point, Mortimer wrote to Purdue's new general counsel, Marc Kesselman, along with Mary Jo White and several others, to request some statistics that he thought might be helpful in making the family's case. He wanted to know whether it was possible to assemble information about people who had overdosed—like the victims cited in the Massachusetts case—in order to figure out if they had life insurance policies. Someone had told him that such policies often pay out for "accidental drug overdoses" but not for suicides. And this had gotten Mortimer thinking. "I believe it is fair to assume that some portion of overdoses are actually suicides," he wrote.

Mortimer also made quiet appeals to powerful people in New York, looking for support. "I am meeting with Michael Bloomberg tomorrow," he informed executives at Purdue at one point, saying that one topic for discussion would be "current narrative vs the truth." The family had been trying to refocus the discussion to heroin and fentanyl; perhaps Bloomberg would have some ideas. They met in Bloomberg's offices, and the former mayor advised Mortimer on messaging, saying that the family should develop a list of ten talking points to repeat. (After the meeting, Mortimer outsourced this project to Purdue's communications staff, instructing them to come up with a list for his review.)

Another person to whom Mortimer made an overture in this period was George Soros. He wanted advice from the billionaire financier and philanthropist, who had become a target of wild (and often anti-Semitic) conspiracy theories that made him out to be an all-powerful global puppet master. Maybe Soros would recognize some of his own struggles in the plight of the Sacklers and offer guidance on how to navigate this storm of negative publicity. Mortimer made his case to someone in Soros's organization, asking to schedule a conversation with the man himself. But Soros declined to take the call.

✢ ✢ ✢

At a certain point, David and Joss decided to sell their New York apartment on East Sixty-Sixth Street and move to Florida. "I'm not a fearful person," Joss said, invoking her mountaineering bona fides. "If K2 doesn't scare me, Florida does not scare me." (She had not climbed K2.) "Sacklers Fleeing NYC," the gossip columns blared. The couple purchased a mansion near Boca Raton for $7.4 million. The litigation against the Sacklers had become so comprehensive, by this stage, that

David and Joss were moving out of New York, a jurisdiction that was suing the family, and down to Palm Beach County, which was suing them, too.

It was a measure of just how intense the opprobrium had become that a New Jersey man, who happened also to be named David Sackler, initiated a lawsuit of his own against a number of media outlets that had used a photograph of him, instead of the other David Sackler, in stories about the family. Being taken "for the wrong David Sackler has undermined his reputation," the lawsuit contended, mentioning that this David Sackler had been reduced to adopting a pseudonym to get a table in a restaurant. Not to be left out, Purdue University, in West Lafayette, Indiana, issued a press release clarifying that it "has never been affiliated in any way with Purdue Pharma."

The story had reached a tipping point. The late-night host Stephen Colbert did a segment on the Sacklers, joking that they had amended the Hippocratic oath to "First, do no harm. Unless harming is incredibly profitable." He displayed a photograph of Richard, Jonathan, Raymond, and Beverly, "seen here not giving a fuck." John Oliver, of the satirical news program *Last Week Tonight*, also aired a segment on the family. The long-standing invisibility of the Sacklers "feels deliberate," Oliver mused. He pointed out that Richard Sackler never gave interviews. But the litigation was providing "glimpses of the depths of Richard's involvement." Oliver mentioned Richard's leaked Kentucky deposition, and he articulated a subtle point: because only the transcript had leaked, and not the video, it was difficult to do much with the deposition on the nightly news. How do you illustrate words on a page?

The show devised a diabolically creative solution. Oliver enlisted a series of prominent actors to deliver dramatic renditions of Richard's deposition and correspondence. The actor Michael Keaton, with an indifferent scowl, reenacted the moment when Richard was sent an article saying that fifty-nine people from a single state had died from overdoses, and responded, "This is not too bad." Bryan Cranston, who played the meth kingpin Walter White in *Breaking Bad*, delivered a rendition of Richard's speech at the OxyContin launch at the Wigwam. Michael K. Williams, who played Omar Little in *The Wire*, offered a third interpretation, his features twisted into a bloodless grimace. And a fourth actor, Richard Kind, did a comedic send-up of all the many times Sackler replied to questions about his company and his own conduct with the words "I don't know." Oliver told viewers that he had set up a website, sacklergallery.com, where they could watch more of these clips. He'd chosen the web address, he said, because "they love having their name on fucking galleries."

The family had learned, in advance, that *Last Week Tonight* was preparing a segment. Mortimer's wife, Jacqueline, panicked. In an overture to the producers, representatives for the family suggested that Jacqueline would like to meet with John Oliver personally, to plead her case. But Oliver did not generally meet with the subjects of his program, and declined to take the Sacklers up on this offer. Jacqueline sent an irate email to others in the family. "This is my son's favorite show," she wrote. "He watches it every week with all of his friends. This situation is destroying our work, our friendships, our reputation and our ability to function in society. And worse, it dooms my children. How is my son supposed to apply to high school in September?"

Like her husband and others in the family, Jacqueline felt a vivid sense of persecution, an angry conviction that she and her relatives were being made to suffer. "I'm done having our family serving as the nation's punching bag for problems that existed long before OxyContin and will exist long afterwards," she wrote. "I have yet to see ANYTHING illegal or even immoral that this company has done." This vilification was a "punishment" that was "being handed out to every man, woman and child, past present and future for an entire family," Jacqueline Sackler proclaimed. "Lives of children are being destroyed."

Chapter 28

THE PHOENIX

ONE DAY IN AUGUST 2019, David Sackler flew to Cleveland to represent his family at a summit of the many attorneys involved in the multidistrict litigation. He had come with a proposal. David was stocky and bearish, with dark brown hair, the light eyes of his grandfather Raymond, the heavy jawline of his father, Richard, and a beard that was flecked with gray. He had become a central player in his family's efforts to address the litigation. David was somewhat more socially adept than Richard was, but no more apologetic. He was angry: angry at the prosecutors and plaintiffs' lawyers suing his family, angry at the press, angry at the museums that were rejecting Sackler gifts. The family's great generosity, he felt, had suddenly been "turned against us."

David was adamant that the Sacklers had done nothing wrong. The science had evolved, he liked to say. People's understanding of addiction had changed. This was a complex business. The pharmaceutical industry was very *complicated*. The FDA had approved everything that the Sacklers did. And anyway, all of their competitors did the same thing. David felt that the family should be more forthright about telling their own story. In fact, just recently, he had given an interview to Bethany McLean, a veteran financial journalist who wrote for *Vanity Fair*. It was the first time in six decades of Sackler ownership of Purdue that any member of the family had granted a substantial interview about the business. David vented to McLean about the "vitriolic hyperbole" and "endless castigation" that his family had been subjected to. "I have three young kids," he said. "My four-year-old came home from nursery school and asked, 'Why are my friends telling me that our family's work is killing people?'"

David fired through the standard talking points. The lawsuits were premised on the notion that the Sacklers had actually been in charge of Purdue, and that was "just so not true." Purdue's own McKinsey consultants might have concluded, privately, that the Sacklers were "involved in all levels of decision-making on a weekly basis." But now David claimed that as a board member from 2012 to 2018 he had done little more than vote on "information I was given." It wasn't as if the family were actually *calling the shots*. "We didn't cause the crisis," he said flatly. In fact, the biggest misstep he was prepared to acknowledge was the Sacklers' failure to correct the erroneous narrative that they *were* the cause. He was speaking now, he said, as part of a campaign to "begin humanizing ourselves as a family."

But this might not have worked out quite the way David intended. McLean was a formidable reporter who, as a young journalist at *Fortune*, had written the first big article to cast doubts about Enron, then gone on to chronicle the company's collapse. She was not the sort of journalist who was likely to just take David's word for it. In her article, she carefully went through each of his arguments, taking it seriously, considering it, then explaining why it was wrong. The notion that less than 1 percent of patients got addicted to opioids had not, in fact, been some kind of scientific consensus, as David suggested. For him to point to the fact that the FDA signed off on Purdue's decisions was to overlook the degree to which the FDA had been compromised by Big Pharma in general and Purdue Pharma in particular. Asked about the lawsuits against the company, David dismissed them with a wave, suggesting that the complaints boiled down to " 'Oh, you shouldn't have marketed these things at all,' " to which he could only say, impatiently, "I guess that's a hindsight debate one can have."

At this point, nearly every state in the union was suing Purdue. Two dozen states had joined Massachusetts and New York in also suing the Sacklers personally. Then there were the thousands of other cases brought by cities and counties and hospitals and school districts and tribes. When California filed suit earlier in the summer, the state's attorney general called out David's father in particular, saying that Richard had "started the fire." Richard had been deposed by a new set of lawyers, in Stamford earlier that year. He looked old and had lost some of his vigor. But he did not appear to have softened his views. Asked whether he should have felt any obligation, before he put a narcotic on the market and claimed that it was less likely to be abused, to have some scientific basis for believing that might actually be true, he delivered a fragmentary soliloquy that could have been written by

David Mamet: "I think, in retrospect, you could—every misfortune in life, you're asking a question, if you knew what would happen, what would you—wouldn't you have done something to prevent it? The answer is: of course. But we didn't expect any such event."

Asked about the fact that the company had conducted no studies on addiction or abuse liability before marketing OxyContin as less addictive and subject to abuse, Richard reflected, "With the fullness of time, maybe that would have been a good idea. Maybe it would have prevented some...some misfortune. But that's speculative. I don't know."

The same month as Richard's deposition, Purdue settled with one of the states, agreeing to pay Oklahoma $270 million, most of which would go toward funding a center for addiction studies and treatment. The Sacklers likely felt that they had no choice: a trial date had been set, and the intention was for the trial to be televised, with testimony that would have been horrendously damaging for Purdue. Besides, juries are unpredictable. They had been known to hand down outlandish penalties in cases featuring sympathetic mom-and-pop plaintiffs and corporate fat-cat defendants. Nevertheless, the Sacklers made it clear in a statement that the Oklahoma deal was not a viable "financial model for future settlement discussions."

"You're talking two thousand cases," Mary Jo White said. "How long will that take to go through the system?" The family did not want to fight these cases individually, or to fight them at all, for that matter. For nearly a quarter of a century, the Sacklers had thrived on their ability to keep cases *out* of court. What the clan wanted now was something White described as a "global resolution." Purdue was scheduled to face another trial, this one in Ohio, starting in October—unless they could strike a deal first.

So David Sackler had been deputized to travel to Cleveland and make an offer on the family's behalf. Ten or so state attorneys general had gathered for the meeting, which took place at a federal courthouse downtown. David and his legal team presented their proposal. The states had all brought their suits separately, but what the Sacklers suggested was an overall resolution that would sweep in all of the plaintiffs in all the different suits. The concept that David and his team outlined was that the Sacklers would relinquish control of Purdue and turn the company into a public trust, and the family would donate a large sum of money to address the opioid crisis. In exchange, the Sacklers would be granted immunity from "all potential federal liability" related to OxyContin. It was a grand bargain, a single negotiated pact that would resolve all of the cases at once and deliver the Sacklers the peace of mind of knowing that they would not spend the rest of their lives in litigation. Almost as soon as the offer had been made, the terms leaked to the press. A wave of headlines announced the news: "Purdue Pharma Offers $10–12 Billion to Settle Opioid Claims."

This seemed like a genuinely significant figure—far more than any sum that had been bandied about in the past. It might not be enough to fully address the costs of the opioid epidemic, far from it, but it would represent the lion's share of the Sacklers' remaining wealth. The offer appeared, at first glance, to signal a major victory for Maura Healey in Massachusetts, and Letitia James in New York, and the lawyer Mike Moore, and all the many plaintiffs and their attorneys. But as further specifics of the Cleveland proposal emerged, the Sacklers' offer turned out to be more complicated and considerably less spectacular. The plan was for Purdue to declare bankruptcy and then be converted into a "public benefit trust." According to Purdue's lawyers, the trust would include more than $4 billion in new drugs to treat addiction and counteract overdoses, which would be provided as an in-kind gift. That would be supplemented by an additional $3 or $4 billion in drug sales by the version of Purdue that would emerge from bankruptcy as a public trust. So the personal contribution of the Sacklers would be not $10 billion (much less $12 billion) but $3 billion. And even that money would not come out of pocket. Instead, the Sacklers suggested that their contribution be financed by selling off Mundipharma, the global pharmaceutical concern that had continued to cultivate new markets for opioids abroad. As a concession, the Sacklers indicated that they *might* be willing to kick in an additional $1.5 billion, bringing their total contribution to $4.5 billion. But only if they managed to sell Mundipharma for more than $3 billion. There was also one very notable nonmonetary provision. Under the terms of the deal that David Sackler offered, his family would admit to no wrongdoing whatsoever.

The initial press coverage presented this proposal as if it signified some kind of unconditional surrender. But to Maura Healey and her attorneys, the deal seemed deeply flawed. "It's a joke," Healey's lead prosecutor, Gillian Feiner, said. The proposal was premised on a number of big contingencies, Feiner pointed out. And it seemed significant that the Sacklers, having been exposed as paragons of rapacious greed, remained unprepared to contribute any money of their own beyond what could be generated from the sale of Mundipharma. (By way of comparison, between 2008 and 2016 alone the family had paid itself nearly $4.3 billion in OxyContin proceeds.) But also, on a more symbolic level, Feiner was struck by the fact that in a legal controversy about how destructive the rampant sale of OxyContin had been, one major plank of David Sackler's proposal was that after Purdue was set up as a charitable trust, the plaintiffs would raise money to address the opioid crisis through ongoing proceeds from Purdue—which is to say, by selling the very drug that had started the crisis in the first place. This would create a perverse incentive in which the states, having inherited the company, would suddenly find themselves in the opioid business. "That would be the ultimate victory for the Sacklers," Feiner's colleague Sandy Alexander observed. "If the states step into their shoes and sell the same drugs to the same patients using the same doctors, and people keep dying at the same rate, the Sacklers would present that as a very compelling exoneration for them."

Letitia James, the attorney general of New York, did not mince words, deriding David's offer as "an insult, plain and simple." To Maura Healey, it seemed highly significant that the proposal involved no admission of wrongdoing. That would effectively allow the Sacklers to buy silence, just as they had always done in the past. "It's critical that all the facts come out about what this company and its executives and directors did, that they apologize for the harm they caused, and that no one profits from breaking the law," Healey said. At one point during the negotiations in Cleveland, she and her deputy, Joanna Lydgate, were heading to an elevator when they crossed paths with David Sackler and his entourage. He introduced himself and said, "I'm really glad you could make it." He had an air of self-importance, Healey thought, as if he was used to commanding respect.

"Well, David," Healey said curtly, "your family hurt a lot of people." Then she and Lydgate entered the elevator without shaking his hand.

Some of the negotiators made a counterproposal to the Sacklers, suggesting that they pledge more of their own personal money. They wanted the family to commit to the additional $1.5 billion up front, rather than make it contingent on a higher sale for Mundipharma. But the Sacklers wouldn't budge. "Almost all states would agree to the deal if the Sackler family would guarantee it 100%," said North Carolina's AG, Josh Stein, who negotiated with the family. But the Sacklers' position, Stein said, was "Take it or leave it."

This recalcitrance left the negotiators on the plaintiffs' side feeling openly disgusted. "I think they are a group of sanctimonious billionaires who lied and cheated so they could make a handsome profit," Pennsylvania's attorney general, Josh Shapiro, said. "I truly believe that they have blood on their hands."

Judge Polster, who was presiding over the negotiations, indicated that he wanted at least thirty-five states on board with the settlement. Unless the Sacklers could get the parties to sign on, they would face the trial in Ohio in the fall. But the family had one powerful piece of leverage. Because Purdue had never really developed another successful product after OxyContin, and because the company had been hemorrhaging money to pay its astronomical legal bills, and because the Sacklers had been taking money *out* of the business at every opportunity, Purdue Pharma's coffers were nearly empty. Having sold some $35 billion worth of OxyContin over two decades, the company might now be down, according to press reports, to as little as $500 million in cash. On August 19, Purdue sent a letter to former sales reps informing them that the firm might not be able to fund their retirement benefits.

If the states did not want to sign off on their generous offer, the Sacklers indicated, then Purdue would just declare bankruptcy without a deal in place. Doing so would have one big near-term advantage for the Sacklers: after a company files for bankruptcy, the judge handling the process will generally freeze all litigation against the company so that it can be restructured. The Sacklers did not want Purdue to go to trial in October. If their settlement proposal wouldn't keep the company out of the courtroom, then bankruptcy would. And if Purdue did go bankrupt, it would leave virtually every state and all the other entities that had filed suit against the company with no choice but to fight over its remaining assets in bankruptcy court. Take the money now, Mary Jo White warned, or the alternative would be to "pay attorneys' fees for years and years and years to come."

This was a threat wrapped in velvet. In urging the plaintiffs to sign off on the Cleveland proposal, Purdue's lawyers told them that the total amount they might hope to recover in a bankruptcy proceeding (and then somehow divvy up) could be as little as $1 billion. It was true that

Purdue was simply not worth that much money anymore. The Sacklers had managed to extend the patent exclusivity of OxyContin again and again since 1996, far longer than anyone had ever thought possible. But the cliff was finally approaching: the patents for the reformulated Oxy-Contin were soon set to expire. "The party's over," one former Purdue executive said. "The public declaration is, 'Okay, society. You've won.' But to me, it almost seems like this was the plan all along."

On September 8, press reports indicated that talks between the two sides had broken down. The family refused to commit more money, and too many of the state prosecutors were opposed to the deal. The Sacklers had rejected two alternative offers from the states about how payments could be handled, and they declined to offer counterpropos-als. "As a result, the negotiations are at an impasse," the plaintiffs' nego-tiators said, "and we expect Purdue to file for bankruptcy protection imminently."

✢ ✢ ✢

The next day, as people watching the case waited to see if Purdue would declare bankruptcy, Joss Sackler arrived at the Bowery Hotel, in lower Manhattan, for the runway show of the spring 2020 collection of her label LBV. It was Fashion Week in New York, and Joss was excited to present her new line. She had hired an actual designer, Elizabeth Kennedy, who had previously worked at Isaac Mizrahi and other nota-ble labels. The two women had met at one of Joss's wine soirees, and Kennedy signed on to design her collection, saying, "Joss and I are try-ing to create something new and fresh." Kennedy felt no scruples about taking Joss's money, saying that the label "doesn't have anything to do with" OxyContin. Joss arrived at the Bowery in a sleeveless red frock, escorted by two private security guards. Her husband might have been embroiled in the delicate process of trying to get a quorum of thirty-five states to sign off on the Sacklers' settlement proposal. He might have been beta testing a new public posture of somber compassion (the Sacklers felt empathy, he insisted to *Vanity Fair*, "so much empathy"). But Joss was not going to let any of this noise interfere with her moment. Invitations to the show, which were distributed widely to media and fashion types, described Joss Sackler as "the undeterred 'phoenix.'" She had not taken part in the *Vanity Fair* interview; the family's han-dlers might have feared she would say something impolitic. But Joss did manage to appear in the accompanying photograph, posing in profile; standing, statuesquely, by her man, while David glowered directly into the camera. Joss posted the photo on Instagram and wrote, "Powerful words by my husband."

In advance of the show, *Page Six* had crowed, "Fashionistas 'Skipping' Joss Sackler's New York Fashion Week Show." But Joss and her staff (she had a staff) had been working overtime to persuade people to come. They did this by offering free car service and hair and makeup to a variety of influential young fashion personalities, some of whom had never heard of the Sackler controversy, much less Joss herself. It was not unusual, at such events, for designers to seek out famous people who could sit in the front row, generating publicity and conferring an implicit endorsement. One celebrity whom Joss was angling to bring to the show was the singer, tabloid icon, and fabled hell-raiser Courtney Love. Her staff sent an invitation to Love, saying that Joss and Elizabeth Kennedy were both "huge fans" and that Love personified the kind of "strong and undeterred" woman that LBV was made for. As an inducement, they offered Love $100,000 and a "custom-made 'Phoenix' dress from LBV embroidered with 24-carat gold thread."

Courtney Love was no stranger to this type of invitation, and $100,000 seemed like a more than reasonable sum for sitting through a twenty-minute fashion show. But when Love discovered who exactly Joss Sackler was, she was shocked. In an email, Joss's representatives had stressed that "the brand has no relation to Purdue…other than Joss is married to the family." But that did seem like a relation! And what was so strange about Joss Sackler (of all people) inviting Courtney Love (of all people) to her fashion show was that Love, famously, had a more than incidental relation to opioids herself. Kurt Cobain, her late husband and the father of her daughter, had been addicted to heroin. He killed himself in 1994. Love had struggled with addiction herself, to heroin—but also to OxyContin. When Joss invited her to the LBV show, she had been sober for barely a year. The irony was almost too much to contemplate.

Just as Nan Goldin, when she came out of recovery, had directed her righteous anger at the family whose drug had put her in there, Courtney Love now lashed out herself. "I am one of the most famous reformed junkies on the planet," she told Joss's nemesis, *Page Six*. "What is it about me that says to Joss Sackler, 'I will sell out to you?'" She mocked Joss's wine club (with its "philanthropic arm") and pilloried her fashion line. "This request from Joss Sackler is shameless and offensive after everything I, many of my friends, and millions of other addicts have been through with OxyContin," she proclaimed. "I'm sober, but I will always be an opioid addict." In the end, Love said, the moral stain on the Sackler family could not be covered up by any amount of "24 carat gold thread."

Love was not in attendance when the music started booming and models, perched on precarious heels, began to saunter up and down an improvised runway on the terrace of the Bowery. David Sackler wasn't either. But many friends and supporters of Joss did show up, and when questioned by reporters about the controversy, they tended to describe Joss's business in the language of women's empowerment. "It's unfair," one attendee told the *Daily Beast*. "She's her own woman and people should see the line before they open their mouths. All she's seen as is a man's wife. For her to run a business is amazing." This was Joss's perspective, too. She traded barbs with Courtney Love on Instagram and quoted the singer's own lyrics back to her: "Slow your troll @courtney love. I do not work for Purdue, I never did. Aren't these your very words 'we are not who we fuck?'" When the show was over, Joss beamed triumphantly, flanked by her security guards. "This was such a success," she said.

✤ ✤ ✤

Six days later, Purdue Pharma filed for bankruptcy. One peculiarity of American bankruptcy law is that a corporation can effectively pick the judge who will preside over the case. One day the previous March—six months before the company actually filed for bankruptcy—Purdue had paid a $30 fee to change its address for litigation documents to an anonymous office building in White Plains, New York. There is a federal courthouse in White Plains, and only one bankruptcy judge presided there, a man named Robert Drain. Before his appointment to the bench in 2002, he had worked as a partner at the corporate law firm Paul, Weiss. The company selected Drain carefully. He would now exert tremendous control over the endgame for the Sacklers and Purdue.

The first thing that Drain could be expected to do, which was customary in any bankruptcy case, was to freeze all of the lawsuits against

Purdue, pending resolution of the bankruptcy proceedings. Now the company would be spared from the sequence of trials that had been about to commence in Ohio. But in a hastily organized press conference in Boston, Maura Healey urged people to think, for a moment, about how precisely this once mighty company could have found itself in bankruptcy. "The Sacklers have done a pretty good job of sucking the life out of Purdue," she said. "Year after year, month after month, they were draining hundreds of millions of dollars." All that was left at this point, she said, was "essentially a shell."

Healey made no effort to conceal the indignation she felt at the thought that the Sacklers would push their company into bankruptcy now that it was no longer of any use to them, then waltz off with the billions they had taken out of it. Lawyers for the Sacklers emphasized that their proposal for a global settlement was still very much on the table. But Healey was skeptical of their assurances about all the good the family would do if the states would just accept their plan. "They've had ample opportunity for years to do something constructive," she pointed out. But instead, "they continue to fight us every step of the way." The members of the family were still "working on their brand," she scoffed. But the sort of careful image management at which the family had long excelled was simply no longer viable. "We know who the Sacklers are," Healey concluded.

Nevertheless, she was struggling to maintain her coalition of states opposing the family's settlement proposal. The challenge was that while many of the attorneys general found the offer to be insultingly low when considered alongside the Sacklers' fortune or the magnitude of their culpability, it was nevertheless a great deal of money. Many states, reeling from the epidemic and desperate for resources, were tempted to take what they could get. "It is, I think, the best deal that can be obtained," said Dave Yost, the attorney general in Ohio. Tennessee's attorney general, Herbert Slatery, agreed, pointing out that the plan "would secure billions" to address the epidemic and "result in the Sackler family divesting themselves of their business interests in the pharmaceutical industry forever."

Curiously, a partisan divide emerged among the state prosecutors. Red state AGs were more inclined to go along with the deal the Sacklers were proposing, whereas blue state prosecutors wanted to fight for more. Some speculated that this might be due to how dire the need for emergency funds was in the red states, or to different political cultures—Republicans more inclined to accommodate corporate interests, Democrats more given to redistributionist zeal. But another factor might have been that behind the scenes the Sacklers were actively whipping votes. The family had long understood the physics of political influence and the value of a well-connected fixer. When they needed to make the threat of felony charges go away back in 2006, they deployed the former federal prosecutor Rudy Giuliani. Now that they were facing a cohort of angry attorneys general, they put a new fixer on the payroll: a former U.S. senator from Alabama, Luther Strange, who had previously served as state AG. Until 2017, Strange had been the chairman of a national group called RAGA, or the Republican Attorneys General Association. In the past, Purdue had donated generously to this group, and to its Democratic counterpart, giving the two organizations a combined $800,000 between 2014 and 2018. Remarkably, the company continued to contribute to both groups, even after declaring bankruptcy and even as virtually every state attorney general, Democrat or Republican, was suing them. During the summer of 2019, Luther Strange took part in a RAGA meeting in West Virginia as an emissary for the Sacklers and personally lobbied the Republican AGs in attendance to support a settlement.

To further complicate matters, the plaintiffs' lawyers, like Mike Moore, who had brought suits against Purdue on behalf of local governments and served as key allies for those trying to hold the Sacklers to account, seemed inclined to accept the settlement as well. Plaintiffs' lawyers work on a contingency basis, taking up to a third of any final settlement in fees, which means that they sometimes have incentives of their own to seize a multibillion-dollar settlement when it is on the table, rather than take the gamble of pushing for a larger and more just result and ending up with nothing. These attorneys also regarded the Purdue case as one piece of a larger litigation puzzle, in which they were pursuing separate suits against other drugmakers, wholesalers, and pharmacies. Some of the lawyers involved in the bankruptcy suspected that Mike Moore himself might have played a hand, behind the scenes, in conceiving the deal that the Sacklers proposed in Cleveland. It would be a compromise, in which the states would get some much-needed funds to address the crisis, the Sacklers would achieve an outcome they could live with, and the plaintiffs' lawyers would collect hundreds of millions in fees. These suspicions proved correct: Moore acknowledged, in a subsequent interview, that working with another plaintiffs' lawyer, Drake Martin, he had "put this deal together" for Purdue.

✦ ✦ ✦

One major sticking point for the Democratic prosecutors was that Purdue might be crying poverty, but the Sacklers remained one of the wealthiest families in the United States. "When your illegal marketing campaign causes a national crisis, you should not get to keep most of the money," Healey's coalition of non-consenting states wrote in a filing, arguing that what the Sacklers were offering simply "does not match what they owe."

This was the premise of New York's lawsuit against the Sacklers— that the family had looted its own company—and even as the bankruptcy proceeding played out, Letitia James wanted to gather more detailed information on their finances. The Sackler fortune was dispersed in a vast global web of hundreds of shell companies and trusts and LLCs, many of them established in tax havens and jurisdictions with powerful bank secrecy laws. The structure of their financial arrangements could seem deliberately obscure, with an infinity of anonymous corporate entities, all nested like Matryoshka dolls. In August, Letitia James had subpoenaed records from thirty-three financial institutions and investment advisers that had ties to the family. She was pursuing a legal theory of "fraudulent conveyance," arguing that the family had deliberately hidden money in order to evade potential creditors. The subpoenas went to big institutions like Citibank, Goldman Sachs, and HSBC but also to smaller holding companies that were linked to the family and registered in offshore tax havens like the British Virgin Islands and the isle of Jersey.

The Sacklers fought the subpoenas, suggesting that they amounted to a form of "harassment." A spokesman for Mortimer released a statement blasting the gambit as "a cynical attempt by a hostile A.G.'s office to generate defamatory headlines." But a judge approved the subpoenas, and within weeks Letitia James had already acquired telling information. The response from a single financial institution allowed her office to track roughly $1 billion in wire transfers by the Sacklers, including funds that Mortimer himself had funneled into Swiss bank accounts.

When Judge Drain halted all litigation against Purdue, it seemed to Maura Healey that she and Letitia James and other state prosecutors should be able to proceed with their cases against the Sacklers. After all, the *family* wasn't filing for bankruptcy. The Sacklers had "extracted nearly all the money out of Purdue and pushed the carcass of the company into bankruptcy," Josh Stein, the North Carolina AG, said. "Multi-billionaires are the opposite of bankrupt." But on September 18, Purdue made a special appeal to Judge Drain. Having maintained the ruse, for decades, that the Sacklers and Purdue were separate, their lawyers now argued that the Sacklers were "inextricably twined" in any lawsuits against their company. For the moment, the Sacklers were prepared to carry through on the deal that they had proposed in Cleveland, their legal team suggested. But should Judge Drain permit the legal proceedings against their family to continue, they might be forced to reconsider and become "unwilling" to deliver even the $3 billion.

It wasn't just the implicit threat that rankled Maura Healey. It was the fact that the Sacklers were playing a shell game: they were throwing their lot in with Purdue when it suited them to do so and distancing themselves from the company when it didn't. They wanted none of the responsibility that comes with owning a corporation and serving on its board of directors but all of the protections. It would be one thing to request a shield from litigation if their own money were at issue in the bankruptcy proceedings, but they *weren't declaring bankruptcy!* Instead, the family was attempting to game the bankruptcy rules in an effort "to avoid their own individual accountability," Healey and other AGs wrote in a brief to the court. "The Sacklers want the bankruptcy court to stop our lawsuits so they can keep the billions of dollars they pocketed from OxyContin and walk away without ever being held accountable," Healey said. "That's unacceptable."

❖   ❖   ❖

There was some precedent, in bankruptcy law, for this kind of maneuver. In 1985, a Virginia pharmaceutical corporation, the A. H. Robins Company, filed for bankruptcy. It had manufactured a contraceptive intrauterine device called the Dalkon Shield, which turned out to be extremely dangerous, causing a range of injuries and death and giving rise to thousands of lawsuits seeking hundreds of millions of dollars from the company. Like Purdue, A. H. Robins was a family-owned business, and there were charges that members of the Robins family had known about and concealed evidence relating to the danger of their product. The Robins clan was known for its philanthropy; at the University of Richmond, both the athletic center and the business school were named after members of the family. As evidence accumulated that their product was hurting people, the company maintained that the device was safe and effective "when properly used." (Confronted by reports that the Dalkon Shield was causing uterine infections, company lawyers sought to undermine the women who experienced these effects, suggesting that the problem was not the device but rather their own "hygienic habits" and "promiscuity.") When the Robins company declared bankruptcy, the Robins family did not. Yet the bankruptcy court agreed to stay all litigation not just against the company but against the family as well. In Massachusetts, Sandy Alexander, the attorney who worked for Maura Healey, discovered an out-of-print book about the Dalkon Shield case. He bought ten used copies and distributed them to his colleagues as an indication of the paradigm they might be forced to contend with in White Plains. The title of the book was *Bending the Law*.

As it happened, Judge Drain had dealt with this issue on at least one prior occasion himself. In a 2014 bankruptcy case, he had granted a similar release to third parties who were not actually declaring bankruptcy. It was tempting to wonder whether Drain's demonstrated openness to the concept was not part of Purdue's rationale for selecting him in the first place. In a filing, the Raymond wing of the family suggested to Drain that if he would just agree to halt all proceedings against the Sacklers, that might provide the family with some "breathing room," allowing them to finalize their deal with the states. In a court hearing, one company lawyer said, "Litigation against the Sacklers *is* litigation against Purdue."

On October 11, 2019, Judge Drain sided with the Sacklers. It was an "extraordinary" step, he acknowledged from the bench, but he thought it was appropriate. The attorneys had argued over the issue for hours, during which Drain often showed signs of impatience with the lawyers opposing the move. He granted the Sacklers a temporary reprieve, but with the possibility of extension. In a statement, Purdue celebrated the decision, suggesting that it would be "for the ultimate benefit of the American public."

Chapter 29

UN-NAMING

TWO MONTHS AFTER PURDUE Pharma declared bankruptcy, in November 2019, a team of economists released a fascinating study. "Overdose deaths involving opioids have increased dramatically since the mid-1990s, leading to the worst drug overdose epidemic in U.S. history," they wrote. But there is "limited empirical evidence on the initial causes." What they wanted to figure out, in an academically rigorous manner, was how the crisis had actually started. There were different theories about the catalyst. People generally agreed that a sea change in the culture of prescribing by American doctors was an important factor, but it could be difficult to pinpoint what prompted that change. In recent years, some observers had begun to suggest that the opioid crisis was actually just a symptom of a deeper set of social and economic problems in the United States, that suicide and alcohol-related deaths were also on the rise, and that all of these fatalities should be understood as part of a larger category of "deaths of despair."

But these economists—Abby Alpert at the Wharton School, William Evans and Ethan Lieber at Notre Dame, and David Powell at Rand—were specifically interested in the role of Purdue Pharma. Many public health experts and journalists and prosecutors like Maura Healey had suggested, in an anecdotal way, that it was Purdue's marketing of OxyContin that sparked the crisis. The economists wanted to see if the data actually bore that out.

But how could you do that? There were so many social, medical, and economic variables that could have contributed. How could you possibly isolate the impact of OxyContin? The economists were curious about the role of drug marketing, and when they obtained some internal Purdue documents, which had been unsealed in litigation, they made an interesting discovery. When it first started marketing the drug back in 1996, Purdue identified a significant barrier to entry in a handful of U.S. states. Some states had what was known as "triplicate" programs: a policy that required doctors to fill out special triplicate prescription forms anytime they wanted to prescribe Schedule II narcotics. A copy of each form would be filed with the state, which allowed state agencies to maintain a prescription database, in order to monitor for diversion or other irregularities. These programs started decades before the opioid crisis; the first was established in California in 1939 because of concerns, even then, about diversion of opium-based pharmaceuticals. The triplicate programs were eventually phased out altogether in 2004. But at the time OxyContin was released, five states had these restrictions: California, Idaho, Illinois, New York, and Texas.

When the economists consulted Purdue's documents, they discovered numerous references to the triplicate programs. The company had identified them as a problem. Focus groups suggested that physicians in triplicate states avoided writing opioid prescriptions because they regarded the paperwork as cumbersome and they "did not want to give the Government an excuse to monitor their activities." Staff reported that "doctors in the triplicate states were not enthusiastic about the product." So during the initial launch of OxyContin, Purdue chose to limit its marketing efforts in these states, instead concentrating its resources in other states with laxer regulations, where the company could expect a higher return on investment. As a consequence of this comparatively moderate marketing rollout (and of the triplicate restrictions themselves), the academics determined that the distribution of OxyContin ended up being about 50 percent lower than average in these five states during the years following the launch.

This seemed like a promising data set from which to draw some solid empirical conclusions about the impact of the drug. The states had nothing in common geographically. They comprised four of the most populous states, but also one of the least. Their economies were different. There was no common thread that connected these five states (but none of the others) which might have any explanatory value, in other words, apart from the triplicate programs and the related fact that OxyContin was much less widely available during the early years in these states than it was everywhere else. So how did their experience of the opioid crisis compare with what happened in the rest of the country?

Prior to 1996, the triplicate states actually had a higher rate of over-

dose deaths than the rest of the nation. But what the team of economists discovered was that shortly after the launch of OxyContin, that
relationship suddenly flipped. Overdose rates everywhere else started
to climb much faster than in the triplicate states. Those five states were
sheltered, enjoying "uniquely low" growth in overdose deaths, the
scholars found. In fact, even after the triplicate programs were discon-
tinued several years later, "their initial deterrence of OxyContin promotion and adoption had long-term effects on overdose deaths in these
states." By contrast, states with more exposure to OxyContin during
the years immediately after it was introduced "experienced higher
growth in overdose deaths in almost every year since 1996."

Other studies had already drawn a causal connection between the
reformulation of OxyContin in 2010 and the rise in the abuse of heroin
and fentanyl. But the economists found that in the five states that had
triplicate programs in place back when OxyContin was introduced,
heroin and fentanyl deaths rose much less dramatically. In fact, even
in 2019, nearly a quarter of a century after the original "blizzard of
prescriptions," overdose deaths in the triplicate states, from *all* opioids,
were some of the lowest in the nation. These disparities could not be
explained away by other factors, such as unrelated drug control policies
or economic considerations, the scholars concluded. "Our results show
that the introduction and marketing of OxyContin explain a substantial share of overdose deaths over the last two decades."

It made David Sackler extremely angry to think about New York's
attorney general, Letitia James, describing the drug that his father,
Richard, introduced as the "taproot" of the opioid epidemic. "You can
make that argument," he would say, "but you have to prove it." Here,
though, was something that looked a lot like proof. In their private
emails, the Sacklers complained that they were being blamed for heroin
and fentanyl overdoses, when all they ever did was sell a legal, FDA-
regulated drug. They strategized with the company's spin doctors
about how to change the subject and refocus the conversation around
fentanyl. But a separate study, by a pair of economists from Rand and
the University of Southern California, found that the 2010 reformulation, while it might have caused a decline in the abuse of OxyContin,
"increased overall overdose rates." Purdue had created a generation of
people who were addicted to opioids, through the careful and relentless
cultivation of demand for the drug. When the reformulation happened,

that demand did not go away: it just found another source of supply. The paper established that even the boom in illicit fentanyl, like the rise in heroin before it, "was driven by demand considerations existing years prior to the entry of fentanyl." Synthetic opioid abuse was disproportionately high in states that had high rates of OxyContin misuse. Nor did the knock-on effects of the reformulation dissipate after a few years, the authors of this study concluded. Instead, they grew over time as markets developed and innovated, leading to a public health emergency.

In its earliest known iterations, in the poetry of Hesiod, the Greek myth of Pandora grew out of a parable about technology. Prometheus defied the gods by stealing fire from Mount Olympus and giving it to humankind. Fire is a volatile gift, capable of creation and destruction, but humans learned to tame it, and it became the basis for civilization. As punishment for this insubordination, the gods sent a "beautiful evil," Pandora. She was said to be the first woman, and she carried with her a jar (or, as it has been translated, a "box"). The jar contained all that is evil, disease and other terrors, "harsh toil" and "grievous sicknesses that are deadly to men." Prometheus had warned the humans to be wary of any gifts from the gods. But they did not heed his warning, and Pandora opened her jar. In some versions of the story, Pandora can seem malevolent, deliberately unleashing a whirlwind of torment. In other tellings, she is naive, her greatest sin simply curiosity. As they sought to hide from a historic crisis of their own creation, the Sacklers could sometimes seem like Pandora, gazing, slack-jawed, at the momentous downstream consequences of their own decisions. They told the world, and themselves, that the jar was full of blessings, that it was a gift from the gods. Then they opened it, and they were wrong.

✢ ✢ ✢

Early one morning, employees of Purdue Pharma showed up for work at One Stamford Forum to discover that a giant piece of sculpture had been deposited, overnight, on the sidewalk in front of the building. It was an enormous steel spoon. It weighed eight hundred pounds, and the handle had been bent over backward, evoking the "spoon and shoot" tests that Purdue had run on OxyContin prior to releasing the drug. The bowl of the spoon was stained, to symbolize burned heroin. This sculpture was the work of Domenic Esposito, an artist who had a personal connection to the issue: his brother had started on OxyContin and ended up addicted to heroin. "It's a symbol of what's basically the albatross of my family," Esposito said, explaining that his mother would find this kind of spoon "every time my brother relapsed." The owner of a local Stamford gallery had thought it would be appropriate to install the sculpture directly in front of Purdue headquarters. But somebody called the cops, and they arrested the gallery owner for "obstructing free passage." Within a couple of hours, the relevant authorities had been summoned to remove the spoon. They had to bring a bulldozer to do it.

There was more security around the building, lately. Some days, cars were searched when they arrived. Protesters had started showing up, sometimes in ones and twos, sometimes by the dozen. Often, mothers would come, clutching blown-up photographs of their dead children. They looked like the Mothers of the Disappeared in Argentina. Some chanted their loved ones' names; others just stood there silently, bearing stark witness, embodying, with an awful steadfast dignity, the idea that Nan Goldin kept repeating about how a generation of people had been wiped out.

Goldin showed up herself to protest, wearing sunglasses and holding her SHAME ON SACKLER banner. The family no longer came to work on the ninth floor. With bankruptcy proceedings under way, they had finally extricated themselves, more or less, from the inner workings of the company. But they still owned the building. And given the family's affinity for the arts, it seemed poignantly apt that some of the protesters were artists. For a time, there was a Massachusetts man named Frank Huntley who would show up with a sculpture of a skeleton that he had fashioned out of three hundred pill bottles and a plastic skull. Huntley was a painter and wall paperer who had been prescribed OxyContin after an injury in 1998. All those prescription bottles in the sculpture had been his. "This was me for 15 years," Huntley said of the skeleton. "This drug controlled me every day."

For two decades, the glass headquarters in Stamford had been surrounded by signs emblazoned with Purdue's distinctive ringed and underlined logo. But eventually the company determined that it would probably be a prudent idea to take the signs down. Goldin derived some satisfaction from this furtive acknowledgment of Purdue's ignominy. But she was still hell-bent on seeing the Sackler name come down, too.

Many cultural and educational institutions had started a process, during this period, of rethinking their willingness to carry the names of morally questionable benefactors. In 2017, the president of Yale had announced that the university would rename a residential college that was named after John C. Calhoun, because Calhoun's legacy as a white supremacist was in fundamental conflict with Yale's "mission and values." At Oxford, a Rhodes scholar from South Africa had helped to spearhead a campaign to take down a statue of Cecil Rhodes.

Yet numerous universities, among them Yale itself, continued to accept Sackler donations in 2018, even as the lawsuits and press scrutiny intensified and other institutions were distancing themselves. It was not until 2019 that Yale cut ties with the Sacklers, announcing that it would not take any more gifts from the family. But the university had no intention of shedding the Sackler name where it was associated with gifts that had been given in the past. Harvard took a similar stance. The presidential candidate Elizabeth Warren, who had taught at Harvard prior to joining the U.S. Senate, had urged the university to remove the Sackler name. But Harvard's president, Lawrence Bacow, responded that it would be "inappropriate" to remove the name, because Arthur Sackler had endowed the Sackler Museum before OxyContin was invented. In any case, Bacow pointed out, "legal and contractual obligations" would prevent the university from taking such a step.

Goldin was not satisfied. On July 1, 2019, she showed up in Paris to launch a protest at the Louvre. The museum's Sackler Wing had been supported by the family of Mortimer Sackler. The wing consisted of twelve rooms full of marvelous Near Eastern antiquities. As hundreds of tourists and trinket sellers looked on, Goldin and a band of forty or so supporters swarmed the central plaza by the entrance to the Louvre. Goldin stepped into a fountain by the great glass pyramid that was the centerpiece of the courtyard and shouted, "Take down the Sackler name!" The Sacklers might have enjoyed considerable clout in France, where both Mortimer and Raymond had been recognized with the Legion of Honor. But Goldin had a credibility of her own. Her photographs hung in the Louvre. She had been named a Commander of the Order of Arts and Letters by the French government. (For fun, she wore the medal to the protest.) Some members of her group PAIN had also discovered that there was a special circumstance at the Louvre that might allow them to make a breakthrough. Consulting the museum's bylaws, they learned that the Louvre reserved the right to sunset any naming agreements after twenty years. And the Sackler Wing had carried the name for more than two decades. Within two weeks of Goldin's protest, the president of the Louvre, Jean-Luc Martinez, announced that the wing would "no longer carry the Sackler name." The museum claimed that this decision had nothing to do with Purdue Pharma or OxyContin or Nan Goldin's protest, and was instead just a routine housecleaning. The rooms weren't being "*de-baptized*," a spokeswoman insisted—just updated. But nobody was under any illusions, and overnight all the engraved signage announcing the *Aile Sackler des Antiquités Orientales* and listing the names of Mortimer's seven surviving children—Ilene, Kathe, Mortimer, Samantha, Marissa, Sophie, Michael—came off the walls, and references to the family were scrubbed from the museum's website. "The Sacklers wanted everything that Nan has in terms of the art world," Goldin's fellow activist Megan Kapler said. "And she stepped in and said, 'No. This is my world. You don't get to be in it.'"

✤ ✤ ✤

Arthur's widow, Jillian, had started telling people that she was reluctant to use her own last name. She resented the "blanket designation 'the Sackler family'" and continued her rearguard effort to "disentangle" Arthur's name from that of his brothers, engaging press flacks to fire off shrill letters to news outlets demanding "clarifications." She coined a new locution, "OxySacklers," which she hoped could distinguish the families of Raymond and Mortimer. But after years of silence in the face of the ravages of OxyContin, it might have been too late for people like Jillian or Arthur's daughter Elizabeth to convincingly adopt the moral high ground. Jillian acknowledged that her campaign was "like spitting in the wind." Nevertheless, she insisted, had Arthur been alive, he would have intervened to stop his brothers from marketing OxyContin so aggressively. ("Does anyone believe that?" Nan Goldin asked. "How cynical is that?")

Notwithstanding the best efforts of Jillian and Elizabeth, the Smithsonian, to which Arthur had awarded his collection after his years of flirtation with the Met, on the understanding that he would get a museum with his name on it, now ended up subtly distancing itself from the family as well. Contractually, the museum could not remove the

Sackler name. Instead, it announced a decision to "re-brand," renaming the Sackler and Freer galleries as the National Museum of Asian Art. Henceforth, the museum would minimize its use of the Sackler name whenever it could, rolling out a new logo and burying any reference to the Arthur M. Sackler Gallery in small print. Arthur's son, Arthur Felix, paid a visit to his cousin Richard, in Connecticut, and lambasted him for sullying the family name. Jillian wondered if her late husband's reputation would "ever recover."

✦   ✦   ✦

Perhaps the most thorough reckoning with the Sackler legacy took place at Tufts. The relationship between the Sacklers and Tufts dated back to 1980, when Arthur, Mortimer, and Raymond made a major donation with the understanding that the School of Graduate Biomedical Sciences would be named after the family. A gift agreement at the time spelled out precisely where and in what manner the Sackler name would be displayed. Three years later, Arthur made a separate agreement to have Tufts name its medical school building after him. In 1986, the Arthur M. Sackler Center for Health Communications was established, and Arthur was celebrated at a black-tie gala. At the time, he likened the center that would carry his name to "the Alexandrian library, but of the twenty-first century." Over the decades, the family continued to give money to Tufts, donating some $15 million altogether and sponsoring research in cancer, neuroscience, and other fields. In 2013, Raymond was awarded an honorary PhD. The degree was conferred in a private ceremony at Purdue's offices because of Raymond's advanced age. "It would be impossible to calculate how many lives you have saved," the university's president, Anthony Monaco, told Raymond. "You are a world changer." To mark the occasion, the university included a biography of Raymond on its website that detailed his many philanthropic contributions but made no mention of Purdue whatsoever.

When Purdue pleaded guilty to the federal charges of misbranding in 2007, nobody at Tufts had raised any particular concerns. When Sam Quinones published *Dreamland* in 2015, the medical school made a quiet decision to scuttle the book from its reading list for incoming students. In fact, it was only in 2017, after the near simultaneous articles in *The New Yorker* and *Esquire,* that questions arose about the propriety of

Tufts's relationship with the family. Medical students began to express discomfort at attending lectures in buildings named after the Sacklers or earning degrees from the Sackler school. Some of them started to organize, much as Nan Goldin had, establishing a group called Sack Sackler. One first-year med student, Nicholas Verdini, made an impassioned entreaty to the university's board of trustees in which he informed them that his own sister had been addicted to opioids and had died of a heroin overdose two years earlier. She was twenty-five and left behind two daughters.

Maura Healey, in her complaint against the Sacklers, singled out Tufts as an example of the malign tentacles of the family's influence. Richard had served on an advisory board at the School of Medicine from 1999 until 2017. The family had offered what was described as "a more targeted gift" to establish a new master's program in "Pain, Research, Education, and Policy," and Richard enjoyed a warm relationship with the professor, Dr. Daniel Carr, who was appointed to run the program. "Our continued collaboration is a top priority for me," Carr told Richard in 2001. When the controversy surrounding Oxy-Contin arose, Carr assured Richard that he should blame not himself but "the perpetrators who victimize us, for their harmful misdeeds." In 2002, Carr appeared in a Purdue advertisement in *The Boston Globe*, dressed in a white coat, praising the company for "doing something" about the opioid crisis. The pain program appointed a new adjunct professor—David Haddox—and he touted his Tufts credential as a sign of his academic independence. In lectures to Tufts students, Haddox used Purdue-branded materials. According to *The Tufts Daily*, as late as 2010 one of the topics that he lectured on was "pseudo-addiction."

After the outcry from students, Tufts engaged a former federal prosecutor, Donald Stern, to conduct an internal review. When the review was complete, in December 2019, President Monaco and the chairman of the board sent an email to the Tufts community. "Our students, faculty, staff, alumni, and others have shared with us the negative impact the Sackler name has on them each day," they wrote. The response that they announced was a radical one: the university would remove the name, stripping it from five facilities and programs. "Our students find it objectionable to walk into a building that says Sackler on it," Harris Berman, the dean of the School of Medicine, said, explaining that they found the name "incongruous with the mission of the school and what we're trying to teach them." It was not just OxyContin that was problematic, Berman continued, but Arthur's legacy as well. "The Sackler name is a problem, whether it's the Arthur Sackler name, or all the Sackler names," he said.

The student activists were jubilant. "What our faculty and our deans are teaching us every day is that we take care of patients and respect patients and treat people with dignity, and walking into the office with the Sackler name on your building seems pretty hypocritical," one medical student, Mary Bridget Lee, said. By taking such a clean-cut moral stand, she suggested, Tufts might "set a precedent for other institutions."

Fearful, perhaps, of precisely that possibility, the Sacklers aggressively resisted the move. Jillian expressed her indignation that Arthur was "being blamed for actions taken by his brothers and other Oxy-Sacklers." As for the OxySacklers, a family attorney, Daniel Connolly, deplored the decision by Tufts as "intellectually dishonest" and pointed out that the Sacklers had "made gifts in good faith." Connolly threatened legal action, demanding that the move be "reversed." The family sent Tufts a letter accusing the university of breach of contract. It was a graphic measure of the Sacklers' vanity, and of their pathological denial, that the family was prepared to debase itself by trying to force its name back onto a university where the student body had said, quite explicitly, that they found it morally repugnant. But the administrators at Tufts held firm.

When he heard the news, Nicholas Verdini was in the cafeteria, and he ran outside to watch as workmen removed the Sackler name. He was a little stunned. Around him, people were clapping. Verdini thought of his sister. This felt "like a big win for her."

In places where the Sackler name was painted on walls, workmen used rollers to erase it with a fresh coat of paint. In places where raised brass lettering announced the name, they used a hammer and chisel to pry the letters off one by one, until all that was left were ghost marks, the faint, grubby outline where the name used to be.

✧ ✧ ✧

The Sacklers might have become social pariahs, but in White Plains their handpicked bankruptcy judge, Robert Drain, was proving to be an excellent choice. A declaration of bankruptcy conjures images of failure and shame, but for the Sacklers, Drain's courtroom had become a safe harbor. He renewed the injunction on any lawsuits against the family, then renewed it again, over objections from Letitia James that the Sacklers were receiving "the benefits of bankruptcy protection without filing for bankruptcy themselves."

As a bankruptcy judge, Drain seemed to regard himself as a creative technocrat, a deal maker whose chief concern was efficiency. He frequently invoked the great expense of the bankruptcy process—with scores of attorneys for the company, the Sacklers, and the various creditors, all billing by the hour—and sought to streamline the proceedings, citing the needs of those who had suffered from the opioid crisis and suggesting that whatever limited value Purdue still had should go toward helping people struggling with addiction, rather than toward enriching lawyers.

With such a deliberately narrow conception of his own assignment, Drain exhibited little interest in larger questions of justice and accountability, as if these were theoretical concepts that were extraneous to the negotiation at hand. In fact, at times he evinced frustration with state prosecutors and attorneys representing victims who had lost loved ones to the crisis, expressing impatience with their insistent demands to hold the company and the family to account. The offer by the Sacklers to settle all claims was still on the table, and in one hearing Drain suggested that the continued refusal by Maura Healey and other AGs to take them up on it was political grandstanding; the notion that they would "hold up something that is good for all" was "almost repulsive," Drain said.

One major source of contention in the White Plains proceedings was discovery: the ability of the state prosecutors and lawyers representing Purdue's creditors to gather information about the company and about the finances of the Sacklers. How much money did the Sacklers still have? How could anyone expect to achieve a just resolution, Letitia James wondered, without some sense of "how much has been stashed away"? There was a dark absurdity in the spectacle of Judge Drain and all of these bankruptcy lawyers arguing self-seriously about how to divvy up what was left of Purdue Pharma—which now amounted to cash and assets of roughly $1 billion—when the Sacklers were looking on from the sidelines, apparently untouchable, and holding on to so much more. According to deposition testimony by one of Purdue's own experts, the family had taken as much as $13 billion out of the company.

One legal scholar, reflecting on the case, noted that bankruptcy experts can occasionally behave as if their specialized field were "the Swiss Army knife of the legal system." Judge Drain appeared adamant that his courtroom was the ideal venue in which to resolve any and all outstanding issues relating to the role that Purdue and the Sacklers played in the opioid crisis. He spoke the same lingo as the bankruptcy lawyers arguing the case, a bloodless idiom of "efficiency," "consensus," "maximizing value," achieving a "deal." When it came to discovery, Drain told the bankruptcy lawyers to "keep an eye on" the attorneys in the case who *weren't* bankruptcy lawyers, to make sure they understood that any information gathered from Purdue or the Sacklers should be regarded not as "discovery for purposes of a trial" but as "due diligence" for an eventual deal. Drain didn't really believe in trials. "They are not some form of public truth serum," he said dismissively. He preferred "negotiations that lead to agreements."

Some of the attorneys involved were troubled by the distinctly clubby ethos of the proceedings. The Sacklers inhabited an elite milieu. They hired attorneys who attended elite law schools and now worked at elite firms, to represent them in cases where the lawyers opposing them were often products of those same elite institutions, and the judges were, too. This gave rise, in the words of one of the lawyers suing Purdue, to "a collusive atmosphere." The bankruptcy bar is especially small and insular. Purdue's new board chairman, a restructuring expert named Steve Miller, had known Judge Drain for years. In a 2008 memoir, he recounted a humorous anecdote about how he once took a nap in Drain's chambers. Kenneth Feinberg, the victim compensation expert who was appointed to be one of the two mediators in the bankruptcy, had previously worked for Purdue, and been paid some $12 million. Everyone seemed to know everyone. One night, Gillian Feiner, the lead lawyer from the Massachusetts attorney general's office, was staying overnight in White Plains for a hearing. She got a government rate at the Ritz. A lot of lawyers involved in the case stayed there; it was a short walk from the courthouse. Feiner spoke to a couple of her fellow prosecutors from other states that were suing the company, and learned that they were planning on having dinner that evening with

Mark Kesselman—the general counsel of Purdue. Feiner didn't join them. She dined alone, at the hotel bar, instead. "Just me and my principles," she texted a friend.

For Nan Goldin and the activists from PAIN, it was intensely frustrating to realize that this might be the venue in which the Sacklers would play their endgame. It wasn't just that the bankruptcy process prized economic compromise over all other values; it was that bankruptcy law is so technical and antiseptic that it is difficult for non-lawyers to grasp. "We're fighting on their terms now," one of the PAIN activists, Harry Cullen, complained. "The court speaks in terms of numbers. Everything is *fungible*." Early on, the group staged die-ins on the steps of the courthouse. But after the arrival of the COVID-19 pandemic in March, Drain stopped holding hearings in person, shifting to telephone conferences, which robbed the protesters of a theater in which to stage their actions. "It chops us off at the knees," Cullen said. "How are we supposed to hold them accountable?" Goldin actively intervened in the proceedings, helping start a committee of victims to push for greater accountability in the bankruptcy. They created a petition asking for an independent examiner to be assigned to the case, someone who could serve as a check on Judge Drain. This had been a feature in several high-profile bankruptcy cases, such as Enron and WorldCom, that included allegations of serious corporate misconduct. But Drain didn't think it was necessary in this one.

One day that summer, *The New York Times* published an op-ed by a journalist, Gerald Posner, and a bankruptcy scholar, Ralph Brubaker, which suggested that the Sacklers might "get away with it," keeping most of their fortune and facing no meaningful retribution. When a lawyer invoked the op-ed at a hearing, Judge Drain exploded. "It doesn't matter what some numbskull Op-Ed writer puts in," he sputtered. He urged the lawyers in attendance not to "buy or click on" publications like *The New York Times* and announced that he did not "want to hear some idiot reporter or some bloggist quoted to me again in this case."

✢ ✢ ✢

Drain's fit of pique notwithstanding, it seemed increasingly likely, with every passing month, that the Sacklers might indeed get away with it. One question that hung over the bankruptcy proceeding was whether the Department of Justice might file charges of its own against the company—or against the family. Federal prosecutors in multiple jurisdictions had been investigating Purdue for the past several years, quietly issuing subpoenas and gathering evidence. Judge Drain had set a deadline of July 30 for any claimants who felt they should be "creditors" of Purdue in the bankruptcy to file papers with the court. More than a hundred thousand people filed individual claims, arguing that Purdue's opioids had upended their lives and that they should be entitled to some compensation. Insurance companies filed claims as well. A single insurer, United Health, submitted a stunning filing, revealing that when it commissioned an analysis of how many of its policyholders had been prescribed Purdue opioids and then subsequently diagnosed with an opioid use disorder, the result was in the "hundreds of thousands." So much for the idea that people didn't get addicted under a doctor's care.

Just before the deadline, the Department of Justice filed a claim of its own, disclosing that multiple civil and criminal investigations had revealed that between 2010 and 2018, Purdue sent sales reps to call on prescribers the company knew "were facilitating medically unnecessary prescriptions." Purdue also purportedly paid kickbacks to prescribers, motivating them to write more prescriptions; to an electronic medical records company, so that it would create a digital alert that prompted physicians to recommend opioids while meeting with patients; and to specialty pharmacies, to induce them to dispense prescriptions that other pharmacies refused to fill. All of this conduct, Justice officials maintained, "gives rise to criminal liability."

What was most galling about this inventory of misdeeds was that it so resembled the general flavor of wrongdoing to which Purdue had pleaded guilty back in 2007. The details had changed, but the gist was the same: the company had been fraudulently pushing its opioids with rank indifference to the dangers they posed. The federal government itself might become a creditor of Purdue's, the DOJ filing suggested, in the event that the company ended up getting convicted of any of these allegations, or settled the charges. Given that critics of the 2007 deal had suggested that a $600 million fine was not enough of a deterrent—and that Purdue now appeared to be a *recidivist*, committing the same types of crimes—some observers wondered whether this time around the feds might actually charge some executives with felonies. By coincidence, in another recent case, the Justice Department had done just that: in January 2020, John Kapoor, who had served as CEO and board chairman of the pharma company Insys, had been sentenced to five and a half years in prison for his role in promoting and marketing his own dangerous opioid, a fentanyl product called Subsys. Would Craig Landau, Purdue's CEO, be next?

He would not. As it turned out, Mary Jo White and other attorneys for the Sacklers and Purdue had been quietly negotiating with the Trump administration for months. Inside the DOJ, the line prosecutors who had assembled both the civil and the criminal cases started to experience tremendous pressure from the political leadership to wrap up their investigations of Purdue and the Sacklers prior to the 2020 presidential election in November. A decision had been made at high levels of the Trump administration that this matter would be resolved quickly and with a soft touch. Some of the career attorneys at Justice were deeply unhappy with this move, so much so that they wrote confidential memos registering their objections, to preserve a record of what they believed to be a miscarriage of justice.

One morning two weeks before the election, Jeffrey Rosen, the deputy attorney general for the Trump administration, convened a press conference in which he announced a "global resolution" of the federal investigations into Purdue and the Sacklers. The company was pleading guilty to conspiracy to defraud the United States and to violate the Food, Drug, and Cosmetic Act, as well as to two counts of conspiracy to violate the federal Anti-kickback Statute, Rosen announced. No executives would face individual charges. In fact, no individual executives were mentioned at all: it was as if the corporation had acted autonomously, like a driverless car. (In depositions related to Purdue's bankruptcy which were held *after* the DOJ settlement, two former CEOs, John Stewart and Mark Timney, both declined to answer questions, invoking their Fifth Amendment right not to incriminate themselves.) Rosen touted the total value of the federal penalties against Purdue as "more than $8 billion." And, in keeping with what had by now become a standard pattern, the press obligingly repeated that number in the headlines.

Of course, anyone who was paying attention knew that the total value of Purdue's cash and assets was only around $1 billion, and nobody was suggesting that the Sacklers would be on the hook to pay Purdue's fines. So the $8 billion figure was misleading, much as the $10–$12 billion estimate of the value of the Sacklers' settlement proposal had been misleading—an artificial number without any real practical meaning, designed chiefly to be reproduced in headlines. As for the Sacklers, Rosen announced that they had agreed to pay $225 million to resolve a separate civil charge that they had violated the False Claims Act. According to the investigation, Richard, David, Jonathan, Kathe, and Mortimer had "knowingly caused the submission of false and fraudulent claims to federal health care benefit programs" for opioids that "were prescribed for uses that were unsafe, ineffective, and medically unnecessary." But there would be no criminal charges. In fact, according to a deposition of David Sackler, the Department of Justice concluded its investigation without so much as interviewing any member of the family. The authorities were so deferential toward the Sacklers that nobody had even bothered to question them.

When Rosen opened the press conference up for questions, a reporter pointed out that the $225 million the Sacklers were being forced to pay was "a little over 2 percent of that $10 billion they took out of the company," and asked, "Why have you let them keep all that money?"

Rosen replied that in his view the Sacklers were paying a "very steep price."

"Did you ever try to pursue that money?" another reporter asked.

"There is no law that says if you've done something wrong we should just simply strip somebody of their assets," Rosen said defensively. "That's not how it works."

Why hadn't the government pursued criminal charges against the Sacklers? a third reporter inquired. Rosen declined to answer.

❖ ❖ ❖

"It's like 2007 all over again," Barry Meier reflected, following the press conference. In the Virginia case, thirteen years earlier, prosecutors had amassed huge amounts of incriminating evidence, only to have the Sacklers deploy their high-powered lawyers to appeal to the political leadership at Justice and undermine the case. Just as the 2007 case had included a prosecution memo brimming with detailed allegations, there were traces, in this case, of the righteous work of line prosecutors. The official settlement documents cited specific instances of Purdue reps calling on obviously problematic doctors, including one who was nicknamed "Candyman," according to the filing, "because she will immediately put every patient on the highest dose." Lawyers for the Sacklers had argued that the family didn't take money out of the company in preparation for some future day of reckoning, claiming, "No reasonable person would have believed that Purdue would face a meaningful number of opioid-related lawsuits or judgments before 2017." But the settlement agreement included emails between the Sacklers from 2007 in which they acknowledged the likelihood that future lawsuits might "get through to the family" and discussed their intention to take money out. The Sacklers might have agreed to pay a $225 million penalty, but they refused to acknowledge any personal wrongdoing, even as their company pleaded guilty to felony charges.

"Here we are, so many years later when the Justice Department has a second chance to do it right—and once again they let them off the hook," Maura Healey said in an interview on MSNBC. "There's no one going to jail. There's no justice. The Sacklers face no admissions of guilt," she continued. The settlement amounted to little more than "a guilty plea against a company that is already in bankruptcy."

In Healey's office, Gillian Feiner and Sandy Alexander had gotten approval from Judge Drain to depose members of the Sackler family. Feiner questioned David Sackler in August, but the rest of the interviews—of Kathe, Mortimer, and Richard—were scheduled to stretch into November, past the election. Feiner and Alexander were hoping that the federal government would have no choice but to postpone any settlement so long as the Sacklers were still being deposed. After all, what if some damning new evidence came to light? But instead, at a certain point, DOJ lawyers just stopped attending the depositions. "I am not done with Purdue and the Sacklers," Healey vowed, saying that the Sackler depositions would go on, notwithstanding the settlement. "We're going to continue to press our state claims in court."

She and other state AGs were still constrained, however, by Judge Drain's decision to suspend their cases. And as Drain discussed his vision for the final resolution of the bankruptcy, he made it clear that what he really wanted to do was take that temporary bar on litigation against the Sacklers and make it permanent. When the Sacklers settled their cases in Kentucky and Oklahoma, they had stipulated that the family get a full release from all future liability. They were prepared to pay money to make a case go away, but only if they got an ironclad guarantee that it was going away for good. In the term sheet for the settlement proposal that David Sackler presented in Cleveland back in 2019, the family had indicated that they were prepared to supply the $3 billion and give up control of Purdue, but only in exchange for a full release from civil and criminal liability. The Sacklers didn't want to be looking over their shoulders for the rest of their lives. And Judge Drain, with his singular fixation on conserving value in the bankruptcy, appeared to be sympathetic to this consideration. At an early hearing, in February 2020, he suggested that the only way to achieve "true peace" was to have what he called a "third-party release," a ruling that would grant not just Purdue but also the Sackler family freedom from any future opioid-related lawsuits. This was a controversial issue, given that two dozen states were poised to resume their cases against the Sacklers just as soon as the bankruptcy concluded, and Drain indicated that he was raising the matter early, because in some parts of the country it would be illegal for a federal bankruptcy judge to enjoin state authorities from bringing their own lawsuits against a third party, like the Sacklers, who had not even declared bankruptcy in his court. The case law was evolving, Drain said.

A Purdue lawyer, Marshall Huebner, assured the judge that his firm, Davis Polk, was tracking the case law "with an electron microscope."

"You may need to do more than track," Drain said, slipping into a register that sounded strangely like legal advice. "You may need to file an amicus"—a friend-of-the-court brief—"to counteract some of the..." He trailed off. "Well, I'm just leaving it at that."

Huebner, displaying a self-awareness that Drain seemed to lack, said, "I don't know if the world wants a Purdue Pharma amicus." He added, "But we'll have to take that one under advisement."

In a filing to the court in March, the states opposing the Sacklers' settlement terms made the obvious point that such treatment at the hands of the legal system is an exclusive prerogative of the rich and "sends the wrong message to the public about the fairness of our courts."

Yet there was precedent for this, too. In the Dalkon Shield bankruptcy case involving the dangerous contraceptive device, the family that owned the company had ended up making precisely such a deal. Having halted any litigation against the Robins family during the bankruptcy proceedings (even though the family had not declared bankruptcy), the judge presided over a settlement in which the family contributed $10 million. He then barred any and all future lawsuits against the family and the company related to their faulty device. When women who had been injured by the Dalkon Shield came to the court-house, asking to speak, they were forcibly removed by court marshals. After the bankruptcy concluded, the Robins company was acquired by American Home Products. The Robins family made $385 million in the transaction. It seemed a virtual certainty now that the Sacklers would end up paying a few billion dollars but walking away with vastly more. They would evade any further charges against them. And they would never admit wrongdoing.

In the final bankruptcy hearing of 2020, Judge Drain was convers-ing over the teleconference line with the attorneys in the case about the starchy particulars of some procedural motion, when a man's voice broke in. "My name's Tim Kramer," he said. "I got a few things I'd like to say."

"Are you representing someone?" Drain asked. "What is your role in the case?"

"My role is, my fiancée died," Kramer said. "I became the guardian of her daughter." Purdue and the Sacklers "owe my stepdaughter," he said, "because they made the drugs that killed my fiancée."

"Okay, so, Mr. Kramer, the particular matter that is on the calendar first today is a motion to extend the debtors' time, which they have exclusively, to file a Chapter 11 plan," Drain said. "So, I guess I can understand your confusion, particularly given that you're not a lawyer, but this motion really doesn't directly relate to or address your or your daughter-in-law's claims in this case." Kramer had been speaking on behalf of his stepdaughter, not his daughter-in-law, but no matter; he would be afforded an opportunity to have his claim against Purdue reviewed at some later date, Drain said. Whatever he might want to say now was not calendared for the current hearing.

"Oh," Kramer said, in the apologetic tone of someone who has been put in his place. "Should I hang up then? Or should I stay on the line?"

"Whatever you want, sir," Drain said. "You don't have to stay on the line." Kramer volunteered that he would mute his line and "just listen to what you guys have to say."

The hearing proceeded, but before long, there was another interjec-tion. "Your honor? Excuse me," a woman said. She introduced herself as Kimberly Krawczyk, and said she would like to speak "in memory of my brother." Her voice constricted as she fended off a sob. She had sent the judge a letter, she said. "Would you like me to read the letter," she asked, or "just speak in his memory?"

"Well, ma'am, I…" Drain paused. For a long time, there was just silence on the line. "I have to say, ma'am…" He paused again. For more than a year, Drain had presided over the case, and periodically, he would pay lip service to the many victims of the opioid crisis, who existed somewhere outside the courtroom, like an abstraction. But now, when they broke into the proceedings asking to be heard, and he was confronted with the actual human beings whose suffering he had so frequently and casually invoked, he seemed unsettled, and eager to retreat back into the comforting obfuscations of the law. "I hold hearings on what is scheduled before me," Drain said. "There are literally hundreds of thousands of people who have lost dear family members because of opioids." Another pause. "I… um… I don't think that this is the proper forum to do this." Krawczyk tried to interject, but Drain kept going. The hurt and suffering of families like hers was "front and center in my mind," he assured her—and in the minds of the "lawyers and financial people," too. But "we simply can't turn these hearings into something that the law really doesn't contemplate," he concluded. "So I'm not going to let you speak further on this." He did not blame Krawczyk for thinking that she might have had an opportunity to speak, he said. "It's completely understandable. I'm not faulting you. You're not a lawyer."

"My apologies," she said. "At some point, I would like to speak. He was my last family member, and my entire family has been affected through this epidemic, and through Purdue Pharma's family. So I really would like to speak from the pain that it has created and me being left behind with no family."

✣ ✣ ✣

In the decades after they graduated from Columbia and went off to medical school, Richard Kapit and Richard Sackler would occasionally reconnect. Kapit became a psychiatrist and worked for many years at the FDA. He watched his old roommate's rise as the impresario behind OxyContin with great interest, even awe. He still found it amazing to consider that this person with whom he had once been so close had

gone on to launch a drug that transformed the pharmaceutical industry, made him a billionaire many times over, and triggered a crisis of
addiction and death. The thing about Richard that had always struck
Kapit was his enthusiasm. It was so bold, so infectious, yet ultimately
so reckless as well. That's how Kapit would always remember him, as
"this character that gets carried away," he said. "I followed him so often.
I got carried away following him. I guess the term is 'salesman,' but that
doesn't really capture it." He had a hubris, a blindness to consequences,
an unshakable certainty in his own convictions. If there was one attribute that Richard shared with his uncle Arthur—apart from a common
name, a genius at marketing, and a sense of unquenchable ambition—it
was the stubborn refusal to admit doubt, even in the face of contrary
evidence, and a corresponding ability to delude himself into a blink-
ered faith in his own virtue.

A few weeks after Purdue Pharma declared bankruptcy, Beverly
Sackler died. She was the last of the old generation, not counting Jillian
and Theresa, the much younger third wives of Arthur and Mortimer.
Before Raymond died, Beverly used to come to company functions in
Stamford and speak with employees. They found her warm and charming. She still wore the plain gold band from their wedding in 1944. She
and Raymond had so little money in those days, she would tell people,
it was all they could afford.

At a certain point during the bankruptcy proceedings, Richard
Sackler moved back in to his parents' home, the mansion on Field Point
Circle in Greenwich, looking out on the Long Island Sound. The place
was vast and lonely, mostly unchanged since the death of his parents.
Jonathan and his wife, Mary, lived nearby, but Jonathan was struggling
with cancer, and in the summer of 2020 he died, too. His obituaries
looked markedly different from those of his father and uncles. They led
with OxyContin and barely mentioned philanthropy at all.

Richard was mostly alone now. He remained close with his children, but because the bankruptcy proceedings were predicated on a
formal separation between Purdue and the family that owned it, one
of the great passions of his life—micromanaging the business—was
suddenly no longer available to him. He was bitter, and frustrated,
watching, like a benched athlete, as other pharma companies raced to
pioneer a cure for COVID, unable to marshal what was left of Purdue
in the effort, or even to make donations in support of such research,

because at this point nobody wanted his money. He had few friends left, apart from his many paid advisers. When he did talk to people about his struggles, he maintained that OxyContin was a safe product and insisted, all evidence to the contrary be damned, that it was "vanishingly rare" for people to become addicted to the drug when they took it in a doctor's care. The family continued to suggest that few had done as much as they had to *combat* the opioid crisis. One of Richard's lawyers described the 2010 reformulation of OxyContin as the "most ambitious and impactful" measure that Purdue and the Sacklers had taken in this regard. But in September 2020, the FDA released the results of a decade's worth of studies and, citing the tendency of people who were already addicted to OxyContin to switch to heroin and other drugs, held that the reformulation could not be said to have "reduced opioid overdoses" overall. The FDA stopped short of concluding, as other studies had, that the reformulation actually *caused* the heroin crisis. But having analyzed all of the available data, the agency said that it was "unclear" whether reformulated OxyContin had any "net public health benefit" whatsoever.

The day after the Department of Justice resolution was finalized, NYU Medical School, where Richard had received his degree, announced plans to strip the Sackler name from its Institute of Graduate Biomedical Sciences "and other named programs." Tufts was no longer an outlier in removing the name altogether, and the calculus was changing, practically in real time, at other institutions. A day after the NYU decision, the Metropolitan Museum of Art said that the name of the famous Sackler Wing, home of the Temple of Dendur and site of Nan Goldin's first protest, was now officially "under review." Three days after that, Harvard announced the formation of a committee on "renaming," noting that some of the family names that adorned the buildings on its campus were associated with behaviors that "many members of our community would today find abhorrent" and indicating that changes would be coming in due course.

Nan Goldin and her allies in PAIN, who had spent so much of the past year feeling hamstrung by the bankruptcy and the COVID pandemic, experienced a surge of energy and hope. They would redouble their efforts, at the universities, at the Guggenheim, and especially at the Met. They were determined to keep fighting until they saw the name come down.

✢ ✢ ✢

In the final weeks of 2020, a sudden prospect emerged of some form of reckoning for the Sacklers. The Committee on Oversight and Reform of the U.S. House of Representatives announced that it would hold a hearing on "The Role of Purdue Pharma and the Sackler Family in the Opioid Epidemic"—and extended an invitation to Richard, Kathe, Mortimer, and David Sackler to participate. If the Justice Department and a federal bankruptcy court were going to give the Sacklers a pass, perhaps Congress, at least, could hold them to account. This seemed to mark an opportunity, for the lawmakers, to revive the iconic moment in 1994 when the heads of the seven major tobacco companies were hauled in front of Congress and grilled about what they knew and when they knew it on the subject of the addictiveness of cigarettes.

Attorneys for the Sacklers waited a week after the invitation was issued, then sent a polite reply saying: Thank you for this opportunity; we are going to decline. Behind the scenes, members of the family's legal team lobbied furiously to get the committee to call off the hearing, or to have representatives from the company, rather than the family, do the talking, as they had always done in the past. But Caroline Maloney, the New York congresswoman who chaired the committee, sent a letter on December 8 indicating that if the family did not voluntarily accept her invitation, she would be forced to subpoena them.

Nine days later, the hearing was convened. The proceedings would be held remotely, due to the Coronavirus pandemic, and that morning, David Sackler, dressed in a dark suit and sitting in a featureless fluorescent space that looked like a borrowed office, raised his right hand and was sworn in. When the family realized that some of them would have no choice but to appear, they had negotiated, offering David and Kathe, along with Craig Landau from Purdue. Six decades earlier, when Senator Kefauver was holding his congressional hearings, Félix Martí-Ibáñez had claimed an infirmity in order to avoid testifying and Bill Frohlich had said he was inaccessible, somewhere in Germany. Now, according to one person familiar with the negotiations, attorneys for Mortimer Sackler said that he was unable to appear because he would be in "a remote part of Asia." Even when he was running Purdue, Richard Sackler had always preferred to let other people do his talking for him. Faced with the prospect of a brutal public inquiry—one which was likely to focus largely on his own conduct and remarks—he chose not to step up and account for himself, but to send his own son to speak on his behalf.

"I want to express my family's deep sadness about the opioid crisis," David began. He had shaved his beard and combed a schoolboy part in his hair, so, though he was forty now, he looked younger. "What you have heard from the press about the Sacklers is almost certainly wrong and highly distorted."

Prior to his testimony, the committee had invited a series of people to speak about the harrowing impact of OxyContin on their lives. A mother from California, Barbara Van Rooyan, spoke about losing her son, Patrick, after he took a single OxyContin pill and stopped breathing, in 2004. "The first year, I woke each morning wishing that I, too, were dead," she said. "Grief from the loss of a child is not a process. It is a lifelong weight upon one's soul. A weight for which I hold Purdue and the Sacklers responsible." Nan Goldin appeared, a copy of Barry Meier's book positioned prominently on the shelf behind her. "My addiction destroyed my relationships with my friends and family and almost ended my career," she said. "Now I try to speak for the half a million who no longer can."

This was probably quite a novel experience for David—to come face to face with individuals whose lives had been ruined by his family's drug, and be forced to listen to them. "I am deeply and profoundly sorry that OxyContin has played a role in any addiction and death," he said. "Though I believe the full record, which has not been publicly released yet, will show that the family and the board acted legally and ethically, I take a deep moral responsibility for it because I believe our product, OxyContin, despite our best intentions and best efforts, has been associated with abuse and addiction."

These talking points had been carefully engineered. The family would perform compassion, even sorrow—but not acknowledge wrongdoing. "I relied on Purdue's management to keep on top of medical science and ensure the company was complying with all laws," David said. With lawyerly syntax, he kept suggesting that OxyContin had been "associated" with addiction. But the representatives weren't buying it. "You are using the passive voice there, when you say it has been 'associated' with abuse," Jamie Raskin, of Maryland, observed. "Which implies somehow that you and your family were not aware of exactly what was taking place."

Clay Higgins, who prior to running for Congress had been a cop in Louisiana, pointed out that everyone "on the street" knew that Oxy-Contin was addictive. How could the *Sacklers* not have known? Another representative, Kelly Armstrong of North Dakota, remarked that at this point any notion of plausible deniability was difficult to credit. The family could have found evidence of the burgeoning national crisis "just by looking at your own balance sheet."

One after another, the representatives hammered David. "We don't agree on a lot on this committee in a bipartisan way," the ranking member, James Comer, of Kentucky, said. "But I think our opinion of Purdue Pharma and the actions of your family, I think we all agree, are sickening."

At times, David seemed comically out of touch, not just from the details of the opioid crisis but from the quotidian realities of American life. Asked if he had ever visited Appalachia and taken the measure of OxyContin's impact on the region, he replied that he *had* been there—not for any "fact finding" purposes, however, but on vacation, with Joss. At one point, the Illinois congressman Raja Krishnamoorthi put onto the screen a photo of the Los Angeles mansion that David and Joss had acquired in 2018. "This is your home in Bel Air, California, correct?"

"No," David said. "I've never even spent a night there."

To David, this must have seemed downright exonerating. It was a mere investment property, after all. But Krishnamoorthi was confused. Do you own the house? Or don't you?

"The trust for my benefit owns it," David clarified, adding, "As an investment property."

"Oh, the *trust* owns that," Krishnamoorthi said. Of course. The trust. "Yes, Mr. Sackler, the *trust* bought this. For $22 million in an all cash deal." A lot of Americans got addicted to OxyContin, Krishnamoorthi said. "I would submit, sir, that you and your family are addicted to money."

✢ ✢ ✢

When Kathe Sackler appeared, she looked old and drawn. Some of this may have been for show; during a recent deposition in the bankruptcy case, she had insisted on using a magnifying glass to read the documents that were placed in front of her. She began her prepared remarks with a surprising personal aside. "Nothing is more tragic than the loss of a child," she said. "While every family tragedy is unique, I do know how deeply it hurts. I lost my brother Robert to mental illness and suicide," she said. "I have learned from my own experience that our loved ones are not to blame for their mental illness or addiction."

This was a surprising turn. In all the years since 1975, the family had never spoken publicly of Bobby's death—or, for that matter, of his life. Yet now, Kathe chose to do so. One consideration for Kathe may have been that she had been informed, several weeks prior to her testimony, that the details of Bobby's death would soon be published in this book. In any case, whether this disclosure was a bid for sympathy or a genuine expression of compassion, it fell flat. In the rest of her testimony, Kathe employed the same evasive circumlocution that David had. It "distresses" her, she said, to think that OxyContin had become "associated" with so much human suffering.

Peter Welch, of Vermont, mentioned the Mexican drug kingpin Joaquín "El Chapo" Guzmán, who had recently been convicted in a New York federal court. "El Chapo got a life sentence, and he is going to forfeit $12 billion," Welch pointed out. "The Sackler family through Purdue has three felony convictions, but no one is going to jail, and it has its billions still."

"Excuse me," Kathe said, suddenly animated, even testy. "The *Sackler* family doesn't have a felony conviction. Purdue *Pharma* has a felony conviction. I am an individual person." The truth was, Kathe said, she was not very happy with the family business. "I'm angry that some people working at Purdue broke the law," she continued, acknowledging that this had happened more than once. "I'm angry about it from 2007 and I'm angry about it now, again, in 2020."

Maloney asked Kathe if she would apologize, not in some generic "I'm sorry you're upset" sort of way, but genuinely apologize, "for the role *you* played in the opioid crisis."

"I have struggled with that question," Kathe began. "I have tried to figure out: is there anything that I could have done differently, knowing what I knew then, not what I know now?" But on reflection, she concluded, "I can't. There is nothing that I can find that I would have done differently."

David had talked about his desire to "humanize" his family, but one problem for the Sacklers was that, unlike a lot of human beings, they didn't seem to learn from what they saw transpiring in the world around them. They could produce a rehearsed simulacrum of human empathy, but they seemed incapable of comprehending their own role in the story, and impervious to any genuine moral epiphany. They resented being cast as the villains in a drama, but it was their own stunted, stubborn blindness that made them so well suited to the role. They couldn't change.

There was something undeniably ritualistic about the hearing that morning. If the community could not hold the family accountable, it would subject them to a ceremonial shaming. It likely seemed, to Kathe and David, that the whole exercise was theater: that the lawmakers were performing outrage, just as they had performed compassion. But the proceeding was also, in some fundamental way, an expression of democracy: OxyContin had visited destruction on so many communities, and now, the representatives of those communities had gathered to give voice, like some awful Greek chorus, to all of their collective indignation.

One member of the panel was Jim Cooper, a veteran congressman from Tennessee, a state that had been ravaged by the drug. He had a courtly demeanor and spoke slowly, selecting his words with a careful, professorial cadence. On the subject of the family's implacable refusal to recognize what they had done, Cooper said, "I think Upton Sinclair once wrote that a man has difficulty understanding something if his salary depends on his not understanding." He continued, his voice soft and deliberate, "Watching you testify makes my blood boil. I'm not sure that I'm aware of any family in America that's more evil than yours."

✣ ✣ ✣

The 2020 pandemic and the attendant economic collapse only intensified the opioid crisis as social isolation and economic stress caused people to relapse, and overdose fatality rates spiked in many parts of the country. Not long after David and Joss fled New York, Mortimer and Jacqueline quietly sold their East Seventy-Fifth Street town house, in an off-market transaction, for $38 million. They were rumored to be moving to London, a city long favored by oligarchs with unsavory fortunes, which might offer them a more congenial base of operations.

Maura Healey made a point of speaking, on a regular basis, with families who had lost loved ones to opioids. They often felt a tremendous sense of indignation, but what they wanted, many of them told her, was not money but truth. In a filing with the bankruptcy court, the states had estimated the total cost of the crisis to be more than $2 trillion. "What we're trying to do is tell the story, so there's a reckoning," Healey said. To gather evidence and tell the story—the true story, the whole story, the story that had for so long been suppressed—had a value of its own. "We will never be able to collect enough money to account for the damage of this crisis perpetrated by members of the family," Healey pointed out. No amount of money would be enough. But at the same time, she continued, there was no sum the Sacklers could spend to erase the history of what they had done. Nearly a century earlier, during the height of the Depression, Isaac Sackler told his three sons that if you lose a fortune, you can always earn another, but if you lose your good name, you can never recover it. Sounding very much like Isaac Sackler, Maura Healey concluded, "They can't buy their reputations back."

One odd feature of the DOJ resolution was that it endorsed the Sacklers' bid to turn Purdue into a so-called public-benefit corporation, which would continue to sell opioids but distribute the proceeds to the states so they could fight the opioid crisis. None of the public commentary made note of it, but there was irony in the Sacklers proposing that Purdue be turned into a charitable trust. Back in the 1940s, on a snowy street corner in New York, Arthur, Mortimer, and Raymond had made a pact with their best friend, Bill Frohlich. They would work together so closely it would be difficult to say where one man's interests ended and another's began. They would share their businesses and support one another so that the whole enterprise became greater than the sum of its parts, and when the last man died, he would turn all of their assets into a charitable trust.

To Richard Leather, the attorney who formalized that agreement nearly six decades earlier, it was infuriating to watch the family hold out the promise of such an arrangement as a carrot to fend off litigation. "This agreement was not designed to make Richard Sackler rich," Leather said. "It was designed to achieve a gift to humanity. To benefit the public."

In 1947, when Richard Sackler was still a toddler, his father and his uncles incorporated one of their first family foundations "in memory of Isaac Sackler as a tribute by his sons to a man whose love knew no ends and whose interests and vision were limitless." Their aim was to "advance the ideals he cherished," the brothers wrote, and "to help alleviate man's suffering."

AFTERWORD

ONE AFTERNOON AS I was writing this book, in the summer of 2020, I left the house with my wife and children to run an errand. We were getting into our car when a neighbor from a few houses away approached. "I don't want to freak you out," she said. "But there's a guy in an SUV up the street who has been sitting there all day, and I think he's been watching your house."

I live in the suburbs outside New York City, on a sleepy residential street where there's not much reason for random cars to park. So this was unnerving. We thanked the neighbor, piled into our car, then drove up the street, directly past the SUV, and saw a heavyset man of about fifty behind the wheel. As we passed, he grew suddenly absorbed with his phone. We drove off but then made a loop and doubled back, thinking we could surprise him. He must have gotten out of his car as soon as we left, because this time when we approached, the man was standing by the rear bumper, stretching. He was wearing flip-flops. We took his photo.

This was an upsetting encounter for my sons, who are in elementary school, but we tried to make the most of it. We bought binoculars, and they stood vigil at the window to see if he would return. We never saw the man again, though he did come back on at least one other occasion: a different neighbor, who had also noticed him the first time, told us that the man had spent another day watching the house. He was driving a different car this time, a sedan. But it was definitely the same man. There was a tree that he seemed to like to park under, which afforded shade from the sun. In August, a fierce tropical storm hit New York, with winds of seventy miles an hour. We ended up losing power. After the rain stopped, I ventured outside with my boys, carefully avoiding the downed power lines. We walked up the street and saw that the shade tree had been completely uprooted by the storm. I hoped the man would come back now, see that his tree had been violently ripped out of the ground, and wonder whether some higher power wasn't trying to tell him something. But if he did return, we didn't see him.

Of course when this visitor initially appeared, the first thing I thought of was Nan Goldin and the private investigator who had staked out her home in Brooklyn and trailed her fellow activist Megan Kapler. She had no definitive evidence that this man had been hired by the Sacklers. These things are difficult to prove. Private investigators are generally sub-subcontractors, hired by intermediaries, like law firms or crisis management specialists, in part for the purposes of deniability. Often, the investigator himself doesn't know who his ultimate client is. But it seemed like more than a coincidence that Goldin, Kapler, and I had all had the same experience. When I asked Purdue Pharma about this surveillance, the company emphatically denied having any knowledge of it. When I posed the same question to the Sacklers, a family representative made no similar denial, and instead declined to comment. At the time of these visits, I was living in quarantine, due to COVID. I wondered what an investigator could possibly hope to learn from surveilling a writer who never leaves the house. Then it occurred to me that the purpose was almost certainly not to learn anything but to intimidate.

When I started working on this project, in 2016, I came to it indirectly. For several years, I had been writing about the illicit drug trade between Mexico and the United States. In particular, I'd been trying to understand the Mexican drug cartels not just as criminal organizations but as businesses. I wrote a long article that was a sort of business school case study of a drug syndicate, exploring the ways in which the Sinaloa cartel was a dark mirror of a legal commodities enterprise. One thing I noticed, in this research, was a new emphasis, among the cartels, on heroin. That led me to OxyContin. The cartels had been reviled, rightly, for their willingness to sell an addictive product and destroy lives. But I was astonished to discover that the family that presided over the company that made OxyContin was a prominent philanthropic dynasty with what appeared to be an unimpeachable reputation. I read *Dreamland*, by Sam Quinones, then *Pain Killer*, by Barry Meier, and the investigative reporting on Purdue in the *Los Angeles Times*. I was familiar with the Sackler name. It was synonymous, in my mind, with philanthropy. Until reading up on the opioid crisis, I had known nothing of the family's business activities.

I spent the better part of the next year researching and writing the article that was published in *The New Yorker* in 2017. As I learned the fascinating history of the original three brothers and came to understand how Purdue, under Richard Sackler's leadership, marketed Oxy-Contin, I was struck by the echoes of Arthur Sackler's career in all that came later. The family had never spoken publicly at that point about its role in the opioid crisis. I wondered what they would say. But my efforts to secure interviews with the Sacklers were met with frosty silence.

As a journalist, most stories you write don't make a ripple. They chronicle reality, but only rarely change it. The *New Yorker* article did make a difference, in ways that I had not anticipated. I received hundreds of notes from readers who had discovered the Sackler story because they, or someone they knew, had struggled with opioids. Nan Goldin was one of the people I heard from, and I watched, from a distance, as she created a movement.

At the time, I didn't think it would be possible to write a book about the Sacklers, because the family was so secretive, and Purdue, as a privately held company, remained impenetrable. But I started to hear from people who had worked at Purdue, or known the Sacklers, and who wanted to tell their stories. And in January 2019, Maura Healey unveiled her complaint in the Massachusetts case, which was full of the family's private correspondence.

✤ ✤ ✤

There are many good books about the opioid crisis. My intention was to tell a different kind of story, however, a saga about three generations of a family dynasty and the ways in which it changed the world, a story about ambition, philanthropy, crime and impunity, the corruption of institutions, power, and greed. As such, there are aspects of the public health crisis that this book gives scant attention to, from the science of addiction to the best strategies for treatment and abatement to the struggles of people living with an opioid use disorder. The issue of pain and appropriate pain management is enormously complex, and while this book is highly critical of the mass marketing of opioids for moderate pain, it does not explore at any length the harder question, which is currently a matter of heated debate, about the long-term therapeutic value of opioids for severe chronic pain. I have heard from many readers who suffer from chronic pain and worry that my investigative reporting on the misdeeds of Purdue might jeopardize their access to appropriate medication, by stigmatizing opioids and the patients who rely on these drugs to live their lives. I have no desire to contribute to the very real stigmatization of people who take OxyContin and other opioids, whether they do so legally or illegally. Having said that, as I hope this book demonstrates, Purdue Pharma and the Sackler family have for decades invoked the interests of pain patients as a fig leaf for their own avarice, and I think it would be a mistake to give them a pass, on those grounds, today.

As I make clear throughout the book, OxyContin was hardly the only opioid to be fraudulently marketed or widely abused, and my choice to focus on Purdue is in no way a suggestion that other pharmaceutical companies do not deserve a great deal of blame for the crisis. The same could be said for the FDA, the doctors who wrote prescriptions, the wholesalers that distributed the opioids, and the pharmacies that filled the prescriptions. There's plenty of blame to go around. I do share the view, however, of many doctors, public officials, prosecutors, and scholars that Purdue played a special role, as a pioneer.

All three branches of the Sackler family were unenthusiastic about the prospect of this book. Arthur's widow and children declined repeated requests to speak with me, as did the Mortimer wing of the family. The Raymond wing opted for a more actively antagonistic role, hiring an attorney, Tom Clare, who has a boutique law firm, based in Virginia, that specializes in threatening journalists in an effort to "kill" stories before they are published. Clare's opening salvo, which arrived before I had even started writing, in the summer of 2019, was a fifteen-page, single-spaced letter to *The New Yorker* accusing me of "pervasive bias" against his clients and demanding a series of corrections to the article I had published nearly two years earlier. The opioid crisis is driven by "illicit fentanyl smuggled into the United States from China and Mexico," Clare insisted. *The New Yorker* engaged a fact-checker to recheck the article, in response to Clare's critique. But this review turned up no factual errors, and the magazine did not change a word. Next, Clare wrote to me directly to say that the Sacklers were considering "potential litigation" and to formally instruct me not to destroy any "evidence" in anticipation of such a lawsuit. It was a measure of Clare's moxie that he marked all of these letters **"Confidential, Off-the-Record, Not for Publication or Attribution,"** even though anyone with even a passing knowledge of how journalism works would know that he would need my agreement for such a condition, and that unilateral pronouncements are meaningless, even in bold type.

Over the next eighteen months, Clare sent several dozen letters and emails to *The New Yorker* and to Doubleday, the publisher of this book. As I studied the way Arthur Sackler used his powerful lawyer Clark Clifford to manage the Kefauver commission, and how the family consigliere Howard Udell tried to manage *The New York Times,* and how Purdue and the Sacklers used Mary Jo White to undermine one federal investigation in 2007 and then another in 2020, I was struck by the continuities in the family's tactics. I'm married to a lawyer. Many of my close friends are lawyers. I went to law school myself. But I marveled (naively, you might say) at the mercenary willingness of a certain breed of ostensibly respectable attorney to play handmaiden to shady tycoons. At one point Joanna Lydgate, the deputy attorney general in Massachusetts, invoked an adage she first heard from a professor in law school: "Everyone is entitled to a lawyer, but it doesn't have to be you."

After NYU announced its decision to remove the Sackler name, following Purdue's guilty plea in the autumn of 2020, one of the family lawyers, Daniel Connolly, said, "As soon as Purdue documents are released they will show the company's history and that members of the Sackler family who served on the board of directors always acted ethically and lawfully." This struck me as an odd posture to take. The documents that had emerged so far looked so bad for the Sacklers; if the family had *other* documents that were exculpatory and told a different story, why wait? I wrote to Tom Clare, telling him that I would love to see those documents, in order to incorporate them into this book. He replied that because his clients did not believe I would "engage responsibly" with such evidence, they did not want to grant me "preferred access to new materials."

One theme that struck me as I interviewed dozens of former Purdue employees—sales reps, doctors, scientists, executives—was a fog of collective denial. There were stories that the company (and the Sacklers) told, back in the early days of OxyContin, about how it was only people who abused the drug that became addicted, and it was only a handful of errant sales reps who mis-marketed it, and the company was driven only by a selfless desire to help people suffering from pain. Those stories, like the stories that Arthur had told about the drugs he marketed, became unsustainable when you took a hard look at the facts. Yet many at Purdue appear to have gone on believing them, persisting, for decades, in a state of denial. "We were complicit. For monetary reasons," Nicholas Primpas, who worked as a regional account manager for Purdue from 1987 to 2005, told me. "We were slow to catch on. And that might have been greed." But many former employees, whether they loved the Sacklers or hated them, were reluctant to concede even that much.

There is a notable absence of whistleblowers in the OxyContin story. This may be due to the fact that when people did attempt to blow the whistle, Purdue did its best to crush them, as company lawyers did to Karen White, the Florida saleswoman who lost her lawsuit against Purdue in 2005. But I came to believe that it was also a function of denial. I would spend hours talking with intelligent people who had worked at the company, and they could acknowledge all sorts of infirmities in the corporate culture and make astute observations about the personalities involved, but when it came to OxyContin's role in the opioid crisis, they would do their best to explain it away. Even in the face of voluminous evidence, of guilty pleas to felony charges, of thousands of lawsuits, of study after study, of so many dead, they retreated to the old truths, about abuse versus addiction, about heroin and fentanyl. I wondered if, for some of these people, it was just too demoralizing to take a sober measure of their own complicity, if it was simply too much for the human conscience to bear.

✢ ✢ ✢

One day I drove out to the village of Amagansett, close to the tip of Long Island, to meet a man I'll call Jeff. We met at a restaurant, and he told me about his struggles with addiction. A decade earlier, when he was a teenager, he had started abusing opioids. They were "everywhere," he recalled. He particularly liked OxyContin for the clean high that it provided. After sucking the pill's red coating off, he would crush the rest with the edge of a cigarette lighter, then snort it. He didn't inject. "When I was growing up, I always told myself, 'I'll never stick a needle in my arm,'" he said.

In a soft, unflinching tone, Jeff recounted the next decade of his life: he kept abusing painkillers, met a woman, fell in love, and introduced her to opioids. One day, his dealer was out of pills and said, "I'll sell you a bag of heroin for twenty bucks." Jeff was reluctant, but then withdrawal set in, and he acquiesced. At first, he and his girlfriend snorted heroin. "But you build up a tolerance, just like with the pills," he said, and eventually they started injecting it. They were high when they got married. Jeff's wife gave birth to a baby boy who was born with an opioid dependency. "The doctors weaned him off with droplets of morphine," Jeff said.

After a long stretch in rehab, Jeff had gotten sober and stayed that way for more than a year. His baby was healthy, and his wife was sober, too. Looking back, Jeff said, he felt that an impulsive youthful decision to snort pills had set him on a path from which he could not deviate. "It was all about the drug," he said. "I just created a hurricane of destruction."

We paid for our lunch and walked out of the restaurant and strolled along a leafy side street that was flanked by grand houses. Amagansett is a summer colony for many wealthy New York families. During the worst years of Jeff's addiction, he had worked as a tradesman in the area. I'd asked him to show me a particular property he had serviced, and on a quiet road we stopped by the entrance to an immense estate that was mostly hidden behind dense shrubbery. It was the summerhouse of Mortimer and Jacqueline Sackler. Jeff had known, even when he was working for them, about the family business. The irony was not lost on him. The Sacklers had always seemed insulated by the fact that the destruction caused by their drug wasn't happening in their own backyard. Yet there was Jeff, literally in their backyard. "I couldn't tell you how many times I was on that property, sitting in a work truck, snorting a pill," he said.

We reached an ornamental wooden gate, beyond which was a yard dominated by a stately weeping willow. As I was admiring the tree, Jeff said that for the people who maintained the grounds, it was "a pain in the ass." Whenever the wind picks up, he explained, branches break and scatter all over the lawn. "But the place has to be flawless," he said. "There can't be a leaf on the ground." So a crew would sweep through regularly, to clear away the mess.

ACKNOWLEDGMENTS

My first thanks go to all those who so generously gave their time to speak with me over the past two years and who trusted me to tell their stories. There are too many to thank by name, and some I cannot name at all. But you know who you are. Thank you. Thanks also to the staffs of the archives I consulted, all of which are listed in the notes. Thanks to the International Consortium of Investigative Journalists, for granting me access to a trove of leaked banking information, which included details about the Sacklers' accounts. Thanks to Katie Townsend and her colleagues at the Reporters Committee for Freedom of the Press, who intervened in the bankruptcy case to unseal filings containing some very revealing evidence.

This book started as an article in *The New Yorker,* and I'm deeply indebted, as ever, to my longtime editor Daniel Zalewski, who has taught me so much of what I know about how to tell a story. Thanks to E. Tammy Kim and Nicolas Niarchos, who checked the original piece, to Peter Canby, who oversaw the checking (and rechecking), and to Fabio Bertoni. Thanks also to David Remnick, for making so many hard things look so easy, and for managing to be a great boss on top of everything else, as well as to Dorothy Wickenden, Henry Finder, Pam McCarthy, Deirdre Foley-Mendelssohn, Mike Luo, David Rohde, Linnea Feldman Emison, Sean Lavery, Alexander Barasch, Ave Carrillo, Natalie Raabe, and all of my other colleagues at the magazine. Thanks to my friend Philip Montgomery, whose searing photo essay "Faces of an Epidemic" ran alongside my piece in *The New Yorker.*

I feel extraordinarily lucky to be publishing another book with Bill Thomas at Doubleday, who took a chance and signed me up to write *The Snakehead* back in 2006. Bill understood what this book should be from our first conversations about it and has been a steadfast ally and a deeply perceptive interlocutor at every step along the way. A huge thanks to Daniel Novack, my tireless lawyer at Doubleday, who some-how manages to be neurotically punctilious and unflappably laid-back at the same time. Thanks also to the wonderful Michael Goldsmith, and to Todd Doughty, Anke Steinecke, Maria Massey, Ingrid Sterner, Lydia Buechler, Kathy Hourigan, Khari Dawkins, John Fontana, and everyone else at Doubleday. Thea Traff helped with the photos. Oliver Munday designed the beautiful cover. Kimon de Greef wrangled the endnotes on a brutal deadline. Julie Tate fact-checked the book, with incredible attention, care, and good cheer. Any errors that remain are entirely my own.

I owe more to Tina Bennett, my agent of almost twenty years, than I can say. At WME, I'm grateful to Tracy Fisher, Svetlana Katz, Matilda Forbes Watson, Eric Simonoff, Ben Davis, Anna DeRoy, and Chris-tina Lee. I'm grateful also to Ravi Mirchandani and his colleagues at Picador.

Thanks, for various reasons, to Rachel Aviv, Joel Lovell, Raffi Khatchadourian, Andrew Marantz, Henry Molofsky, David Grann, Tyler Foggatt, Micah Hauser, Victoria Beale, Phil Keefe, Jim Keefe, Laura Poitras, Daniel Gorman, Sravya Tadepalli, Sam Rosen, David De Jong, Naomi Fry, Nick Paumgarten, Bart Gellman, Tim Weiner, Paul DeMarco, Jennifer Kinsley, Paulina Rodríguez, Peter Smith, Pauline Peek, Scott Podolsky, David Juurlink, Andrew Kolodny, Ed Bisch, David Fein, David Segal, Larissa MacFarquhar, Jillian Fenni-more, Evan Hughes, Lily Bullitt, Ed Conlon, Mark Rosenberg, Oriana Hawley, Mark Bomback, Andy Galker, Jason Burns, Dave Park, Noah Harpster, Micah Fitzerman-Blue, Will Hettinger, Eric Newman, Alex Gibney, Svetlana Zill, John Jordan, Jed Lipinski, Mike Quinn, Sarah Margon, Sarah Stillman, Ed Caesar, Sheelah Kolhatkar, Ben Taub, Gideon Lewis-Kraus, Sai Sriskandarajah, and "the Michaels," as my kids call them: Michael Wahid Hanna and Michael Shtender-Auerbach. A big special thanks, also, to Alex Godoy.

Writing this book, I thought a lot about family—what holds a family together or tears it apart, what it means to carry a family name—and the experience left me feeling deeply fortunate to have been born into the one that I was. Thanks to my parents, Jennifer Radden and Frank Keefe, for their endless support and their enduring example, and to my in-laws, Tadeusz and Ewa. A particular thanks to my sister, Beatrice, and my brother, Tristram. Even as we live far-flung lives with our own careers and families, I am who I am today because of the childhood we shared, and I love and admire you both, and your families, beyond measure. This book is dedicated to you.

I wrote the manuscript during COVID, on lockdown with my wife, Justyna, and our sons, Lucian and Felix. It's strange to say, but I learned something about adaptability by watching my children recalibrate, in real time, to the catastrophe unfolding around them. We were fortunate, all things considered, and the small ways in which the pandemic tested us are not worth mentioning, in light of what others experienced. But I was inspired by the resilience of my children. It gave me hope at a time when I needed it.

Justyna has informed me that this acknowledgment had "better be good," and that's a decent example, actually, of what I love about her— her unsentimental wit, her total allegiance on the big things, combined with vocal skepticism on all the little ones. To get to share a laugh and a glass of wine and a life and two children with Justyna is all I could ever hope for. It still feels like a coup.

A NOTE ON SOURCES

The Sackler family did not cooperate with my efforts to research this book. None of the Sacklers who feature prominently agreed to grant interviews. Tom Clare, the attorney, responded to my repeated requests for interviews with Richard and David Sackler by writing, "until Mr. Keefe acknowledges (and corrects) the errors in his prior reporting for *The New Yorker* . . . we have no reason to believe Mr. Keefe will give my clients a fair shake in any interview." Apart from generally disputing the very premise of the article, and offering their standard inventory of unpersuasive rebuttals, the Sacklers seemed most exercised about the business involving the pediatric indication for Oxy-Contin, and were demanding that I append a correction to the article asserting, erroneously, that they had not voluntarily sought the pediatric indication but had taken the step only because the FDA compelled them to do so. Much as I would have liked to speak directly with Clare's clients, this was not a condition that I was prepared to meet.

Instead, Clare proposed a meeting with the family's lawyers and PR handlers, at which I would notify them in detail of what I intended to write in the book, and they could tell me more about the alleged errors in my past reporting. I was certainly prepared to hear them out, but Clare's position seemed to shift over time, and my publisher's offers to arrange a meeting went ignored for months. In one email to me, Clare wrote that the Sacklers had been "forced," by my refusal to make changes to *The New Yorker* article, to deal with me "in this manner (in writing and through lawyers)."

As I was completing the book, I sent a list of detailed queries to the Raymond and Mortimer wings of the family. Clare had been adamant that his clients would need ample time to respond to any fact checking inquiries. So I gave them a month.

Just prior to the deadline, Clare arranged a briefing of Doubleday's in-house lawyer, who was responsible for vetting the manuscript, by an attorney for the family and PR representatives for both the Raymond and Mortimer wings. None of these spokespeople would consent to be quoted by name, but they delivered a PowerPoint presentation, in which they claimed that OxyContin only ever represented a tiny fraction of the market for opioids, that it is exceedingly rare for people who take OxyContin as prescribed by doctors to become addicted, and that the Sackler board members played no meaningful role in the management of their company.

One of my sources, who worked as a senior executive at Purdue, once told me that part of the problem for the company was its relationship with the FDA. "The FDA for many years didn't accept that it, too, had missed things," the executive said. When it came to Purdue's opioids, the agency had a long and negligent history of permissiveness. But the attitude in Stamford, the executive continued, was that so long as the company had the FDA's blessing, then its behavior must be okay. Over the years, that dynamic "gave too much comfort to Purdue." In their presentation, the Sackler representatives returned again and again to the FDA. To rebut the charge that Michael Friedman and Paul Goldenheim lied to Congress when they said, in testimony, that there had been no substantial abuse of MS Contin, the representatives pointed to a statement in 2002 by an FDA official saying much the same thing. But there is no reason to think that the FDA would know better than the company itself to what extent the company's drug was being abused, and it seems entirely likely that when he testified in 2002, the FDA official was relying on the earlier sworn testimony of Purdue's own executives. Nor could the Sacklers' handlers, or a representative for Purdue, explain the internal company emails suggesting that the drug had indeed been widely abused, and that the company had received reports of that abuse "all the time, and from everywhere." Similarly, the family lawyer asserted in his briefing for Doubleday that OxyContin is consistently effective on a 12-hour dosing cycle—notwithstanding the abundant evidence to the contrary—because the FDA continues to sign off on the Purdue labelling that says it is.

On the day that the answers to my fact checking inquiries were due, Clare announced that the two wings of the family were working together on their responses—but that they would need more time. At this point, I was bracing for a voluminous reply, and ready to incorporate the family's comments and denials into the body of the book. But when Clare sent their formal response, five days later, it was just a page and a half long. Noting that I had still "not corrected errors from your first piece about the Sackler family," the statement alleged that my fact checking queries had been "replete with erroneous assertions built on false premises about: the Sackler family's business dealings, political affiliations, homes, studies, conduct during board meetings (including false assertions of improper use of medicine)"—this appeared to be a specific denial of the incident in which Richard Sackler was said to have popped an OxyContin pill in front of colleagues, though as the story had been related to me, it was not a board meeting—"and board memberships, involvement in medicine development, emails clearly meant in jest or involving people who had never worked at Purdue, claims about OxyContin's potency and other errata." In fact, the "multitude of errors" left them with "no reassurance that the book as a whole will in any way accurately present the facts," and as such, the family had decided to boycott the fact checking process altogether, and offer no denials to the many specific allegations I had presented. I had sent over a hundred queries, relating to both wings of the family, and to the business. I'd given them plenty of time. But in the end they chose not to respond.

Nevertheless, this account is substantially built on the family's own words. Because Purdue, and to a lesser extent the Sacklers themselves, have been involved in litigation for decades, the most significant source for this book is tens of thousands of pages of court documents: depositions, affidavits, briefs, complaints, court transcripts, and hundreds of emails, memos, and other confidential materials that have been produced in discovery. All of this material is cited in the notes. A prosecution memo or a legal complaint is by its nature an accusatory document, but rather than accept the charges of state and federal authorities at face value, I have depended instead on the evidence that they have unearthed, and used that evidence to tell my own story. In a number of places, my interpretation of the evidence differed from that of state attorneys general, just as it differed, quite considerably, from the interpretation set forth in the various defenses offered up by Purdue and the Sacklers.

When I quote emails or letters, they are referenced in a number of ways, which for clarity and transparency I want to spell out here.

In some instances, I am citing a communication that I possess in its entirety, because it has been produced in discovery or leaked to me. Other times, I quote documents that I do not possess but that are referenced in legal filings; in such cases, I cite to the original document, to the extent that it is identified, and then add, "quoted in the Massachusetts Complaint" or the like, to make clear that I am relying on a characterization in court papers and do not have the underlying document myself.

This is a work of narrative nonfiction: no details are invented or imagined; in instances in which I attribute thoughts or feelings to people, it is because they have described them to me or to someone else, or I am relying on a characterization by someone who knew them. I have employed pseudonyms in two instances: for Howard Udell's legal secretary, whom I am calling Martha West, and for the man in the afterword whom I call Jeff. In putting the book together, I was grateful for the groundbreaking work of scholars and journalists who have explored different aspects of this story, particularly John Lear, Scott Podolsky, David Herzberg, Andrea Tone, Richard Harris, Adam Tanner, Barry Meier, Sam Quinones, David Armstrong, Christopher Glazek, Beth Macy, Chris McGreal, Bethany McLean, Gerald Posner, and the reporting team at the *Los Angeles Times:* Lisa Girion, Scott Glover, and Harriet Ryan.

I conducted interviews with more than two hundred people, many of whom have worked for the Sacklers, at Purdue or in some other capacity; have known the family socially; or have investigated them. A great many of these interviews were on the record. There were numerous sources, however, who for one reason or another would speak only on the condition that I not use their names. On-the-record sources are cited in the endnotes; in instances in which I have relied upon an anonymous source, there is no note. The book is comprehensively endnoted, so if you encounter a quotation or assertion in the text and do not find a corresponding note in the back of the book, that means it comes from an unnamed source. Dozens of sources were interviewed multiple times over a two-year period, and I vetted their recollections—crosschecking with other sources, seeking out documentary corroboration, testing people's memories. In addition, the book has been independently fact-checked, and the checker knew the actual identity of each source and checked each quotation and assertion against interview transcripts and in many cases conducted additional interviews with those unnamed sources for checking purposes.

In book 1, I relied heavily on a memoir that Marietta Lutze privately published in 1997. Only 225 copies were printed; I bought one online. Lutze had a strong point of view, and I sought to corroborate her account through interviews with people who knew Arthur and his family at the time. I also relied on a biography of Arthur M. Sackler, written by a devoted protégé and published in 2012 by the AMS Foundation for the Arts, Sciences, and Humanities. It casts Arthur as a hero of almost mythical proportions, but it was nevertheless very helpful. Arthur's columns in the *Medical Tribune*, which I consulted at the College of Physicians in Philadelphia, furnished additional detail and a sense of Arthur's voice. The Sackler brothers were far too secretive to have left their letters to any archive, but many of their friends did just that, so I was able to gather letters and artifacts from the donated papers of their associates and confidants. I consulted a dozen archives, which are indicated in the notes, but special mention goes to the Félix Martí-Ibáñez Papers at Yale, which were essential in understanding the Sackler brothers and Bill Frohlich and getting a feel for the texture of their life in the 1960s.

The National Archives has a vast repository of files from the Kefauver investigation—some forty boxes in total, a number of which, unless I am mistaken, I was the first researcher to consult. A huge amount of new information about Arthur and his brothers is drawn from the files of that investigation. The voluminous records associated with the battle over Arthur's estate, which I combed through at a courthouse on Long Island, included depositions with family members, minutes of family meetings, and other documents that were full of vivid details.

In writing book 2, I was lucky to connect with Richard Kapit, Richard Sackler's college roommate, and with two friends from Roslyn, one of whom shared with me the letters Sackler wrote in college. I also interviewed dozens of former Purdue employees who worked at the company in every decade since the 1960s. Court documents were critical: two depositions by Richard Sackler, totaling nearly eight hundred pages of testimony; the deposition by Kathe Sackler; a dozen depositions from other Purdue employees; and reams of internal emails and other files. Some of these documents came out through court proceedings; others were leaked to me by people who thought that they should be made public.

One evening as I was in the late stages of writing this book, I received an envelope in my mailbox at home. It had no return address, just a thumb drive and a slip of paper with a quotation from *The Great Gatsby:* "They were careless people ... they smashed up things and creatures and then retreated back into their money or their vast carelessness or whatever it was that kept them together, and let other people clean up the mess." The thumb drive contained thousands of pages of depositions, law enforcement files, and internal records that had been produced in a number of lawsuits against Purdue. I had also sued the FDA, under the Freedom of Information Act, forcing the agency to produce thousands of pages of its own internal records. This was not as fruitful as I might have hoped—the agency informed me that Curtis Wright's emails could "not be located" (!)—but nevertheless shed light on the FDA's approval of OxyContin.

The Department of Justice prosecution memo prepared by Rick Mountcastle in the Western District of Virginia was a crucial source. My hope is that one day this document will be made public in its entirety. I would publish the whole thing myself, but there were conditions placed upon me by the person who shared it, which prevent me from doing so, at least for now. In an email to me, an attorney for Paul Goldenheim claimed that Goldenheim did not lie in his congressional testimony about OxyContin and that everything he said was "not misleading, verifiably accurate, and truthful." I found this claim decidedly unpersuasive, for reasons I detail in the notes. (I also made extensive efforts to contact Michael Friedman, but without success.)

For book 3, I relied on many interviews with people who have worked at Purdue or known the Sacklers in some other capacity. I found, in my reporting, that there is a category of employee who might have seemed almost invisible to the family—from doormen and housekeepers to yoga instructors and administrative assistants—but who often possess a unique, and surprisingly intimate, vantage point on their employers. I was also able to obtain numerous private emails from some family members that have not been made public through litigation but were shared with me. In the bankruptcy proceeding, a forty-eight-page log of a private WhatsApp chat among the heirs of Mortimer Sackler provided a fascinating window into the way in which some family members strategized about how to respond to my reporting in *The New Yorker* and to the wider controversy that soon engulfed them.

As a reporter, I put a lot of stock in documents—in the idea that a stack of paper can be more valuable, sometimes, than an interview. But this was the first project I've ever undertaken in which there were really *too many* documents. I felt like the prosecutors in Abingdon, Virginia, when they were putting together their case against Purdue: overwhelmed by paper. Even so, what I was able to access is a small fraction of what will eventually come out. It appears that the bankruptcy in White Plains will result in a repository of Purdue documents that could run to the tens of millions of pages. If that is the case, then this book will hardly be the last word on these people and events. But my hope is that it can provide a road map for future reporters and researchers to delve through the much larger corpus of documents that will eventually be unsealed, and inspire them to bring the whole truth of this important story to light.

NOTES

PROLOGUE: THE TAPROOT
1 $1 billion in annual revenue: "Debevoise & Plimpton Posts Record Revenue, Profits," Yahoo Finance, March 12, 2019.
1 Mary Jo White entered the building: Unless otherwise noted, the account of Kathe Sackler's deposition is derived from two people who were in the room that day and from the transcript of Kathe Sackler Deposition, *In re National Prescription Opiate Litigation*, MDL No. 2804, Case No. 1:17-MD-2804, April 1, 2019 (hereafter cited as Kathe Sackler Deposition).
1 White sometimes joked: "Interview with Mary Jo White," *Corporate Crime Reporter*, Dec. 12, 2005.
2 She represented the big dogs: Mary Jo White Executive Branch Personnel Public Financial Disclosure Report, Feb. 7, 2013.
2 "Do the right thing": "Street Cop," *New Yorker*, Nov. 3, 2013.
2 White's clients were "arrogant assholes": "A Veteran New York Litigator Is Taking On Opioids. They Have a History," STAT, Oct. 10, 2017.
3 one of the twenty wealthiest families: "The OxyContin Clan," *Forbes*, July 1, 2015.
3 likened the family to the Medicis: "Convictions of the Collector," *Washington Post*, Sept. 21, 1986.
4 difficult to connect the family name: Thomas Hoving, *Making the Mummies Dance: Inside the Metropolitan Museum of Art* (New York: Simon & Schuster, 1993), 93.
4 biggest blockbusters in pharmaceutical history: "OxyContin Goes Global," *Los Angeles Times*, Dec. 18, 2016.
4 The numbers were staggering: "Understanding the Epidemic," CDC website.
5 Mary Jo White sometimes observed: Mary Jo White Oral History, ABA Women Trailblazers Project, Feb. 8 and March 1, 2013, July 7, 2015.
5 Company executives were hauled before Congress: "Cigarette Makers and States Draft a $206 Billion Deal," *New York Times*, Nov. 14, 1998.
5 "the taproot of the opioid epidemic": First Amended Complaint, *State of New York v. Purdue Pharma LP et al.*, Index No.: 400016/2018, March 28, 2019 (hereafter cited as New York Complaint).
5 "a single family made the choices": First Amended Complaint, *Commonwealth of Massachusetts v. Purdue Pharma LP et al.*, C.A. No. 1884-cv-01808 (BLS2), Jan. 31, 2019 (hereafter cited as Massachusetts Complaint).
5 White had other ideas: "Purdue's Sackler Family Wants Global Opioids Settlement: Sackler Lawyer Mary Jo White," Reuters, April 23, 2019.

CHAPTER I: A GOOD NAME
11 in the summer of 1913: Arthur was born on August 22. "Dr. Arthur Sackler Dies at 73," *New York Times*, May 27, 1987.
11 more squarely American-sounding Arthur: Entry for Abraham M. Sackler, U.S. Census, 1920.
11 There's a photo: Photograph in Marietta Lutze, *Who Can Know the Other? A Traveler in Search of a Home* (Lunenberg, Vt.: Stinehour Press, 1997), 167.
11 Sophie Greenberg had emigrated from Poland: Entry for Sophie Sackler, U.S. Census, 1930.
11 Isaac was an immigrant himself: According to a 1910 census form, Isaac arrived in 1904. His parents and several of his siblings had arrived a year earlier; one of his brothers, Mark, had come in 1897. Entry for Isaac Sackler, U.S. Census, 1910.
11 Isaac was a proud man: Lutze, *Who Can Know the Other?*, 166.
11 descended from a line of rabbis: Miguel Angel Benavides Lopez, *Arthur M. Sackler* (New York: AMS Foundation, 2012), 11.

11 They called it Sackler Bros.: Isaac Sackler World War I Draft Registration Card, 1917–1918; "Food Board Fines Bakers and Grocers," *Brooklyn Daily Eagle,* Nov. 2, 1918.

12 all three brothers shared a bed: "Raymond Sackler: Obituary," *Times* (London), July 21, 2017.

12 Isaac did well enough in the grocery business: Lutze, *Who Can Know the Other?,* 166.

12 Flatbush was considered middle class: Beth S. Wenger, *New York Jews and the Great Depression: Uncertain Promise* (Syracuse, N.Y.: Syracuse University Press, 1999), 89.

12 "practically Gentiles": Alfred Kazin, *A Walker in the City* (New York: Harcourt, 1974), 9.

12 Isaac invested in real estate: Lopez, *Arthur M. Sackler,* 12.

12 He began working: Lutze, *Who Can Know the Other?,* 167.

12 she would never fully master written English: Ibid.

12 spoke Yiddish at home: Entries for Isaac and Sophie Sackler, U.S. Census, 1920.

12 They kept kosher: Lopez, *Arthur M. Sackler,* 11.

12 Sophie's parents lived with the family: Lutze, *Who Can Know the Other?,* 166.

12 everyone staked their dreams on him: Ibid., 110.

12 Erasmus Hall High School: Lopez, *Arthur M. Sackler,* 12.

13 accelerated program for bright students: Lutze, *Who Can Know the Other?,* 167.

13 Erasmus was an intimidating institution: Janna Malamud Smith, *My Father Is a Book: A Memoir of Bernard Malamud* (Berkeley, Calif.: Counterpoint, 2013), 40. Bernard Malamud was a classmate of Arthur's at Erasmus, though they only became friends in later life.

13 The school had science labs: Herbert Jacobson, "How I Rigged the Elections at Erasmus Hall," fragment of an unpublished memoir (1976), in Bernard Malamud Papers, 11.7, Harry Ransom Center, University of Texas.

13 teachers had PhDs: Malamud Smith, *My Father Is a Book,* 40.

13 some eight thousand students: Jacobson, "How I Rigged the Elections at Erasmus Hall."

13 suits and red ties: Philip Davis, *Bernard Malamud: A Writer's Life* (Oxford: Oxford University Press, 2007), 34.

13 "Hollywood cocktail party": Jacobson, "How I Rigged the Elections at Erasmus Hall."

13 Arthur loved it: Lopez, *Arthur M. Sackler,* 11.

13 one club or another being convened: Jacobson, "How I Rigged the Elections at Erasmus Hall."

13 "the big dream": "An Open Letter to Bernard Malamud," *Medical Tribune,* Nov. 14, 1973.

13 Sophie would prod him: Lopez, *Arthur M. Sackler,* 11.

14 selling advertising for school publications: Ibid., 12; "The Name of Arthur M. Sackler," *Tufts Criterion* (Winter 1986).

14 liked to bet on himself: Lopez, *Arthur M. Sackler,* 12.

14 their advertising manager: Ibid.

14 "program cards": Ibid.

14 rulers branded with the company name: Lutze, *Who Can Know the Other?,* 168; "Name of Arthur M. Sackler."

14 to help support his family: Lopez, *Arthur M. Sackler,* 12.

14 to his brother Morty: Ibid., 168.

14 "Let the kid enjoy himself": Lutze, *Who Can Know the Other?,* 14.

14 generated a nice commission: "Raymond Sackler: Obituary," *Times* (London), July 21, 2017.

14 had contributed funds to Erasmus: *The Chronicles: A History of Erasmus Hall High School from 1906 to 1937* (Brooklyn: Erasmus Hall High School, 1937), 17.

15 a stained-glass window: Ibid., 49.

15 the ghost of Virgil: Jacobson, "How I Rigged the Elections at Erasmus Hall."

15 his father's fortunes began to slip: Lopez, *Arthur M. Sackler,* 12.

15 He delivered flowers: "Erasmus Hall Jobs Bureau Now Helps Parents Find Work," *Brooklyn Daily Eagle,* May 10, 1932; Lopez, *Arthur M. Sackler,* 12.

15 he never took a holiday: Lopez, *Arthur M. Sackler,* 11.

16 marvel at the artworks: Ibid., 13.

16 peer through brightly lit windows: "Art Collector Honored Guest at Philbrook Opening," *Tulsa World,* Dec. 8, 1975; Lopez, *Arthur M. Sackler,* 12.

16 He loved the sensation: Lopez, *Arthur M. Sackler,* 12.

16 Isaac Sackler's misfortune intensified: Lutze, *Who Can Know the Other?,* 167.

16 The employment agency at Erasmus:

"Erasmus Hall Jobs Bureau Now Helps Parents Find Work."

16 "a good name": "Name of Arthur M. Sackler."

16 take their temperature: "The Temple of Sackler," *Vanity Fair,* Sept. 1987.

17 wanted them to be doctors: Lopez, *Arthur M. Sackler,* 11.

17 "My parents brainwashed me": "Name of Arthur M. Sackler."

17 a noble profession: "Raymond Sackler: Obituary," *Times* (London), July 21, 2017.

17 new scientific discoveries: John C. Burnham, "American Medicine's Golden Age: What Happened to It?," *Science,* March 19, 1982.

17 enrolled as a premed student: Lopez, *Arthur M. Sackler,* 13.

17 often falling apart: "Name of Arthur M. Sackler."

17 studied hard: Lopez, *Arthur M. Sackler,* 11.

17 art classes at Cooper Union: "Name of Arthur M. Sackler."

17 "arms the student with an outlook": Arthur M. Sackler, editor's note, *Medical Violet,* New York University College of Medicine, 1937.

17 soda jerk in a candy store: Lopez, *Arthur M. Sackler,* 13.

17 coached his brothers: Ibid.

18 "kid brothers": Lutze, *Who Can Know the Other?,* 168.

18 a cruise around Lower Manhattan: Lopez, *Arthur M. Sackler,* 15.

18 store for his parents: Ibid., 14.

18 medical school at NYU: The May 1936 edition of the *Medical Bulletin* lists Arthur as editor at the top of the masthead. *Medical Bulletin* 1, no. 3 (May 1936).

18 the picture is clearly staged: The photo accompanies an editor's note by Arthur in the *Medical Violet,* the school yearbook, in 1937.

18 "reveal its secrets": This phrase is from Arthur's inaugural column in the *Medical Tribune,* Aug. 2, 1972.

18 "A physician can do anything": "Of Dreams and Archaeology, of Methylmercury Poisoning," *Medical Tribune,* Oct. 24, 1973.

19 "medicine is a hierarchy": The description of this episode is drawn from a column that Arthur wrote about it. "We Are Our Brother's Keeper," *Medical Tribune,* Sept. 17, 1975.

19 selling apples on the street: "Raymond

Sackler: Obituary," *Times* (London), July 21, 2017; Lutze, *Who Can Know the Other?,* 167.

CHAPTER 2: THE ASYLUM

20 Marietta was twenty-six: Lutze, *Who Can Know the Other?,* 65.

20 would need to do two internships: Ibid., 95–97.

20 she was trailed by catcalls: Ibid., 98.

20 a pair of young interns from Brooklyn: Ibid., 99.

20 had lighter hair: FBI file for Raymond Raphael Sackler, June 23, 1945, Federal Bureau of Investigation file 100-NY-73194-1, obtained through the Freedom of Information Act.

21 perceived imbalance prompted sharp restrictions: Leon Sokoloff, "The Rise and Decline of the Jewish Quota in Medical School Admissions," *Bulletin of the New York Academy of Medicine* 68, no. 4 (Nov. 1992).

21 marked with an *H,* for "Hebrew": "In a Time of Quotas, a Quiet Pose in Defiance," *New York Times,* May 25, 2009.

21 he boarded a ship: "Biography of Mortimer Sackler," University of Glasgow website. The detail about steerage is from "Dr. Mortimer Sackler," *Telegraph,* April 28, 2010.

21 grew to love the warmth: "Raymond Sackler," Obituary, *Herald* (Glasgow), July 28, 2017.

21 finding places at Middlesex University: Lopez, *Arthur M. Sackler,* 16.

21 "Raymond was a peacemaker": Interview with Richard Leather.

21 swap places at the hospital: Lutze, *Who Can Know the Other?,* 100.

21 throw a little party: The fact that the party was at the hospital is from ibid., 206.

22 crooning: Ibid., 99.

22 His name was Arthur Sackler: Lutze, *Who Can Know the Other?,* 168.

22 Arthur liked to joke: Lopez, *Arthur M. Sackler,* 11.

22 asking her on a date: Ibid., 99.

22 she declined: Ibid., 100.

22 Marietta called Arthur Sackler: Ibid.

22 a sprawling asylum: "The Lost World of Creedmoor Hospital," *New York Times,* Nov. 12, 2009.

23 terribly overcrowded: Susan Sheehan, *Is There No Place on Earth for Me?* (New York: Vintage, 1982), 9. By the late 1940s, there were just under six thousand patients. Annual Report, Creedmoor State Hospital,

1947. The overcrowding is addressed in the Annual Report of Creedmoor State Hospital, 1950.

23 Some patients were simply comatose: Lutze, *Who Can Know the Other?*, 124.

23 patients roaming the grounds: The detail about straitjackets is from Sheehan, *Is There No Place on Earth for Me?*, 9.

23 arrived at Creedmoor in 1944: "New Hope for the Insane," *Pageant*, Oct. 1951. The hospital was Lincoln Hospital. Lopez, *Arthur M. Sackler*, 15.

23 worked thirty-six-hour shifts: Lopez, *Arthur M. Sackler*, 15.

23 white-haired Dutch psychoanalyst: "New Hope for the Insane." See also "From Waltzing Mice to MBD," *Medical Tribune*, July 6, 1977; and "A Sentimental Journey," *Medical Tribune*, Aug. 9, 1978.

23 "Freud's favorite disciple": "Breaking Ground at the Site Where American Psychoanalysis and the Space Age Were Launched," *Medical Tribune*, July 13, 1983.

23 Arthur called him "Van O": Lopez, *Arthur M. Sackler*, 16.

23 "mentor, friend, and father": H. P. J. Stroeken, "A Dutch Psychoanalyst in New York (1936–1950)," *International Forum of Psychoanalysis* 20, no. 3 (2011).

23 "a rather derelict career": The contemporary was the Canadian psychiatrist Heinz Lehmann. Quoted in Andrea Tone, *The Age of Anxiety: A History of America's Turbulent Affair with Tranquilizers* (New York: Basic Books, 2009), 89.

23 Psychiatrists made less money: Ibid.

23 Arthur found a job: Lopez, *Arthur M. Sackler*, 16.

23 For a salary of $8,000: FBI Memo on the Schering Corporation, June 23, 1942, Federal Bureau of Investigation, 65-HQ-4851, v. 3 Serial 73, obtained through the Freedom of Information Act.

24 he started a new residency: Lopez, *Arthur M. Sackler*, 16.

24 the novelist Virginia Woolf: Virginia Woolf, "On Being Ill," *Criterion*, Jan. 1926.

24 segregate such sorry cases: Anne Harrington, *Mind Fixers: Psychiatry's Troubled Search for the Biology of Mental Illness* (New York: Norton, 2019), 48–50.

24 an expensive and bespoke solution: Robert Whitaker, *Mad in America: Bad Science, Bad Medicine, and the Enduring Mistreatment of the Mentally Ill* (New York: Basic Books, 2002), 84, 147.

24 female patients outnumbered male patients: Annual Report, Creedmoor State Hospital, 1952.

24 assigned to R Building: "New Hope for the Insane"; Lopez, *Arthur M. Sackler*, 18.

25 assaulted him with a metal spoon: Lopez, *Arthur M. Sackler*, 18.

25 "the limbo of the living dead": Testimony of Arthur M. Sackler, Hearing Before the Subcommittee of the Committee on Appropriations, U.S. Senate, March 15, 1950 (hereafter cited as AMS 1950 Testimony).

25 Arthur reflected at the time: Ibid.

25 Van O believed: Ibid.

25 consign them to a kind of death: Testimony of Johan H. W. van Ophuijsen, Hearing Before the Subcommittee of the Committee on Appropriations, U.S. Senate, March 15, 1950.

25 growing at a faster rate: AMS 1950 Testimony.

25 remove a patient's teeth: Harrington, *Mind Fixers*, 48–49.

25 kill more than a hundred of them: Whitaker, *Mad in America*, 80–82.

26 The treatment had been invented: Harrington, *Mind Fixers*, 65–68; Whitaker, *Mad in America*, 96–97; Edward Shorter, *A History of Psychiatry: From the Era of the Asylum to the Age of Prozac* (New York: Wiley, 1997), 219.

26 Others felt profoundly shaken: Whitaker, *Mad in America*, 99.

26 relief to many patients: Shorter, *History of Psychiatry*, 207–8.

26 mitigate the symptoms: Ibid., 221.

26 The therapy was first used: Annual Report, Creedmoor State Hospital, 1947; Annual Report, Creedmoor State Hospital, 1948.

26 "a great jolt drubbed me": Sylvia Plath, *The Bell Jar* (New York: Harper, 2006), 143.

26 The singer Lou Reed: Anthony DeCurtis, *Lou Reed: A Life* (New York: Little, Brown, 2017), 32.

26 a widely used treatment: Shorter, *History of Psychiatry*, 208.

26 every patient building was outfitted: Annual Report, Creedmoor State Hospital, 1952.

27 They were disgusted: "New Hope for the Insane."

27 "Nothing to it": Shorter, *History of Psychiatry*, 228.

27 they had black eyes: Whitaker, *Mad in America*, 132.

27 for depression: Ibid. Lobotomy was introduced to Creedmoor in 1952. Sheehan, *Is There No Place on Earth for Me?*, 9.

27 could not fully account for mental illness: Lopez, *Arthur M. Sackler*, 18.

27 Arthur set to work: "New Hope for the Insane."

27 a doctor named Harry LaBurt: LaBurt became director at Creedmoor in 1943 and held the position until 1969. "Harry A. LaBurt, 91, Ex-chief of Creedmoor," *New York Times*, Oct. 6, 1989.

28 was always locked: Sheehan, *Is There No Place on Earth for Me?*, 13.

28 "a six thousand bed jail": Donald F. Klein, interview in *An Oral History of Neuropsychopharmacology: The First Fifty Years, Peer Interviews*, ed. Thomas A. Ban and Barry Blackwell (Brentwood, Tenn.: ACNP, 2011), 9:205.

28 one of Creedmoor's annual reports: Annual Report, Creedmoor State Hospital, 1953.

28 did not have a good relationship: Interview with Rachel Klein.

28 in derangements of brain chemistry: AMS 1950 Testimony.

28 Marietta found Arthur waiting: Lutze, *Who Can Know the Other?*, 100.

28 Marietta recounted her experiences: Ibid.

28 little idea of the horrors: Ibid., 72–73.

28 became hostile: Ibid., 97.

29 the marriage dissolved: Ibid., 79–81.

29 worked for a German-owned company: FBI Report on the Schering Company, with Arthur Sackler's name listed in the leadership, July 18, 1941, Federal Bureau of Investigation, 65-HQ-4851 v. 1 Serial 21.

29 penchant for secrecy: Lutze, *Who Can Know the Other?*, 100.

29 to express his ardor: Ibid., 101.

30 His sheer focus felt overwhelming: Ibid., 100.

30 releasing histamine into the bloodstream: "New Hope for the Insane."

30 The Sacklers started conducting experiments: "Recoveries Double in Mental Cases Using Histamine," *Globe and Mail*, May 12, 1949.

31 nearly a third of them improved: "New Treatment with Hormones Aids Psychotics," *New York Herald Tribune*, May 15, 1950.

31 *did* respond to histamine: "New Hope for the Insane."

31 "the chemical causes of insanity": Ibid.

31 "The doctors think they have found":

"Biochemical for Emotional Ills," *Philadelphia Inquirer Public Ledger*, June 12, 1949.

31 double the number of patients: "If You Live to Be a Hundred," *Maclean's*, Dec. 1, 1951.

31 "the chemical activity theory": "A Shot You Take to Help You 'Take It,'" *Better Homes and Gardens*, April 1950.

31 neighborhood boys made good: "Three Brothers, Doctors All, Join in Winning Award," *Brooklyn Daily Eagle*, May 21, 1950.

31 reinforced when Isaac Sackler died: Lopez, *Arthur M. Sackler*, 25.

31 he'd had a heart attack: The account of Isaac's death is drawn from ibid., 18, and "To Live and Die with Dignity," *Medical Tribune*, March 10, 1976.

32 "by grants made in the memory": See, for instance, "A Three-Year Follow-Up Study of Nonconvulsive Histamine Biochemotherapy, Electric Convulsive Posthistamine Therapy, and Electric Convulsive Therapy Controls," *Psychiatric Quarterly* 27 (Jan. 1953).

32 accepting a prize: "Three New York Brothers Honored for Medical Research," *New York Herald Tribune*, May 13, 1950; "New Treatment with Hormones Aids Psychotics."

32 "prevent insanity": "New Hope for the Insane."

32 Arthur had been married: Deposition of Else Sackler, *Matter of Sackler*, Surrogates Court, Nassau County, N.Y. (hereafter cited as EJS Deposition). The copy of this deposition that I retrieved from the courthouse was undated.

32 was an émigré: Petition for Naturalization of Jans Jorgensen (Else's father), U.S. District Court, Los Angeles, No. 123391 (1945).

32 They had been introduced: Emma Zakin Affidavit, Dec. 5, 1990, *Matter of Sackler*, Surrogates Court, Nassau County, N.Y.

32 Arthur kept it a secret: Lopez, *Arthur M. Sackler*, 15.

32 They moved into a furnished unit: EJS Deposition.

32 took her to an Italian restaurant: Lutze, *Who Can Know the Other?*, 101.

33 He wrote love letters: Arthur Sackler to Marietta Lutze, quoted in ibid., 106–7.

33 inherited the family drug company: Lutze, *Who Can Know the Other?*, 103–5.

33 "forced a decision": Ibid., 107.

CHAPTER 3: MED MAN

34 an unusual advertisement: *Medicine Ave.: The Story of Medical Advertising in America*

(Huntington, N.Y.: Medical Advertising Hall of Fame, 1999), 23.

34 For nearly a century: Joseph G. Lombardino, "A Brief History of Pfizer Central Research," *Bulletin of the History of Chemistry* 25, no. 1 (2000).

34 Until World War II: David Herzberg, *Happy Pills in America: From Miltown to Prozac* (Baltimore: Johns Hopkins University Press, 2010), 22.

34 When the war broke out: Federal Trade Commission, *Economic Report on Antibiotics Manufacture* (Washington, D.C.: U.S. Government Printing Office, 1958), 6.

34 the business model: Herzberg, *Happy Pills in America*, 22.

34 not particularly lucrative: Scott H. Podolsky, *The Antibiotic Era: Reform, Resistance, and the Pursuit of a Rational Therapeutics* (Baltimore: Johns Hopkins University Press, 2015), 19.

34 sell at a higher price: Ibid.

34 the era of the "miracle drug": Lopez, *Arthur M. Sackler*, 18.

35 almost every week: L. W. Frohlich, "The Physician and the Pharmaceutical Industry in the United States," *Proceedings of the Royal Society of Medicine*, April 11, 1960.

35 The president of Pfizer: Tom Mahoney, *The Merchants of Life: An Account of the American Pharmaceutical Industry* (New York: Harper, 1959), 237–38.

35 a new antibiotic called Terramycin: Podolsky, *Antibiotic Era*, 23.

35 might really take off: Mahoney, *Merchants of Life*, 243.

35 boutique agency in New York: Podolsky, *Antibiotic Era*, 25.

35 "You give me the money": "Becker, Corbett, Kallir: An Industry Comes to Life," *Medical Marketing and Media*, Jan. 1997.

35 William Douglas McAdams: "W. D. M'Adams, 68, Advertising Man," *New York Times*, Aug. 16, 1954.

35 cod liver oil: Herzberg, *Happy Pills in America*, 29–30.

35 marketed directly to doctors: "McAdams Forms Division to Focus on Latest Drugs," *New York Times*, Dec. 16, 1991.

35 focus exclusively on the pharmaceutical sector: "Advertising: Generic Drugs and Agencies," *New York Times*, Sept. 12, 1985; Herzberg, *Happy Pills in America*, 29–30.

35 he hired Arthur Sackler: Arthur Sackler prepared statement and biography, Hearings Before the Subcommittee on Antitrust and

Monopoly of the Committee on the Judiciary, U.S. Senate, Jan. 30, 1962.

36 for half his life: "The Name of Arthur M. Sackler," *Tufts Criterion* (Winter 1986).

36 did the same with McAdams: Arthur Sackler to Félix Martí-Ibáñez, Aug. 27, 1954, Félix Martí-Ibáñez Papers, Sterling Memorial Library, Yale University (hereafter cited as FMI Papers).

36 "largely a closed club": Lopez, *Arthur M. Sackler*, 18.

36 pass for a gentile: In his 2020 book, *Pharma*, Gerald Posner quotes Arthur's attorney Michael Sonnenreich telling Arthur, "If there is a pogrom, I don't care what you tell them you are, you are going to be in the same cattle car as I am. Stop the games... You could marry all the Christian girls you want, it ain't going to work. They are still going to put you on the train." Gerald Posner, *Pharma: Greed, Lies, and the Poisoning of America* (New York: Avid Reader, 2020), 287.

36 sensitive to anti-Semitism: "The Temple of Sackler," *Vanity Fair*, Sept. 1987.

36 on nights and weekends: Lopez, *Arthur M. Sackler*, 18.

36 most prescription drugs had been generic: *Medicine Ave.*, 16.

36 "I would rather place myself": Arthur M. Sackler, *One Man and Medicine: Selected Weekly Columns (1972–1983) by the International Publisher of "Medical Tribune"* (New York: Medical Tribune, 1983), 29.

37 "Sackler's ads had a very serious": Interview with Kallir.

37 One Terramycin ad: Adam Tanner, *Our Bodies, Our Data: How Companies Make Billions Selling Our Medical Records* (Boston: Beacon Press, 2017), 23–24.

37 president of the company: Arthur Sackler prepared statement and biography, Hearings Before the Subcommittee on Antitrust and Monopoly of the Committee on the Judiciary, U.S. Senate, Jan. 30, 1962.

37 "the lion's den": Arthur Sackler to Félix Martí-Ibáñez, Aug. 27, 1954, FMI Papers. The 11 Bartlett Street address is from the letterhead of John McKeen, included in the files of the investigation into monopoly drug pricing conducted by the Subcommittee on Antitrust and Monopoly of the U.S. Senate Committee on the Judiciary, which are now housed at the National Archives and Records Administration. (This archive will hereafter be cited as Kefauver Files.)

37 "an unparalleled idea man": The contemporary was William G. Castagnoli. "Remembrance of Kings Past," *Medical Marketing and Media*, July 1996.

37 coined by advertisers: According to Scott Podolsky, "The term 'broad-spectrum' itself appears to have entered the literature with Pfizer's initial advertisement for Terramycin by name in July 1950. Previously, the University of Washington's William Kirby, at the General Scientific Meetings of the American Medical Association in June 1950, had spoken of the 'broad spectrum of activity of the newer antibiotics.'" See Scott H. Podolsky, "Antibiotics and the History of the Controlled Clinical Trial, 1950–1970," *Journal of the History of Medicine and Allied Sciences* 65, no. 3 (2010).

38 But until Arthur Sackler used it: *Medicine Ave.*, 22. This might have been an instance in which necessity was the mother of invention, as Arthur *couldn't* have mentioned the name of the drug at this stage, because he had not yet received formal approval from the American Medical Association to do so. See Podolsky, *Antibiotic Era*, 206n70; and Federal Trade Commission, *Economic Report on Antibiotics Manufacture*, 141.

38 one press account at the time: "Pfizer Put an Old Name on a New Label," *Business Week*, Oct. 13, 1951; Podolsky, *Antibiotic Era*, 25.

38 they would have two thousand: Podolsky, *Antibiotic Era*, 25.

38 "Arthur invented the wheel": "Advertising: Generic Drugs and Agencies," *New York Times*, Sept. 12, 1985.

38 "The doctor is feted and courted": John Pekkanen, *The American Connection: Profiteering and Politicking in the "Ethical" Drug Industry* (Chicago: Follett, 1973), 89.

38 Roche: Ibid.

39 golf tournaments: Ibid., 91.

39 "more and more physicians are specifying": "News of the Advertising and Marketing Fields," *New York Times*, Feb. 28, 1954.

39 "Is the public likely to benefit": Charles D. May, "Selling Drugs by 'Educating' Physicians," *Journal of Medical Education* 36, no. 1 (Jan. 1961).

39 one unpublished polemic: Unpublished essay by Arthur Sackler, "Freedom of Inquiry, Freedom of Thought, Freedom of Expression: 'A Standard to Which the Wise and the Just Can Repair': Observations on Medicines, Medicine, and the Pharmaceutical Industry," FMI Papers.

39 "turn back the hands": Ibid. See also

Jeremy A. Greene and Scott H. Podolsky, "Keeping the Modern in Medicine: Pharmaceutical Promotion and Physician Education in Postwar America," *Bulletin of the History of Medicine* 83 (2009).

40 bought the agency from McAdams: "Advertising: Generic Drugs and Agencies."

40 "old and tired": Harry Zelenko, email.

40 Medical Advertising Hall of Fame: *Medicine Ave.*, 18.

40 Creedmoor Institute for Psychobiologic Studies: Lutze, *Who Can Know the Other?*, 112. Arthur junior was born on February 9, 1950, the same day that the new center was formally dedicated.

40 H Building: Annual Report, Creedmoor State Hospital, 1951.

40 sixty-two rooms: AMS 1950 Testimony.

40 devoted to: "Psychobiologic Institute Is Dedicated," *Psychiatric Quarterly* 24, no. 1 (Jan. 1950).

40 operate behind the scenes: Ibid.

40 Four hundred people: "UN President Dedicates New Unit at Creedmoor," *Long Island Star-Journal*, Feb. 10, 1950.

40 president of the United Nations General Assembly: Annual Report, Creedmoor State Hospital, 1950.

40 Even Harry LaBurt: "Psychobiologic Institute Is Dedicated."

40 "a golden era in psychiatry": "UN President Dedicates New Unit at Creedmoor."

40 Marietta Lutze was in labor: Lutze, *Who Can Know the Other?*, 112.

41 A privately published account: Lopez, *Arthur M. Sackler*, 25. The book was published by the AMS Foundation for the Arts, Sciences and Humanities, which is overseen by Arthur's third wife, Jillian Sackler. This is a characterization that Else's children would almost certainly disagree with.

41 Arthur would not settle: Lutze, *Who Can Know the Other?*, 115.

41 an old Dutch farmhouse: Ibid., 116. A number of accounts suggest that the house was actually built in the 1920s, using timbers, doors, and other elements of an eighteenth-century farmhouse in Flushing that had been damaged in a fire. See "Rare in Nassau: A Large Tract with Right Zoning," *New York Times*, July 27, 1997; Michael J. Leahy, ed., *If You're Thinking of Living In . . .* (New York: Times Books, 1999), 255.

41 surrounded by boxwood trees: Lutze, *Who Can Know the Other?*, 115.

41 disapproved of the marriage: Ibid., 108.

41 "fled the Nazis in Germany": This line is used in Lopez, *Arthur M. Sackler*, 25. While Lopez is the author of the book, it is a privately published, largely hagiographic account by a protégé of Arthur's who describes the project as having been culled from Arthur's own remarks and writings.

41 "I was seen as the intruder": Lutze, *Who Can Know the Other?*, 108.

42 birth that day to a baby boy: Ibid., 113.

42 elected to give up work: Ibid., 109.

42 wait for him to come home: Ibid., 117.

42 took on more projects than ever: Lopez, *Arthur M. Sackler*, 23.

42 laboratory for therapeutic research: Ibid., 20.

42 fill that gap: AMS 1950 Testimony.

42 He would tell people: Lopez, *Arthur M. Sackler*, 23.

42 thought of her new husband as Atlas: Lutze, *Who Can Know the Other?*, 110.

43 He thrived on power: Ibid., 125.

43 a sophisticated mid-Atlantic diction: John Kallir, who met him in the 1950s, told me, "I certainly was not aware of a Brooklyn accent. He had a smooth, soft voice." I was also able to hear Arthur's voice in a 1984 episode of the television program *Smithsonian World*, titled "Filling in the Blanks." Smithsonian Institution Archives, Accession 08-081, box 10.

43 appeared before a Senate subcommittee: AMS 1950 Testimony.

44 Word had spread in advertising circles: "Becker, Corbett, Kallir: How It Began," *Medical Marketing and Media*, Nov. 1996.

44 "Sackler had a soft spot": Interview with Wolff.

44 flirted with communism: Lopez, *Arthur M. Sackler*, 15; Sam Quinones, *Dreamland: The True Tale of America's Opiate Epidemic* (New York: Bloomsbury, 2015), 28.

45 member of the Communist Party: FBI File No. 100-HQ-340415, obtained from the National Archives through the Freedom of Information Act.

45 "McAdams had many politically dubious people": Interview with Kallir.

45 cartoonist Charles Addams: Ibid.

45 Andy Warhol: Interview with Wolff.

45 McAdams used one of his cat pictures: "Becker, Corbett, Kallir: An Industry Comes to Life."

45 "controversial, unsettling, and difficult": "Remembrance of Kings Past."

45 no compunction about micromanaging: Harry Zelenko, email.

45 Arthur would refuse, citing: Interview with John Kallir. When John Kallir left McAdams, Arthur sued him for breach of contract, in a case that was ultimately settled out of court. I was able to corroborate Kallir's impressions. Another former employee of Arthur's, Hara Estroff Marano, told me a remarkably similar story about Arthur's hiring of communists. "All the blacklisted writers," she said. "Sackler hired them—and then exploited them."

45 job offer from Eli Lilly: Interview with Kallir.

45 "We weren't paid terribly well": Interview with Wolff.

46 "It sort of helped his image": Ibid.

46 "Artie could be quite charming": Zelenko, email.

46 one obvious rival: Ibid. Harry Zelenko, an associate art director who started working at the firm when McAdams himself was still running it, told me that Haberman "expected to run the agency" but that Arthur "pushed this woman out." Interview with Zelenko.

46 Haberman wrote a novel: Helen Haberman, *How About Tomorrow Morning?* (New York: Prentice-Hall, 1945), 11, 13.

46 "Artie outsmarted her": Zelenko, email.

46 "He wasn't a backslapper": Interview with Keusch.

47 Frohlich was a debonair German: "L. W. Frohlich, the Gay Jewish Immigrant Whose Company Sells Your Medical Secrets," *Forward*, Jan. 12, 2017.

47 Frohlich boasted: Frohlich to John Talbott, July 28, 1959, Kefauver Files.

47 "We are living in the midst": Frohlich, "Physician and the Pharmaceutical Industry in the United States."

47 had once worked for Sackler: Tanner, *Our Bodies, Our Data*, 23; *Medicine Ave.*, 18.

47 "He started out being an art director": EJS Deposition.

47 opened his own agency: *Medicine Ave.*, 22. There is some disagreement over whether he opened the firm in 1943 or 1944.

47 fixture at the opera: Interview with Kallir.

47 at his beach house: "L. W. Frohlich, the Gay Jewish Immigrant Whose Company Sells Your Medical Secrets."

47 controlled and disciplined: Interview with Kallir.

47 "a competitive zeal": Frohlich, "Physician and the Pharmaceutical Industry in the United States."

47 Sackler acknowledged this competitive reality: Arthur Sackler testimony, Hearings Before the Subcommittee on Antitrust and Monopoly of the Committee on the Judiciary, U.S. Senate, Jan. 30, 1962.

47 described the rivalry: "Critics Fail to Inhibit Ethical Drug Ad Growth," *Advertising Age*, Feb. 1, 1960.

47 "Frohlich and McAdams dominated": Interview with Kallir.

48 investigated Frohlich during the war: Tanner, *Our Bodies, Our Data*, 26.

48 Frohlich was Jewish: "L. W. Frohlich, the Gay Jewish Immigrant Whose Company Sells Your Medical Secrets."

48 friends and associates did not know: Ibid.

48 scrupulously closeted life: Ibid.

48 "The momentum of the business": Arthur Sackler to Félix Martí-Ibáñez, Aug. 27, 1954, FMI Papers.

48 able to reintroduce matches: Sheehan, *Is There No Place on Earth for Me?*, 10.

48 "patients out of mental hospitals": Thorazine advertisement, *Mental Hospitals* 7, no. 4 (1956).

48 declined for the first time: Tone, *Age of Anxiety*, 80.

48 deinstitutionalization of the mentally ill: Harrington, *Mind Fixers*, 103. Harrington offers a more complex account of the deinstitutionalization of the mentally ill, arguing that it would be an oversimplification to attribute this development exclusively, or even chiefly, to medication. She cites other factors, such as new regulations, costs, and alternative community-based forms of treatment. See ibid., 113.

49 "Helping schizophrenics would be": Tone, *Age of Anxiety*, 80–81.

49 The *Times* later maintained: "1957 | When Pfizer and the Times Worked Closely," *New York Times*, Nov. 27, 2015.

49 gave half of the stock: EJS Deposition.

49 "It was very, very important": Tanner, *Our Bodies, Our Data*, 24.

50 lifelong friends: Interview with Richard Leather.

50 always denied it: Tanner, *Our Bodies, Our Data*, 25. Also see "An Art Collector Sows Largesse and Controversy," *New York Times*, June 5, 1983.

50 Arthur was the controlling force: Posner, *Pharma*, 618n10.

50 the "musketeers": Interview with Richard Leather.

50 late into the night: Lutze, *Who Can Know the Other?*, 117.

50 According to Richard Leather: Interview with Leather.

50 a significant commitment: Interview with Leather.

50 all married, with kids: "2 Doctors to Be Privates," *New York Times*, May 8, 1953.

51 researching the effects of burns: Annual Report, Creedmoor State Hospital, 1952.

51 "communist cell": Interview with Kallir.

51 investigating the Sackler brothers: FBI Files for Raymond and Beverly Sackler, 100-NY-73194-1.

51 fired from Creedmoor: "2 Doctors Dismissed over Oath," *New York Herald Tribune*, May 8, 1953; "2 Doctors to Be Privates."

51 speak of the harm: Louis Lasagna remembrance of Arthur Sackler, *Studio International* 200, supplement 1 (1987).

51 A *New York Times* article: "2 Doctors to Be Privates."

51 "Arthur was a wonderful buffer": Interview with Leather.

52 bought the company for $50,000: In a deposition nearly seventy years later, Richard Sackler was asked, "Do you know how much the family paid to acquire Purdue?" "I actually do," he replied: "$50,000." Deposition of Richard Sackler, *In re National Prescription Opiate Litigation*, MDL No. 2804, U.S. District Court for the Northern District of Ohio, March 8, 2019 (hereafter cited as RDS 2019 Deposition).

52 Purdue Frederick: "Norwalk Firm Finds Niche Among Pharmaceutical Giants," *Hartford Courant*, July 23, 1992.

CHAPTER 4: PENICILLIN FOR THE BLUES

53 a chemist named Leo Sternbach: Tone, *Age of Anxiety*, 120.

53 a "major" tranquilizer: Pekkanen, *American Connection*, 60.

53 a less powerful medication: Tone, *Age of Anxiety*, 131.

53 tranquilizer called Miltown: Ibid., 124.

53 it became a blockbuster: "Adventurous Chemist and His Pill," *Washington Post*, Jan. 20, 1980.

53 party drug in Hollywood: Tone, *Age of Anxiety*, 78.

53 other companies now set out: Ibid., 124.

54 Make something different enough: "Adventurous Chemist and His Pill."

54 his father had been a chemist: Ibid.

54 Hoffmann-LaRoche did not: Tone, *Age of Anxiety*, 145.

54 "endangered species": "Adventurous Chemist and His Pill."

54 he had a breakthrough: Ibid.

54 Roche compound No. 0609: Herzberg, *Happy Pills in America*, 40.

54 carefully recording in his notebook: "Adventurous Chemist and His Pill."

54 they turned to Arthur Sackler: Interview with John Kallir.

55 Arthur assigned Kallir: Interview with Rudi Wolff.

55 an astonishing range of afflictions: Pekkanen, *American Connection*, 71.

55 FDA regulations forbade: Jeremy Greene and David Herzberg, "Hidden in Plain Sight: Marketing Prescription Drugs to Consumers in the Twentieth Century," *American Journal of Public Health* 100, no. 5 (May 2010).

55 *Life* magazine carried a story: "New Way to Calm a Cat," *Life*, April 18, 1960.

55 planted by Roche: Pekkanen, *American Connection*, 74–75.

56 $2 million marketing Librium: Tone, *Age of Anxiety*, 136.

56 critique published in a medical newsletter: Pekkanen, *American Connection*, 75–76.

56 more than $2 million a year: Ibid., 82.

56 an almost clairvoyant grasp: Gerson went on to run McAdams. "Looking Back, Looking Forward," *Medical Marketing and Media*, April 1998.

56 "The Age of Anxiety": This was one of a series of advertisements for Librium and Valium that ran in heavy rotation in the *Medical Tribune* (and numerous other medical publications) during the 1960s. Old copies of the *Medical Tribune* are difficult to find, but the College of Physicians in Philadelphia has the fullest run I could locate, and I consulted these in person.

56 One study found: Herzberg, *Happy Pills in America*, 51.

56 it really took off: Pekkanen, *American Connection*, 75.

56 1.5 million new prescriptions: Tone, *Age of Anxiety*, 137–38.

56 fifteen million Americans: Pekkanen, *American Connection*, 75.

57 They called it Valium: "Adventurous Chemist and His Pill."

57 "Arthur was in pretty heavy": Interview with Wolff.

57 prescribed for "psychic tension": "The Tranquilizer War," *New Republic*, July 19, 1975.

57 use it in sports medicine: Pekkanen, *American Connection*, 79.

57 "When do we *not* use this drug?": Herzberg, *Happy Pills in America*, 40. The original citation is H. Angus Bowes, "The Role of Diazepam (Valium) in Emotional Illness," *Psychosomatics* 6, no. 5 (1965).

58 "One of the great attributes": "Looking Back, Looking Forward."

58 "35, single and psychoneurotic": Tone, *Age of Anxiety*, 157. This is a Valium ad that ran in the *Archives of General Psychiatry* 22 (1970).

58 An early ad for Librium: "Valium and the New Normal," *New York Times*, Sept. 30, 2012. Librium ad that ran in the *Journal of the American College Health Association* 17, no. 5 (June 1969).

58 as the historian Andrea Tone observed: Tone, *Age of Anxiety*, 156.

58 the drug could alleviate fears: Pekkanen, *American Connection*, 80.

58 tens of millions of tablets: Tone, *Age of Anxiety*, 153.

58 most prescribed drug in America: Ibid.

58 in the top five: Herzberg, *Happy Pills in America*, 40.

58 reached sixty million: "Adventurous Chemist and His Pill."

58 one of the most profitable companies: Tone, *Age of Anxiety*, 154.

59 escalating series of bonuses: It has occasionally been suggested that Arthur received a commission on each pill sold, but according to an interview that Barry Meier conducted with Arthur's lawyer Michael Sonnenreich, this was not the case. Sonnenreich maintains that Arthur received an escalating series of bonuses rather than a royalty. Barry Meier, *Pain Killer: An Empire of Deceit and the Origin of America's Opioid Epidemic* (New York: Random House, 2018), 199.

59 "penicillin for the blues": Pekkanen, *American Connection*, 60.

59 Arthur was present for the birth: Lutze, *Who Can Know the Other?*, 126–27.

59 carried a big briefcase: Miriam Kent Affidavit, *Matter of Sackler*, May 29, 1992.

59 "The *Medical Tribune* was his baby": Interview with Keusch.

59 reached millions of doctors: Lopez, *Arthur M. Sackler*, 23.

59 elaborate multipage spreads: I reviewed nearly two decades of issues of the *Medical Tribune* at the College of Physicians in Philadelphia. Large ads for both Librium and Valium appear in almost every issue.

60 his tendency to remain obscure: "An Art Collector Sows Largesse and Controversy," *New York Times,* June 5, 1983.

60 "Dr. Sackler and I remained close": Affidavit in Support of Else Sackler's Motion for Partial Summary Judgment on Claim for Payment on Promissory Note, File No. 249220, *Matter of Sackler,* New York State Surrogate's Court, 1990.

60 the firm's only shareholders: "Both Dr. Sackler and I were officers and directors of McAdams and, for many years, its only shareholders. In 1978, Dr. Sackler transferred two of his shares of stock to our daughters, thereby equalizing our respective holdings to 44 shares each." Ibid.

60 time with Else: Else Sackler to Stanley Salmen, Dec. 18, 1959, Columbia University Central Files, box 507. (This archive will hereafter be cited as CUCF.)

60 not just friends but confidants: Interview with Michael Rich and a confidential interview with a close friend of the family.

60 "We talked on a daily basis": EJS Deposition.

60 "a very private person": "The Sackler Collection, Cont'd," *Washington Post,* July 30, 1982.

60 could open up to her: Zakin Affidavit.

61 Marietta felt quite alone: Lutze, *Who Can Know the Other?,* 123, 120.

61 a predictable rhythm: Ibid., 117.

61 She got a little dog: Ibid., 122.

61 a kindly gardener: Ibid., 115.

61 "Play with me, Daddy": Interview with Michael Rich.

61 wouldn't be home at all: Lutze, *Who Can Know the Other?,* 117.

61 brunch with his other family: EJS Deposition.

62 seemed to be living a double life: Interview with Kallir.

62 Roche had informed doctors: Tone, *Age of Anxiety,* 146.

62 never conducted a single study: Herzberg, *Happy Pills in America,* 109.

62 unpleasant withdrawal symptoms: Tone, *Age of Anxiety,* 141–42.

62 When Hollister informed Roche: Ibid., 142.

62 Roche was anything but chastened: Ibid., 146.

63 offered a different interpretation: Ibid.

63 just have addictive personalities: Herzberg, *Happy Pills in America,* 110–12.

63 "There are some people who just get addicted": "A Psychiatrist Discusses What's Good About Tranquilizers," *Vogue,* April 1, 1976.

63 syndicated ask-the-doctor column: "The Constant Griper," *Pittsburgh Sun-Telegraph,* March 14, 1957.

63 treated as controlled substances: "Tranquilizer War." Also see "U.S. Acts to Curb 2 Tranquilizers," *New York Times,* Aug. 16, 1973.

63 devastating for his bottom line: Lopez, *Arthur M. Sackler,* 13; Posner, *Pharma,* 262–63.

63 FDA adviser would speculate: "Tranquilizer War."

64 twenty million Americans: "Adventurous Chemist and His Pill."

64 even though it was prescribed: Tone, *Age of Anxiety,* 142.

64 "a nightmare of dependence and addiction": "Abuse of Prescription Drugs: A Hidden but Serious Problem for Women," *New York Times,* April 19, 1978; Hearing on the Use and Misuse of Benzodiazepines, Subcommittee on Health and Scientific Research, Committee on Labor and Human Resources, U.S. Senate, Sept. 10, 1979.

64 Roche stood accused: "Americans Are Spending Almost Half a Billion Dollars a Year on a Drug to Relieve Their Anxiety—a Fact That Is in Itself Considerable Cause for Anxiety," *New York Times,* Feb. 1, 1976.

64 The Rolling Stones: "Mother's Little Helper," Rolling Stones, 1966.

64 "Valium changed the way": "Looking Back, Looking Forward."

64 "that drug worked": Quinones, *Dreamland,* 30.

65 Arthur often railed: See, for instance, "On a Deadly Hazard," *Medical Tribune,* Jan. 10, 1979.

65 addictive personalities of the patients: "The Other Sackler," *Washington Post,* Nov. 27, 2019.

65 $1 for each of the patents: "Adventurous Chemist and His Pill."

65 $10,000 bonus for each drug: Sternbach was not bitter. He said he was not "a victim of capitalistic exploitation. If anything, I am an example of capitalistic enlightenment . . . I was grateful to the company for bringing us over from Europe, for providing my family with a certain security." Tone, *Age of Anxiety,* 138.

65 no expensive hobbies: Ibid., 138–39.
65 He felt no moral responsibility: "Adventurous Chemist and His Pill."

CHAPTER 5: CHINA FEVER

66 visit to the cabinetmaker's shop: Lutze, *Who Can Know the Other?*, 149.
66 distinctive rosewood table: Ibid., 150. According to Sackler's own account, he began collecting art after graduating from medical school in the 1940s. Initially, "he focused on pre- and early renaissance and French Impressionist and post-Impressionist Paintings. At this time he also actively supported contemporary American painters. Then in the 1950's he started collecting Chinese art." Biography of Arthur Sackler, provided by Jillian Sackler to Harry Henderson, Oct. 1, 1986, Harry Henderson Papers, Penn State University.
66 His name was Bill Drummond: "East Meets West in LI Ranch House," *Newsday*, July 17, 1963.
66 forced to relocate: The brother was Robert Drummond. "Ex–Oak Parker Heads Chinese Furniture Shop," *Chicago Daily Tribune*, Feb. 24, 1957.
67 American spy in China: "The Smithsonian's Mystery Building," *Washington Post*, Aug. 30, 1987.
67 imposed an embargo: "East Meets West in LI Ranch House."
67 "proud of his 'eye'": Draft of a tribute to Arthur Sackler by Harry Henderson, Henderson Papers.
67 decided, on an impulse, to buy them: Lutze, *Who Can Know the Other?*, 150.
67 awaken something inside him: Ibid.
67 "It was at that time": Draft of a tribute to Sackler by Henderson.
67 had always appreciated art: Lutze, *Who Can Know the Other?*, 154.
68 half his fortune on art: Jean Strouse, *Morgan: American Financier* (New York: Random House, 1999), xii.
68 a large "corpus of material": Lutze, *Who Can Know the Other?*, 154.
68 stack of scholarly literature: Ibid., 153.
68 seeking out the Chinese galleries: Ibid., 160.
68 pronounce all of the Chinese names: Hoving, *Making the Mummies Dance*, 95.
68 New Jersey doctor named Paul Singer: Lutze, *Who Can Know the Other?*, 151.
68 a self-taught expert: "Trove of Asian Art Is Left to the Smithsonian," *New York Times*, Sept. 9, 1999.
68 "I've bought all the things": "In Memoriam," *Studio International* 200, supplement 1 (1987).
68 "let's eliminate the middleman": "The Temple of Sackler," *Vanity Fair*, Sept. 1987.
68 precious Chinese artifacts: Karl Meyer and Shareen Blair Brysac, *The China Collectors: America's Century-Long Hunt for Asian Art Treasures* (New York: Palgrave, 2015), 339–40.
68 "I met a very eager pupil": "In Memoriam," *Studio International* 200, supplement 1 (1987).
69 "it was like an electric charge": "Temple of Sackler."
69 arousal and release: Lutze, *Who Can Know the Other?*, 152.
69 saw this in her husband: Ibid., 153.
69 their rarest treasures: Ibid., 151.
69 Dai Fubao: Ibid., 153.
69 the Ch'u Manuscript: Li Ling, *The Chu Silk Manuscripts from Zidanku, Changsha (Hunan Province)*, vol. 1, *Discovery and Transmission* (Hong Kong: Chinese University of Hong Kong, 2020), 167.
69 refused to take no for an answer: Lutze, *Who Can Know the Other?*, 160.
69 Arthur paid it: Ling, *Chu Silk Manuscripts from Zidanku*, 1:167.
69 natural sense of secrecy: "Art Collector Honored Guest at Philbrook Opening," *Tulsa World*, Dec. 8, 1975.
69 "They were handshake deals": Minutes of an executors' meeting from July 22, 1987, cited in Affidavit of Gillian T. Sackler, Index No. 249220, *Matter of Sackler*, June 13, 1990.
70 registered under a false name: "Temple of Sackler."
70 Arthur had money: Hoving, *Making the Mummies Dance*, 93.
70 purchase the whole inventory: "Temple of Sackler."
70 "whole collections seemingly with a glance": Hoving, *Making the Mummies Dance*, 94.
70 a zealous negotiator: Ibid.
70 "of maximizing each deal": Lutze, *Who Can Know the Other?*, 164.
70 New boxes would arrive: Ibid., 155.
70 getting a Yorkshire terrier: Ibid., 164.
70 "put him on the world stage": Ibid., 156–57.
70 greatest collections of Chinese art: Hoving, *Making the Mummies Dance*, 93–94.

71 "the possibility of immortality": Lutze, *Who Can Know the Other?*, 156–57.
71 "the Sackler Gift": Grayson Kirk to Arthur Sackler, Jan. 8, 1960, CUCF.
71 "the Sackler Fund": Arthur Sackler to Stanley Salmen, Dec. 10, 1959, CUCF.
71 the Frick Collection: "700 See Treasures of Frick Gallery," *New York Times*, Dec. 12, 1935.
72 "no personal publicity": Arthur Sackler to Stanley Salmen, Dec. 10, 1959.
72 "Dr. Sackler is quite particular": Robert Harron to Davidson Taylor, Feb. 26, 1964, CUCF.
72 as part of "the Sackler Collection": Arthur Sackler to Stanley Salmen, Dec. 10, 1959.
72 he hated that expression: "Art Collector Honored Guest at Philbrook Opening."
72 "members of my family": Arthur Sackler to Stanley Salmen, Dec. 10, 1959.
72 approximately $70,000: "Meeting with Professor Mahler and Professor Baughman," Memorandum, Oct. 5, 1960, CUCF.
72 came not from Arthur: Raymond Sackler to William O'Donoghue, Dec. 14, 1959; Marietta Lutze Sackler to Stanley Salman, Dec. 17, 1959; Else Sackler to Stanley Salmen, Dec. 18, 1959, CUCF.
72 within four days of one another: "Arthur M. Sackler," Memorandum, Dec. 1, 1961, CUCF.
72 represented by the same accountant: Goldburt's name comes up repeatedly in the correspondence at Columbia. He was a longtime accountant for all three Sackler brothers. Interview with Richard Leather.
73 he was anxious: Lutze, *Who Can Know the Other?*, 158.
73 help decorate their home: Lutze, *Who Can Know the Other?*, 158.
73 Arthur wrote an introduction: Exhibition program for *The Ceramic Arts and Sculpture of China: From Prehistoric Times Through the Tenth Century A.D.*, CUCF.
73 "seems to be a tax gimmick": File Memorandum, April 25, 1961; Confidential Memorandum, March 1, 1965, CUCF.
73 "I hope you can make an inquiry": Stanley Salmen to Arthur Sackler, Aug. 23, 1960, CUCF.
74 "if you put your name on something": Posner, *Pharma*, 280.
74 plaque for Low Library: Grayson Kirk to Trustees Committee on Honors, memorandum, Feb. 19, 1964, CUCF.

74 "all photographs of Sackler objects": Arthur Sackler to Stanley Salmen, Dec. 17, 1965, CUCF.
74 regarded Arthur as difficult: "Sackler Funds," Confidential Memo, March 1, 1965, CUCF.
74 he wanted to build a Sackler museum: Arthur Sackler to Grayson Kirk, Dec. 12, 1967, CUCF.
74 "I have no doubt": Arthur Sackler to Grayson Kirk, Dec. 12, 1967, CUCF.
75 the province of packing lists: Lutze, *Who Can Know the Other?*, 155.
75 He collected relentlessly: Ibid., 148.
75 keep up with his own collecting: Ibid., 162.
75 "a conflagration": "In Memoriam," *Studio International* 200, supplement 1 (1987).
75 "Each purchase overshadowed the last": Lutze, *Who Can Know the Other?*, 156.

CHAPTER 6: THE OCTOPUS

76 Fourth Annual Symposium on Antibiotics: "Antibiotic Symposium for 1957," Memo from Welch to George Larrick, March 8, 1957, Kefauver Files.
76 first day of the conference: Testimony of Warren Kiefer, Hearings Before the Subcommittee on Antitrust and Monopoly of the Committee on the Judiciary, U.S. Senate, June 1, 1960 (hereafter cited as Kiefer Testimony).
76 authority in the field: "Drug Aide Quits; Blames Politics," *New York Times*, May 20, 1960; Testimony of Gideon Nachumi, Hearings Before the Subcommittee on Antitrust and Monopoly of the Committee on the Judiciary, U.S. Senate, June 1, 1960 (hereafter cited as Nachumi Testimony).
76 equivalent of a war hero: "Defends FDA Aide's Outside Pay: Drug Maker Says It Was OK'd," *Chicago Tribune*, Sept. 13, 1960. Welch had been a semipro baseball catcher. Oral history of Dr. Lloyd C. Miller, History of the U.S. Food and Drug Administration, Jan. 27, 1981; "Drug Aide Quits; Blames Politics."
76 Welch had received a telegram: Telegram from Dwight D. Eisenhower, in *Antibiotics Annual, 1956–1957* (New York: Medical Encyclopedia, 1957).
77 a psychiatrist by training: "Dr. Félix Martí-Ibáñez Is Dead; Psychiatrist and Publisher, 60," *New York Times*, May 25, 1972; Herman Bogdan, "Félix Martí-Ibáñez—Iberian Daedalus: The Man Behind the Es-

says," *Journal of the Royal Society of Medicine* 86 (Oct. 1993).

77 closely with the Sackler brothers: "3 Brothers Find Insanity Clews by Blood Test," *New York Herald Tribune,* Nov. 2, 1951.

77 "There is no man in medicine": Arthur Sackler to Henry Welch, Feb. 28, 1956, Kefauver Files.

77 fashioned himself a Renaissance man: "Physician Is Top Expert," *Atlanta Constitution,* Jan. 5, 1960; "Dr. Félix Martí-Ibáñez Is Dead; Psychiatrist and Publisher, 60."

77 columns in popular magazines: "The Romance of Health," *Cosmopolitan,* July 1963.

77 working for Arthur: "Advertising News: Madness in the Method," *New York Herald Tribune,* March 4, 1955.

77 company that he'd established: Bogdan, "Félix Martí-Ibáñez—Iberian Daedalus."

77 glossy magazine about medicine: "Doctors' Pains," *Newsweek,* June 20, 1960.

78 letters with comical doodles: Martí-Ibáñez to Welch, Jan. 16, 1957, Kefauver Files.

78 "Welch had strong opinions": Testimony of Barbara Moulton, Hearings Before the Subcommittee on Antitrust and Monopoly of the Committee on the Judiciary, U.S. Senate, June 2, 1960 (hereafter cited as Moulton Testimony).

78 They "felt obliged": Oral history of Dr. Lloyd C. Miller, Jan. 27, 1981.

78 paid for by the journals: "Antibiotic Symposium for 1957," Memo from Welch to George Larrick, March 8, 1957.

78 In a letter to Welch: Richard E. McFadyen, "The FDA's Regulation and Control of Antibiotics in the 1950s: The Henry Welch Scandal, Félix Martí-Ibáñez, and Charles Pfizer & Co.," *Bulletin of the History of Medicine* 53, no. 2 (Summer 1979).

78 "private and confidential aspects": Martí-Ibáñez to Welch, quoted in "Public Health at 7½ Percent," *Saturday Review,* June 4, 1960.

78 "We are now in the third era": Welch, opening remarks at Fourth Annual Antibiotics Symposium, published in *Antibiotics Annual, 1956–1957.*

79 expressed unease at the spectacle: Moulton Testimony.

79 *The Washington Post* declared: "Some of Deadliest Ills Defeated by Antibiotics," *Washington Post,* Oct. 19, 1956.

79 a press release: Kiefer Testimony.

79 purchased a new home: Lutze, *Who Can Know the Other?,* 137.

79 abandoning her career: Ibid., 123–24.

79 Marietta oversaw the relocation: Ibid., 138.

80 combining the two: Ibid., 137–38.

80 an urban safari: Ibid., 138.

80 tending to their mother, Sophie: Ibid., 118.

80 initiated into the faith: Ibid., 142–43.

81 Gray's Glycerine Tonic: Gray's Glycerine Tonic bottle, exhibit at the National Museum of American History.

81 winking joke at the company: "New in Town: Purdue for Pain," *U.S. 1,* May 8, 2002.

81 laxative called Senokot: "Arabian Remedy Yields New Drug," *Maryville (Mo.) Daily Forum,* July 22, 1955.

81 "Have you considered the possibility": Martí-Ibáñez to Mortimer and Raymond Sackler, memorandum, Sept. 28, 1955, FMI Files.

81 developing his own mania: Mortimer Sackler to Martí-Ibáñez, Feb. 7, 1960, FMI Files.

81 "the occasional moment or two": Arthur Sackler to Martí-Ibáñez, Aug. 11, 1958, FMI Files.

81 Sackler headquarters under surveillance: "Sackler Brothers," Memorandum from John Blair to Paul Rand Dixon, March 16, 1960, Kefauver Files.

82 nuclear attack on New York City: "Hiroshima, U.S.A.," *Collier's,* Aug. 5, 1950.

82 One night in the late 1950s: Podolsky, *Antibiotic Era,* 70–71. Podolsky speculates that the unnamed research physician was Maxwell Finland.

82 Lear had dinner: Richard Harris, *The Real Voice* (New York: Macmillan, 1964), 19.

82 brochure that had been sent to doctors: "Taking the Miracle Out of the Miracle Drugs," *Saturday Review,* Jan. 3, 1959.

82 written to each of the named physicians: Harris, *Real Voice,* 19.

83 Lear wrote to the doctors: Ibid.

83 produced by Arthur Sackler's agency: "Public Health at 7½ Percent."

83 *Saturday Review* article: "Taking the Miracle Out of the Miracle Drugs."

83 Lear got him on the phone: "The Certification of Antibiotics," *Saturday Review,* Feb. 7, 1959.

83 they spoke for two hours: Ibid.

84 met with a couple of staffers: Harris, *Real Voice,* 25.

84 rawboned public servant: "Crime: It Pays to Organize," *Time,* March 12, 1951; Harris, *Real Voice,* 10.

84 a southern liberal: "Crime: It Pays to Organize."

84 full-time staff of thirty-eight: Harris, *Real Voice*, 25–26.

84 groundbreaking investigation of the Mafia: "Crime: It Pays to Organize."

85 unprecedented ratings: "The Senator and the Gangsters," *Smithsonian*, April 18, 2012.

85 "the greatest TV show": "Kefauvercasts Prove a Real Tele Bargain," *Billboard*, March 31, 1951.

85 put the senator on the cover: *Time*, March 12, 1951, March 24, 1952, Sept. 17, 1956.

85 "These drug fellows": This line has commonly been misattributed to Kefauver himself. In fact, it was said by Paul Rand Dixon. Harris, *Real Voice*, 47.

85 could corrupt government: "Crime: It Pays to Organize."

85 regulatory agencies can be hoodwinked: Harris, *Real Voice*, 106.

85 convening hearings: Ibid., 41.

85 unrelenting pressure from the drug companies: Moulton Testimony.

86 the inquiry reoriented: Jeremy A. Greene and Scott H. Podolsky, "Keeping the Modern in Medicine: Pharmaceutical Promotion and Physician Education in Postwar America," *Bulletin of the History of Medicine* 83 (2009).

86 patient but persistent interlocutor: Harris, *Real Voice*, 58, 117.

86 "You have blitzed the medical profession": Testimony of John McKeen, Hearings Before the Subcommittee on Antitrust and Monopoly of the Committee on the Judiciary, U.S. Senate, May 4, 1960.

87 insinuated its own ad copy: Nachumi Testimony.

87 entitled to half of any income: "Drugmakers and the Govt.—Who Makes the Decisions?," *Saturday Review*, July 2, 1960.

87 "It was a standing joke": Kiefer Testimony.

88 "During the course of the drug investigation": "Sackler Brothers," Memorandum from John Blair to Paul Rand Dixon, March 16, 1960, Kefauver Files.

88 Kefauver's staff attempted to tally: Ibid.

89 diagram the sprawling web: Ibid.

89 article in the *Saturday Review*: "Public Health at 7½ Percent."

89 "the first real link": Lear to Blair, May 24, 1960, Kefauver Files.

89 He found a document: "Public Health at 7½ Percent."

89 according to one of his informants: Lear to Blair, May 24, 1960.

90 Lear sent the clipping: Lear to Blair, letter and enclosed cartoons, June 27, 1961, Kefauver Files.

90 investigators were most interested: "Further Information Concerning M.D. Publications and the Sackler Brothers," Memorandum from John Dixon to John Blair, May 17, 1960, Kefauver Files.

90 uncover some direct link: Ibid.

90 "if you have to carry me in": "Senators Study Income of High Food-Drug Aide," *Washington Post*, May 18, 1960; Statement of Michael F. Markel, Hearing Before the Subcommittee on Antitrust and Monopoly of the Committee of the Judiciary, United States Senate, May 17, 1960.

90 "Dr. Welch was said to be in danger": "U.S. Scientist Held Outside Jobs, Flemming Tells Drug Inquiry," *New York Times*, May 18, 1960.

90 letter marked "Personal and confidential": Martí-Ibáñez to Frohlich, March 2, 1960, Kefauver Files.

91 7.5 percent of all the advertising: "Public Health at 7½ Percent."

91 Welch earned a salary of $17,500: Ibid.

91 $287,142 from his publishing ventures: "Dr. Henry Welch Earnings from Editorship of M.D. Publications, Journals and from Medical Encyclopedia, Inc., 1953 Through March 1960," Memorandum, Kefauver Files.

91 "Once those figures get out": "Senators Study Income of High Food-Drug Aide."

91 resigned from the FDA: "Welch Resigns as Head of FDA; Denies Wrong," *Washington Post*, May 20, 1960.

91 maintain his innocence: "Drug Aide Quits; Blames Politics."

91 retired to Florida: "Henry Welch, FDA Ex-official, Dies," *Washington Post*, Oct. 29, 1982.

91 announced a review: "FDA Plans Second Look at Drugs OK'd by Welch," *Chicago Tribune*, June 4, 1960.

91 Frohlich declined to testify: Hearings Before the Subcommittee on Antitrust and Monopoly of the Committee on the Judiciary, U.S. Senate, Jan. 31, 1962.

91 one final witness: "Kefauver Subpoenas Advertising Records," UPI, Dec. 24, 1961.

91 Marietta had always noticed: Lutze, *Who Can Know the Other?*, 125.

92 He despised Kefauver: Lopez, *Arthur M. Sackler*, 24.

92 dismissed any such suggestion: Arthur Sackler to Welch, Feb. 28, 1956, Kefauver Files.

92 noises of protest: Exchange of letters between Perrin H. Long and Martí-Ibáñez, May 1957, Kefauver Files.
92 "dear and admired friends": Martí-Ibáñez to Perrin H. Long, May 9, 1957, Kefauver Files.
92 "I used to be pleased": "Doctors' Pains."
92 "This was the era of McCarthyite witch-hunts": Lopez, *Arthur M. Sackler*, 24.
92 hired Clark Clifford: Ibid.
92 "The committee will come to order": Unless otherwise noted, this scene is drawn from a transcript of the Hearings Before the Subcommittee on Antitrust and Monopoly of the Committee on the Judiciary, U.S. Senate, Jan. 30, 1962.
93 They had been war-gaming: Draft of a script of questions and potential answers, Kefauver Files.
93 "He seemed to parade his voice": Hoving, *Making the Mummies Dance*, 95.
95 "I was very glad to have": Welch to Arthur Sackler, "Personal and Confidential," Feb. 23, 1956, Kefauver Files.
95 "I would very much like to meet you": Arthur Sackler to Welch, Feb. 28, 1956, Kefauver Files.
95 "I would like to tell you at a time": Arthur Sackler to Welch, March 9, 1959, Kefauver Files.

CHAPTER 7: THE DENDUR DERBY
96 A small temple: Dieter Arnold, *Temples of the Last Pharaohs* (New York: Oxford University Press, 1999), 244.
96 decorated with carved depictions: Dieter Arnold and Adela Oppenheim, "The Temple of Dendur: Architecture and Ritual," available on the Metropolitan Museum's website.
96 converted into a Christian church: "642 Stones Will Soon Regain Form as an Egyptian Temple," *New York Times*, Nov. 29, 1974.
96 Luther Bradish visited the temple: "The Boomerang Graffito (or Bad, Bad, Luther B!)," NPR, June 7, 2013.
96 Félix Bonfils: "642 Stones Will Soon Regain Form as an Egyptian Temple."
97 build a dam: "Imperiled Heritage," *Hartford Courant*, March 13, 1960.
97 "new pyramid": Ibid.
97 three-hundred-mile lake: "Floating Laboratories on the Nile," *Unesco Courier*, Oct. 1961; "Metropolitan Due to Get Temple of Dendur," *New York Times*, April 25, 1967.
97 offered to give the Temple of Dendur:

"Cairo Offers U.S. a Temple Saved from Aswan Flooding," *New York Times*, March 27, 1965.
97 eight-hundred-ton temple: "Metropolitan Due to Get Temple of Dendur."
97 incorporated in 1870: Michael Gross, *Rogues' Gallery: The Secret Story of the Lust, Lies, Greed, and Betrayals That Made the Metropolitan Museum of Art* (New York: Broadway Books, 2010), 24.
97 started with a private art collection: Calvin Tomkins, *Merchants and Masterpieces: The Story of the Metropolitan Museum of Art* (New York: Dutton, 1970), chap. 3.
98 The Met would be free: A state law in 1893 governing support for the Met maintained that the museum "shall be kept open and accessible to the public free of all charge." "The Met Files a Formal Proposal to Charge Admission to Out-of-State Visitors," *New York Times*, May 5, 2017.
98 "Think of it, ye millionaires": Winifred Eva Howe, *A History of the Metropolitan Museum of Art* (New York: Metropolitan Museum of Art, 1913), 200.
98 record $2.3 million: "Museum Gets Rembrandt for $2.3 Million," *New York Times*, Nov. 16, 1961.
98 museum could hardly afford: "To Keep the Museums Open," *New York Times*, Jan. 9, 1961.
98 "a painting is worth the price": "Attendance Soars at Museums Here," *New York Times*, Nov. 27, 1961.
98 none of them were paying: Ibid.
98 The Met's director: "James Rorimer of Metropolitan, Duncan Phillips, Collector, Die," *New York Times*, May 12, 1966.
98 He announced a goal: "Museum Sets 1964 as Building Date," *New York Times*, Oct. 22, 1961.
99 turned for help to Arthur Sackler: "James Rorimer of Metropolitan, Duncan Phillips, Collector, Die"; Hoving, *Making the Mummies Dance*, 95.
99 "They were proud that they had escaped": Interview with Leather.
99 Thirty of them: "James Rorimer of Metropolitan, Duncan Phillips, Collector, Die."
99 pledging $150,000: Hoving, *Making the Mummies Dance*, 95.
100 gaming the tax code: Ibid.
100 would actually *make* money: Ibid.; Gross, *Rogues' Gallery*, 344.
100 museum needed cash: Gross, *Rogues' Gallery*, 344.

100 "That's four thousand years old": "James Rorimer of Metropolitan, Duncan Phillips, Collector, Die."

100 Arthur liked Rorimer: "The Met's Sackler Enclave: Public Boon or Private Preserve?," *ARTnews,* Sept. 1978.

100 "We'd talk for hours": Hoving, *Making the Mummies Dance,* 95.

101 private "enclave" in the museum: "The Temple of Sackler," *Vanity Fair,* Sept. 1987.

101 Rorimer signed off: Gross, *Rogues' Gallery,* 344.

101 arrangement was kept secret: "Temple of Sackler."

101 Arthur would suggest: Hoving, *Making the Mummies Dance,* 95.

101 *another* enclave at a different institution: Frederick Dookstader to Arthur Sackler, May 31, 1996, Smithsonian/Museum of the American Indian Files.

101 had a heart attack: "James Rorimer of Metropolitan, Duncan Phillips, Collector, Die."

101 Hoving was a publicity hound: "A Happening Called Hoving," *New York Times Magazine,* July 10, 1966.

102 a rubble of 642 sandstone bricks: "Metropolitan Due to Get Temple of Dendur."

102 "We have not been campaigning": "Feud over a Temple Boils into a Tempest," *New York Times,* Sept. 29, 1966.

102 Twenty cities put together bids: "A Panel of 5 Will Choose Site in U.S. for Temple of Dendur," *New York Times,* Jan. 23, 1967.

102 what about Cairo, Illinois?: "Suggested for Art Museum," *Chicago Tribune,* April 25, 1967.

102 "the Dendur Derby": "Metropolitan Due to Get Temple of Dendur."

102 "in as naturalistic a way": "Feud over a Temple Boils into a Tempest."

103 one Met official proclaimed: "Metropolitan Due to Get Temple of Dendur"; "Feud over a Temple Boils into a Tempest."

103 "I'll light the temple up": "Charity Fund-Raisers Know the Value of Art," *New York Times,* May 21, 1967.

103 resistance from conservationists: "Museum Wing Will Cost $15 Million," *New York Times,* Jan. 23, 1973.

103 one day it dawned on him: Hoving, *Making the Mummies Dance,* 240–42.

104 Nobody could say that he had: Ibid., 95.

104 difficult to track down: In his correspondence with Félix Martí-Ibáñez, Arthur

is forever apologizing for not writing more or being in better touch. This is also echoed in the recollections of Marietta Lutze.

104 But within thirty minutes: Hoving, *Making the Mummies Dance,* 241.

104 "I'll do it," Arthur said: Ibid., 240–42.

104 "their office hours": Gross, *Rogues' Gallery,* 345.

105 construction got under way: "Drills Sing in Park as Museum Flexes Wings," *New York Times,* March 28, 1974.

105 "thanks largely to a recent gift": "642 Stones Will Soon Regain Form as an Egyptian Temple."

105 forced to raise more funds: Gross, *Rogues' Gallery,* 345.

105 chipping in $1.4 million: "Drills Sing in Park as Museum Flexes Wings."

105 for eleven years: "642 Stones Will Soon Regain Form as an Egyptian Temple."

105 "an apothecary shop": "Temple of Sackler."

105 "He was touchy, eccentric": Hoving, *Making the Mummies Dance,* 95.

105 officials at the Met chafed: "An Art Collector Sows Largesse and Controversy," *New York Times,* June 5, 1983.

105 when it came to the old-line burghers: "Temple of Sackler."

106 "I gave the Met exactly": Ibid.

106 "an anti-Semitic place": Ibid.

106 ran out of old rich WASPs: Gross, *Rogues' Gallery,* 345–46.

106 "the Sackler wing is a generous gift": "Art Collector Sows Largesse and Controversy."

106 described Arthur as "slippery": Hoving, *Making the Mummies Dance,* 94.

106 "Throw him out": This line appears in the typescript manuscript for *Making the Mummies Dance,* which is held in the Hoving Papers at Princeton, but not in the book.

106 unveiled the Sackler Wing: "King's Treasures Open at Museum," *Asbury Park Press,* Dec. 12, 1978.

106 the names Arthur, Mortimer, and Raymond: "Treasures of Tut Glitter in Daylight," *New York Times,* Dec. 12, 1978.

106 "the goddess of modern dance": "King's Treasures Open at Museum"; "Weekend Notes," *Newsday,* Oct. 4, 1985; "Dance: Miss Graham 'Frescoes,'" *New York Times,* April 23, 1980.

107 performed in the temple: "King's Treasures Open at Museum."

107 He had become friends with Arthur:

"The Mayor's 'Stroke Diary,'" *Newsday*, Aug. 13, 1987.

107 "And what greater way to mark it": "Exhibit of King Tut Expected to Draw 1.3 Million Visitors," AP, Sept. 19, 1978.

107 cocktails and a dance band: "Martha Graham Opens New Dance Work," AP, Dec. 11, 1978.

107 Even as the brothers celebrated: "Sackler Brothers," Memorandum from John Blair to Paul Rand Dixon, March 16, 1960, Kefauver Files.

CHAPTER 8: ESTRANGEMENT

108 an impressive woman: "Muriel L. Sackler," Obituary, *New York Times*, Oct. 9, 2009; "Miriam [*sic*] Sackler," Petition for Naturalization No. 413227, Southern District of New York, 1942. According to this document, Muriel's birth name might have been Miriam; the name is not a typo—she writes "Miriam" in longhand on the signature line.

108 Gertraud Wimmer: "Two Looks, Two Lives," *Savvy*, Sept. 1981.

108 started a relationship: Gertraud "Geri" Wimmer was thirty-five years old in September 1981, so she was born around 1946. Ibid.

108 "the *bellissima* Geri": Martí-Ibáñez to Mortimer Sackler, July 30, 1969, FMI Papers.

108 Sophie resented this: Lutze, *Who Can Know the Other?*, 164.

108 she died, of cancer, in 1965: Ibid., 143.

109 "The Cote D'Azur this year is not as mobbed": Mortimer Sackler to Martí-Ibáñez, Aug. 13, 1966, FMI Papers.

109 oversaw the purchase: "Dr. Mortimer Sackler," Obituary, *Telegraph*, April 27, 2010.

109 "Calm down. Take a tranquilizer": Interview with Panagiotis "Taki" Theodoracopulos; "Mortimer Sackler and Me," *Spectator*, April 4, 2019.

109 screenwriter Paul Gallico: "Paul Gallico, Sportswriter and Author, Is Dead at 78," *New York Times*, July 17, 1976; Mortimer Sackler to Martí-Ibáñez, Aug. 6, 1968, FMI Papers; Paul Gallico interview from 1973, in *Publishers Weekly, The Author Speaks: Selected "PW" Interviews, 1967–1976* (New York: R. R. Bowker, 1977), 54–57.

109 developed the Mediterranean tendency: Mortimer Sackler to Martí-Ibáñez, Aug. 13, 1966, FMI Papers.

109 "The sun is with us daily": Mortimer Sackler to Martí-Ibáñez, July 24, 1968, FMI Papers.

109 "I was expecting Bobby": Mortimer

Sackler to Martí-Ibáñez, Aug. 13, 1966, FMI Papers.

109 "Geri and I are expecting": Mortimer Sackler to Martí-Ibáñez, July 24, 1968.

110 a daughter, Samantha: Martí-Ibáñez to Mortimer Sackler, July 30, 1969, FMI Papers.

110 they were married: Ibid.; Mortimer D. Sackler Affidavit, *Mortimer Sackler v. Gertraud Sackler*, Supreme Court of the State of New York, July 31, 1984 (hereafter cited as MDS Affidavit).

110 purchased a beautiful villa: Maureen Emerson, *Riviera Dreaming: Love and War on the Côte d'Azur* (London: I. B. Tauris, 2008), 19, 120, 139.

110 "The house is far from finished": Mortimer Sackler to Martí-Ibáñez, July 2, 1969, FMI Papers.

110 purchased an enormous town house: Interview with Elizabeth Bernard, who was Mortimer's housekeeper; Martí-Ibáñez to Mortimer Sackler, Dec. 11, 1972, FMI Papers; dinner invitation from Geri and Mortimer Sackler to Martí-Ibáñez, Dec. 13 [year not specified], FMI Papers. The invitation lists the address as 10 East Sixty-Fourth Street.

110 maintained a grand apartment: MDS Affidavit.

110 also bought a home: Mortimer Sackler to Martí-Ibáñez, Oct. 4, 1963, FMI Papers.

110 he had become a "swinger": Mortimer Sackler to Martí-Ibáñez, June 6, 1967, FMI Papers.

110 "a full and vigorous life": Mortimer Sackler to Martí-Ibáñez, March 1967, FMI Papers.

110 "While books and the written word": Mortimer Sackler to Martí-Ibáñez, April 15, 1966, FMI Papers.

110 Geri gave birth to a second child: Birth announcement for Mortimer D. Alfons Sackler, May 9, 1971, FMI Papers.

110 "the new family": Mortimer Sackler to Martí-Ibáñez, April 15, 1966.

110 renounced his American citizenship: MDS Affidavit.

111 for tax reasons: Barry Meier, *Pain Killer: A "Wonder" Drug's Trail of Addiction and Death* (Emmaus, Pa.: Rodale, 2003), 217. There are two editions of *Pain Killer*, which I will differentiate in the notes by year, the original (2003) and revised (2018).

111 never seen Mortimer so happy: Mortimer Sackler to Martí-Ibáñez, May 11, 1972, FMI Papers.

111 someday becoming a doctor: Martí-

Ibáñez to Mortimer Sackler, June 8, 1971, FMI Papers.

111 father and son grew tempestuous: Mortimer Sackler to Martí-Ibáñez, July 2, 1969.

111 "My sense is that Arthur": Interview with Rich.

111 He still intervened: Interview with Richard Leather.

112 very much intermingled: Interview with John Kallir. I consulted two decades of *Medical Tribune* issues, and advertisements for Senokot, Betadine, and other Purdue Frederick products appear in virtually every issue.

112 embarrass his brothers: Interview with John Kallir.

112 "Ray was quiet": Ibid.

112 raised two sons: Interview with Richard Kapit; Martí-Ibáñez to Mortimer Sackler, June 8, 1971, FMI Papers.

112 "I have never been so 'out of contact'": Arthur Sackler to Martí-Ibáñez, Aug. 11, 1958, FMI Papers.

112 close touch with Raymond: Mortimer Sackler to Martí-Ibáñez, April 4, 1966, FMI Papers.

112 "let Morty be our guide": Raymond Sackler to Martí-Ibáñez, Oct. 5, 1963, FMI Papers.

112 Purdue Frederick budget meetings: Raymond and Mortimer Sackler to Martí-Ibáñez, Sept. 10, 1971, FMI Papers.

112 black-tie dinners: Dinner invitation from Geri and Mortimer Sackler to Martí-Ibáñez, Dec. 13 [year not specified], FMI Papers; birthday invitation, Dec. 7 [year unspecified], FMI Papers.

112 "Arthur, Mortimer and Raymond": Arthur, Mortimer, and Raymond Sackler to Martí-Ibáñez, June 19, 1969, FMI Papers.

112 Martí-Ibáñez praised Mortimer: Mortimer Sackler to Paul Ghalioungui, Jan. 3, 1967, FMI Papers.

113 "It seemed to me that her strong": Lutze, *Who Can Know the Other?*, 143.

113 "I tried to interest my son": "Of Dreams and Archaeology, of Methylmercury Poisoning," *Medical Tribune*, Oct. 24, 1973.

113 Marietta began to fear: Lutze, *Who Can Know the Other?*, 145.

113 enormously proud: Interview with Rich.

113 Marietta increasingly resented: Lutze, *Who Can Know the Other?*, 164.

113 he and Else would frequent museums: Zakin Affidavit.

113 holidays with Else: Reply Affidavit of Else Sackler, *Matter of Sackler*, March 1, 1991.

113 by Monet: The painting was *Les Peupliers*, painted in 1891. The Sackler family sold it at Christie's in 2000 for $22 million.

113 "to find a Monet for Else": Zakin Affidavit.

114 named Jillian Tully: The third wife of Arthur Sackler has spelled her first name a number of ways—Gillian, Jill, and Jillian. For the sake of ease and clarity, I will refer to her only as Jillian, except in instances in which the name is spelled differently in primary documents.

114 "I met Dr. Sackler in 1967": "The Other Sackler," *Washington Post*, Nov. 27, 2019.

114 Arthur told Jillian: Affidavit of Gillian T. Sackler, *Matter of Sackler*, Index No. 249220, Surrogate's Court of the State of New York, Nassau County, June 13, 1990 (hereafter cited as GTS Affidavit).

114 moved to New York: "Other Sackler."

114 she officially changed her name: GTS Affidavit.

114 split into two: "Other Sackler."

114 "This was not a family": Interview with Rich.

115 Arthur allowed Frohlich to be: Tanner, *Our Bodies, Our Data*, 30.

115 $40 million in revenue: Ibid., 28.

115 "most beautiful villa": Mortimer Sackler to Martí-Ibáñez, Aug. 29, 1969, FMI Papers.

115 then pass out: Tanner, *Our Bodies, Our Data*, 28.

115 immediately took charge: Interview with Richard Leather.

115 diagnosed with a brain tumor: Tanner, *Our Bodies, Our Data*, 28.

115 secret agreement: Ibid., 29.

115 known as a tontine: Interview with Richard Leather; Tanner, *Our Bodies, Our Data*, 29.

116 four-way musketeers agreement: Interview with Richard Leather.

116 two written agreements: Ibid.

116 obscuring their brother's involvement: Tanner, *Our Bodies, Our Data*, 29.

116 $37 million: Ibid.

116 "Four people founded IMS": RDS 2019 Deposition.

116 "I knew very little": Tanner, *Our Bodies, Our Data*, 29.

116 "gave away his rights to IMS": Minutes of an Estate Meeting, Aug. 7, 1987.

117 "They moved the company out": Minutes of an Estate Meeting, July 29, 1987.

117 "Dad came up with the idea": Minutes of an Estate Meeting, Aug. 7, 1987.

117 "the beginning of the whole rift": Minutes of an Estate Meeting, July 29, 1987; Minutes of an Estate Meeting, Aug. 7, 1987.

117 "You are entering life": Martí-Ibáñez to Robert Sackler, Oct. 14, 1964, FMI Papers.

117 He maintained an apartment: Interview with Elizabeth Bernard. Much later, Bernard filed an unsuccessful lawsuit against Purdue over employee benefits that she claimed she had been denied. But having worked for the family for nearly three decades, she had nothing but warm and vivid memories when it came to Mortimer D. Sackler and I found her to be entirely credible.

118 "Robert was very distraught": Interview with Welber.

118 "I have friends. Relatives": Kathe Sackler Deposition.

118 PCP was rejected for human use: "Teen-Age Use of 'Angel Dust' Stirs Concern," New York Times, Nov. 10, 1977.

118 "he freaked out": Interview with Bernard.

118 "She was complaining": The account of Bobby's suicide is based on an interview with Ceferino Perez, who was an eyewitness. Elizabeth Bernard, who was called by the family to come and clean up Muriel's apartment afterward, corroborated most of the details of Perez's recollection, with one exception: Bernard does not remember the window being broken. She thinks that Bobby might have opened the window and jumped out. Of the two of them, Perez seems to possess the clearer memory of the suicide, which he witnessed himself, so I have rendered the scene from his point of view.

CHAPTER 9: GHOST MARKS

120 His collecting must be driven: Lutze, Who Can Know the Other?, 165.

120 Arthur was traveling more: Ibid., 176.

120 he were in a race with time: Ibid., 171.

120 enrolled in psychotherapy: Ibid., 174.

120 Arthur opposed this decision: Ibid., 174–75.

120 retrain as a psychotherapist: Ibid., 175.

120 come to feel like "conquest": Ibid., 171.

120 Arthur lost interest: Ibid., 178.

121 she pleaded with him: The precise timing of this revelation is difficult to pin down: in her memoir, Marietta does not give a year but describes this conversation as happening prior to Arthur's sixtieth birthday party,

which took place in 1973, but after she and Arthur bought the apartment at UN Plaza, which they did in 1970. In an affidavit, Jillian Sackler writes that she and Arthur first met in 1967, and at that point Arthur was already, in his telling, "estranged" from Marietta. According to two people who knew Marietta during this period, she might have been in denial over the obvious signs that her marriage was ending. In the end, however, she and Arthur remained formally married until December 1981.

121 "I love somebody else": Ibid., 178.

121 Marietta drove in from Long: Ibid., 180.

121 more "open" arrangement: Ibid., 179.

121 maintain the outward appearance: Ibid.

121 Marietta delivered the speech: Ibid., 181.

122 at the Goya show: "Royalty & Raves at a Sparkling World Premiere," Washington Post, Nov. 17, 1986.

122 feting a visiting French marquise: "Series of Bubbly Parties Salutes a New Champagne," Los Angeles Times, Sept. 23, 1982.

122 Medical Tribune column: "Tenor Talks of Loving the Public and His Favorite Opera Composers," Medical Tribune, Nov. 1, 1978; "Pavarotti Talks of Sex and Sunshine," Medical Tribune, Nov. 15, 1978; "The Quiet Scholar: King of Sweden," Medical Tribune, Nov. 1, 1972.

122 "What passes for news": The quotation is from Sidney Wolfe. "A Financial Man and the Fogg," Boston Globe, Feb. 16, 1982.

122 art collector Edward Warburg: "The Temple of Sackler," Vanity Fair, Sept. 1987.

122 "Good heavens": "Art Collector Honored Guest at Philbrook Opening," Tulsa World, Dec. 8, 1975.

122 "I am one of the few men": Ibid.

122 He loved air travel: "The Chariots of the Gods—and the 747," Medical Tribune, Oct. 3, 1973.

122 requested a seat in the back: "Remembrance of Kings Past," Medical Marketing and Media, July 1996.

123 piece of jade: "Sadat Urges U.S. to Back Liberation of the Third World," AP, Aug. 8, 1981; "Koch and City Lionize Sadat," Newsday, Aug. 8, 1981.

123 "I knew a lot of geniuses": Gail Levin, Becoming Judy Chicago (Oakland: University of California Press, 2007), 363.

123 Arthur became friends: "A Halo and a Vision," Medical Tribune, July 25, 1973; "The Colors of Love—I," Medical Tribune, April

12, 1978; "The Colors of Love—II," *Medical Tribune,* April 26, 1978; "An Open Letter to Bernard Malamud," *Medical Tribune,* Nov. 14, 1973.

123 Reflecting on the friendship: Interview with Janna Malamud Smith.

123 practically a rite of passage: See, for instance, "FDA Chief Defends Position on Package Inserts," *Medical Tribune,* Feb. 11, 1976.

123 death notice to the *Times:* "Sackler— Robert, M.," *New York Times,* July 6, 1975.

123 cut off the ends of their neckties: Interview with Elizabeth Bernard.

123 memorial scholarship fund: In a paid death notice for Mortimer D. Sackler in 2010, Tel Aviv University noted, "The Robert M. Sackler Memorial Scholarship Fund will continue to transform lives far into the future." Interestingly, however, there is no public information associated with this fund: it is a "memorial" scholarship without any description of the individual being memorialized.

124 shoebox of old photographs: Interview with Judith Schachter.

124 Mortimer Sackler had been in France: Interview with Elizabeth Bernard.

124 account in the tabloids: MDS Affidavit; "Suzy Says," *New York Daily News,* Sept. 13, 1977.

124 younger than Mortimer's daughters: She was born in 1949, so thirty-one or thereabouts when they married in 1980. "Drugs Mogul with Vast Philanthropic Legacy," *Financial Times,* April 23, 2010.

124 white stucco mansion: The address is 67 Chester Square. See "Meet the Chester Square Candys," *Telegraph,* March 8, 2016.

124 fall/winter couture show: "Valentino's Art Presented at Met Museum," *Los Angeles Times,* Sept. 24, 1982.

125 three hundred guests were invited: "A Party at the Museum...," *New York Daily News,* Sept. 22, 1982.

125 Muhammad Ali performed magic tricks: "'Waiting for Valentino' in New York," *Desert Sun* (Palm Springs), Sept. 27, 1982; "Valentino's Art Presented at Met Museum."

125 adorned with white flowers: "'Waiting for Valentino' in New York."

125 Arthur Sackler was disgusted: Notes by Thomas Hoving on Arthur Sackler in the Thomas Hoving Papers, Princeton University Library (hereafter cited as Hoving Notes).

125 did not get along: Ibid.

125 "It was kind of like that last scene": Interview with Rich.

125 existence of the secret arrangement: "The Met's Sackler Enclave: Public Boon or Private Preserve?," *ARTnews,* Sept. 1978.

126 "He offered me several gifts": "Temple of Sackler."

126 *ARTnews* published a story: "Met's Sackler Enclave"; interview with Charles Brody.

126 submit to a deposition: "The Sackler Collection, Cont'd," *Washington Post,* July 30, 1982.

126 Administrators at the Met: Gross, *Rogues' Gallery,* 346.

126 Arthur had been very open: "Arthur Sackler's Inner Resources," *Washington Post,* June 7, 1987.

126 candid about his ambitions: "Financial Man and the Fogg."

126 seeking to punish him: Hoving Notes.

126 Why couldn't he take that seat?: Ibid.

126 denied him any credit: "An Art Collector Sows Largesse and Controversy," *New York Times,* June 5, 1983.

127 invitation to spend an afternoon: Arthur Sackler to Pauling, June 21, 1980, Ava Helen and Linus Pauling Papers, Oregon State University. (This archive will hereafter be cited as Pauling Papers.)

127 It was a business deal: Posner, *Pharma,* 280.

127 "Arthur's new toy": Jillian Sackler to Pauling, June 21, 1983, Pauling Papers.

127 "didn't have time for Arthur": Gross, *Rogues' Gallery,* 347.

127 aired his grievances: Hoving Notes.

127 "Dear Doctor Sackler": Ripley to Arthur Sackler, March 10, 1980, Smithsonian Institution Archives. (This collection will be cited hereafter as Smithsonian Files.)

127 "a major gift to the nation": Arthur Sackler to Ripley, April 4, 1980, Smithsonian Files.

127 "a mixed blessing": Memorandum for the Record, by James McK. Symington, April 8, 1980, Smithsonian Files.

128 "Your very generous offer": Ripley to Arthur Sackler, Sept. 18, 1980, Smithsonian Files.

128 his "unshakeable" position: Memorandum for the Record, by Ripley, Oct. 6, 1981, Smithsonian Files.

128 Arthur prevailed: Arthur Sackler/ Smithsonian Institution Contract, Fifth

Preliminary Draft, April 1982, Smithsonian Files.

128 roughly $75 million: Ripley letter (this copy does not have a recipient but went to multiple people), Aug. 10, 1982, Smithsonian Files.

128 museum would open to the public: Smithsonian Institution, news release, April 1986, Smithsonian Files.

128 "Disappointed? The disinherited always": "Sackler Collection, Cont'd."

128 squad of curators: "Art Collector Sows Largesse and Controversy."

128 It seemed to Marietta: Lutze, *Who Can Know the Other?,* 181.

129 in a letter: Ibid., 181–82. This is an instance in which Marietta's telling of the story may not be entirely reliable, because, according to a family friend, she *did* come away from the marriage with a lot of valuable paintings. She ended up with a Braque, a Picasso, a Kandinsky, and others. "*She* may not have asked for them," the friend said. "But her lawyers did."

129 driving her mad: Ibid., 182.

129 grabbed the sleeping pills: Ibid.

130 The pills tasted bitter: Ibid., 185.

130 "How could you do this to me?": Ibid.

130 the divorce was finalized: The divorce became final on December 28, 1981. Jillian and Arthur were married the next day. GTS Affidavit.

130 Marietta got the apartment: Lutze, *Who Can Know the Other?,* 202.

CHAPTER 10: TO THWART THE INEVITABILITY OF DEATH

131 the same stage: Sanders Theatre webpage, Office of the Arts, Harvard University.

131 "President Bok": "A New Millennium Begins," Dedicatory Address, Harvard University, Oct. 18, 1985.

131 opening of the Arthur M. Sackler Museum: Program for "Lectures Celebrating the Dedication of the Arthur M. Sackler Museum," Oct. 18, 1985; Invitation to the Dedication of the Arthur M. Sackler Museum, Oct. 18, 1985, Louis Lasagna Papers, University of Rochester.

131 canceled the project: "The Miracle on Quincy Street," *Harvard Crimson,* Oct. 17, 1985.

131 $10 million: "The Man Who Made It Real," *Harvard Crimson,* Oct. 17, 1985.

132 Itzhak Perlman: "Arty Party," *Harvard Crimson,* Oct. 17, 1985.

132 *The Boston Globe:* "Architecture," *Boston Globe,* Sept. 8, 1985.

132 "all species were at the mercy": "New Millennium Begins."

132 press release: Smithsonian Institution, news release, April 1986, Smithsonian Files; Program for the Grand Opening of the Arthur M. Sackler Center for Health Communications at Tufts University, Feb. 20, 21, 1986.

132 "spent the greatest part": Arthur Sackler to colleagues at McAdams, Dec. 28, 1967.

132 no mention of McAdams: Smithsonian Institution, news release, April 1986.

133 Security was tight: Thomas Lawton to Milo Beach, May 12, 1993, Smithsonian Files.

133 "a very privileged moment": "Digging Museums," *Washington Post,* June 22, 1983.

133 The plan: Thomas Lawton to Milo Beach, May 12, 1993.

133 "$175 million plus": "Convictions of a Collector," *Washington Post,* Sept. 21, 1986; "Forbes 400," *Forbes,* Oct. 1986. (If you look closely at the cover of the magazine, the name "Arthur Mitchell Sackler" is right there, in a cursive font, alongside the others.)

133 list of "firsts": "During Medical Tribune's Life Span," *Medical Tribune,* May 7, 1980.

133 three-day "Festschrift": Jillian Sackler to Harry Henderson, Oct. 1, 1986, Henderson Papers.

133 "list of achievements": Jillian Sackler to Harry Henderson, Oct. 18, 1986, Henderson Papers.

133 "His agenda would have required": Louis Lasagna, *Studio International* 200, supplement 1 (1987).

133 "is my greatest enemy": "Of Time and Life, Part I," *Medical Tribune,* April 2, 1975.

134 a punishing schedule: "Art Collector Sows Largesse and Controversy," *New York Times,* June 5, 1983.

134 to keep up: "The Other Sackler," *Washington Post,* Nov. 27, 2019.

134 Arthur fell ill: EJS Deposition. It was the fall of 1986. Thomas Lawton to Tom Freudenheim, Dec. 12, 1986, Smithsonian Files.

134 giant cake: An entry on the website worldofsugarart.com features photos of the cake. Scott Clark Woolley, email.

134 rejected the plans: "Party Palace," *New York,* Jan. 9, 1989.

134 changing her last name: Interview with Michael Rich.

134 lunch together: Lutze, *Who Can Know the Other?*, 207.

135 "to take over responsibility": Arthur Sackler to Gillian Sackler, memorandum, April 15, 1987.

136 planning an exhibition: The exhibit ran from May 1 through June 28, 1987. "Jewels of the Ancients," *RA: The Magazine for the Friends of the Royal Academy*, no. 14 (Spring 1987).

136 more than two hundred pieces: "Jewels with a Frown," *Sunday Times* (London), May 3, 1987.

136 essay to promote the show: "In the Shadow of the Ancients," *RA: The Magazine for the Friends of the Royal Academy*, no. 15 (Summer 1987).

136 third millennium B.C.: Alice Beckett, *Fakes: Forgery and the Art World* (London: Richard Cohen Books, 1995), 106.

136 "pleased to find myself almost": Ibid.

136 "jewels so delicate as the wreaths": Ibid., 109.

136 published a shocking story: "Jewels with a Frown."

136 "I would be very, very surprised": Beckett, *Fakes*, 113.

136 "there was a unanimous opinion": "Experts Query Jewels," *Sunday Times* (London), July 5, 1987; Beckett, *Fakes*, 113–14.

136 The scandal was devastating: "Doctor's Collection Is a Prescription for Controversy," *Independent*, Nov. 3, 1988.

137 "Man proposes, but God disposes": "Of Dreams and Archaeology, of Methylmercury Poisoning," *Medical Tribune*, Oct. 24, 1973.

137 always hated being sick: Lutze, *Who Can Know the Other?*, 207.

137 chose not to inform his family: Interview with Michael Rich; Lutze, *Who Can Know the Other?*, 207.

137 under a pseudonym: Interview with Michael Rich.

137 he was already dead: Lutze, *Who Can Know the Other?*, 207.

137 Marietta could not believe it: Ibid.; "Dr. Arthur Sackler Dies at 73," *New York Times*, May 27, 1987.

137 star-studded ceremonies: Program for a Memorial Service to Celebrate the Life of Arthur Mitchell Sackler, M.D., Harvard University, Memorial Church, Oct. 5, 1987.

137 memorial concert at the Kennedy Center: Invitation to the Friends of Arthur M. Sackler Concert, Kennedy Center, Sept. 12, 1987, Henderson Papers; "The Fanfare of Friends," *Washington Post*, Sept. 14, 1987.

137 Ed Koch: Program for Memorial Service for Arthur M. Sackler, June 17, 1987, Henderson Papers.

137 "How can I find words": Jillian Sackler eulogy for Arthur Sackler, Memorial Service for Arthur M. Sackler, M.D., Sackler Wing, Metropolitan Museum of Art, June 17, 1987.

138 they were barely speaking: "Other Sackler."

138 "What is so ironic": "In Memoriam," *Studio International* 200, supplement 1 (1987).

138 Arthur Sackler had a precept: Levin, *Becoming Judy Chicago*, 362.

CHAPTER 11: APOLLO

143 Richard Kapit first encountered: Unless otherwise noted, details relating to the friendship between Richard Kapit and Richard Sackler are derived from multiple interviews with Kapit.

145 Richard was in the geometry club: Roslyn High School 1960 Yearbook.

145 had his own car: Barbara Schaffer, email.

145 Margie was smart and worldly: Obituary of Dr. Marjorie Ellen Yospin Newman, Legacy.com.

145 "The rigor is stupefying": Richard Sackler to a Roslyn friend, Oct. 26, 1963.

145 complained about the work: Richard Sackler to a Roslyn friend, May 5, 1964.

146 "gaping ass-hole": Richard Sackler to a Roslyn friend, May 5, 1964.

146 liked to talk about sex: In the May 5, 1964, letter, he wrote to his Roslyn friend, "A couple of orgies, sexual and otherwise, should do a lot to straighten warped values and appendages, the wrath of which have been turned upon themselves too long."

146 "His enthusiasm was infectious": Richard Kapit, email.

148 shards of protective casing: This sequence is based on footage of the splashdown, which is widely available online.

148 solution that the frogmen used: "NASA Turned to Norwalk Firm to Kill Potential Moon Germs," *Hartford Courant*, July 23, 1992; "Scientists Cannot Rule Out Possibility of Germs on Moon," *Chicago Tribune*, July 14, 1969.

148 had acquired Physicians Products: "Local Firm Acquired by Purdue Frederick," *Progress-Index* (Petersburg, Va.), March 30, 1966.

148 a Purdue Frederick advertisement: Betadine advertisement.

148 Richard brought Kapit on trips: Kapit

remembers the offices being in Connecticut, but in the late 1960s they were in Yonkers. (They moved to Norwalk in 1972.) Interview with Bob Jones.
150 he went to SUNY Buffalo: RDS 2019 Deposition.
150 "My dearest nephew and colleague": Martí-Ibáñez to Richard Sackler, June 7, 1971, FMI Papers.

CHAPTER 12: HEIR APPARENT
151 W. T. Grant died: "William T. Grant, Store Founder, Dies," *New York Times,* Aug. 7, 1972.
151 "there are not many buyers": "Buyers Scarce When the Price Is $1.8 Million, Hospital Finds," *New York Times,* Jan. 21, 1973.
152 When the *Times* reporter called: "W. T. Grant Estate Sold," *New York Times,* June 3, 1973.
152 Purdue Frederick would now consolidate: The building at 50 Washington Street in Norwalk was built in 1970.
152 Two hundred employees: "Drug Company Moving to Norwalk," *Hartford Courant,* Nov. 30, 1972.
152 internship in internal medicine: "A Family, and a Transformative Legacy," Medicine@Yale, July/Aug. 2014.
152 assistant to the president: Statement from Robert Josephson to *New Yorker,* Oct. 19, 2017. In his 2019 deposition, Richard was asked to confirm this and said that while he could not recall having started at Purdue as Raymond's assistant, "it doesn't do violence to any contrary memory."
152 other humdrum remedies: "A Financial Man and the Fogg," *Boston Globe,* Feb. 16, 1982. Cerumenex had been sold by the company dating back to the 1950s. Purdue Frederick advertisement, *Medical Tribune,* July 2, 1962.
152 "old world": Interview with Francine Shaw.
153 a "conservative" company: Nelson to Hon. James P. Jones, July 11, 2007.
153 "It felt very small": Interview with Olech.
153 Greenwich mansion for tennis: Interview with Carlos Blanco.
153 "An integral part of our philosophy": Mundipharma International Group brochure.
153 sold Sophie's jewelry: "Sharing Ideas," *Boston Globe,* Feb. 16, 1986.
153 reporter from *The Jerusalem Post:* "Psy-

chiatrists Give $3M. to T.A. Medical School," *Jerusalem Post,* Oct. 19, 1972.
154 house in Greenwich: Interview with Carlos Blanco.
154 avid skier: "Skiers Covet Clear Skies, Warm Weather," *Salt Lake City Tribune,* Dec. 25, 1985.
154 University of Pennsylvania: "Penn Speaker Hails U.S. Achievements," *Philadelphia Inquirer,* May 23, 1972; "Beth M. Bressman," *Item of Millburn and Short Hills* (Millburn, N.J.), Nov. 6, 1969.
154 PhD in clinical psychology: "Ph.D. Degree Is Awarded Beth Sackler," *Item of Millburn and Short Hills* (Millburn, N.J.), March 20, 1980.
154 married in 1979: According to the Connecticut Marriage Index, they were married June 3, 1979.
154 never obtained a degree: Official biography of Richard Sackler, which previously appeared on the webpage of the Koch Institute for Integrative Cancer Research at MIT but has since been removed.
154 still owned three ways: Kathe Sackler Deposition.
154 "I had a lot of ideas": RDS 2019 Deposition.
154 more than a dozen patents: U.S. Patent and Trademark Office website.
154 pick up the phone: RDS 2019 Deposition.
155 an entitled dilettante: Ibid.
155 helicopter and rooftop heliport: Advertisement for 50 Washington Street, "the only luxury office building in Conn with helicopter and heliport for exclusive use of its tenants," *Bridgeport Post,* March 28, 1972.
156 difficult taskmaster: Interview with Cobert.
157 grown up in Brooklyn: "Pain Relief," *Corporate Counsel,* Sept. 2002.
157 joined Purdue as vice president: "The Simple Things in Life Are Fine but Howard Udell Loves Complexity," article in an internal Purdue brochure (Fall 1999); "Pain Relief."
157 "Corporate attorneys can do one of two things": Interview with Cobert.
157 "the company can't do what it needs": "Simple Things in Life Are Fine but Howard Udell Loves Complexity."
158 "He was always looking": Interview with Larry Wilson.
158 director of clinical research: "Takesue Named," *Bernardsville (N.J.) News,* Sept. 11,

1975; "Dr. Edward Takesue," *Morristown (N.J.) Daily Record*, June 4, 1985.

158 "Watch out": Interview with Cobert.

158 "waltzed in and out": Ibid.

158 "My legal residence is Switzerland": MDS Affidavit.

158 he divided his time: Ibid.

158 Sacklers did not speak of it: Interview with Carlos Blanco.

158 budget of $140,000: MDS Affidavit.

159 Mortimer retained his own apartment: Ibid.

159 this felt like an invasion: Ibid.; interview with Elizabeth Bernard.

159 commune of photographers and models: MDS Affidavit.

159 kicked the squatters out: MDS Affidavit.

159 took her to court: Ibid.

159 Arthur Sackler liked to opine: Lutze, *Who Can Know the Other?*, 205.

159 Napp had been acquired: Mundipharma International Group brochure.

159 "Only one in ten": "Dr. Mortimer Sackler," *Times* (London), April 13, 2010.

160 narcotics in palliative care: Twycross to the author, email. It has occasionally been suggested that Mortimer Sackler himself might have somehow been involved in the early dialogue with St. Christopher's, but Twycross had no memory of that, and I could find no indication of direct involvement by the Sacklers in the papers of Cicely Saunders at Kings College London.

160 called the system Continus: The asthma drug was Uniphyl. "Thrust Under Microscope," *Hartford Courant*, Sept. 2, 2001.

160 morphine would slowly release: "Mortimer Sackler Dies at 93," *Los Angeles Times*, March 8, 2014.

160 become known as MS Contin: The original name in the U.K. was MST. MS Contin was the brand name in the United States.

160 "MS Contin really was": Kathe Sackler Deposition.

160 the London *Times:* "Morphine Making a Welcome Return," *Times* (London), Sept. 15, 1983.

160 delivery system had "revolutionized": Mundipharma International Group brochure.

160 "We have no intention": Napp Laboratories Advertisement/Job Posting, *Guardian*, Oct. 27, 1988.

161 "Before this goes into effect": Interview with Cobert.

162 FDA sent a letter: "Purdue Frederick Will Submit NDA for MS Contin," *Pink Sheet*, July 8, 1985.

162 The FDA's commissioner: Ibid.

162 "FDA will not interfere": "Purdue Frederick MS Contin Continued Marketing," *Pink Sheet*, July 15, 1985.

162 dwarfing anything that Purdue: "Thrust Under Microscope."

CHAPTER 13: MATTER OF SACKLER

163 in the summer of 1987: Unless otherwise noted, details of this meeting of the executors in the building at Fifty-Seventh Street come from Minutes of the Estate of Arthur M. Sackler, July 29, 1987. These minutes, along with minutes of other executors' meetings, were found in the file for *Matter of Sackler*, in the courthouse in Mineola.

163 remained in the family: GTS Affidavit.

163 flinty and sharp: Interview with Michael Rich.

163 trophy wife and a floozy: Interview with Rich, and with another close family friend.

163 Arthur's "dearest friend": Jill Sackler remarks at Memorial Service for Arthur M. Sackler, Metropolitan Museum of Art, June 17, 1987.

163 cut her out: Interview with Michael Rich.

164 Arthur had debts: Minutes of the Estate of Arthur M. Sackler, July 29, 1987.

164 her 49 percent ownership stake: Memorandum by Edward J. Ross to Hon. C. Raymond Radigan, "Estate of Arthur M. Sackler—Index No. 249220," June 16, 1988 (hereafter cited as Ross Memo).

164 "cash cow": The lawyer was Michael Sonnenreich. Minutes of a meeting of family attorneys, July 8, 1987.

164 "Just do good things": EJS Deposition.

164 the handshake deal: Meeting minutes of the Estate of Arthur M. Sackler, July 22, 1987, cited in GTS Affidavit.

164 "that the Sackler name not be tarnished": GTS Affidavit.

164 what obligations: Minutes of the Estate of Arthur M. Sackler, July 29, 1987.

165 nonsensical rationale: Verified Answer of Carol Master, Else Sackler, Arthur F. Sackler, and Elizabeth Sackler in *Matter of Sackler*, File No. 249220. The version of this document that I retrieved in the Mineola files is undated. "Before and during her marriage to Dr. Sackler, Gillian seldom accompanied Dr. Sackler during his visits with his children and grandchildren. Dr. Sackler explained to Else and Arthur separately that because he did not wish to have any more children, he thought it would be insensitive for him to involve Gillian with his children and grandchildren."

165 regarded Jillian as a usurper: Interview with Michael Rich and with a friend of the family who spoke with several of Arthur's children at the time.

165 would go to Jillian: Affidavit of Thomas J. Schwarz, File No. 249220, May 8, 1990, *Matter of Sackler.*

165 took over the town house: GTS Affidavit.

165 estranged from "the brothers": "The Other Sackler," *Washington Post,* Nov. 27, 2019; Minutes of the Estate of Arthur M. Sackler, July 29, 1987.

165 Morty had already inquired: Minutes of the Estate of Arthur M. Sackler, July 29, 1987.

165 This would be a delicate process: Ibid.

166 pay off Arthur's debts: Ibid.

166 a no-win situation: Minutes of a meeting of the attorneys for the Estate of Arthur M. Sackler, July 9, 1987.

166 "Your father did the same thing": Minutes of the Estate of Arthur M. Sackler, July 29, 1987.

167 "There's something about looking": Ibid.

167 "There were promises, verbal promises": Ibid.

167 Else approached Jillian: Reply Affidavit of Else Sackler, *Matter of Sackler,* March 1, 1991.

167 actually on loan: Respondent Else Sackler's Memorandum of Law in Support of Her Motion for Summary Judgment Dismissing the Proceeding, *Matter of Sackler.* The version of this memo that I found in the Mineola files is undated.

167 "She offered no proof": Jill Sackler to J. Kartiganer, March 6, 1989.

168 one of Else's attorneys insinuated: GTS Affidavit.

168 warehouse on the Upper East Side: "Doctor's Collection Is a Prescription for Controversy," *Independent,* Nov. 3, 1988.

168 "smear" campaign: Response to Memorandum Submitted in Behalf of Executors Carol Master and Arthur F. Sackler, *Matter of Sackler,* Sept. 25, 1992; GTS Affidavit.

168 She confided to a friend: Jill Sackler to Linus Pauling, April 27, 1991, Pauling Papers.

168 "inspired variously by greed": Memo-

randum by attorneys for Arthur F. Sackler and Elizabeth Sackler, quoted in Response to Memorandum Submitted in Behalf of Executors Carol Master and Arthur F. Sackler, *Matter of Sackler,* Sept. 25, 1992.

168 forced to cancel: "Feud Spoils Christie's Bid Day," *Times,* Jan. 13, 1993.

168 more than $7 million: "Depositions of Smithsonian Employees in Litigation Concerning the Estate of Arthur M. Sackler," Memorandum from Ildiko D'Angelis to Constance B. Newman, May 24, 1993, Smithsonian Files.

168 closely with a personal curator: GTS Affidavit.

168 Katz was affronted: Ibid.

168 taking over the management: Katz to Elizabeth Sackler, Nov. 18, 1988.

169 named Miss Vermont: "She's Here for the Summer," *Burlington (Vt.) Free Press,* June 13, 1968.

169 Elizabeth went to the final competition: Levin, *Becoming Judy Chicago,* 376–77; "The Girl Who Won the Title," *Brattleboro (Vt.) Reformer,* Aug. 31, 1968.

169 bragged about his beauty queen: Interview with Michael Rich.

169 "I gave up explanations": "The Princess and the Porcupine Quills," *Medical Tribune,* Nov. 29, 1972.

169 "My father loved his passions": "The Temple of Sackler," *Vanity Fair,* Sept. 1987.

169 her father's "genius": Elizabeth Sackler remarks given at the National Portrait Gallery, Nov. 18, 1996, Henderson Papers.

169 But Elizabeth objected: The Smithsonian attempted to split the difference, using the short version ("The Singer Collection") on an introductory panel and the longer version ("The Dr. Paul Singer Collection of Chinese Art of the Arthur M. Sackler Gallery") as a credit line for each individual object. Milo Beach to Elizabeth Sackler, Sept. 21, 1999. Elizabeth was not satisfied. "Because the content of the panel is misleading, erroneous, and insulting as well as a breach of the Settlement Agreement I am dismayed that two relatively significant events, a reception and a dinner, have already taken place at the Sackler Gallery since the installation of the Singer material and horrified by the news that the Visiting Committee will arrive to be greeted by it," she wrote. Elizabeth Sackler to Milo Beach, Sept. 30, 1999. Smithsonian Files.

170 "If the bunch of Arthur's heirs": Singer

to M. M. Weller, March 24, 1996, Smithsonian Files.

170 charitable trust: Interview with Leather.

170 "four-way agreement": Minutes of Executors Meeting, July 22 and Aug. 7, 1987; EJS Deposition.

170 "a business relationship": EJS Deposition.

171 "a fraud": Interview with Leather.

171 Arthur got nothing: Minutes of the Estate of Arthur M. Sackler, June 24, 1987.

172 Arthur did the same thing: Minutes of the Estate of Arthur M. Sackler, July 29, 1987.

172 "The main thing I'm worried about": Ibid.

172 "I don't really know what Napp is": Minutes of an Estate Meeting, July 29, 1987.

172 "Is the price right?": Minutes of a meeting of the attorneys for the Estate of Arthur M. Sackler, July 9, 1987.

172 for $22 million: Ross Memo.

CHAPTER 14: THE TICKING CLOCK

173 "the fuel of interest": Catherine L. Fisk, "Removing the 'Fuel of Interest' from the 'Fire of Genius': Law and the Employee-Inventor, 1830–1930," *University of Chicago Law Review* 65, no. 4 (Fall 1998).

174 "nonstop news and editorial campaign": "An Uphill Fight for Generics," *Newsday*, March 18, 1986.

174 investigation by *The New York Times*: "Drug Makers Fighting Back Against Advance of Generics," *New York Times*, July 28, 1987.

174 Bill Frohlich had declared: L. W. Frohlich, "The Physician and the Pharmaceutical Industry in the United States," *Proceedings of the Royal Society of Medicine*, April 11, 1960.

174 "the patent cliff": "Cliffhanger," *Economist*, Dec. 3, 2011.

175 sponsored by Purdue: *Advances in the Management of Chronic Pain: International Symposium on Pain Control* (Toronto: Purdue Frederick, 1984), 3.

175 Richard personally wrote: "Dr. Romagosa on Symposium in Toronto," *Lafayette (La.) Daily Advertiser*, Aug. 19, 1984.

175 Robert Kaiko: Kaiko delivered a talk and chaired another session. *Advances in the Management of Chronic Pain.*

175 Kaiko had a PhD: Biography of Robert Kaiko, PhD, Scientific Advisory Board, Ensysce.

175 "Pain is the most common symptom":

Richard Sackler Deposition in *Commonwealth of Kentucky v. Purdue Pharma LP et al.*, Aug. 28, 2015 (hereafter cited as RDS 2015 Deposition).

175 Bonica was a colorful figure: Latif Nasser, "The Amazing Story of the Man Who Gave Us Pain Relief," TED talk, March 2015. Bonica arrived in the United States in 1927, according to *The New York Times*; some other sources suggest that he came in 1928. "John J. Bonica, Pioneer in Anesthesia, Dies at 77," *New York Times*, Aug. 20, 1994.

176 published a seminal book: "John Bonica Devoted His Life to Easing People's Pain," *University of Washington Magazine*, Dec. 1, 1994; John J. Bonica, *Management of Pain* (Philadelphia: Lea & Febiger, 1953).

176 development of epidural anesthesia: "John J. Bonica, Pioneer in Anesthesia, Dies at 77," *New York Times*, Aug. 20, 1994.

176 undiagnosed chronic pain: "Conquering Pain," *New York*, March 22, 1982.

176 "no medical school": "An Interview with John J. Bonica M.D.," *Pain Practitioner* (Spring 1989).

176 "epidemic of pain": "Conquering Pain."

176 it had been stigmatized: RDS 2015 Deposition.

176 "Addiction does *not* occur": *Advances in the Management of Chronic Pain*, 36.

177 "to counteract numerous myths": "Medical Essays," *Lafayette (La.) Advertiser*, Feb. 4, 1997; "Morphine Safest to Control Pain," *Lafayette (La.) Advertiser*, Feb. 17, 1985.

177 "Many of these myths": "Morphine Safest to Control Pain."

177 "revolutionizing the Canadian narcotic": *Advances in the Management of Chronic Pain*, 3.

177 "generous and sustained release": Ibid., 150.

177 "Morphine is the safest and best drug": "Morphine Safest to Control Pain."

178 "I hope sales weren't off": Interview with Larry Wilson.

178 "MS Contin may eventually face": Kaiko to Richard Sackler, memorandum, July 16, 1990, cited in Expert Report by David Kessler, Multidistrict Opiate Litigation, 1:17-md-02804-DAP, July 19, 2019 (hereafter cited as Kessler Report).

179 hit a lawyer: "OxyContin Made the Sacklers Rich. Now It's Tearing Them Apart," *Wall Street Journal*, July 13, 2019.

179 had similar handwriting: Kathe Sackler Deposition.

179 "I was not invited": Ibid.
180 constantly discuss the possibilities: "The Secretive Family Making Billions from the Opioid Crisis," *Esquire,* Oct. 16, 2017.
180 Kathe suggested using oxycodone: Kathe Sackler Deposition.
180 According to Kathe: Ibid.
180 a different recollection: RDS 2019 Deposition.
180 Kaiko had suggested oxycodone: Kaiko to Richard Sackler, memorandum, July 16, 1990, cited in Kessler Report.
181 Wilson liked him: Interview with Wilson.
181 "He worked hard": Ibid.
181 would call you at home: Massachusetts Complaint.
181 single-minded devotion: RDS 2019 Deposition.
181 Richard officially joined: New York Complaint.
181 signaled the ambition: "Thrust Under a Microscope," *Hartford Courant,* Sept. 2, 2001.
181 "Purdue Frederick was the original company": RDS 2015 Deposition.
182 "a new aggressiveness": "OxyContin: The Most Significant Launch in Purdue History!," *Teamlink* (internal Purdue newsletter) (Winter 1996).
182 senior vice president: "On the Move," *New York Daily News,* March 5, 1993.
182 OxyContin Project Team memo: Oxy-Contin Project Team Memo, Dec. 14, 1993, quoted in RDS 2015 Deposition.
182 Brooklyn-born executive: Mark F. Pomerantz and Roberto Finzi to Hon. James P. Jones, July 16, 2007.
182 after sitting next to him: Meier, *Pain Killer* (2018), 105.
182 at the Holocaust Museum: Mark F. Pomerantz and Roberto Finzi to Hon. James P. Jones, July 16, 2007.
182 "Big Red": "OxyContin: The Most Significant Launch in Purdue History!"
182 Friedman wrote a memo: "Product Pipeline and Strategy—VERY CONFIDENTIAL," Memo by Michael Friedman, Dec. 24, 1994.
183 Friedman told the Sacklers: Ibid.

CHAPTER 15: GOD OF DREAMS
185 someone figured out: Martin Booth, *Opium: A History* (New York: St. Martin's Press, 1996), 15.
185 Assyrian medical tablets: Ibid., 16.
185 Hippocrates himself suggested: Ibid., 18.

185 carried certain dangers: Ibid., 20.
185 In parts of Europe: See, generally, Althea Hayter, *Opium and the Romantic Imagination: Addiction and Creativity in De Quincey, Coleridge, Baudelaire, and Others* (New York: HarperCollins, 1988).
186 broad range of maladies: Booth, *Opium,* 58.
186 apothecary's assistant in Prussia: Ibid., 68–69.
186 In his book *Opium: A History:* Ibid., 78.
186 produced a generation of veterans: Ibid., 74.
186 By one estimate: "How Aspirin Turned Hero," *Sunday Times* (London), Sept. 13, 1998.
186 "the most pernicious drug": "Uncle Sam Is the Worst Drug Fiend in the World," *New York Times,* March 12, 1911.
186 team of chemists in Germany: Lucy Inglis, *Milk of Paradise: A History of Opium* (London: Picador, 2018), 240–41; Booth, *Opium,* 77–78.
186 Bayer proceeded to sell: Walter Sneader, "The Discovery of Heroin," *Lancet,* Nov. 21, 1998; Booth, *Opium,* 78.
186 Bayer claimed: Booth, *Opium,* 78.
186 addictive after all: John Phillips, "Prevalence of the Heroin Habit," *Journal of the American Medical Association,* Dec. 14, 1912.
187 medical use of heroin declined: Booth, *Opium,* 78.
187 Bayer stopped making the drug: "How Aspirin Turned Hero."
187 rumored to have become addicted: John H. Halpern and David Blistein, *Opium: How an Ancient Flower Shaped and Poisoned Our World* (New York: Hachette, 2019), 174.
187 "I'll die young": Booth, *Opium,* 84.
187 He did die young: "What Lenny Bruce Was All About," *New York Times,* June 7, 1971.
187 "You won't believe how committed": Richard Sackler, email, May 22, 1999, cited in RDS 2015 Deposition.
187 "You need a vacation": Friedman to Richard Sackler, email, Dec. 23, 1996, quoted in RDS 2019 Deposition.
188 "the first time that we have chosen": "OxyContin: The Most Significant Launch in Purdue History!," *Teamlink* (internal Purdue newsletter) (Winter 1996).
188 company market research memo: Purdue Pharma Market Research Memo, July 9, 1992, quoted in Kathe Sackler Deposition.
188 pointed out to Richard in an email: Friedman, email, in a chain with Richard

Sackler, from May 28, 1997, cited in RDS 2015 Deposition.

189 outlined in a series of emails: Ibid.

189 minutes of an early Purdue team meeting: Launch Team Meeting Minutes, March 31, 1995.

189 the company's estimates: Testimony of Paul Goldenheim, Committee on Health, Education, Labor, and Pensions, U.S. Senate, Feb. 12, 2002 (hereafter cited as Goldenheim 2002 Testimony).

190 Department of Pain Medicine and Palliative Care: Declaration of Russell K. Portenoy, MD, *State of Oklahoma v. Purdue Pharma et al.,* Jan. 17, 2019 (hereafter cited as Portenoy Declaration).

190 Portenoy argued that the suffering: "A Pain-Drug Champion Has Second Thoughts," *Wall Street Journal,* Dec. 17, 2012.

190 "gift from nature": Ibid.

190 early and enduring relationship: Portenoy Declaration.

190 co-authored an influential article: Russell Portenoy and Kathleen Foley, "Chronic Use of Opioid Analgesics in Non-malignant Pain: Report of 38 Cases," *Pain,* May 1986.

190 Portenoy would later explain: Portenoy Declaration.

190 Portenoy shared Richard's view: Ibid.

191 described the fear of opioids: "Pain-Drug Champion Has Second Thoughts."

191 rose by 75 percent: "The Alchemy of OxyContin," *New York Times,* July 29, 2001.

191 "Until last week, our belief": Memorandum from Richard Sackler, Nov. 30, 1991, quoted in Kathe Sackler Deposition.

192 article in the local newspaper: "Norwalk Firm Finds Niche Among Pharmaceutical Giants," *Hartford Courant,* July 23, 1992.

193 modern system of FDA approval: See Jeremy A. Greene and Scott H. Podolsky, "Reform, Regulation, and Pharmaceuticals—the Kefauver-Harris Amendments at 50," *New England Journal of Medicine* 367, no. 16 (Oct. 2012).

193 "Things are changing faster": "Oxy-Contin: The Most Significant Launch in Purdue History!"

193 he was the main regulator: Deposition of Curtis Wright, *In re National Prescription Opiate Litigation,* MDL No. 2804, U.S. District Court, Northern District of Ohio, Dec. 19, 2018 (hereafter cited as Wright 2018 Deposition).

193 Instead, Purdue argued: Purdue pre-launch submissions to the FDA, quoted in

Prosecution Memorandum Regarding the Investigation of Purdue Pharma, L.P. et al., United States Attorney's Office, Western District of Virginia, Sept. 28, 2006 (hereafter cited as Prosecution Memo). A Purdue training manual instructed sales reps to inform physicians that "abuse is less likely with OC because it is more difficult to extract the oxycodone from the controlled-release system."

194 "care should be taken": Overall Conclusion to 1995 FDA Review, Curtis Wright, Oct. 1995. Cited in Massachusetts Complaint.

194 had "very strong opinions": March 19, 1993, teleconference, cited in Kessler Report.

194 Michael Friedman wrote: Friedman to Mortimer, Raymond, and Richard Sackler, memorandum, 1994 (no more specific date provided), quoted in RDS 2015 Deposition.

194 "once a company gets approval": Interview with Wilson.

194 "the Bible for the product": RDS 2015 Deposition.

195 "a more potent selling instrument": "OxyContin: The Most Significant Launch in Purdue History!"

195 promotional language would have to go: 1996 Executive Summary for Purdue Research Center, quoted in RDS 2019 Deposition.

195 "agreed to more such informal contacts": Project Team Contact Report, Sept. 17, 1992, cited in Prosecution Memo.

195 "how far we have come": Richard Sackler, email, quoted in Kathe Sackler Deposition (no date specified).

195 According to a confidential memo: Project Team Contact Report, Reder & Wright, Dec. 28, 1994, cited in Prosecution Memo.

195 new line of text: "How One Sentence Helped Set Off the Opioid Crisis," *Marketplace,* Dec. 13, 2017.

196 implying that Purdue must have: Deposition of Curtis Wright, Multidistrict Opiate Litigation, MDL No. 2804, Dec. 1, 2018 (hereafter cited as Wright 2018 Deposition).

196 Robert Reder suggested: "How One Sentence Helped Set Off the Opioid Crisis."

196 Wright allowed: Wright 2018 Deposition. "Q. Okay. Do you recall ever proposing that language to Robert Reder? A. I don't remember specifically doing so, but I could have."

196 "Sounds like B.S. to me": Schnitzler to Wright, email, Nov. 21, 1995, cited in Prosecution Memo.

196 "Actually, Diane, this is": Wright to Schnitzler, Nov. 21, 1995.

196 "This didn't just 'happen'": "OxyContin: The Most Significant Launch in Purdue History!"

196 "had a lot to do with": Richard Sackler, email, quoted in Wright 2018 Deposition.

196 credited the "unparalleled teamwork": "OxyContin: The Most Significant Launch in Purdue History!"

196 package of nearly $400,000: Purdue to Wright, Oct. 9, 1998, cited in Prosecution Memo.

196 Wright denied making any overtures: Wright 2018 Deposition.

196 one of Wright's first calls: Wright 2018 Deposition: "Q. So does this reflect your calling Robert Reder at Purdue less than ten days after you've left the Food and Drug Administration? A. Probably."

196 subsequent sworn deposition: RDS 2015 Deposition.

CHAPTER 16: H-BOMB

198 Calixto Rivera woke: Details about Calixto Rivera's life and death are drawn from press coverage in The Record, as cited in the following notes. I tried to track down Rivera's family, or people who knew him, but without success. "Lodi: Explosion, Human Drama Both Developed Gradually," Hackensack (N.J.) Record, May 28, 1995.

198 out into the rain: "Communications Glitch Before Lodi Blast?," Hackensack (N.J.) Record, April 24, 1995.

198 state's biggest industry: "Tougher Chemical Pushed," Associated Press, April 24, 1995.

198 fourteen just in Lodi: "A Preventable Tragedy," Hackensack (N.J.) Record, April 27, 1995.

198 sprawling, two-story complex: "Company Plans Not to Rebuild Its Lodi Plant," New York Times, April 28, 1995.

198 turn-of-the-century dye works: "Chemical Plant Explosion Kills 4 in New Jersey Town," New York Times, April 22, 1995.

198 purchased the Lodi property in 1970: "Lodi Betrayed the People's Trust," The Hackensack (N.J.) Record, Oct. 18, 1995.

198 shut the plant down: "Chemical Plant Explosion Kills 4 in New Jersey Town."

199 made them nervous: "Chemical Plant Has History of Problems," Hackensack (N.J.) Record, April 27, 1995.

199 working at Napp for nine years: "As

Grief Replaces Shock, Families Mourn Four Victims of Plant Explosion," New York Times, April 24, 1995.

199 a hard worker: "'Our Friends Are Dead; Our Jobs Are Gone,'" Hackensack (N.J.) Record, April 30, 1995.

199 started mixing chemicals: "Lodi: Explosion, Human Drama Both Developed Gradually."

199 new and unfamiliar chemicals: "Napp: Investigation Finds Chain of Errors Before Fatal Blast," Hackensack (N.J.) Record, Oct. 17, 1995.

199 particularly volatile chemicals: "Lodi Chemical Blast Had Many Facets," Hackensack (N.J.) Record, May 28, 1995.

199 something was clearly off: EPA/OSHA Joint Chemical Accident Investigation Report, Napp Technologies Inc., Oct. 1997 (hereafter cited as Lodi Report).

199 cited for numerous violations: "Chemical Plant Has History of Problems."

199 known to hire people: "Napp: Investigation Finds Chain of Errors Before Fatal Blast."

200 Patterson Kelley blender: Lodi Report.

200 mixing the Rhode Island chemicals: "Lodi: Explosion, Human Drama Both Developed Gradually."

200 emanate from the mixer: Lodi Report.

200 couldn't tell a good smell: "Napp: Investigation Finds Chain of Errors Before Fatal Blast."

200 signs in the mixing room: "Lodi: Explosion, Human Drama Both Developed Gradually."

201 gauges on the mixer: Ibid.

201 chemicals were smoldering: "Lodi: No Charges, but a Reprimand," Hackensack (N.J.) Record, April 26, 1995.

201 smelled like a dead animal: Lodi Report.

201 gauge on the tank kept rising: Ibid.

201 staff did not alert them: "Chemical Plant Explosion Kills 4 in New Jersey Town."

201 plant was being evacuated: Lodi Report.

201 veteran of the plant: "Coffee Break Saved Worker's Life," Hackensack (N.J.) Record, April 25, 1995.

201 Everybody was standing around: "Lodi: Explosion, Human Drama Both Developed Gradually."

201 could smell it outside: "Lodi: No Charges, but a Reprimand."

201 the men go back: Lodi Report.

201 Don't go, Calixto told him: "Coffee Break Saved Worker's Life."

201 company would later maintain: "Lodi: Explosion, Human Drama Both Developed Gradually."

201 eerily quiet: Ibid.

202 one chemist would subsequently observe: Ibid.

202 empty the smoldering chemicals: Ibid.

202 exploded in every direction: Ibid.

202 hurled it fifty feet: "Lodi: No Charges, but a Reprimand"; Lodi Report.

202 firestorm engulfed the space: "Lodi: Explosion, Human Drama Both Developed Gradually."

202 Flaming debris rained down: "Chemical Plant Explosion Kills 4 in New Jersey Town."

202 his friend was inside: "Lodi: Explosion, Human Drama Both Developed Gradually."

202 his skull crushed: Ibid.

202 identified only by dental records: "'Our Friends Are Dead; Our Jobs Are Gone.'"

202 die in the hospital: "Lodi: No Charges, but a Reprimand."

202 Forty people were injured: "Chain of Errors Left 5 Dead," *Hackensack (N.J.) Record,* Oct. 17, 1995.

202 the sun: "Lodi: Explosion, Human Drama Both Developed Gradually."

202 runoff oozed out: "Green Liquid Leaks in Lodi," *Hackensack (N.J.) Record,* May 2, 1995.

202 pollution fed into the Passaic: "Chemical Plant Explosion Kills 4 in New Jersey Town."

202 fish went belly up: "Toxic Spill in Lodi Blast Killed Thousands of Fish, EPA Says," *New York Times,* April 24, 1995; "Company Plans Not to Rebuild Its Lodi Plant."

203 bringing manslaughter charges: "State Rules Out Manslaughter in Lodi Chemical Plant Blast," *New York Times,* March 15, 1996.

203 "the facilities or the technical people": "Napp: Investigation Finds Chain of Errors Before Fatal Blast."

203 "They never asked questions": Ibid.

203 "We will not go": "Chemical Plant Owners Won't Rebuild in Lodi," *Camden (N.J.) Courier-Post,* April 28, 1995.

203 Sacklers assiduously distanced themselves: Jonathan Goldstein to Hon. James P. Jones, July 9, 2007.

203 had originally been hired: "Napp Chemicals Appoints Boncza," *Passaic (N.J.) Herald-News,* Dec. 27, 1969.

203 issued strict orders: "Company Officials Failed Repeatedly," *Hackensack (N.J.) Record,* Oct. 17, 1995.

203 "a coverup": "Napp: Investigation Finds Chain of Errors Before Fatal Blast."

203 "They're a family of American tycoons": "Lodi Plant Owners Known for Wealth, Philanthropy," *Hackensack (N.J.) Record,* April 27, 1995.

204 tried to solicit a comment: "Executive: Napp Put Safety First," *Hackensack (N.J.) Record,* Nov. 8, 1995.

204 "It's an honor": "Connecticut Man to Be Knighted by the British," Associated Press, Oct. 20, 1995.

CHAPTER 17: SELL, SELL, SELL

205 great blizzard: "Coastal Blizzard Paralyzes New York and Northeast," *New York Times,* Jan. 8, 1996.

205 official launch: Weather report, *Arizona Republic,* Jan. 9, 1996; "OxyContin: The Most Significant Launch in Purdue History!," *Teamlink* (internal Purdue newsletter) (Winter 1996).

205 formally approved: Robert F. Bedford (FDA) to James H. Conover (Purdue Pharma), approval letter, Dec. 12, 1995.

205 various prizes: "Taking Home the 'Wampum'! Wigwam Contest Winners," *Teamlink* (internal Purdue newsletter) (Winter 1996).

205 Sackler stepped up: "Where Cactus Is Par for the Course," *New York Times,* March 10, 1991.

206 prepared speech: "OxyContin: The Most Significant Launch in Purdue History!"

207 In Richard Sackler's view: RDS 2015 Deposition.

208 "I sold Betadine antiseptics": Deposition of Stephen Seid, National Prescription Opiate Litigation, MDL No. 2804, Dec. 12, 2018 (hereafter cited as Seid Deposition).

208 "Your priority is to *sell*": Purdue Sales Bulletin, Jan. 25, 1999.

208 parrot the language: Interview with Steven May.

209 instructed by Purdue: Ibid.

209 *"Discussed side effects":* Note from Purdue rep Carol Neiheisel, visiting Nancy Swikert, Jan. 11, 2000.

209 *"Worried re addiction w/Oxy":* Notes from Purdue rep Holly Will, visiting Richard Gruenewald, July 12, 1997.

209 *"Seemed to hear the Oxy message":* Note from Purdue rep John Bullock, visiting Raymond Timmerman, July 19, 1997.

209 *"with both hands":* Note from Purdue rep John Wethington, visiting Wal-Mart #689, July 20, 1997.

209 one study in particular: Seid Deposition.

209 The study had been published: Jane Porter and Hershel Jick, "Addiction Rare in Patients Treated with Narcotics," *New England Journal of Medicine,* Jan. 10, 1980.

210 co-opted his work: "Sloppy Citations of 1980 Letter Led to Opioid Epidemic," NPR, June 16, 2017.

210 study was irresistible: Interviews with multiple former Purdue sales reps. A subsequent study found more than six hundred citations to the letter. See Pamela T. M. Leung et al., "A 1980 Letter on the Risk of Opioid Addiction," *New England Journal of Medicine,* June 1, 2017.

210 "non-branded" literature: Interviews with Steven May and Dodd Davis; "The Alchemy of OxyContin," *New York Times Magazine,* July 29, 2001.

210 speakers bureau: RDS 2015 Deposition.

210 "pain management seminars": "OxyContin Abuse and Diversion and Efforts to Address the Problem," Report by the U.S. General Accounting Office, Dec. 2003 (hereafter cited as GAO Report).

210 the company sponsored seven thousand: "Sales of Painkiller Grew Rapidly, but Success Brought a High Cost," *New York Times,* March 5, 2001.

210 The marketing of OxyContin: Interview with Steven May.

210 this conflict of interest: New York Complaint.

210 subsidized by Purdue: Ibid.

211 "no other company had previously": Portenoy Declaration.

211 wily strategies: Interview with Steven May.

211 A 2016 study found: Colette DeJong et al., "Pharmaceutical Industry–Sponsored Meals and Physician Prescribing Patterns for Medicare Benefits," *JAMA Internal Medicine* 176 (2016). See also Scott E. Hadland et al., "Association of Pharmaceutical Industry Marketing of Opioid Products to Physicians with Subsequent Opioid Prescribing," *JAMA Internal Medicine* 178 (2018).

211 as much as $9 million: Budget Information, June 16, 2014, cited in Massachusetts Complaint.

211 "physicians who attended the dinner": Richard Sackler to Friedman, Oct. 23, 1996.

211 "The primary goal of medical practice": Interview with David Juurlink.

212 "hope in a bottle": Purdue marketing materials cited in Complaint, *State of Tennessee v. Purdue Pharma LP,* Circuit Court of Knox County, Tennessee, Sixth Judicial District, Case No, 1-173-18, May 15, 2018 (hereafter cited as Tennessee Complaint).

212 "All indications are that": "Awaken the Sleeping Giant!," *Teamlink* (internal Purdue newsletter) (Winter 1996).

212 "We felt like we were doing": Interview with May. Steven May subsequently initiated a whistleblower lawsuit against Purdue; it was dismissed on procedural grounds.

212 three weeks: Goldenheim 2002 Testimony. May did not have an exact recollection of how long the training lasted, but according to Goldenheim's testimony it generally involved "three weeks of classroom training at the home office."

213 one of seven hundred: "In 1996, the 300-plus Purdue sales representatives had a total physician call list of approximately 33,400 to 44,500. By 2000, the nearly 700 representatives had a total call list of approximately 70,500 to 94,000 physicians." GAO Report.

213 "What Purdue did really well": Interview with May.

213 They targeted certain regions: Interview with Rick Mountcastle.

213 "We focused our salesmen's attention": RDS 2015 Deposition.

213 doctors as "whales": Interview with May.

213 Purdue also explicitly instructed: Interviews with multiple former sales representatives; Massachusetts Complaint.

213 To May, it seemed: Interview with May.

213 Headquarters advised: Phase II OxyContin Tablets Team Meeting Minutes, June 13, 1997.

213 "It is important that we": Mike Cullen, email, June 1997, cited in RDS 2015 Deposition. The same exchange is also quoted in the Massachusetts Complaint.

214 the most extraordinary letters: Interview with Robin Hogen.

214 "We may need to start": Richard Sackler, email, Jan. 11, 1997. According to the Prosecution Memo of the U.S. Attorney's Office for the Western District of Virginia, "The genesis of the idea for these videos appears to have been company president Richard Sackler."

214 produced a promotional video: *I Got My Life Back,* Purdue video, 1998.

215 Friedman was delighted: Mike Cullen,

email, Dec. 15, 1997, cited in Prosecution Memo. It was indeed screened at the January 1998 National Sales Meeting.

215 Jonathan, discussed it: Email between Jonathan Sackler, Michael Friedman, and Mark Alfonso, Oct. 28–29, 1998.

215 twenty thousand copies of the video: Prosecution Memo.

215 "sell itself": Jim Lang, "Sales & Marketing Update," *Teamlink* 11, no. 1 (Winter 1996): "The product is perceived as being so good it will sell itself." In an anonymous post on the CafePharma forum, a onetime Purdue employee attributed a similar sentiment to Lang: "I remember him telling the Sacklers at one of those 'dog and pony' year end shows. He told them 'OxyContin, it sells itself.'" CafePharma post, Feb. 12, 2018.

215 offered free samples: Walter Sneader, "The Discovery of Heroin," *Lancet*, Nov. 21, 1998.

215 eighty-two million: "Down for the Downers," *Maclean's*, Feb. 18, 1980.

215 thirty-four thousand free prescriptions: GAO Report. A Purdue spokesperson confirmed this figure.

215 "160 was a bit too much": Purdue Pharma, "Long-Acting OxyContin® Tablets Now Available in 160 mg Strength to Relieve Persistent Pain," press release, July 9, 2000; interview with Larry Wilson.

215 they doubled again: Table 2: Total OxyContin Sales and Prescriptions from 1996 Through 2002, in GAO Report.

216 "I am pleased to report": Friedman to Raymond, Mortimer, and Richard Sackler, memorandum, Oct. 13, 1999.

216 "There is no sign": Highlights of the keynote speech by Dr. Richard Sackler, Jan. 24, 2000, National Sales Meeting.

216 "He just cannot understand": "'We Didn't Cause the Crisis': David Sackler Pleads His Case on the Opioid Epidemic," *Vanity Fair*, June 19, 2019.

216 "After the initial launch phase": Richard Sackler to Cornelia Hentzsch, email, May 29, 1999.

216 "un-controlled" medication in Germany: Email exchange between Richard Sackler and Paul Goldenheim, March 14, 1997, quoted in RDS 2015 Deposition.

216 "I'm very concerned": Kaiko to Richard Sackler, Feb. 27, 1997, quoted in RDS 2015 Deposition and Massachusetts Complaint.

217 "How substantially would it improve": Richard Sackler to Walter Wimmer, email,

March 2, 1997, quoted in RDS 2015 Deposition and Massachusetts Complaint.

217 "If OxyContin is uncontrolled": Kaiko to Richard Sackler, Feb. 27, 1997, quoted in RDS 2015 Deposition and Massachusetts Complaint.

217 "I thought it was a good idea": Richard Sackler to Walter Wimmer, email, date unclear, quoted in RDS 2015 Deposition.

217 under constant pressure: Interview with May; interview with Dodd Davis.

217 "What materials could we pull together": Richard Sackler to Friedman, April 22, 1997, quoted in RDS 2015 Deposition.

217 "This was a pretty special company": Interview with May.

218 "You are part of a legend": Highlights of the keynote speech by Dr. Richard Sackler, Jan. 24, 2000, National Sales Meeting.

218 "has outperformed our expectations": RDS 2015 Deposition.

218 "$$$$$$$$$$$$$ It's Bonus Time": Memo to sales reps, Aug. 19, 1996, reproduced by *Los Angeles Times*, May 15, 2016.

218 program called Toppers: RDS 2015 Deposition.

218 There was fierce competition: "Awaken the Sleeping Giant!"

218 $170,000 in three months: Anonymous CafePharma post, July 25, 2018.

218 $1 billion in sales: "Sales of Painkiller Grew Rapidly, but Success Brought a High Cost."

218 doubled its sales force: RDS 2015 Deposition.

218 company paid $40 million: GAO Report.

218 quarter of a million: New York Complaint.

218 Friedman informed the Sacklers: Friedman, email, Oct. 13, 1999.

219 a dream come true: Interview with May.

219 overdosed on OxyContin: Ibid.

CHAPTER 18: ANN HEDONIA

221 litigation against big tobacco: "Cigarette Makers and States Draft a $206 Million Deal," *New York Times*, Nov. 14, 1998.

221 It was an epic story: Interview with Meier.

222 an inadvertent how-to: The 2003 GAO Report noted that this language "may have inadvertently alerted abusers to a possible method of misusing the drug."

222 "They're coming in and promoting": Interview with Meier.

222 Friedman warned colleagues: Friedman, email, Nov. 30, 2000, cited in Massachusetts Complaint.
222 Mortimer Sackler added: Mortimer D. Sackler, email, Dec. 1, 2000, cited in Massachusetts Complaint.
222 "deflects attention": Ibid. For the attribution to Friedman specifically, see Complaint in *State of Delaware, ex rel. v. Richard Sackler et al.*, Case No. N19C-09-062 MMJ, Superior Court of Delaware, Sept. 9, 2019 (hereafter cited as Delaware Complaint).
222 a front-page story: "Cancer Painkillers Pose New Abuse Threat," *New York Times*, Feb. 9, 2001.
223 cranking out pills: "Pain Pill Is Meal Ticket, Problem for Drug Maker," *Hackensack (N.J.) Record*, July 8, 2001.
223 Richard wrote back immediately: Richard Sackler to Friedman, email, June 17, 1999, quoted in Massachusetts Complaint.
223 Richard was appointed president: Presentation of Defenses, *In re Purdue Pharma LP et al.*, filed with the bankruptcy court (and then withdrawn) by Joseph Hage Aaronson LLC, Counsel to Raymond Sackler Family, Dec. 20, 2019 (hereafter cited as B Side Defenses).
223 were now vice presidents: Massachusetts Complaint.
223 "They are so spry": "Thrust Under Microscope," *Hartford Courant*, Sept. 2, 2001.
223 still drove to work: Interview with Nancy Camp.
224 "the heart and soul": Ronald D. Levine to Hon. James P. Jones, May 28, 2007.
224 took the drug himself: Mary T. Yelenick to Hon. James P. Jones, June 26, 2007.
224 subsequent testimony by Martha West: Deposition of "Martha West" (I am not including the full information on court documents related to Martha West, in order to protect her privacy.)
225 "a way of life": Jeffrey Udell to Hon. James P. Jones, July 1, 2007.
225 West noticed that her boss: West Deposition.
225 "so that we are feared": Richard Sackler, email, Sept. 3, 1996.
225 "picked up references to abuse": Udell, email, summer 1999, cited in New York Complaint.
225 Udell issued instructions: Prosecution Memo.
225 called it "Disappearing Ink": West Deposition.

225 applying for a patent: U.S. Patent Application 20030126215, Aug. 12, 2002.
225 "It didn't really work": Kathe Sackler Deposition.
225 "We got to get you on OxyContin": West Deposition.
226 The abuse spread: "The Alchemy of OxyContin," *New York Times*, July 29, 2001.
226 fertile terrain for OxyContin: Interview with May; interview with Rick Mountcastle.
226 problems with prescription drug abuse: Interview with Rick Mountcastle; "Alchemy of OxyContin."
226 "the Cadillac high": Beth Macy, *Dopesick: Dealers, Doctors, and the Drug Company That Addicted America* (New York: Little, Brown, 2018), 35.
226 shadow OxyContin sales force: "Alchemy of OxyContin."
226 spiral of dependence: See, for instance, Macy, *Dopesick*, 49.
227 sent a letter to thousands: Testimony of Jay P. McCloskey, Hearings Before the Committee on the Judiciary, U.S. Senate, July 31, 2007.
227 "some overly zealous prosecutor": "Pain Relief," *Corporate Counsel*, Sept. 2002.
227 highest consumers of OxyContin: "Cancer Painkillers Pose New Abuse Threat."
227 Udell and Friedman acknowledged: Transcript of an interview Meier conducted with Udell, Friedman, and Paul Goldenheim, Aug. 24, 2001.
227 "We've got to figure out": "Pain Relief."
227 later testify under oath: RDS 2015 Deposition.
227 find hundreds of references: RDS 2019 Deposition.
227 "I feel like we have a credibility issue": Jim Speed, email, Nov. 30, 1999.
228 "The best ones for snorting": Mark Alfonso, email, Sept. 21, 1999, quoted in RDS 2019 Deposition.
228 "I was trained as a physician": RDS 2019 Deposition.
228 sensitive to concerns: Richard Sackler, email, Jan. 14, 1997.
228 "I hate this": Friedman, email, May 10, 2000, quoted in RDS 2019 Deposition.
228 "Eventually, these stories will appear": Email exchange between Robin Hogen and Mark Alfonso, June 2000, quoted in RDS 2019 Deposition.
228 "Statements were made that OxyContin": Joseph Coggins, email, Jan. 26, 2001, cited in Massachusetts Complaint.

229 shared a press article: Mortimer D. A. Sackler, email, Feb. 8, 2001, cited in Massachusetts Complaint.

229 "This is not too bad": Richard Sackler to Robin Hogen and David Haddox, Feb. 8, 2001. In the B Side Defenses, attorneys for Richard suggest that he was saying not that the *number of deaths* was "not too bad" but that the article, in its entirety, was "not as bad as anticipated."

229 many letters from patients: Edward Mahony to Hon. James P. Jones, July 11, 2007.

229 understandably proud: Interview with Robin Hogen.

229 "My son was only 28": Letter cited in Massachusetts Complaint.

229 "[We] need a strategy": RDS 2019 Deposition.

229 he made a telling distinction: "The Other Sackler," *Washington Post*, Nov. 27, 2019.

230 "hammer on the abusers": Richard Sackler, email, Feb. 1, 2001, cited in Massachusetts Complaint.

230 "Most employees felt that we": Interview with Ritchie.

230 "We are losing sales": "Thrust Under Microscope."

230 "Abusers aren't victims": 2001 email exchange between Richard Sackler and an acquaintance, quoted in Amended Complaint, *State of Connecticut v. Purdue Pharma LP et al.,* No. X07 HHD-CV-19-6105325-S, May 6, 2019 (hereafter cited as Connecticut Complaint).

231 "We think she abused drugs": Interview with Marianne Skolek Perez; "A Chilling Attempt at Damage Control," *Star Ledger,* March 5, 2003.

231 Hogen subsequently apologized: Interview with Hogen.

231 the first patients to use OxyContin: "'You Want a Description of Hell?': Oxy-Contin's 12-Hour Problem," *Los Angeles Times,* May 5, 2016.

232 letter writers described taking Oxy-Contin: [Redacted] to Kevin McIntosh, May 14, 2001; [Redacted] to Purdue Pharma, April 16, 2001.

232 "As a salesperson, you're saying": Interview with Davis.

232 By 2001, the company: "Based on [Purdue's] own internal documents, including IMS Health data, the company was aware as early as 1998 that 12.1% of all OxyContin prescriptions were written q8h or more fre-

quently. This trend of prescribing outside the recommended dosing schedule continued to increase over succeeding years, moving to 14% in 2000, 20.2% in 2001, before dropping slightly to 18% in 2002." Petition to Require Purdue Pharma LP to Revise the Labeling of OxyContin® Tablets to Strengthen Warnings of the Greater Potential for Developing Side Effects and Adverse Drug Reactions due to Prescribing Dosing Frequencies in Excess of the Recommended Guidelines, Submitted by Richard Blumenthal to the Food and Drug Administration, Jan. 23, 2004. A company spokesperson denied this claim, asserting that it was based on a "small qualitative survey . . . which did not include anesthesiologists and pain medicine physicians," but offering no alternative figures. In his petition, Blumenthal indicated that if anything, these figures were likely an *under*-estimate. He cites another study reviewing OxyContin dosing frequencies which "indicated that 86.8% of patients taking OxyContin were dosed q8h or more frequently."

232 "These numbers are very scary": Ibid.

232 "add to the current negative press": Agreed Statement of Facts, *United States v. The Purdue Frederick Company Inc., Michael Friedman, Howard Udell, Paul Goldenheim,* U.S. District Court for the Western District of Virginia, May 9, 2007.

232 so-called black box: "FDA Strengthens Warnings for OxyContin," FDA Talk Paper, July 25, 2001.

232 "I found that it didn't work": West Deposition.

233 "Unlike many drug companies": "Sales of Painkiller Grew Rapidly, but Success Brought a High Cost," *New York Times,* March 5, 2001.

233 "I grew up among the mining": Testimony of David Haddox, Prescription Drug Abuse Hearing, Hartford, Dec. 11, 2001.

233 "If I gave you a stalk of celery": "Deadly OxyContin Abuse Expected to Spread in U.S.," AP, Feb. 9, 2001.

233 "typically involved multiple factors": "Cancer Painkillers Pose New Abuse Threat."

233 "A lot of these people say": "Maker of Often-Abused Painkiller Faces Suits over Addiction, Deaths," AP, July 27, 2001.

234 coined a term, "pseudo-addiction": David Weissman and J. David Haddox, "Opioid Pseudoaddiction," *Pain* 36, no. 3 (1989).

234 "seems similar to addiction": "Dispelling the Myths About Opioids," brochure for physicians, produced by Partners Against Pain, 1998.

234 "There's no difference": West Deposition. In an October 19, 2017, statement to *The New Yorker,* the Purdue spokesman Robert Josephson acknowledged, "Patients who take OxyContin in accordance with its FDA-approved labeling instructions will likely develop physical dependence."

234 insider who wanted to talk: Interview with Meier.

235 Meier was astonished: Ibid.

235 Meier decided to write a story: Ibid.; Meier, *Pain Killer* (2003), 299.

235 "It is not unusual": "At Painkiller Trouble Spot, Signs Seen as Alarming Didn't Alarm Drug's Maker," *New York Times,* Dec. 10, 2001.

235 "Oh, there are a lot of old people": Interview with Meier.

236 "immediate danger to public health": "At Painkiller Trouble Spot, Signs Seen as Alarming Didn't Alarm Drug's Maker."

236 awful irony was beginning to emerge: Interview with Meier.

236 After the terrorist attacks: Macy, *Dopesick,* 70. This is a famous episode in Purdue lore, which is related by various ex-employees and described in anonymous posts on the CafePharma discussion board.

236 "The whole thing is a sham": 2001 email exchange between Richard Sackler and an acquaintance, quoted in Connecticut Complaint.

237 "At some point, I became addicted": West Deposition.

237 West eventually sued Purdue: Complaint in a lawsuit filed by West against Purdue.

237 was subsequently confirmed: The memo is cited in the Prosecution Memo. A Purdue spokesperson also corroborated its existence in response to a fact checking inquiry from me.

237 to produce a 160-milligram OxyContin: Purdue Pharma, "Long-Acting OxyContin® Tablets Now Available in 160 mg Strength to Relieve Persistent Pain," press release, July 9, 2000.

238 "What are you doing?": West Deposition.

238 pulling the 160-milligram pill: Richard Silbert to Hon. James P. Jones, July 13, 2007; Jay McCloskey to Hon. James P. Jones, July 9, 2007.

238 "I was angry at the time": West Deposition.

CHAPTER 19: THE PABLO ESCOBAR OF THE NEW MILLENNIUM

239 hearing in a municipal building: "Prescription Abuses Turn a New Drug Bad," *Philadelphia Inquirer,* July 29, 2001.

239 familiar ritual for the trio: "Pain Relief," *Corporate Counsel,* Sept. 2002.

240 "enamored of Harvard": Interview with Cobert.

240 advertisement that Purdue placed: Purdue Pharma advertisement, *Philadelphia Daily News,* March 27, 2003.

240 "We have a tiger by the tail": Goldenheim, email, Jan. 16, 1997.

240 "tamperproof" prescription pads: "Painkiller Maker Fights Back," *Hartford Courant,* July 18, 2001.

241 Friedman, Goldenheim, and Udell also suggested: This is still an argument that the Sacklers make today: in an email to *The New Yorker* on October 4, 2020, Davidson Goldin disputed the suggestion that OxyContin ignited the opioid crisis by pointing to evidence of rising levels of prescription drug abuse prior to the introduction of the drug.

241 sponsored an advertising campaign: "The Maker of OxyContin, a Painkiller That Is Addictive, Sponsors a Campaign on Drug Abuse," *New York Times,* Sept. 4, 2003.

241 the company had known: Prosecution Memo.

242 "enough to keep a person busy": Mark Alfonso to Jim Lang, cc: Michael Friedman, email, Oct. 3, 1997, cited in Prosecution Memo.

242 "it is imperative": Michael Friedman to Richard Sackler, Feb. 16, 2001.

242 in separate testimony: Goldenheim 2002 Testimony. In response to a request for comment, an attorney for Paul Goldenheim claimed that "None of the communications concerning incidents of diversion and abuse that you cite detract even slightly from the truthfulness of Paul Goldenheim's testimony concerning the level of abuse of MS Contin and that the abnormal and unexpected increase in diversion and abuse of Oxycontin was not known until early 2000." But he offered no explanation for the abundant evidence that Purdue was aware well prior to 2000 of widespread and significant problems with OxyContin, and with reports of extensive MS Contin abuse which came, in the words of Mark Alfonso, "all the time, and from everywhere." Noting that the Justice Department had investigated Goldenheim, the lawyer claimed that they "did not find that the testimony was false or misleading." In fact, the prosecution memo prepared by Justice concluded exactly that, stating that Goldenheim and Friedman testified "falsely and fraudulently" on these two points. Michael Friedman has never spoken publicly about these events since his guilty plea in 2007. My extensive efforts to contact him were unsuccessful.

242 report describing the abuse: Prosecution Memo.

242 "the most common source": Kaiko to Mortimer Sackler et al., email, March 3, 1997, cited in Prosecution Memo.

242 memo to Friedman: Law Department Memorandum from Udell to Mortimer D. Sackler et al., March 19, 1998, cited in Prosecution Memo. The original article was "Prescription Drugs Marked Up 5,000% on B.C. Black Market," *Ottawa Citizen*, Feb. 16, 1998.

242 *another* press account: Law Department Memorandum from Udell to John Stewart, cc: Michael Friedman, Dec. 10, 1998, cited in Prosecution Memo. The original article is "Chasing the Dragon's Tail," *Calgary Herald*, Aug. 29, 1998.

243 Udell acknowledged to Friedman: Law Department Memorandum from Udell to John Stewart, cc: Friedman, Jan. 5, 1999, cited in Prosecution Memo.

243 "Look, we stipulate—*I* stipulate": "OxyContin: Its Use and Abuse," Hearing Before the Subcommittee on Oversight and Investigations, Committee on Energy and Commerce, U.S. House of Representatives, Aug. 28, 2001.

246 "Virtually all of these reports": Goldenheim 2002 Testimony.

246 "fail to address the fundamental": Blumenthal to Richard Sackler, July 31, 2001.

246 "While we have the highest regard": Udell to Blumenthal, Aug. 10, 2001.

247 a menacing voice mail: Meier, *Pain Killer* (2018), 185. Transcript of voice mail message from Hogen, March 15, 2001, cited in Prosecution Memo.

247 In 2002, Udell announced: "Drug Maker Tied to Fatal Overdoses Avoids Blame," *Daily Report* (Fulton County, Ga.), April 30, 2002.

247 Numerous lawsuits had been filed: "Pain Relief," *Corporate Counsel*, Sept. 2002.

247 pressures of coterie politics: For more on this phenomenon, see Jesse Eisinger, *The Chickenshit Club: Why the Justice Department Fails to Prosecute Executives* (New York: Simon & Schuster, 2017).

248 "We have to be politically Machiavellian": "Pill Maker Attacks Negative Publicity," *Orlando Sentinel*, Oct. 21, 2003.

248 $50 million in assets: "A Rocky Road to Riches," *Los Angeles Times*, Jan. 25, 2008.

248 Giuliani was "uniquely qualified": Ibid.

248 "Government officials are more comfortable": Ibid.

248 "would not take an assignment": "Under Attack, Drug Maker Turned to Giuliani for Help," *New York Times*, Dec. 28, 2007.

248 enlist the very prosecutors: "Ex-prosecutor Became Adviser to OxyContin," *Courier-Journal*, Nov. 23, 2001.

248 "understand the company's corporate culture": Testimony of Jay P. McCloskey, Committee on the Judiciary, U.S. Senate, July 31, 2007.

249 "We can get virtually every senator": RDS 2019 Deposition.

249 wrote to Richard Sackler: Foley to Richard Sackler, email, April 4, 2001.

249 "the pain community": Foley to Hon. James P. Jones, July 2, 2007. The American Academy of Pain Medicine was a slightly older group; it was founded in 1983.

250 government relations executive for Purdue: "Pro-painkiller Echo Chamber Shaped Policy amid Drug Epidemic," AP, Sept. 19, 2016.

250 "We are in the middle of a real": Richard Sackler to Jonathan Sackler, email, May 28, 2001, quoted in RDS 2019 Deposition.

250 "to bind these organizations": Richard Sackler to Goldenheim, April 13, 2001.

250 "If they want our bucks": Hogen to David Haddox, Aug. 5, 2000, quoted in Kessler Report.

250 report about the origins: "Fueling an Epidemic: Exposing the Financial Ties Between Opioid Manufacturers and Third Party Advocacy Groups," Ranking Member's Office, Homeland Security and Governmental Affairs Committee, U.S. Senate, Feb. 2018.

251 report in *BusinessWeek*: "The Pit Bull of Public Relations," *BusinessWeek*, April 17, 2006.

251 column he had managed: "Heroic Dopeheads?," *New York Post*, Aug. 1, 2001.

251 "The anti-story begins": Dezenhall to Hogen, Udell, and Friedman, Aug. 1, 2001.

251 worked closely with a psychiatrist: "Inside Purdue Pharma's Media Playbook: How It Planted the Opioid 'Anti-story,'" ProPublica, Nov. 19, 2019.
251 company called Kroll: Dezenhall to Udell, Aug. 3, 2001. Apparently unaware of this email, or unaware that I had it, a Purdue spokesperson said, "Any suggestion that Eric Dezenhall retained the services of Kroll to conduct such an investigation is false."
251 shadowy international company: "The Secret Keeper," *New Yorker,* Oct. 19, 2009.
252 Udell was convinced: "Pain Relief."
252 Udell gloated: "They Haven't Got Time for the Pain," *Corporate Counsel,* Feb. 1, 2004.
252 "These dismissals strengthen our resolve": Meier, *Pain Killer* (2018), 144.
252 White filed suit: "Saleswoman Sues OxyContin Maker over Dismissal," *Tampa Tribune,* Feb. 1, 2005.
252 White's attorney told the jury: Ibid.
253 "It behooved us to call on": Karen White Deposition, Dec. 17, 2003, quoted in Kessler Report.
253 "The company was all about": "Did Drug Maker Know of OxyContin Abuse?," ABC News, Oct. 5, 2007.
253 "Ma'am, have you ever": Deposition of Karen White in *Karen White v. Purdue Pharma LP,* U.S. District Court, Middle District of Florida, 8:03-CV-1799-7: T-26MSS, May 5, 2004.
254 White's attorney made a motion: Plaintiff's Motion in Limine, *Karen White v. Purdue Pharma LP,* U.S. District Court, Middle District of Florida, 8:03-CV-1799-7: T-26MSS, Jan. 13, 2005.
254 $138,000 in lost pay: "Saleswoman Sues OxyContin Maker over Dismissal."
254 "I was definitely the underdog": Ibid.
254 ended up naming: "How Florida Ignited the Heroin Epidemic," *Palm Beach Post,* July 1, 2018.
254 "we're going to be watching them": "Purdue Fights Back with Media Blitz, Legal Offensive," *Orlando Sentinel,* Oct. 21, 2003.
255 block their release: "OxyContin Maker Sues to Get Plans Back," *Orlando Sentinel,* Dec. 14, 2002; Attorney General's Memorandum of Law in Opposition to Verified Emergency Complaint for Temporary and Permanent Injunction, *Purdue Pharma LP v. State of Florida,* Case No. 02-23184 CACE 02, Circuit Court, Broward County, Fla., Dec. 23, 2002.
255 service that Dezenhall offered: Eric

Dezenhall, *Glass Jaw: A Manifesto for Defending Fragile Reputations in an Age of Instant Scandal* (New York: Twelve, 2014), 32.
255 abused drugs in the past: "Right Too Soon," *Columbia Journalism Review,* Aug. 23, 2017.
255 bringing a libel action: Timothy Bannon to Hon. James P. Jones, July 12, 2007.
255 major retraction: Ibid.; "Inside Purdue Pharma's Media Playbook."
255 Bloodsworth's flawed execution: "Right Too Soon."
255 article in *Slate:* "The Accidental Addict," *Slate,* March 25, 2004.
255 "set the record straight": "Sentinel Finishes Report About OxyContin Articles," *Orlando Sentinel,* Feb. 22, 2004.
256 "We, until early 2000, didn't really know": Transcript of Meier interview with Udell, Friedman, and Goldenheim, Aug. 24, 2001. The transcript, which was created by Purdue and subsequently turned over to prosecutors in discovery, does not specify the precise speakers when it quotes the three executives. The attributions that I am making here are based on Barry Meier's recollection of who was saying what.
256 a stern letter: Udell to Meier, Jan. 9, 2003. In Udell's June 20 letter to Steven Murphy, he mentions that he reiterated the offer in another letter to Meier on June 5.
256 "Both of our companies": Howard Udell to Steven Murphy, June 20, 2003.
256 "Hang in there Richard": Wettlaufer to Richard Sackler, July 27, 2001.
256 "Thanks for your support": Richard Sackler to Wettlaufer, July 29, 2001.
256 "I'd like to try an argument": A second email from Richard Sackler to Wettlaufer, July 29, 2001.
257 "I do not believe most": Wettlaufer to Richard Sackler, July 29, 2001.
257 "I understand what you": Richard Sackler to Wettlaufer, July 30, 2001.
257 "Poor people in the inner city": Wettlaufer to Richard Sackler, July 30, 2001.
257 "Don't make that bet": Richard Sackler to Wettlaufer, July 30, 2001.
257 "a designer drug": Email cited in Amended Complaint, *State of Connecticut v. Purdue Pharma,* No. X07 HHD-CV-19-6105325-S, May 6, 2019. Further details about the email and the sender in RDS 2019 Deposition.
258 sent an email to some members: Email chain quoted in Kathe Sackler Deposition.

258 "In terms of narcotic firepower": Meier, *Pain Killer* (2003), 12.

258 "seemed unable or unwilling to take": Ibid., 293–94.

258 one of the greatest challenges: "Correcting the Record: Times Reporter Who Resigned Leaves Long Trail of Deception," *New York Times,* May 11, 2003.

259 two top editors resigned: "The Times Chooses Veteran of Magazines and Publishing as Its First Public Editor," *New York Times,* Oct. 27, 2003.

259 "stepping on a land mine": "Repairing the Credibility Cracks," *New York Times,* May 4, 2013.

259 its first "public editor": "Times Chooses Veteran of Magazines and Publishing as Its First Public Editor."

259 "if the reader has been dealt with straight": Ibid.

259 wrote an article: "The Delicate Balance of Pain and Addiction," *New York Times,* Nov. 25, 2003.

259 "sensationalized and skewed account": "The Public Editor: You Can Stand on Principle and Still Stub a Toe," *New York Times,* Dec. 21, 2003.

259 They appealed directly to Okrent: Interview with Okrent.

260 Udell asserted that: Interview with Meier.

260 an egregious conflict: "Public Editor: You Can Stand on Principle and Still Stub a Toe."

260 "It was hugely frustrating": Interview with Meier.

261 strong-armed by corporate thugs: Ibid.

CHAPTER 20: TAKE THE FALL

262 John Brownlee was: Unless otherwise noted, details about John Brownlee are drawn from an interview with Brownlee.

262 announced guilty pleas: "7 Plead Guilty to Selling OxyContin," *Staunton (Va.) News Leader,* Sept. 20, 2001.

262 Who was *making* it?: Chris McGreal, *American Overdose: The Opioid Tragedy in Three Acts* (New York: PublicAffairs, 2018), 137.

262 "We know he gave some": "Doctor Who Dispensed OxyContin Is Indicted," AP, Feb. 2, 2002.

263 had already opened an investigation: Interviews with Rick Mountcastle, Brownlee, and another prosecutor who worked for Brownlee at the time.

263 "We were sitting around talking": Interview with Mountcastle.

263 stories about the aggressiveness: Interview with Mountcastle.

264 a subpoena to Connecticut: Statement of John L. Brownlee Before the Committee on the Judiciary, U.S. Senate, July 31, 2007 (hereafter cited as Brownlee Testimony).

264 pickup team of borrowed hands from: Interview with Mountcastle.

264 Mountcastle figured that the company: Ibid.

264 photo of the evidence room: Photo provided to the author by Brownlee.

265 six hundred different subpoenas: Brownlee Testimony.

265 the "revolving door": For more on this phenomenon, see Jesse Eisinger, *The Chickenshit Club: Why the Justice Department Fails to Prosecute Executives* (New York: Simon & Schuster, 2017).

265 "rein in the Western District": Deposition of Howard Shapiro, *Commonwealth of Kentucky v. Purdue Pharma LP et al.,* Civil Action No. 07-CI-01303, April 15, 2015 (hereafter cited as Shapiro Deposition).

266 "Go back to Virginia": Interviews with Mountcastle and Brownlee; Brownlee Testimony.

266 devise little tricks: Interview with Mountcastle.

266 three hundred interviews: Brownlee Testimony.

266 Howard Udell's legal secretary: West Deposition.

267 "When I was a manager": Alfonso to Hogen, cc: Friedman, email, forwarded to Udell, June 19, 2000, cited in Prosecution Memo.

267 its own internal studies: The results of this study were included in Curtis Wright's Medical Officer Review of Purdue's submissions to the FDA. But when he was later questioned about why the evidence of withdrawal was not reflected in the original package insert, which he approved, Wright could not offer any explanation, saying that he was unable to recall when, how, or why the final language ended up in the insert. Prosecution Memo.

267 final package insert: Prosecution Memo.

267 completely surprised to learn: Transcript of Barry Meier interview with Friedman, Goldenheim, and Udell, Aug. 24, 2001.

267 spoon and shoot study: Prosecution Memo; Brownlee Testimony.

267 trained sales reps: Prosecution Memo.

267 uncovered troubling clues: Project

Team Contact Report, Sept. 17, 1992, cited in Prosecution Memo.
267 March 1995 email: Reder to Udell and others, email, March 24, 1995, cited in Prosecution Memo.
268 "I think there was a secret deal": Interview with Mountcastle.
268 "The defense in a case like this": Interview with Brownlee.
268 sales reps continuing to call: Prosecution Memo.
268 "street value of OC": Sales call notes from Patricia Carnes, Jan. 20, 1999, cited in Prosecution Memo.
268 "I mean we have an OC pill": Transcription of Fleishman-Hillard interview with Friedman, May 12, 1999, cited in Prosecution Memo.
269 "He now takes methadone": Spanos to Adam Rodriguez, June 16, 1999.
269 Johnny did appear: *I Got My Life Back, Part II,* Purdue Pharma promotional film, 2000.
269 report in the *Milwaukee Journal Sentinel:* "What Happened to the Post Children of OxyContin?," *Milwaukee Journal Sentinel,* Sept. 8, 2012.
270 pills in his pocket: Ibid.
270 incapacitated by his dependence: Ibid.
270 planning a big celebration: Kathe Sackler Deposition.
270 $1 billion a year: According to the GAO, OxyContin sales in the United States reached $1.5 billion in 2002. When you factor in Purdue's other products in the United States and revenue from its international businesses, the total revenue of the entire enterprise was likely around $2 billion.
270 the Legion of Honor: President Jacques Chirac to Mortimer Sackler, April 4, 1997.
270 knighted by the British queen: "Drugs Mogul with Vast Philanthropic Legacy," *Financial Times,* April 23, 2010.
270 the magazine *Harpers & Queen:* "Blessed Are the Very, Very Rich," *Harpers & Queen,* Feb. 1992.
271 "I was an active executive": RDS 2019 Deposition.
271 "Dr. Richard has to back off": Russell Gasdia, email, March 8, 2008, cited in Massachusetts Complaint.
271 "He and Michael were very close": Interview with Hogen.
271 "frequent interactions with my subordinates": Friedman to Richard Sackler, email,

2006, cited in Complaint in *State of Oregon v. Richard S. Sackler et al.,* Circuit Court of the State of Oregon, No. 19CV22185, Aug. 30, 2019.
271 step down as vice presidents: Declarations of Jonathan Sackler, Kathe Sackler, and Mortimer Sackler, cited in Massachusetts Complaint.
271 "those moves were for show": Massachusetts Complaint.
272 "I will strenuously protest": Kathe Sackler to Mortimer Sackler, quoted in Kathe Sackler Deposition.
272 Brownlee bought and read: Interview with Brownlee.
272 "He was very personable": Interview with Mountcastle.
272 "He's not a magician": Interview with Brownlee.
273 prosecution memo: Prosecution Memo.
273 on the table was $1.6 billion: Shapiro Deposition. Rick Mountcastle did not dispute this number.
273 federal prosecutors bring a criminal case: Interviews with Paul Pelletier, Rick Mountcastle, and other former officials involved in the case.
274 "reported directly to The Family": Prosecution Memo.
274 memo of his own: Ogrosky to Steve Tyrrell and Paul Pelletier (Criminal Division, Department of Justice), internal memorandum, Oct. 6, 2006.
275 not be difficult to convict: Ibid.
275 Shapiro filed in: Shapiro Deposition.
275 subsequently plead guilty: "Top Justice Official Admits Abramoff Fueled His Regal Life," McClatchy, April 22, 2008.
276 a robust presentation: Shapiro Deposition; interviews with Mountcastle, Brownlee, and one other attorney who was in the meeting.
276 "I did not make or overrule": Interview with Alice Fisher.
276 John Brownlee recalled: Interview with Brownlee.
276 But in an interview: Interview with Paul McNulty.
277 "This is the reason we *have*": Interview with Pelletier.
277 subsequent deposition by Howard Shapiro: Shapiro Deposition.
277 continued to fight: John Brownlee to Andrew Good, Mark F. Pomerantz, and Mary Jo White, October 18, 2006. One indi-

cation that the deputy attorney general *was* involved in signing off in this matter is that one of the recipients of this letter, cc'd along with Alice Fisher, Rudy Giuliani, and others, is Ronald Tempas, who was the associate deputy attorney general.

277 Brownlee issued an ultimatum: Brownlee Testimony.

278 felt he was "inquiring": Ibid.

278 "It's Mary Jo White": Interview with Paul McNulty.

278 refused to roll over: Brownlee Testimony.

278 people who knew Brownlee: Interviews with Pelletier and Mountcastle.

278 he got word: Brownlee Testimony.

279 Brownlee later testified: Ibid.

279 a guilty plea: "Ruling Is Upheld Against Executives Tied to OxyContin," *New York Times,* Dec. 15, 2010.

280 sentence of three years: "Three Executives Spared Prison in OxyContin Case," *New York Times,* July 21, 2007.

280 $600 million fine: Statement of U.S. Attorney John Brownlee, May 10, 2007.

280 photographer snapped pictures: Photographs by Don Petersen for the *Times.* "Narcotic Maker Guilty of Deceit over Marketing," *New York Times,* May 11, 2007.

280 said nothing to him: Interview with Meier.

280 "Purdue Pharma acknowledged in the court": "In Guilty Plea, OxyContin Maker to Pay $600 Million," *New York Times,* May 10, 2007.

280 "You are responsible": Lynn Locascio Testimony, *United States v. Purdue Frederick et al.,* U.S. District Court, Western District of Virginia, 1:07CR29, July 20, 2007.

281 "Please do not allow": Ed Bisch Testimony, *United States v. Purdue Frederick et al.,* U.S. District Court, Western District of Virginia, 1:07CR29, July 20, 2007.

281 "I am one of the patients": Kenny Keith Testimony, *United States v. Purdue Frederick et al.,* U.S. District Court, Western District of Virginia, 1:07CR29, July 20, 2007.

282 $34 million in fines: Statement of U.S. Attorney John Brownlee, May 10, 2007.

282 "Certain employees made or told": Howard Shapiro remarks, *United States v. Purdue Frederick et al.,* U.S. District Court, Western District of Virginia, 1:07CR29, July 20, 2007.

282 "The media have done him": Ira Friedman to Hon. James P. Jones, June 7, 2007.

282 Goldenheim's wife: Anne Goldenheim to Hon. James P. Jones, July 16, 2007.

282 "Simply put (and with apologies to my parents)": Silbert to Hon. James P. Jones, July 13, 2007.

282 "endured the slings and arrows": Jeffrey Udell to Hon. James P. Jones, July 1, 2007.

282 on display was galling: Interview with Mountcastle.

283 "this is a case of unusual": McCloskey to Hon. James P. Jones, July 9, 2007.

283 "There is no evidence at all": Mary Jo White remarks, *United States v. Purdue Frederick et al.,* U.S. District Court, Western District of Virginia, 1:07CR29, July 20, 2007.

283 "Purdue and its executives": Statement of John Brownlee on the Guilty Plea of the Purdue Frederick Company and Its Executives for Illegally Misbranding OxyContin, May 10, 2007.

283 stepping down as U.S. Attorney: "Brownlee Resigns; May Run for Office," *Roanoke (Va.) Times,* April 17, 2008; "Brownlee Announces Run for Attorney General," *Richmond Times-Dispatch,* May 20, 2008.

283 shell game of corporate nomenclature: Interview with Mountcastle.

284 Purdue Frederick would take the charge: Board Minutes, Feb. 14, 2008, cited in Massachusetts Complaint.

284 protecting the family: Board Minutes, Oct. 25, 2006, cited in Massachusetts Complaint.

284 "accept responsibility for the misconduct": Silbert to Hon. James P. Jones, July 13, 2007.

284 "took responsibility on themselves": Kathe Sackler Deposition.

284 "Those three guys basically": Interview with Ritchie.

284 Friedman $3 million: Board Minutes, Feb. 14, 2008, cited in Massachusetts Complaint.

284 Udell got $5 million: Board Minutes, Nov. 21, 2008, cited in Massachusetts Complaint.

284 pay themselves $325 million: Board Minutes, Nov. 6, 2008, cited in Massachusetts Complaint.

284 "just another move": Gary Harney Testimony, *United States v. Purdue Frederick et al.,* U.S. District Court, Western District of Virginia, 1:07CR29, July 20, 2007.

285 subsequent congressional hearing: State-

ment of Senator Arlen Specter, Committee on the Judiciary, U.S. Senate, July 31, 2007.

285 "That's been in the bank": Interview with Camp. Purdue fired Camp in 2014, and she subsequently complained about the terms of her dismissal, but I cross-checked much of what she told me over the course of several long interviews and found her credible.

285 voted to expand Purdue's sales force: Board Minutes, Feb. 8, 2008.

285 Sackler was later asked: RDS 2015 Deposition.

CHAPTER 21: TURKS

289 called Amanyara: "Rainmakers and Amanyara Villas," *New York Times*, Sept. 14, 2007.

290 Geri's dubious description: "Two Looks, Two Lives," *Savvy*, Sept. 1981. Geri's company was called Colturae Inc.

290 Mortimer ended up: Mortimer D. A. Sackler biography, website of the Vitality Institute.

290 Jacqueline Pugh: "Wild at Heart," *Vogue*, Oct. 2013.

290 "Mortimer and his family are involved": "The New Dot.com Society," *Vogue*, April 2000; "Wild at Heart."

290 estate in Amagansett: "Wild at Heart."

290 upsized their Manhattan home: "Sackler Family Member Sells Upper East Side Townhouse for $38 Million," *New York Times*, Jan. 31, 2020.

290 Turks and Caicos retreat: Unless otherwise noted the description of Amanyara is based on interviews with a friend of Mortimer's who visited him there and a yoga instructor the family brought with them to Amanyara. "Inside Amanyara, a Peaceful Sanctuary in Turks and Caicos," *Vanity Fair*, May 15, 2018.

291 a place of peace: "Inside Amanyara, a Peaceful Sanctuary in Turks and Caicos"; "First Look at Amanyara," *Travel + Leisure*, April 2, 2009.

291 thirty-nine different countries: "First Look at Amanyara."

291 approximately five to one: Interview with the yoga instructor.

291 Amanyara was dedicated: "First Look at Amanyara."

292 the whole staff would mobilize: Interview with the former yoga instructor; "Moment of Silence Held by Country Leaders for Drowned Haitians," *Magnetic Media*, Jan. 25, 2017.

292 budding society hostess: "Donatella's New York State of Mind," *Women's Wear Daily*, Feb. 7, 2006.

292 "The mechanical bulls are fantastic": "Cocktails for Arts: Museums Compete for Young Patrons," *International Herald Tribune*, Jan. 13, 2006.

292 "Even though we have different": Kathe Sackler Deposition; B Side Defenses.

293 "The pharmaceutical industry has become": Feb. 2008 email from Mortimer D. A. Sackler to Richard and Jonathan Sackler, cited in Amended Complaint, *State of Connecticut v. Purdue Pharma LP et al.*, No. X07 HHD-CV-19-6105325-S, Connecticut Superior Court, May 6, 2019.

293 of $3 billion: "At Purdue Pharma, Business Slumps as Opioid Lawsuits Mount," *Wall Street Journal*, June 30, 2019. In response to a fact-checking query, Purdue Pharma told me that OxyContin revenue peaked in 2009 at just $2.3 billion, but given rebates and other complications the accounting for this sort of a figure can be done a number of ways.

294 agreement committing to improve: Statement of John Brownlee on the Guilty Plea of the Purdue Frederick Company and Its Executives for Illegally Misbranding OxyContin, May 10, 2007.

294 the company boasted: Representatives of the Sackler family and Purdue have stressed to me repeatedly since 2017 that this period was characterized by tremendous compliance.

294 revived the old manner: The Massachusetts Complaint lays out numerous instances of this behavior.

294 to distribute literature: See, for instance, *Clinical Issues in Opioid Prescribing*, Purdue pamphlet, 2008, cited in Massachusetts Complaint, and "Providing Relief, Preventing Abuse," also distributed by Purdue, cited in Tennessee Complaint. In court papers, a former Purdue employee who joined the company in 2009 and worked as a sales rep for six years said, "I also discussed pseudoaddiction with doctors." Declaration of Sean Thatcher, *State of Montana v. Purdue Pharma LP et al.*, Case No. ADV-2017-949, Montana First Judicial Court, Feb. 16, 2018.

294 "Always Be Closing": Notes from Purdue sales representatives' training notebooks, dating from 2009 and 2012, reproduced in Tennessee Complaint.

294 "key messages that work": Pamela Tay-

lor, email, May 16, 2008; Executive Committee notes, April 16, 2008; presentation by Luntz, Maslansky Strategic Research, April 16, 2008, cited in Massachusetts Complaint.
294 distributed a pamphlet: "Providing Relief, Preventing Abuse" (2008), cited in Massachusetts Complaint.
294 a separate campaign: In the Face of Pain website, cited in Massachusetts Complaint.
294 board meeting that fall: Board Report, Oct. 15, 2008, cited in Massachusetts Complaint.
295 the actor Heath Ledger: "Unnecessarily Dangerous Drug Combo Caused Heath Ledger's Death," Wired, Feb. 6, 2008.
295 Biden called a hearing: Senator Joe Biden Opening Statement, Hearing on Prescription and Over-the-Counter Drug Abuse, Subcommittee on Crime and Drugs, Committee on the Judiciary, U.S. Senate, March 12, 2008.
295 crime ring in Los Angeles: Complaint in City of Everett v. Purdue Pharma, Case No. 17 2 00469 31, Superior Court of the State of Washington, Jan. 19, 2017; "More Than 1 Million OxyContin Pills Ended Up in the Hands of Criminals and Addicts. What the Drugmaker Knew," Los Angeles Times, July 10, 2016.
295 prescribed seventy-three thousand pills: "More Than 1 Million OxyContin Pills Ended Up in the Hands of Criminals and Addicts."
295 A shady operation: Ibid.
295 Michele Ringler: Ringler to Jack Crowley, Sept. 2, 2009; "More Than 1 Million OxyContin Pills Ended Up in the Hands of Criminals and Addicts."
296 "I feel very certain": Ringler to Jack Crowley, Sept. 2, 2009.
296 "Shouldn't the DEA be contacted": Ringler to Jack Crowley, Sept. 1, 2009.
296 "As far as reporting to DEA": Crowley to Ringler, Sept. 1, 2009.
296 complaints—nearly a dozen: "More Than 1 Million OxyContin Pills Ended Up in the Hands of Criminals and Addicts."
296 Crowley would later acknowledge: Ibid.
296 "Region Zero": "OxyContin Closely Guards Its List of Suspect Doctors," Los Angeles Times, Aug. 11, 2013.
296 the company did nothing: "More Than 1 Million OxyContin Pills Ended Up in the Hands of Criminals and Addicts."
296 "a long time to catch up": Ibid.
296 defended the company's conduct: Ibid.

296 an investigation by the Los Angeles Times: Ibid.
297 "quantification of their negative impact": Kathe Sackler to Ed Mahony et al., March 11, 2008, cited in Massachusetts Complaint and reproduced in B Side Defenses.
297 Udell had continued to work: Burt Rosen Deposition, In re National Prescription Opiate Litigation, U.S. District Court, Northern District of Ohio, 1:17-MD-2804, Jan. 16, 2019 (hereafter cited as Rosen Deposition).
297 the three executives: "Let Me Stay in the Game: Purdue's Ex-G.C. Fights a Prohibition Against Working with the Government," Corporate Counsel, Feb. 1, 2011.
297 a legal services organization: Howard Udell Obituary, New York Times, Aug. 5, 2013.
297 opioids to American servicemen: Massachusetts Complaint.
298 "Many veterans of Operation Enduring Freedom": Derek McGinnis, Exit Wounds: A Survival Guide to Pain Management for Returning Veterans and Their Families (Washington, D.C.: Waterford Life Sciences, 2009), 5.
298 opioids are still "underused": Ibid., 106.
298 "Long experience with opioids": Ibid., 107.
298 "the most amazing redemption": "Howard Udell: Helped Hundreds of Veterans with Legal Problems," Hartford Courant, Sept. 3, 2013.
298 Udell never felt: Ibid.
298 "which amounted to remarks": Ibid.
299 Kathe Sackler once described: Kathe Sackler Deposition.
299 "He had a number of roles": Ibid.
300 memo to his relatives: This language appears to have originated in a memo to Richard from F. Peter Boer, re: CEO CONSIDERATIONS, dated April 12, 2008. However, the Massachusetts Complaint suggests that Richard himself endorsed this language, presumably by amending or signing off on the memo. Significantly, in the B Side Defenses, attorneys representing Richard quote the relevant language in the Massachusetts Complaint and do not dispute the characterization of Richard having "written" the memo. (The "defenses" raised by Richard's attorneys in this instance are that the CEO loyalty discussion came up in the context of a possible sale of Purdue and was "unrelated to deceptive marketing allegations.")
300 served on the board: Robert Josephson to New Yorker, email, Oct. 19, 2017; Massachusetts Complaint.

300 board met frequently: Massachusetts Complaint.

300 "Mortimer camp": Jonathan Sackler to Theresa Sackler, June 23, 2016.

301 "Why are you BOTH reducing": Mortimer D. A. Sackler, emails, Nov. 23 and 24, 2010, cited in Massachusetts Complaint.

301 pressing for greater distributions: Email exchange between David, Jonathan, and Richard Sackler, Nov. 12, 2014.

301 ten-year plan: Purdue Pharma 10-Year Plan, June 24, 2010, cited in Massachusetts Complaint.

301 Mortimer personally directed: "In 2011, Mortimer D. A. Sackler demanded that the 2012 budget reduce research and development expenses: 'we must cut spending and R&D investment back to an appropriate level given the actual sales that we have and our lack of diversification of those sales.'" Complaint in *State of Oregon v. Richard S. Sackler et al.,* Circuit Court of the State of Oregon, No. 19CV22185, Aug. 30, 2019.

301 Jonathan Sackler characterized: Jonathan Sackler to Richard Sackler et al., email, Oct. 12, 2014, cited in Settlement Agreement between the United States Department of Justice and Dr. Richard Sackler, David Sackler, Mortimer D. A. Sackler, Kathe Sackler, and the Estate of Jonathan Sackler, Oct. 21, 2020 (hereafter cited as DOJ Sackler Settlement).

302 company sued Endo: "Judge Says Maker of OxyContin Misled Officials to Win Patents," *New York Times,* Jan. 6, 2004.

302 Paul Goldenheim admitted: Opinion and Order, *Purdue Pharma LP v. Endo Pharmaceuticals Inc.,* 00 Civ. 8029 (SHS), Southern District of New York, Jan. 5, 2004.

302 run might be over: Edward Mahony to Hon. James P. Jones, July 11, 2007.

302 restore its monopoly: Opinion, *Purdue Pharma LP et al. v. Endo Pharmaceuticals,* U.S. Court of Appeals for the Federal Circuit, Feb. 1, 2006.

302 maximize the windfall: The legal and business history is too complex to fully rehearse here, but briefly: Endo challenged the validity of Purdue's patent for OxyContin and won the judgment invalidating Purdue's patent exclusivity in 2004. Following that ruling, Endo and several other companies launched generic versions of OxyContin. But Purdue won a judgment from an appeals court in 2006 vacating that decision and ultimately settled with the other companies

(which withdrew the generic versions from the market) and regained its patent exclusivity. See "Endo Defiant over Generic Oxy-Contin Knockback," *Pharma Times,* Feb. 7, 2006; "Purdue Fends Off Generic OxyContin Competition," Law360, Aug. 29, 2006; Settlement Agreement, Aug. 28, 2006, signed by Mortimer Sackler, Michael Friedman, and others, SEC Archives.

302 engaged with the consulting firm: Interview with Nancy Camp.

302 beginning to flatten: Mike Innaurato, email, Dec. 3, 2009, cited in Massachusetts Complaint.

302 Ed Mahony: Mahony, email, Feb. 26, 2008, cited in Massachusetts Complaint.

302 Richard convened a meeting: Richard Sackler, email, July 12, 2009, cited in Massachusetts Complaint.

302 He demanded weekly status: Richard Sackler, email, Oct. 8, 2009, cited in Massachusetts Complaint.

303 new kind of weekly sales report: Robert Barmore, email, Oct. 8, 2009; Dipti Jinwala, email, Oct. 8, 2009; David Rosen, email, Oct. 8, 2009, all cited in Massachusetts Complaint.

303 series of recommendations: "Identifying Granular Growth Opportunities for OxyContin: Addendum to July 18th and August 5th Updates," McKinsey & Company to John Stewart and Russ Gasdia, confidential memo, Aug. 8, 2013.

303 "the best possible chance": McKinsey Presentation, Sept. 11, 2009, cited in Massachusetts Complaint.

303 For these outside consultants: Jonathan Cain to McKinsey colleagues, email, Oct. 16, 2008.

303 He still jetted: "Dr. Mortimer Sackler," *Times* (London), April 13, 2010.

303 last night of 2009: "Choir's on Song as Star Cricketer Makes His Catch," *South Wales Evening Post,* Jan. 6, 2010.

303 The bride was twenty-seven: Ibid.

303 grown up in London: "Inside the Sackler Scandal," *Tatler,* March 22, 2019.

303 arranged for seventy members: "Choir's on Song as Star Cricketer Makes His Catch."

304 stayed up reveling: "Dr. Mortimer Sackler," *Times* (London), April 13, 2010.

304 obituary in *The New York Times:* "Mortimer D. Sackler, Arts Patron, Dies at 93," *New York Times,* March 31, 2010.

304 Another extensive obituary: "Dr. Mortimer Sackler," *Times* (London), April 13,

2010. Some published versions of this obituary did include a reference to OxyContin; others did not.

CHAPTER 22: TAMPERPROOF

305 new kind of OxyContin: William N. Evans, Ethan Lieber, and Patrick Power, "How the Reformulation of OxyContin Ignited the Heroin Epidemic," *Review of Economics and Statistics* 101, no. 1 (March 2019).

306 "a very large proportion": Interview with Craig Landau.

306 "Purdue should be leading the charge": Mortimer Sackler, email, Feb. 12, 2008, cited in Massachusetts Complaint.

306 obtaining several patents: See for instance U.S. Patent No. 7727557, "Pharmaceutical Formulation Containing Irritant," filed September 22, 2006, United States Patent and Trademark Office.

306 He even weighed in: Complaint in *State of Oregon v. Richard S. Sackler et al.*, Circuit Court of the State of Oregon, No. 19CV22185, Aug. 30, 2019.

306 granted Purdue permission: FDA, "FDA Approves New Formulation of Oxy-Contin," news release, April 5, 2010.

307 permitted a claim: "Purdue Pharma L.P. Statement on FDA Approval of New Label for Reformulated OxyContin® (Oxycodone HCL Controlled-Release) Tablets CII and Citizen Petition Regarding Withdrawal of Original Formulation due to Safety," April 18, 2013.

307 "the extent to which the new": FDA, "FDA Approves New Formulation of Oxy-Contin." The new formulation was approved in 2010; the new language about the abuse deterrent properties was approved in 2013. But the studies, which were initially announced in 2010, had hardly been concluded by the time the new label was approved; in fact, it was not until 2020 that FDA released the full results of these studies.

308 "evergreening": Roger Collier, "Drug Patents: The Evergreening Problem," *Canadian Medical Association Journal,* June 11, 2013.

308 "close the door to the competition": Alfonso to Friedman, Jan. 25, 2001.

308 set to expire in 2013: See "OxyContin Maker Guards Exclusivity," *Wall Street Journal,* June 27, 2012; "Purdue Pharma Is Taking Advantage of Patent Law to Keep OxyContin from Ever Dying," *Quartz,* Nov. 18, 2017.

308 filed papers with the FDA: Purdue Pharma LP Citizen Petition, No. FDA-2012-

P-0760 (July 13, 2012), arguing that if generic versions of OxyContin were allowed, "abuse of extended release oxycodone could return to the levels experienced prior to the introduction of reformulated OxyContin." In case there was any uncertainty about the company's motives, a Purdue consultant explained to the FDA that if the agency permitted generic versions of OxyContin, it would "substantially reduce" the "incentives to invest in the significant research and development necessary to bring tamper-resistant products to market." Complaint in *State of Washington v. Purdue Pharma, L.P. et al.,* Sept. 28, 2017.

308 "no longer outweigh" the risks: "Abuse-Deterrent Properties of Purdue's Reformulated OxyContin (Oxycodone Hydrochloride) Extended-Release Tablets," Memorandum from Douglas Throckmorton to Janet Woodcock, April 16, 2013; "FDA Bars Generic OxyContin," *New York Times,* April 16, 2013.

308 "Purdue is gratified": "Purdue Pharma L.P. Statement on FDA Approval of New Label for Reformulated Oxycontin® (Oxycodone HCL Controlled-Release) Tablets CII and Citizen Petition Regarding Withdrawal of Original Formulation due to Safety."

309 He demanded "intelligence": Richard Sackler to Gasdia, Jan. 30, 2011.

309 calculations of his own: Delaware Complaint.

309 "Who have you chosen for me": Richard Sackler to Gasdia, June 16, 2011.

310 Gasdia sounded a quiet alarm: Gasdia to Weinstein, June 16, 2011.

310 "LOL," Weinstein replied: Weinstein to Gasdia, June 16, 2011.

310 opted not to make the trip: Memorandum of Law in Support of the Individual Directors' Motion to Dismiss for Lack of Personal Jurisdiction, *Commonwealth of Massachusetts v. Purdue Pharma LP et al.,* Civil Action No. 1884-CV-01808(B), April 1, 2019; the B Side Defenses note that Richard did "one ride-along in 2011 in Fairfield County," adding that he did not *personally* "engage in promotion or marketing."

310 "Anything you can do": Gasdia to Stewart, March 7, 2012.

310 "I work on this virtually": Stewart to Gasdia, March 8, 2012.

310 "implies a danger of untoward": Richard Sackler, email, July 20, 2011, cited in Massachusetts Complaint.

310 "Do you share my disappointment?":
Richard Sackler, email, March 9, 2011, cited
in Massachusetts Complaint.

311 "What else more can we do": Richard
Sackler to Russell Gasdia, email, March 16,
2011.

311 joined his cousin in expressing concern:
Mortimer Sackler, emails, April 5 and 8,
2011, cited in Massachusetts Complaint.

311 staff reported: Executive Committee
Notes, May 12, 2011, cited in Massachusetts
Complaint.

311 In Richard's view: Richard Sackler to
Gasdia, June 16, 2011.

311 "It's been hard to convince": Gasdia,
email, Feb. 27, 2014, cited in Massachusetts
Complaint.

311 the Sacklers fired him: Richard Sackler,
email, June 10, 2014, cited in Massachusetts
Complaint.

311 continued to sell well: Board Presentation, April 14, 2011, cited in Massachusetts
Complaint.

311 their staff informed them: Stuart Baker,
email, Aug. 16, 2010; Presentation by Paul
Coplan, Aug. 19, 2010.

311 "will not stop patients": Stewart to
Richard Sackler, Feb. 22, 2008, cited in Massachusetts Complaint.

311 showed the board data: Massachusetts
Complaint.

311 users swapped stories: "Drug Is Harder
to Abuse, but Users Persevere," *New York
Times*, June 15, 2011.

312 a subsequent study: Tara Gomes et al.,
"Reformulation of Controlled-Release Oxycodone and Pharmacy Dispensing Patterns
near the US-Canada Border," *Open Med*,
Nov. 13, 2012.

312 maintains that it alerted authorities:
Robert Josephson, email, Oct. 19, 2017.

312 to diminish: Evans, Lieber, and Power,
"How the Reformulation of OxyContin Ignited the Heroin Epidemic."

312 Centers for Disease Control would ultimately conclude: "CDC Guidelines for Prescribing Opioids for Chronic Pain," Centers
for Disease Control and Prevention, March
18, 2016.

312 "evidence was not robust": In 2020, the
FDA released the results of "postmarket"
studies into the effectiveness of reformulated
OxyContin in curbing abuse. "OxyContin Abuse Deterrent Formulation (ADF),"
FDA Briefing Document, Joint Meeting
of the Drug Safety and Risk Management
(DSaRM) Advisory Committee and Anesthetic and Analgesic Drug Products Advisory Committee (AADPAC), Sept. 10–11,
2020.

312 a research abstract: Howard Chilcoat et
al., "Changes in Prescriptions of OxyContin
and Opana After Introduction of Tamper
Resistant Formulations Among Potentially
Problematic and Comparator Prescribers,"
Drug and Alcohol Dependence, July 1, 2014. A
Purdue spokesperson confirmed this figure.

312 tout the investment: Interview with
Craig Landau.

313 According to court documents: DOJ
Sackler Settlement.

313 "It should not clear": "Drug Is Harder
to Abuse, but Users Persevere."

314 In the book *Dreamland*: Quinones,
Dreamland, 65.

315 call attention to precisely this transition: Statement from the Sackler family (both
the Raymond and the Mortimer wings), sent
by Davidson Goldin, a representative for the
Raymond wing, who coordinated with representatives from the Mortimer wing, Oct. 1,
2020. ("The family members have great sympathy for those suffering from addiction and
are fully committed to contributing to solutions to the nation's complex crisis of opioid
abuse. According to U.S. government data,
the rise in opioid-related deaths is driven
overwhelmingly by heroin and illicit fentanyl smuggled by drug traffickers into the
U.S. from China and Mexico.")

315 Sackler Professorship in Internal Medicine: "A Family, and a Transformative Legacy," *Medicine@Yale*, July/Aug. 2014.

316 four out of five people: *Opioid Addiction:
2016 Facts & Figures*, American Society of
Addiction Medicine.

316 A survey of 244 people: Theodore J. Cic-
ero and Matthew S. Ellis, "Abuse-Deterrent
Formulations and the Prescription Opioid
Abuse Epidemic in the United States: Lessons Learned from OxyContin," *JAMA Psychiatry* 72, no. 5 (2015).

316 "The reason heroin *happened*": Interview
with Davis.

316 "rapid rise in the heroin death rate":
Evans, Lieber, and Power, "How the Reformulation of OxyContin Ignited the Heroin
Epidemic." Of course there were other factors that might have contributed to the rise
in heroin abuse—the tightening of prescribing by doctors, the closure of pill mills, the
increased supply described by Quinones.

But supply-side arguments cannot account for the sudden rate of increase in 2010, coinciding so precisely with the reformulation. In 2020, the FDA released the findings of a decade's worth of study of the OxyContin reformulation, concluding that there was insufficient evidence to infer that the reformulation caused a reduction in overall Oxy-Contin abuse (because people continued to abuse it orally) and—under the category of "unintended adverse consequences"—that "any decreases in prescription opioid overdose... may have been offset, or more than offset, by increases in illicit opioid overdose due to substitution." Christina R. Greene, "Literature Review: Impact of Reformulated OxyContin on Abuse and Opioid-Related Morbidity and Mortality," FDA, Sept. 10–11, 2020.

CHAPTER 23: AMBASSADORS

317 "I think we can do much better": "Democrats Reap $91,000 from Charter Schools Advocate and His Family," *Hartford Courant*, June 21, 2014.

317 fund a charter network: "Sackler Family Opioid Fortune Backed CT Charter Schools," *New Haven (Conn.) Register*, March 9, 2019; 2017 Form 990 Tax Returns for the Bouncer Foundation.

317 she loved photography: "The 'Dangerous' Filmmaking of Madeleine Sackler," *Backstage*, July 8, 2014.

318 interview on C-SPAN: "Q&A: Madeleine Sackler," C-SPAN, June 24, 2010.

318 short-listed: Documentary short list, 2010 Academy Awards.

318 "It's kind of the flip side": "A Prison Film Made in Prison," *New Yorker*, Jan. 29, 2018.

318 Wright had visited Pendleton: Interview with Jeffrey Wright.

319 acquired by HBO: "Prison Film Made in Prison."

319 "to elevate the voices": Madeleine Sackler biography, from her personal website.

319 $3 million in cash: "OxyContin Heiress Madeleine Sackler Pays Cash on L.A.'s Eastside," Dirt.com, Jan. 30, 2020.

319 longtime director: Massachusetts Complaint.

319 scoff at the suggestion: "Prison Film Made in Prison."

320 increasing since 2010: "Indiana—Opioid-Involved Deaths and Related Harms," National Institute of Drug Abuse, April 2020.

320 116 opioid prescriptions: U.S. Opioid Prescribing Rate Maps for 2015, CDC website.

320 In the very prison: David Bursten (Indiana Department of Public Correction) to *The New Yorker*, email.

320 the prison's own statistics: Ibid.

320 African Americans had been spared: "A 'Rare Case Where Racial Biases' Protected African-Americans," *New York Times*, Dec. 6, 2019.

320 reinstating a mandatory minimum: "Pence Reinstates Mandatory Minimum Prison Terms for Some Drug Crimes," *Times of Northwest Indiana*, March 21, 2016.

320 82 percent of those charged: "Quick Facts: Heroin Trafficking Offenses," U.S. Sentencing Commission.

320 she would state vaguely: "Madeleine Sackler's Films Praised, but She Faces Scrutiny over Opioid Wealth," *Guardian*, May 2, 2018.

321 followed press coverage: Jonathan Sackler to Kathey Walsh, Jan. 2, 2014, reproduced in B Side Defenses.

321 He had expressed concerns: Zach Perlman, email, Dec. 9, 2015, cited in Massachusetts Complaint.

321 Raymond would still inquire: Delaware Complaint.

321 Jonathan was also particularly keen: Jonathan Sackler, email, Jan. 2, 2014, cited in Massachusetts Complaint.

321 a generous profile: "Prison Film Made in Prison."

322 when the *O.G.* premiered: "Prison Film Made in Prison"; "The Premiere of 'O.G.,' the Film Made Inside an Indiana Prison," *New Yorker*, April 24, 2018.

322 posed for photographs: Getty Images from "'The O.G.' Experience," an event hosted by HBO at Studio 525 on February 23, 2019.

322 Wright had sent Madeleine an email: Jeffrey Wright to Madeleine Sackler, October 26, 2017.

322 Madeleine never responded: Interview with Jeffrey Wright.

323 interned at Purdue: The Raymond Sackler Family's Opposition to the Official Committee of Unsecured Creditors' Exceptions Motion, *In re Purdue Pharma LP et al., Debtors*, U.S. Bankruptcy Court, Southern District of New York, Chapter 11, Case No. 19-23649 (RDD), Oct. 14, 2020.

323 15 East Sixty-Second Street: Moab

Partners LP, U.S. Securities and Exchange Commission, Form D.

323 David took a seat: Massachusetts Complaint.

323 "I think my dad's vision": "'We Didn't Cause the Crisis': David Sackler Pleads His Case on the Opioid Epidemic," *Vanity Fair*, June 19, 2019.

323 provided by the company: "Cash Transfers of Value Analysis," Dec. 16, 2019, audit conducted by AlixPartners and submitted to the bankruptcy court in White Plains.

323 subsequent court filing: Ibid.

323 "Richard would say": Interview with Camp.

324 Mortimer sought the counsel: These talking points are included in an email from Mortimer D.A. Sackler to Kerry Sulkowicz, July 16, 2017.

325 disdainful of his cousin: All of these quotes and details are from David Sackler to Richard, Beth and Joss Sackler, June 12, 2015.

326 Madeleine's brother: "Inside the Room Where Tech Actually Vies for Military Jobs," *Wired*, March 12, 2019; Clare Sackler website.

326 His other daughter, Marianna: Deposition of Marianna Sackler, *In Re: Purdue Pharma LP et al., Debtors*, United States Bankruptcy Court, Southern District of New York, Case No. 19-2649 (RDD), September 2, 2020.

326 "no career": David Sackler to Richard, Beth, and Joss Sackler, June 12, 2015.

326 $12 million home: Tuija Catalano to Rich Hillis of the San Francisco Planning Commission, re: 2921 Vallejo Street, Oct. 16, 2017 (citing a complaint by Marianna and her husband, James Frame, in a property dispute).

326 chain of restaurants: "Hedge Fund Tosses Family That Controls Maker of Oxy-Contin," *Wall Street Journal*, March 7, 2019; "On Hospitality with Jeff Lefcourt of the Smith and Jane," OpenTable, April 2, 2016.

326 £26 million home: "Homes Gossip," *Evening Standard*, July 20, 2010.

326 financing company called Rooks Nest: "How Family Fortune Bankrolls London Arts," *Evening Standard*, March 19, 2018.

326 "non-profit incubator": Details on Marissa Sackler are from "Marissa Sackler: Busy Bee," *W*, May 19, 2014. The assessment of her manner of speaking is based on a number of speeches she has delivered, which are available on YouTube.

327 a gala opening: "New Serpentine Sackler Gallery Opens as Michael Bloomberg Steps In as Chairman," *Evening Standard*, Sept. 25, 2013.

327 windows in Westminster: Westminster Abbey website.

327 more than $100 million: "How Family Fortune Bankrolls London Arts."

327 Prince of Wales Medal: 2011 Honouree: Theresa Sackler. Arts and Business Cymru.

327 modern office building: The address of Mundipharma House is 14 Par La Ville Road, Hamilton HM 08, Bermuda.

328 according to one former financial adviser: Interview with a former financial adviser to the family. Also see "The Sackler Files: How the Tax Haven of Bermuda Played Key Role in £10 Billion Family Fortune," *Evening Standard*, May 11, 2018.

328 company representatives announced: "OxyContin Goes Global," *Los Angeles Times*, Dec. 18, 2016.

329 "You show up, do a presentation": Ibid.

329 "the tools you need to properly address": Ibid.

329 the same discredited literature: Ibid.

329 "is exceptional and ahead of forecast": Draft Note to the Board, in Richard Sackler to David Sackler, Nov. 12, 2014.

329 "smart and diligent around emerging markets": Jonathan Sackler to Richard Sackler et al., email, Oct. 12, 2014, cited in DOJ Sackler Settlement.

329 "This is where the growth": "China Rises as Key Market for Leading Opioid Producer," *Nikkei Asian Review*, Jan. 25, 2019.

330 grew 800 percent: "OxyContin Goes Global."

329 alternative to cheap, Indian-made morphine: "How Big Pharma Is Targeting India's Booming Opioid Market," *Guardian*, Aug. 27, 2019.

329 "China is so critical to our trajectory": "China Rises as Key Market for Leading Opioid Producer."

330 By 2025, he hoped: "Fake Doctors, Pilfered Medical Records Drive Oxy China Sales," AP, Nov. 20, 2019.

330 The *China Medical Tribune*: Ibid.

330 aggressive incentive structure: Ibid.

330 The company claimed: Ibid.

330 investigation by the Associated Press: Ibid.

330 series of flashy promotional videos: "OxyContin Goes Global."

330 informed the Sackler board: Board

Presentation on Abuse Deterrent Strategy, March 21, 2013, cited in Massachusetts Complaint.

331 felt it should show "deference": Report and Recommendations Concerning the Relationship of the Sackler Family and Purdue Pharma with Tufts University, Prepared by Yurko, Salvesen & Remz, PC, for Tufts University, Dec. 5, 2019 (hereafter cited as Tufts Report).

331 "I'm glad they picked": RDS 2019 Deposition.

331 "sat down and...did an inventory": Ibid.

331 "I'm quite pleased": Damas, email, Oct. 20, 2014, quoted in Vermont Complaint.

CHAPTER 24: IT'S A HARD TRUTH, AIN'T IT

332 commissioned a demographic study: Memorandum in Support of Purdue's Motion to Change Venue, *Commonwealth of Kentucky v. Purdue Pharma LP,* Pike Circuit Court, Division II, Civ. Action No. 07-CI-01303, June 10, 2013.

332 fiercely resisted the idea: Interviews with Mitchel Denham and Tyler Thompson.

333 Bobbitt had a fondness: "Professor Bobbitt," *New York Observer,* Oct. 14, 2008.

333 "Our major problem has been": Draft Note to the Board, in Richard Sackler to David Sackler, Nov. 12, 2014.

334 complained to his father: David Sackler to Jonathan and Richard Sackler, Nov. 12, 2014.

334 He mocked the bizarrely "bureaucratic" manner: David Sackler to Jonathan and Richard Sackler, Oct. 7, 2014, reproduced in B Side Defenses.

334 forwarded him a memo: Raymond Sackler to Richard, Jonathan, and David Sackler, May 5, 2014. The attached memo itself is not included with the email that I have, but is characterized in the Delaware Complaint and the Massachusetts Complaint.

335 "The room was filled with only family": Arnab Ghatak to McKinsey colleagues, email, Aug. 23, 2013.

335 "'moving forward fast'": Martin Elling to Rob Rosiello, email, Aug. 24, 2013.

335 turned seventy: Richard was born on March 10, 1945.

335 shifted in his chair: Video recording of RDS 2015 Deposition.

335 "We were face-to-face with the guy": Interview with Denham.

335 led by Tyler Thompson: Unless otherwise specified, the depiction of Richard's Kentucky deposition is drawn from a transcript and video of RDS 2015 Deposition.

336 "A smirk and a so-what attitude": Interview with Thompson.

337 $24 million to settle: "OxyContin Maker to Pay State $24 Million to Settle Claim It Marketed Powerful Painkiller Improperly," *Lexington (Ky.) Herald-Leader,* Dec. 23, 2015.

338 requests to seal records: "How Judges Added to the Grim Toll of Opioids," Reuters, June 25, 2019.

338 directed the prosecutors: Agreed Judgment and Stipulation of Dismissal with Prejudice, *Commonwealth of Kentucky v. Purdue Pharma et al.,* Civil Action No. 07-CI-01303, Commonwealth of Kentucky, Pike Circuit Court, Dec. 22, 2015.

338 have Richard's deposition unsealed: "STAT Goes to Court to Unseal Records of OxyContin Maker," STAT News, March 15, 2016.

338 ruled in STAT's favor: Order, *Boston Globe Life Sciences Media LLC, d/b/a STAT v. Purdue Pharma LP et al.,* Action No. 07-CI-01303, Commonwealth of Kentucky, Pike Circuit Court, May 11, 2016.

338 immediately appealed: "Purdue Pharma Files Appeal of Decision to Unseal OxyContin Records," STAT News, May 17, 2016.

338 a major story: "OxyContin Maker Closely Guards Its List of Suspect Doctors," *Los Angeles Times,* Aug. 11, 2013.

339 "Nobody *needed* to call on": Interview with Davis.

339 doctors are a "gold mine": "OxyContin Maker Closely Guards Its List of Suspect Doctors."

339 sent an update: Damas, email, June 30, 2014, cited in Massachusetts Complaint.

339 Richard demanded to see: Scott Glover, email, Aug. 14, 2014, cited in Massachusetts Complaint.

339 "Why are all the alerts": Richard Sackler to Damas, Nov. 18, 2013, cited in Massachusetts Complaint.

339 Damas offered to reconfigure: Damas, email, Nov. 18, 2013, cited in Massachusetts Complaint.

339 another big story: "'You Want a Description of Hell?': OxyContin's 12-Hour Problem," *Los Angeles Times,* May 5, 2016.

340 third investigative piece: "OxyContin Goes Global," *Los Angeles Times,* Dec. 18, 2016.

340 open letter to the World Health Organization: Katherine Clark et al. to Dr. Margaret Chan, May 3, 2017.

341 more than 165,000 Americans: "CDC Guidelines for Prescribing Opioids for Chronic Pain—United States, 2016," CDC website, March 18, 2016.

341 surpassed car accidents: "OxyContin Maker Closely Guards Its List of Suspect Doctors."

341 midyear update: Midyear Update, June 8, 2016, cited in Massachusetts Complaint.

342 "A New Narrative: Appropriate Use": Board of Directors: Purdue Midyear Preread, June 2017, cited in Massachusetts Complaint.

342 rejected the proposal: Ibid.

343 The family refused: Ibid.

343 "Did I teach about pain management": "A Pain-Drug Champion Has Second Thoughts," *Wall Street Journal*, Dec. 17, 2012.

343 "It's obviously crazy to think": Ibid.

343 "Did you read any articles": 2016 email from Richard Sackler, cited in Amended Complaint, *State of Connecticut v. Purdue Pharma LP et al.*, No. X07 HHD-CV-19-6105325-S, Connecticut Superior Court, May 6, 2019.

344 "Sackler family members hold no": Robert Josephson, email, Nov. 3, 2016, cited in Massachusetts Complaint.

344 staff amended it: Robert Josephson, email, Nov. 28, 2016, cited in Massachusetts Complaint.

344 "The statement will come out of Singapore": Robert Josephson and Raul Damas, email, Dec. 1, 2016, cited in Massachusetts Complaint.

344 2001 meeting with Purdue: Minutes of a meeting on OxyContin between representatives of Purdue Pharma and the FDA, April 23, 2001.

344 "great mistakes of modern medicine": "Former FDA Head: Opioid Epidemic One of the 'Great Mistakes of Modern Medicine,'" CBS News, May 9, 2016.

345 it wasn't the FDA at all: Interview with Tom Frieden.

345 an epidemic: CDC, "Prescription Painkiller Overdoses at Epidemic Levels," press release, Nov. 1, 2011.

345 "CDC does not want to hear": Rosen to Purdue colleagues, Sept. 9, 2015.

345 David Haddox replied: Haddox to Purdue colleagues, Sept. 9, 2015.

346 study by the Associated Press: "Pro-painkiller Echo Chamber Shaped Policy amid Drug Epidemic," AP, Sept. 19, 2016.

346 roughly eight times: "Pharma Lobbying Held Deep Influence over Policies on Opioids," AP, Sept. 18, 2016.

346 spent $4 million: Ibid.

346 a "stranglehold": "Opioid Epidemic: Ex-DEA Official Says Congress Is Protecting Drug Makers," *Guardian*, Oct. 31, 2016.

346 also fought measures: David Haddox, "Pain, Analgesics, and Public Policy," a position paper drafted for the Pain Care Forum and the CDC, Jan. 11, 2012.

346 tracked these developments: Massachusetts Complaint.

346 "provide for some unified direction": Rosen to Udell, Alan Must, and Pamela Bennett, Jan. 7, 2005; Rosen Deposition.

346 "We know of no other medication": Thomas R. Frieden and Debra Houry, "Reducing the Risks of Relief—the CDC Opioid-Prescribing Guideline," *New England Journal of Medicine*, April 21, 2016.

346 "primed" to start using: "New Vital Signs Report—Today's Heroin Epidemic," CDC Briefing, July 7, 2015.

346 "It was no less addictive": Interview with Frieden.

346 The draft guidelines: CDC Guidelines for Prescribing Opioids for Chronic Pain, 2016.

347 a position paper: Haddox, "Pain, Analgesics, and Public Policy."

347 the Pain Care Forum attacked them: "Pro-painkiller Echo Chamber Shaped Policy amid Drug Epidemic."

347 important to Richard Sackler: Alan Must Deposition, *In re National Prescription Opiate Litigation*, MDL No. 2804, Case No. 1:17-MD-2804, U.S. District Court, Northern District of Ohio, March 14, 2019 (hereafter cited as Must Deposition), citing a document in which Richard Sackler says "it was important" for both the American Pain Foundation and for Purdue "that APF be seen as independent."

347 "I don't recall being involved": Rosen Deposition.

348 larger-than-usual contribution: Must Deposition. In response to a fact-checking inquiry, a Purdue representative maintained that the payments were larger in 2016 "because they were for 2016 and 2017."

348 "consensus guidelines": "Pro-painkiller Echo Chamber Shaped Policy amid Drug Epidemic."

348 "As a civilization we somehow managed": "Painkiller Politics," AP, Dec. 18, 2015.
348 The industry had taught: For a deeply nuanced, thoughtful, and accessible exploration of this dilemma, see Travis Rieder, *In Pain: A Bioethicist's Personal Struggle with Opioids* (New York: HarperCollins, 2019).
349 his business plan: Landau Presentation, May 2, 2017, cited in Massachusetts Complaint.
349 One innovative idea: "High Impact Interventions to Rapidly Address Market Access Challenges: Innovative Contracts," confidential Purdue slide deck, Dec. 2017. Also see "McKinsey Proposed Paying Pharmacy Companies Rebates for OxyContin Overdoses," *New York Times*, December 1, 2020.
349 "He worked the day before": RDS 2019 Deposition.

CHAPTER 25: TEMPLE OF GREED
350 Nan Goldin: Unless otherwise noted, material relating to Nan Goldin comes from multiple interviews with her.
350 "Most of all, my father cared": "Nan Goldin's Life in Progress," *New Yorker*, June 27, 2016.
350 When Nan was eleven: Nan Goldin, *Soeurs, saintes et sibylles* (Paris: Regard, 2005).
350 Barbara was troubled: Ibid.
350 "Tell the children": Ibid.
350 Nan left home: Stephen Westfall, "Nan Goldin," *BOMB*, Oct. 1, 1991.
350 her first show: Ibid.
351 "all the denial": "Downtown Legend Richard Hell Interviews Nan Goldin About Art, Opioids, and the Sadness of Life on the Fringes," Artnet News, Nov. 8, 2018; interview with Goldin.
352 Goldin's friend Cookie Mueller: "Nan Goldin on Art, Addiction, and Her Battle with the Sacklers," *Financial Times*, Nov. 8, 2019.
352 for an installation: "A Voyeur Makes Herself at Home in the Louvre," *New York Times*, Dec. 8, 2011.
352 "a padding between you and the world": "Nan Goldin Survived an Overdose to Fight the Opioid Epidemic," *T Magazine*, June 11, 2018.
353 only one in ten: "Receipt of Services for Substance Use and Mental Health Issues Among Adults: Results from the 2016 National Survey on Drug Use and Health," NSDUH Data Review, National Survey on Drug Use and Health, Sept. 2017.

353 $2,000 a day: According to the Fernside/McLean Hospital website, the fee is $1,985 per day, and no insurance or third-party reimbursement is accepted.
353 past 200,000: Pujah Seth et al., "Quantifying the Epidemic of Prescription Opioid Overdose Deaths," *American Journal of Public Health* 108, no. 4 (April 2018).
353 latest figures from the CDC: CDC, "Opioid Overdoses Treated in Emergency Departments," press briefing, March 6, 2018.
354 The *New Yorker* article: "Empire of Pain," *New Yorker*, Oct. 23, 2017.
354 *Esquire* published a piece: "House of Pain," *Esquire*, Oct. 16, 2017.
355 "is morally abhorrent to me": "Elizabeth A. Sackler Supports Nan Goldin in Her Campaign Against OxyContin," *Hyperallergic*, Jan. 22, 2018.
355 "would not have approved": "Meet the Sacklers," *Guardian*, Feb. 13, 2018.
355 a dense CV: "Joss and Jillian Sackler on OxyContin Scandal and Opioid Crisis Accusations," *Town & Country*, May 16, 2019.
356 "Sackler founded a dynasty": Lopez, *Arthur M. Sackler*, 122.
356 "initiated fact-based medical advertising": "Dr. Arthur M. Sackler, 1913–1987," biography on www.sackler.org.
356 "I survived the opioid crisis": Nan Goldin, "Pain/Sackler," *Artforum*, Jan. 2018.
356 "I admire Nan Goldin's courage": Elizabeth Sackler, letter to the editor, *Artforum*, Feb. 2018.
356 "he was the architect": "'Direct Action Is Our Only Hope': Opioid Crisis Activist Nan Goldin on Why People Need to Go Offline to Fight for Their Beliefs," Artnet News, Sept. 4, 2018.
357 letter to *The New Yorker*: Tom Clare to Fabio Bertoni, July 10, 2019. The insincerity of this assertion is amply demonstrated by Purdue's own documents indicating that the company was more interested in securing a patent extension than in selflessly "complying" with the FDA's requests. In a conversation with the attorney vetting this book at Doubleday, representatives for the Sacklers cited the Pediatric Research Equity Act, but when pressed on whether or not Purdue had any discretion when it came to spending millions of dollars on clinical trials, or whether the company had lodged any protest or request for a waiver with the agency, they declined to comment. In reality, the company did have some discretion. Indeed, when the

FDA *originally* asked Purdue to conduct pediatric trials for OxyContin, over a decade earlier, the company initiated trials but then abandoned them, citing the high cost, thus refusing to accommodate the agency. So the notion that Purdue had no choice but to comply is at odds with the actual history. It was only as the expiration of the OxyContin patents approached that Purdue revived the initiative. See "After Delay, OxyContin's Use in Young is Under Study," *New York Times,* July 6, 2012.

357 his "goals and objectives": Landau, email, describing his "goals and objectives" for the coming year, Jan. 5, 2011, cited in Massachusetts Complaint.

358 a budget presentation: Purdue Pharma LP Budget Presentation 2010, Nov. 2 and 3, 2009.

358 "the extension from doing pediatric trials": Mortimer Sackler to Ed Mahony et al., Sept. 28, 2009.

358 he proposed to Purdue: Jonathan Sackler, email, Nov. 21, 2017, cited in Massachusetts Complaint.

358 "I think we need to find": Paul Madeiros, email, April 10, 2018, cited in Massachusetts Complaint.

359 CDC had recently announced: "Assessing Benefits and Harms of Opioid Therapy for Chronic Pain," CDC website, Aug. 3, 2016.

359 The patent application: U.S. Patent No. 9,861,628 ("Buprenorphine-Wafer for Drug Substitution Therapy"), assigned to Rhodes Pharmaceuticals LP, April 22, 2016.

359 "Abuse and Addiction market": Project Tango Presentation Slides, Sept. 12, 2014.

359 "Pain treatment and addiction": "BDC Meeting—Project Tango," slide deck for a presentation at Purdue, Sept. 12, 2014.

359 "the opioid addiction space": Project Tango Presentation Slides, Sept. 12, 2014.

359 board voted not to proceed: Davidson Goldin to *New Yorker,* email, Oct. 1, 2020.

360 "But few institutions seem concerned": "Gifts Tied to Opioid Sales Invite a Question: Should Museums Vet Donors?," *New York Times,* Dec. 1, 2017.

360 Oxford University was similarly steadfast: "How Family Fortune Bankrolls London Arts," *Evening Standard,* March 19, 2018.

361 quietly coordinating: Unless otherwise noted, the account of the Met action is drawn from multiple interviews with Goldin, Megan Kapler, and Harry Cullen.

361 "Temple of greed!": Video footage of the protest.

361 Goldin had started a group: "Opioid Protest at Met Museum Targets Donors Connected to OxyContin," *New York Times,* March 10, 2018.

CHAPTER 26: WARPATH

363 Tasmanian Alkaloids facility: "Shake-up on Opium Island," *New York Times,* July 20, 2014.

363 genetically engineered: "How an Island in the Antipodes Became the World's Leading Supplier of Licit Opioids," *Pacific Standard,* July 11, 2019.

363 85 percent of all the thebaine: "Shake-up on Opium Island."

363 a 1998 agreement: Michael B. Kindergan (Noramco of Delaware Inc.) to Ed Miglarese (PF Laboratories), Oct. 15, 1998.

363 encourage local farmers: "How Johnson & Johnson Companies Used a 'Super Poppy' to Make Narcotics for America's Most Abused Opioid Pills," *Washington Post,* March 26, 2020.

364 "give them a 747": Ibid.

364 raised thirty-six times: Ibid.

364 A subsequent report: "Review of the Drug Enforcement Administration's Regulatory and Enforcement Efforts to Control the Diversion of Opioids," Office of the Inspector General, U.S. Department of Justice, Sept. 2019.

364 the Sacklers protested: Tom Clare to Fabio Bertoni, July 10, 2019.

365 the company knew: Steve Zollo to David Domann et al., Feb. 21, 2001.

365 "We are not the only company": "'We Didn't Cause the Crisis': David Sackler Pleads His Case on the Opioid Epidemic," *Vanity Fair,* June 19, 2019.

365 In legal papers: Purdue's Memorandum of Law in Support of Its Motion to Dismiss Amended Complaint, *Commonwealth of Massachusetts v. Purdue Pharma LP et al.,* Civil Action 1884-CV-01808 (BLS2), March 1, 2019.

365 the smallness of Purdue: "Data Touted by OxyContin Maker to Fight Lawsuits Doesn't Tell the Whole Story," ProPublica, Sept. 9, 2019.

365 representatives were incentivized: In Tennessee, for instance, Purdue trained its sales staff to "develop a specific plan for systematically moving physicians to move to the next level of prescribing behavior." Tennessee Complaint.

365 market-leading 27 percent: "Purdue Led Its Opioid Rivals in Pills More Prone to Abuse," *Wall Street Journal*, Sept. 19, 2019.

365 a separate analysis: "Data Touted by OxyContin Maker to Fight Lawsuits Doesn't Tell the Whole Story."

366 Purdue pointed a finger: "The Lawyer Who Beat Big Tobacco Takes On the Opioid Industry," *Bloomberg Businessweek*, Oct. 5, 2017.

366 "OxyContin was introduced": Robert Josephson statement to *New Yorker*, Oct. 19, 2017.

366 to some who worked at Purdue: New York Complaint.

366 Rhodes Pharmaceuticals: "RI Is Home to Major Oxycodone Manufacturer and Marketing—State Is Suing Parent Company," GoLocal Prov, Sept. 11, 2018.

366 uncovered by the *Financial Times:* New York Complaint; "Billionaire Sackler Family Owns Second Opioid Drugmaker," *Financial Times*, Sept. 9, 2018.

366 set up as a "landing pad": "How Purdue's 'One-Two' Punch Fuelled the Market for Opioids," *Financial Times*, Sept. 10, 2018.

366 seventh-largest opioid manufacturer: Ibid.

366 immediate-release oxycodone: Deposition of Richard J. Fanelli, *In re National Prescription Opiate Litigation*, MDL No. 2804, U.S. District Court for the Northern District of Ohio, Dec. 7, 2018 (hereafter cited as Fanelli Deposition).

366 In one internal email: Baumgartner to Richard Fanelli, email, cited in Fanelli Deposition.

366 active role in Rhodes: New York Complaint.

367 Purdue itself acknowledged: Kessler Memo.

367 presentation for Johnson & Johnson: "Duragesic Disease Modeling," McKinsey Presentation for Johnson & Johnson, April 29, 2002.

367 "the main culprit": Interview with Moore.

367 up-and-coming figure: Carrick Mollenkamp et al., *The People vs. Big Tobacco* (New York: Bloomberg Press, 1998), 28.

367 By his own admission: "Lawyer Who Beat Big Tobacco Takes On the Opioid Industry."

368 take on Big Tobacco: Mollenkamp et al., p. 30.

368 got rid of Joe Camel: "Tobacco Industry Still Has Many Advertising Weapons Available," *New York Times*, June 21, 1997.

368 landmark fine: "Big Tobacco in the Balance," *Guardian*, May 6, 2000.

368 $20 billion settlement from BP: "Mike Moore vs. the Opioid Industry," *60 Minutes*, June 30, 2019.

368 nephew who was addicted: "Lawyer Who Beat Big Tobacco Takes On the Opioid Industry."

368 series of civil cases: Ibid.

369 fundamentally libertarian view: Ibid.

369 Collaborating with a loose consortium: Interview with Moore.

370 According to the CDC: "CDC Foundation's New Business Pulse Focuses on Opioid Overdose Epidemic," CDC website, March 15, 2017.

370 a court hearing in January: Transcript of Proceedings, *In re National Prescription Opiate Litigation*, MDL No. 2804, Jan. 9, 2018.

370 20 percent of the total population: Complaint in *Ohio v. Purdue Pharma LP et al.*, Court of Common Pleas, Ohio, May 31, 2017.

370 opioid-addicted parents: "Lawyer Who Beat Big Tobacco Takes On the Opioid Industry."

370 coroners had run out of room: "Amid Opioid Overdoses, Ohio Coroner's Office Runs Out of Room for Bodies," *New York Times*, Feb. 2, 2017.

371 proposed a plan: "Confidential Program Recommendation," Matt Well (Herald Group) to Josie Martin and Keith Wood (Purdue Pharma), June 20, 2017. A Purdue spokesperson denied that the company had hired the Herald Group, but allowed that a "third party" might have hired them "on the company's behalf."

371 "pad their budgets": "State AGs Target Painkiller Makers to Pad Their Budgets," *Wall Street Journal*, July 31, 2017; Matt Well to Alan Must, August 1, 2017, email.

371 "worked with" the writer: Matt Well to Alan Must, August 1, 2017, email.

371 "a huge pocket": "Litigation over America's Opioid Crisis Is Heating Up," NPR, July 25, 2019.

371 "the Sacklers have not been named": "Meet the Sacklers," *Guardian*, Feb. 13, 2018.

372 eulogized Jonathan's father: Statement by Research!America President and CEO Mary Woolley on the Passing of Philanthropist Raymond Sackler, July 19, 2017.

372 Jonathan wrote: Mary Woolley and one

of the two recipients who protested, Mark Rosenberg, both corroborated this account in interviews with me.

372 "We should be prepared": Jonathan Sackler, email, Feb. 26, 2018.

372 the South London Gallery: "South London Gallery Returned Funding to Sackler Trust Last Year," *Art Newspaper,* March 22, 2019.

372 actor Mark Rylance: "How Family Fortune Bankrolls London Arts," *Evening Standard,* March 19, 2018.

372 "a domino effect": Jonathan Sackler, email, March 5, 2018.

373 the website STAT: "Purdue's Sackler Embraced Plan to Conceal OxyContin's Strength from Doctors, Sealed Deposition Shows," STAT, Feb. 21, 2019.

373 embarrassed by these revelations: "OxyContin Made the Sacklers Rich. Now It's Tearing Them Apart," *Wall Street Journal,* July 13, 2019.

373 "I don't know what I can say": "New Jersey Is About to Hit Opioid Makers with a Major Lawsuit," NJ.com, Oct. 4, 2017.

373 Sacklers stepped down from the board: Massachusetts Complaint.

373 a "hit list": Interview with Megan Kapler.

373 In April 2018: "Nan Goldin Survived an Overdose to Fight the Opioid Epidemic," *T Magazine,* June 11, 2018.

374 article in the paper: "Guggenheim Targeted by Protesters for Accepting Money from Family with OxyContin Ties," *New York Times,* Feb. 9, 2019.

374 the Guggenheim announced: "Guggenheim Museum 'Does Not Plan to Accept Any Gifts' from the Sackler Family," *Hyperallergic,* March 22, 2019; "Guggenheim Museum Says It Won't Accept Gifts from Sackler Family," *New York Times,* March 22, 2019.

374 the National Portrait Gallery in London: "British Gallery Turns Down $1.3 Million Sackler Donation," *New York Times,* March 19, 2019.

375 "seek or accept further donations": "Tate Galleries Will Refuse Sackler Money Because of Opioid Links," *New York Times,* March 21, 2019.

375 "We do not intend to remove": Ibid.

375 Guggenheim let it be known: "Guggenheim Museum Says It Won't Accept Gifts from Sackler Family."

375 "I will not do the show": "Nan Goldin Threatens London Gallery Boycott over

£1M Gift from Sackler Fund," *Observer,* Feb. 17, 2019.

375 "I congratulate them": "British Gallery Turns Down $1.3 Million Sackler Donation."

375 "I would like to address": " 'Like Being Married to a Serial Killer': Hito Steyerl Denounces Sackler Sponsorship of Museums," *Art Newspaper,* April 10, 2019.

375 The museum promptly announced: Ibid.

375 One night, one of Goldin's close deputies: Interviews with Goldin, Kapler, and Harry Cullen.

376 Metropolitan Museum of Art: "The Met Will Turn Down Sackler Money amid Fury over the Opioid Crisis," *New York Times,* May 15, 2019.

376 "Do you know who made this film?": Interview with Kapler.

376 "She presents herself as a social activist": "Madeleine Sackler's Films Praised, but She Faces Scrutiny over Opioid-Linked Wealth," *Guardian,* May 2, 2018.

376 "took the money": Interview with Goldin.

376 "more than full-time": "Madeleine Sackler's Films Praised, but She Faces Scrutiny over Opioid-Linked Wealth."

377 "The Sackler name has become synonymous": Ibid.

377 the company had announced: "OxyContin Maker Purdue Pharma Stops Promoting Opioids, Cuts Sales Staff," Reuters, Feb. 10, 2018.

377 the company had already calculated: The States' Notice of Public Health Information to Protect Purdue Patients, *In re Chapter 11 Purdue Pharma LP et al.,* 1 Case No. 19-23649, U.S. Bankruptcy Court, Southern District of New York, Dec. 9, 2019.

377 eliminating its sales force: "OxyContin Maker Purdue Pharma Cuts Remaining Sales Force," Reuters, June 20, 2018.

377 witness against Purdue: Portenoy Declaration.

377 a legal complaint: Massachusetts Complaint.

CHAPTER 27: NAMED DEFENDANTS

378 married to his son, David: Unless otherwise noted, details in this paragraph are from "Joss and Jillian Sackler on OxyContin Scandal and Opioid Crisis Accusations," *Town & Country,* May 16, 2019.

378 or "Poppi": David Sackler to Richard, Beth and Joss Sackler, June 12, 2015.

378 Her dissertation was about: Jaseleen Ruggles, "The Degree of Certainty System in Written Spanish in Mexico" (PhD diss., City University of New York, 2014).

378 club for young rich women: LBV website.

378 "winemaking bulldogs": "Joss and Jillian Sackler on OxyContin Scandal and Opioid Crisis Accusations."

379 "Joss is a threat assessor": Joss Sackler biography, LBV website.

379 turn LBV into a fashion brand: "Last Sackler Standing," *Air Mail*, Aug. 17, 2019.

379 "my own women's initiative": Open letter to Matthew Schneier, posted on Facebook (and since deleted) by Joss Sackler.

379 fashion reporter from *The New York Times:* "Uptown, Sackler Protests. Downtown, a Sackler Fashion Line," *New York Times*, Feb. 19, 2019.

379 indignant web post: Open letter to Matthew Schneier, posted on Facebook (and since deleted) by Joss Sackler.

379 She threw parties: "Joss and Jillian Sackler on OxyContin Scandal and Opioid Crisis Accusations."

380 mansion in Bel Air: "OxyContin Heir David Sackler Scores Dope $22.5 Mil Bel-Air Mansion," *TMZ*, March 8, 2018.

380 "I support my family": "Joss and Jillian Sackler on OxyContin Scandal and Opioid Crisis Accusations."

380 emoji of a middle finger: "Joss Sackler Flips Off Page Six," *New York Post*, Aug. 22, 2019.

380 first openly gay attorney general: Interview with Healey; "Maura Healey Setting Her Course as Attorney General," *Boston Globe*, Nov. 12, 2014; "Massachusetts AG Maura Healey May Send Your Gay Marriage Story to SCOTUS," MSNBC, March 3, 2015.

380 Healey had started investigating: Interview with Maura Healey and Joanna Lydgate.

381 He cross-checked those names: Interview with Alexander; Massachusetts Complaint.

381 Healey held a press conference: "AG Healey Sues Purdue Pharma, Its Board Members and Executives for Illegally Marketing Opioids and Profiting from Opioid Epidemic," Office of Massachusetts Attorney General Maura Healey, June 12, 2018.

381 "The public deserves answers": Attorney General Maura Healey, press conference, June 12, 2018.

381 This did not strike Healey: Interview with Healey and Joanna Lydgate.

382 "a whole lot of finger pointing": See Jennifer D. Oliva, "Opioid Multidistrict Litigation Secrecy," *Ohio State Law Journal*, vol. 80 (2019).

382 some twelve million documents: Interview with Sandy Alexander.

382 Purdue's lawyers intervened: Joint Motion to Impound Amended Complaint, *Massachusetts v. Purdue Pharma Inc. et al.*, 1884-CV-01808, Dec. 3, 2018.

382 "My antennae go up": Transcript of a hearing in *Massachusetts v. Purdue Pharma Inc. et al.*, 1884-CV-01808, Massachusetts Superior Court, Dec. 21, 2018.

383 invoked a dark precedent: Memorandum of Decision and Order on Emergency Motion to Terminate Impoundment, *Massachusetts v. Purdue Pharma Inc. et al.*, Civ. No. 1884-01808-BLS2, Massachusetts Superior Court, Jan. 28, 2019.

383 an emergency appeal: "How Judges Added to the Grim Toll of Opioids," Reuters, June 25, 2019.

383 "I'm not very happy": Transcript of Proceedings, *In re National Prescription Opiate Litigation*, Civil Action Number 1:17MD02804, Jan. 30, 2019.

383 Big Tobacco litigation: See the Truth Tobacco Industry Documents archive, hosted by the University of California, San Francisco library, at www.industrydocuments.ucsf.edu.

383 274-page complaint: Massachusetts Complaint.

383 warned the Sacklers: "That same month, staff contacted Richard Sackler and Jonathan Sackler because they were concerned that the company's 'internal documents' could cause problems if investigations of the opioid crisis expanded." Delaware Complaint.

384 "their own 'beach type' folding chairs": "Pain Doctor Who Prescribed Large Amounts of Oxycodone Pleads Guilty to Fraud," *Boston Globe*, March 15, 2017; Department of Justice, "Physician Sentenced to Prison for False Billing Scheme," press release, Feb. 6, 2019.

384 Purdue's top prescriber: Massachusetts Complaint.

385 "Purdue took advantage of addiction": Ibid.

385 derided Healey's filing: Statement of the Raymond Sackler and Beacon Company in Support of the Debtors' Motion for a Pre-

liminary Injunction, U.S. Bankruptcy Court, Southern District of New York, Chapter 11, Case No. 19-23649 (RDD), Oct. 8, 2019.

385 "inaccurate and misleading": "NYC Society Shuns Sackler Family over OxyContin Fortune," *New York Post,* May 11, 2019.

385 Sacklers put together their own filing: Respondents Richard Sackler, MD's and Kathe Sackler, MD's Motion to Dismiss the Division's Notice of Agency Action and Citation, In the Matter of Purdue Pharma LP et al., DCP Legal File No. CP-2019-005, DCP Case No. 107102, April 9, 2019.

385 seized on an email: Memorandum of Law in Support of the Individual Directors' Motion to Dismiss for Lack of Personal Jurisdiction, *Commonwealth of Massachusetts v. Purdue Pharma LP et al.,* Civil Action No. 1884-CV-01808(B), April 1, 2019.

386 motion to dismiss the case was denied: The judge in Massachusetts, Janet Sanders, denied both Purdue's motion to dismiss and a separate motion to dismiss by the Sacklers and other directors. Memorandum of Decision and Order on the Defendant Purdue's Motion to Dismiss, *Commonwealth of Massachusetts v. Purdue Pharma LP and Others,* Massachusetts Superior Court, Civil Action No. 1884CV01808, Sept. 16, 2019; Memorandum of Decision and Order on the Defendant Directors' and Executives' Rule 12(b)(2) Motion to Dismiss, *Commonwealth of Massachusetts v. Purdue Pharma LP and Others,* Massachusetts Superior Court, Civil Action No. 1884CV01808, Oct. 8, 2019.

386 Healey posted a video: Interviews with Sandy Alexander and Feiner; Instagram video posted by Healey on Oct. 8, 2019.

386 James described OxyContin: New York Complaint.

386 as far back as 2007: DOJ Sackler Settlement.

387 "We've taken a fantastic amount": Jonathan Sackler to Mortimer D. A. Sackler, Sept. 8, 2014, cited in DOJ Sackler Settlement.

387 "eliminating all our documents": Martin Elling to Arnab Ghatak, email, July 4, 2018.

387 "Will do": Arnab Ghatak to Martin Elling, email, July 4, 2018.

387 "press attention that these legal cases": "Museums Cut Ties with Sacklers as Outrage over Opioid Crisis Grows," *New York Times,* March 25, 2019.

387 "Five years ago, the Sackler family":

"NYC Society Shuns Sackler Family over OxyContin Fortune."

387 Achievement First: "Charter Network Says No to Further Donations from Opioid-Linked Sackler Family," Chalkbeat.org, June 6, 2019.

387 Hildene Capital Management: "Hedge Fund Tosses Family That Controls Maker of OxyContin," *Wall Street Journal,* March 7, 2019.

387 Even Purdue's banker: "'We Didn't Cause the Crisis': David Sackler Pleads His Case on the Opioid Epidemic," *Vanity Fair,* June 19, 2019.

387 private family WhatsApp: These passages are taken from a log, which was produced in the bankruptcy proceedings, of a WhatsApp group maintained by members of the Mortimer Sackler family between October 2017 and May 2019.

388 "The media is eager to distort": Jonathan Sackler to Davidson Goldin, Ted Wells, and David Bernick, Feb. 17, 2019.

388 "We have not done a good job": "'We Didn't Cause the Crisis.'"

388 engaged in a "battle": Mortimer D. A. Sackler to Craig Landau et al., Nov. 11, 2018.

388 talk about "drug abuse": Mortimer D. A. Sackler to Jonathan Sackler et al., Feb. 17, 2019.

389 wrote to Purdue's new general counsel: Mortimer Sackler Jr. to Kesselman et al., Dec. 18, 2018.

389 "I am meeting with Michael Bloomberg": "When the Billionaire Family Behind the Opioid Crisis Needed PR Help, They Turned to Mike Bloomberg," ProPublica, Feb. 27, 2020.

389 sell their New York apartment: "The Year Ended with Another Big Sale at 220 Central Park South," *New York Times,* Jan. 3, 2020.

389 "If K2 doesn't scare me": "Last Sackler Standing." Joss does appear to be a genuinely accomplished climber who has summited other mountains and who occasionally wears a baseball cap that says "K2." She did get as far as base camp, in the summer of 2019, but collapsed and had to return home, in an episode she attributes to an autoimmune disease. Ibid.

389 "Sacklers Fleeing NYC": "Sacklers Fleeing NYC Following Family's OxyContin Scandal," *Page Six,* May 20, 2019.

389 become so comprehensive: Memorandum of Law in Support of the Individual

Directors' Motion to Dismiss for Lack of Personal Jurisdiction, *Commonwealth of Massachusetts v. Purdue Pharma LP et al.*, Civil Action No. 1884-CV-01808(B), April 1, 2019; "Sackler Family Company Pays $7 Million for Mansion near Boca Raton," *Palm Beach Post*, Oct. 25, 2019.

390 "for the wrong David Sackler": "This David Sackler Wants the World to Know He's Not That David Sackler," *Crain's*, June 3, 2019.

390 Purdue University: "Purdue University Statement RE: Purdue Pharma," March 7, 2019.

390 Stephen Colbert did a segment: *The Late Show with Stephen Colbert*, Sept. 14, 2018. The actual expletive is bleeped and you can't see Colbert's mouth when he says it, so I should acknowledge, for you sticklers checking the endnotes, that there's a possibility what he actually said was "not giving a *shit*." Colbert could … not be reached for comment.

390 John Oliver, of the satirical: *Last Week Tonight with John Oliver*, HBO, April 14, 2019.

391 "This is my son's favorite show": Jacqueline Sackler to Maura Kathleen Monaghan et al., April 10, 2019.

CHAPTER 28: THE PHOENIX

392 He was angry: "'We Didn't Cause the Crisis': David Sackler Pleads His Case on the Opioid Epidemic," *Vanity Fair*, June 19, 2019.

392 David was adamant: "Purdue Offers $10–12 Billion to Settle Opioid Claims," NBC News, Aug. 27, 2019.

392 interview to Bethany McLean: "'We Didn't Cause the Crisis.'"

392 Purdue's own McKinsey consultants: Jonathan Cain to McKinsey colleagues, email, October 22, 2008.

393 first big article: "Is Enron Overpriced?," *Fortune*, March 5, 2001.

393 nearly every state: According to a fact-checking email from a representative of Purdue Pharma on October 1, 2020, twenty-nine states and Washington, D.C., ultimately named individual Sacklers as defendants.

393 called out David's father: "Purdue Pharma: OxyContin Maker Faces Lawsuits from Nearly Every U.S. State," *Guardian*, June 4, 2019.

393 deposed by a new set of lawyers: RDS 2019 Deposition.

394 "With the fullness of time": Ibid.

394 pay Oklahoma $270 million: "Purdue Pharma Begins Resolution of Opioid Cases

with $270 Million Deal," *Wall Street Journal*, March 26, 2019.

394 "global resolution": "Sackler Family Want to Settle Opioids Lawsuits, Lawyer Says," *Guardian*, April 25, 2019.

394 scheduled to face another trial: "Exclusive: OxyContin Maker Prepares 'Free-Fall' Bankruptcy as Settlement Talks Stall," Reuters, Sept. 3, 2019.

394 make an offer: "Purdue Offers $10–12 Billion to Settle Opioid Claims."

395 "public benefit trust": Ibid.

395 According to Purdue's lawyers: "Purdue Pharma in Talks over Multibillion-Dollar Deal to Settle More Than 2,000 Opioid Lawsuits," *Washington Post*, Aug. 27, 2019.

395 but $3 billion: "Purdue Offers $10–12 Billion to Settle Opioid Claims."

395 "It's a joke": Interview with Feiner.

396 nearly $4.3 billion: "Purdue Pharma in Talks over Multibillion-Dollar Deal to Settle More Than 2,000 Opioid Lawsuits."

396 "That would be the ultimate victory": Interview with Alexander.

396 "an insult, plain and simple": "Attorney General James' Statement on Opioid Discussions," New York Attorney General's Office, Sept. 11, 2019.

396 To Maura Healey: "Purdue Pharma Tentatively Settles Thousands of Opioid Cases," *New York Times*, Sept. 11, 2019.

396 crossed paths with David Sackler: Interview with Maura Healey and Joanna Lydgate.

396 a counterproposal to the Sacklers: "Purdue Pharma Tentatively Settles Thousands of Opioid Cases," *New York Times*, Sept. 11, 2019.

396 the Sacklers wouldn't budge: "Email: Opioid Talks Fail, Purdue Bankruptcy Filing Expected," AP, Sept. 8, 2019.

396 "Almost all states would agree": "Luther Strange's Role in the Purdue Pharma Opioid Settlement Embraced by GOP States," AP, Sept. 14, 2019.

397 "I think they are a group": "Email: Opioid Talks Fail, Purdue Bankruptcy Filing Expected."

397 coffers were nearly empty: "Exclusive: OxyContin Maker Prepares 'Free-Fall' Bankruptcy as Settlement Talks Stall." After Purdue filed for bankruptcy, it emerged that the company actually had $1 billion or so in cash.

397 Purdue sent a letter: "Purdue Pharma in Talks over Multibillion-Dollar Deal to Settle More Than 2,000 Opioid Lawsuits."

397 declare bankruptcy: "Exclusive: Oxy-Contin Maker Prepares 'Free-Fall' Bankruptcy as Settlement Talks Stall."

397 Mary Jo White warned: "Sackler Family Want to Settle Opioids Lawsuits, Lawyer Says."

397 Purdue's lawyers told them: "Exclusive: OxyContin Maker Prepares 'Free-Fall' Bankruptcy as Settlement Talks Stall."

398 press reports indicated: "Email: Opioid Talks Fail, Purdue Bankruptcy Filing Expected."

398 Kennedy felt no scruples: "Can a Fashion Line Backed by Joss Sackler Ever Find Success Without Controversy?," Fashionista .com, Sept. 10, 2019.

398 "so much empathy": "'We Didn't Cause the Crisis.'"

398 Invitations to the show: Invitation to Elizabeth Kennedy for LBV c/o Joss Sackler runway presentation, Sept. 9, 2019.

399 Joss posted the photo: Joss Sackler Instagram post, June 19, 2019.

399 In advance of the show: "Fashionistas 'Skipping' Joss Sackler's New York Fashion Week Show," New York Post, Sept. 7, 2019.

399 invitation to Love: "OxyContin Heiress Offered Ex-opioid Addict Courtney Love $100K to Attend Fashion Show," Page Six, Sept. 8, 2019.

399 "the brand has no relation": Ibid.

399 "I am one of the most famous": Ibid.

400 "It's unfair": "Supporters Back Joss Sackler, OxyContin Heiress, as She Stages NYFW Show: 'What Scandal?,'" Daily Beast, Sept. 9, 2019.

400 traded barbs: Instagram post by Joss Sackler, Oct. 6, 2019.

400 flanked by her security guards: "Security Detail Was Out in Force for LBV's Ready-to-Wear Debut," Women's Wear Daily, Sept. 9, 2019.

400 filed for bankruptcy: Voluntary Petition for Non-individuals Filing for Bankruptcy by Purdue Pharma LP, U.S. Bankruptcy Court for the Southern District of New York, Sept. 15, 2019.

400 pick the judge: "Purdue's Choice of NY Bankruptcy Court Part of Common Forum Shopping Strategy, Experts Say," Washington Post, Oct. 10, 2019.

400 change its address: Certificate of Change, filed by Norton Rose Fulbright on behalf of Purdue Pharma Inc., New York State Department of State, March 1, 2019.

400 Robert Drain: "Purdue Pharma, Maker of OxyContin, Files for Bankruptcy," New York Times, Sept. 15, 2019.

401 press conference in Boston: Attorney General of Massachusetts, press conference, Sept. 16, 2019.

401 struggling to maintain her coalition: "Partisan Divide Grows over Opioid Settlement Plan," NPR, Oct. 20, 2019.

401 Many states, reeling from the epidemic: "Purdue Pharma Tentatively Settles Thousands of Opioid Cases."

401 a partisan divide: "Partisan Divide Grows over Opioid Settlement Plan."

402 donated generously: "Opioid Firms Kept Donating to State AGs While Negotiating Settlements," NBC News, Sept. 9, 2019.

402 continued to contribute: "Purdue Pharma Made Political Contributions After Going Bankrupt," Intercept, July 7, 2020.

402 lobbied the Republican AGs: "Partisan Divide Grows over Opioid Settlement Plan."

403 "put this deal together": Interview with Moore.

403 major sticking point: "Purdue Pharma's Bankruptcy Plan Includes Special Protection for the Sackler Family," Washington Post, Sept. 18, 2019.

403 "When your illegal marketing campaign": The Non-consenting States' Voluntary Commitment and Limited Opposition in Response to Purdue's Motion to Extend the Preliminary Injunction, In re Purdue Pharma LP et al., Debtors, U.S. Bankruptcy Court, Southern District of New York, Case No. 19-23649 (RDD), March 12, 2020.

403 vast global web: "A Pharmaceutical Fortune, Dispersed in a Global Labyrinth," AP, Aug. 29, 2019.

403 records from thirty-three financial institutions: "New York Subpoenas Banks and Financial Advisers for Sackler Records," New York Times, Aug. 15, 2019.

403 fought the subpoenas: "New York Uncovers $1 Billion in Sackler Family Wire Transfers," New York Times, Sept. 13, 2019.

404 "extracted nearly all the money": Josh Stein, North Carolina Attorney General's Office, press release, Oct. 4, 2019.

404 a special appeal: Memorandum of Law in Support of Motion for a Preliminary Injunction, Chapter 11, Case No. 19-23649, Sept. 18, 2019.

404 in a brief: The States' Coordinated Opposition to the Debtors' Motion for Preliminary Injunction of States' Law Enforcement Actions Against the Sacklers, *In re Purdue Pharma LP et al.,* Chapter 11, Case No. 19-23649 (RDD), U.S. Bankruptcy Court, Southern District of New York, Oct. 4, 2019 (hereafter cited as States' Coordinated Opposition to Preliminary Injunction).

404 "The Sacklers want the bankruptcy court": Massachusetts Attorney General's Office, "AG Healey Urges Court to Reject Purdue Pharma's Request to Stop Lawsuits Against the Company and the Sacklers," press release, Oct. 4, 2019.

404 filed for bankruptcy: "A. H. Robins Files Bankruptcy Petition," *Washington Post,* Aug. 22, 1985.

404 the Dalkon Shield: Richard B. Sobol, *Bending the Law: The Story of the Dalkon Shield Bankruptcy* (Chicago: University of Chicago Press, 1991), x.

405 the company maintained: Ibid., 11.

405 undermine the women: Ibid., 13.

405 stay all litigation: Ibid., 64.

405 a similar release: "Purdue Bankruptcy Venue May Be Part of Strategy Seeking Favorable Ruling, Experts Say," *Washington Post,* Oct. 10, 2019.

405 In a filing: Statement of the Raymond Sackler and Beacon Company in Support of the Debtors' Motion for a Preliminary Injunction, U.S. Bankruptcy Court, Southern District of New York, Chapter 11, Case No. 19-23649 (RDD), Oct. 8, 2019.

405 In a court hearing: "Judge Grants Purdue Pharma, Sackler Family Pause in Civil Lawsuits," *Washington Post,* Oct. 11, 2019.

405 acknowledged from the bench: Transcript in *Purdue Pharma LP, Debtor,* U.S. Bankruptcy Court, Southern District of New York, Case No. 19-23649 (RDD), Oct. 11, 2019; "Judge Grants Purdue Pharma, Sackler Family Pause in Civil Lawsuits."

405 "for the ultimate benefit": "Judge Grants Purdue Pharma, Sackler Family Pause in Civil Lawsuits."

CHAPTER 29: UN-NAMING

406 a fascinating study: Abby E. Alpert et al., "Origins of the Opioid Crisis and Its Enduring Impacts" (National Bureau of Economic Research Working Paper 26500, Nov. 2019).

406 had actually started: Interview with David Powell, of Rand, one of the authors.

406 "deaths of despair": See, for instance, "The Media Gets the Opioid Crisis Wrong.

Here Is the Truth," *Washington Post,* Sept. 12, 2017; "The Age of American Despair," *New York Times,* Sept. 7, 2019; Anne Case and Angus Deaton, *Deaths of Despair and the Future of American Capitalism* (Princeton, N.J.: Princeton University Press, 2020).

408 "You can make that argument": "'We Didn't Cause the Crisis': David Sackler Pleads His Case on the Opioid Epidemic," *Vanity Fair,* Aug. 2019.

408 a separate study: David Powell and Rosalie Liccardo Pacula, "The Evolving Consequences of OxyContin Reformulation on Drug Overdoses" (National Bureau of Economic Research Working Paper, April 2020).

409 myth of Pandora: Dora Panofsky and Erwin Panofsky, *Pandora's Box: The Changing Aspects of a Mythical Symbol* (Princeton, N.J.: Princeton University Press, 1991), 7.

409 said to be the first woman: Hesiod, *Works and Days,* 91–92, in *Hesiod: Theogony and Works and Days,* trans. M. L. West (Oxford: Oxford University Press, 1999).

409 deposited, overnight: Interview with Domenic Esposito.

410 "It's a symbol": "Protesters Place Giant Heroin Spoon Outside Stamford's Purdue Pharma," *Stamford Advocate,* June 22, 2018.

410 more security: "Hedge Fund Tosses Family That Controls Maker of OxyContin," *Wall Street Journal,* March 7, 2019.

410 Protesters had started showing up: "Hundreds Protest Outside Purdue Stamford HQ," *Stamford Advocate,* Aug. 21, 2018.

410 "This was me for 15 years": "OxyContin Maker Purdue Pharma Takes Down Signs at Stamford HQ," *Stamford Advocate,* May 13, 2019.

410 take the signs down: Ibid.

411 president of Yale had announced: "Yale Changes Calhoun College's Name to Honor Grace Murray Hopper," *Yale Daily News,* Feb. 11, 2017.

411 statue of Cecil Rhodes: "Rhodes Must Fall Activist Accepts £40,000 Rhodes Scholarship to Study at Oxford University," *Independent,* Jan. 24, 2017.

411 accept Sackler donations: "Prestigious Universities Around the World Accepted More Than $60M from OxyContin Family," AP, Oct. 3, 2019.

411 cut ties with the Sacklers: "Yale Won't Accept Sackler Donations," *Yale Daily News,* Sept. 25, 2019.

411 Elizabeth Warren: "Elizabeth Warren,

Unveiling Opioid Plan, Says Sackler Name Should Come Off Harvard Buildings," *New York Times,* May 8, 2019.

411 Lawrence Bacow, responded: "Tufts Removes Sackler Name over Opioids: 'Our Students Find It Objectionable,'" *New York Times,* Dec. 5, 2019.

411 protest at the Louvre: Interviews with Goldin and Megan Kapler; "Artist Nan Goldin Protests Against Sackler Wing at the Louvre," *Guardian,* July 1, 2019.

412 sunset any naming agreements: Interview with Goldin and Kapler.

412 "no longer carry the Sackler name": "Louvre Removes Sackler Name from Museum Wing amid Protests," *Guardian,* July 17, 2019.

412 *de-baptized,* a spokeswoman insisted: "The Louvre Museum Has Removed the Sackler Name from Its Walls and Website Following Protests by Nan Goldin's Activist Army," Artnet News, July 17, 2019.

412 "The Sacklers wanted everything": Interview with Kapler.

412 reluctant to use her own last name: "Joss and Jillian Sackler on OxyContin Scandal and Opioid Crisis Accusations," *Town & Country,* May 16, 2019.

412 "blanket designation": "Stop Blaming My Late Husband, Arthur Sackler, for the Opioid Crisis," *Washington Post,* April 11, 2019; "The Other Sackler," *Washington Post,* Nov. 27, 2019.

412 "like spitting in the wind": "Other Sackler."

412 she insisted: Ibid.

412 "Does anyone believe that?": Ibid.

412 subtly distancing itself: "Don't Call It the Freer/Sackler. Call It the National Museum of Asian Art," *Washington Post,* Dec. 4, 2019.

413 lambasted him for sullying: "OxyContin Made the Sacklers Rich. Now It's Tearing Them Apart," *Wall Street Journal,* July 13, 2019.

413 late husband's reputation would "ever recover": "Other Sackler."

413 back to 1980: Tufts Report.

413 "the Alexandrian library": "A Historical Opening for Tufts' New Sackler Center," *Tufts Criterion* (Winter 1986).

413 $15 million altogether: "'We Owe Much to the Sackler Family': How Gifts to a Top Medical School Advanced the Interests of Purdue Pharma," STAT, April 9, 2019.

413 in a private ceremony: "The Secretive Family Making Billions from the Opioid Crisis," *Esquire,* Oct. 16, 2017.

413 included a biography: "'We Owe Much to the Sackler Family.'"

413 scuttle the book: Tufts Report.

413 only in 2017: Ibid.

414 One first-year med student: Interview with Verdini; Obituary of Katelyn Marie Hart, Conway Cahill-Brodeur Funeral Home.

414 on an advisory board: "'We Owe Much to the Sackler Family.'"

414 "Our continued collaboration": Tufts Report.

414 appeared in a Purdue advertisement: "Inside the Purdue Pharma–Tufts Relationship," *Tufts Daily,* May 19, 2019.

414 David Haddox: Tufts Report.

414 Purdue-branded materials: "Inside the Purdue Pharma–Tufts Relationship."

414 "Our students, faculty, staff": Peter R. Dolan and Anthony P. Monaco to the Tufts community, Dec. 5, 2019.

414 "Our students find it objectionable": "Tufts Removes Sackler Name over Opioids."

415 "What our faculty and our deans": Ibid.

415 "being blamed for actions": Ibid.

415 "intellectually dishonest": Ibid.

415 letter accusing the university: "Sackler Family Members Fight Removal of Name at Tufts, Calling It a 'Breach,'" *New York Times,* Dec. 19, 2019.

415 workmen removed the Sackler name: Interview with Verdini.

415 all that was left: "Tufts Has Purged the Sackler Name. Who Will Do It Next?," *Boston Magazine,* Dec. 6, 2019.

416 "the benefits of bankruptcy protection": Statement by Letitia James, April 7, 2020.

416 in one hearing Drain suggested: Hearing transcript, *Purdue Pharma LP, Debtor,* U.S. Bankruptcy Court, Southern District of New York, Case No. 19-23649 (RDD), March 18, 2020.

416 "how much has been stashed away": Statement by Letitia James, May 13, 2020.

417 deposition testimony: Deposition of Jesse DelConte of AlixPartners, cited in States' Coordinated Opposition to Preliminary Injunction. In the B Side Defenses, the family of Raymond Sackler offers a more conservative (but still pretty significant!) estimate of $10.3 billion taken out of the company between 2008 and 2017.

417 "the Swiss Army knife": Tweet from Professor Melissa B. Jacoby (@melissabjacoby), Oct. 7, 2020.

417 Drain appeared adamant: Hearing transcript, *Purdue Pharma LP, Debtor,* U.S. Bankruptcy Court, Southern District of New York, Case No. 19-23649 (RDD), Aug. 26, 2020. Also see the transcript for July 23, in which Drain expresses the same view.

417 "negotiations that lead to agreements": Hearing transcript, *Purdue Pharma LP, Debtor,* U.S. Bankruptcy Court, Southern District of New York, Case No. 19-23649 (RDD), Sept. 30, 2020.

417 In a 2008 memoir: Steve Miller, *The Turnaround Kid: What I Learned Rescuing America's Most Troubled Companies* (New York: Harper Business, 2008), 223.

417 had previously worked for: "Purdue Pharma Paid Kenneth Feinberg Millions Before Seeking to Hire Him as Mediator," *Wall Street Journal,* Feb. 28, 2020.

417 One night, Gillian Feiner: Interview with Gillian Feiner.

418 "We're fighting on their terms": Interview with Cullen.

418 asking for an independent examiner: "We Demand Accountability and Transparency from Purdue and the Sacklers!" Change.org petition. This proposal was echoed in a 2019 letter signed by several law professors. Jonathan Lipson to William Harrington, November 5, 2019.

418 published an op-ed: "The Sacklers Could Get Away with It," *New York Times,* July 22, 2020.

418 "It doesn't matter what some numbskull": Hearing transcript, *Purdue Pharma LP, Debtor,* U.S. Bankruptcy Court, Southern District of New York, Case No. 19-23649 (RDD), July 23, 2020.

418 might file charges: "Purdue Pharma in Talks with Justice Department to Resolve Criminal, Civil Probes," *Wall Street Journal,* Sept. 6, 2019.

419 a hundred thousand people filed: Personal Injury Claim Summary (Claims processed as of 12/7/2020), *Purdue Pharma LP, Debtor,* U.S. Bankruptcy Court, Southern District of New York, Case No. 19-23649 (RDD), July 30, 2020.

419 a stunning filing: Attachment to Proof of Claim, United HealthCare Services Inc., filed in *Purdue Pharma LP, Debtor,* U.S. Bankruptcy Court, Southern District of New York, Case No. 19-23649 (RDD), July 30, 2020.

419 Department of Justice filed a claim: Proof of Claim, U.S. Department of Justice, filed in *Purdue Pharma LP, Debtor,* U.S. Bankruptcy Court, Southern District of New York, Case No. 19-23649 (RDD), July 30, 2020.

420 John Kapoor: U.S. Attorney for the District of Massachusetts, "Founder and Former Chairman of the Board of Insys Therapeutics Sentenced to 66 Months in Prison," press release, Jan. 23, 2020.

420 pressure from the political leadership: "The Sackler Family's Plan to Keep Its Billions," *New Yorker,* Oct. 4, 2020.

420 a press conference: Department of Justice, press conference, Oct. 21, 2020; Plea Agreement between the Department of Justice and Purdue Pharma, Oct. 20, 2020.

420 two former CEOs: Deposition of John Stewart, *In Re: Purdue Pharma LP et al., Debtors,* United States Bankruptcy Court, Southern District of New York, Case No. 19-2649 (RDD), Oct. 27, 2020; Deposition of Mark Timney, *In Re: Purdue Pharma LP et al., Debtors,* United States Bankruptcy Court, Southern District of New York, Case No. 19-2649 (RDD), Oct. 30, 2020.

420 "more than $8 billion": Department of Justice, press conference, Oct. 21, 2020; Department of Justice, "Justice Department Announces Global Resolution of Criminal and Civil Investigations with Opioid Manufacturer Purdue Pharma and Civil Settlement with Members of the Sackler Family," press release, Oct. 21, 2020.

420 obligingly repeated that number: "OxyContin Maker Purdue Pharma to Plead to 3 Criminal Charges in $8 Billion Settlement," AP, Oct. 21, 2020; "OxyContin Maker Purdue Pharma Reaches $8 Billion Settlement in Opioid Crisis Probe," *Forbes,* Oct. 21, 2020.

421 "knowingly caused the submission": DOJ Sackler Settlement.

421 nobody had even bothered: Deposition of David Sackler, *In Re: Purdue Pharma LP et al., Debtors,* United States Bankruptcy Court, Southern District of New York, Case No. 19-2649 (RDD), Aug. 28, 2020.

421 "a little over 2 percent": The journalist was Kadhim Shubber from the *Financial Times.*

421 "Did you ever try to pursue": This was Hannah Kuchler, also of the *Financial Times.*

421 a third reporter inquired: This was Jef Feeley of Bloomberg News.

421 "It's like 2007 all over again": Interview with Meier.

421 official settlement documents: DOJ Sackler Settlement.

422 "No reasonable person would have": B Side Defenses.

422 emails between the Sacklers: David Sackler to Jonathan and Richard Sackler, May 17, 2007, cited in DOJ Sackler Settlement. The Sacklers and their attorneys would continue to assert, unconvincingly, that the family had no serious expectation of widespread litigation before 2017. But other internal documents that were subsequently unsealed suggest otherwise. See "Sackler Family Debated Lawsuit Risk While Taking Billions From Purdue," *Wall Street Journal*, Dec. 22, 2020.

422 "Here we are, so many years": Healey interviewed on *The Rachel Maddow Show*, MSNBC, Oct. 23, 2020.

422 Alexander had gotten: Interviews with Feiner and Alexander.

422 "I am not done with Purdue": Maura Healey on Twitter, Oct. 21, 2020.

422 "We're going to continue to press": Healey interviewed on *The Rachel Maddow Show*, MSNBC, Oct. 23, 2020.

422 cases in Kentucky and Oklahoma: Settlement Agreement and General Release, *Commonwealth of Kentucky v. Purdue Pharma, LP et al.*, Pike Circuit Court, Division II, Civil Action No. 07-CI-01303, Dec. 22, 2015; Consent Judgment as to the Purdue Defendants, *State of Oklahoma v. Purdue Pharma, LP, et al.*, District Court of Cleveland County, Case No. CJ-2017-816, March 26, 2019.

422 In the term sheet for the settlement: Summary Term Sheet for a proposed comprehensive settlement.

423 early hearing: Hearing transcript, *Purdue Pharma LP, Debtor*, U.S. Bankruptcy Court, Southern District of New York, Case No. 19-23649 (RDD), Feb. 21, 2020.

423 "sends the wrong message": The Non-consenting States' Voluntary Commitment and Limited Opposition in Response to Purdue's Motion to Extend the Preliminary Injunction, *In re Purdue Pharma LP et al., Debtors*, U.S. Bankruptcy Court, Southern District of New York, Case No. 19-23649 (RDD), March 12, 2020.

423 In the Dalkon Shield: Sobol, p. 180.

424 "I got a few things": Transcript in *Purdue Pharma LP, Debtor*, U.S. Bankruptcy Court, Southern District of New York, Case No. 19-

23649 (RDD), Dec. 15, 2020. (The official transcript does not note the long pauses in Drain's delivery; I was dialed into the hearing as well and listened to it live.)

426 "this character that gets carried away": Interview with Kapit.

426 His obituaries: "Jonathan Sackler, Co-owner of Purdue Pharma, Dies," AP, July 6, 2020; "Jonathan Sackler, Joint Owner of Opioid Maker Purdue Pharma, Dies Aged 65," *Guardian*, July 6, 2020.

427 "most ambitious and impactful": Tom Clare to Fabio Bertoni, July 10, 2019.

427 But in September 2020: OxyContin "Abuse Deterrent Formulation (ADF)," FDA Briefing Document, Joint Meeting of the Drug Safety and Risk Management (DSaRM) Advisory Committee and Anesthetic and Analgesic Drug Products Advisory Committee (AADPAC), Sept. 10–11, 2020.

427 plans to strip the Sackler name: Robert I. Grossman to the NYU Langone community, email, Oct. 22, 2020.

427 Metropolitan Museum of Art said: "After Purdue Pharma Reached a $225 Million Settlement with US Authorities, the Met Says the Name of Its Sackler Wing Is 'Under Review,'" Artnet News, Oct. 23, 2020.

427 Harvard announced: "Charge to the Committee to Articulate Principles on Renaming," Office of the President, Harvard University, Oct. 26, 2020.

428 "The Role of Purdue Pharma": Memorandum re. Hearing on "The Role of Purdue Pharma and the Sackler Family in the Opioid Epidemic," Committee on Oversight and Reform, U.S. House of Representatives, Dec. 14, 2020.

429 "deep sadness about the opioid crisis": "The Role of Purdue Pharma and the Sackler Family in the Opioid Epidemic," Hearing before the House Oversight And Reform Committee of the U.S. House of Representatives, Dec. 17, 2020.

432 intensified the opioid crisis: "The Opioid Crisis, Already Serious, Has Intensified During Coronavirus Pandemic," *Wall Street Journal*, Sept. 8, 2020; "'The Drug Became His Friend': Pandemic Drives Hike in Opioid Deaths," *New York Times*, Sept. 29, 2020.

432 sold their East Seventy-Fifth Street town house: "Israel Englander Buys Sackler Townhouse for $38M," Real Deal, Jan. 7, 2020.

433 In a filing: Attachment to Consolidated

Proof of Claim of States, Territories, and Other Governmental Entities, *Purdue Pharma LP, et al, Debtors,* United States Bankruptcy Court, Southern District of New York, Case No. 19-23649 (RDD), July 30, 2020.

433 "We will never be able to collect": Interview with Healey.

433 "This agreement was not designed": Interview with Leather.

434 "to help alleviate man's suffering": Sackler Foundation filing, 1947, quoted in Martin L. Friedman, of Chapman, Wolfsohn, and Friedman (attorneys for Purdue Frederick and Mortimer and Raymond Sackler), to Senator Estes Kefauver, Nov. 28, 1961, Kefauver Files.

AFTERWORD

436 emphatically denied: Fact checking responses from Purdue Pharma, Dec. 14, 2020.
436 made no similar denial: Fact checking responses from the Raymond and Mortimer Sackler families, Dec. 18, 2020. I had asked if any members of either family had knowledge of the investigators sent to monitor Nan Goldin, Megan Kapler, or myself, and whether the family or any entity working on their behalf had arranged for this surveillance. In their response to me, the family did offer denials relating to several other queries, but elected (rather conspicuously, it seemed to me) to leave this one unanswered.

436 I wrote a long article: "How a Mexican Drug Cartel Makes Its Billions," *New York Times Magazine,* June 17, 2012.

438 an attorney, Tom Clare: "New York Times, NBC, and '60 Minutes' Bigwigs Hired These Media Assassins to Fight #MeToo Stories," *Daily Beast,* July 20, 2018.

438 Clare's opening salvo: Clare to Fabio Bertoni, July 10, 2019.

439 "Everyone is entitled to a lawyer": Interview with Lydgate.

439 "acted ethically and lawfully": "NYU to Remove Sackler Name Following Purdue Pharma Deal," AP, Oct. 22, 2020.

439 "engage responsibly": Clare to the author, Oct. 29, 2020.

440 "We were complicit": Interview with Primpas.

INDEX

sealing evidence from case in, 337–8
settlement paid by Purdue, 337–8
Keusch, Phil, 46, 59
Koch, Ed, 107, 137
Kroll investigation firm, 251–4

Landau, Craig, 344–5, 349, 360
late-night show segments on Sacklers,
   390–1, 509n390
lawsuits/litigation:
   Agreed Statement of Facts in guilty plea,
      281–4, 285
   agreement to improve conduct after
      guilty plea, 294
   bankruptcy declaration and settlement
      agreement, 400–3, 404, 405, 422–5,
      451–2
   criminal charges in Virginia case, 272–7,
      421
   damage control role of Udell, 224–5,
      237–8, 241–2, 256, 259–61
   deceptive marketing cases, 332, 334–5,
      370, 421–2
   deposition of Kathe, 1–4, 5–7
   deposition of Richard, 332, 334–8, 372–3
   final bankruptcy hearing, 424–5
   fines paid in Virginia case, 280, 282–5,
      294
   fining corporations and licenses for
      misconduct, 284–5
   guilty pleas and sentencing in Virginia
      case, 279–84, 293–4, 297, 299–300, 369
   litigation threat over book, 438–9, 446–7
   misbranding charges, 273, 276, 279, 413
   multidistrict litigation, 370, 377, 382
   multidistrict litigation settlement
      proposal, 392–8, 422–3
   Oklahoma case settlement, 394, 422
   OxyContin litigation, 5–7, 247–50, 251–2
   OxyContin patent challenges, 225
   private lawsuits, 297
   public relations efforts to counter, 370–1,
      387–9
   Purdue lawsuits brought by Moore, 367,
      368–71
   Purdue litigation record, 252
   scapegoating Sacklers in, 5–6
   sealing evidence from Kentucky case,
      337–8
   settlement preference over litigation,
      338, 369, 370
   swagger of Richard and Udell related
      to, 225
   tobacco industry cases, 5, 221, 299, 368
   White wrongful termination lawsuit,
      252–4, 440

Lear, John, 82–4, 85, 89–90, 95, 269
Leather, Richard, 50, 116, 170–1, 299, 433–4
Librium:
   abuse of and addiction to, 62–5
   development of, 53–4
   marketing of, 54–6, 57–9, 183, 206,
      462n56
   Medical Tribune ads for, 59
   naming of, 54
   patent on, 63–4, 65
   success of, 55, 56–7, 58–9, 206
Los Angeles Times coverage of Purdue, 314,
   338–40
Louvre, 3, 304, 352, 411–12
Love, Courtney, 399–400
Lutze, Marietta, see Sackler, Marietta Lutze
L. W. Frohlich agency:
   Arthur as silent partner in, 49–50, 89,
      115
   closing after death of Frohlich, 115
   competition between McAdams and,
      45–7, 49
   conflict of interest in Sackler-Frohlich
      arrangements, 49–50, 89, 116
   success of, 115

Maine:
   consumption of OxyContin in, 227
   McCloskey letter warning of abuse
      dangers, 227, 228, 241, 283
   McCloskey resignation and work for
      Purdue, 248–9, 283
   OxyContin abuse and overdoses in, 222,
      226, 227
Martí-Ibáñez, Félix:
   appearance of, 77
   background and career of, 77
   congressional subpoena for, 90
   friendship with Arthur, 77, 88
   as front man for Sacklers, 90
   investigation of, 88–91
   job for Welch, inquiry about, 90
   letter to Bobby on Sackler name, 117
   letter to Richard on Sackler name, 150,
      326
   McAdams work of, 77
   MD Publications role of, 77, 87, 88, 147
   relationship with Welch, 77–8, 84, 90–1,
      195
Massachusetts:
   complaint document against Sacklers,
      382–6
   family members named in lawsuit in, 377
   impounding documents in, 382–3
   lawsuit against Sackler family in, 5, 377,
      380–6, 393, 395